SECOND CANADIAN EDITION

Forensic Psychology

STEPHEN PORTER

University of British Columbia Okanagan

LAWRENCE S. WRIGHTSMAN

University of Kansas

NELSON EDUCATION

NELSON EDUCATION

Forensic Psychology, Second Canadian Edition

by Stephen Porter and Lawrence S. Wrightsman

Vice President, Editorial Higher Education:
Anne Williams

Executive Editor:
Lenore Taylor-Atkins

Marketing Manager:
Ann Byford

Developmental Editor:
Leah Blain

Photo Researcher:
Sandra Mark

Permissions Coordinator:
Sandra Mark

Production Service:
Integra Software Services Pvt. Ltd.

Copy Editor:
Karen Rolfe

Proofreader:
Erin Moore

Indexer:
Jeanne Busemeyer, Hyde Park Publishing Services

Manufacturing Manager:
Joanne McNeil

Design Director:
Ken Phipps

Managing Designer:
Franca Amore

Interior Design:
Peter Papayanakis

Cover Design:
Alexandra Moroz

Cover and Chapter Opener Images:
andipantz/Getty Images; Massimo Merlini/Getty Images

Compositor:
Integra Software Services Pvt. Ltd.

Printer:
Edwards Brothers Malloy

Library and Archives Canada Cataloguing in Publication Data

Porter, Stephen, 1970-
   Forensic psychology / Stephen Porter, Lawrence S. Wrightsman. —2nd Canadian ed.

Order of authors' names reversed on previous edition.
Includes bibliographical references and index.
ISBN 978-0-17-650936-1

   1. Forensic psychology—Textbooks. I. Wrightsman, Lawrence S II. Title.

RA1148.W74 2013   614'.15
C2012-906921-3

ISBN-13: 978-0-17-650936-1
ISBN-10: 0-17-650936-4

Dedication

This book is dedicated to my beautiful son Soren Porter.

Stephen Porter, Ph.D.

Brief Contents

Contents

CHAPTER 9

Criminal Responsibility and Competency to Stand Trial 207

CHAPTER 10

Intimate Partner Violence, Homicide and Stalking 232

CHAPTER 11

Sex Offenders 256

CHAPTER 12
The Psychology of Child and Adult Sexual Assault Victims   280

CHAPTER 13
Psychopathy: History, Assessment, Etiology, and Its Association with Violence   312

CHAPTER 14
The Role of Psychology in Sentencing, Parole, and Dangerous Offender Hearings in Canada   336

CHAPTER 15

The Promising Future of Forensic Psychology in Canada   351

Preface

The terms "forensic psychology" and "psychology and law" are commonly heard in our society. A quick Google search of "forensic psychology" yields almost three million hits. We frequently hear references to forensic psychology in the news media, movies, and popular television shows. More importantly, the science of forensic psychology is increasingly prominent in leading academic journals, and more and more students are seeking information about university courses relating to this fascinating area. But what *is* forensic psychology? While the term has been around for decades, there is controversy over what it means or which professional activities would be subsumed under the heading (as we explore in Chapter 1). In this book, we adopt a broad definition of forensic psychology, and the material we explore should be of interest to anyone who works at—or is interested in—the fascinating intersection of psychology and the legal system, from students and academic researchers to psychologists who engage in various activities in the legal system. It also is relevant to nonpsychology professionals, such as law enforcement officers, judges and lawyers, social workers, parole officers, and victims services staff, who deal with people who have contact with the legal system (suspects, defendants, offenders, crime victims).

This book has two major foundations. One is the original text by Lawrence Wrightsman, among the most well-respected, scholarly, and popular books in the area. Dr. Wrightsman based his text on a course he was teaching in the early 1990s in response to students' great desire for knowledge about the activities of forensic psychologists and the opportunities for training in the field. The second is the First Canadian Edition (Wrightsman & Porter, 2005) developed from the Wrightsman text almost a decade ago. It was one of the first forensic psychology textbooks written from a Canadian perspective. In that book, I endeavoured to build upon the high quality of Dr. Wrightsman's original text, updating and revising in light of the new developments in the field and trying to better meet the needs of students and professors in Canada.

While teaching a forensic psychology course from 1998 to 2004 (when the First Canadian Edition was released), I had chosen to use a collection of readings rather than an existing textbook heavy on American legal content. As such, the First Canadian Edition highlighted the great differences that exist between Canada and the United States in terms of our legal systems, the practices by forensic psychologists in the two countries, and our cultural landscapes in general. The First Canadian Edition emphasized the uniquely Canadian perspective, while discussing our field in its full international context.

While continuing in the spirit of those two original texts, the current textbook was intended to make major advancements over its predecessors in major ways. In this Second Canadian Edition, Nelson Education offered me the freedom to make substantial general and specific content changes. Some of the major general changes included replacing most of the American legal case material with Canadian content, increasing the use of relevant Canadian legal case descriptions, generating profiles of leading Canadian researchers, highlighting emerging debates in the field, and building an even stronger scientific basis for our observations and conclusions. Further, I hope the stylistic changes witnessed throughout this edition make it a more enjoyable read! Another intention—while maintaining the Canadian legal focus—was to make this a truly international textbook in terms of exploring the topics that now are widely considered to be of major interest in our field around the world. To do this, I consulted with experts in forensic psychology around the world and surveyed the major journals in our field, such as *Law and Human Behaviour, Criminal Justice and Behaviour,* and *Legal and Criminological Psychology.* I also perused the forensic content in journals in other areas of psychology such as the *Journal of Personality and Social Psychology* and generalized journals such as *Psychological Science* and *Psychological Bulletin.* Ultimately, this led to numerous specific content changes from the book's earlier versions. I decided to include some completely new chapters, including those on "Sex Offenders"; "Psychopathy"; "Intimate Partner Violence, Homicide and Stalking"; and "The Role of Psychology in Sentencing, Parole, and Dangerous Offender Hearings in Canada." Other chapters from the First Canadian Edition were completely overhauled, such as those on detecting deception, remembering crime, and jury decision making. I hope that readers agree that this new material makes for a much better textbook.

In my course, as in this Second Canadian Edition, the content reflects several key beliefs:

1. *"Knowledge" within, and the practice of, forensic psychology should be firmly based in empirical research.* As Leonardo da Vinci—arguably the first scientist/practitioner—stated, "Science is the captain, practice the soldier." When psychologists venture into the legal system, their claims and conclusions must be based on sound research, not simply their own personal opinions (as often happened in the past). Throughout this textbook, there is an emphasis on the relevant research findings that can best inform the practices of psychologists in the legal arena.

2. *Forensic psychology, as a field, is in a dynamic state of formulation and development.* For some professionals in our field, forensic activities evolve from the applied or clinical roles of the psychologist; for others, an experimental, applied cognitive, or social psychological background leads to involvement in forensic work research when they testify as an expert witness in court or act as a consultant to the police. Thus, the contents of a book entitled *Forensic Psychology* should be broad, inclusive, and self-reflective. In this book, the reader will find a broad array of topics from deception detection to criminal interrogations, from criminal responsibility to competency to stand trial, from domestic violence to eyewitness testimony, from psychopathy to posttraumatic stress disorder. Because of the evolving nature of forensic psychology, the development of "knowledge" via "hot" debates in our field are encouraged. These discussions include ethical concerns about the increasing presence of neuroscience in the courts, assumptions about gender and violence, the effectiveness of offender treatment programs, and the ability of juries to make accurate decisions about guilt and innocence.

3. *Forensic psychology is a profession.* This book is oriented around the variety of roles for the forensic psychologist and is directed toward the student who is curious about the day-to-day activities of forensic psychologists, whether academic researchers or practising psychologists (or for many of us, like myself, both!). Specific chapters, focusing on activities such as police psychology or the nature of sex offenders, describe how the psychologist can be useful (or sometimes problematic!) to the legal system and, specifically, to the body of knowledge, techniques, and instruments available to the psychologist. The ethical considerations in applying this material to the legal system's questions are emphasized throughout the book.

4. *The forensic psychologist is a participant in the legal system and as such must be aware of the legal system's "rules of the game."* When psychologists move from their academic offices or clinical examining rooms to practise as forensic psychologists, they are on a different turf, with different rules and expectations. Judges, police officers, trial lawyers, and others have expectations for the forensic psychologist that may conflict with what the psychologist can ethically or realistically provide. A textbook on forensic psychology should consistently consider the temptations and responsibilities when psychologists venture into the legal system, and how to resolve various ethical dilemmas with which they may be confronted.

5. *Sources of information about forensic psychology are rich, varied, and extensive.* A text focusing on forensic psychology should not only reflect psychological science and be heavy on empirical evidence, but also include anecdotal or legal evidence in the form of descriptions of real cases that provide provocative illustrations of the phenomena under consideration. Such a text should try to capture the vitality of a field that constantly confronts new inquiries and issues. Thus, each chapter includes examples and legal cases relevant to the topic under study, as well as suggested readings selected to complement the text material for the interested reader. The References section at the end of the book, with roughly 2000 entries, includes academic papers in leading psychological journals, as well as information from court cases and popular periodicals. Further, a list of relevant websites is included on the Companion website

(http://www.forensicpsych2.nelson.com). Most cases described here are Canadian court cases, from an animal cruelty case in a provincial court in Corner Brook, Newfoundland (Chapter 7), to numerous cases in the Supreme Court of Canada, the authority with the final say on a psycholegal issue.

6. *A book about a popular topic such as forensic psychology should be as user-friendly as possible.* In addition to the extensive list of references and the suggested readings, each chapter of the book contains an introductory outline, a closing summary of its contents, and a list of key terms. Each key term is printed in boldface when introduced in the text. Boxes in each chapter provide further exploration of specific topics, case examples, and summaries of research findings.

ANCILLARIES

The **Nelson Education Teaching Advantage (NETA)** program delivers research-based instructor resources that promote student engagement and higher-order thinking to enable the success of Canadian students and educators.

Instructors today face many challenges. Resources are limited, time is scarce, and a new kind of student has emerged: one who is juggling school with work, has gaps in his or her basic knowledge, and is immersed in technology in a way that has led to a completely new style of learning. In response, Nelson Education has gathered a group of dedicated instructors to advise us on the creation of richer and more flexible ancillaries that respond to the needs of today's teaching environments. Whether your course is offered in class, online, or both, Nelson is pleased to provide pedagogically driven, research-based resources to support you.

In consultation with the editorial advisory board, Nelson Education has completely rethought the structure, approaches, and formats of our key textbook ancillaries. We've also increased our investment in editorial support for our ancillary authors. The result is the Nelson Education Teaching Advantage.

NETA Presentation has been developed to help instructors make the best use of PowerPoint® in their classrooms. With a clean and uncluttered design developed by Maureen Stone of StoneSoup Consulting, NETA Presentation features slides with improved readability, more multimedia and graphic materials, activities to use in class, and tips for instructors on the Notes page. A copy of *NETA Guidelines for Classroom Presentations* by Maureen Stone is included with each set of PowerPoint slides.

NETA Presentation: Microsoft® PowerPoint® lecture slides for every chapter have been created by Dr. Stephen Porter, the first author. There is an average of 30 slides per chapter. NETA principles of clear design and engaging content have been incorporated throughout.

The **Test Bank** was written by Dr. Stephen Porter, the first author. There is an average of 25 multiple choice questions and 5 true/false questions per chapter. It also includes questions for class discussion and/or essay examinations that will help time-pressed instructors more effectively communicate with their students and also strengthen the coverage of course material. Test Bank files are provided in Word format for easy editing and in PDF format for convenient printing whatever your system.

DayOne—ProfInClass is a PowerPoint® presentation that you can customize to orient your students to the class and their text at the beginning of the course.

Go to NelsonBrain.com to access these resources for your text.

Companion Website

The book-specific companion website is available at **http://www.forensicpsych2.nelson.com.** It features links to Canadian and international resources that are relevant to forensic psychology. This site also includes study resources and information on degrees and careers in psychology.

ACKNOWLEDGMENTS

If this book were solely the product of the authors, it would be very different from the one you are reading. I am greatly indebted to a number of people who contributed to the final version of this work.

Many thanks to Lawrence Wrightsman, whose classic original text provided an excellent foundation for this book. The writing of this adaptation was facilitated by the support and assistance of numerous individuals at Nelson Education. First and foremost, I am greatly indebted to Executive Editor Lenore Taylor-Atkins and Developmental Editor Leah Blain, for supporting me throughout the writing period. I also thank Karen Rolfe, the freelance editor on this project; her fine editing job on an earlier draft led to an improved final product. I also had a large group of students who contributed a great amount of their time and hard work in contributing in substantial ways to the new and revised chapters found in the book. The first UBC—Okanagan Psychology Ph.D. graduate (2012), Leanne ten Brinke, contributed significantly to the preparation of the "Deception Detection in the Legal System" chapter. Leanne has received numerous prestigious awards and accolades and quickly is becoming recognized as a world expert in the use of facial expressions in credibility assessment. Her work has been profiled all over the world, but notably on CBC's *Quirks and Quarks*! My doctoral student Julia Shaw contributed her fine efforts to the preparation of the chapters on "Police Interrogations and Confessions" and "Psychopathy: History, Assessment, Etiology, and Its Association with Violence." Julia is establishing herself on an international level in forensic psychology, having recently (2012) edited the *Psychology & Law Factbook* published by the European Association of Psychology and Law Student Society. My former honours (and eventual Master's) student Alysha Baker contributed to the preparation of the "Deception Detection in the Legal System" and "Remembering Crime" chapters. In 2012, Alysha had a first-author paper on emotional intelligence and deception detection published in *Legal and Criminological Psychology* and has been accepted into the Master's program in forensic psychology at UBC—Okanagan. My former honours student Natasha Korva contributed to the preparation of the "The Police: Selection, Training, and Evaluation" and "The Psychology of the Jury" chapters. Natasha has won major awards including the Diversity Award of the American Psychology and Law Society (APLS), and herself has a first-author publication on jury decision making in *Psychiatry, Psychology and Law*. Natasha is now a graduate student in the Master's of Experimental Psychology program at Carleton University. Finally, my Ph.D. student Pamela Black has been an unstoppable force in the development of this new text. Pamela contributed significantly to the preparation of the "Criminal Profiling," "Criminal Responsibility and Competency to Stand Trial," "The Psychology of Child and Adult Sexual Assault Victims," and "Sex Offenders" chapters. Without Pamela's excellent and untiring assistance and feedback over the two years of writing, this new edition never could have happened. Pamela's career in forensic psychology is taking off, and she has a first-author paper on treating trauma in adolescents being published in *Canadian Psychology*. Thank you for your motivation, hard work, support, and constant good humour. You were, and continue to be, my "dream team."

Further appreciation is extended to my colleagues at the CAPSL—Drs. Michael Woodworth, Zachary Walsh, and Jan Cioe—for creating an inspirational work environment and being the best of colleagues and friends.

I'd also like to thank the following experts in the field who kindly reviewed and provided feedback on earlier drafts of various chapters in the book (among others who wish to remain anonymous):

- Jody Bain, University of Victoria
- Catherine Marion, Sheridan College, Davis Campus
- Deborah Matheson, Vancouver Island University
- Marc Patry, St. Mary's University
- Ravi Ramkissoonsingh, Niagara College
- Veronica Stinson, St. Mary's University
- Oliver Stoetzer, Fanshawe College

The suggestions of these reviewers were greatly appreciated and contributed greatly to the quality of the text. I also thank my production editor Susan Calvert, and proofreader Erin Moore. They were an inspirational team with which to work.

STEPHEN PORTER

Dr. Stephen Porter received his Ph.D. in forensic psychology at UBC and currently is a researcher and consultant in the area of psychology and law. After working as a prison psychologist, Dr. Porter spent a decade as a psychology professor at Dalhousie University where he initiated the first undergraduate forensic psychology specialization in Canada. In 2009, he transferred to the UBC campus in Kelowna where he assumed a position as a professor of psychology and the codirector of the Centre for the Advancement of Psychological Science & Law (CAPSL). Dr. Porter has published numerous scholarly articles on psychopathy and violent/predatory behaviour, deceptive communication and interviewing, and forensic aspects of memory, with funding from the Social Sciences and Humanities Research Council of Canada (SSHRC) and the Natural Sciences and Engineering Research Council of Canada (NSERC). As a registered forensic psychologist, Dr. Porter is consulted by Canadian courts and has been qualified as an expert witness in various areas, including "dangerousness and risk for violence" and "memory and the factors involved in credibility assessments." He has been consulted by police in serious crime investigations and provides training to law enforcement, mental health professional groups, government agencies, journalists, trial judges, and other adjudicators. Most recently, he has become part of the RCMP crisis negotiation team (e.g., hostage negotiations) in the Okanagan region.

Website: stephenporter.ca

LAWRENCE WRIGHTSMAN

Lawrence S. Wrightsman (Ph.D., University of Minnesota, 1959) was professor of psychology at the University of Kansas, Lawrence. Wrightsman authored or edited ten other books relevant to the legal system, including *Psychology and the Legal System* (4th edition, coauthored with Michael T. Nietzel and William H. Fortune), *The American Jury on Trial* (coauthored with Saul M. Kassin), and *Judicial Decision Making: Is Psychology Relevant?* He was invited to contribute the entry on the law and psychology for the recently published *Encyclopedia of Psychology,* sponsored by the American Psychological Association and published by Oxford University Press. His research topics included jury selection procedures, reactions to police interrogations, and the impact of judicial instructions. He also served as a trial consultant and testified as an expert witness. Wrightsman is a former president of both the Society for the Psychological Study of Social Issues and the Society of Personality and Social Psychology. In 1998 he was the recipient of a Distinguished Career Award from the American Psychology-Law Society. This award has been made on only six occasions in the 30-year history of the organization; the preceding awardee was U.S. Supreme Court Justice Harry Blackmun.

An Analysis of the Field of Forensic Psychology

> *The longstanding recognition that psychiatric or psychological testimony also falls within the realm of expert evidence is predicated on the realization that in some circumstances the average person may not have sufficient knowledge of or experience with human behaviour to draw an appropriate inference from the facts before him or her.*
>
> —Chief Justice of Canada Beverley McLachlin (*R. v. D. D.*, 2000)

WHAT IS FORENSIC PSYCHOLOGY?

The term *forensic psychology* has become increasingly salient in the first decades of the 21st century. For 20 years now, there has been increasing interest among undergraduate and graduate students in studying forensic psychology. The field itself has progressed and matured over the decades, with the development of interdisciplinary journals such as *Behavioral Sciences and the Law, Criminal Justice and Behavior,* the *International Journal of Forensic Mental Health, Legal and Criminological Psychology,* and *Law and Human Behavior.* Leading mainstream journals such as *Assessment, Psychological Assessment, Journal of Applied Psychology, Journal of Consulting and Clinical Psychology, Psychological Bulletin* and *Psychology, Public Policy, and Law* have been publishing more and more articles that we would refer to as forensic in nature (Heilbrun & Brooks, 2010). Further, The American Psychology–Law Society (AP-LS), the leading interdisciplinary scientific organization in North America, holds annual conferences and sometimes coordinates joint meetings with the European Association of Psychology and Law and the Australian and New Zealand Association of Psychiatry, Psychology, and Law.

But what is forensic psychology? As a beginning definition, this textbook proposes that forensic psychology is any research or practice at the intersection of psychological science and the legal system. Psychologists interested in this line of work may be found working in universities (studying things such as violent behaviour, psychopathy, risk assessment, legal decision making, eyewitness memory, deception detection, mental disorder and crime, and confessions), prisons, jails, police departments, law firms, government agencies, or in private practice,

to name just a few. They may work with lawyers, offenders, victims, and psychiatric clients in various capacities. As such, our working definition encompasses a broad definition. **Forensic psychology** is any scientific inquiry at the intersection of psychology and the legal system, or the application of such scientific knowledge in forensic contexts. Thus, it is both (1) the research endeavour that investigates aspects of human behaviour directly related to the legal process (e.g., jury decision making, deception detection, eyewitness testimony, investigative interviewing, or criminal behaviour), and (2) the professional practice or application of psychology within or in consultation with a legal system that includes both criminal and civil law and their numerous areas of intersection (Bartol & Bartol, 1999, 2011). Thus, forensic psychology encompasses activities as wide ranging as conducting research on any human behaviour within or relating to the criminal justice system, and applied activities such as conducting risk assessments, assessing competency to stand trial, criminal profiling, serving as an expert witness, and more. If you go on to specialize in forensic psychology, you will find yourself engaging in fascinating, meaningful work and it is likely that your services will be in high demand.

Consider the following five real-life examples:

- Leanne ten Brinke recently received her Ph.D. in experimental forensic psychology from the University of British Columbia (UBC). She is already an internationally renowned expert in behavioural analysis and deception, and has consulted with police investigators in serious crime cases. Her research has been published in various respected journals, including *Psychological Science* and *Law and Human Behavior.* She has found her passion in creating theories, designing experiments, and sharing new knowledge with other researchers and professional groups that can apply it to their work to make more effective decisions. Leanne hopes to continue her work in deception detection, first impressions, and human decision making in an academic setting, as an assistant professor.

- Dr. Robert Hare is professor emeritus at UBC and the world's leading expert in the psychopathic personality. He and his former students and colleagues conduct research on the issue of psychopathy and how this construct informs our understanding of criminal behaviour and decision making in legal settings. They also provide training internationally on the application of the Psychopathy Checklist—Revised (PCL—R) (Hare, 2003).

- Dr. Diane Sirkia is a forensic psychologist working full time as a psychologist in a medium-security prison in British Columbia. She works with a group of psychologists all of whom engage in a variety of activities, including writing risk assessments and providing crisis intervention and short-term counselling to inmates. Further, she has conducted research in the area of psychopathy and risk in collaboration with academic researchers.

- Dr. Barry Cooper was trained as a forensic psychologist. He has worked in various prisons for the Correctional Service of Canada, conducting assessments on violent offenders and serving as a member of the research committee and clinical supervisor for the Critical Incident Stress Management team. He currently works at the Forensic Psychiatric Hospital in Port Coquitlam, British Columbia, providing treatment, conducting assessments, and doing research with people who have been found unfit to stand trial or not criminally responsible for their actions. He is a clinical instructor in the Department of Psychiatry at the University of British Columbia and Director of Research and Development of the Forensic Alliance. He provided evidence at British Columbia Review Board hearings and testified in court for the prosecution and defence in relation to his research and clinical-forensic interests.

- Dr. Paul Ekman is the world's leading expert in emotional expressions and credibility assessment. Dr. Ekman is professor emeritus of psychology at the University of California, San Francisco, and has authored or edited 15 books, most recently *Emotions Revealed* in 2007, and

is co-author with the Dalai Lama on *Emotional Awareness: Overcoming the Obstacles to Psychological Balance and Compassion,* published in 2008. He has consulted with federal and local law enforcement, national security agencies, corporate sales departments, negotiators, health and education professionals, and animators at some of the largest animation studios in the world. The American Psychology Association identified him as one of the 100 most influential psychologists of the 20th century. *Time Magazine* selected him as one of the 100 most influential people of 2009, and he was the scientific adviser to the dramatic television series on Fox TV, *Lie to Me,* which was inspired by Dr. Ekman and his research. In addition, he is the president of the Paul Ekman Group (PEG), a small company based in San Francisco that is active in research, development, and production of online training tools and workshop training relevant to emotional skills, and evaluating truthfulness and credibility.

THE PROMISE AND PROBLEMS OF FORENSIC PSYCHOLOGY

These examples reflect the variety of activities that may fall under the label of "forensic psychology." They were chosen for several reasons. First, note that the training and past experiences of these professionals differ greatly, depending on their role. A forensic psychologist who does court-ordered risk assessments (such as Dr. Sirkia) comes from a background in clinical or applied forensic psychology. A forensic psychologist who works full time in a prison also may have been trained in clinical or forensic psychology, but with more concentration on psychopathology and the use of tests and other assessment devices to measure competency and credibility assessment/malingering (faking a serious mental disorder, often to avoid punishment). Other forensic psychologists, such as expert witnesses on child eyewitnesses, may have been trained as experimental psychologists or social psychologists. Some psychologists such as Dr. ten Brinke spend most of their time devising experiments to test scientific theories and generate findings of relevance in the legal system. A psychologist such as Dr. Ekman may spend years conducting basic research on human emotion and deception and then ultimately apply this work through training and consultation to various professional groups (e.g., police or airport security staff). Any of these forensic psychologists could be asked to testify as an expert witness in court. All of the key undergraduate and graduate university forensic programs in Canada rely heavily on the scientist-practitioner model, in which relevant scientific findings inform practice in the field. Subsequent chapters will detail the diverse activities of forensic psychologists, including detecting deception, criminal profiling, police selection, and evaluating criminal responsibility and competence, as well as those illustrated above. But even though their day-to-day activities may differ, forensic psychologists share common challenges and temptations, explored in Chapter 2.

Although our proposition that forensic psychology is *any* application of psychology to the legal system may sound straightforward, there are controversies within the field regarding who is a forensic psychologist and the nature of the training that would lead to such a designation (see Heilbrun & Brooks, 2010). The development of doctoral training programs with *forensic psychology* (such as the University of British Columbia and Carleton) or *psychology and law* (such as Simon Fraser University) in their title have undergone significant changes over the past few decades. Not all observers would agree that each of the five examples above reflects their definition of forensic psychology. Students, judges, and even the past president of the Canadian Psychological Association (CPA), James Ogloff, have observed the problems in trying to define this field. Ogloff (2004) noted that "While some attention has been paid to defining our field, variously known as 'forensic psychology,' 'psychology and law,' 'law and psychology,' and 'legal psychology,' there is still little agreement on appropriate definitions" (p. 84).

In examining the definitions of forensic psychology offered in the professional literature, one can separate them into broad and narrow types. The definition offered at the start of this chapter, of course, is a broad one; narrow definitions (as are often used in Great Britain, for example) limit the focus of forensic psychology to clinical and professional practice issues, such as assessing criminal responsibility (or insanity) or competency to stand trial, conducting child custody evaluations, and other activities that rely upon professional training as a clinical psychologist. This type of definition excludes scientific research, as well as many specific applied activities, including those in which

research psychologists engage, such as testifying as an expert witness on child witnesses or risk for violence (activities in which the first author has engaged as a "forensic psychologist" e.g., *Children's Aid Society of Halifax v. P. M. H.,* 2006: N.S. Supreme Court; *R. v. Miller,* 2005: Supreme Court of B.C., respectively). Psychologists trained in experimental, social, cognitive, or developmental psychology but who lack clinical training would not be eligible for this designation. Thus, it must be recognized that for many psychologists, forensic psychology solely is a specialization of clinical psychology (a position with which we disagree). As an illustration, forensic workshops offered at the annual conference of the Canadian Psychological Association (CPA) typically are focused on clinical psychology topics, such as risk assessment or treatment for offenders.

Therefore, much disagreement exists over how encompassing the definition should be. Right now, many psychologists are left in, to use John Brigham's (1999) term, a "definitional limbo." Consider Brigham's own situation: A social psychologist and a professor, he has no training in clinical psychology. He carries out research on eyewitnesses' memory and sometimes provides expert testimony in criminal trials. If asked in court, "Are you a forensic psychologist?" he has said:

My most accurate current response would seem to be, "Well, it depends. ..." And, in my experience, judges *hate* responses of that sort, which they see as unnecessarily vague or evasive. (Brigham, 1999, p. 280, italics in original)

As more and more graduate students seek training in forensic psychology, the lack of an agreed-upon definition increases the magnitude of the problem. One manifestation of the issue is to question whether the CPA should certify a "specialty" or proficiency in forensic psychology as the American Psychological Association (APA) has done. Although it is true that the purpose of a **specialty designation** is to evaluate specific graduate-school training programs and not to credential individuals, a concern exists that in the future such labels may be applied to individual psychologists. So should a training program that seeks a specialty designation as forensic psychology include only clinical training or should it be broader? Or should such a specialty designation even be sought?

Throughout the above discussion, the issue has been presented as an either-or question. That is, should training for forensic psychology be limited to clinical psychology or should it include more? Some forensic psychologists have suggested a richer, less adversarial, conception of what training in forensic psychology should be. Kirk Heilbrun (described in Brigham, 1999 and Heilbrun & Brooks, 2010) has offered a model, presented in Table 1.1, that reflects three training areas and two approaches.

Heilbrun's model is comprehensive, and the boundaries of forensic psychology used in this book are in keeping with his conceptualization. Note that among the training topics in his model are consultation in jury selection and in litigation strategy, policy and legislative consultation, and expert testimony on the state of the science, as well as traditional topics such as forensic assessment (all topics covered in various chapters throughout this textbook).

More recently, Heilbrun and Brooks (2010) proposed that forensic psychology should be incorporated into a more interdisciplinary field of *forensic science*. At UBC—Okanagan, there currently is a plan to develop such a program with collaboration between forensic biologists, chemists, anthropologists, and psychologists. With a common goal of improving criminal justice and solving crime through scientific research and analysis, it makes sense for these professionals to begin working together and educating students in a formal university program. Next, we explore the history and current state of forensic psychology science, training, and practice in Canada.

FORENSIC PSYCHOLOGY IN CANADA

In whatever manner we choose to define forensic psychology, many Canadians are recognized as international leaders in the field (Helmus, Babchishin Camilleri, & Olver, 2011). In the foreword of a 1997 text by Chris Webster and Margaret Jackson, John Monahan at the University of Virginia, a towering figure in the field, commented on "the remarkably strong international presence of Canada in forensic psychology and psychiatry, a presence out of proportion to relative population size, not to mention relative crime rate" (Monahan, 1997, pp. x–xi). Ogloff (2004), now based at Monash University in Australia, noted that:

There are prominent research groups or individuals at the University of Victoria, the University of British Columbia, Simon Fraser University, the University of Saskatchewan, the University of Regina, Queen's University, the University of Toronto, Ryerson University, University of Guelph, Université de Montréal, Dalhousie University, and the University of New Brunswick. ... In addition to prominence as researchers and clinicians, Canadians have distinguished themselves as editors of key journals in the field. (p. 84)

Once widely viewed as a subfield of psychology in which one might "end up working," forensic psychology now is one of the most highly respected areas of psychology. As one of the authors noted

Table 1.1   **Heilbrun's Conceptualization of Training in Forensic Psychology**

	LAW AND PSYCHOLOGY INTEREST AREAS (WITH ASSOCIATED TRAINING)		
	Clinical (clinical, counselling, school psychology)	**Experimental** (social, developmental, cognitive, human experimental psychology)	**Legal** (law, some training in behavioural science)
Research/ Scholarship	1. Assessment tools 2. Intervention effectiveness 3. Epidemiology of relevant behaviour (e.g., violence, sexual offending) and disorders	1. Memory 2. Perception 3. Child development 4. Group decision making	1. Mental health law 2. Other law relevant to health and science 3. Legal movements
Applied	1. Forensic assessment 2. Treatment in legal context 3. Integration of science into practice	1. Consultation re jury selection 2. Consultation re litigation strategy 3. Consultation re "state of science" 4. Expert testimony re "state of science"	1. Policy and legislative consultation 2. Model law development

From Brigham, John C. "What Is Forensic Psychology, Anyway?", *Law and Human Behavior*, 23, 1999, p. 283. Published by American Psychological Association. Reprinted by permission of Kirk Heilbrun.

in a special issue of the CPA journal *Canadian Journal of Behavioural Science* devoted to forensic psychology, much of the ground-breaking research in major areas of forensic psychology, including eyewitness testimony, risk assessment, deception detection, victimology, psychopathy, and criminal behaviour, was and is conducted in Canada (Porter, 2004). In addition, Canadian researchers are having a major impact in society. For example, both the National Judicial Institute (NJI) and the Correctional Service of Canada (CSC) rely heavily on training provided by psychologists for their staff. Researchers such as Rod Lindsay at Queen's University have been contracted by the NJI to educate the judiciary in several areas, including eyewitness testimony and assessing credibility. These types of applications in Canada provide an excellent example of bridging the gap between our basic science and applied practice in the field. On the other hand, there is not enough specialized training in forensic psychology offered in Canada, given our reputation and the great demand for our services. For example, whereas in 1995, Simourd and Wormith found that 24 universities in Canada (64 percent

of those surveyed) offered some training, by 2011 more than half of the departments had decreased their educational opportunities in forensic psychology (Helmus et al., 2011). Correctional psychology positions have been greatly understaffed for years (Olver et al., 2011). Thus, while the interest in and need for forensic psychology has been rising, training opportunities have been declining. There seems to be an assumption in Canadian psychology departments that training in standard clinical psychology programs is sufficient to prepare new psychologists to deal with the complexities of work in forensic contexts. We could not disagree more! At present, according to the survey by Helmus et al. (2011), there are four structured forensic psychology graduate programs in Canada: Carleton, Dalhousie, Québec à Trois-Rivières, and Simon Fraser. Also, some good news: since the survey was conducted, a new program was started at UBC—Okanagan, with three new forensic psychology faculty hires. The result was the creation of the Centre for the Advancement of Psychological Science and Law (CAPSL). The CAPSL is committed to devising specialized training—at both the

The CAPSL faculty members: Clockwise from left – Drs. Michael Woodworth, Stephen Porter, Jan Cioe, and Zachary Walsh

undergraduate and graduate levels—in forensic psychology (see Box 1.1 and http://capsl.ca).

THE CONFLICT BETWEEN PSYCHOLOGY AND THE LAW

Disagreement within the field of psychology regarding the limits of forensic psychology is not the only problem we face. When psychology seeks to apply its findings to the legal system, it faces the task of working with another discipline, that of the law. Lawyers—including judges, trial lawyers, and legal scholars—are trained to look at human behaviour in a way that is quite different from the perspective of psychologists. A goal of this chapter is to examine the nature of these conflicts between the law and psychology (and other social sciences). Only after that exploration may we move to a more extensive description of the various roles of forensic psychologists, in Chapter 2.

Laws and Values

Laws are human creations that evolve from the need to resolve disagreements. In that sense, laws reflect values, and values are basic psychological concepts. **Values** may be defined as standards for decision making, and thus laws are created, amended, or discarded because society has established standards for what is acceptable and unacceptable behaviour. Society's values can change,

leading to new laws and new interpretations of existing laws. For example, 100 years ago society looked the other way when a married man forced his wife to have sexual relations against her will, but has become increasingly aware of and concerned with spousal sexual assault, and now Canada and other countries have laws that prohibit such actions. Further, we have new laws relating to technology, such as online child pornography and other computer-related crimes.

Each discipline approaches the generation of knowledge and the standards for decision making in a different way. A lawyer and a social scientist will see the same event through different perspectives due to their specialized training. Judges may rely on procedures and concepts that are in stark contrast with those of psychology in forming their opinions. It is not that one approach is correct and that the other is wrong; rather, they have different goals.

Some lawyers consult with psychologists in evaluating and planning their case evidence, and Canadian courts now accept psychologists as expert witnesses on a variety of topics. But obstacles stand in the way of full application, and many of them are at the most basic level—the level of values and goals. Conflicts between the values of psychology and the values of the legal system serve as a focus for this chapter, because they play a role in evaluating the topics covered in subsequent chapters, especially in the degree to which psychology is successful in influencing the decisions of the legal system.

| BOX 1.1 | CENTRE FOR THE ADVANCEMENT OF PSYCHOLOGICAL SCIENCE AND LAW (CAPSL) AT THE UNIVERSITY OF BRITISH COLUMBIA |

The Centre for the Advancement of Psychological Science and Law (CAPSL) was established in 2009 to conduct research and provide training focused on issues at the intersection of psychology and the legal system. CAPSL consists of four core faculty members; Drs. Stephen Porter, Michael Woodworth, Zach Walsh, and Jan Cioe, as well as numerous research associates and graduate and undergraduate students. CAPSL research focuses on four key areas: (1) individual differences that predispose individuals to crime and antisociality, with a focus on personality and aggression; (2) investigative psychology, with a focus on

deceptive behaviour, credibility assessment, and memory; (3) legal decision making; and (4) the development and refinement of interventions to reduce recidivism among perpetrators of violence and assist with the recovery of crime victims. The CAPSL is outfitted with a range of high-tech research equipment, including sophisticated audio and video recording, an eye-tracker, physiological recording equipment, and face-reading software. Ultimately, the CAPSL's aims are to inform legal/investigative reforms, advance clinical practice, and improve training for forensic professionals.

There are many ways to distinguish these contrasting goals and values; John Carroll put it as follows:

The goals of the law and the goals of social science are different and partially in conflict. The law deals in morality, social values, social control, and justifying the application of abstract principles to specific cases. In day-to-day operation, the system values efficiency and expediency. ... In contrast, social science deals in knowledge, truth, and derives abstract principles from specific instances. These are thought to be value free. In operation, the scientific method values reproducible phenomena and underlying concepts and causes rather than the specifics or form in which these appear. (Carroll, 1980, p. 363)

The response of the CPA to "repressed" memories following several legal cases is an example of the expression of psychology's values. Since the 1980s, some allegations of crime have been based on memories "recovered" in psychotherapy or highly leading police interviews (see Porter, Peace, Douglas, & Doucette, 2011). For example, Donna Cole (pseudonym) recovered memories of being sexually abused by her father at the age of 18 months. Her outlandish claims included that her father placed both her and her brother in a roasting pan in the oven, dismembered and buried a female hitchhiker, and raped the family dog after mutilating the animal. Her testimony led directly to her father's conviction. Such cases led the CPA to produce a position paper (spearheaded by Dr. James Ogloff) questioning the accuracy of recovered memory evidence in legal cases, based on increasing empirical evidence for the existence of false memories. For example, in 1994 Canadian researchers Stephen Lindsay and Don Read published a widely cited paper that examined memories of childhood sexual abuse as "recovered" in therapy and concluded that many were likely to be mistaken. Moreover, in 1999, Canadian researchers established that false memories for potentially traumatic childhood events (such as serious accidents, medical procedures, etc.) could be implanted in adult subjects with suggestive interviewing (Porter, Yuille, & Lehman, 1999; Porter, Birt, Yuille, & Lehman, 2000). Ultimately, the CPA recommended to Anne McLellan, then the federal Minister of Justice, that a full judicial inquiry be conducted into all Canadian convictions stemming from such

evidence. McLellan rejected the recommendation and many people remain in prison as a result of such evidence. Perhaps her reaction to the CPA was not surprising given the politics involved. Nonetheless, the approach taken by the CPA was an **empirical** rather than a political or subjective one in attempting to apply psychological science in the legal system.

The Legal System's Reliance on Intuition over Empiricism

Psychologists are trained that the best way to answer a question about human behaviour is to collect relevant data. A conclusion about behaviour is not accepted until the observations are objectively measurable, they show **reliability** (they are consistent over time), and they possess **replicability** (different investigators can produce similar results). In contrast, judges and lawyers are more willing to rely on their own experience, their own views of life, and their intuition or "gut feelings" (ten Brinke & Porter, 2011). J. Alexander Tanford (1990), a professor of law, proposed that courts tend "to approve legal rules based on intuitive assumptions about human behaviour that research by psychologists has shown to be erroneous" (p. 138).

For example, judges long have believed that they have special insight into deciding a witness is lying or telling the truth based on "demeanour evidence" (Porter & ten Brinke, 2010). A strategy commonly relied upon by Canadian judges is to consider whether testimony has "the ring of truth" (see *R. v. Mervyn*, 2003; *R v. Roble*, 2004; *R. v. S. (R.D.)*, 1997). In *R. v. Lifchus* (1997), Justice Cory encouraged the use of intuition among jurors, noting:

... there may be something about a person's demeanour in the witness box which will lead a juror to conclude that the witness is not credible. It may be that the juror is unable to point to the precise aspect of the witness's demeanour which was found to be suspicious ... A juror should not be made to feel that the overall, perhaps intangible, effect of a witness's demeanour cannot be taken into consideration in the assessment of credibility (para. 29).

Despite this argument, no social scientific evidence substantiates that the use of intuition is valid in evaluating credibility. However, there is growing evidence shows that judges may not be well equipped to identify liars on the stand. Ekman and O'Sullivan (1991) found that judges and other groups performed at chance in judging the honesty of videotaped speakers. A major problem in evaluating the credibility of witnesses is a widespread reliance on cues to lying that lack validity. Porter, Birt, and Woodworth (2000) found that many faulty credibility judgments are based on misleading strategies, such as relying on a single dominant cue or one's "gut instinct." Whereas judges may associate lying with speech disturbances, longer pauses, gaze aversion (believing that a liar will not look you in the eye), body movements, and shifting positions, liars seem to show the opposite pattern (e.g., Vrij, 2008). There is evidence that Canadian judges may use the wrong approach to identify liars (from case transcripts). For example, in the Canadian case *R. v. Jabarianha* (2001), the judge stated: "Mr. Corkum and Mr. Jabarianha were less than believable. Each exhibited classic signs of discomfort when challenged. … Each was evasive at times or his eyes shifted around. Thus in certain points of the story each displayed signs of untruthfulness" (para. 29). Porter and ten Brinke (2009) reviewed survey evidence to suggest that Canadian judges rely on gaze aversion and nervous behaviour to make decisions about a witness's credibility. One might argue that it is our responsibility as students of forensic psychology to attempt to counteract the legal system's reliance on intuition over research evidence. As such, the NJI's approach of inviting researchers to lead some of its training sessions with Canadian judges is a step in the right direction.

Illustrations from the Courtroom

Two illustrations from the courtroom decisively reflect the conflict in values between the legal profession and scientific psychology. The first, a Canadian example, demonstrates the debate over whether psychologists should give expert testimony in the courtroom. In the other, an American example, the court's opinion was consistent with the position of the psychologist who testified as an expert witness, but the effect of the psychologist's testimony in influencing the outcome was unclear. These two examples reflect the difference of opinion both between disciplines and within each discipline.

© iStockphoto.com/spxChrome

How do judges and juries come to conclusions about guilt and innocence?

A Canadian Example

In Canada, there has been much debate over when expert testimony should be admitted as evidence, and what defines an "expert." Do psychologists possess knowledge that would qualify as expert evidence?

In the landmark 1994 case *R. v. Mohan*, detailed principles for assessing the admissibility of expert opinion were offered by the late Justice Sopinka. He established four criteria for admitting expert evidence: (1) relevance, (2) necessity, (3) absence of any exclusionary rule, and (4) qualification of the expert. Concerning relevance, the trial judge must assess the expert's relevance to the issue at hand, as well as the value of the expert's information versus the possible prejudicial (biasing) effect it may have on legal decision making. The court made it clear that the expert evidence must be more than simply "helpful." The higher standard requires that expert evidence be necessary and provide information "that is likely to be outside the experience and knowledge of a judge or jury" (summary para. 4), but not likely to distort the fact-finding process.

Does psychological testimony ever meet these criteria? Despite disagreement from some legal professionals, in *R. v. Lavallee* (1990) (a domestic violence case), it was determined that expert testimony by both psychiatrists and psychologists "falls within the realm of expert evidence." The next question concerns what types of expert psychological testimony are acceptable to courts in Canada.

The Canadian law makes it clear that expert evidence must go beyond "common sense" and can never replace (or "usurp") the function of judges and juries (neither of whom are compelled to accept an expert's opinion). However, it is clear that the application of this principle can be problematic. For example, courts somewhat arbitrarily have decided that certain types of psychological evidence are "common sense" and others are not. Supreme Court of Canada judgments have decided in favour of expert evidence concerning the behaviours of sexually abused persons (*R. v. Burns*, 1994), and the behaviour of battered women (*R. v. Lavallee*, 1990). In *Lavallee*, expert evidence on the psychological effects of domestic assault was viewed as both relevant and necessary because of the average person's negative reaction to a spouse who stays in an abusive relationship and because of the need to dispel inaccurate assumptions.

On the other hand, Canadian courts have resisted allowing expert testimony on eyewitness testimony or other aspects of witness credibility, with the apparent assumption that the evaluation of problem of testimony is a matter of "common sense." The problem of relying on the common sense of the trier of fact in judicial decision making was demonstrated by University of Guelph researcher Dan Yarmey (1986) in his test of the standards outlined by the courts for the assessment of eyewitness accuracy. Despite some of the court's common sense notions for determining the accuracy of a given witness, he found that the accuracy of the witness's prior description of the accused and the witness's level of confidence at the time of the incident were not good predictors of accuracy. Many of the difficulties that arise during eyewitness testimony contradict the common sense beliefs held by judges and laypersons about eyewitness memory (Yarmey, 2001).

The complexities here are clearly highlighted in the type of abuse cases mentioned above in which someone reports that he or she "recovered" a memory for a crime after repressing it for decades. To date, Canadian courts have no consistent approach to deciding whether such evidence is valid or determining the value of relevant expert evidence. In the case of *R. v. Francois* (1994), Francois was convicted of repeatedly raping a 13-year-old girl. The only evidence at trial was the complainant's testimony that she had "blocked out" the sexual assaults until her memory returned in a flashback years later. When Francois appealed his conviction to the Supreme Court of Ontario, it was upheld. The judge rationalized that:

It was ... for the jury to determine, on the basis of *common sense* and *experience* [italics added], whether they believed the complainant's story of repressed and recovered memory, and whether the recollection she experienced in 1990 was the truth. The jury's acceptance of the complainant's evidence concerning what happened to her cannot, on the basis of the record, be characterized as unreasonable. In sum, the verdict was not illogical or speculative or inconsistent with the main body of evidence. (summary para. 4)

On appeal, Francois' conviction was set aside.

Although the judge's comments convey a belief that jurors can readily determine the credibility of recovered memory evidence based on common sense, in reality the jury had been asked to act as experts on a very complex psychological issue. Most psychologists would agree that the judge contradicted the principle asserted in *R. v. Mohan* (1994) that psychological testimony can and should be admitted as evidence in situations where the issue at hand is beyond the experience and knowledge of judges and juries.

Another example in the Canadian context involves expert testimony relating to false confessions. A group of psychologists based at St. Mary's University in Halifax recently reviewed the Canadian courts' response to such expert testimony (Smith, Stinson, & Patry, 2010). They noted that judges in Canada have been reluctant to allow expert testimony on confession issues. In two cases in which expert testimony on false confessions was offered by the defence (i.e. , *R. v. Osmar*, 2007 and *R. v. Bonisteel*, 2008), the judge excluded it because it was deemed to be unnecessary to assist the jury, again seemingly based on the assumption that jurors can use their common sense to evaluate confessions.

In the case of *R. v. Osmar* (2007), two men were murdered approximately one month apart in Thunder Bay, Ontario. In the early morning hours of January 16, 1998, Raymond Greenwood was killed in his hotel room. At the time, the accused, Timothy Osmar, was working as a taxi driver. The Crown's theory was that at some point Osmar went to the hotel, entered Greenwood's room, and repeatedly stabbed him to death, presumably as part of a robbery. On February 25, 1998, Theodore Keeper was murdered in a manner similar to Mr. Greenwood. While there was no evidence to connect Keeper to this killing, the police believed that both killings were committed by the same person, and focused their investigation on Osmar. After the investigation led to no incriminating evidence after several months, the police began an intensive "Mr. Big" operation (see Smith et al., 2009 and an in-depth exploration of Mr. Big cases in Chapter 7), that eventually led to a confession by Osmar to people whom he believed were part of a serious crime syndicate. The defence argued that Osmar had falsely confessed as a result of this police operation. They called Dr. Richard Ofshe, a social psychologist and a leading expert on the phenomenon of false confessions, as an expert to testify about the reasons that suspects falsely confess and the proper method of evaluating the reliability of a confession. On a "voir dire", Ofshe explained that (1) "where the reasons not to confess are sufficiently reduced by making the suspect believe that resistance is hopeless and that some advantage may come from confession, both the likelihood of confession and the risk of false confession will rise"; (2) "that, while the phenomenon of false confessions is very well known to social psychologists, most people presume that innocent people will not confess falsely"; and (3) "the way to evaluate the reliability of the confession is to compare the details in the confession with the facts of the murder not given to the suspect by the police." The trial judge held that Ofshe's evidence was not admissible as it did not meet the test for admission of expert evidence and that his evidence was neither relevant nor necessary to assist with jurors' decision making. Yet there is a great deal of scientific evidence to suggest that laypersons (e.g., jurors) do not have a "natural" understanding of either the plausibility of or the factors that can lead to false confessions (e.g., Kassin, 2008) and that Dr. Ofshe's three main points were valid from a scientific point of view.

What are we to make of this conflict between the perspectives of psychological science and the judiciary? First, we need to note that the goals of researchers and judges are different. Psychologists derive the truth from empirical evidence. For example, as the CPA asserted to Anne McLellan, it has been shown in numerous studies that many recovered memories are actually false memories (e.g., Frenda, Nichols, & Loftus, 2011; Porter et al., 2011), and that their assessment goes beyond the knowledge of most laypersons. Judges, on the other hand, wish to establish the truth through an evaluation of the evidence in a particular case and with certain assumptions about human decision making based on their own observations.

Both positions can be defended. As psychologists, we have been trained to believe that empirical results define the truth, and that data have power. In contrast, judges believe that each case is unique, that laypersons can figure out the truth via their common sense, and that accumulated data may not be relevant in a single case.

An American Civil Case: *Price Waterhouse v. Hopkins* (1989)

The previous discussion concerned court decisions regarding whether psychological testimony was relevant to specific types of cases and the extent to which it should be admitted. But what about the impact of such testimony once it does enter the courtroom? In the American case *Price Waterhouse v. Hopkins* (1989), the U.S. Supreme Court acknowledged the presence of sex discrimination in a civil suit after reviewing the testimony of a psychologist about the nature of stereotyping. But how much difference did the testimony of the psychologist make?

Ann Hopkins was in her fourth year as a very successful salesperson at Price Waterhouse, a leading accounting firm. She had brought in business worth US$25 million, her clients raved about her, and she had more billable hours than any other person proposed for partner that year (Fiske, Bersoff, Borgida, Deaux, & Heilman, 1991). But she was not made a partner—not that year and not the next year. Price Waterhouse apparently rejected her because of her heavy-handed managerial style and her "interpersonal skills problems." She was described as "macho," lacking "social grace," and needing "a course at charm school." A colleague didn't like her use of profanity. Another reportedly advised her that she would improve her chances if she would "walk more femininely, talk more femininely, dress more femininely, wear make-up, have her hair styled, and wear jewellery" (p. 1117). She was caught in a double bind; women were censured for being aggressive even though aggressiveness was, in reality, one of the job qualifications (Chamallas, 1990).

Hopkins took the firm to court, claiming sex discrimination. The above information, although disturbing, was not enough; she had to demonstrate that the stereotypic remarks, quoted above, were evidence of discrimination in the decision to reject her as a partner. Thus, social psychologist Susan Fiske was asked to testify as an expert witness. She agreed, because she felt the case fit with the scientific literature on sex stereotyping in organizations to a striking degree.

An account by Fiske and her colleagues describes the nature of her testimony in the case:

[The testimony] drew on both laboratory and field research to describe antecedent conditions that encourage stereotyping, indicators that reveal stereotyping, consequences of stereotyping for out-groups, and feasible remedies to prevent the intrusion of stereotyping into decision making. Specifically, she testified first that stereotyping is most likely to intrude when the target is an isolated, one- or few-of-a-kind individual in an otherwise homogeneous environment. The person's solo or near-solo status makes the unusual category more likely to be a salient factor in decision making. (Fiske et al., 1991, p. 1050)

Of 88 candidates proposed for partner status in 1982, Hopkins was the only woman; of 662 partners at Price Waterhouse, only seven were women.

Among many relevant matters, Professor Fiske also testified that subjective judgments of interpersonal skills—apparently essential in the partnership decision—are quite vulnerable to stereotypic biases, and decision makers should be alert to the possibility of stereotyping when they employ subjective criteria. She concluded that sexual stereotyping played a major role in the firm's decision to deny Hopkins a partnership.

In the Price Waterhouse decisions on partners, the opinions of persons with limited hearsay information were given the same weight as the opinions of those who had more extensive and relevant contact with Hopkins (Fiske et al., 1991, 1993), and Price Waterhouse had no policy prohibiting sex discrimination. As Fiske and her colleagues observed, "consistent with this failure to establish organizational norms emphasizing fairness, overt expressions of prejudice were not discouraged" (Fiske et al., 1991, p. 1051). in her testimony, Professor Fiske noted that many of Price Waterhouse's practices could be remedied if the firm applied psychological concepts and findings.

At the original trial, the judge expressed some frustration over the psychologist's testimony. He seemed to have difficulty understanding what the psychologist was saying, and "at times he undermined her position by changing the meaning of her statements and then challenging her to explain

herself more clearly" (Chamallas, 1990, p. 110). But after considering all the evidence, the judge ruled in favour of Hopkins claim, writing that an "employer that treats [a] woman with [an] assertive personality in a different manner than if she had been a man is guilty of sex discrimination" (p. 1119). Not surprisingly, Price Waterhouse appealed the decision and, in doing so, argued that the social psychologist's testimony was "sheer speculation" of "no evidentiary value" (p. 467). After the decision was upheld, Price Waterhouse asked the U.S. Supreme Court to review the case, and because various appellate court decisions in *Hopkins* and other similar cases had been in conflict, the Court accepted the case for review. In 1989, the U.S. Supreme Court handed down its decision to uphold a significant portion of the decision.

Thus, it would appear that the testimony of a research psychologist had a significant impact on the judge's decision in a landmark case. But some of the justices were hostile to Professor Fiske's message; in his dissenting opinion, Justice Anthony Kennedy questioned her ability to be fair, implying that Fiske would have reached the same conclusion *whenever* a woman was denied a promotion. Even the majority opinion by Justice William Brennan downplayed the impact of the expert witness's testimony; the majority opinion stated:

Indeed, we are tempted to say that Dr. Fiske's expert testimony was merely icing on Hopkins' cake. It takes no special training to discern sex stereotyping in a description of an aggressive female employee as requiring "a course at charm school." Nor ... does it require expertise in psychology to know that, if an employee's flawed "interpersonal skills" can be corrected by a soft-hued suit or a new shade of lipstick, perhaps it is the employee's sex and not her interpersonal skills that has drawn criticism. (p. 1793)

Fiske and her colleagues had the following reaction to this comment:

One can interpret this comment in various ways; as dismissive, saying that the social science testimony was all common sense; as merely taking the social psychological expertise for granted; or as suggesting that one does not necessarily require expert witnesses to identify stereotyping when the evidence is egregious. (Fiske et al., 1991, p. 1054)

© iStockphoto.com/arfo

Do people "choose" to commit crimes or is crime strictly a product of the offender's background and brain functioning?

While any of these is a possibility, none is congruent with a claim that the social science evidence really made a difference in the U.S. Supreme Court's opinion.

Further, not all psychologists have endorsed the application of Fiske's conclusions (Barrett & Morris, 1993). Not only do judges disagree with one another, but also there is less than unanimity among psychologists. In fact, the lack of agreement within the field creates problems for the establishment of agreed-upon procedures for forensic psychologists. For example, is there sufficient scientific evidence to justify a psychologist's testifying that a murder defendant's behaviour reflected battered-woman syndrome?

THE HISTORY OF THE RELATIONSHIP BETWEEN PSYCHOLOGY AND THE LAW

We have seen the diversity of activities by contemporary forensic psychologists and have begun to identify the complex interaction between modern-day psychology and the law. How did we get where we are today? What was the relationship of the two fields when they began to interrelate? How have matters changed?

The division between contemporary psychologists who conduct research (mostly in laboratories) in search of scientific observations and those who work assessing and/or "treating" individuals can be traced back to the beginnings of the 20th century, and the distinction is certainly relevant to the origin of forensic psychology. On the one hand, the courts have faced the challenge of dealing with

people, who, because of mental disturbance or a criminal tendency, do not conform their behaviour to legal requirements. On the other hand, psychologists in laboratories have studied various phenomena and psychological conditions that may be relevant to understanding criminal behaviour. In the modern context, courts must grapple with the appropriate punishment for people who have committed murder by their own free will or choice. Often this decision is facilitated by practising clinical psychologists and psychiatrists who give their opinion about the relation between mental disorder and the crime. Recently, research psychologists and neuroscientists have been entering the courtroom arguing that certain murderers—particularly psychopaths—have brain anomalies (especially relating to the prefrontal cortex and amygdala) that reduce their culpability or ability to control their behaviour (e.g., Gazzaniga, 2011). These are two very different types of forensic psychologists offering very different testimony but with a common goal of determining criminal responsibility.

Origins of the first approach can be traced to Cesare Lombroso (1836–1909), an Italian considered to be the father of modern criminology, because he sought to understand the causes of crime. The development of separate juvenile courts in the United States—first in Illinois in 1899—led William Healy, a physician, to initiate a program of study of the causes of juvenile delinquency. In doing so, he sought the advice of prominent academic psychologists such as Edward G. Thorndike, William James, and James R. Angell. Healy's founding of the Juvenile Psychopathic Institute in 1909, with a staff that included psychologist Dr. Grace M. Fernald, led to increased emphasis on the foundations of criminal behaviour. Dr. Fernald was one of the first psychologists to specialize in the diagnosis and treatment of juvenile delinquency (Bartol & Bartol, 2011).

Also, during the late 1800s and early 1900s Sigmund Freud was developing his theory of personality, and his writings about psychopathology influenced thinking about the causes of criminal behaviour. In a speech in 1906 to a group of judges, Freud proposed that psychology could be of practical use to their field (Horowitz & Willging, 1984).

The Role of Hugo Munsterberg

The other thread can be traced to academic psychology. Consider the following quotation from a prominent psychology-and-law researcher regarding his building facilities: "… visiting friends [would find], with surprise, twenty-seven rooms overspun with electric wires and filled with (equipment), and a mechanic busy at work" (Munsterberg, 1908, p. 3). Five pages later, this psychologist wrote, "Experimental psychology has reached a stage at which it seems natural and sound to give attention to its possible service for the practical needs of life" (p. 8).

Those statements are from *On the Witness Stand* (1908), written by Hugo Munsterberg almost a century ago. After receiving a Ph.D. from Leipzig University and studying with world-renowned Professor of Psychology Wilhem Wundt, Munsterberg came from Germany to the United States in September 1892 to establish—at William James's invitation—the psychological laboratory at Harvard University. Three months later, at the APA's first annual meeting, a dozen papers were presented, of which Munsterberg's was the last. In it, he criticized his colleagues' work as "rich in decimals but poor in ideas" (Cattell, 1894).

Despite the fact that interests in psycho-legal issues captured only a small portion of his professional time, Munsterberg's impact on the field was so great that it is appropriate to call him the founder of forensic psychology. His choices of what to study are still somewhat reflected in current research activities of psychologists interested in the legal system. For example, the chapter topics of Munsterberg's 1908 book—memory distortions, eyewitness accuracy, confessions, suggestibility, hypnosis, crime detection, and the prevention of crime—in varying degrees define what some psychologists think of as topics for contemporary forensic psychology.

Munsterberg was by no means the sole instigator of a movement. In some ways, he was a less-than-ideal symbol; he was arrogant and pugnacious and he often engaged in self-important posturing. Even William James later described him as "vain and loquacious" (Lukas, 1997, p. 586). More importantly, there were other pioneers, too. Even before Munsterberg's book, Hermann Ebbinghaus (1885), using himself as a subject, had demonstrated the rapid rate of early memory loss. In France, as early as 1900 Alfred Binet was seeking to understand children's competence as eyewitnesses (Yarmey, 1984). In Germany, Louis William Stern began publishing eyewitness research as early as 1902; during the next year he was admitted to German courts of law to testify as an expert witness on eyewitness identification. Stern (1903) established

a periodical dealing with the psychology of testimony. Although it is true that much of the early work published there was classificatory (e.g., six types of questions that might be asked of an eyewitness), other contributions were empirical; for example, he compared the memory abilities of children and adults. Wells and Loftus (1984) observed: "Not surprisingly, the early empirical work was not of the quality and precision that exists in psychology today" (p. 5). Yet the foundation was set.

In a series of *Psychological Bulletin* articles, Guy Montrose Whipple (1909, 1910, 1911, 1912) brought the *Aussage* (or eyewitness testimony) tradition into English terminology, introducing American audiences to classic experiments relating testimony and evidence to perception and memory. Even prior to World War I, "law was acknowledged as a fit concern for psychology and vice versa" (Tapp, 1976, pp. 360–361).

But Munsterberg was the psychologist who pushed his reluctant American colleagues into the practical legal arena (Bartol & Bartol, 2011), and thus he had the greatest impact—for good or bad. Some of the topics that first received illumination by Munsterberg and his contemporaries continue to remain in the limelight. Especially with regard to the accuracy of eyewitness identification, the immense interest in recent times can be directly traced back to Munsterberg's work.

Munsterberg's Goals for Psychology and the Law

Munsterberg's mission has been described as raising the position of the psychological profession to one of importance in public life (Kargon, 1986), and the legal system was one vehicle for doing so. Loftus (1979) commented: "At the beginning of the century, Munsterberg was arguing for more interaction between the two fields, perhaps at times in a way that was insulting to the legal profession" (p. 194). "Insulting" is a strong description but it is true that Munsterberg wrote things like this: "It seems astonishing that the work of justice is carried out in the courts without ever consulting the psychologist and asking him for all the aid which the modern study of suggestion can offer" (1908, p. 194). At the beginning of the 20th century, chemists and physicists were routinely called as expert witnesses (Kargon, 1986). Why not psychologists? Munsterberg saw no difference between the physical sciences and his own.

Munsterberg's Values

A description of Munsterberg's specific views toward the court system will help us understand the actions he took. More importantly, an examination of his views will cause us to ask: How different are our values and beliefs from his?

The jury system rests on a positive assumption about human nature, that a collection of reasonable people are able to judge the world about them reasonably accurately. So, one of the pillars of society is a legal system that makes fair and accurate decisions concerning guilt and innocence. As Kalven and Zeisel (1966) put it, the justice system:

> recruits a group of twelve lay [people], chosen at random from the widest population; it convenes them for the purpose of a particular trial; it entrusts them with great official powers of decision; it permits them to carry out deliberations in secret and report out their final judgment without giving reasons for it; and, after their momentary service to the state has been completed, it orders them to disband and return to private life. (p. 3)

Despite the centuries-old assumption that our courts live up to this expectation, there are good reasons to question its validity, as outlined recently by Porter and ten Brinke (2010):

1. It is not possible to empirically evaluate the accuracy of trial outcomes.
2. The courts, like science, do not hold the expectation of infallibility in their decisions. However, whereas psychological science has long relied on an acceptable error rate of 5 percent, the courts maintain the mysterious "beyond a reasonable doubt" criterion. The imprecision of this definition acknowledges that doubt is permissible, but only to the extent that it would be unreasonable to conclude otherwise. The definition also recognizes that errors will occur in "some" proportion of cases.
3. In numerous contexts, human decision making is highly irrational (e.g., Kahneman & Tversky, 1982). Thus, to maintain the assumption that legal decision making is generally sound, one must accept that its accuracy is not testable, that the reasonable-doubt standard ensures that only few errors occur, and that judges and jurors have the knowledge and ability to overcome normal biases to make rational decisions.

As his biographer, Matthew Hale, Jr., saw it, Munsterberg predicted our view a century earlier and took a very different view of society from the justice system: "The central premise of his legal psychology ... was that the individual could not accurately judge the real world that existed outside him, or for that matter the nature and processes of his own mind" (Hale, 1980, p. 121). Thus police investigations and courtroom procedures required the assistance of a psychologist (who, in Munsterberg's view, could be more objective than other persons).

Three Types of Activities

Munsterberg reflected his desire to bring psychology into the courtroom by carrying out three tasks:

1. Demonstrating the fallibility of memory, including time overestimation, omission of significant information, and other errors.
2. Publishing *On the Witness Stand*, a compilation of highly successful magazine articles. As a result of these articles, he was, after William James, North America's best-known psychologist (e.g., Lukas, 1997). His goal in these *McClure's Magazine* pieces was to show an audience of laypersons that "experimental psychology has reached a stage at which it seems natural and sound to give attention also to its possible service for the practical needs of life" (1908, p. 8).
3. Offering his testimony as expert witness in highly publicized trials. Perhaps most controversial was his intrusion in the Idaho trial, in 1907, of the labour leader "Big Bill" Haywood (Hale, 1980; Holbrook, 1957). The IWW (Industrial Workers of the World) leader was charged with conspiracy to murder Frank Steunenberg, a former governor of Idaho and a well-known opponent to organized labour. On December 30, 1905, in Caldwell, Idaho, Steunenberg had opened the gate to his modest home and was blown apart by a waiting bomb. The murder trial transformed Haywood into an international symbol of labour protest; Clarence Darrow offered his services as defence lawyer, and people such as Eugene V. Debs and Maksim Gorky rallied support (Hale, 1980).

The case against Haywood rested on the testimony of the mysterious Harry Orchard, a one-time IWW organizer who—after a four-day interrogation—confessed to committing the bombing (as well as many other crimes) at the behest of an "inner circle" of radicals, including Haywood. Munsterberg firmly believed that one of psychology's strongest contributions was in distinguishing false memories from true ones. Thus, he examined Orchard in his cell, during the trial, and conducted numerous tests on him over a period of seven hours, including some precursors of the polygraph. In Munsterberg's mind, the most important of these was the word association test. Upon returning to Cambridge, Munsterberg permitted an interview with the Boston *Herald* (July 3, 1907), which quoted him as saying, "Orchard's confession is, every word of it, true" (Lukas, 1997, p. 599). This disclosure, coming before a verdict had been delivered, threatened the impartiality of the trial, and Munsterberg was rebuked by newspapers nationwide. Still, the jury found Haywood not guilty, as the state did not produce any significant evidence corroborating Orchard's confession, as Idaho law required. Two weeks later, Munsterberg amended his position by introducing the concept of "subjective truthfulness." His free association tests, he now concluded, revealed that Orchard genuinely believed he was telling the truth, but they couldn't discern the actual facts of the matter.

Despite the adverse publicity, Munsterberg maintained his inflated claims for his science. In a letter to the editor he wrote: "To deny that the experimental psychologist has indeed possibilities of determining the 'truth-telling' process is just as absurd as to deny that the chemical expert can find out whether there is arsenic in a stomach or whether blood spots are of human or of animal origin" (quoted by Hale, 1980, p. 118). His claims were couched in exaggerated metaphors; he could "pierce the mind" and bring to light its deepest secrets.

In fairness, it should be noted that Munsterberg did not limit his advocacy to one side in criminal trials. In one case he felt the defendant's confession was the result of a hypnotic induction and hence false, so Munsterberg offered to testify for the defence. In the Idaho case his conclusions (which, if not derived from his political ideologies, were certainly in keeping with his antipathy to anarchy and union protest) supported the prosecution.

Munsterberg, like most true believers committed to their innovative theories, may have exaggerated claims in order to get attention and convince himself of their merits. His biographer, Matthew Hale (1980), has made a strong case that Munsterberg "deceived himself with alarming frequency, and his distortions in certain cases bordered on outright falsification" (p. 119).

Reaction of the Legal Community

Not surprisingly, Munsterberg's advocacy generated a negative reaction from the legal community. One attack, titled "Yellow Psychology" and written by Charles Moore, concluded that the laboratory had little to lend to the courtroom and expressed skepticism that Munsterberg had discovered a "Northwest Passage to the truth" (quoted in Hale, 1980, p. 115).

The article by John Henry Wigmore (1909), a law professor and a leading expert on evidence (cast in the form of a trial against Munsterberg during which lawyers cross-examined him for damaging assertions), was in the words of Wallace Loh, "mercilessly satiric" (1981, p. 316); it suggested that experimental psychology, at the time, lacked enough knowledge to be practical (Davis, 1989). Further, Wigmore argued that the jury system distrusted those outside interferences, such as Munsterberg's, that intruded upon their common sense judgments. But Wigmore made a telling point in this article. As Loftus (1979) reminded us, in Wigmore's courtroom drama, "Before the jurors left the courtroom to go home, the judge took a few moments to express his personal view. He said essentially this: In no other country in the civilized world had the legal profession taken so little interest in finding out what psychology and other sciences had to offer that might contribute to the nation's judicial system" (p. 203).

A Period of Inactivity

Perhaps for these reasons—exaggeration by Munsterberg and avoidance by legal authorities—research by scientific psychology applicable to the courts languished from the First World War until the latter half of the 1970s. There were contributions in the 1930s, 1940s, 1950s, and 1960s, but they were infrequent. Historical treatments of the development of the field (e.g., Bartol & Bartol, 2011; Davis, 1989; Foley, 1993; Kolasa, 1972; Yuille,

Daylen, Porter, & Marxsen, 1996) note that a few works examined the legal system from the psychological perspective; those included books such as Burtt's *Legal Psychology* in 1931 and Robinson's *Law and the Lawyers* in 1935 and some speculative reviews in law journals (Hutchins & Slesinger, 1928a, 1928b, 1928c; Louisell, 1955, 1957). But until the 1960s, more work on the legal field was done by anthropologists, sociologists, and psychiatrists (Tapp, 1977).

The relationship between eyewitness confidence and accuracy is an example of the gap in research activity. Munsterberg conducted perhaps the first empirical test of this relationship (Wells & Murray, 1984). He had children examine pictures for 15 seconds and then write a report of everything they could remember. Subsequently they were required to underline those parts of their report of which they were absolutely certain. Munsterberg reported that there were almost as many mistakes in the underlined sentences as in the rest. Other studies in the first years of the 20th century, by Stern and by Borst, were reported by Whipple (1909). Paradoxically, no further empirical interest surfaced until almost 65 years later (Wells & Murray, 1984).

Resurgence in the 1970s

Resurgence in forensic interest by experimental psychologists and social psychologists did not occur until the 1970s. Two Canadian researchers who began to tackle the accuracy of eyewitness identification at this time were John Yuille at the University of British Columbia (e.g., Yuille, 1980) and Dan Yarmey at the University of Guelph. In 1979, Yarmey published one of the first important modern texts on eyewitnesses, *The Psychology of Eyewitness Testimony*, which inspired numerous other researchers to start their own work in the area. Yarmey completed his book while on sabbatical at the University of Tennessee and then the University of Toronto. Early in his sabbatical, he was contacted by a lawyer from Michigan who had read his articles on facial recognition and wanted advice in a case. Yarmey decided to visit the law library to see what lawyers knew about eyewitness identification and concluded that they knew very little. He then decided to write his book, which went on to have a great impact in forensic psychology.

Why the rise of forensic psychology in the 1970s? A renewed emphasis on the necessity to make observations in natural contexts in order to understand social behaviour and memory was one reason, according to Wells and Loftus (1984). More generally, social psychology in the 1970s responded to a crisis about its relevance by extending its concepts to real-world topics, including health and the law (Davis, 1989). Nagel (1983) went so far as to claim: "The contemporary law and psychology movement has been the direct outgrowth of social psychologists' self-reflection on the failure of their discipline to advance social policy: it was an explicit rejection of the academically effete nature of much social psychological curiosity and an attempt to become more 'action-oriented'" (1983, p. 17). James H. Davis (1989) took a different approach:

It is tempting to draw a general parallel between the temporal sequence of the past: Munsterberg's proposals; reaction and critique of other scholars, disenchantment among social psychologists; and finally, abandonment of efforts at application of psychology to law. But something different happened "the next time around." The general disenchantment that was characteristic of the latter "crisis" period was not followed by an "abandonment phase." Rather, we have seen a continuous evolution and strengthening of some new developments during the succeeding years—a period in which *applied research in social psychology came to be recognized in its own right.* (1989, p. 201, italics in original)

The Present

Where do we stand now? Psychologists do research on a number of topics relevant to the real world of the legal system. Beyond the extensive work on jury decision making, psychologists have studied diverse phenomena such as sentencing decisions, deception detection, children's abilities as eyewitnesses, risk assessment, psychopathy, false confessions, and the impact of expert testimony.

At the same time, judges, trial lawyers, police, and other representatives of the legal system are making real-world decisions—about the competency of a defendant, which jurors to dismiss, and how to interrogate a suspect. Applied psychologists sometimes have an influence on such decisions as well as the thousands of others made daily in the legal system.

An argument in this book is that it is time for psychologists to move beyond their laboratories and seriously ask how their perspective can improve the decisions made in law offices and courtrooms. In doing so, we need to face the obstacles discussed earlier in this chapter. Each profession and each discipline has its own way of doing things, its own way of seeing the world and defining the experiences in it. Police operate out of shared assumptions about the nature of the world; the experience of going through law school socializes lawyers to emphasize certain qualities; judges learn certain values and emphasize them in their decisions. Forensic psychologists must recognize these values (as well as their own) as they attempt to have an impact.

THE PERSPECTIVES OF PSYCHOLOGY AND THE LAW

If forensic psychology can succeed in the legal system in any systematic way, it must first confront the conflicts between the goals and values of the legal profession and those of psychology. The following paragraphs examine some of these conflicts in depth (see also Box 1.2).

What Determines Truth?

The most fundamental conflict between psychology and law arises from the attempt to define what is true—in itself perhaps the most elusive and challenging quest. Suppose we ask a psychologist, a police officer, a trial lawyer, and a judge the same question: How do you know that something is true? Each might say, "Look at the evidence," but for each the evidence is defined differently. As noted earlier, psychologists base their answers on empirical observations. They are trained that speculation and armchair reasoning are not enough; such approaches may convince others but not the research psychologist. Even psychological theories, influential as they may be in directing the choice of research topics and procedures, are not accepted until they are validated by replicated research findings. "Being empirical" is the *sine qua non* of scientific psychology.

For the police officer, personal observation is a strong determinant of the truth. Police take pride in their ability to detect deception and their interrogative skills as ways of separating truth telling from falsification. Gisli Gudjonsson (1992), a psychologist and a former police officer, noted that many police interrogators have blind faith in the use of nonverbal signs of deception. (A considerable amount of research has since shown that police officers essentially flip a coin in trying to decide if a suspect is telling the truth; e.g., Vrij, Granhag, & Porter, 2011). Certainly they also rely on physical measures; speeding is determined by the reading on the radar gun; alcohol level by the blood-alcohol test. However, crime investigation may reflect either inductive or deductive

---

methods of reasoning; see examples of this distinction, developed by Frey (1994), in Box 1.3.

As the police example above suggests, a belief in the validity of intuition is a part of a police officer's evidence evaluation. Hays (1992), a 20-year veteran of the Los Angeles Police Department, wrote: "Most cops develop an instinct for distinguishing the legitimate child abuse complaints from the phony ones" (p. 30). Police are willing to use a broader number of methods to determine truth than are psychologists. For example, a substantial number of police departments are willing to use psychics to help them solve crimes, whereas most psychologists would be appalled if someone argued that psychics could offer any valid avenues toward knowledge.

In a 1994 murder case in British Columbia, eight-year-old Mindy Tran was abducted while riding her bicycle outside her Kelowna home. She was found by 68-year-old Rex Fitzgerald of Nova Scotia. Fitzgerald, who had been contacted by the RCMP (because of his experience in similar cases), was able to solve a mystery that had confounded more than 400 searchers. He quickly was able to find Mindy's remains in a shallow grave with the use of a "divining rod" (usually used to find water)

and a strand of her hair. He later said that he is not a psychic, but "It's just that I have the ability to work a divining rod. I don't know why. I feel it's an energy of some sort" (*Calgary Herald News*, August 11, 1999).

A lucky coincidence? A prearranged discovery? Most psychologists would reject the use of psychics, "divining rods," and so forth, in criminal investigation, but some police, at least in "last-resort" cases, will be amenable to any source of possible assistance.

What about lawyers and judges—what determines truth for them? Within the courtroom, for some lawyers, truth may be irrelevant. Probably for more judges and trial lawyers, the assumption is that the adversary system will produce truths or at least fairness. The nature of the adversary system leads some trial lawyers to value conflict resolution over the elusive quest for the truth. Another conception sometimes offered by critics of the legal system is that trials are not conducted to find out what happened—the police, the prosecutor, and the defence lawyer all probably know what happened—but as a game to persuade the community that the proof is strong enough to justify punishment.

BOX 1.3   **INDUCTIVE VERSUS DEDUCTIVE METHODS OF REASONING**

Induction and deduction are two contrasting methods used to solve a problem. *Deduction* requires the application of rules or a theory, whereas induction requires the generation of rules or a theory. Usually, deduction refers to going from the general to the specific, whereas *induction* refers to a process of using several specifics to generate a general rule.

In a creative analysis, Bruce Frey contrasted the ways that two popular fictional detectives solved crimes. Sherlock Holmes's investigative procedure was to examine a set of clues, develop a number of possible solutions, and eliminate them one by one. "When you have eliminated all the possibilities but one, that remaining one, no matter how improbable, must be the correct solution"–so goes his credo. (Further examples of Holmes's approach can be found in Chapter 4). Frey (1994) labelled this the "inductive process" because it examined many possibilities and used observations to create a theory and infer a conclusion.

In contrast, Miss Jane Marple, the heroine of many of Agatha Christie's mysteries, used quite different, deductive skills. A polite elderly woman who lived in the village of St. Mary Mead, she possessed an intimate knowledge of human interactions and behaviours among the inhabitants of her hometown. Her procedure when entering a problem-solving situation was to use the model of St. Mary Mead as a template and to apply that model to whatever the specific facts were.

We know that both detectives were quite successful (their authors made sure of that). And neither procedure has a clear superiority over the other. Do these approaches distinguish between the problem-solving styles of the psychologist and the lawyer? Psychology as a science relies on the deductive method; a general theory leads to specific hypotheses; the testing of these hypotheses leads to results that confirm, disconfirm, or revise the theory. With its emphasis on *precedent* and previous rulings, the law would seem, in a broad sense, to be inductive. But each discipline is multifaceted, and specific psychologists, legal scholars, and lawyers might follow either procedure.

But if trial lawyers and, especially, judges focus on the assessment of truth in a court-related context, evidence and the law are determinants. Legal authorities rely heavily on precedents in reaching decisions. The principle of **stare decisis** ("let the decision stand") has a weight, for judges, equivalent to that of experimentation for scientific psychologists. This is not to say that the courts always ignore social science research when that research can help clarify or resolve empirical issues that arise in litigation. Tomkins and Oursland (1991), among others, have observed that the historic tension between social science and the law does not mean that social science has been excluded from the courts.

The Nature of Reality

In the novel *Body of Evidence* (1991), author Patricia D. Cornwell (an expert on medical forensics) has a character express the opinion that "Everything depends on everything else" (p. 13); that is, you can't identify cause and effect, as variables interact with each other in undecipherable ways. To what extent do people give credence to such a view? Psychologists are trained to disabuse this notion; the experimental method emphasizes an analytic nature of the world. Psychologists assume that each quality of a stimulus has a separate, discernible influence on our response or behaviour. None of the other professions or disciplines holds so adamantly to this conception of the world.

Although the field of psychology assumes that the world is composed of separable variables that act independently or interactively on other variables, it also is more tolerant of ambiguity than is the legal field. In fact, the approach of psychology can be labelled probabilistic, for several reasons. Psychologists express "truths" as "statistically significant" at a numeric level, for example, the .05 level (which means that if a result occurs in less than 5 out of 100 comparisons it is not significant in that it may have occurred by chance or coincidence). Based on the statistics their research yields, psychologists will conclude that there is or is not a likelihood—not a certainty—that a real effect or difference exists.

Even more basic is psychology's assumption that people think in terms of probabilities and likelihoods. If you examine the instruments used by research psychologists, you find that they often will ask subjects, "What is the likelihood that …?" or similar questions. In contrast, the courts,

lawyers, and people in general may well think in yes-or-no, right-or-wrong categories.

The research of Kahneman, Slovic, and Tversky (1990; Tversky & Kahneman, 1974, 1983) and a book by Robyn Dawes (1988) provide numerous examples of the lay public's misunderstanding of probabilities and inability to apply probabilistic reasoning; for example, the adherence to the "gambler's fallacy," ignorance of regression-to-the-mean effects, and failure to pay attention to base rates.

Ten Brinke and Porter (2010) reviewed evidence that irrational thinking permeates legal decision making. One example relates to the influence of a defendant's appearance on the perceived likelihood that he or she committed the crime. The Dangerous Decisions Theory (DDT) (Porter & ten Brinke, 2009) predicts that interpersonal judgments of trustworthiness occur instantaneously upon seeing a face, which subjectively may be experienced as "intuition." This rapid process of trustworthiness assessment likely was originally intended to reduce the danger to our human ancestors. However, in the modern context, the impression can lead to biased (or "dangerous") decisions concerning the target. In the courtroom, the initial impression of a defendant's trustworthiness has an enduring subconscious influence on the manner in which new information concerning the target is assimilated by judges and jurors. Specifically, the initial intuitive evaluation will influence subsequent inferences concerning the defendant (or other witness) by making decision making about him or her increasingly irrational (Kahneman & Tversky, 1982). Decisions also will be influenced by an observer's experience and personal schemas about deceptive behaviour and heuristics for detecting lies. This will generate a noncritical, "tunnel vision" assimilation of potentially ambiguous or contradictory evidence concerning the defendant.

In the first study to empirically test the validity of DDT directly, Porter, Gustaw, and ten Brinke (2008) presented mock jury participants with vignettes of the same crimes accompanied either by a photo of a defendant whose face previously had been rated as appearing highly trustworthy or untrustworthy. It was found that participants required less evidence (and less incriminating evidence) before finding an untrustworthy defendant guilty of murder. Further, when presented with major exonerating evidence (e.g., DNA implicating someone else), participants changed their verdict to not guilty 84 percent of the time for trustworthy-looking defendants but only 42 percent of the time for untrustworthy-looking ones.

These findings are buttressed by wrongful convictions exemplified by the Canadian case of Steven Truscott—a poignant example of DDT in action, as presented in credibility assessment training workshops (e.g., Porter & ten Brinke, 2011).

In our legal system, proof is based "on showing direct cause and effect: action A caused (or at least in measurable ways contributed to) result B; Jones pulled the trigger and Smith died; Roe violated the contract and as a consequence Doe lost money" (Rappeport, 1993, p. 15). In contrast, psychologists are more concerned with the probability that A is related to B.

THE LEGAL SYSTEM'S CRITICISMS OF PSYCHOLOGY

If psychology wants to make a contribution to the functioning of the legal system, then it must self-reflect and consider its criticisms, some of which are explained in the following paragraphs.

The Lack of Ecological Validity of Psychological Research

The oldest criticism, originating back to Wigmore's response to Munsterberg's work, involves the **ecological validity** of studies; that is, the question of whether results found in controlled or laboratory conditions will also occur in real life. The procedures and subjects of psychological research studies and the procedures and participants in the actual legal system may be dissimilar. For example, jury research has served as a significant source of such criticism, both by lawyers and by some psychologists (Nuñez, McCrea, & Culhane, 2011). It is erroneous to assume that because a manipulation has an effect in the laboratory, it will have the same effect on jurors in the courtroom (Tanford & Tanford, 1988). As John Yuille (1989), a founder of one of the first forensic psychology programs in Canada, noted, there are two fundamental problems for psychologists in the role of expert:

First, the types of assessments clinicians are asked to make (e.g., concerning the accused's mental state at the time of committing the offense) may exceed the capacity of the discipline. Second, the research foundation that psychologists employ in court does not always apply to the court situation in the way experts imply; the application of laboratory research

findings to real world contexts is sometimes premature. It is concluded that psychologists should adopt a more conservative response to requests to provide expert evidence. (p. 181)

Yuille's concern seems to be validated in a recent study by Keller and Weiner (2011) who examined legal decision making among university students (the typical group studied by jury researchers) and community participants. Their results showed that the two groups held different biases that led to differences in how they decided on a defendant's culpability (guilt likelihood, convincingness of prosecutor's arguments, convincingness of defendant's arguments, and the defendant's criminal intentions) in sexual assault and homicide case scenarios. The results also showed that student mock jurors were more lenient when assigning guilt in homicide cases than were community members. As such, researchers must strive to examine relevant populations in order to generalize their findings to the courtroom setting.

Going Beyond the Data to Make Moral Judgments

Many Canadian judges have chastised certain psychologists and other "experts" for going beyond their data and venturing beyond their expertise to make moral judgments, or even to act as "hired guns." For example, psychologists may be encouraged to testify in court about theories and findings that lack validity. These and other temptations are examined in detail in Chapter 2. Throughout this book the quality of the scientific evidence supporting the conclusions of forensic psychologists will be examined, as this problem is, perhaps, the most important to overcome if the relationship between psychology and law is to improve. In a positive development, there have been recent changes in the manner in which psychologists are expected to testify as experts in Canada to increase their impartiality and "stick to the data." For example, the Ontario Rules of Civil Procedure were changed in January 2010 to require experts to acknowledge their duty is "to provide opinion evidence that is fair, objective and non-partisan." This acknowledgement of expert duty, known as Form 53, also states that experts are expected to provide evidence related only to matters within their area of expertise and to provide "such additional assistance as the court many reasonably require."

THE FUTURE OF THE RELATIONSHIP BETWEEN PSYCHOLOGY AND THE LAW

Courts have sometimes been sympathetic to psychological research; sometimes they have not. Can we detect why? Can we predict the future of this relationship?

Tanford (1990) reviewed two types of theories of the interaction between social science and the law. One type predicts that the obstacles to the use of social science research in the courts can be overcome and that science will eventually assume a prominent role in legal policy making. This view notes that modern Western culture has elevated science to a prominent position. In contrast, the other approach predicts that social science will not have much of an impact on the law in the foreseeable future. This position is based on the current reluctance of the courts to rely on empirical research. Tanford (1990) offers six reasons for this reluctance:

1. Judges are conservative and perceive social scientists to be liberal.
2. Judges are self-confident and do not believe that they need any assistance from non-lawyers.
3. Judges are human, and it is human nature to be unscientific.
4. Judges are ignorant of, inexperienced with, or do not understand empirical social science.
5. Judges perceive science as a threat to their power and prestige.
6. Law and social science are rival systems with competing logics (Tanford, 1990, p. 152).

Any of these reasons for reluctance to accept forensic psychology can surface in a specific case. Chapter 2 examines some of the roles for psychologists in the legal system and some of the ways that psychologists may abuse their opportunities, thus contributing to the conflict between the two disciplines.

SUMMARY

Forensic psychology may be broadly defined as any application of psychological knowledge or methods to a task faced by the legal system. This definition implies that forensic psychologists can play many roles: from criminal profiler to child-custody evaluator, from police counsellor to prison psychologist, from expert witness to evaluation researcher. But other definitions of forensic psychology limit it to clinical and professional applications of psychology to the legal system. Current training programs reflect these diverse definitions, and Canada is considered to be a world leader in many areas of psychological research and application in the legal system.

In their attempts to apply their knowledge to the legal system, forensic psychologists need to be aware of the history of the relationship and the conflicting values between the scientific and legal approaches. In the 100-year-old history of the relationship, influences can be traced from criminology and from experimental psychology. Hugo Munsterberg, a professor and director of the Psychological Laboratory at Harvard University in the first two decades of the 20th century, may be considered the founder of forensic psychology because of his research on such contemporary topics as eyewitness accuracy and memory, his influential articles for the lay public, and his involvement in several prominent trials. But he was only one of a number of experimental psychologists who were active in applying their knowledge to the courts during the period from 1900 to 1920. For various reasons, the relationship between the two fields languished for 50 years, until the mid-1970s. Since that time there has been an explosion of research and also a similar expansion in the application of psychological concepts and findings to diverse legal issues such as eyewitness memory, deception detection, risk assessment, psychopathy, legal decision making, and many others.

But psychology has not always had the effects it sought. Court decisions in both Canada and the United States illustrate the conflict between psychology and the law with regard to their bases of decision making. Some conflicts are fundamental, dealing with the nature of truth and reality. Others are not necessarily rooted in the philosophy of each discipline; for example, the legal system is uninformed about and hence unsympathetic to the methods used in psychology, and the methods of psychological research are sometimes unsatisfactory when dealing with real-world problems.

KEY TERMS

deduction, p. 19

ecological validity, p. 21

empirical approach, p. 8

forensic psychology, p. 2

induction, p. 19

precedent, p. 19

reliability, p. 8

replicability, p. 8

specialty designation, p. 4

stare decisis, p. 20

values, p. 7

SUGGESTED READINGS

Gazzaniga, M. (2011). Neuroscience in the courtroom. *Scientific American, 304,* 54–59.

This paper explores the controversies around the new practice of bringing psychologists and neuroscientists as experts in the court to describe brain scans of violent offenders. The author suggests the need for great caution in adopting such findings from neuroscience in court.

Heilbrun, K., & Brooks, S. (2010). Forensic psychology and forensic science: A proposed agenda for the next decade. *Psychology, Public Policy, and Law, 16,* 219–253.

This paper is of special value to those considering further training in forensic psychology. The authors review the progress of our discipline over the last three decades and offer a novel "forensic science" framework for future training and research.

Hess, A. K., & Weiner, I. B. (Eds.). (2006). *Handbook of forensic psychology* (3rd ed.). New York: John Wiley.

This updated collection of comprehensive and detailed reviews of many of the topics explored in this book includes lie detection, testifying in court, assessing competency, and police consultation.

Munsterberg. H. (1908). *On the witness stand.* Garden City, NY: Doubleday.

This book is worth extracting from stuffy library stacks to determine just how prescient it is for the forensic psychology of the 21st century.

Roles and Responsibilities of Forensic Psychologists

> *We can't trust prison shrinks. I got a high score on your fucking test because the psychologist has a beef against me. He screwed me because in a group session I said he was full of crap. So now he says I'm a flaming psychopath, and you can't treat me. So what the fuck do you do with me?*
>
> —Canadian inmate quoted by R. Hare (1998, p. 114)

THE MULTITUDE OF ROLES

In introducing Chapter 1, we described five professionals whose professional activities qualify them to be called forensic psychologists, even though their day-to-day work differs dramatically. The activities of these five psychologists by no means encompass the entire range of those subsumed under forensic psychology. For example, consider two different tasks, each reflecting **assessment** as a primary responsibility of many forensic psychologists. Neuropsychologists engage in forensic activities when they examine a defendant to determine whether he or she has damage to the right hemisphere of the brain or the amygdala, affecting judgment and impulse control (e.g., Bigler & Brooks, 2009; Wahlund & Kristiansson, 2009). In their forensic capacity, neuropsychologists carry out a comprehensive evaluation of brain functioning, with an emphasis on the measurement of deficits in psychological functioning. A number of tests have been developed to assess normal versus impaired brain functioning, and several textbooks review these procedures (for example, Horton & Hartlage, 2010, and Goldstein & Incagnoli, 1997). The assessment of the psychological, as well as the neurological, characteristics of offenders also is an important task for forensic psychologists. One example is psychopathy (as described in depth in Chapter 13). Although 0.6 percent to 1 percent of the general population may be classified as psychopaths (e.g., Coid, Yang, Ullrich, & Hare, 2009; Neumann & Hare, 2008), they comprise 15 percent to 25 percent of the prison population and are responsible for a disproportionate amount of violent and sadistic crime (Mokros, Osterheider, Hucker, & Nitsche, 2011; Shaw & Porter, 2012). Psychopathy incorporates the following characteristics: an emotional void, impulsivity,

a lack of guilt or remorse, pathological lying and manipulativeness, and a continual willingness to violate social norms. Psychopaths also perpetrate much of the premeditated, instrumental violence in society, as established by Michael Woodworth and colleagues in their investigations regarding the characteristics of homicide offenders (Porter & Woodworth, 2007; Woodworth & Porter, 2002; also see Flight & Forth, 2007; Reidy, Shelley-Tremblay, & Lilienfeld, 2011; Walsh, Swogger, & Kosson, 2009). Forensic psychologists have developed instruments to assess psychopathy that have been widely adopted by legal and correctional organizations including Correctional Service Canada (CSC) with regards to deciding on security levels, treatment needs, and parole recommendations. Among the most prominent is the PCL-R, developed by Robert Hare, a professor emeritus at the University of British Columbia and a consultant with the FBI. The PCL-R employs a 20-item rating scale, completed on the basis of a semistructured interview and on other information about the subject (Hare, 2003). Sample characteristics to be rated by the psychologist include lack of realistic long-term goals and callous lack of empathy. Each item is rated on a three-point scale, according to specific criteria.

A considerable amount of research and theory development concerning psychopathy used by forensic psychologists have been conducted by Canadian researchers at the University of British Columbia, Simon Fraser University, Queen's University, and Carleton University. These researchers have pointed out that because of pressures from the legal system, forensic psychologists must be careful to remain objective when using such assessment tools (e.g., Hare, 1998; Sadoff, 2011). Additionally, forensic psychologists are placed in the unique (and often conflicting) dual roles of treatment provider and organizational consultant

Promising Too Much

Sometimes forensic psychologists who are hired by lawyers or the courts promise a level of success they cannot guarantee. The types of assessments utilize assessment tools that are not infallible. The accuracy of the test results depends on numerous factors beyond the training and abilities of the psychologist; these include the standard error of measurement (the average level of error associated with the test), the honesty of the person being tested, and the setting in which the tests are administered. Psychologists need to concede the potential fallibility of their assessments, while using tools with a strong empirical basis (in the context of risk assessments, tools such as the PCL-R, Violence Risk Appraisal Guide (VRAG) (Quinsey et al., 2006), and the Historical-Clinical-Risk Management-20 (HCR-20) (Webster, Douglas, Eaves, & Hart, 1997) and describing such strengths for the court. In particular, the psychologists who have developed the tests and other instruments that are used in forensic assessments may be tempted (consciously or unconsciously) to claim a greater level of validity than is warranted in real-life situations.

Some forensic psychologists may become committed to the use of certain tests such as the MMPI-II or the Rorschach even in situations where their applicability is questionable. For example, in institutions run by the Correctional Service of Canada, the MMPI-II is almost always used during intake assessments (assessments that occur soon after incarceration) with criminal offenders, when, in fact, there is little evidence for its predictive validity in that context. While such tests may provide useful "clinical" information concerning an offender, the limits on their ability to predict future criminal behaviour should be made clear to everyone reading the psychological assessment report.

Substituting Advocacy for Scientific Objectivity

When psychologists become **expert witnesses** in Canada, they usually are hired by one side in an adversarial proceeding. In such a situation, most psychologists are conscientious and try to be ethical, to the point of fully describing the limits of their opinion and even empirical evidence that supports the opposite view. But it may be

that can lead to ethical dilemmas. In other words, forensic psychologists often work *with* offenders but *for* corrections (e.g., Birgden & Perlin, 2009). Thus, this chapter emphasizes the ethical responsibilities of psychologists as they respond to the sometimes conflicting demands of the legal system. In doing so, we will investigate specific activities of psychologists, some of which will be further developed in subsequent chapters.

THE TEMPTATIONS OF FORENSIC PSYCHOLOGISTS

Although there are diverse roles for psychologists in the legal system, limits have been placed on the application of psychology in this setting by professional organizations, including the Canadian Psychological Association (CPA) and Division 41 of the American Psychological Association (APA), the latter known as the American Psychology-Law Society (AP-LS). These groups have developed specific guidelines as to what is acceptable behaviour in legal contexts, described later in this chapter. The law itself also sets controls on the contributions of psychologists, whether they are expert witnesses asked to testify at trial or consultants conducting pretrial assessments.

Despite such guidelines from psychological governing bodies and the legal system, forensic psychologists, for various reasons, may sometimes exceed what is acceptable in their profession and what the law practically permits them to do. The following are some of the potential temptations tempting to play the **advocate role**, to take sides, to become sympathetic to the arguments of the side that is paying the psychologist, and to slant the testimony in that direction. The shift toward partisanship may be subtle, even unconscious. Some lawyers contribute to the problem by "shopping around" until they find an expert who will say what they want (Spencer, 1998). Many people, including some judges, see the expert witness as a **hired gun**, willing to say whatever his or her hiring client needs to be said. An apparent example of a hired gun on the stand occurred in the trial of John Demjanjuk, the alleged "Ivan the Terrible," a Nazi concentration camp guard, at his eventual trial in Israel. A handwriting expert who was testifying in Demjanjuk's defense concluded that a signature on a document was probably not Demjanjuk's, but the prosecution confronted him with an earlier public statement of his that had expressed the opposite conclusion. The expert refused to explain the inconsistency on the grounds that he had a "contractual relationship" with the Demjanjuk Defense Fund, which would sue him if he explained further (Spencer, 1998). A recent, widely discussed book by experimental psychologist Margaret Hagen (1997) has served as a broadside attack on psychologists as hired guns; see Box 2.1.

BOX 2.1 **ARE PSYCHOLOGISTS "WHORES OF THE COURT"?**

With its bright yellow book jacket and its provocative title, *Whores of the Court*, splashed across the entire cover, Margaret Hagen's book was bound to attract attention. But it is the book's contents that have generated the strongest reaction. For Hagen, an experimental psychologist on the faculty of Boston University, the whores are those forensic psychologists, psychiatrists, and social workers who mislead judges and juries about child sexual abuse, criminal responsibility or insanity, psychological disability, and a variety of other topics—hence the book's subtitle: *The Fraud of Psychiatric Testimony and the Rape of American Justice*.

Those concerned with the powerful temptations of forensic psychology will find much to applaud in the book. Hagen expresses the caution that should be the basis of forensic applications when she questions whether mental health professionals can distinguish between real victims of posttraumatic stress disorder and those who fake symptoms. She describes (on p. 262) how a professional staff member at a trauma clinic testified that no one could fake traumatic memories or fool psychiatric tests. She has been justifiably critical of psychologists who serve as hired guns in child custody disputes.

But she weakened her case by overreaction, exaggeration, and stereotyping. Saul Kassin (1998a), in a thoughtful review, summarized:

> Underlying much of Hagen's attack are three underlying themes, or stereotypic portraits, of forensic clinical psychologists. One is that they are simply not competent on the basis of science (not to mention their lack of education in such areas as neuroscience, learning, memory, development, and behavior in social groups) to testify as they do. Second is that many clinical psychologists are driven by missionary liberal motives. ... The third theme is that forensic clinical psychologists are economically motivated by the almighty dollar. ... This last motive is what gives rise to the image of psychologists as "whores" of the court. (p. 322)

Some of Hagen's statements are wildly divergent from the present authors' experience as expert witnesses; for example, she wrote:

> For the whole clinical psychological profession in whatever guise, the increase in power and prestige in the civil litigation arena has been dizzying. Just think of it. Judges genuflecting before your sagacious testimony, and changing the law to fit your word. ... It is a compelling picture of a powerful profession flexing its muscles as never before. (Hagen, 1997, p. 255)

Neither of us can recall a judge "genuflecting"—more likely, when testifying, other types of judicial nonverbal behaviour were pointed in our direction. Thus we agree with another thoughtful review of her book, by Solomon Fulero (1997), that noted that she has committed

continued

the same mistakes that she attributed to forensic psychologists:

> I agree here that while Hagen's essential point is well-taken—that is, a number of psychological experts are offered in courts to testify about shaky theories, questionable ideas, and conclusions without solid empirical evidence—the manner in which this point is presented "throws out the baby with the bathwater," obscuring valid comments about the proper types and uses of psychological expert testimony with anecdotes, errors, flaming overgeneralizations, and inflammatory charges.

> Further, the presentation of the essential point in such a manner will actually make it more difficult to rein in the very excesses Hagen deplores. (p. 10)

Thus, Hagen's book reminds readers that forensic psychologists can succumb to the temptations of exaggeration and falsification when they respond to the pressures of the legal system. But the book fails to acknowledge the more typical efforts of people in our field to represent the field in an ethical and objective manner. Nonetheless, even if "hired guns" are rare, we should carefully consider their potential impact in the courtroom.

In *R. v. Samra* (1998), the Ontario Court of Appeal considered the issue of "hired gun" testimony. On March 18, 1982, the appellant Kuldip Samra entered Courtroom 4 at Osgoode Hall in Toronto armed with a gun and ammunition. Although Samra would later claim that he went into the courtroom to commit suicide, he walked directly to the front of the room, where he shot and killed two men and wounded a third victim. Samra then left the scene and fled Canada. Eight years later, he was arrested in India and extradited back to Canada in 1992. The defence introduced expert testimony by Dr. Allan Long, a psychologist, and Dr. Jerry Cooper, a psychiatrist. These experts were called to support the theory that Samra was in an "altered state" at the time of the shootings and was incapable of formulating a plan to murder someone.

When the defence lawyer attempted to have Dr. Cooper qualified as an expert, the Crown prosecutor challenged his expertise and was allowed to cross-examine him (in front of the jury) on material from a *Globe and Mail* article. The following parts of the article were read to Dr. Cooper (see *R. v. Samra*, 1998):

[According to Dr. Andrew Malcolm,] some of my colleagues have apparently decided to play the game and become courtesans, court prostitutes, experts of easy virtue. In that case, let themselves be employed by either one of the adversaries and then pack a pile of lies on top of their genuine credentials for all the world to see.

It is hard to find a more flexible expert witness than Toronto psychiatrist Jerry Cooper, who, unlike many of his colleagues who seem to testify with great reluctance, loves the battle as no other.

He says candidly, "When I look at a case, I always ask the lawyer what he wants. When a lawyer is happy and his client is happy, then I'm happy."

But he shudders when it is suggested that sounds like ammunition for the hired gun theory.

Mr. Greenspan says he has noted an "institutional bias": Psychiatrists who work in the world of the mentally ill have a tendency to see mental illness in various degrees wherever they look.

Dr. Cooper appears to give him credence when he says, "Depending on the defence [a lawyer wishes to offer], I can find anyone insane." (para. 70)

Although Dr. Cooper denied telling the reporter that he could find anyone insane, his credibility was greatly undermined by the suggestion from the article that he may be a hired gun. In the end, Samra was convicted of two counts of first-degree murder and one count of attempted murder, and the Ontario Court of Appeal dismissed his appeal.

The proper role for a psychologist as an expert witness is that of a friend of the court, an objective scientist who reports *all* the data and conflicting findings, even if he or she makes a less supportive case for the side that hired the psychologist (Cutler & Kovera, 2011; Yuille, 1989). But it is hard to avoid the seduction of taking sides. Sometimes, when the advocate role becomes paramount, the psychologist or psychiatrist may create a diagnosis to fit the behaviour when no proof exists for the validity of the diagnostic construct.

Take the example of Karla Homolka, who along with her husband Paul Bernardo, took part in the rapes and murders of Leslie Mahaffy and Kristen French. In one of the most notorious plea bargains in Canadian legal history, Homolka entered into a deal with the Ontario Crown on May 14, 1993, in which she agreed to plead guilty to two counts of manslaughter in return for a 12-year sentence (see Galligan Report, 1996). At sentencing, evidence was presented that she had played a direct role in the drugging, sexual assault, and death of her 15-year-old sister Tammy. Prior to the plea bargain, Homolka had been assessed by several mental health professionals. In March 1993, she was admitted to a Toronto hospital where she remained for over six weeks of evaluations by two psychiatrists and two psychologists selected by the Crown prosecutor. Reports from this stay include a mix of various diagnoses and sometimes colourful clinical descriptions, including stress, anxiety, depression, learned helplessness, posttraumatic stress disorder, "psychic numbing" (Galligan Report, p. 152), lack of affect, and other indicators of "battered woman syndrome," whereas no evidence was found for psychosis or sexual deviance. Her domestic abuse and domination by Bernardo supposedly had left her similar to a "concentration camp survivor," and was seen as having contributed to her involvement in the murders (Galligan Report, 1996). In explaining battered-woman syndrome, expert witness psychologist Peter Jaffe testified that such women feel powerless and can develop maladaptive behaviour, potentially contributing to the commission of criminal acts.

Battered-woman syndrome? Concentration camp survivor? Psychic numbing? Learned helplessness? None of these are psychiatric disorders. Although battered-woman syndrome is a valid legal defence, did Homolka really show evidence for such a syndrome? The true extent of Homolka's involvement or culpability in the Mahaffy and French cases was evident from six homemade videotapes later recovered. Her claims of being under Bernardo's control, central to the plea bargain, appeared to be false as she (reportedly) actively conversed with and enthusiastically sexually assaulted the victims with a coy smile on her face. The descriptions provided by the psychologists and psychiatrists arguably deterred justice in this case. Karla was released from prison in 2005, after she completed her online Bachelor's degree in Psychology from Queen's University, and was shortly thereafter deemed to pose no risk to the community. Although Homolka was able to fly below the radar for many years, she was recently tracked to

the Caribbean, where she was found living with her husband and three children (*Vancouver Sun*, 2012). We will never fully understand her actions or the ill-conceived reasoning adopted by the psychologists assigned to her legal proceedings.

In order to deal with the problems associated with contradictory or biased experts, the Canadian courts recently introduced new guidelines; the Canadian Federal Court Rules changed how expert witnesses and their testimony will be dealt with in Federal Court proceedings (interested students can find details of the changes at the Government of Canada website at http://gazette.gc.ca/rp-pr/p2/2010/2010-08-18/html/sor-dors176-eng.html≠a). Some of the highlights include:

1. All expert witnesses will be provided a new Code of Conduct applicable specifically to expert witnesses. The expert will also need to sign a certificate acknowledging that he or she agrees to be bound by the Code.
2. Streamlining the process of qualifying expert witnesses.
3. Opposing expert witnesses may be ordered by the Court to confer among themselves and potentially testify as a panel (dubbed "hot tubbing"). These discussions are confidential and will not be disclosed to the Court.
4. The parties can nominate a single joint expert, but only on consent of all parties, in order to reduce the problem of the "battle of the experts.". The notion of reducing conflicting expert testimonies by having experts agree on a joint statement before appearing in court is a dramatic change and a positive one, from our perspective. While this process is likely to be difficult for experts with conflicting views, it is intended to simplify the information presented by experts to judicial decision makers who can become frustrated by contradictory expert testimonies.

Letting Values Overcome Empirically Based Findings

None of us can escape our values as influences on the ways that we perceive the world. Sometimes there may be an unconscious temptation for our values to determine our conclusions in a court of law. Let's consider some examples.

A forensic psychologist is asked to do an evaluation of a pair of parents who are divorcing in order to assist the judge in making a custody decision that is in the best interests of the child. The psychologist discovers that one of the parents—on rare occasions when the child has uttered an expletive—washes out the child's mouth with soap. There may be nothing illegal about this, and probably nothing physically harmful, but the psychologist is repulsed by the behaviour. No empirical data exist that inform the general question of appropriateness for custody, but the psychologist's recommendation is affected by it. Or let us assume that one parent smokes and the other does not; should such factors influence a recommendation about custody?

In an American case (*Barefoot v. Estelle*, 1983), two psychiatrists went beyond the research conclusions regarding the difficulty of predicting dangerousness by testifying that they "knew" that the defendant would commit crimes in the future (Lavin & Sales, 1998). In subsequent cases, the courts made explicit their recognition that predictions of future behaviour given by psychologists or psychiatrists are far from infallible. For example, in the Canadian case *Re Moore and the Queen* (1984), Justice Ewaschuk stated:

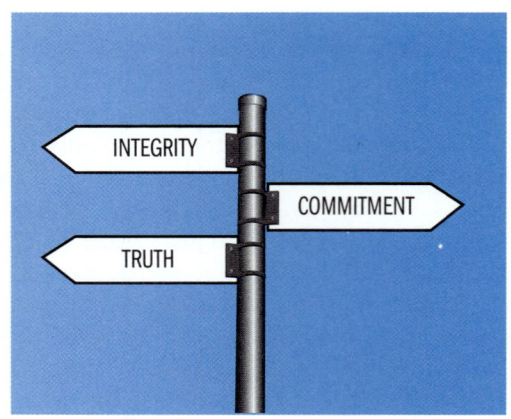

I accept the submission that the evidence of a psychiatrist, psychologist or criminologist is at times highly speculative and in certain instances a lay person is in as good a position to make a prediction as to future dangerousness. In the final say, the court, however, must be so satisfied and not the expert witnesses. That is not to say that experts may not assist the court, especially as to whether the offender currently suffers from a psychological disorder, e.g., psychopathy, which may be relevant to the likelihood of future dangerous conduct.

In our view, at all times psychologists must strive to maintain objectivity in the courtroom and make sure that they do not make statements that move beyond what science has established on any legal issue. Perhaps the legal system would be best served if we fill an "education" role rather than an advocacy role (Porter, Campbell, Birt, & Woodworth, 2003b), although some would disagree, as we shall see.

The Problem of Cursory or Unreliable Forensic Assessments

In the Canadian correctional system, we have seen many cases in which the reliability of the forensic

assessment is questionable. Problems with the assessment of psychopathy provide a good example. As mentioned earlier, the best-validated tool used to determine whether an offender is psychopathic is the PCL-R (Hare, 2003), an observer-rated instrument based on a thorough review of collateral information and complemented, if possible, by an interview with the offender. Despite the high validity and reliability of the PCL-R, problems have occasionally arisen with its use. The PCL-R's creator, Robert Hare, has outlined some of the misuses he has observed (Hare, 1998; see also Martens, 2008):

1. *Assessments by unqualified raters.* Hare notes that individuals with insufficient qualifications and training have sometimes utilized and applied the PCL-R in their assessments. He argues that clinicians who apply the PCL-R should possess an advanced degree in the social, medical, or behavioural sciences (such as a Ph.D., D.Ed. or M.D.) and have adequate training and experience in the use of the PCL-R. These recommended qualifications were endorsed in the Canadian courts by Justice MacKay in *Pinkney v. Canada (Attorney General)* (1998).

2. *Confusing psychopathy with antisocial personality disorder (APD).* Hare points out that many clinicians continue to confuse these diagnoses and their implications for predicting the behaviour of an offender (e.g., psychopathy is much more predictive of future criminal acts than is APD).

3. *Overreliance on "clinical opinion."* Some clinicians make the mistake of ignoring or downplaying the PCL-R definitions given in the manual in favour of their own clinical

opinions ("I know what shallow affect means. I don't need to keep referring to the scoring criteria.").

4. *Unauthorized or blatant misuse.* Occasionally, a PCL-R assessment has been conducted by someone with no credentials to do so whatsoever. Hare gives the example of a judge who himself decided to score an offender on the PCL-R and gave a considerably lower score than the score provided by an expert psychiatrist.

Perhaps nowhere could the misuse of the PCL-R have more severe consequences than in the context of a "dangerous offender" hearing. Section 752 of the Criminal Code of Canada has a category of dangerous offenders for those offenders who are very likely to reoffend violently or inflict severe psychological violence, warranting an indefinite sentence (Discussed in detail in Chapter 14). Typically, during the hearing for such a determination, both the defence and Crown are expected to present reports and/or testimony concerning risk factors from their own psychiatrists or psychologists. Psychopathy now is considered to be one of the most important considerations in this regard due to its strong association with risk for future violence (Shaw & Porter, 2012). Very often, the reports for the two sides differ in conclusions about PCL-R scores (and the dangerousness of the offender), suggesting the possibility of the problems discussed by Hare.

The potential unreliability of psychiatric diagnoses will recur as an issue throughout this book, but the temptation of concern here is being less than thorough and professional in one's work for the courts or other authorities.

Maintaining Dual Relationships and Competing Roles

A psychologist who is evaluating a divorced couple for child custody accepts an invitation to have dinner with the female partner. Another psychologist who is seeing a man as a psychotherapy client attempts to initiate a romantic relationship with him. These are examples of **dual relationships**, in this case, a situation that is clearly unethical according to the CPA ethical guidelines (see CPA website for ethical guidelines; link provided at the end of the chapter). A less obvious conflict of interest occurs when the forensic psychologist is engaged in more than one type of professional activity with the same individual.

When a child reports having been sexually abused, the court may request a psychologist to do an evaluation. If the psychologist has served as a psychotherapist for the child or someone in the child's family, it is inappropriate for the same psychologist to serve as an evaluator of the claims of abuse. The forensic evaluator has to maintain a stance of absolute impartiality, whereas the therapist often serves as an advocate for his or her client (Lawlor, 1998; McCarron & Stewart, 2011). But what happens if the evaluation is required in a small town with only one psychotherapist (the same one giving the child in question therapy)? A similar temptation to fill two competing roles may occur in child-custody decisions or in situations in which a psychologist treats individual clients in sex offender therapy at a prison, and later is asked to evaluate their risk to reoffend in the community. These are tricky situations and it is clear that psychologists in training must be well versed in how to work through such dilemmas to make the best ethical decision. Recently, Canadian psychologists have advocated the use of case vignettes (scenarios in which an ambiguous ethical dilemma is presented) to gain the required skill to become ethical practitioners (McCarron & Stewart, 2011).

SPECIFIC ROLES: TRIAL AND POLICE CONSULTING

To further examine issues around ethical professional behaviour in legal settings, this chapter considers several specific roles for forensic psychologists. For each role, a salient question that must be answered by the forensic psychologist is: "Who is my client?" In this context, forensic psychologists normally are paid by a lawyer and his or her client, and this team has expectations of the psychologist. But psychologists also have ethical responsibilities to promote human welfare, and, hence, shouldn't society in general be construed as a "client"? Because of these various pressures, conflicts can emerge in each of the roles, as illustrated below.

Duties

Increasingly, trial lawyers rely on psychologists and other social scientists to help them prepare for the trial. This role typically has been called a **trial consultant** or psycho-legal consultant. Further, police in Canada often hire forensic psychologists as consultants in their investigations. At present, no province licenses or certifies such consultants, so it is up to the lawyer or police investigator to decide whom to consult in a trial or investigation, respectively. Psychological consultants in our legal system have diverse backgrounds in cognitive, social, child, forensic (clinical, investigative), and other areas of psychology.

What do psychologists hired as trial consultants do? The consultant may be hired by a lawyer to assist in identifying the major issues in a case and/or prepare witnesses for trial. Trial consultants also may be asked to comment on the validity of expert reports from the opposing side and advise on how to effectively cross-examine an opposing expert. In addition, an increasingly common use of trial consultants in Canada is to give an opinion on the quality of the psychological evidence available in the case. Was a police interrogation coercive or suggestive? Was an interview by a police officer or social worker with a child overly leading? Were inappropriate methods used in therapy that may have led to a mistaken recovered memory and allegation? Were the psychological tests used by a mental health professional to evaluate an offender's future risk to reoffend valid and appropriate? Is the behaviour of the defendant consistent with someone who commits a particular crime? For example, UBC psychologist Dr. Donald Dutton, a researcher who specializes in spousal violence, was consulted by the prosecution team in the O.J. Simpson case concerning the factors that can lead to spousal homicide (such as previous domestic violence, jealousy, estrangement, stalking, and threats) and whether Simpson's profile was consistent with that of a wife killer.

Police hire psychologists as consultants in their investigations for many purposes. For example, the first author of this textbook has been consulted by the police to assist in planning suspect interviewing, to generate a psychological profile of a known suspect (or suspects), to evaluate the credibility of sexual assault allegations, and to evaluate the credibility of suspect alibis/denials in murder investigations.

In Canada, although there seem to be wide regional differences, trial and police consulting are becoming increasingly important activities for forensic psychologists. Later chapters describe the duties of such consultants in more detail. Because of growth in this area, relevant educational opportunities for psychology students who intend to go on to work as forensic consultants are critical. At UBC—Okanagan, the first author teaches a graduate-level course in forensic consulting (Psychology 508), intended for students who plan to pursue a career as an academic or a clinical psychologist and who plan to have a consulting practice. The course begins with an overview of the Canadian legal system with consideration of the various applications of psychology at its various levels. Next, we consider basic practical issues in acting as a consultant in the legal system (e.g., deciding whether your expertise is relevant, communicating with lawyers/police/courts, fee arrangements, contracts, report writing, being subpoenaed). The course then considers specific relevant science, empirically informed practice, and controversies in the following areas: (1) ethical issues (confidentiality, defining the "client"); (2) expert testimony; (3) mental disorder and crime (the concept of mens rea, psychological legal defences (e.g., automatism, provocation, not criminally responsible by reason of mental disorder [NCRMD]); (4) assessing credibility/deception; (5) eyewitness testimony/recovered memories; and (6) assessing confession evidence. A major course component is the use of role-plays in which students act as consulting psychologists. These role-plays are diverse, including a courtroom scenario (e.g., cross-examination); initial consultation, meeting, negotiations, and contract agreement with a demanding defence lawyer; consultation by police in an investigation; and the decision to break confidentiality with a client. Students find this acting approach helpful in developing their ethical and professional skills as psychological consultants.

Clientele

Because we owe confidentiality and our services to the client, the question is "who is the client?" is critical one for all forensic psychologists. The clientele of proximal concern to the trial consultant is the lawyer or police force that hires the consultant, and, secondarily, their client (usually a defendant) who hired the defence. A special type of ethical issue emerges here because trial consultants not only are social scientists, but also contractors because they may advertise and market their services. Larger firms in the United States distribute glossy brochures extolling their various services. In Canada, on the other hand, the trial consultant typically works alone with little advertising. For example, an academic who does work in the area of child witnesses might be hired by the defence to discuss how the child's testimony may have been tainted by improper questioning by police or social workers (and how to cross-examine such witnesses). Nonetheless, because the service is paid for by the client, there often is external or even unconscious pressure to provide an opinion in line with the client's needs. This is something the consultant must always try to keep in mind; however, the consultant must remain as objective as possible. The psychologist hired by the police as a consultant views the police themselves as the only client (not, for example, the suspect or complainant as the subject of an investigation). Because the police have hired the psychologist to assist in the investigation, usually there would not be the same pressure to provide a particular opinion as when acting as a trial consultant. However, there can be challenges in this role as well (see nearby "Ethical Responsibilities"). Sometimes, the client comprises a number of investigators who may have differing views of psychologists and of what one can contribute to an investigation.

Conflicts with the Legal System

Conflicts between trial consultants and their lawyer clients can be classified as "procedural" or "substantive". With regard to procedures, consultants always need to keep in mind that they are employed by the lawyers and should defer to them with regard to decisions involving the case. For example, a trial consultant may believe that questions about a complainant's history of psychotherapy are necessary to investigate the possibility of a false memory. However, the lawyer may feel that such questions are inappropriate invasions of privacy or could lead to a jury perception of unfair treatment of the complainant. The police investigator client may disagree with a psychologist's recommendation for a nonconfrontive, sympathetic approach to interview a criminal suspect. Substantive conflicts can arise over any topic: the appropriate theory of the case, how witnesses should present themselves, which witnesses should be presented first, or the opinion that a serial killer is operating in a particular region. As an example of the latter, Dr. Kim Rossmo, a former Vancouver police officer who obtained his Ph.D. in criminology at SFU in the 1990s had warned the Vancouver Police Department (VPD) that the hordes of women who had gone missing on Vancouver's East

Side had likely been killed by a single individual. The VPD ignored his opinion and ultimately missed a chance to cut short serial killer Robert Pickton's ability to kill 49 women, according to his own self-report (Cameron, 2010).

Ethical Responsibilities

The dual occupational nature of the consultant—applied scientist plus contractor—makes for challenging ethical responsibilities. As an applied researcher, the consultant must follow the standard guidelines for ethical research, which take the form of a list of moral imperatives:

1. Thou shall not fake or exaggerate data.
2. Thou shall not plagiarize.
3. Thou shall not make false conclusions on the basis of your data.

Further, the consultant has the moral responsibility not to break the law, even when the consultant's client encourages it. The consultant may be faced with a situation in which he or she knows that a witness is lying about important case facts but the lawyer wants the consultant to help the witness appear as credible as possible. As strange as it may sound, lawyers may not wish to hear the truth from their clients, preferring that a story be maintained even it is a lie. As Winnipeg defence lawyer Greg Brodsky says, "I don't want my client telling me exactly what happened, because I can't put on a defence I know to be perjured in court" (Dotto, 2004, p. 45). When a court requires it, the consultant must break confidentiality with the client to avoid breaking the law.

A good idea is for consultants to never suggest that their services will help win a case for their client or solve a case. In fact, the psychologist should discuss with the lawyer or the police in the first consultation that a psychological conclusion rendered about the client may or may not be favourable for their case or help solve the case. For example, if a psychologist is approached by the defence to conduct a risk assessment for a sentencing hearing, he or she should always remind the lawyer that the client may be found to be a high risk. In this outcome, the lawyer would likely not request that the expert testify, which brings up serious ethical concerns.

Confidentiality is a special concern for trial consultants, with the recognition that it is essential that trial consultants keep all information about a particular case private and confidential, unless the consulting lawyer and client have agreed in writing to forego confidentiality or the trial consultant is legally required via a court order to do so. That is, the lawyer/lawyer's client "owns" the information/opinion the consultant generates, and the consultant owes him or her the same confidentiality that a psychotherapist owes to his or her therapy client.

This is quite different from a forensic psychologist who works in a Canadian prison setting and can expect that information collected for a risk assessment will not be kept confidential and will be shared with many relevant parties, including the National Parole Board of Canada, for example. In that context, the paying client is considered to be the Correctional Service of Canada, a government organization representing Canadian society at large. As such, the psychologist has no obligation of confidentiality to the offender and his or her lawyer during any type of prerelease assessment. On the other hand, a psychologist who is providing mental health services (such as treating a depressed offender) should be expected to keep personal information from therapy sessions confidential (unless the material pertains to risk for violence to self or others). This is because the offender is best construed as the client in that context. Obviously, deciding who is the client is critical but can be complicated!

"WELL, I'VE NEVER CALLED AN EXPERT WITNESS ON EXPERT WITNESSES BEFORE..."

www.CartoonStock.com

SPECIFIC ROLES: THE EXPERT WITNESS

Academic psychologists as well as practising forensic psychologists may be called on to provide expertise in court. A different type of ethical issue may surface in this role. The lawyer who is paying the psychologist may want the psychologist to draw conclusions that are not warranted from research or clinical findings.

Duties

During a trial, each side may ask the judge to permit expert witnesses to testify on its behalf. In contrast to other witnesses (called **fact witnesses**), who can testify about only what they've observed or what they know as fact, expert witnesses may express opinions, with the assumption that they possess special knowledge about a topic that is beyond that of an average juror. The judge must be convinced that the testimony that any expert will present reflects his or her requisite knowledge, skill, or experience in a certain field and that the testimony will help resolve the dispute and lead jurors toward the truth.

The topics for which a psychology expert may be called as an expert witness are extensive. Box 2.2, containing examples from Nietzel and Dillehay (1986), describes a number of these topics. Most reflect some form of clinical expertise, and many (including criminal responsibility, eyewitness identification, and children's custody) are evaluated in detail in subsequent chapters. The purpose of this section is to examine the conflicts and ethical issues that cut across specific topics.

Clientele

Although traditionally an expert witness was asked to serve the court rather than the litigants, now expert witnesses are contracted by trial lawyers or crown prosecutors. Nevertheless, the judge must determine the expert witness's appropriateness for a particular trial. In Canada, experts must be formally "qualified" in the court prior to entering evidence. During the qualification process, lawyers from the two sides have the opportunity to examine the credentials (education, training, and experience) of the psychologist as they pertain to the psychological issue at hand. The judge then determines whether to admit the psychologist as an expert and allow him or her to give an expert opinion.

As far as the presiding judge is concerned, the expert witness serves as a witness but not as an advocate or decision maker. Like other witnesses, experts must agree to give honest testimony while on the stand. Nevertheless, some judges are dubious about expert testimony. One decision by the Supreme Court of British Columbia is typical:

The issue of the impugned medical opinions raises a matter of concern which has been addressed by the courts of this Province on numerous occasions. The proliferation of competing expert reports in civil litigation is increasingly becoming a problem of costs to the litigants and delays and cost in the court process. This problem of proliferation is exacerbated by an even greater concern that experts called upon by litigants to assist the court and then given deference by the court often abandon their legitimate and valued role and descend to advocacy. (*Houseman [Guardian of] v. Sewell*, 1997, para. 18)

As noted in Box 2.1, it is not only judges who are critical of expert witnesses. In the Canadian case *R. v. Lavallee* (1990), the Crown prosecutor brought an application to have expert evidence concerning "battered woman syndrome" withdrawn from the jury. He stated that the jury was perfectly capable of deciding the issue and that expert evidence was therefore "unnecessary and superfluous." The trial judge denied the application, stating that the Crown's concerns could be met through an appropriate charge to the jury.

Testimony on Eyewitness Accuracy

Among the various topics in Box 2.2, judges are perhaps most inconsistent in their reaction to the admissibility of psychologists testifying on the accuracy of eyewitnesses (Cutler, 2009; Penrod, Fulero, & Cutler, 1995). In fact, in trials in which the testimony of an eyewitness is potentially pivotal and the eyewitness's accuracy is an issue, psychologists often have been denied the opportunity to testify. Robert Buckhout (1983) reported that in New York, "I have testified before juries in about 10 cases and been kept out too many times to count' (p. 67). Solomon Fulero (1988) concluded that psychologists had been allowed to testify

---

BOX 2.2	EXAMPLES OF TOPICS FOR PSYCHOLOGISTS AS EXPERT WITNESSES
1. Criminal responsibility	What is the relationship between the defendant's mental condition at the time of the alleged offence and the defendant's responsibility for the crime with which the defendant is charged?
2. Competence to stand trial	Does the defendant have an adequate understanding of the legal proceedings?
3. Sentencing	What are the prospects for the defendant's rehabilitation? What deterrent effects do certain sentences have? What is the defendant's level of risk for reoffence?
4. Eyewitness identification	What are the factors that affect the accuracy of eyewitness identification? How is witness confidence related to witness accuracy?
5. Trial procedure	What effects are associated with variations in pre-trial and/or trial procedures?
6. Civil commitment	Does a mentally ill person present an immediate danger or threat of danger to self or others that requires treatment no less restrictive than hospitalization?
7. Psychological damages in civil cases	What psychological consequences has an individual suffered as a result of another individual's conduct? How treatable are these consequences? To what extent are the psychological problems attributable to a pre-existing condition? Is post-traumatic symptomology related to another person's behaviour?

continued

8. Trademark litigation	Is a certain product name or trademark confusingly similar to a competitor's? Are advertising claims likely to mislead consumers?
9. Class action suits	What psychological evidence is there that effective treatment is being denied or that certain testing procedures are discriminatory against minorities in the schools or in the workplace?
10. Guardianship and conservatorship	Does an individual possess the necessary mental ability to make decisions concerning living conditions, financial matters, health, etc.?
11. Child custody	What psychological factors will affect the best interests of the child whose custody is in dispute? What consequences are these factors likely to have on the family?
12. Adoption and termination of parental rights	What psychological factors affect the child whose parents' disabilities may render them unfit to raise and care for the child?
13. Professional malpractice	Did the defendant's professional conduct fail to meet the standard of care owed to the plaintiffs?
14. Social issues in litigation	What are the effects of pornography, violence, spouse abuse, etc., on the behaviour of a defendant who claims that his or her misconduct was caused by one of these influences?

NIETZEL, M.T., *Psychological Consultation in the Courtroom*, 1st Edition, © 1986, p. 100–101. Reprinted by permission of Pearson Education, Inc., Upper Saddle River, NJ.

about eyewitness accuracy for the defence in at least 450 cases in 25 states, but many states still prevent them from doing so.

In Canada, judges generally have disallowed expert testimony concerning eyewitness testimony. For example, in the Toronto robbery case *R. v. McIntosh and McCarthy* (1997), the defence lawyer attempted to have the testimony of prominent University of Guelph researcher Dr. Dan Yarmey admitted as evidence. Yarmey was to testify on several aspects of eyewitness identification, including the accuracy of recall, the effect of postevent information, cross-racial identification, and factors at the time of the robbery that could have influenced the memory of the witnesses. When considering this evidence, the judge refused to admit Dr. Yarmey's testimony, stating, "I do not agree, based on the evidence I've heard from Dr. Yarmey, that the science has advanced that far away from the common experience of jurors" (para. 25). A major development since the case challenges this judicial viewpoint. In the 2001 inquiry into Thomas Sophonow's wrongful murder conviction in Manitoba, Justice Cory stated that injustices have resulted from errors by "honest, right-thinking eyewitnesses," and strongly advocated the need for a better understanding of eyewitness memory among

the judiciary. He stated that he "would recommend that judges consider favourably and readily admit properly qualified expert evidence pertaining to eyewitness identification. This is certainly not **junk science**. Careful studies have been made with regard to memory and its effect upon eyewitness identification" (Sophonow Inquiry Report, 2001). Therefore, we may see more expert testimony on this issue in coming years. In fact, a judge in *R. v. Henderson* (2010) admitted expert testimony on eyewitness memory, stating that "I am satisfied that Dr. Loftus has the appropriate credentials to allow her to give expert testimony in the fields of human perception, memory formulation and development, and memory recall as it pertains to eyewitness identification" (para 53).

Why have so few psychologists been permitted to testify in this area in the past? According to Benton and colleagues (2007), "… one of the most commonly cited reasons used by trial courts for excluding the testimony of eyewitness experts, (is) that the information the experts have to offer is common sense to the average juror" (p. 454). If expert reports are viewed as common sense, expert testimony is unnecessary. In reality, it has been demonstrated that judges and jurors typically endorse many misconceptions that can deter their ability to offer a fair trial (Borgida & Fiske, 2008), suggesting that experts present information far beyond the common sense of most legal decision makers. Additionally, many judges may fear that an expert witness's testimony will be so powerful that it will usurp the jury's role as the fact finders in the case.

Judges also may fear a "battle of the experts," and believe that psychologists do not possess information beyond the common knowledge of ordinary persons and may only confuse the jury with their opposing theories on the topic. These last two reasons can be combined because one factor that contributes to the court's suspicion of the quality and reliability of psychologists' testimony is disagreement within the field about psychological phenomena, with respected researchers coming to contradictory conclusions in some areas, and the controversy among psychologists over the appropriateness of testifying in court as an expert witness. Each of these issues is discussed below.

Kassin, Hosch, and Memon (2001) surveyed 64 experts on eyewitness testimony. At least 80 percent agreed that research results on each of the following topics were sufficiently reliable to present in court: the wording of questions, lineup instructions, confidence malleability, postevent information, and the accuracy–confidence correlation, as well as other topics. Experts made sharp distinctions between topics considered well established and those that were still undergoing research. Accordingly almost none of the experts were willing to testify when they felt that a body of research was inconclusive. Unlike in previous decades, partly because of developments in DNA exonerations and a wealth of new research on the subject, few psychologists today would dispute that there is sufficient empirical background to justify the use of expert testimony in eyewitness cases.

As mentioned, many judges believe that eyewitness memory is within the purview of common sense. The problem with relying on the common sense of the trier of fact in judicial decision making was shown by Yarmey (1986) in his test of the standards outlined by the U.S. Supreme Court for the assessment of eyewitness accuracy. Despite some of the court's "common sense" standards for determining eyewitness accuracy, he found that the accuracy of the witness's description of the accused and the witness's level of confidence at the time of incident were not important predictors of accuracy. In a subsequent review of the role of

eyewitness experts in the courtroom published in *Canadian Psychology*, Yarmey (2001) argued that many of the difficulties arising with eyewitness testimony contradict the common sense beliefs held by lay persons and lawyers about eyewitness memory. This view was reiterated by Justice Cory in the Sophonow Inquiry (Sophonow Inquiry Report, 2001).

Another conflict concerns the role of the expert witness. We saw in Chapter 1 that Munsterberg did not hesitate to take sides; he played the role of advocate. In contrast, contemporary psychologists have been trained to be impartial scientists. Which role is appropriate? Elizabeth Loftus posed it this way:

Should a psychologist in a court of law act as an advocate for the defense or an impartial educator? My answer to that question, if I am completely honest, is *both*. If I believe in his innocence with all my heart and soul, then I probably can't help but become an advocate of sorts. (Loftus & Ketcham, 1991, p. 238, italics in original)

As John Brigham responded, "Loftus's implication that one will become an advocate could prove destructive in the creative hands of an aggressive lawyer who is seeking to destroy an impartial expert witness's credibility" (Brigham, 1992, p. 529). Further, in the survey by Kassin, Hosch, and Memon (2001), the experts said that they were as willing to testify for the prosecution as for the defence. In response to an article by Loftus (2003), the first author and colleagues argued that "it is not our role as psychologists to make policy decisions for the legal system, just as it is not our role to comment on whether recovered memory evidence should be admissible in the courtroom. We argue that this is simply not our question to answer" (Porter, Campbell, et al., 2003b, p. 213). On the other hand, our role as researchers should be to provide relevant scientific data to legal decision makers to help them in their cases.

Ethical Responsibilities

In 1986, a psychic testified in court that a CAT scan had caused her to lose her psychic powers, and a physician—testifying as an expert witness—supported her claim. The jury awarded her US$1 million in damages (the award was later overturned). The expert witness in a trial has a great opportunity to influence case decisions; however, "it is virtually impossible to prosecute an expert witness for perjury" (*Sears v. Rutishauser*, 1984, p. 212). Michael Saks concluded that an expert witness who manages to overlook contrary findings or who commits errors "still is likely to remain safe from any formal penalty" (1992, p. 193). This includes protection from civil liability. Testimony given in court is privileged; "a witness may say whatever he or she likes under oath, and no private remedies are available to persons who may be harmed as a result" (Saks, 1992, p. 193). One problem is to decide whether an expert is deliberately deceitful or simply incompetent. Unless evidence for dishonesty exists, the court must conclude that the defendant was "only" incompetent.

Suppose that an expert witness, at the end of extended testimony, looks at the jury intently and says:

I guess you noticed that I withheld some information from the court, stretched other information, and offered an opinion that sounded more certain than our field's knowledge really permits. I did that because I am committed to making the world a better place, and I think it will be better if the court reaches the outcome I want to see in the case. (Saks, 1992, pp. 187–188)

In reality, such actions do happen, even if they are not acknowledged by the experts, who may disregard contradictory evidence, or exaggerate their own credentials. Every expert witness must consider the question: Do I tell the court things that will undercut my own seemingly authoritative knowledge? And, as is considered in detail later in this chapter, every expert must make a personal decision about what the standard should be for reporting on a particular finding or the validity of a specific diagnostic tool.

Saks (1992) identified three different ways to resolve this conflict:

1. *The conduit-educator.* As a **conduit-educator**, the expert's own field becomes his or her first priority. The thinking might go like this:

My first duty is to share the most faithful picture of my field's knowledge with those who have been assigned the responsibility to make the decisions. To do this may be to be a mere technocrat, rather than a complete human being concerned with the moral implications of what I say and with the greatest good of society. The central difficulty of this role is whether it is all right for me to contribute hard-won knowledge to causes I would just as soon see lose. (Saks, 1992, p. 189)

---

2. *The philosopher-ruler/advocate.* If the expert witness views him- or herself as a kind of **philosopher-ruler/advocate**, the oath of telling "the whole truth" is of less concern than it is in the conduit-educator role. Hans described it as follows:

Some experts chose a legal-adversary stance, in which they volunteered only research evidence that supported their side, de-emphasized or omitted the flaws in the data, or refrained from discussing opposing evidence. In the words of one expert: "I understand the partisan nature of the courtroom and I realized that I would be on the stand arguing for a position without also presenting evidence that might be contrary to my … side. But, you see, that didn't bother me, because I knew that the other side was also doing that." (Hans, 1989, p. 312)

---

3. *The hired gun.* Although somewhat similar to philosopher-ruler/advocates in their bias toward one side, hired guns serve their employer's values rather than advance their own (Saks, 1992). Their motivation is to help the person who hired them. However, the CPA's ethical guidelines assert that psychologists are responsible for attempting to prevent the distortion, misuse, or suppression of psychological data, and that they must present scientific findings in a balanced way.

Saks has suggested one test of how well the expert has assumed the honest educator's role is to ask the witness: "Please tell the court everything you know about this case that the party who called you to the witness stand hopes does not come out during your cross-examination" (Saks, 1992, p. 191).

The courts of course, have, established some standards for admissibility of proposed experts, as we introduced in Chapter 1. The first guidelines were known as the **Frye test** (*Frye v. United States*, 1923), and were established in the United States more than 80 years ago. The Frye test stated that the well-recognized standards regarding principles or evidence for any particular field should determine the admissibility of expert testimony. In the United States, additional guidelines were established in 1975 with the adoption of the Federal Rules of Evidence, which specified, among other determinants, that qualified experts can testify "if scientific, technical, or other specialized knowledge will assist the trier of fact to understand the evidence or to determine a fact in issue" (quoted by Bottoms & Davis, 1993, p. 14).

In Canada, the classic statement of the role of expert evidence is found in *Kelliher (Village of) v. Smith* (1931), in which the Supreme Court of Canada concluded that in order for testimony to be considered "expert," "the subject matter of the inquiry must be such that ordinary people are unlikely to form a correct judgment about it, if unassisted by persons with special knowledge" (p. 684). As described earlier, in *R. v. Mohan* (1994), the Supreme Court stated that expert evidence must be both *necessary* in assisting the trier

of fact and *relevant*. Again, while in some ways these requirements have been interpreted liberally, it is apparent that experts would not be allowed to testify about matters that the court felt were "common sense," such as eyewitness testimony.

SPECIFIC ROLES: THE PREPARATION OF SCIENTIFIC BRIEFS FOR THE COURTS

The efforts of Munsterberg and his contemporaries to bring scientific psychology into the courts sought to produce results that would be influential at the trial level. Munsterberg apparently never tried to influence the decision of a court of appeals. This role, specifically the preparation of **amicus curiae briefs** to accompany appeals, is an important example of the role of forensic psychologists in the United States (Collins, 2004). *Amicus curiae* briefs are arguments by a third party (in this case a

psychologist or group of psychologists) to the dispute that seek as a "friend of the court" to inform judges on matters relevant to the dispute.

In Canada, the use of *amicus curiae* briefs in this way is rare. However, courts do accept analogous submissions from psychologists about the need for certain information to be disclosed before trial. For example, a lawyer in Halifax recently requested a written submission from a forensic psychologist (the first author of this textbook) pertaining to the general importance of examining therapy notes in evaluating the credibility of recovered memories, while not speaking to the particular evidence in the case. In addition, in the mid-1990s the CPA adopted a similar role by submitting a report to the federal justice minister recommending that a full judicial inquiry be conducted into all Canadian convictions stemming from recovered memory evidence. Although this recommendation ultimately was rejected, such an action is similar in purpose to the American *amicus curiae* brief in that its intention is to alter the legal system through scientific advocacy concerning psychological evidence.

The development of *amicus curiae* briefs in part may be a result of the uncertain impact of social science on the law (Roesch, Golding, Hans, & Reppucci, 1991), leading to more activist interventions. But in doing so, psychologists force an issue we visited earlier with expert witnesses: Are we reporters of research or advocates? A second issue is—once again—the lack of agreement among psychologists on the desirability of submitting such *amicus curiae* briefs. Because *amicus curiae* briefs give an example of the strong impact psychologists can have in the legal system, we now turn to a famous historical American case in which an *amicus curiae* brief was used.

Brown v. Board of Education (1954)

In the historic decision that racially segregated schools were "inherently unequal" (*Brown v. Board of Education,* 1954), the U.S. Supreme Court cited research by psychologists Kenneth Clark and Mamie Clark and a statement by a group of prominent social scientists titled "The Effect of Segregation and the Consequences of Desegregation: A Social Science Statement." It is uncertain just how much the justices, in overturning school segregation, were influenced by the social scientists' statement (Cook, 1984). However, consider statements such as "[T]he policy of separating the races is usually interpreted as denoting the inferiority of the

Negro group," or "A sense of inferiority affects the motivation of a child to learn." These statements from the Court's opinion are consistent with the conclusions drawn from the well-publicized doll study by Kenneth Clark and Mamie Clark (1952). Consistent with conclusions, yes, but how consistent with results?

The Clarks showed a set of dolls to 134 black children (ages six to nine) in the segregated schools of Pine Bluff, Arkansas, and to 119 black children in unsegregated schools in Springfield, Massachusetts. The children were requested to do certain things, such as:

Give me the doll you like the best.

Give me the doll that looks like you.

Give me the doll that looks bad.

The segregated Southern children, the Clarks wrote, were "less pronounced in their preference for the white doll." When asked to hand their questioner "the doll that looks like you," 39 percent of the unsegregated Springfield children picked the white doll compared with only 29 percent in the segregated Arkansas schools. When asked for the nice doll, 68 percent of the Springfield children chose the white doll, while only 52 percent of the Pine Bluff children did. Which doll "looked bad"? More than 70 percent of the desegregated children chose the black doll, whereas only 49 percent of the segregated children did. What are we to make of these findings? Do they, as the Clarks concluded, show invidious effects of segregation? The straightforward interpretation of the data, for critics of the Clarks' conclusions (see van den Haag, 1960), was that if the tests demonstrate damage to black children, then they demonstrate that the damage is *less* with segregation and *greater* with desegregation.

Kenneth and Mamie Clark's interpretation of the results, as you might expect, was completely opposite. Essentially, the Clarks believed that "black children of the South were more adjusted to the feeling that they were not as good as whites, and because they felt defeated at an early age, did not bother using the device of denial" (quoted by Kluger, 1976, p. 356). Surely the Clarks' interpretation is not the most parsimonious. Did they predict this finding before the data were collected? The research report does not say. The Clarks stated that some children, when asked which doll they resembled, broke down and cried. This type of behaviour, they reported, "was more prevalent in the North than in the South" (1952, p. 560). Research results that are subject to conflicting interpretations—especially when the result is not consistent with a desired explanation—demand that the researchers begin with a theory that produces testable hypotheses. Fortunately, the U.S. Supreme Court in 1954 concluded that school segregation is inherently unequal and did not have to rely on research data for its conclusion.

If the data thus were subject to a multitude of interpretations, why did the Court not simply note that school segregation, on the face of it, induced an assumption of inferiority leading to a response of humiliation? It may have been:

> precisely because the Court knew it was backing a firm precedent and entering a heated debate, that it wished to garner *all* the supporting evidence that was available. Without data, there was a danger that the arguments on both sides might merely have become so much moral posturing and empty assertions. (Perkins, 1988, p. 471).

As Thurgood Marshall noted in 1952, the earlier separate-but-equal "doctrine had become so ingrained that overwhelming proof was sorely needed to demonstrate that equal educational opportunities for Negroes could not be provided in a segregated system" (quoted in Rosen, 1972, p. 130).

Turning from Clark and Clark's data to the statement by the social scientists that was part of the *Brown amicus* brief, we should note that some psychologists also disagree about the statement's desirability. Stuart Cook (1979), 25 years later, concluded that the information in it was sound, but Harold Gerard (1983) felt that the statement was based "not on hard data but mostly on well-meaning rhetoric" (p. 871).

Differences between Psychologists

Should a psychologist become an expert witness or aid in the preparation of scientific briefs for the courts? What accounts for the differences in the sometimes-volatile reactions of psychologists on specific issues and specific cases?

Kassin and Wrightsman (1983) proposed that jurors contemplating evidence in a criminal trial possessed varying degrees of either pro-prosecution or pro-defence biases. They found that a measure constructed to assess juror bias could predict the direction of the juror's verdict in most types of criminal trials. This analysis may be extended to differences in psychologists' reactions to involvement in the court system. How consistent should a phenomenon be to declare it reliable? And how is consistency measured: a box score of different studies' results, the percentage of variance accounted for, a meta-analysis? Monahan and Walker (1988) proposed that the same standard should exist for presenting results to the public as for peer evaluation; there should be only one standard. Elliott sought a high **standard of reliability**, or degree of consistency, in research findings; in his view, psychologists should reflect "organized skepticism" (Elliott, 1991, p. 75). Self-labels to describe those who insist on an exceedingly high standard of reliability include "cautious" and "prudent." It would seem that for such psychologists, the state of knowledge in a particular area must approach certainty. Does this mean that there is no situation in which they would endorse involvement with the courts? Elliott's response:

> The claim made here is not that scientific organizations should not or may not (or should or may) take moral positions. Rather, it is that, if they do so, they should not affect to base them on scientific foundations when such foundations are insufficient to bear the argument constructed on them. (1991, p. 74).

In contrast, psychologists who have testified and submitted *amicus* briefs or similar reports,

"I SEE YOU GOT A 74 IN YOUR CHEMISTRY FINAL, AND STILL YOU CALL YOURSELF AN EXPERT WITNESS."

www.CartoonStock.com

while demanding a clear pattern of research findings, do not have the same standards regarding reliability. Many of them endorse the "best available evidence" argument, which proposes that it is appropriate for psychologists to testify even if their conclusions must be tentative. Yarmey (1986) argued that an expert's statements should conform to the criterion of scientific respectability, but that absolute certainty is not required. He suggested the criterion: Is the evidence clear, convincing, reliable, and valid, or is it sufficiently ambiguous that experts could find support for whatever position they wished to defend?

Other representations of what might be called "the clear and convincing" standard of proof: Phoebe Ellsworth, in response to Elliott, wrote, "to keep silent until our understanding is perfect is to keep silent forever" (1991, p. 77), and "I think we should file briefs when we believe that we have something to say that would improve the quality of the courts' decision making" (p. 89).

Bersoff (1987) has asked what state of the data would ever be strong enough to persuade critics and skeptics to testify? This question leads to a consideration of a second dimension. Psychologists differ in their perception and weighing of conflicting facts, just as jurors do. Bermant (1986) proposed that these assessments of the strength of the available evidence are the basis for any decision about the propriety of expert testimony. Part of the difference in evidence interpretations results from the degree to which psychologists show **sympathy for the defendant** and a concern about avoiding erroneous convictions. The state of mind of the testifying psychologist, of course, varies from case to case, but individual differences in general predispositions may also be present.

As Ring (1971) observed more than four decades ago, most social psychologists are politically liberal. Social scientists who empathize with the defendant tend to be skeptical that the defendant truly committed the crime, or that the eyewitnesses' testimony is accurate or that the confession was voluntary. A major concern of politically liberal psychologists is that some defendants will be wrongfully convicted, imprisoned, and executed. Their critics do not share this concern. For example, McCloskey and Egeth (1983) argue that wrongful convictions from mistaken eyewitness testimony reflected only a "small fraction of the 1% of cases in which defendants were convicted at least in part on the basis of eyewitness testimony" (p. 552). Konecni and Ebbesen approvingly quoted

the above, and concluded from it "that in the state of California one person is wrongfully convicted approximately every three years because of mistaken eyewitness testimony" (1986, p. 119).

The second dimension of the differences in psychologists' willingness to intervene is the question: How many errors of omission are we willing to make to avoid making one error of commission? Konecni and Ebbesen (1986) conclude:

One wrongful conviction every three years because of mistaken identification in a state the size of California (if the estimates given above are correct) may be one wrongful conviction too many, but most reasonable people would probably regard it as well within the domain of 'acceptable risk'—acceptable because no workable system of justice is perfect. (p. 119)

Other psychologists would disagree; the magnitude of error, they would say, is much greater. But for politically liberal psychologists one wrongful conviction *really is* too many; it is unacceptable. In that regard, they seek a standard of perfection in some ways similar to the standard of perfect research consistency sought by their critics. Both seek "zero defects." The *amicus* brief directed to the U.S. Supreme Court has been a frequent mechanism by which the American Psychological Association seeks its goals to promote and advance human welfare (Grisso & Saks, 1991). In several instances this device has been effective (Tremper, 1987). But in notable cases the Court decided in a direction contrary to the conclusions supported by psychological theory and findings (*McCleskey v. Kemp*, 1987; *Schall v. Martin*, 1984).

At first it may appear that psychology's intervention was unsuccessful in such cases. But in such cases, the court's references to scientific data did not challenge the facts that the psychologists had demonstrated; it simply said that "the psychological data were not sufficient grounds upon which to decide the legal questions" (Grisso & Saks, 1991, p. 207). The Court appeared to listen to the evidence and took it seriously enough to discuss it.

Thus, in Grisso and Saks's (1991) view, these briefs may be making two important contributions to forensic psychology. First, "they may reduce the likelihood that judicial use of spurious, unsubstantiated opinions about human behavior will establish precedent for future cases" (p. 207). Second, the briefs may, to put it crudely, "keep the Court honest," or to quote Grisso and Saks, "psychology's input may compel judges to act like judges, stating clearly the fundamental values and normative premises on which their decisions are grounded, rather than hiding behind empirical errors or uncertainties" (p. 208). In this light, psychology's efforts in these controversial cases appear to be more effective.

When psychology seeks to influence the courts, it needs to go more than halfway. In a study of the court's use of social science research in cases involving children, Hafemeister and Melton (1987) concluded that when secondary social science sources were cited, they typically were works published in law reviews or government reports, not in psychology journals. The moral is clear: If you want to influence judges, publish your conclusions in the periodicals they read.

Ethical Considerations

What is the appropriate stance for psychologists who seek to influence court decisions? We have mentioned some of the dangers. Roesch, Golding, Hans, and Reppucci (1991), a group of Canadian and American collaborators, posed these choices:

Should social scientists limit themselves to conducting and publishing their research and leave it to others to apply their research findings? Or do they have an ethical obligation to assist the courts and other social groups in matters relating to their expertise? If an activist role for social scientists is appropriate, what are the comparative advantages of brief writing, expert testimony, and other mechanisms of approaching the courts? (p. 2)

When psychology as an organized profession seeks to influence the law through an *amicus curiae* brief to an appellate court, it can do so for a variety of reasons. For example, the APA may perceive a shared interest in the outcome with one of the parties in the litigation—usually this interest relates to economic benefits, powers, or prerequisites for its members (Saks, 1993). For example, in 1993, the APA filed an *amicus curiae* brief in conjunction with a court case involving the confidentiality of unfunded grant applications, such as personal details and original research ideas (Adler, 1993). This "guild" interest is not consistent with the neutral stance of some conceptions of the *amicus*

brief. Roesch et al. (1991) noted that this advocacy brief contrasts with the **science-translation brief**, that is, an objective summary of a body of research similar to the one the CPA submitted to the justice minister concerning repressed memories.

The science-translation brief reflects the second role, as an honest broker. It is offered when the psychological body possesses knowledge the court otherwise might not have and that might assist the court in deciding the case before it. Saks argued that taking this role "minimizes the temptation to fudge, maximizes the value of the knowledge to the public interest" (1993, p. 243) and helps protect the integrity of psychology.

Even a science-translation brief will reflect the perspective and values of its writers (Roesch et al., 1991). How much interpretation should a brief contain? Melton and Saks suggested that both the advocacy brief and the science-translation brief:

---

can end up misleading a reader, especially a lay reader, which is what judges are when they read these kinds of briefs. The solution, we think, is in approaching the writing with an honest desire to share with the courts a faithful picture of the available psychological knowledge, and to interpret the research only to the extent that doing so will clarify its meaning. (1990, p. 5)

Because controversy is inevitable in science, any science-translation brief will generate some disagreement by social scientists. But "in preparing briefs, social scientists should strive to ensure, at a minimum, that briefs represent a consensual view of social scientists (i.e., what *most* experts in the field would conclude)" (Roesch et al., 1991, p. 6). Alternative explanations should be included, when appropriate.

Guidelines for Forensic Psychologists

As interest in forensic psychology continues to grow, systematic concern about codifying the ethical guidelines has increased. The CPA provides general guidelines concerning issues such as confidentiality (see Box 2.3), dual relationships, and test administration for psychologists working in legal contexts, whereas the American Psychology-Law Society has developed a more specific set of guidelines for forensic psychologists, under the direction of Stephen L. Golding, Thomas Grisso, and David Shapiro, than are generally accepted in Canada. These *Specialty Guidelines for Forensic Psychology* were originally developed and published in 1991, and revised in 2011 because of continued development in the field and practitioners' need for updated ethical and practical guidelines. These guidelines focus on several aspects of forensic work, including the relationship between psychologists and litigating parties and procedures in preparing forensic evaluations. The Committee on the Revision of the Specialty Guidelines for Forensic Psychology (2011) explains:

> The goals of these *Guidelines* are to improve the quality of forensic psychological services;

enhance the practice and facilitate the systematic development of forensic psychology; encourage a high level of quality in professional practice; and encourage forensic practitioners to acknowledge and respect the rights of those they serve. (p. 1)

The updated guidelines are readily available on the AP-LS website (www.ap-ls.org). In another way of certifying competence, the American Board of Forensic Psychology offers a diploma in forensic psychology, indicating that the recipient is at the highest level of excellence in his or her field of forensic competence. Many Canadian forensic psychologists have been certified in this manner.

BOX 2.3 CONFIDENTIALITY AND PSYCHOTHERAPISTS

When a person consults with a psychologist, there is an assurance from professional ethics codes that information shared within the meeting will remain confidential. In this context, confidentiality means that nothing will be shared with a third party, except for other medical or mental health professionals (and then only as required). A privileged communication extends even beyond the ethical expectation of confidentiality into a legal obligation. In general, a person involved in the contract of a privileged communication cannot be compelled to disclose the privileged information in the courtroom. Examples of such relationships include lawyers and clients, spouses, doctors and patients, and religious advisers and their followers.

It is noteworthy that there is a legal precedent on the matter of duty to warn in the Canadian case *Smith v. Jones* (1999). In this case, Jones underwent a psychiatric assessment (by Smith) requested by the defence for the purpose of sentencing. During the assessment, Mr. Jones disclosed his intent to kidnap, rape, and kill prostitutes. Dr. Smith informed the defence counsel of the threats, and was instructed to maintain confidentiality as the disclosures were bound under the solicitor-client privilege. Dr. Smith pursued a civil action entitling him the legal right to disclose the threat, and to force the lawyer to present this information to the courts in the sentencing hearing. This case was appealed through to the Supreme Court of Canada, which held that lawyer-client privilege is limited in the circumstance that public safety is at risk. The court ruled that a breach of solicitor-client confidentiality was warranted when (1) there is a

clear risk to an identifiable class of victims; (2) there is a risk of serious bodily harm or death; and (3) the danger is imminent. However, the dissenting position stated that confidentiality should be maintained in all other circumstances in order to promote confidence in legal and therapeutic relationships. Within this context, dangerous individuals may be more likely to disclose the danger they pose, and seek treatment, rather than acting on these impulses (*Smith v. Jones*, 1999). This case provides the legal backbone requiring Canadian mental health professionals to breach confidentiality and fulfill their ethical duty to warn and protect third parties from harm (Glancy, Regehr, Bryant, & Schneider, 1999).

But what of evidence of past crimes? Is confidentiality provided? Consider the U.S case of Lyle and Erik Menendez, who were charged with killing their parents. In this case, the police were informed by a former lover of the brothers' psychotherapist (Beverly Hills psychologist L. Jerome Oziel) that tapes existed on which the brothers had confessed to their parents' murders. So a further question arose: Can psychologist–client privilege be broken by a third party?

In 1992, two years after the brothers' arrest, the California Supreme Court suppressed the tape from evidence as an invasion of therapist–client privilege. But when (in late 1993) the trial started, the brothers presented their mental state as an issue in the trial. The trial judge then ruled that the client privilege was waived. The judge acknowledged that his ruling had little precedent and that it was "a unique situation not addressed by any other case in any other court" (quoted by Associated Press, 1993, p. A7).

SUMMARY

The roles of forensic psychologists in the legal system are diverse, but they share certain temptations, including promising too much, substituting advocacy for scientific objectivity, letting values overcome empirically based conclusions, doing a cursory job, and maintaining dual relationships and competing roles.

Psychologists differ about the degree to which the field should apply its findings to solutions of legal problems. Some believe that psychologists do not possess findings that are sufficiently reliable to be applied to real-life decisions. Others are critical of the majority of their colleagues, who because of their politically liberal orientations,

tend to sympathize with the defendant in criminal cases. Psychologists active in legal intervention respond by noting that the information from that field, although not perfectly consistent, improves the quality of decision making in the legal system. The courts have entered this controversy by considering just what the standard should be in admitting scientific evidence at trial. In pivotal decisions, the courts have applied standards of scientific acceptance (i.e., publication in a peer-reviewed journal, replicability) to determine the admissibility of psychologists as expert witnesses, and the roles to be assumed by forensic psychologists in court.

KEY TERMS

advocate role, p. 27

amicus curiae briefs, p. 39

assessment, p. 25

conduit-educator, p. 38

confidentiality, p. 33

dual relationships, p. 31

expert witness, p. 26

fact witness, p. 34

Frye test, p. 38

hired gun, p. 27

junk science, p. 36

philosopher-ruler/advocate, p. 38

science-translation brief, p. 43

standard of reliability, p. 41

sympathy for the defendant, p. 42

trial consultant, p. 31

SUGGESTED READINGS

Brodsky, S. L. (1991). *Testifying in court: Guidelines and maxims for the expert witness.* Washington, DC: American Psychological Association.
This relentlessly readable book by one of the United States' most respected forensic psychologists includes a wealth of practical suggestions, succinctly put. An example: "With indifferent attorneys be assertive. With incompetent attorneys, decline the case or educate them" (p. 197).

Committee on the Revision of the Specialty Guidelines for Forensic Psychology (2011). *Specialty guidelines for forensic psychology.* Retrieved from http://www.ap-ls.org/aboutpsychlaw/SpecialtyGuidelines.php
It is important that we understand the roles and responsibilities forensic psychologists are expected to assume.

Gottlieb, M. C., & Coleman, A. (2012). Ethical challenges in forensic psychology practice. In S. J. Knapp, M. C. Gottlieb, M. M. Handelsman, L. D. VandeCreek, S. J. Knapp, M. C. Gottlieb, ... L. D. VandeCreek (Eds.), *APA handbook of ethics in psychology, Vol 2: Practice, teaching, and research* (pp. 91–123). Washington, DC: American Psychological Association.
This chapter in the most recent volume of the *APA Handbook of Ethics* focuses on the roles that psychologists play in the legal system. It includes discussions about the additional obligations that forensic psychologists face and the ethical dilemmas they must resolve. All forensic psychologists should keep up to date on the *Handbook of Ethics*!

Hagen, M. A. (1997). *Whores of the court: The fraud of psychiatric testimony and the rape of American justice.* New York: HarperCollins.
A few forensic psychologists love it, more hate it, and some of us say, "Yes, but ..." (see Box 2.1 on pages 27–28). Certainly the most talked-about book in recent years.

Melton, G., Petrila, J., Poythress, N. G., & Slobogin, C. (2007). *Psychological evaluations for the courts* (3rd ed.). New York, NY US: Guilford Press.

This book is a great source of information about conducting assessments and writing up psychological reports for the courts. It not only provides useful information about the nature and content of a wide variety of psychological reports, but also offers best practice guidelines and sample reports. This is a must-read for any psychologist who plans to conduct psychological assessments for the courts.

Ziskin, J. (1995). *Coping with psychiatric and psychological testimony* (Vol. 1–3, 5th ed.). Los Angeles: Law and Psychology Press.

Few of us have had such an impact that our names have become verbs within the lingo of a certain profession, but that is true of the late Jay Ziskin. When trial lawyers "Ziskinize" psychologists or psychiatrists who are testifying, they challenge them by cross-examining them intensively with regard to the accuracy of their statements and the validity of the procedures they have used. This three-volume set (earlier editions were prepared with David Faust) assesses the validity of a number of forensic topics; any forensic psychologist who anticipates being an expert witness needs to consult these volumes.

WEBSITE

Canadian Code of Ethics for Psychologists, Third Edition: **http://www.cpa.ca/cpasite/userfiles/Documents/Canadian%20Code%20of%20Ethics%20for%20Psycho.pdf**

The Police: Selection, Training, and Evaluation

> *Looking in the rear view mirror, I want to state unequivocally that this organization is solidly on the right road and is making excellent progress.*
>
> —Royal Canadian Mounted Police Commissioner Giuliano Zaccardelli (RCMP 2004/2005 Directional Statement)

> *I am very concerned about these very troubling reports . . . We expect all members of the RCMP to carry out their duties with integrity and professionalism. Our government is committed to providing all women in the RCMP a workplace free of sexual harassment. I will be raising this issue with the new commissioner very shortly.*
>
> —Public Safety Minister of Canada Vic Toews regarding a large number of cases of sexual harassment against women by RCMP officers in 2011

PSYCHOLOGY'S ROLE IN POLICE WORK

This chapter explores the manner in which psychology can play a significant role in many aspects of police work, from the selection of recruits, through the training of police and other law enforcement officers, to the evaluation of their work performance. Forensic psychologists can assist in responding to the major types of complaints about the police—corruption, racism, sexual harassment, and brutality. Further, psychology and the other social sciences have evaluated recent changes in police procedures, such as **team policing,** or the assignment of police officers to particular neighbourhoods so that they become familiar with local concerns and priorities. The main purpose of this chapter is to examine what psychology has to offer in attaining the goal of improving law enforcement procedures.

WHO ARE THE CLIENTS?

In terms of both public perception and officer morale the last several years have been awful for the RCMP and other police forces in Canada (see Perrott & Kelloway, 2011). There have been numerous scandals involving police corruption and brutality, and allegations of systemic sexual harassment against female officers. In June 2010 a public inquiry evaluating the use of Tasers in British Columbia greatly criticized the RCMP's use of the weapons, particularly in the notorious case of Robert Dziekanski, a Polish immigrant who arrived at the Vancouver International Airport to meet his mother on October 14, 2007. He died after being Tasered five times by a group of four RCMP officers, in a terrifying incident that was caught on cell phone video by observers. As of 2012, all four officers have been charged with perjury for lying about the circumstances of the Tasering incident. The case is ongoing. In November 2011, Corporal Catherine Galliford, a former spokeswoman for the BC RCMP, came forward to claim that she had been the victim of chronic sexual harassment throughout her 20-year career. In 2004, the largest investigation into police corruption in Canadian history was ongoing in Toronto, with allegations of serious criminal activity against at least 12 members (Seglins, 2008). As of June 2012, five former drug squad officers have been convicted of attempting to obstruct justice. In January 2004, the Halifax Police Department publicly apologized to boxer Kirk Johnson for treating him unfairly due to his race. In June 2010 there were numerous allegations of police brutality and civil rights violations by police officers during the G8/G20 summit protests in Ontario. In January 2011, Kelowna RCMP officer Geoff Mantler was videotaped apparently kicking a man in the head after he was on the ground and had already surrendered to the officer. (Mantler has been charged with aggravated assault.) This incident made media headlines all over Canada, and caused citizens to question the morality of their country's police officers. Did these incidents come out of the blue? Are these simply a "few bad apples"? Not according to famed Canadian police psychologist Mike Webster who had worked for the RCMP on contract for over 30 years (see Mason, 2009). After Robert Dziekanski's death, Webster spoke publicly about the RCMP's systemic problems and ultimately lost most of his contract work (Mason, 2009). Webster (2009 as reported by *The Globe and Mail*'s online edition) stated:

I hold the RCMP executive responsible for this attitude and indirectly responsible for Robert's death. Tragically, the four policemen were doing what they had been trained to ... the RCMP must accept that they are not an elite group above and separate from the community ... the RCMP is in need of significant transformational change ... Changing bits and pieces of its infrastructure ... will not suffice. These kinds of changes focus on the outdated core values and culture ... most of the resistance comes from the top.

Less acknowledged is the other side of the coin: the acts of heroism by law enforcement officers and the risk of officers' death or injury and mental health problems. On March 3, 2005, four RCMP officers were shot and killed by James Roszko in Mayerthorpe, Alberta, during an operation to recover stolen property and investigate a possible marijuana grow-op. One of the officers had been on the job for less than three weeks. According to a CBC report, a total of 222 RCMP officers and those from the RCMP's predecessor the North West Mounted Police have been killed in the line of duty since the 1870s (CBC News, 2011). Further, stresses on the police can take a terrible toll; in a 2006 Canadian report, the Standing Senate Committee on Social Affairs, Science and Technology observed that **police stress** often leads to mental health problems such as depression, substance abuse, burnout, and even suicide (report available on Parliament of Canada's website [see end of chapter for link]). These problems may be especially prevalent in the scandal-ridden RCMP. A recent study of a group of 129 RCMP constables found that they perceived themselves to be less in control, to have less workplace social support, and to experience greater levels of psychological distress than a control group of 60 municipal constables in Nova Scotia (Perrott & Kelloway, 2011).

According to Loo (1986), 35 RCMP officers committed suicide between 1960 and 1983. Between 1975 and 1999, 22 members of the Toronto Police Service committed suicide, a far higher rate than the general population (Schaer, 1999). According to a 2010 CBC news report, an internal RCMP staff survey suggested that nearly 60 percent of officers and staff in British Columbia considered quitting the force last year because of frustrations in the workplace, lack of recognition, and unrealistic expectations.

In identifying the possible contributions of psychology to policing, we begin by asking: Who are the **clients**? To whom are forensic psychologists responsible when they seek to apply psychological knowledge in the policing context? While a practising forensic psychologist might be hired by a police department—most often as a consultant although sometimes as a staff member—the psychologist also has an ethical responsibility to respond to the public's concerns about the police. As we will see, meeting both of these responsibilities at the same time often is extremely challenging.

The Public

What does the public expect of police officers? Common expectations might include fairness,

The internationally-revered RCMP has been severely criticized in the past several years for various reasons described in this chapter.

respect, and a lack of prejudice against specific groups. However, not surprisingly in light of the above scandals, the public does not believe that the police always meet these standards. After several stories about alleged incidents of police brutality in British Columbia (especially in Vancouver), the Ipsos-Reid Group polled citizens of the province in October 2003, and found that about 26 percent of residents considered incidents of police brutality to be "common." A desire for police fairness and an equal treatment of all citizens is typical among citizens (Tyler & Folger, 1980; Vermunt, Blaauw, & Lind, 1998). A frequent complaint about Canadian police is their discrimination against visible-minority groups such as Aboriginal Canadians, blacks, and others. For decades, members of visible-minority groups have perceived themselves to be unjustly victimized by police officers (Decker & Wagner, 1982). Blacks believe they are discriminated against by the police far more than are whites in several ways, including being roughed up unnecessarily, being stopped and searched without justification, and being subjected to abusive language.

This perception was given credibility in a case in Halifax, in 2003. Heavyweight boxer Kirk Johnson claimed he was discriminated against because of his ethnic background when Halifax police pulled him over and seized his car in 1998. The Nova Scotia Human Rights Commission ruled in Johnson's favour in December 2003, ordering police to pay him $10 000 in damages. It found that officers had "acted on a stereotype."

Despite the fact that several years have passed since the Johnson incident, visible minority Canadian residents still feel that they are treated worse than white residents. Although several years have passed since the Johnson incident, visible-minority Canadian residents still feel they are treated worse than white residents. Wortley and Owusu-Bempah (2011) explored police stop-and-search activity using a 2007 survey of Toronto residents. The results suggested that blacks were 3.3 times more likely than whites to report having been stopped and searched by the police. The researchers also found that males and younger individuals were more likely to be stopped and searched by the police compared with females and older people, which suggests that Canadian police officers may be acting on racial, sexist, and ageist stereotypes.

Another unforgettable incident of police brutality involving race is the case of Amadou Diallo (Williams, 2007). On February 5, 1999, Guinean immigrant Amadou Diallo was confronted in his New York City home by four police officers because he fit the description of a rape suspect. When Diallo proceeded to pull out his wallet and identification to prove that he was innocent, the police shot him 41 times. Because of this extreme, excessive violence against a black individual, racism was believed to have contributed to the incident. In an experimental investigation, Kahn and Davies (2011) assessed shooting reflexes when community participants were presented with either a black or white man with a gun/wallet in his hand (in video game format). They found that when the black man had either a wallet or a gun in his hand, he was much more likely to be shot than a white man, suggesting increased danger to blacks and intensifying racial bias.

So great are these concerns that victims sarcastically use the crime-classification expression **DWB** ("driving while black") to reflect the tendency of some patrol officers to concentrate on visible minorities as possible offenders. While until recently the problem was much more apparent in the United States, inquiries into policing and the legal system in Nova Scotia, Manitoba, and Ontario have indicated the presence of police bias against various visible-minority groups in Canada (Rudin, 2000). Indeed, the Canadian courts have acknowledged the existence of **racial profiling**. For example, in April 2003, the Ontario Court of Appeal stated in *R. v. Brown* (2003):

In the opening part of his submission before this court, counsel for the appellant (the Crown) said that he did not challenge the fact that the phenomenon of racial profiling by the police existed. This was a responsible position to take because, as counsel said, this conclusion is supported by significant social science research (note 4 at 165).

A 2003 report by the Ontario Human Rights Commission called "Paying the Price: The Human Cost of Racial Profiling" concluded that a major problem existed with "the entire criminal justice system's" treatment of Aboriginal people (p. 58). The report noted that Aboriginal people are vastly overrepresented in the correctional system, from arrest by police to incarceration in prison. While making up only 2.8 percent of Canada's population, Aboriginal people comprise 17 percent of the federal offender population. In fact, adult

Aboriginal people are incarcerated at more than six times the national rate, and they are denied parole at a higher rate than other offenders. In a 2007 survey of Toronto residents, They (2011) found that black respondents are more likely to view racial profiling as a major problem in Canada than whites or Asians. They also found that the black community's concern with racial profiling may be justified; black respondents were much more likely to report being stopped and searched by the police in the two years preceding the survey than respondents of other racial backgrounds.

What can be done to resolve this problem? Does psychology have anything to offer? Although this topic deserves more attention, one intervention is the use of a psychologist to assist in community involvement in **police selection**. Often, the goals in selection by police departments reflect traditional criteria but fail to recognize the goal of diversity in the makeup of law enforcement agencies, specifically the hiring of visible minorities and women.

Katherine W. Ellison (1985) is a community psychologist who was invited to develop a new procedure for selecting police officers for a New Jersey police department. In doing so, she capitalized on the concept of **stakeholders**, people who have a special knowledge and interest, or a stake, in running the department. Stakeholders included, as you would expect, officers from the department, especially patrol officers. Members of the township council and other township officials, as well as members of the local media, the clergy, and other opinion leaders were included as well. But Ellison also solicited interviews from a stratified quota sample of 100 citizens from the community and included community representatives in the specific panel that interviewed candidates for police training. A side benefit, in addition to selecting officers who reflected community demographics, was an increase in the communication between the police and members of the community. Recent research exploring characteristics, qualities, and skills that stakeholders view as most important when hiring police chiefs found that personal traits (including integrity, strong morality, and leadership traits), political knowledge, communication skills, and being "inspirational" were the most desired characteristics (O'Leary, Resnick-Luetke, & Monk-Turner, 2011). Recent empirical research has examined the relation between such personal

features and actual job performance. Ono et al. (2011) examined the extent to which cognitive ability, the Big Five factor personality dimensions, and emotional intelligence were related to training and job performance of U.S. federal criminal investigators. While conscientiousness was modestly related to training performance, cognitive ability and emotional intelligence were significant predictors of job performance and neuroticism was negatively correlated with job performance.

A second community concern is **police corruption**. Alpert and Smith (1994) found that one third of all police force complaint incidents involved excessive force, suggesting that police brutality and police corruption—police misconduct specifically for personal gain (e.g., financial profit)—are commonplace. Deviant behaviour by police can vary along a continuum of seriousness (a categorization is offered in Box 3.1). Canadians were astonished in January 2004 when six officers in the Toronto Police Department were charged with robbery, assault, perjury, and conspiracy. After a lengthy delay, finally the trials began in 2012. The officers allegedly concocted informants, stole hundreds of thousands of dollars, and helped to launder money. Court documents also revealed that some officers pretended to get tips from false informants and used this fabricated information to obtain search warrants (CBC News Online, 2004, January 20). Modern corruption by police officers is different from that of earlier times, when some officers were bribed to ignore rampant examples of gambling, prostitution, or liquor violations. Now, the corruption is manifested in officers who are active participants in the crime; some, in the words of the former police commissioner of New York City, William Bratton, have "truly become predatory figures" (quoted by Johnson, 1998, p. 8A).

In some cases, officers who engage in corrupt behaviour do so partly because of difficulties in achieving professional success. Big city police who are given the task of capturing drug dealers often must rely on informants, but when the police slip informants money for information (usually $10 to $20), their supervisors ridicule their requests for reimbursement, telling them that's just part of doing business (Kramer, 1997). But temptations to become lawbreakers also are a part of chasing drug dealers. One police officer, convicted of corruption, told a reporter:

So when we hit a place, we'd take some money to reimburse our informant payments. After a while, with so much dough sitting around, you just take more, and then you begin to get used to it. Unless you're completely nuts, you're careful. If you find 10 grand, say, you take only three or four. You can't raid a drug house and come back and not turn in some money. That'd be a sure tipoff. (quoted by Kramer, 1997, p. 83)

Why does such corruption occur, given the extensive screening that is demanded of potential candidates? Are these behaviours the result of personality characteristics, or do they develop from the presence of a subculture (a local precinct, a squad of officers) prone to corruption? These are important questions that have not received sufficient study. O'Connor (2005) suggested that police deviance is viewed as a slippery slope, in which social moral inhibitions gradually deteriorate with time on the job. Skolnick (1966) concluded that a process of informal socialization—specifically, interactions with experienced officers—was perhaps more important than police-academy training in determining how rookies viewed their work and the public. In his classic analysis of police life, Niederhoffer (1967) argued that the police subculture transformed a police officer into an authoritarian personality, and several studies of changes that take place during the passage from being a recruit to an experienced police officer support such a tendency (Carlson & Sutton, 1975; Genz & Lester, 1976; Hageman, 1979; McNamara, 1967). Role demands may lead to increased authoritarianism and a greater willingness to use force; working in high-crime areas seemed to foster authoritarianism in the police (Brown & Willis, 1985). One empirical study to determine whether authoritarianism scores of police officers were related to the number of times they had been disciplined found no significant relationship (Henkel, Sheehan, & Reichel, 1997), but the approach needs to be extended. Expressions of brutality and corruption may well reflect an interaction between a predisposition to law breaking within the individual officer and being in a subculture that makes such actions easy to do and easy to get away with doing—a subculture that may even have norms that encourage such behaviour. However, with increasing technology (e.g., cell phone cameras) and greater potential for posting representations of police misconduct on public websites (e.g., Youtube, Facebook), police are under tighter surveillance and encouraged to present themselves on their best behaviour (Goldsmith, 2010). This new visibility has been brought on by incidents such as the 2007 Robert Dziekanski case in Vancouver, and the 2010 G20 summit "Officer Bubbles" case in which a Toronto police officer was caught on video threatening to arrest a protestor for simply blowing bubbles. Similar incidents include the 2011 Kelowna

---

BOX 3.1 | **TYPES OF POLICE DEVIANCE BY CATEGORY AND EXAMPLE**

Higher-Level Corruption

Violent Crimes: The physical abuse of suspects, including torture and nonjustifiable homicide

Denying Civil Rights: "Routine" schemes to circumvent constitutional guarantees

Criminal Enterprise: The resale of confiscated drugs, stolen property, and so forth

Major Bribes: Accepting, for example, $1000 to "overlook" contraband shipments and other law violations

Property Crimes: Burglary, theft, and so forth

Lower-Level Corruption

Role Malfeasance: Destroying evidence, offering biased testimony, and protecting "crooked" cops

Being "Above" Inconvenient Laws: Speeding, smoking marijuana

Minor Bribes: Accepting, for example, $20 to "look the other way" on a parking or moving violation

Playing Favourites: Not ticketing friends, family, and so forth

Gratuities: Accepting free coffee, meals, and so forth

SCHMALLEGER, FRANK J., *Criminal Justice Today: An Introductory Text for the 21st Century*, 8th Edition, © 2005, p. 330. Reprinted by permission of Pearson Education, Inc., Upper Saddle River, NJ.

Mantler case and the Ian Tomlinson case in London, England, during which police assaulted Tomlinson—without reason—during a peaceful protest, and Tomlinson ultimately died.

The Police Department

A second client of the forensic psychologist, of course, is the police department itself, as exemplified by Canadian psychologist Mike Webster, described earlier, who worked for the RCMP for more than three decades. A psychologist can assist police departments and other law enforcement agencies in answering a number of important questions, such as:

- What should be included in the training program for recruits? Does success in a training program predict effectiveness as a police officer?
- Are there ways to prevent or reduce police burnout? What are effective ways to deal with the stresses of police work?
- How effective are different strategies for combating crime? Are foot patrols more effective than police cars? Does saturated patrolling work?
- What kinds of techniques work best when solving criminal cases?

Ensuing sections of the chapter examine psychology's responses to these questions and identify conflicts between the approaches of psychology and the police. More detailed information relevant to these questions can be found in books on the topic of police psychology, including those by Blau (1994), Kurke and Scrivner (1995), Miller (2006), and Kitaeff (2011).

THE SELECTION OF POLICE

What should be the goals of a program to select candidates for law enforcement training? Foremost for police chiefs has been the screening out of mentally ill applicants rather than the selection of those with a desirable profile (Reiser, 1982c). Some psychologists (e.g., Smith & Stotland, 1973) have proposed that we should move beyond this focus on gross pathology. For example, what are the characteristics of an ideal law enforcement officer, and how best are they measured (Fruyt et al., 2009)? Psychology has made strides toward answering these questions over the last 80 years but definitive answers remain elusive, partly because

of the lack of agreement about the ideal and partly because some desired traits cannot be reliably measured (Ainsworth, 1995).

Attainment of the goal of selecting desirable police officers for training is especially tantalizing because the initial pool is typically a large one. However, Hadley (2009) indicates that the number of applicants has declined across Canada in recent years partly because qualified candidates are less attracted to the policing career. The selection of recruits for the RCMP in Canada is rigorous. Police recruits are required to write the **RCMP Police Aptitude Test (RPAT)**, a multiple-choice 144-question test designed to evaluate one's aptitude for police work. Seven psychological competencies are measured that are seen by the RCMP as essential to perform as a police officer: composition (spelling, grammar, and vocabulary), comprehension, memory, judgment, observation, logic, and computation. Applicants who score high enough on the RPAT then must pass a Physical Abilities Requirement Evaluation (PARE). Applicants who succeed in the PARE then must participate in an **interview** to assess their communication and knowledge competencies as well as their potential to obtain a security clearance. Following this stage, candidates undergo a background investigation, several personality measures, a pre-employment polygraph test to confirm their prior history, and, finally, basic cadet training. Obviously, one must be highly motivated to go through such a gruelling application process!

A History of Psychology and Police Selection

Psychologists' involvement in the evaluation of police characteristics extends back to Lewis Terman, the author of the widely used Stanford-Binet intelligence test. Terman (1917), publishing in the very first issue of the *Journal of Applied Psychology,* tested the intelligence of 30 police and firefighter applicants in San José, California. Finding that their average IQ was 84, he recommended that no one whose IQ fell below 80 should be accepted for those positions (Spielberger, 1979).

Several decades later, the emphasis shifted to personality characteristics. In the 1940s an attempt was made to use the Humm-Wadsworth Temperament Scale as a basis to select police applicants in Los Angeles (Humm & Humm, 1950), despite the lack of evidence for its validity (Ostrov, 1986). Since then, a variety of procedures has been employed by psychologists to enhance the selection of optimal recruits. Personality inventories continue to be used, but interviews and situational tests also become prioritized as tools. Each of these approaches is evaluated in the next sections.

TOOLS FOR PSYCHOLOGICAL SELECTION

The Interview

As in the selection of persons for most professional positions, the personal interview has been a central part of the selection process for law enforcement officers throughout North America. In some areas, a clinical psychologist or psychiatrist conducts a brief interview, with a traditional goal of searching for psychopathology (Silverstein, 1985). But, more recently, emphasis has shifted to the use of the interview to assess such desirable qualities as social maturity, stability, and skill in interpersonal relations (Janik, 1993). Chandler (1990) viewed the interview as addressing issues about "military bearing," sense of humour, and absence of anger. The interview can provide information on interviewee characteristics not visible through other procedures; these include body language, appropriateness of emotions expressed, insight into one's own behaviour, and an ability to convey a sense of self (Silverstein, 1985).

Nevertheless, as a selection device, the interview is fraught with problems. The purpose of the clinical interview (an interview conducted by a clinician to assess the mental health of the applicant) traditionally has been not so much to predict behaviour but to gain an in-depth understanding of the individual. Validity often was assessed by comparing one clinician's judgment with that of other clinicians. The literature from industrial/organizational psychology on the use of the clinical interview gives no indication that it is valid as a predictor of job performance (Ulrich & Trumbo, 1965), one issue being that self-presentation tactics often are successful (e.g., Barrik, Shaffer, & DeGrassi, 2009) and observers often are unduly influenced by physical appearance and demeanour (e.g., Porter & ten Brinke, 2009).

Although interviews have been steadily improving with the addition of structure since the early 1960s (Jacobs, Cushenbury, & Grabarek, 2011), there still is no agreed-upon format for the interview. However, some urge that the interview be standardized so that it always covers issues relevant to the job criteria (Hibler & Kurke, 1995), and modern interview practices that are employed today attempt to incorporate individual questions that are applicable to key requirements of the job (Jacobs et al., 2011). A structured approach also permits comparisons between applicants, but other psychologists and psychiatrists prefer the opportunity to probe topics of concern as these emerge from the responses of the individual candidate. Regardless of the procedures used, it is essential that the interview be conducted fairly and equitably (Jones, 1995). Members of visible-minority ethnic groups who are applicants are sensitive to possibilities of racial bias by interviewers, and some commentators (Jones, 1995; Milano, 1989) have suggested that a form be prepared, specifying the topics covered in the interview. Today, careful attention is given to factors that might affect an interviewee's performance (e.g., interviewer tone of voice, interview environment, etc.), and all of these features are thought to increase the reliability of the interview (Chapman & Zweig, 2005).

An article by Hargrave and Hiatt (1987) cites studies related to psychiatric interviews (the assessment of the applicant's mental health) for selection of police officers. One of the problems they note is the strong tendency for people to portray themselves more positively in face-to-face interviews than on personality tests (e.g., Barrik et al., 2009), resulting in an increase in the number of **false positives** (poor risks who are hired) and no impact on the goal of reducing **false negatives** (those not hired who would have displayed acceptable performance).

Two particular problems obstruct the attainment of validity for interviews in police selection, neither specific to this particular occupation (Spielberger, 1979). The first is the lack of criteria against which to judge predictors (Hargrave & Hiatt, 1987); police and other law enforcement officers have a great deal of autonomy in their activities and the number of activities they carry out daily may be quite diverse. Second, screening of applicants via a clinical interview leads to an elimination of those considered unqualified; the resulting studies thus have a restricted range of candidates, from whom individual differences in effectiveness are compared with their interview results.

Hargrave and Hiatt (1987) aimed to deal with the second problem by capitalizing on a rather unusual situation. Two classes of police academy trainees (n = 105) were individually tested and interviewed by two clinical psychologists who each rated them on suitability for the job. However, these ratings were not used to exclude any candidate from training. The trainees were rated on the following: personality characteristics (anxiety, mood, anger, antisocial characteristics, and ability to accept criticism), interpersonal effectiveness (ability to communicate, assertiveness, self-confidence, and ability to get along with others), and intellectual characteristics (judgment and verbal skills). The interview used a five-point rating scale, ranging from 1 = unsuitable to 5 = excellent, in order to assess overall psychological suitability for the job.

The trainees then completed a five-month law enforcement course at the academy. At the end of training, three performance criteria were examined: (1) attrition during training, (2) ratings of psychological suitability given by the training officers, and (3) peer evaluations. Correlations were determined between each of these and the ratings by each clinician. The correlations follow:

	CLINICIAN A	CLINICIAN B
Academic attrition	.24**	.14
Instructors' ratings	.19	.27*
Peer evaluations	.09	.13
Composite criterion	.26**	.24**

*$p < .05$
**$p < .01$

Although some of these correlation coefficients are statistically significant, the relationships are relatively weak and are certainly too low to make confident predictions about the success of individuals.

An analysis of clinicians' dichotomized ratings of "suitable" versus "unsuitable" with the goal criterion of "successful" versus "unsuccessful" found that Clinician A correctly classified 67 percent of the subjects, and Clinician B 69 percent; an analysis of trainees who were rated by the clinicians as "suitable" but were "unsuccessful" on the composite criterion indicated that all but one were unsuccessful due to attrition.

Psychological Tests

Although the administration of psychological tests to police trainees is a frequent selection strategy, recent research has found that age and attitude are bigger predictors of job performance than personality traits (Sanders, 2007). Psychological tests can be group administered, computer scored, and easily interpreted. But do they have any validity?

The MMPI and the CPI. General personality measures such as the **Minnesota Multiphasic Personality Inventory (MMPI)** (Hathaway & McKinley, 1983) and the California Psychological Inventory (CPI) (Gough, 1975) are staples of such testing. The MMPI originally was designed in the early 1940s to identify persons with psychotic or neurotic problems. As Blau (1994) observed, it has been the workhorse of paper-and-pencil personality assessment for more than half a century. It consists of 550 true-or-false items and usually takes an hour to complete. In the late 1980s, the MMPI-2 was developed out of a need to update and restandardize the original instrument (Butcher, Dahlstrom, Graham, Tellegen, & Kaemmer, 1989). Whether the MMPI-2 was an improvement over the original MMPI has generated much discussion (see Blau, 1994) One study that administered both scales to 166 police officers found that 70 percent of them produced normal profiles on both tests (Hargrave, Hiatt, Ogard, & Karr, 1993). But individual respondents did not always score the highest on the same subscale from one form of the test to the other. Caillouet et al. (2010) found that among a sample of more than 400 police officers, the MMPI-2 profiles had little predictive validity in terms of police performance or misconduct.

The **California Psychological Inventory (CPI)** is similar in format to the MMPI, but its subscales reflect personal traits such as dominance, sociability, and flexibility, in contrast to the diagnostic categories (e.g., Psychopathic Deviate, Hypomania) of the MMPI. A survey of 72 major law enforcement agencies (Strawbridge & Strawbridge, 1990) found that the MMPI was by far the most frequently used instrument—in 33, or 46 percent, of the departments. The next most frequent were the CPI (in 11 departments) and the Inwald Personality Inventory (used in five departments), discussed below. The Rorschach Inkblot Technique was used by two departments, and two used a human-figure drawings test (some departments used multiple tests.) Thirty-seven (or 51 percent) of the departments used no test at all. This Strawbridge & Strawbridge survey is more than 20 years old and, because more departments have sought accreditation by the Commission on Accreditation for Law Enforcement

Agencies (CALEA) (Blau, 1994), the percentage of departments using tests has increased since then. In a recent study by Cochrane, Tett, and Vandecreek (2003), it was found that more than 90 percent of 155 police agencies now use psychological screening. The CALEA has given accreditation to several Canadian police services, including those in Camrose, Edmonton, and Lethbridge, Alberta; Brandon and Winnipeg, Manitoba; and Brantford, Ontario. Other Canadian agencies (e.g., Alberta Transportation and Inspection Services) also have been accredited by CALEA (CALEA, 2004).

When reviewing the use of psychological tests in police selection, Hargrave and Hiatt (1987) reported studies finding significant relationships between MMPI scales and police officers' job tenure, automobile accidents, supervisors' ratings, and job problems. Although the CPI has been used less often, scale scores were closely related to trainees' academy performance and to supervisors' ratings. (Specific studies cited are listed in Hargrave and Hiatt, 1987, p. 110, and Bartol, 1991, p. 127.) In another review, Bartol (1991) was less sanguine, describing the track record of the MMPI in screening and selection of law enforcement personnel as "mixed." But despite its limitations, the MMPI continues to be the most commonly used personality measure for the selection of police. More research has recently found the predictive validity of the MMPI-2 in the psychological screening of officer candidates to be supported, suggesting the MMPI-2 as a better screening procedure than the CPI (Detrick, Chibnall, & Rosso, 2001; Sellbom, Fischler, & Ben-Porath, 2007; Sun, Liu, & Wang, 2006). More specifically, Sellbom et al. (2007) analyzed data from 291 male police officers including complaints about the officers, involuntary termination, and supervisory ratings. The researchers' results indicated the RC scales that had the best predictive validity (RC3, RC4, RC6, RC8) of behavioural problems, and that lower cutoff scores maximized the prediction of officer misconduct.

In the study of trainees described earlier that evaluated the predictive validity of the clinical interview, Hargrave and Hiatt also administered the MMPI and CPI to 105 police trainees on their first day of training. The clinicians then interpreted each trainee's scores to classify his or her suitability. They compared these ratings with the same criteria as the interview data, with these results:

	CLINICIAN A	CLINICIAN B
Academic attrition	.24**	.15
Instructors' ratings	.25**	.27*
Peer evaluations	.36*	.13*
Composite criterion	.34**	.24**

*p < .05
**p < .01

Clinician A correctly classified 66 percent of the trainees; Clinician B 67 percent. These latter predictions were not significantly different from those by the interview data, although the correlations between test results and individual criteria are somewhat higher than the interview. Again, the results are not sufficiently strong to make decisions about individual applicants.

Although some of these correlations are significant, once more, the relationships are not especially impressive. In a follow-up study, Hargrave and Hiatt (1989) tested 579 trainees with the CPI and found that CPI profiles distinguished between those suitable and unsuitable for training. These authors concluded that CPI profiles have a more consistent relationship with job performance by police than with police academy variables. In general, the higher-rated police officers scored higher on the measures from the so-called Class II and Class III on the CPI (Class II consists of measures of socialization, responsibility, intrapersonal values, and character; Class III consists of measures of achievement potential). The other two classes of variables on the CPI showed no replicated relationship with police performance; these are Class I (measures of poise, ascendancy, self-assurance, and interpersonal adequacy) and Class IV (measures of intellectual and interest modes).

A second approach by Hargrave and Hiatt (1989) capitalized on the evaluations given to police on the job. A total of 45 officers from three municipal law enforcement agencies, all of whom had experienced serious job problems, were compared with 45 matched controls who had not received disciplinary notices for serious job problems. (The groups were matched on gender, race, education, and length of employment; their average age was 27 years and most had some college and had been on the job three years.) The kinds of job-related difficulties experienced by the problem group included providing drugs to prisoners, conviction for use of illegal drugs, unnecessary use of force, physical confrontations with other officers, and violations of departmental procedures that resulted in the escape of prisoners. All of these police had taken the CPI as part of the job-selection process. Only on the CPI Class II scales were there significant differences between the two groups; recall that Class II measures maturity, personal values, self-control, and sense of responsibility. Individuals who score higher on the scales in Class II are seen as careful, cautious, controlled, and as having a sense of duty and a reluctance to take risks. Those scoring low (less than 40) are more carefree, but also are opportunistic risk takers.

The nonproblem group scored higher on the CPI scales of So (Socialization), Sc (Self-Control), and Wb (Sense of Well-Being). Compared to nonproblem officers, there were four times as many problem officers with scale scores at or below a T score of 40 (meaning they scored at least one standard deviation under the mean). Thus, it appears that qualities of impulsivity, risk taking, boredom, lack of objectivity, and willingness to break rules contribute to problems among officers (Hargrave & Hiatt, 1989).

Derived from the 434-item CPI, the CPI-260 is an instrument specifically developed to assess the interpersonal skills, self-management, self-discipline, disposition at work, motivations and thinking styles, as well as personal characteristics and personal orientations of business executives. Research has found that law enforcement leaders scored similarly to business leaders, suggesting that the CPI-260 is an effective tool in the training of leadership for law enforcement officers (Miller, Watkins, & Webb, 2009).

Hargrave and Hiatt (1987) used a similar procedure to assess the predictive validity of the MMPI. They followed 55 urban police officers who had received at least one performance evaluation. Those rated as unsatisfactory scored significantly higher on two MMPI scales: Pa (Paranoia) and Ma (Hypomania). Building on this procedure, Bartol (1991) followed 600 police officers from 34 small-town police departments over a 13-year period to determine which officers were terminated. He concluded that an **immaturity index** consisting of a combination of the MMPI scales of Pd (Psychopathic Deviate), Ma (Hypomania), and the L Scale (discussed below) was a strong predictor of termination.

Bartol suggested that an immaturity index cutoff score of 49 (combination of the Pd and Ma scores plus the L score) is *suggestive* of possible problems" (1991, p. 131, italics in original),

especially if the Ma scale is highly elevated. Of the terminated officers, 70 percent received immaturity scores of 49 or above, compared with 23 percent of the retained group. (If an immaturity score of 54 was used as the cutoff, 53 percent of the terminated group would be correctly identified, and compared to 95 percent of the retained group.)

It should be noted that the typical interpretation given a high Ma score on the MMPI is consistent with a low score on the CPI Class II—impulsive, moody, and having a low frustration tolerance. Bartol wrote: "Police administrators and peers of high Ma officers often describe them as hyperactive individuals who seek constant activity" (1991, p. 131). One terminated police officer reportedly had developed the off-duty habit of locating speed traps and then driving by at a high speed to test other officers' alertness and effectiveness in high-speed chases (Bartol, 1991).

Bartol concluded that the Pd scale from the MMPI, alone, had limited predictive power; it was more useful when combined with a high Ma score. In general, this combination—in MMPI lingo, a 4-9 code—in individuals reflects "a marked disregard for social standards and values. They frequently get into trouble with the authorities because of antisocial behaviour" (Graham, 1987, p. 109).

The 4-9 code (Psychopathic deviate mania) had appreciable predictive power for Bartol's sample only when merged with the **L Scale**. When the MMPI was originally developed, the purpose of the L Scale was to detect a deliberate and unsophisticated attempt on the part of respondents to present themselves in a favourable light (Graham, 1987). (Items scored on the L Scale include the test taker portraying him- or herself as someone who does things such as "read every editorial in the newspaper every day," which most people would like to say they do but in all honesty cannot say they do.) Bartol (1991) noted that "police administrators continually report that high-L-scoring police officers demonstrate poor judgment in the field, particularly under high levels of stress. They seem to be unable to exercise quick, independent, and appropriate decision making under emergency or crisis conditions. They become confused and disorganized" (1991, p. 131). Based on 15 years of working with police supervisors, Bartol considered an L score above 8 (out of 15 items) to be one of the best predictors of poor performance as a police officer. However, he offered a titillating addition: "More recently, we have also discovered that extremely low L Scale scores (0 or 1) also forecast poor performance, suggesting that the L Scale may be curvilinear in its predictive power" (1991, p. 131).

More recent research has examined the MMPI-2 scales and their prediction on behavioural misconduct among police officers. Davis, Rostow, Pinkston, Combs, and Dixon (2004) examined the aggressiveness and immaturity indices of more than 1400 officer candidates and found several significant positive correlations between these measures and supervisor-rated misconduct and termination cases. Cullen, Ones, Drees, Viswesvaran, and Langkamp (2003) found that L and K scales predicted overall job performance, and K and certain clinical scales (4, 5, 6, 9, 0) predicted disciplinary problems. Sellbom, Fischler, and Ben-Porath (2007) found consistent results in that scores on several of the MMPI-2 scales predicted behavioural misconduct among police officers. Although some research has indicated the predictive validity of the MMPI-2 and the L scale/K scale, other research (Weiss, Weiss, Cain, & Manley, 2009) has suggested that participants or officers engage in considerable impression management when taking the test, and thus have elevated scores, specifically on the L scale and K scale. Therefore, the authors suggest that a higher cutoff than normal on the MMPI-2 should be used when eliminating officers from the applicant pool.

The Inwald Personality Inventory. Whereas the MMPI and the CPI are generalized psychological tools intended to be used in various contexts, the **Inwald Personality Inventory (IPI)** was developed for a more specific and limited purpose: to measure the suitability of personality attributes and behaviour patterns of law enforcement candidates (Inwald, 1992; Inwald, Knatz, & Shusman, 1983). This instrument is a 310-item, true-false questionnaire consisting of 26 scales (25 original scales and one validity scale) designed to measure, among other things, stress reactions and deviant behaviour patterns, including absence and lateness problems, interpersonal difficulties, antisocial behaviour, and alcohol and drug use. Suspicious, anxious, and rigid characteristics are also measured by IPI subscales. This test usually takes about 45 minutes to complete.

Another key difference between the IPI and the MMPI and CPI is that the IPI was developed "with the express purpose of directly questioning public safety/law enforcement candidates and documenting their admitted behaviours, rather than inferring those behaviours from statistically derived personality indicators" (Inwald,

1992, p. 4). As Blau (1994) noted, it is essentially a "screening out" test that seeks to assess antisocial behaviour and emotional maladjustments that might adversely affect police performance.

The IPI items measure both personality characteristics and behaviour patterns. The scales contain statements that assess both the unusual types of behaviour patterns that reflect severe problems and those that reflect less extreme adjustment difficulties. They are designed to identify, for example, "a highly guarded but naive individual as having hyperactive or antisocial tendencies based strictly on behavioral admissions" (Inwald, 1992, p. 3). The scales also have a goal of differentiating between individuals who express socially deviant attitudes and those who act on them (Inwald, 1992). The IPI contains a validity scale (Guardedness) related to some of the validity scales on other inventories. But in contrast to the MMPI L Scale, the 19 statements on the Guardedness scale contain minor shortcomings common to almost all people. Inwald notes: "When a candidate denies such items, a strong need to appear unusually virtuous is indicated" (1992, p. 4).

The IPI items were developed by Inwald after reviewing more than 2500 pre-employment interviews with candidates for law enforcement positions. The emerging characteristics not only include qualities related to effective police functioning, but also self-revealing statements made by applicants during actual interviews.

A factor analysis (Inwald, 1992) of the IPI scales, using 2397 male and 147 female police officer candidates, to determine what is common to the responses to different items, found the following:

- Factor 1, for both sexes, measured rigid, suspicious, and antisocial behaviours. It included Rigid Type, Undue Suspiciousness, and Antisocial Attitudes.
- For the males, Factor 2 was composed of two scales, Substance Abuse and Hyperactivity, reflecting risk taking and impulsive behaviour. For the female sample, Alcohol and Depression scales also contributed to this factor.
- For the third factor, even greater sex differences emerged; for the men, Phobic Personality, Lack of Assertiveness, Depression, and Loner Type scales loaded on the factor (were strongly related to Factor 3), but for females, these were replaced with Job Difficulties and Absence Abuse.

An early effort to validate the IPI compared it to the MMPI in a study of 716 male correctional officer recruits; criterion measures included job retention or termination, absence, lateness, and disciplinary measures in the first ten months of service (Shusman, Inwald, & Landa, 1984). This study concluded that for most criteria, the IPI scales predicted the status of officers better than did the MMPI scales and that the combination of IPI and MMPI scales increased accuracy of classification. The improved performance when the two scales are used together is a consistent observation of the validation studies reported in the test manual (Inwald, 1992), along with the relative strength of the IPI over the MMPI (Scogin, Schumacher, Howland, & McGee, 1989). Further validation studies (Inwald & Shusman, 1984; Shusman & Inwald, 1991a) used 329 police recruits and 246 correctional officers; again, it was concluded that more IPI than MMPI scales discriminated the successful and less successful officers. For example, the IPI and MMPI yielded 82 and 69 percent correct classifications for absenteeism, respectively. When combined, the two scales achieved an accuracy rate of 85 percent. Especially useful as predictors of problematic behaviour were IPI scales measuring trouble with the law, previous job difficulties, and involvement with drugs. Using a different methodology known as a cross-validation, Shusman, Inwald, and Knatz (1987) first studied 698 male police officers who completed six months of training in the police academy. The researchers examined the usefulness of the most predictive criteria in this original sample and then investigated their predictiveness in a second sample of 421 officers. In the validation sample, the IPI scales assigned from 61 to 77 percent of the officers into correct group membership, based on eight performance criteria, whereas the MMPI scales identified only between 50 and 70 percent. In the cross-validation sample, slightly more shrinkage (i.e., a lower rate of correct classifications) was observed for the IPI than for the MMPI in regard to most of the criteria. But even with this somewhat greater degree of shrinkage, the cross-validation classification rates for the IPI were equal to or greater than the original validation percentages from the MMPI alone for all but one of the eight criteria.

Several of the IPI items ask for admissions of behaviours that at the least, are socially unacceptable, and often are violations of laws. Would applicants for positions in law enforcement readily admit to such behaviours? A clever study by Ostrov (1985) (a police psychological consultant) provided a provocative answer. Two groups of approximately 200 applicants each (all "serious candidates") were screened by the Chicago Police Department, using the IPI. Each candidate also was asked to provide a urine sample for analysis of drug use following completion of the IPI. While Ostrov was skeptical that candidates would truthfully answer questions about drug use or past criminal acts, a comparison of urine analysis results with the IPI results indicated that a high percentage were truthful. In both groups, about one of five of the police candidates flunked the urine test. These individuals were found to differ from other candidates on several of the Drug Scale items relating both to marijuana and hard drug use. Surprisingly, most "guilty" individuals admitted to their "guilt" on the psychological test.

The "Big Five" Personality Traits and Policing

Another approach has been to examine the "Big Five" personality features (openness to new experience, conscientiousness, agreeableness, extraversion, and neuroticism or "OCEAN") in relation to police job performance. These five traits are thought to represent the five "fundamental" features of the human personality (e.g., McCrae & Costa, 1997). Ono et al. (2011) examined the extent

"YOU HAVE THE RIGHT TO REMAIN SILENT."

to which cognitive ability, the Big Five factor personality dimensions, and emotional intelligence are related to training and job performance of U.S. federal criminal investigators. Training performance measures were collected during a 17-week training program. Job performance measures were collected one year after the investigators completed the training program. Conscientiousness—which shows consistent relations with all job performance criteria for numerous occupational groups (Barrick & Mount, 1991)— was modestly related to training performance. Cognitive ability and emotional intelligence were positively correlated with job performance. Neuroticism was negatively correlated with job performance. Other research examining the Big Five among police recruits showed that certain personality types are attracted to the profession. Saulters-Pedneault, Ruef, and Orr (2010) found that police recruits scored higher than firefighters on gregariousness, a facet of extraversion, and on conscientiousness. Compared to the general population, police and firefighters both scored higher on excitement seeking, a facet of extraversion.

Situational Tests

A third approach to screening potential law enforcement officers uses **situational tests**, that is, placing the testee in a simulated police situation to evoke samples of the behaviour he or she will show on the job. One example of such testing is the work of Dunnette and Motowidlo (1976), who sought to define the critical dimensions of job performance for each of four police jobs: (1) general patrol officer, (2) patrol sergeant, (3) detective (investigator), and (4) intermediate-level commander. Finding little in the way of assessing these specific dimensions when they began their work in the early 1970s, they designed a series of simulations and standardized situational tasks, such as role-playing exercises on behaviours believed to be representative of critical police tasks. They used these tools to assess how the recruits would respond to activities that form the criteria for effective police work. For example, they asked recruits to intervene in a domestic dispute carry out a burglary investigation, and aid a man injured at a hotel. Selection of candidates for police training was based on performance on these and other kinds of tasks.

On other occasions, situational tests have been used in police selection (see Jacobs, Cushenbery, & Grabarek, 2011). One example is the work of Mills, McDevitt, and Tonkin (1966), who administered three tests intended to simulate police tasks to a group of Cincinnati police candidates. The Foot Patrol Observation Test required candidates to walk a six-block downtown route and then answer questions about what they remembered having just observed. In the Clues Test, candidates were given ten minutes to investigate a set of planted clues about the disappearance of a hypothetical city worker from his office. They were observed as they performed this task and were graded on the information they assembled. The Bull Session was a two-hour group discussion of several topics of importance in police work. Performance on the Clues Test correlated significantly with class ranking in the police academy, but the scores from the Foot Patrol Observation test did not. Although independent grades for the Bull Session measure were not derived, it was viewed as an important measure of emotional and motivational qualities. Additionally, Mills and colleagues (1966) discovered that the Clues Test was not correlated with intelligence—indicating the advantage of including a measure of nonintellectual abilities in a selection battery.

Despite the fact that situational tests have an intuitive appeal as selection devices, they have not proven to be superior to personality tests (MMPI, CPI, and IPI) as predictors of performance. Because they are time consuming and expensive, they are used mainly to supplement psychological tests.

The Pre-Employment Polygraph

Polygraph screening has been used to screen employees since the 1930s (e.g., Alder, 2007), and is a core component of the RCMP selection approach. Messig and Horvath (1995) conducted a survey on 626 law enforcement agencies in the United States and found that approximately 62 percent of the responding agencies utilized the polygraph in their hiring process. Further, the agencies reported rejecting about a quarter of applicants because of polygraph findings that had not been discovered during prior screening. Messig and Horvath (1995) reported that their polygraph screenings were able to uncover unsolved homicides, perpetration of rape, commission and armed robberies, and illegal drug use. These results suggest that the pre-employment polygraph might be crucial to police screening. While the polygraph may be a useful tool in some circumstances when approached with caution, potential problems can result from misguided policies surrounding the polygraph (Handler, Honts, Krapohl, Nelson, & Griffin, 2009), as described in Chapter 5. Handler et al. (2009) suggested that using the polygraph test alone to eliminate law enforcement applicants is a misguided practice, and that the results should be used in the context of a "whole person" approach to evaluating candidates. They further suggest that the polygraph results might be best understood by having a police psychologist effectively communicate the results and make recommendations for the hiring process. Finally, Hander et al. (2009) also opined that the use of the pre-employment polygraph may actually deter applicants who would not be suitable for police work. Vrij et al. (2011b) and Porter and ten Brinke (2010) associated the polygraph with major problems, particularly the false positive problem, in which people are identified as being guilty of various transgressions of which they are actually innocent. The extent of this problem in police selection contexts is not known, but certainly we assume that many deserving recruits are screened out unfairly via polygraph testing.

THE TRAINING OF POLICE

All law enforcement agencies have some form of training programs for their recruits. What roles do psychologists play in such training programs, and what does our clientele want from psychologists in this regard?

A forensic psychologist with training in organizational psychology can evaluate a police training program to see whether it is consistent with the responsibilities and responses of police as they carry out their tasks. The typical training program has been criticized for emphasizing "narrowly defined aspects of the job dealing with criminal activity, understanding relevant laws, effective firearms training, self-defense, and other survival techniques" (Stratton, 1980, p. 38). Although these skills are important, psychologists urge departments to include in training the strategies necessary for coping with job-related stress and other interpersonal and communication skills. Police department administrators have become increasingly aware that police need to have human-relations skills, including awareness of diversity and the ability to communicate effectively.

THE PSYCHOLOGIST'S ACTIVITIES IN A POLICE DEPARTMENT

In Canada, some police forces have a full-time psychologist on the force. However, it is more common for psychologists to be consulted by police on an as-needed basis. For example, Dr. Mike Webster, a former RCMP officer, is a well-known psychologist in private practice in BC, who has dealt almost exclusively with law enforcement agencies, including the RCMP and the FBI (Webster, 2004). He has taught at the British Columbia Police Academy, the Canadian Police College, and the FBI Training Academy. As mentioned earlier, Webster has been somewhat ostracized by the RCMP after speaking out about its failures in various scandals. The Law Enforcement Behavioural Sciences Association (LEBSA), formed by a group of psychologists who work with police, and a section of Division 18 of the American Psychological Association (Division of Psychologists in Public Service), called the Police Psychology Section, were developed to address the concerns of police psychologists. These organizations sponsor presentations and workshops at national conventions and share procedures, experiences, and data with each other.

Martin Reiser was the first full-time police psychologist, beginning his service as department psychologist with the Los Angeles Police Department in 1968. He observed that psychologists usually are asked to participate in police training programs in two ways: as teachers and as consultants (Reiser, 1972). As teachers, they may be asked to instruct recruits on handling mentally ill persons, human relations, criminal psychology, and relationships with authority figures, among other topics. As a consultant, "the psychologist is expected to have some practical know how and expertise about educational processes, teaching techniques, learning systems, and technology" (Reiser, 1972, p. 33).

Psychologists serving as consultants to police generally are available and on call to anyone in the department. Requests might include the following:

- The police chief wants a survey of pursuits and shootings.
- A sergeant asks for help in developing a psychologically based program of driver training to reduce police-involved accidents.
- Homicide detectives want consultation on a bizarre murder, as with cases in which the first

author of this textbook has been consulted. Sometimes, police may wish for a psychological profile, as discussed in Chapter 2, but more often they request advice on how best to interview a known suspect.

- An investigator in a serious crime case asks a psychologist to evaluate the credibility of either a complainant or criminal suspect based on his or her language, body language, and facial expressions by viewing the videotaped interview (e.g., ten Brinke & Porter, 2012). For example, the first author and colleagues have been asked to evaluate the credibility of a person publically pleading for the return of a missing relative (e.g., ten Brinke, Porter, & Baker, 2012).
- An officer needs psychological counselling (e.g., Adams & Buck, 2010; Hickman, Fricas, Strom, & Pope, 2011).

Psychologists acting as consultants to police departments need to be flexible and adaptable; they must modify their frame of reference in order to accommodate the variety of service requests (Reiser, 1982a, 1982b). One of the central problems for the psychologist-consultant is that of identification; is the psychologist a mental health specialist, a social change agent, an organizational staff specialist, or an employee in a hierarchy? Reiser (1982b) has proposed that the level of the organization at which the consultant "gets plugged in" will determine how he or she is seen by other members of the organization, particularly by those in power.

Traditionally, police officers have been wary of, if not downright antagonistic toward, psychologists. They likely have come in contact with a psychologist or another mental health professional in some way that inhibits the development of their respect for the psychological profession. White and Honig (1995) described these interactions as follows:

1. Watching "do-gooder" psychologists testify on behalf of criminals.
2. Observing psychologists seem to protect police officers who are claiming a disability but are perceived by their fellow officers as weak or abusing the system.
3. Viewing psychologists as enemies with the power to keep an officer or potential officer off the force through the psychologist's role in police selection or fitness-for-duty evaluations.

Negative perceptions of police psychologists may be somewhat lessened if the psychologists have a policing background (such as former police officer Mike Webster in BC). However, an initial task for all police psychologists is to listen and learn. They should seek to understand the culture of the police department by participating in **ride-alongs** (in which the psychologist accompanies officers on patrol), asking questions, and in all ways understanding the world of law enforcement rather than "gathering ammunition to change it" (White & Honig, 1995, p. 259). Police administrators may fear that psychologists may somehow usurp the administrator's control or brainwash the police administrator in some way. Reiser (1982b) has emphasized that the personal attributes of a consultant—being pragmatic, showing adaptability—are crucial for success; what a psychologist is able to achieve is "a function of role expectations of the organization, plus what the individual consultant brings to the situation in the form of his [or her] personal attributes" (p. 28).

Each of these responsibilities may have many manifestations. Like many organizations, police departments are susceptible to adopting innovative and unique programs, partly because they are new and different. Often such programs do not receive an adequate internal evaluation, if any evaluation at all. Psychologists can play a useful role in evaluating the effectiveness of such innovations, whether they are team policing, sensitivity training, or community orientation sessions.

THE CURRICULUM OF TRAINING PROGRAMS

A new police chief may ask a psychologist to design a training program for recruits. Central questions the psychologist should ask are: What do police do? What do they need to know and be able to do? Studies of policing consistently have found that the major police role is to provide services and keep peace rather than attend to crime-related activities (Meadows, 1987). Yet, the training provided to the police may be inconsistent with their subsequent duties. Germann (1969) has noted that most entry-level police training is devoted to "crook-catching"—as much as 90 percent of the training time—although police spend only 10 percent to 15 percent of their time on these activities. The RCMP seems to be recognizing this problem and focusing more on the realities of police work in its training. More specifically, law enforcement officers must confront complex social issues, and Napier (2005) suggests that adequate training is required in order for them to respond appropriately. For example, police officers often are faced with situations that deal with youth, which can be challenging. LaMotte et al. (2010) gave patrol officers a training program that was predicted to enhance officers' knowledge about youth behaviour and strategies for interacting with youth. They found that officers who received this training had increased comfort levels with interacting with youth, as well as a more positive attitude toward them.

For about 130 years, RCMP recruits have been trained at the "depot" in Regina, Saskatchewan. Current training strategies emphasize problem-solving exercises, knowledge of the law, cultural diversity and sensitivity, role-plays, performance demonstration, lectures, panel discussions, research discussions, and community interaction. The RCMP's training agenda appears to approach the recommendations of the National Advisory Commission on Criminal Justice Standards and Goals (1973, p. 392), which suggested a training program organized around the following six subject areas:

1. *Introduction to the criminal justice system.* This includes an examination of the foundation and functions of the criminal justice system with specific attention to the role of the police in the system and government.
2. *Law.* This includes an introduction to the development, philosophy, and different types of law including; criminal law; criminal procedure and rules of evidence; discretionary justice. Also, it includes an understanding of the application of federal legislation; the understanding of court systems and procedures and related civil law.
3. *Human values and problems.* This includes public service and noncriminal policing, cultural awareness, the changing roles of the police, human behaviour and conflict management, psychology as it relates to the police function, causes of crime and delinquency, and public relations.
4. *Patrol and investigation procedures.* This includes the fundamentals of the patrol function including traffic, juvenile, and preliminary investigation, reporting and communication; arrest and detention procedures, interviewing, criminal investigation and case preparation, equipment and facility use, and other day-to-day responsibilities and duties.
5. *Police proficiency.* This includes the philosophy of when to use force and the appropriate

determination of the degree necessary, armed and unarmed defence, crowd, riot, and prisoner control, physical conditioning, emergency medical services, and driver training.
6. *Administration.* An understanding of evaluation, examination, and counselling processes, department policies, rules, regulations, organization, and personnel problems.

The commission recommended a distribution of training time as indicated in Box 3.2. Meadows (1987) surveyed 234 police chiefs and 355 criminal justice educators as to the importance of training in each of these categories. Both groups felt a need for increased training in the law and in written and oral communication, implying that police officers may not be doing a good job of communicating with the public.

ON-THE-JOB TRAINING

Once the police officer is credentialled and on the job, the need for training does not end, and law enforcement agencies now are providing more opportunities to police to receive training. With emerging technologies, Donovant (2007, 2009) suggests that online education might be appropriate with regards to specific topic areas. Online education offers police officers the convenience and scheduling flexibility to receive training without taking time away from their job, as well as working from remote locations (for example, the RCMP). Although online education does not allow for the hands-on component of police training, most officers feel it can be of value when it is used to complement other forms of training (Donovant, 2009). To complement police training, research is now demonstrating the advantages that consulting with a mental health professional (psychologist, psychiatrist, etc.) for various reasons can have on overall police performance (Bennell, 2005; Bennell, Jones, & Corey, 2007; Reynold & Miles, 2009; Snook & Mercer, 2010; Storey, Gibas, Reeves, & Hart, 2011; see Canadian Researcher Profile on page 68 for more information about Dr. Bennell). In particular, risk assessments are a critical part of a law enforcement officer's duties, and Storey et al. (2011) found that training in violence risk assessments can improve related knowledge, skills, and attitudes in criminal justice professionals.

White and Honig (1995) discussed the role of the police psychologist in training activities and divided on-the-job training into three categories:

BOX 3.2   CRIMINAL JUSTICE STANDARDS AND GOALS

Commission-Recommended Distribution of Training Time by Percentage by Area

Subject Area	Recommended Percentage of Training Time
Introduction to the Criminal Justice System	8%
Law	10
Human Values and Problems	22
Patrol and Investigation Procedures	33
Police Proficiency	18
Administration	9
Total	100%

(From *Report on Police*, by the National Advisory Commission on Criminal Justice Standards and Goals, 1973, p. 394.)

wellness training, training that provides information or skills, and training that relates the individual to the organization. Each is described in Box 3.3. In addition, police officers may need training in specialized activities; three types are described in the following sections.

Specialized Training: Responses to Intimate Partner Violence and Individuals with Mental Illness

As we explore further in Chapter 10, research in Canada indicates that 6 to 7 percent of spouses report that they have been subjected to violence (pushed, grabbed, shoved, slapped, sexually assaulted, hit with an object, or had a gun or knife used against them) by their partner (Statistics Canada, 2009). However, very few incidents of domestic violence are reported to the police (Statistics Canada, 2009). One reason is that victims do not expect police to be sympathetic or helpful. More surprising is the fact that the percentage of people reporting incidents of domestic violence has decreased from 28 percent in 2004 to 22 percent in 2009 (Statistics Canada, 2009).

The expectation of an apathetic police response to a report of partner violence may be realistic. Levens and Dutton (1980) found that Canadian police had negative attitudes toward intervening in domestic disputes. In 1979, the Oakland, California, Police Department's training

bulletin instructed police that a man should not be arrested for wife assault because he would "lose face" (Paterson, 1979, cited by Jaffe, Hastings, Reitzel, & Austin, 1993). Even with the feminist movement, which pushed for stricter policies of arrest in domestic violence situations, police still may be reluctant to intervene in certain cases for a number of different reasons. For example, research has suggested that domestic assault calls are one of the three most common scenarios in which officers are assaulted (Ellis et al., 1993; Stanford and Mowry, 1990). Johnson (2008) found that on average, 29 officers a year in the United States were either injured or killed after responding to a domestic assault. Given that domestic assault calls are one of the most dangerous situations for police officers to attend (Bard, 1970; Ellis, Choi, & Blaus, 1993; Stanford & Mowry, 1990; Uchida et al., 1987), educating officers about how domestic assaults occur, and developing policies and programs around officer safety in these situations, could encourage officers to be more cautious during domestic violence calls (Johnson, 2008). Johnson (2008) further suggests that police dispatchers should be trained and required to relay pertinent information about the accused abuser (i.e., previous arrests, access to weapons, etc.) before sending officers to the scene. Johnson (2011) recently examined 1951 domestic assault calls and whether the abusers assaulted police officers, and found particular abuser characteristics to successfully

BOX 3.3   TYPES OF ON-THE-JOB TRAINING FOR LAW ENFORCEMENT OFFICERS

Wellness Training

White and Honig stated that the goal of **wellness training** "is assisting the police officer toward improving his or her lifestyle through learning new, health-enhancing behaviours and ideas. Wellness training is based on the concept that how an individual manages his or her life, and the accompanying stressors, will have a significant impact on job performance" (1995, p. 260).

Job stress is recognized as a major problem for law enforcement officers, and **burnout** may be the result. Training that deals with these issues must take into account the police culture that emphasizes the illusion of invulnerability, the suppression of emotion, and the emphasis on mental and physical toughness (Hogan, 1971; Reiser, 1974). In addition to stress management, among the specific topics that are a part of wellness training are the following:

- *Alcohol and drug abuse*. A tradition in law enforcement is drinking with fellow officers after a shift, often known as "choir practice" (White & Honig, 1995).
- *Relationship with one's spouse*. The literature suggests that police, compared to most other occupational groups, have great difficulties in marital relationships (Kroes, Margolis, & Hurrell, 1974; Singleton & Teahan, 1978).
- *Surviving critical incidents*. It is estimated that 60 to 70 percent of law enforcement officers leave the force within five years of an episode in which a fellow officer, witness, or suspect is killed, or the officer is seriously injured (Reese, Horn, & Dunning, 1991; Simpson, Jensen, & Owen, 1988).

Informational and Skill Training

This type of continuing education assists police officers in performing their job duties. All the special topics listed below reflect issues of human behaviour and can benefit from the participation of psychologists.

- Managing persons with mental illness
- Cross-cultural awareness
- Improvement of communication skills
- Working with victims of rape and sexual assault.

Two kinds of specialized topics, responses to spouse assault and negotiating with hostage takers, are considered in this chapter.

Organizational Training

The goal of organizational training is to improve the functioning of the organization as a whole; it is especially useful for officers in supervisory and management roles (White & Honig, 1995). For example, like any organization, police departments may face questions of sexual harassment, grief management, racial discrimination, and substance abuse.

---

predict officer assaults. Johnson (2011) suggests that police should be educated in these findings, and that they should be incorporated into their safety training for domestic assault scenarios. Training of police by psychologists conceivably can improve how police respond and eventually whether victims choose to call for help. The renowned work by Donald Dutton and his colleagues (Dutton, 1981, 1988; Dutton & Levens, 1977) at the University of British Columbia found that training significantly increased the use by police of mediation and referral techniques.

One review (Jaffe, Hastings, Reitzel, & Austin, 1993) suggested that training programs for police should include information on the "social costs of wife assault, statistics on prevalence, information on why victims stay or return, and descriptions of local services" (p. 89). The review also suggested that a manual of resources for victims of domestic violence be available to police and that officers carry business cards printed with the phone numbers of 24-hour hotlines or shelters.

Morrissey, Fagan, and Cocozza (2009) suggested that mental health professionals can aid law enforcement officers in certain cases because a psychologist or psychiatrist can better understand individuals with mental illness (for example, the Robert Dziekanski case in Vancouver described earlier shows the lack of understanding the police had, resulting in the use of excessive physical force). It is important for police officers to be able to identify mental illness so that they can accurately address the situation and respond in the most appropriate manner. The Canadian Mental

Health Association (2004) argues that individuals with mental illness are more likely to be detected and arrested for minor offences and remanded in custody, therefore having more interaction with police. Overall, individuals with mental illness are suggested to be at a higher risk of committing criminal activity and violence as a whole (Modestin, 1998; Paterson, Claughan, & McComish, 2004). The prevalence of mental illness has been a growing concern in correctional settings (see Parker, 2009), and overall, about 10 percent of federal inmates in Canada were diagnosed as having mental illness at the time of admission in 2006–2007 (e.g., see Sinha, 2009). Parker (2009) examined a mental health training program for correctional officers on a prison special housing unit. Parker compared incidents during which officers used force on suspects before and after nine months of training, and found that after ten hours of mental health training over a five-week period, there was a decline in use of force by the officers. The results suggest that an understanding and knowledge of mental health might cause law enforcement officers to behave more appropriately in certain situations.

Negotiating with Terrorists and Hostage Takers

As September 11, 2001, made shockingly clear, terrorism is now a part of modern industrialized society; every time we go through a metal detector at an airport, we may be reminded of the possibility. Psychologists and other social scientists are beginning to study the phenomenon systematically (Crenshaw, 1986; Friedland & Merari, 1985). As the first line of response to terrorism, police and other public-safety agencies play a central role (Greenstone, 1995b; Huq, Tyler, & Schulhofer, 2011; Roberts, 2011). Psychologists have not only begun to study the police response to terrorism, but also have become part of the investigative process itself. Psychologists have been heavily criticized recently for their role in helping plan interrogations with police and the military during wartime (for example, at the notorious Guantanamo Bay prison for military detainees) (Pope & Guthell, 2009). Clearly, as a field, we need to explore the complex ethical dilemmas that accompany such practices.

On nearly a daily basis, we hear about someone taking another person or persons hostage. Law enforcement officers must choose whether to negotiate with the hostage taker or to use force

to protect and free the hostages. An example of this occurred in 2004 with the longest hostage situation in Nova Scotia's history. A three-day-long armed standoff, which began on May 19, 2004, in Halifax, finally ended when a couple left a barricaded home with their five-month-old daughter and a deceased elderly woman (the man's mother) and were arrested by police. Larry Finck and Carline VandenElsen left the house without warning and crossed the street carrying the body of the elderly woman on a makeshift stretcher (she had died of natural causes). Several shots had been fired from the home by Mr. Finck on the first day of the standoff, but no one was hurt. The standoff had started after Finck refused to hand over his daughter to the Children's Aid Society. Police cordoned off the street and began negotiations with the aid of a local psychologist. The police in this case had made the difficult decision not to use force but to wait things out, thankfully with a peaceful conclusion.

Negotiation with terrorists and hostage takers has become a well-established concept and receives great emphasis in policing throughout North America (Grubb, 2010; Webster, 2004). A survey of 34 police departments found that 31 (91 percent) had a designated negotiation team (Fuselier, 1988). More recently, crisis intervention teams and crisis negotiation teams have been developed to assist with law enforcement officers in resolving critical incidents/hostages (Augustin and Fagan, 2011). Van Hasselt et al. (2006) conducted an empirical study on the efficacy of crisis/hostage negotiation training with regards to the FBI, and found that agents were significantly better qualified after training. Despite positive results in internal training programs, training courses on hostage negotiation often recommend consultation with a clinical psychologist (Fuselier, 1988), including in the Canadian context (e.g., Michaud, St-Yves, & Guay, 2008). Brad Kelln (a psychologist who is consulted by Nova Scotia police during hostage negotiations) and McMurtry (2007) argued that there are no specific strategies that can be taught to police negotiators in every hostage scenario.

Who Takes Hostages?

Four basic types of **hostage takers** are differentiated in the law enforcement and clinical literature: the political activist or terrorist, the criminal, the mentally disturbed person, and the prisoner. Hassel (1975, cited by Fuselier, 1988) concluded that the most frequent type of hostage taker is the

Police and psychologists involved in hostage negotiations must negotiate with people in extreme, life-and-death situations.

researcher Dr. Hugues Herve and colleagues (2004) found that among 1200 Canadian federal offenders housed in the Pacific region between the 1960s and 1998, 11.3 percent had committed acts of unlawful confinement. Approximately half of these perpetrators were psychopaths, and the sample scored significantly higher on the PCL-R than offenders in the general prison population.

Why Do People Take Hostages?

There are numerous contexts in which hostage takings occur, from the man who takes his spouse hostage in their home to the inmate taking a correctional officer hostage to a terrorist taking a political hostage. Regarding the latter, Fuselier (1988) suggested the main reasons that political terrorists take hostages: to demonstrate to the public the inability of a government to protect its own citizens, to ensure increased publicity for their political agenda, to create civil discontent indirectly by causing the government to overreact and restrict its citizens, and to demand release of members of their groups who are in custody. Yun and Roth (2008) analyzed 234 cases of terrorist hostage-takings and kidnappings and found that these two situations are patterned and that the behavioural scripts and outcomes can be predicted with some degree of accuracy. They found that particular variables such as the presence of negotiation and the hostage takers' demands predicted the fate of hostage victims. Although more research is needed in this area, Yun and Roth's (2008) findings might provide valuable information to law enforcement officials and negotiation teams to successfully resolve hostage situations. These results reflect the study of planned activities. In contrast, the criminal may spontaneously take a hostage when his or her own freedom is jeopardized, thus reflecting a need for safe passage or a means to escape. Mentally disturbed people take hostages for a variety of reasons, although each stems from the hostage taker's own view of the world. Inmates usually use hostages to protest conditions within the prison. The more recent "new breed" of terrorist is described as highly sophisticated and motivated by political and/or religious beliefs (Albini, 2001). Dolnik and Fitzgerald (2011) suggested that this new terrorist is more likely to execute hostages, and that adjustments need to be made to negotiation strategies in order to improve negotiators' skills in dealing with hostage incidents more effectively.

criminal trapped while committing a crime, and Stratton (1978) has identified political terrorists as the most difficult to negotiate with because of their "total commitment, exhaustive planning, and ability to exert power effectively" (p. 7). Maher (1977) considered the mentally disturbed hostage taker the greatest threat. These contradicting conclusions reflect, for Fuselier (1988), the need for a "systematic nationwide collection or compilation … of information on hostage incidents" (pp. 175–176) by law enforcement agencies.

Recently, psychopathy has emerged as an important psychological condition in understanding some hostage takings. As explored in Chapter 13, much research has established that psychopaths commit an inordinate amount of violence in society (e.g., Forth & Book, 2010; Hare & Neumann, 2009, 2010; Monahan et al., 2001; Shaw & Porter, 2012). They also perpetrate a higher degree of instrumental violence (that is, violence that is planned in advance) (e.g., Cornell et al., 1996; Walsh & Kosson, 2007; Walsh, Swogger, & Kosson, 2009). Thus, it may not be surprising that psychopaths may resort to hostage taking in order to achieve some goal. Canadian

Craig Bennell

After a short career as a social worker with Aboriginal youth gangs in Edmonton, Alberta, Craig Bennell decided to pursue graduate studies in psychology. Having worked alongside the police for some time, he was particularly interested in seeing how psychology could contribute to the field of policing. At the time, there was no better place to study these issues than the Centre for Investigative Psychology at the University of Liverpool, in England. After six years of intensive study under the supervision of Professor David Canter, a well-known psychologist and offender profiler, Craig began his academic career at Carleton University, where he now directs Carleton's Police Research Lab.

With his students, Craig focuses most of his time trying to understand and improve police decision making, especially in stressful situations. Most recently, he has started to explore how stereotypes about race, gender, and age can influence the use-of-force decisions police officers frequently have to make, and how various factors (e.g., scene complexity, background noise, lighting conditions) can either increase or decrease the effect that stereotypes have on behaviour. Given his initial findings, which seem to suggest that stereotypes can have a strong influence on these decisions, much of Craig's future research will likely focus on ways of minimizing the impact of stereotypical thinking, through specially designed training programs.

Craig is also well known for his research on psychologically based investigative techniques, such as criminal profiling. During his time in Liverpool, Craig became increasingly skeptical of what profilers were doing and was shocked at the lack of empirical research supporting many of their activities. Craig and several colleagues have attempted to fill this gap by conducting studies to test the reliability, validity, and usefulness of the techniques that profilers frequently draw on. Many of these studies raise serious concerns about the value of profiling and related studies. Future research in Craig's lab will continue to explore these issues and attempts will be made to better understand the investigative and legal implications of the results.

Currently, Craig is an associate professor in the Department of Psychology at Carleton, where he teaches classes in forensic and police psychology. He is also the co-editor of the *Journal of Police and Criminal Psychology*, and an editorial board member for numerous other journals. He has recently been recognized for his contributions to the field of investigative psychology by being made an Honorary Fellow of the International Academy for Investigative Psychology, and he has received numerous awards, including a Significant Contribution Award from the Canadian Psychological Association (Criminal Justice Section). His time away from campus is spent with his wife, who is also a teacher, and his two young sons (mostly at the hockey arena).

THE ROLE OF THE FORENSIC PSYCHOLOGIST IN HOSTAGE TAKING SITUATIONS

Does the psychologist have something valuable to offer when hostages are taken? The answer seems to be a qualified yes. Police who are well trained in the procedures of hostage negotiations are more likely to bring about a successful resolution of the incident (Augustin & Fagan, 2011; Borum, 1988a; Kelln & McMurtry, 2007). Success in such situations is usually defined as "a resolution in which there is no loss of life to any of those involved in the incident including police, hostage taker, and hostages" (Greenstone, 1995b, p. 358). Psychological considerations are central in evaluating progress in the negotiations. For example, Greenstone (1995b) suggested that if the hostage taker is talking more, is more willing to talk about his or her personal life, and reflects less violence in his or her conversation, progress is being achieved. Further, McMains (1988) identified three roles for psychologists: the professional, who is a source of applicable behavioural science information; the consultant, who develops training programs, materials, and exercises; and the participant-observer, who makes suggestions but recognizes the authority of the law enforcement personnel. However, Call (2008) suggested that the three most common roles for a mental health professional during a critical incident situation are consultation of negotiation techniques, assessment of perpetrators and counselling law enforcement officers after the incident.

However, experts are not in agreement, and several perspectives can be identified:

1. Powitsky (1979) argued that psychologists might perform some relevant duties, such as gathering information to be used in the negotiating strategy, but "the majority of practicing psychologists, especially those who work outside of the criminal justice system, would not be very helpful (and some would be harmful) in a hostage-taking situation" (p. 30).

2. Poythress (1980), who described himself as a "guarded optimist," has offered that "mental health professionals may have something to offer in the hostage situation, but probably less than the field commanders might hope for" (p. 34). He listed three reasons that the responsible police officer should not enlist a psychologist's opinion on the decision to negotiate rather than attack:
   - Psychologists have little formal training on this topic, little research has been done, and few psychologists have had much field experience on it. In the two decades since Poythress wrote this, a modest beginning has occurred in providing assistance to negotiations (e.g., Fowler, De Vivo, & Fowler, 1985; Grubb, 2010; Soskis, 1983; Vecchi, Van Hasselt, & Romano, 2005; and Yonah & Gleason, 1981). The FBI's training academy at Quantico, Virginia, had originally developed a 30-hour Basic Hostage Negotiations training module (Greenstone, 1995a) but now requires all FBI negotiators to complete a two-week training program that must be undertaken at the FBI Academy (Federal Bureau of Investigation, 2012).
   - Predictors of the probable dangerousness of a given person in a given situation are notoriously bad (Poythress, 1980).
   - As Meehl (1954) showed many years ago, statistical (i.e., actuarial) methods are more accurate than clinical judgment in general predictions of outcome.

3. More positive in Poythress's view was Reiser (1982a, 1982b), who saw the psychologist contributing as a backup and adviser to the negotiation team, as well as providing training on the assessment of the hostage taker's motives and personality, the development of communication skills, and the challenge of dealing with stress and fatigue.

4. Fuselier (1988), author of a useful review of the psychologist's role in hostage negotiation, accepted the value of psychologists as consultants, but only after they have received training in hostage negotiation concepts. After attendance at a hostage negotiation seminar, the psychologist "can assist in both determining whether a mental disorder exists and deciding on a particular negotiation approach" (p. 177). But he believes that a psychologist should not be used as the **primary negotiator**; instead, being a consultant allows the psychologist "to maintain a more objective role in assessing the mental status and performance of the negotiator" (1988, p. 177).

5. Ax, Fagan, and Holton (2003); Birge (2002); and Feldmann (2004) are less reluctant and suggest that mental health professionals can provide valuable information about the perpetrator especially when behaviour is motivated by mental illness or extreme emotional states. Further, they feel that mental health workers are important because they can provide support and counselling to the negotiation team members when they become stressed or emotionally unstable. Ax et al. (2003) and Feldmann (2004) also suggest that a mental health worker might be able to access a perpetrator's mental health and substance abuse history much more easily than a law enforcement official. As a critical incident progresses, negotiators might become too involved in their current negotiation tactic/strategy, and a mental health worker might be able to lend an objective perspective on the situation, as well as deliver relevant information more concisely (Morrissey, Fagan, & Cocozza, 2009). Kelln and McMurtry (2008) have argued that psychologists can be very helpful to hostage negotiation in light of their backgrounds and perspective in encouraging flexibility. They assert that a good hostage negotiation model must be flexible enough so that it applies to virtually any situation regardless of the context, subject's state of mind, or other constraints. As such, psychologists can contribute to training in terms of teaching good critical thinking, being open-minded and flexible, as well as offering

particular strategies for dealing with particular types of hostage takers. They also can offer these skills through the provision of advice to law enforcement as the actual situation unfolds. It is clear that more research is needed in this area (Dattilio, Edwards & Fishman, 2010).

Psychologists, if not primary negotiators, can then play a role in offering a postincident critique of the team, as well as counselling police and victims. The effects on police of participation in a hostage negotiation may be similar to those resulting from other stressful situations: anxiety, somatic responses, and a subjective sense of work overload (Beutler, Nussbaum, & Meredith, 1988; Dietrich & Smith, 1986; Zizzo, 1985).

Many traumatic incidents (hostage negotiations, witnessing violence and/or death, etc.) may cause posttraumatic stress disorder (PTSD) and other stress, and those officers affected may require counselling by a psychologist. Work stress in law enforcement has been documented to be significantly associated with negative affects such as depression (Gershon & Lin, 2002), intimate partner abuse (Gershon, Barocas, Canton, Li, & Vlahov, 2009; Johnson, Todd, & Subramanian, 2005), and physical health issues (i.e., heart disease) (Franke, Collins, & Hinz, 1998). Gershon et al. (2009) suggest that interventions that address certain stressors associated with policing and promote effective coping mechanisms will benefit law enforcement officers and minimize stress and associated outcomes in their line of work. Police peer support programs address work-related stress among officers, and have shown to be effective in modifying police stressors (Robinson & Murdoch, 2003). More specifically, Wang et al. (2010) suggest that strategies specifically reducing routine work environment stress (e.g., long shifts, stressful work conditions, time pressures, paperwork, public demands, threat of physical danger, etc.) may decrease depression in law enforcement officers. One method of reducing stress and building resilience in police officers is a training program suggested by Arnetz, Nevedal, Lumley, Backman, and Lublin (2009). Rookie police officers participated in a trial training program for 10 weeks, and after 12 months of receiving the training, significant mood reductions, less heart rate reactivity, and overall better police performance was documented. If more related training programs are implemented, police well-being and job performance may improve.

The Psychologist as Evaluation Researcher

Another role for the psychologist with respect to hostage negotiations is as an evaluation researcher. What works and what doesn't work? Allen, Cutler, and Berman (1993) collected the types of responses used by the police tactical teams to all 130 situations reflecting hostage taking or suicide attempts in Miami, Florida, for five years. They focused on the 48 of these cases in which some form of negotiation was used. Face-to-face negotiation (compared to use of a bullhorn, a public address system, or a telephone) was the least effective method of apprehending the hostage taker and was often seen as a last resort. The analysis also indicated that hostage takers under the influence of drugs were much less likely to come out without violence.

Evaluating Effectiveness of Police Activities

Many evaluations of police activities and innovations in police policies are carried out by persons not trained in the methodology of psychology and the social sciences. We argue that psychologists can play a major role in the evaluation of police activities. Two examples are provided here: one at the level of the individual police officer (the fitness-for-duty evaluation) and the other at the level of general policy innovation (community policing).

Fitness-for-Duty Evaluations

After participating in critical incidents involving the death of a partner or an injury during a chase or shootout, a law enforcement officer may display emotional or behavioural reactions such that a **fitness-for-duty evaluation** is requested by his or her supervisor (Inwald, 1990). Complaints against the officer, such as charges of brutality, may also lead to an investigation of the officer's emotional stability. A psychologist may be called on to conduct the evaluation (Delprino & Bahn, 1988). Robin Inwald (1990) has offered a set of guidelines for such evaluations; these include the following:

1. They shall be done only by qualified psychologists or psychiatrists who are licensed in that geographic region.
2. The evaluator should be familiar with research on testing and evaluation in the field of police psychology.

3. If possible, the evaluation should *not* be done by a psychologist or psychiatrist who provides counselling within the same department.

4. Issues of confidentiality should be made explicit in writing prior to conducting the fitness-for-duty evaluation, and a consent form should be obtained from the officer.

5. The fitness-for-duty assessment should include at least one interview with the officer, a battery of psychological tests; interviews with supervisors, family members, and coworkers; and a review of any past psychological and medical evaluations.

6. The fitness-for-duty evaluator should provide a written report documenting the findings of the evaluation along with specific recommendations regarding continued employment and rehabilitation. (Two examples of such reports may be found in Blau, 1994, pp. 134–138 and pp. 140–142.)

Psychologists and psychiatrists who conduct fitness-for-duty evaluations are making assessments and recommendations that could have a significant affect on the lives and careers of law enforcement professionals, and therefore great care must be taken (Miller, 2009). One method of assessing an officer's fitness for duty is to use the Officer Evaluation Scale. Lopez (2011) assessed the validity and reliability of the scale, and concluded that 10 of the 13 subscales on the scale generated reliable ratings of fitness. The remaining subscales were deemed unreliable possibly because of the methods used in the study. These findings suggest that the Officer Evaluation Scale should be administered more often in fitness-for-duty evaluations because the large majority of the scales were found to be reliable.

COMMUNITY POLICING

The decades of the 1970s and 1980s saw increases in drug usage and related crime, along with the continued decay of many inner cities. Like other concerned institutions, law enforcement agencies sought new ways to deal with these problems. The concept of **community policing** was developed as a response. As the name implies, its goal was to reunite the police with the community (Peak & Glensor, 1996). One definition of community policing is "an extension of the police-community relations concept which envisions an effective working partnership between the police and members of the community in order to solve problems which concern both" (Schmalleger, 1995, p. 200). In community policing, the police department focuses on improving the quality of life and being responsive (even proactively) to citizens' concerns. For example, residents of a neighbourhood are outraged at the intrusion of crack houses on their streets and drug traffickers in the public parks. A community-policing program might respond to this concern by frequently patrolling the parks and establishing surveillance of the crack houses.

However, community policing has been implemented in different ways in different regions (Skolnik & Bayley, 1986). The RCMP provides community-policing services to all provinces and territories except Ontario and Quebec. The manner in which RCMP services are delivered is based on the individual community's policing philosophy. The RCMP rightfully states that this approach helps to identify the particular social needs of the communities, which play a major role in the recognition, development, and determination of their own policing needs. In San Francisco, where police adopted a community policing strategy, officers began riding on city buses; in other cities, police began athletic programs for young people in high-crime areas, established bicycle patrols or re-established foot patrols, or developed neighbourhood police stations. The size of police department has been shown to be a strong predictor of community policing, such that larger organizations are more successful in incorporating it into their communities (Morabito, 2010; Rogers, 2003).

While anecdotal evidence for the effectiveness of these programs was encouraging, a more reliable evaluation was difficult. Often, communities would establish several changes at once and hence not be able to evaluate the separate impact of each. It was unclear just what was the goal of the change—a quicker response by the police to crimes, reduction of crime rates, higher clearance rates (i.e., the percentage of crimes for which an arrest or a conviction is made) for crimes that were committed, police job satisfaction, or greater community satisfaction with the police and reduced fear of crime. Palmiotto and Kingshott (2010) propose that the public should be aware of the goals of the law enforcement because the alliance between the police and their community allows for overall satisfaction. Kingshott (2011) advises that police should be more transparent and open in the media to gain the trust of citizens in their communities. Similarly, Rosenbaum, Graziano, Stephens, and Schuck (2011) suggest that police department websites offering more opportunities to contact police and report crime allow citizens to be aware of law enforcement's objectives and intentions. Perhaps because of lack of communication and openness to the public, some citizens remain suspicious of the police and are not willing to accept a more visible presence of the police in their neighbourhood (Schmalleger, 1995). For example, community policing has had a detrimental effect on the homeless population in Montreal, suggesting that it was implemented solely for police to justify and draw attention away from their prior negative actions by stating that they were only enforcing programs that the community had demanded (when in fact, this was not the case) (Sylvestre, 2010). In addition, some police are more comfortable with traditional law enforcement duties rather than community relations (Sparrow, Moore, & Kennedy, 1990). Further, Glaser and Denhardt (2010) found that officers who doubted the ability of community citizens to rise above self-interest are less likely to make efforts with community policing. The forensic psychologist as an evaluation researcher can assist the police department in designing interventions that permit clearer tests of their effectiveness. The evaluation researcher also can clarify the important outcome measures—how the community weighs the importance of crime control, citizen satisfaction, or job satisfaction of police.

SUMMARY

Forensic psychologists can contribute to many aspects of police work: to the selecting of candidates for training, to the preservice and on-the-job training of officers, to hostage negotiations, to the evaluation of the performance of individual officers, and to the creation and evaluation of innovative programs by law enforcement agencies. In doing so, forensic psychologists have the difficult task of being responsive to the police department as a client, but also recognizing public concerns about police corruption, racism, and brutality. Further, there are temptations for psychologists to contribute to controversial areas of policing such as helping to plan interrogations with terrorist suspects, activities that we traditionally have spent time critiquing in our research (e.g., identifying the problem of false confessions as described in Chapter 7). Such activities are fraught with ethical dilemmas and professional issues that demand further study.

The selection of candidates for law enforcement training is usually a complex and extensive process. The psychologist often plays a role in interviewing candidates and in advising the department about instruments to administer to candidates. Among these, the Minnesota Multiphasic Personality Inventory is the most widely used, but the Inwald Personality Inventory is worthy of consideration, as it was designed specifically for selection of law enforcement officers. The RPAT written examination used in RCMP selection examines a number of psychological competencies including memory and language.

There are both general and specific topics for which psychologists can contribute to the in-service training of police officers. Wellness training is of special importance, given the high rates of stress and resulting alcoholism, burnout, and marital discord among law enforcement officers as an occupational group. Forensic psychologists have also contributed to specialized training in responding to the taking of hostages and to domestic assaults.

The psychologist acts as evaluation researcher when asked to assess the worthiness of a recently adopted policy, such as community policing.

KEY TERMS

SUGGESTED READINGS

Bennell, C., Jones, N. J., & Corey, S. (2007). Does use-of-force simulation training in Canadian police agencies incorporate principles of effective training? *Psychology, Public Policy, and Law, 13*(1), 35–58.
This article discusses the use-of-force simulation training that is incorporated in numerous police agencies in Canada. The authors discuss ways in which police could enhance the effectiveness of this training.

Hogan, J., Bennell, C., & Taylor, A. (2011). The challenges of moving into middle management: Responses from police officers. *Journal of Police and Criminal Psychology, 26*(2), 100–111.
This article explores the importance of police management in achieving organization goals, the key characteristics to effective management and common mistakes that are made, and the concerns around the lack of training.

Kitaeff, J. (Ed.). (2011). *Handbook of police psychology*. New York: Routledge/Taylor & Francis Group.
A comprehensive review of the growing field of police psychology.

Miller, L. (2006). Practical police psychology: Stress management and crisis intervention for law enforcement. Springfield, IL: Charles C. Thomas Publisher.
This comprehensive review analyzes the daily challenges that law-enforcement officers face. The text discusses both community policing and law enforcement personnel as decision makers. More specifically, this review gives an in-depth discussion of tactics employed by the police, as well as the stresses that can be caused by the job, and ways of coping with it.

Sellbom, M., Fischler, G. L., & Ben-Porath, Y. S. (2007). Identifying MMPI-2 Predictors of police officer integrity and misconduct. *Criminal Justice and Behavior, 34*(8), 985–1004.
This article discusses the Minnesota Multiphasic Personality Inventory (MMPI-2) and its ability to predict misconduct in police officers.

WEBSITE

Out of the Shadows at Last—Transforming Mental Health, Mental Illness and Addiction Services in Canada: **http://www.parl.gc.ca/ Content/SEN/Committee/391/soci/rep/pdf/ rep02may06part1-e.pdf**

CHAPTER 4

Criminal Profiling

> *Profilers, especially those who employ typology-based approaches, assume that it is possible to classify crimes into mutually exclusive types and that criminals who commit similar types of crimes will have similar backgrounds [sic] characteristics (and, by extension, criminals committing different types of crimes will have different backgrounds). The current studies failed to find strong empirical support for either of these assumptions.*
>
> —Memorial University of Newfoundland researchers Brandy Doan & Brent Snook (2008)

CRIMINAL PROFILING AND FORENSIC PSYCHOLOGY

In many countries, such as Canada, police sometimes rely on **criminal profiling** to aid their investigations. A criminal profiler is a psychological consultant or investigator who examines evidence from the crime scene, victims, and witnesses in an attempt to construct an accurate description of the person or persons who perpetrated the crime. Although criminal profiling may hold potential as an investigative tool, the empirical foundations of profiling and its assumptions remain questionable, as the quotation at the start of the chapter conveyed.

Is criminal profiling an appropriate topic for a textbook on forensic psychology? On the one hand, many students—some of whom will be the forensic psychologists of the future—are drawn to the field because of their desire to emulate Clarice Starling of *The Silence of the Lambs* or the main characters in television shows such as *Criminal Minds, The Mentalist,* or *The Profiler.* The classification and capture of serial criminals sounds like a fascinating career. On the other hand, the quotation at the beginning of this chapter reflects the views of many forensic psychologists who do not include criminal profiling as a major topic under the rubric of forensic psychology. Here are some of their reasons:

1. Training in criminal profiling has been controlled by the law enforcement, and most graduate programs in forensic psychology do not offer specialized courses on this topic. To date, the only persons who have been eligible for formal training by the FBI are law enforcement officers. In Canada, the RCMP relies on a small number of senior law enforcement officers who have received specialized training from the FBI. The OPP and the QPP also employ criminal profilers to conduct, as it is called in Canada, "criminal investigative analysis" (RCMP, 2011b).

2. The number of criminal profiling jobs is small. Even during its period of most frequent activity in the 1970s and 1980s, the Behavioral Sciences Unit of the FBI was a very small operation, with only a dozen or fewer profilers. Although there are positions in U.S. crime labs and some detectives in large-city police departments may do some profiling, the number of open positions is minuscule compared to the intense level of interest. In Canada, there are few or no openings at any given time.

3. The vast majority of professionals who do profiling did not do graduate work in psychology; rather, they advanced through the ranks of law enforcement, starting out as field agents, or they went through police-academy training. Although one current FBI profiler has a Ph.D. in psychology, he became a profiler because of his extensive FBI work experience, not because of his Ph.D. In Canada, the small number of profilers employed by the RCMP and provincial police forces generally do not have Ph.D.s. (The situation is different in Great Britain, where many profilers are psychologists [Gudjonsson & Copson, 1997]). In Canada, three agencies have a section dedicated to criminal profiling: the RCMP's Special Services and Behavioural Sciences Branch, the Sûreté

du Québec's Behavioural Analysis Service, and the Ontario Provincial Police's (O.P.P.) Behavioural Sciences Section (Marin, 2003). Most of these profilers are police officers who moved up the ranks.

4. Even experienced profilers such as John Douglas (one of the first criminal profilers with the FBI) acknowledge that profiling is an art more than it is a science. All profilers are not in agreement about the appropriate methodology for profiling offenders; for example, some advocate the use of a statistical or actuarial analysis of the crime scene findings while others advocate the use of clinical approaches of single cases to make inferences about the perpetrator's personality processes (Bekerian & Jackson, 1997). Therefore, criminal profiling is a broad, hard-to-pin-down term that covers a variety of procedures and operating assumptions (Woodworth & Porter, 1999).

5. For these and other reasons, expert testimony on profiling is not likely to be admitted in court, as it fails to meet *Mohan* or *Daubert* standards of merit as judged by the scientific community (Bosco, Zappalà, & Santtila, 2010). In fact, a decade ago the Ontario Court of Appeal ruled that "unscientific" criminal profiling should not be allowed as expert opinion evidence (*R. v. Ranger*, 2003). In that case, Detective Kathryn Lines, a manager of the Behavioural Sciences Section of the Ontario Provincial Police, who specializes in criminal profiling gave expert evidence at trial. However, the Court concluded that:

Accepting that criminal profiling may be a useful, albeit potentially dangerous, aid to police investigations, its use as a means of proof in a courtroom is quite another matter ... All aspects of expert opinion testimony of course must meet the same test for admissibility and I am not suggesting that the simple characterization of the evidence answers the question on admissibility. I am simply observing that expert opinion testimony about "WHY" or "WHO" usually raises more concerns. These concerns relate most frequently to two aspects of the *Mohan* test for admissibility: the requirement that the evidence be sufficiently reliable to warrant its admission and the requirement that its probative value exceed its prejudicial effect. (para. 70)

And recall that the *Mohan* case itself involved a consideration of a type of "profiling" (whether the crimes likely had been perpetrated by a pedophile and/or a sexual psychopath).

Despite these disclaimers, using the broad definition of forensic psychology introduced in Chapter 1, profiling is an application of psychological concepts to the legal system, even though the evidence for its effectiveness is less than overwhelming. (In that respect, it shares a quality with topics of some of the other chapters of this book, procedures that are more accepted by many forensic psychologists). Further, for good or bad, criminal profiling is becoming much more commonly applied in the Canadian context and requires much closer scientific scrutiny. Since 1991, the OPP has handled about 3150 requests for service, while the RCMP has responded to approximately 175 requests annually (Bourque, LeBlanc, Utzschneider, & Wright, 2009).

The typical cases for which such referrals were made included homicides, sexual assaults, and child abuse. As Canadian researcher Craig Bennell (2008) observed, the frequency with which profilers have been asked to generate profiles has increased exponentially over the past three decades, while the amount of profiling research has increased at a much slower rate.

It is hoped that a critical analysis of the current state of the field will increase your awareness of both its opportunities and pitfalls. We also hope that a consideration of the current limitations of criminal profiling will inspire researchers—including you as future researchers—to devise ways of improving the investigative technique through innovative science.

WHY DEVELOP CRIMINAL PROFILES?

The Problem of Serial Criminal Behaviour

Serial crimes of a sexual and/or homicidal nature continue to be a major concern to the public. As we know from Canadian cases, violence by serial offenders can escalate to tragic proportions if law enforcement fails to apprehend those offenders quickly. For example, between 1957 and 1981, Clifford Olson (who passed away in 2011 much to the relief of his victims' families)—one of Canada's most notorious serial offenders—was arrested 94 times for both minor and major crimes, including armed robbery and sexual assault (Stanbridge & Kenney, 2009; Woodworth & Porter, 1999). After numerous children were found murdered in British Columbia

TV shows such as *Criminal Minds* appeal to the public's fascination with criminal profiling and suggest — in a highly exaggerated way — that profilers have an uncanny ability to get into the mind of criminals and solve crimes.

Monty Brinton/© CBS/Courtesy Everett Collection

between November 1980 and August 1981, Olson became a suspect and was arrested. However, he was released and continued to murder children until he was rearrested. Olson, a diagnosed psychopath, ultimately was convicted of 11 counts of murder.

Most readers will be aware of another Canadian offender whose crimes increased in severity over many years—Paul Bernardo, known as the "Scarborough Rapist." Bernardo sexually assaulted numerous Ontario women over the course of several years in the early 1990s. Although he was a suspect in the investigation, he was not arrested and his violence escalated until he, along with his wife Karla Homolka, raped and murdered three young women, including Homolka's own sister.

In October 2011, police in British Columbia announced the identity of possibly Canada's youngest serial murderer suspect. Twenty-one-year-old Cody Alan Legebokoff has been charged with the slayings of a teenage girl and four women in the Prince George area over one year. According to published reports, no one who knew Legebokoff could recall any signs of potential trouble in the young man. His grandfather

described "a good upbringing—everything was perfect … I hunted with him. I fished with him. We did everything and he was a perfectly normal child" (see *Vancouver Sun* archives).

Next to crime prevention, crime detection is of the highest priority to the public and to law enforcement agencies. The types of cases described above have made clear the need for Canadian law enforcement to develop better techniques to help prevent and solve serial crimes, especially murders. A common definition of **serial murder** is the killing of three or more people (or the "belief" of the perpetrator that the victims were deceased) with a "cooling off" period between the killings (Holmes & Holmes, 1998; Trojan & Salfati, 2010). There are a number of factors present in serial murder cases that make them especially difficult to solve; notably, there often is no relationship between the killer and victim (Nicole & Proulx, 2007; Porter et al., 2003), whereas in most murder cases the killer and victim are related (e.g., Correctional Service of Canada, 1995; Juodis et al., 2009; Porter & Woodworth, 2006). Further, it may be difficult or impossible to establish a motive in many serial homicide cases (Hazelwood & Burgess, 1995). People who commit consecutive murders are of major societal concern given that they may account for up to a third of all murders (Juodis et al., 2009; Linedecker & Burt, 1990, p. ix). The FBI has reported that nearly 200 serial killers have been identified and imprisoned or killed since 1970 (Youngstrom, 1991). Estimates of the number of serial killers at large in the United States vary widely—from 25 (Associated Press, 1992) to 100 (Holmes & Holmes, 1996, p. 62). In Canada, we have had our share of serial killers in the past two decades. In 1999, when the first author of this textbook worked at a medium-security prison in British Columbia, at least five serial killers were housed there. One of my most interesting and bizarre experiences as a clinical-forensic psychologist was meeting a man who had killed five prostitutes and believed he had "become" his last female victim, and was applying to have a sex change. Serial killer Robert Pickton currently is held at a maximum-security prison in British Columbia. Pickton was convicted of six counts of second-degree murder, although he has confessed to killing 49 women, noting that he wanted to kill another woman in order to make it to 50. A more recent addition to the list of Canadian killers is Russell Williams, the former Canadian Forces colonel. In 2010, he was convicted of first-degree murder among other sex crimes and received a life sentence with no chance of parole for 25 years. In addition, it is believed that there are a number of serial killers who continue to prey on others in Canada. The RCMP in Edmonton firmly believe that it is dealing with a long-time serial murderer who has disposed of at least 13 female victims, many of them sex trade workers, outside the upscale suburb of Sherwood Park.

If we are able to develop valid profiles of criminals, the process would aid both of the above-mentioned goals—detection and prevention.

But what do we mean by a **criminal profile**? A "profile" of what? Some profilers emphasize the personality and motivations of the offender, including characteristic ways of committing crimes and treating victims. But certainly physical characteristics are important—the criminal's age, sex, race, height, and weight. Whether the perpetrator is left-handed or right-handed sometimes is easily determined from an analysis of the *actus reus*. Because these qualities plus other demographic data (e.g., occupation, education) are sought in

addition to a personality sketch of the criminal, some investigators (e.g., Holmes & Holmes, 1996; Palermo & Kocsis, & Slovenko, 2005) prefer to use the term **sociopsychological profile** rather than the more common term, **psychological profile**.

Canadian law enforcement agencies might include computer-based profiling, in which the crime scene characteristics or peculiarities of a current crime are matched with past crimes to identify a common perpetrator. This computer-based approach is known as the Violent Crime Linkage Analysis System or **ViCLAS**. This might also include **geographic profiling**, developed by Dr. Kim Rossmo, a former member of the Vancouver Police Department who received his Ph.D. in criminology from Simon Fraser University. With geographic profiling, the geographic pattern of crimes is used to make a probabilistic estimate of where the offender lives (see Rossmo, 2010, 2011).

Recurring Mysteries

One of the ideal outcomes of criminal profiling, as we shall explore in more detail, is matching crime scene information (**physical evidence**) with characteristics of a specific suspect to help determine whether this suspect did commit the crime.

Knowledge generated from criminal profiling may provide insights into some of the unresolved questions about highly publicized crimes, exemplified in the case of Jeffrey MacDonald. In February 1970, Jeffrey MacDonald was a well-respected doctor, a graduate of Princeton University who had completed a prestigious residency at Northwestern University Medical School before concluding his obligatory military service as a Green Beret in Vietnam. But on the night of February 16, 1970, police alleged that Captain MacDonald:

---

smashed the skull of his pregnant wife several times with a club, and stabbed her 21 times with an icepick; clubbed his 5-year-old daughter Kimberly with three blows, then stabbed her no fewer than ten times; and finally placed his little (age 2) daughter Kristen across his lap, knifed her 17 times, and drove an icepick into her tiny body 15 times. (Noguchi, 1985, p. 61)

MacDonald himself had a superficial knife wound to the ribs. He has steadfastly claimed—for more than 40 years now—that these atrocities were committed by a knife- and club-wielding

Manson Family-style "hippie cult," screaming, "Acid is groovy; kill the pigs," and that one of the cult members scrawled the word pig in blood across the headboard of his bed. Because the crimes occurred on an army base, a military court first processed the case. As a result of this investigatory hearing (which lasted for four months), all charges against MacDonald were dismissed. But nine years later, he was tried in a civilian court and convicted of the murders of his wife and children. Despite numerous appeals that are continuing in 2012, MacDonald remains in prison.

The prosecution in the trial argued that MacDonald had staged the crime scene so that it would appear that he had a violent struggle with the four intruders. It provided the following explanation: MacDonald had fallen asleep on the living-room couch while watching television. When he awoke and went to the bedroom, he found that one of his children had wet her bed. An argument with his wife resulted, escalating into a fight. MacDonald, it was argued, got a club, became angrier, and lost control. When his older daughter came upon the scene, he proceeded to attack and kill her. Realizing the need for a cover story, he continued the grisly acts, stabbing the children frequently to make it appear to be a cultish, Manson-like murder.

For several reasons, the MacDonald case continues to capture attention (Anson, 1998; Potter & Bost, 1995; Slovenko, 2006). MacDonald is an attractive, personable defendant, who continues to claim he is innocent. Further, it was established that some of the evidence was destroyed by the police, and it has been argued that the FBI presentation of crucial evidence was misleading (Noguchi, 1985; Wecht, 1994). The widespread publicity about errors in the FBI's laboratory that surfaced in the late 1990s (see, for example, Kelly & Wearne, 1998) included a claim that an FBI agent misrepresented the results of laboratory analyses of clothing fibres in the MacDonald case. Cyril Wecht, an internationally recognized forensic pathologist, investigated the case and concluded:

As I studied his psychological profile—that of a well-educated, successful, balanced person—I found that it did not fit the profile of a person who would suddenly snap, kill his wife and kids, and then regain his composure enough to try to cover it up ... That kind of person is known to slam a fist into a door, throw household objects, or verbally threaten people.

But Jeffrey MacDonald had never displayed any of those actions either before or after that night in 1970. (Wecht, 1994, pp. 136–137)

The former chief medical examiner of Los Angeles County, Dr. Thomas Noguchi, reviewed the evidence in detail and expressed a similar concern: "If MacDonald destroyed his own loving family, then on this one occasion an otherwise normal man behaved with the almost inconceivable rage and cunning of a psychotic" (1985, p. 87). But to the specific question: Is Jeffrey MacDonald innocent? Noguchi's response was "I do not know" (p. 88), and Dr. Wecht chose not to testify at the trial because his examination of the wounds to MacDonald left him uncertain about whether or not they had been self-inflicted.

This case is illustrative because it includes divergent conclusions drawn from the physical evidence (forensic evidence) versus those drawn from criminal profiling. Physical evidence, such as blood typing and the pattern of knife thrusts through MacDonald's pajama top is highly influential for jurors. But as Wecht (1994) has noted, physical evidence can be misrepresented or misinterpreted. It might be argued that such evidence needs to be weighed against what we know about the character and motivations of Jeffrey MacDonald, including his intelligence, his affable personality, and his decades-long claim of innocence. As of July 2012 MacDonald was being held in the New Hanover County Jail awaiting evidentiary hearings in his upcoming appeal hearing in September.

False Stereotypes and Simplified Assumptions

The Jeffrey MacDonald case makes us confront our assumptions about human nature. Could someone as engaging and dedicated as MacDonald kill his own children "out of the blue" and in cold blood? What was going through your mind as you read the case description? You probably started to quickly make inferences about the facts of the case, perhaps even relating to guilt and innocence. Thus, the case also reinforces that each of us carries around our own assumptions and theories about the motivations or *mens rea* for criminal acts and their perpetrators.

In the novel *Evidence* (Weisman, 1980), an assistant district attorney says to an investigative reporter:

> Most crime is amazingly simple ... You guys always look for some kind of conspiracy. You're always writing about psychological motivation, about role modeling ... [M]ost perps do what they do because it's all they know. They're stupid. They hate, they want, and they do things to other people because that's what they know how to do. Robbers rob. Muggers mug. Rapists rape. That's what they do best. It's their job. All that talk about sociopathic patterns, the messed-up childhoods, the resentment of the father-authority figure, I think it's a crock. The perp is a perp ... They do what they know best. (p. 221)

Perhaps this oversimplified analysis applies in a few instances. But experienced criminal investigators and forensic psychologists alike argue that a sophisticated psychological analysis often is required. Take, for example, the crime of stalking. In Canada, reported incidents of stalking have risen dramatically since 1993 when it was defined as a specific crime ("criminal harassment" in the Criminal Code of Canada. A group of police services noted an estimated 16 percent rise in stalking incidents from 1999 to 2000, and about a 50 percent increase since 1996 (Statistics Canada, 2001a). In 2005, Statistics Canada reported that between 2000 and 2005, 11 percent of females and 7 percent of males aged 15 years and over had been the victim of stalking (see Chapter 10). Although it is hard to know whether this reflects a real increase in stalking behaviour or a greater awareness and reporting of the crime, it does highlight the societal importance of the problem. But stalkers reflect a variety of motives, behaviours, and psychological traits, making it difficult to develop one psychological profile that covers all, or even a majority, of them (Meloy, 1998; Storey, Hart, Meloy, & Reavis, 2009). The process of profiling needs to be applied to the individual stalker, rather than the group.

An assumption that profilers must be careful to avoid relates to widespread false stereotypes held about criminals in the general population. For example, bank robbers are seen by the public as clever, debonair, skillful, and glamorous; in reality, a study of convicted bank robbers found that most were young, impulsive, high on drugs or experiencing a personal crisis, and desperate (Gill & Matthews, 1994; Gill & Pease, 1998). Most of them repeat the crime until they get caught (and most of them are). In contrast to some other types of major crimes, police solve nearly four out of every five bank robberies. Not so clever after all!

Similarly, the crime of embezzlement or other fraud carries a false connotation. Many people assume that embezzlers are old, trusted employees who have steadfastly worked for a single firm for many years. But a survey of 23 men and 39 women convicted of embezzling (Pogrebin, Poole, & Regoli, 1986) concluded that the typical embezzler was a 26-year-old, married white woman with a high school education who earned close to minimum wage and worked in an entry-level position for less than one year. The most frequent motivation expressed by the embezzlers was a marital or family problem.

When asked to describe what an assassin is like, many people would probably describe a deranged but determined madman, a lonely loser who follows up his threats of violence with an act against his sole target (Dedman, 1998). But an analysis by the U.S. Secret Service of all 83 persons who killed or tried to kill American politicians or other nationally known figures between 1949 and 1998 challenged these stereotypes (see Fein & Vossekuil, 1999): "Fewer than half of the assassins showed symptoms of mental illness. Many shifted from one target to another, valuing the act more than the victim. No one had communicated a direct threat to the target or to law-enforcement authorities" (Dedman, 1998, p. A-15).

We also make assumptions about the backgrounds of murderers. As Ressler and Shachtman (1992) observed, a common myth is that murderers come from impoverished or broken homes. Ressler, Burgess, and Douglas (1988) conducted interviews with 36 convicted male murderers; more than half lived initially in a family that appeared to be intact, with both the mother and father living together with the son (also see Langevin et al., 1988) As a group, the murderers were intelligent children; although 7 of the 36 had IQ scores below 90, almost a third (11 of 36) had IQs above 120, and most were at least in the normal range. On the other hand, there were dysfunctional aspects of these families—high rates of alcohol or drug abuse, consistent emotional abuse—but the families often appeared to be "normal." Perhaps the stereotype of the impoverished or abusive background of the murderer is more accurate in relation to sex murderers. Research by Carter and Hollin (2010) and Nicole and Proulx (2007) indicated that sex murderers were more likely to have been victims of sexual and physical abuse in childhood (two-thirds reporting the latter), and have more disturbed relationships with their fathers relative to sexual offenders in general.

There is much evidence that people hold assumptions even about what perpetrators of various crimes look like (Korva et al., 2012). Certain faces are perceived as congruent with specific types of crimes (Bull & McAlpine, 1998; Dumas & Teste, 2006), and there are perceived stereotypical features of rapists, armed robbers, or murderers. Defendants whose faces are congruent with facial characteristics commonly associated with these crimes are more likely to be found guilty in legal settings, regardless of weak evidence (Dumas & Teste, 2006). And defendants with an "untrustworthy"-looking face are convicted of murder (by mock jurors) based on less incriminating evidence than trustworthy-looking defendants (Porter, Gustaw, & ten Brinke, 2010). As such, profilers need to examine their own assumptions about criminals that can influence their inferences in a particular case.

CURRENT NEEDS FOR PROFILING

Criminal profiling is not appropriate as an aid in detection for every serious crime. But for certain types of criminals, criminal profiling "potentially" can be useful.

Arsonists

In 2005, 13 315 incidents of arson were reported in Canada (Gannon, 2005). One of these incidents occurred in Lunenburg, Nova Scotia, when the second-oldest church in Canada (built in 1754) was deliberately torched. A team of 20 investigators was assigned to the still-unsolved case, which has been officially classified as arson. In the fall of 1993, forest fires devastated large sections of Southern California, including Malibu and Laguna Beach; at least five of the 23 fires, it was concluded, were deliberately set, with several others suspected to be arson (Sharn, 1993). The state of California alone has 40 000 suspicious fires a year. In one year in New York City, more than 101 000 fires occurred; 246 people died in these conflagrations. Investigators concluded that 5362 of these fires were deliberately set (Micheels, 1991). As Micheels (1991) noted, "next to war, arson is humanity's costliest act of violence" (p. xv). During 2010 there were 12 241 reported incidents of arson in Canada, a high number, but a 10 percent decrease from the previous year (Statistics Canada, 2010).

What kind of person would do this? Although few arsonists are caught or prosecuted (see

Caudill et al., 2011) because of few witnesses and little evidence, arson takes the lives of hundreds of North Americans every year. Can criminal profiling analysis assist in overcoming these challenges? In their *Crime Classification Manual*, Douglas, Burgess, Burgess, and Ressler (1992) introduced the arsonist profiling process by identifying three types of this crime: serial arson, spree arson, and mass arson. They also classified the motives of arsonists into various types, including vandalism, excitement, revenge, crime concealment, and profit. The FBI's National Center for the Analysis of Violent Crime interviewed 83 convicted serial arsonists; their most frequently reported motive was revenge (Rider, 1980), an eerily similar pattern to that of homicide (Woodworth & Porter, 2002). Micheels provided an example:

The guy is pissed off that his girlfriend is seeing another man. This type of fire setter is probably one of the most dangerous ... In his rage, he'll try to burn her out, or burn the new boyfriend, with a Molotov cocktail or by squeezing flammable liquids under the door, and he won't really care about who sees him or anything else. (1991, pp. 6–7).

One of the most tragic examples of this type was the Puerto Rican Social Club fire on Sunday, October 24, 1975, in the South Bronx, New York. A total of 27 people died, and 22 were seriously injured. The fire was set on the only stairway from ground level to the second-floor club. José Antonio Cordero, who admitted setting the fire, stated that his motive was jealousy (a young woman had attended the dance that night against his wishes). Cordero was sentenced to life in prison.

The profile of the typical arsonist is "a young, white male—most likely a loner with a history of problems" (Sharn, 1993, p. 3A). But as noted above, fires are started for a multitude of reasons. Other characteristics of arsonists are as varied as their motives; a veteran fire investigator observed that "they range from kids to little old ladies, from jilted lovers to Mafia wiseguys, from teenage crack dealers to lawyers and respectable businessmen. Arson is committed by individuals and by groups" (Micheels, 1991, p. xv).

Recently, there has been a significant increase in empirical attention given to characteristics of arsonists. For example, Enayati, Grann, Lubbe, and Fazel (2008) examined all arsonists referred for an inpatient forensic psychiatric examination in Sweden over a five-year period (1997–2001). They found that the most common Axis I diagnoses (the major mental illnesses in the *DSM-IV-TR*) among this group were psychotic illnesses and substance use disorders. Compared with other violent offenders referred for forensic psychiatric examinations, arsonists were more likely to be diagnosed with a learning disability and also, in the men, Asperger's syndrome.

On the other hand, Horley and Bowlby (2011) at the University of Alberta concluded that while arson statistically is associated with an unstable childhood, low socioeconomic status, and negative marital status, when combined with other factors such as alcohol abuse, arsonists on the whole are not much different from other offender groups. In other words, criminal offenders in general share many of the same features (not to suggest causation!) so we shouldn't jump to conclusions about their relation to arson specifically. Similar research by Roe-Sepowitz and Hickle (2011) that examined 217 male and 114 female juveniles charged with arson suggests that there are important differences between male and female arsonists. They found that female arsonists more often than males reported a major crisis within their family in the past. Females also had exhibited greater problems with tardiness or school truancy, and more often reported a history of childhood abuse and higher scores on a suicide ideation scale. Male arsonists were more likely to experience greater mental health problems, report gang involvement, and have a history of delinquency and arsons.

A recent study of Dutch arsonists found that—relative to other psychiatric patients—arsonists had more often received psychiatric treatment in the past and had a history of severe alcohol abuse (Labree, Nijman, van Marle, & Rassin, 2010). In this sample, although the base rate of major psychotic disorders was relatively low (28 percent), delusional thinking of some form was found to play a role in the arson crimes in about half of the cases (52 percent). There may be differences in single-crime versus repeat arsonists, as would be predicted by criminal profiling. Dickens et al. (2009) found that repeat arsonists more often are younger and single, and possess a number of features, including poor school adjustment and wetting the bed, suggesting childhood disturbance. They also are more likely to have a personality disorder and have spent previous time in prison.

So, while there are consistent indications of psychopathology, substance abuse, and a criminal orientation among arsonists that could be useful to criminal profilers, the diversity of arsonists makes it difficult to create a definitive profile. More research on this complex population clearly is needed.

Serial Bombers

Former PEI chemistry teacher Roger Charles Bell served a ten-year sentence for setting off four bombs in Charlottetown, including one in the PEI Supreme Court in 1988 and one in the legislature building in 1995. These and other bombings, such as the Federal Building in Oklahoma City and the World Trade Center in New York, led to instant analyses of the type of persons who commit these acts. This section describes a special type of bomber—the serial bomber—specifically, the so-called Unabomber, who was so named because most of his initial targets were universities, high-tech centres, and airlines (University/Airline Bomber) (Meddis, 1993). (The actions of another serial bomber, the "Mad Bomber," and how profiling was involved in his arrest are discussed later in this chapter.) The Unabomber was linked to 16 bombings all over the United States, causing three deaths and injuries to 23 people. His attacks began in 1978, but became sporadic with no attempts between 1987 and 1993. After a six-year hiatus, he sent one bomb to a genetics professor at the University of California, San Francisco, in June 1993, and another to a computer science professor at Yale University two days later. Then, the next year, he struck again, with a different kind of victim. On December 10, 1994, Thomas Mosser, an advertising executive, was killed by a mail bomb at his suburban New Jersey home. The Unabomber's final victim, a California forestry executive, was killed five months later, in April 1995.

The variety of intended victims, their locations all over the United States, and the time lapse between bombings posed a tough problem for criminal profilers. However, this serial bomber was considered to be a neat, meticulous individual who spent hours making and polishing bomb components (Fernandez, 1993). Behavioural-science specialists at the FBI theorized that "because there are no links between the victims and because many of them have been on the cutting edge of computer sciences, psychology, and genetics, the bomber may select his targets more for symbolic significance than because of any personal animus" (Labaton, 1993b, p. A10). Federal officials noted that the attacks were growing increasingly violent, with the use of very powerful bombs. Even though it was difficult to connect the deaths of the advertising and forestry executives to earlier victims, these bombs were built with similar materials and had a similar, sophisticated design (Levy, 1994). Like the previous ones, the explosives were made from scratch, without any traceable store-bought parts.

Interestingly, at least four of his targets, including the two in June 1993, had been featured in articles in *The New York Times* that characterized them as leading figures in their fields (Labaton, 1993a). (Another one of these, James McConnell of the University of Michigan, was a psychologist recognized for his successful introductory textbook and his research on memory transfer in invertebrates. Professor McConnell received a large manila envelope at his home; the cover letter —with a Salt Lake City postmark—suggested that McConnell should review "this thesis, which should be of interest" [Reynolds, 1994, p. 148]. McConnell's graduate assistant opened the package, and the blast injured him severely.) The next victim, Thomas Mosser, was featured in a *New York Times* article that appeared five days before he received the deadly bomb; the article described his promotion at the Young and Rubicam advertising agency.

After the attack on Mosser, FBI officials published a sketch of what they thought the Unabomber looked like, based on reports of a shadowy figure spotted in a Salt Lake City parking lot just after a bomb exploded in 1987. They described him as a recluse, a white man in his late 30s or 40s, who had a high school education but some familiarity with university life. They speculated that he mailed his packages from Northern California (Levy, 1994).

In 1994, the FBI suggested it might even know his motivation: a hatred of sophisticated technology, the one link that the FBI saw among his multitude of targets (Perez-Pena, 1994). The investigators stated that the signature that was sometimes used—"F. C."—stood for "an obscene phrase belittling computers" (Perez-Pena, 1994, p. A12), but they didn't say how they had reached that conclusion. As concern mounted in the early 1990s over further attacks, the FBI made some interesting speculations about him. In a magazine article about the Unabomber published six weeks before his December 1994 attack on the advertising executive, an FBI agent was quoted as saying: "I can see him moving away from academic targets. I think he will broaden his horizons and go into a lot of different areas" (Reynolds, 1994, p. 154).

The search for the Unabomber took another turn in the fall of 1995, when the Unabomber promised no further bombings if his 35 000-word manifesto was published in U.S. national newspapers. Analysis of his manuscript led the FBI to conclude the following as part of his criminal profile:

1. He was born and grew up in Morton Grove, Illinois, a northern suburb of Chicago. He almost certainly came from a background of affluence and education. After completing high school in nearby Skokie or Maine Township, he attended Northwestern University but did not graduate.
2. He was a "meticulous grammarian" who produced his efforts on a manual typewriter made in the early 1960s.
3. He was then believed to be living in the San Francisco area.
4. He was a talented machinist who assembled his devices mostly from handmade parts.
5. He was "a loner fixated on detail, the son of an overbearing parent, an egomaniac who is unable to get along with others and probably never married" (Howlett, 1995, p. 2A).

The FBI laboratory was even reported to have a DNA profile of the Unabomber, based on samples of saliva used to mail one of the package bombs. But despite all the information and effort, it took a unique break for a suspect to be located. With the publication of the Unabomber's manifesto, the brother of Theodore Kaczynski noted strong similarities to his brother's writings. After he contacted the FBI, it investigated and eventually arrested Kaczynski in his isolated cabin in Montana. Found in the cabin was an old manual typewriter and the materials used for assembling bombs.

As we know, Kaczynski eventually confessed to the actions, but we can still ask: How well did the profile fit? He is clearly a loner, never married, who had difficulty relating to other people. And he did grow up in the Chicago area. But rather than being a college dropout, he completed his undergraduate education and then received a Ph.D. from Harvard University. He taught mathematics for several years at the University of California at Berkeley before he voluntarily resigned. And, of course, he was living in the mountains of Montana when apprehended although he had lived in the San Francisco Bay area. So the profile was only partially correct. Would it have aided the FBI in apprehending Kaczynski had his brother not come forward? We cannot say, but certainly the eventual identification of the Unabomber was not a sterling example of the usefulness of profiling.

WHAT *IS* CRIMINAL PROFILING?

While the origins of criminal profiling are unclear, for centuries, elements of society have tried to pinpoint the physical or psychological qualities linked to criminal or deviant behaviour (Kocsis, 2007; Pinizzotto, 1984). Even literary works such as Shakespeare's *Julius Caesar* ("yon Cassius has a lean and hungry look") and Edgar Allan Poe's "The Murders in the Rue Morgue" reflected attempts to profile unacceptable behaviours by use of physical attributes (McPoyle, 1981, cited by Pinizzotto, 1984). The documented history of real-life profiling can be traced at least to the publication of the notorious *Malleus Malificarum*, a book from the 1400s written for the Catholic Church and intended to identify witches based on their behaviour and physical characteristics (Woodworth & Porter, 1999).

The first modern example of criminal profiling occurred in the Jack the Ripper case in London, England, in the late 1800s. Dr. George Phillips, the police surgeon involved in the investigation, observed the pattern of wounds on the victims in order to attempt to determine the offender's psychological characteristics. Phillips thought that a careful examination of the evidence could give clues about the personality of the killer (e.g., Turvey, 1999). One of the most famous examples of a successful criminal profile came in 1956 when psychiatrist Dr. James Brussels successfully profiled the New York Mad Bomber (described in greater detail below) for investigators, using a psychoanalytic interpretation of the crime scene and the Mad Bomber's letters (e.g., Wilson, Lincoln, & Kocsis, 1997). In 1972, the FBI Behavioral Science Unit (BSU) was created after several notorious cases of serial and mass homicide in the 1960s (e.g., the Boston Strangler and Richard Speck).

Definitions

Criminal profiling has been described as an educated attempt to provide specific information about a certain type of suspect (Geberth, 1981)

Savage Chickens by Doug Savage

HMMM... JUST LIKE THE OTHERS... DRAINED OF BLOOD, BUT ONLY TWO SMALL PUNCTURE WOUNDS ON THE ANKLE

NIGHT OF THE VAMPIRE CHIHUAHUAS!

www.savagechickens.com © Doug Savage

In a serial murder or rape case, investigators are interested in the perpetrator's "signature," or unique offending pattern across crimes that can be linked and help solve the crime.

and as a biographical sketch of behavioural patterns, trends, and tendencies (Douglas, Ressler, Burgess, & Hartman, 1986). A comprehensive definition was offered in the text edited by Koscis (2007): "the application of psychological theory and behavioral analysis to the investigation and reconstruction of physical evidence that relates to a particular offender's crime scene characteristics, victimology, motivation, and behavior patterns" (p. 62). The basic premise of criminal profiling is that the way a person thinks directs the person's behaviour. It is important to recognize that profiling can never provide the specific identity of the offender (Douglas et al., 1986) (despite its characterization in popular culture), simply the profile of the person most likely to commit such a crime (Crabbé, Decoene, & Vertommen, 2008).

Similarly, not all types of crimes are conducive to successful criminal profiling. Holmes and Holmes (1996) concluded that crimes, even though they may be serial in nature, such as cheque forgery, bank robbery, and kidnapping are not good candidates for profiling. A single act of murder, especially if it is spontaneous, is more difficult to interpret than a series of crimes that reflect similar actions or locations. In the latter instance, the consistencies in crime scenes and manner in which victims were treated by the perpetrator allow the police to get a better handle on the nature of the perpetrator. The nature of the victim's wounds also might give clues to the personality and experience of the attacker. Holmes and Holmes

(1996) even suggested that some serial killers are aware of the "trace" they leave at a crime scene; these psychologists quote the remarkable observations of one such killer, as presented in Box 4.1.

Geberth (1990) stated that the purpose of criminal profiling is:

---

to provide the investigator with a personality composite of the unknown suspect(s) that will aid apprehension. By studying the crime scene from a psychological standpoint, the criminal psychologist is able to identify and interpret certain items of evidence at the scene, which provide clues to the personality type of the individual or individuals who have committed the crime. (p. 492)

Three Approaches to Criminal Profiling

Although the above quotation implies a specific standardized procedure, three different approaches can be included under the rubric "criminal profiling" (or "offender profiling," the term used in Europe to describe this process). Even though each has a different strategy, the general intent is the same. Each is described below.

Profiling Historic and Political Figures

Understanding the behaviour and motivations of individuals who commit serial crimes reflects one goal of profiling. In the nine days between his murder of Gianni Versace and his own suicide, spree killer Andrew Cunanan became the target of widespread questions about his motivations and personality (Orth, 1999). Whether a perpetrator's effects are broad and perversely successful, like Hitler's or Stalin's, or specific and futile, like those of Frank Corder (the man who was killed as he flew his small plane into the trees surrounding the White House), their actions lead us to ask, Why? When a national leader dies suddenly and is replaced by a newcomer—as in the case of North Korea's dictator Kim Jong-il who died in 2011 and was replaced by his son Kim Jong-un—the CIA seeks to develop a personality profile that will predict the behaviour of the new ruler while he or she is in power.

Adolf Hitler. The practical benefits of profiling a specific perpetrator were tested by the World War II effort of the U.S. government's Office of Strategic Services (OSS) to profile the personality of Adolf Hitler. In 1943, a practising psychiatrist, Walter C. Langer, assembled material to provide a psychological description of Hitler's personality, a diagnosis of his mental condition, and a prediction of how he would react to defeat. Almost three decades after the end of the war, a book was published, detailing all these conclusions (Langer, 1972). (Hitler's basic nature remains a controversy among scholars; in fact, two books, by Lukacs

---

BOX 4.1	A KILLER'S VIEW OF HIS OWN CRIMES

R. M. Holmes, a forensic psychologist, has interviewed a number of criminals. The following is the statement of one.

First of all, any investigative onlooker to my crime scene would have immediately deduced that the offender was extremely sadistic in nature. The visible markers of bondage, and the nature of the victims' wounds—the evidence of unhurried, systematic abuse—would have indicated that sadistic acts were not new to the offender; he had committed such brutality in the past, and would likely continue this pattern of victimization in the future.

From these points, it could have then been correctly assumed that, although brutally violent, the offender was nevertheless intelligent enough to attach method to his madness—as well as cautious and aware enough with regard to his surroundings—to make sure he proceeds unseen in the commission of his deeds.

Further, ... such a brutal offense was unprecedented in this area, it could have been correctly assumed that the offender was very new to the city; if he was a drifter, he was at least someone who very possibly could deem to leave town as suddenly as he arrived (which is exactly what I did). (quoted in Holmes & Holmes, 1996, p. 41)

(1997) and by Rosenbaum (1998) dealt with the varying conceptions held by other authors of Hitler's motivations and character.)

Langer conducted a psychoanalytic profile of Hitler, in which the nature of Hitler's childhood relationship with his parents was seen as quite influential on his future behaviour. Apparently, Hitler saw his father as brutally cold and cruel in his relationship with his wife and children. In contrast, Hitler's mother was long suffering and affectionate; young Adolf developed a strong emotional attachment to her. But, while Hitler was still an adolescent, his mother died a painful death from cancer.

Langer concluded that Hitler was unable to develop an intimate relationship with others that sustained adversity because he judged people as fundamentally untrustworthy. At the same time, he saw himself as infallible and omnipotent. In an analysis heavily influenced by the Adlerian notion of the "inferiority complex," Langer held that through Hitler's leadership of a powerful Germany, he could somehow prove his manhood to his deceased mother.

With regard to predictions, the analysis by Langer offered several possibilities for Hitler's approach to adversity. It cast doubt on Hitler's likelihood of seeking refuge in another country; more likely was the possibility that he would lead his troops into a final futile battle. Langer opined correctly the possibility that in the face of inevitable defeat, Hitler would commit suicide. He noted that Hitler had threatened to take his own life on earlier occasions and had said to an associate, "Yes, in the hour of supreme peril I must sacrifice myself to the people" (quoted by Langer, 1972, p. 216). As we know, Langer was right.

It is unlikely that the profile of Hitler transmitted to the U.S. government had any discernible effect on Allied foreign policy or the outcome of the war; even Langer (1972, p. 25) doubted that it did; it simply came too late.

Saddam Hussein. The quest to understand the personality and behaviour of world leaders is never ending. Recently, the world has focused on violent leaders such as the Yugoslavian leader Slobodan Milosevic and Libyan leader Muammar Gaddafi, the latter killed by rebels in October 2011. During the Iraqi conflicts, the U.S. government sought to profile Saddam Hussein, who eventually was captured by American soldiers in 2003. Psychiatrist Jerrold M. Post of George Washington University testified on this matter before the U.S. House of Representatives in December 1990, and his testimony was later published (Post, 1991).

Post disabused the government officials of labels for Saddam Hussein such as "madman of the Middle East." He stated: "[T]here is no evidence that he is suffering from a psychotic disorder. He is not impulsive, only acts after judicious consideration, and can be extremely patient; indeed he uses time as a weapon" (1991, p. 283). However, Post concluded that Hussein often was politically out of touch with reality, that he possessed a "political personality constellation—messianic ambition for unlimited power, absence of conscience, unconstrained aggression, and a paranoid outlook" (1991, p. 285), which made him quite dangerous.

In the wake of the Gulf War of 1991, Post predicted that Saddam Hussein would not "go down to the last flaming bunker" if he had a way out, but that he would "stop at nothing if he is backed into a corner" (pp. 288–289). For a long time, Post's predictions—in light of what has happened in the years since the Gulf War of 1991—seemed accurate. Based on CIA profiles, U.S. policymakers fully expected Saddam Hussein to break under the increasing pressure (Cockburn & Cockburn, 1999), but when he was found by American soldiers in a hole in the ground (with a pistol), he seemed meek and offered no resistance whatsoever, similar to Gaddafi's response when the rebels captured him in 2011.

David Koresh. The analyses of Hitler and Hussein were based on a wealth of material about these public figures, developed over extended periods. Sometimes, in contrast, a crisis develops, requiring a quicker decision.

After a 51-day siege of the Branch Davidian compound in Texas led by David Koresh, the FBI decided to attack, based on reports that children inside were being abused. The result, as we now know, was a disaster. As many as two dozen cult members, including Koresh, were shot as fire began to consume the 86 persons in the compound on April 19, 1993 (Verhovek, 1993).

The actions of Koresh and the people in the compound have brought questions about the adequacy of the psychological profile of Koresh assembled by the FBI. William Sessions, then director of the FBI, was quoted as saying: "We had been assured, both from our own evaluations of David Koresh, from the psychologists, from the psycholinguists, from a psychiatrist, from his writings, from his assertions himself, repeatedly, that he did not intend to commit suicide" (quoted by Lewis, 1993, p. A19).

One of those to whom Director Sessions apparently referred was Murray S. Miron, then a professor of psychology at Syracuse University and a specialist in psycholinguistics. Miron had done forensic analyses of communication for years—he did a quite accurate profile of David Berkowitz, the "Son of Sam"—and, with John Douglas of the Profiling and Consultation Program of the FBI Academy, had published analyses of threats of violence (Miron & Douglas, 1979). Miron was quoted as telling the FBI that suicide "was not part of his (Koresh's) agenda" (*Los Angeles Times*, 1993).

Profiling Criminals' Common Characteristics

Far different from the focus on specific influential individuals is the second approach, in which the profiler looks for consistencies in the personalities, backgrounds, and behaviours of offenders who carry out similar kinds of crimes. Are all bank robbers alike? Do rapists have similar personalities? One benefit of the extensive amount of profiling done in the last 20 years is the generation of new, and sometimes surprising, patterns. For example, as Heilbroner (1993) has noted, serial killing turns out to be a highly sexual process; for many serial killers—including Ted Bundy and Jeffrey Dahmer—their victims are simply bodies on which they enact their sexual fantasies. Porter and colleagues at UBC (Porter et al., 2003; Porter et al., 2010) concluded that a lack of conscience combined with a thrill-seeking motivation promote sexual homicide and the extent of torture and sadistic behaviour evidenced during the homicidal act.

Childhood Experiences

Many methods exist for seeking answers to questions about consistency in criminals' backgrounds. One approach is to determine whether similar childhood experiences characterize offenders of a particular type. For example, do sexual murderers have a history of having been sexually abused as children? Unfortunately, many of the highly publicized answers to this question are based on conclusions drawn from self-reports of convicted rapists and pedophiles. For example, Murphy and Peters (1992) observed that there is a pervasive belief that the majority of sexual offenders have a history of being sexually victimized. When Robert R. "Roy" Hazelwood of the FBI's Behavioral Sciences Unit interviewed 41 men who had raped at least ten times each, he found that 31 of them reported they had been sexually abused as children (reported in Sullivan & Sevilla, 1993).

Ressler, Burgess, Hartman, Douglas, and McCormack (1986) classified 36 murderers as having committed sexually oriented murders, by using observations such as the victim's attire or lack of attire, exposure of sexual parts of the victim's body, positioning of the victim's body in a provocative way, and evidence of sexual intercourse or insertion of foreign objects into the victim's body cavities. When questioned about prior sexual abuse/assault, 43 percent of the sexual murderers indicated they had been the victims of such abuse in childhood, 32 percent in adolescence, and 37 percent as adults (as you can see from the numbers, some offenders reported multiple types of abuse) Approximately 75 percent reported having been psychologically abused, and 35 percent witnessed sexual violence as a child. The murderers who had been abused themselves reported a wider variety of symptoms of maladjustment in childhood, including everything from cruelty to animals to rape fantasies. Those who were sexually abused in childhood tended to mutilate the body after killing, as contrasted with the murderers who raped and then killed. The authors of the study speculated that "undisclosed and unresolved early sexual abuse may be a contributing factor in the stimulation of bizarre, sexual, sadistic behavior characterized in a subclassification of mutilators" (Ressler et al., 1986, p. 282). That is, they concluded that murderers with a history of sexual abuse will first kill the victim to achieve control before they carry out sexual intercourse, masturbation, or other sexually symbolic activities. But differences between the two groups only approached statistical significance, and no effort was made to verify these self-reports by the use of independent sources. Porter and Woodworth (2007) found that many murderers self-reported details about the crime that served to excuse or minimize their responsibility for the crime.

Nevertheless, to presume that having been sexually victimized as a child is a predominant cause of becoming a sexual offender is problematic. While it appears that sexual offenders are more likely than others to have experienced sexual abuse in childhood (e.g., Jespersen, Lalumiere, & Seto, 2009), the vast majority of such victimized children do not become offenders as adults (Murphy & Peters, 1992). Further, some researchers have concluded that sexual killers have a low rate of childhood abuse (Langevin et al., 1988) and that only one in five sexual killers has an established history of childhood sexual abuse (Briken,

Habermann, & Kafka, 2006), suggesting that the relation between sex abuse and sexual offending is a weak one at best.

MMPI Profiles. Another approach, within the search for common characteristics, is the use of personality inventories to develop psychological profiles of offender types. As noted in Chapter 3, the Minnesota Multiphasic Personality Inventory and its revision, the MMPI-2, are the most widely used assessment devices for detecting psychopathology. A number of studies have looked at the typical MMPI profiles of various types of offenders.

How specific and diagnostically accurate are the results of these studies? Much controversy exists around these issues. For example, in the study of child molesters, several researchers have found that such offenders have an elevated score on MMPI Scale 4, which measures Psychopathic Deviance (Langevin, Paitich, Freeman, Mann, & Handy, 1978; Swenson & Grimes, 1969); these results suggest that these offenders were rebellious, impulsive, self-centred, and defiant of authority. On the other hand, studies using the PCL-R (Hare, 2003), find that child molesters have a low base rate of psychopathy (e.g., Olver & Wong, 2006; Porter et al., 2000). Other studies (reviewed by Murphy & Peters, 1992) find no differences between types of offenders, or basically normal profiles.

We also may question how specific the obtained profiles are to one type of offender. Quinsey, Arnold, and Pruesse (1980) compared child molesters to a number of other groups seen in a psychiatric correctional facility; these other groups included rapists, murderers of non–family members, murderers of family members, arsonists, and property offenders. Each group showed an elevation on MMPI Scale 4 and Scale 8 (the Schizophrenia Scale). In general, prison populations and a number of psychiatric populations show elevations on Scale 4 alone or on that scale along with Scale 8 or Scale 9, the Hypomania Scale (Dahlstrom, Welsh, & Dahlstrom, 1972). Further, Davis and Archer (2010) found that while the MMPI Pd (Psychopathic Deviate) scale has shown moderate to large effect sizes when distinguishing sex offender and non–sex offender groups, the relationship may reflect antisocial behaviour in general rather than traits specific to sex offenders.

Another problem is that use of average elevation of each scale may imply greater homogeneity in the group than is actually warranted. Three studies with large groups, reviewed by Murphy and Peters (1992), were consistent in finding the 4-8 profile (indicating that the individual scored high on both Scale 4 (Psychopathic Deviate) and Scale 8 (Schizophrenia) as the most frequent. But the actual percentage of child molesters with this as the elevated profile were found by the following:

1. Erickson, Luxenburg, Walbek, & Seely (1987): n = 498 offenders, 13 percent
2. Hall, Maiuro, Vitaliano, & Proctor (1986): n = 406 offenders, 7 percent
3. Hall (1989): n = 81 offenders, 17 percent

Among these 985 sex offenders, almost every imaginable MMPI profile was found—of the 45 possible Scale-2 elevated profiles, 43 different combinations were observed (Murphy & Peters, 1992). A similar study (Duthie & McIvor, 1990), using a cluster analysis of MMPI profiles of child molesters, found eight identifiable clusters.

Profiling Criminals from Crime Scene Characteristics

Is it possible to draw a profile of the criminal from the psychological or physical characteristics of the crime scene? Stated another way, does the pattern of behaviours in this crime resemble patterns from other cases? This second question reflects the current application of the term *criminal profiling* by the FBI (Ressler & Shactman, 1992). An example and a description of the procedures are provided in the next section, but first we need to recognize that some characteristics extracted from the crime scene or interviews with victims are more diagnostic than others.

Douglas and Munn (1992) made a distinction between the MO (***modus operandi***, or standard procedure) of a criminal and his or her "signature." A burglar may begin his criminal career by breaking a basement window to gain entry. But realizing the danger of being caught as a result of the noise, in subsequent crimes he brings glass-cutting tools; he refines his MO in order to reduce the risk of apprehension. In contrast, a criminal's **signature** reflects unique, personal aspects of the criminal act, often the reflection of a need to express violent fantasies. (See Box 4.2 for John Douglas's elaboration of the distinction.) For example, a rapist may consistently engage in the same specific order of sexual activities with each of his victims. Douglas and Munn (1992) concluded that "the signature aspect remains a constant and enduring part of each offender … it never changes" (p. 5).

CRIMINAL-PROFILING PROCEDURES USED BY THE POLICE AND THE FBI

Contemporary law enforcement seeks to do more than describe the typical murderer or child molester. Rather, investigators use the crime scene to generate hypotheses about the type of person who committed the crime and then seek specific individuals who possess those characteristics.

In some ways the modern criminal profilers resemble the legendary detectives of fiction such as Hercule Poirot, Sherlock Holmes, Charlie Chan, and Miss Marple. As Box 4.3, which presents an example of the deductive skill of Sherlock Holmes, indicates, attention to detail is the hallmark of these investigators (Douglas, Ressler, Burgess, & Hartman, 1986), and not even the smallest clue at the crime scene should escape the attention of the profiler (Douglas & Olshaker, 1995). But, unlike the detectives in novels, criminal profilers must focus on more than one clue. They analyze all clues and crime patterns. Truly, as Rossi (1982) suggested, criminal profiling can be thought of as a collection of leads.

Observers sometimes are bewildered or astounded at the conclusions drawn by profiling specialists, but many of these are simply the result of common sense inferences (Snook et al., 2007). Consider, for example, these conclusions drawn from sets of facts in different cases, examined by John Douglas and other profilers:

- Based on descriptions by her friends and coworkers, the victim was obedient, submissive, and compliant. But the crime scene showed evidence of torture on her body.

  Inference: The offender inflicted pain for its own sake; "that's what he needed to make the crime satisfying" (Douglas & Olshaker, 1998, p. 13).

BOX 4.2 — *MODUS OPERANDI* VERSUS SIGNATURE

John Douglas offers a vivid description of the difference between a criminal's MO and a signature:

> MO is what an offender has to do to accomplish a crime. It's learned behavior and gets modified and perfected as the criminal gets better and better at what he does. For example, a bank robber's accomplice might realize after one or two jobs that he ought to leave the getaway car's motor running during the robbery. This would be an aspect of modus operandi. The signature, on the other hand, is something the offender has to do to fulfill himself emotionally. It's not needed to successfully accomplish the crime, but it is the reason he undertakes the particular crime in the first place. ...
>
> I worked on two cases, with two different offenders working in two different states, yet both did a similar thing during [a bank] robbery. In a case in Grand Rapids, Michigan, the robber made everyone in the bank undress— take off everything—and stay that way until he had left with the money. In another case in Texas, the bank robber also made his victims undress, with one variation: he posed them in degrading sexual positions and then took photographs of them.
>
> ... [T]he first case is an example of an MO, while the second is an example of signature. In the Michigan case, the robber had everyone strip to make them uncomfortable and embarrassed so they would not look at him and be able to make a positive ID later on. Also, once he escaped, they would be preoccupied with getting redressed before calling the police or reacting in any other way. ... So this MO greatly helped the offender accomplish his goal of robbing money from that bank.
>
> In the Texas case, having everyone strip so he could take pictures of them had nothing to do with accomplishing the robbery; in fact, quite the opposite, it slowed him down and made him easier to pursue. But it was something he felt a need to do for his own emotional satisfaction and completeness. This is a signature—something that is special (possibly even unique) to that particular offender. (Douglas & Olshaker, 1998, pp. 90–92)

- A serial rapist was described as wearing work boots.

  Inference: He might be employed at one of the nearby factories. "Since he was able to come and go as he pleased at home (evidenced by the late night/early-morning timing of most [of his] rapes, he was either single, worked shifts, or was the dominant partner in a relationship" (Douglas & Olshaker, 1998, p. 55).

- The victim's body was dumped along the side of a road in a remote location.

  Inference: The offender had access to a vehicle, and the offender was familiar with this specific, isolated area (Oldfield, 1997).

- In a case in which the victim survived, the rapist made himself unidentifiable to the victim.

  Inference: The victim and the offender knew each other (Jackson, van den Eshof, & de Kleuver, 1997).

- A number of people were found separately murdered on isolated hiking trails in the mountains near San Francisco. Each had been a victim of a sudden attack from the rear.

  Inference: In perhaps his most famous (correct) prediction, John Douglas told the local law enforcement officers that the killer had a speech impediment. He later wrote: "The secluded locations where he wasn't likely to come in contact with anyone else, the fact that none of his victims had been approached in a crowd or tricked into going along with him, the fact that he felt that he had to rely on a blitz attack even in the middle of nowhere—all of this told me we were dealing with someone with some condition that he felt awkward or ashamed about. Overpowering an unsuspecting victim and being able to dominate and control her was his way of overcoming this handicap" (Douglas & Olshaker, 1995, p. 156). When the offender, David Carpenter, was eventually captured, it was found that he had a severe stuttering problem.

THE "MAD BOMBER"

The highly popular true-crime books by former FBI profilers such as John Douglas, Robert Ressler, and Roy Hazelwood have convinced many readers of the effectiveness of criminal profiling. Often the case of New York City's "Mad Bomber" is offered as a dramatic demonstration of an accurate profile. But, as in the case of the Unabomber, the successful resolution of this case depended on other factors besides the specifics of the profile.

BOX 4.3	SHERLOCK HOLMES'S DEDUCTIVE SKILLS

Behaviour is there for everyone to see. But the consummate criminal profiler notices and interprets things that others neglect. Sometimes works of fiction can provide examples more clearly than can real life. Sherlock Holmes, for example, once remarked that "Perhaps I have trained myself to see what others overlook" (Doyle, 1891, p. 42). In *The Man with the Twisted Lips*, the challenge to Holmes was to determine the status of a missing husband. A clue surfaces in the form of a letter:

> Holmes: I perceive also that whoever addressed the envelope had to go and inquire to the address.
>
> Mrs. St. Claire: How can you tell?
>
> Holmes: The name, you see, is in perfectly black ink, which has dried itself. The rest is of the grayish color which shows that blotting paper has been used. If it had been written straight off, and then blotted, none would be of a deep black shade. This man has written the name, and there has then been a pause before he wrote the address, which can only mean that he was not familiar with it. (Doyle, 1892, p. 89)

A small point, perhaps, but often an accumulation of details permits the investigator to narrow the possibilities to a manageable area of inquiry.

More recent fictional examples of police investigators using criminal profiling in their work include three novels by Thomas Harris—*The Red Dragon* (1981) is more detailed than the more famous *Silence of the Lambs* (1988) and the more recent *Hannibal* (1999)—as well as Caleb Carr's *The Alienist* (1994) and *The Angel of Darkness* (1997) and Lawrence Sanders's *The Third Deadly Sin* (1981).

For 16 years, starting in 1940, someone was detonating homemade bombs in public places around the city. The first bombs were small and ineffective, and hence little noticed, but as they gradually increased in size, the city grew terrified. The police and the city's newspapers came to label the perpetrator as mad, partly because he had sent letters and made phone calls to the local newspapers; these messages conveyed a mixture of emotions from threat to apology. He admitted, "I am not well" (Brussel, 1968, p. 17).

The first bomb was found on a windowsill of the Consolidated Edison Company's building. The second bomb, also unexploded, was found ten months later, lying on the street (stuffed inside a man's woolen sock) five blocks from Consolidated Edison's headquarters. But within three months (in December 1941) the United States was at war, and, amazingly, the police received a letter, printed in block letters, stating: "I will make no more bomb units for the duration of the war—my patriotic feelings have made me decide this—Later I will bring the Con Edison to justice—They will pay for their dastardly deeds—F.P." (quoted in Brussel, 1968, pp. 15–16). During and immediately following the war (from 1941 to 1946) at least 16 other letters signed "F.P." were received by the electric company, *The New York Times*, and various hotels, theatres, and department stores in Manhattan. But no more bombs were delivered until 1950, when a third unexploded bomb was discovered on the lower level of Grand Central Station. Five more surfaced in the same year, several of which exploded. Miraculously, no one was hurt.

By 1956 citizens were petrified and the police were mystified. In desperation, the police contacted a psychiatrist, James A. Brussel, who had a private practice in New York City and was also the state's assistant commissioner of mental hygiene. Could he provide any suggestions about the type of person who would do this?

Based on his success in this case (and, later, in others), Dr. Brussel came to be known as a modern-day Sherlock Holmes. And in some ways his methods were similar to those of the great fictional detective. He described them as "my own private blend of science, intuition, and hope" (Brussel, 1968, p. 3). By looking at the Mad Bomber's deeds, Brussel tried to deduce what kind of man he might be.

Brussel knew from conferences with the police that the bomber had to know something about metalworking, pipe fitting, and electricity. He might have learned such skills on a job, or perhaps as a hobby. If the latter, he might require space and equipment, a situation that neighbours would notice.

Brussel also analyzed the Mad Bomber's phone calls and letters. The terrorist believed that some grave injustice had been done him by Consolidated Edison, "something which, according to his letters, had rendered him chronically ill" (Brussel, 1968, p. 29). A single fixed belief dominated his thoughts, and had for 16 years. Brussel concluded that the Mad Bomber was suffering from paranoia and that it was steadily getting worse. His grudges moved to delusions—unalterable, systematized, logically constructed delusions.

Next, Brussel focused on the Mad Bomber's physical characteristics. He proposed that the man was "symmetrically built; perpendicular and girth development in good ratio; neither fat nor skinny" (1968, p. 32). These conclusions were based on the body typology first developed by Ernst Kretschmer and later systematized by William Sheldon in his studies of "somatotypes" (the idea that features of one's physical appearance suggest certain personality traits). The relationship of body type and personality has largely been ignored by contemporary criminologists, but Brussel relied on a conclusion of Kretschmer's that roughly 85 percent of paranoiacs have a mesomorphic or athletic body type (Kretschmer, 1925).

Some of Brussel's deductions were considered farfetched by the police. He noticed the odd curved way that the Bomber printed the *W*s in his letters. Brussel also considered the manner in which the Bomber slit the undersides of theatre seats to laboriously stuff his bombs in the upholstery. Brussel later wrote:

This slashing of seats, like the misshapen *W*, was an out-of-pattern fact in the Bomber's otherwise careful, tidy existence. Just like the *W*, therefore, it had to represent the welling-up and breaking-through of some powerful emotion within the man. My deduction was that it was the same feeling in both cases—a feeling related in some way to sex.

I studied the photograph of the slashed seat. I wondered: Why would a man take a knife and slash the *underside*? Could the seat symbolize the pelvic region of the human body? In plunging a knife upward into it, had the Bomber been symbolically penetrating a woman? Or castrating a man? Or both? (1968, p. 37, italics in original)

Through a series of steps, Brussel concluded that the Mad Bomber "obviously" distrusted and despised male authority, including the police and his former employers at Consolidated Edison. This suggested to Brussel that he harboured no love for his father, or even hated him. He concluded that the Mad Bomber had never progressed beyond the Oedipal stage of love for his mother, a common pattern, Brussel had found, in paranoiacs. He wrote:

And now, I thought, I had a plausible explanation for his otherwise unexplainable act of slashing theater seats. In this act he gave expression to a submerged wish to penetrate his mother or castrate his father, thereby rendering the father powerless—or to do both.

Farfetched? Perhaps. But nothing else I could think of seemed to fit with the available facts so well. It fitted the picture of a man with an overwhelming, unreasonable hatred of men in authority—a man who, for at least 16 years, had clung to the belief that they were trying to deprive him of something that was rightfully his. Of what? In his letters he called it justice, but this was only symbolic. His unconscious knew what it really was: the love of his mother. (1968, p. 39)

From all these deliberations, Brussel developed a detailed description of the Mad Bomber:

Single man, between 40 and 50 years old, introvert. Unsocial but not anti-social. Skilled mechanic. Cunning. Neat with tools. Egotistical of mechanical skill. Contemptuous of other people. Resentful of criticism of his work but probably conceals resentment. Moral. Honest. Not interested in women. High school graduate. Expert in civil or military ordnance. Religious. Might flare up violently at work when criticized. Possible motive: discharge or reprimand. Feels superior to critics. Resentment keeps growing. Present or former Consolidated Edison worker. Probably case of progressive paranoia. (1968, p. 47)

Brussel went on to tell the police that the Mad Bomber was "Middle-aged. Foreign-born. Roman Catholic. Single. Lives with a brother or sister. When you find him, chances are he'll be wearing a double-breasted suit. Buttoned" (see Douglas, Ressler, Burgess, & Hartman, 1986, p. 404).

Brussel persuaded the police to put a description of the Mad Bomber in the newspapers, in an effort to prod him out of hiding. And so they did, on Christmas Day 1956. The notice in the newspapers generated a brief, unrevealing phone call from the Mad Bomber to Dr. Brussel and several letters to the papers in which he wrote: "I did not get a single penny for a lifetime of misery and suffering—just abuse …" (quoted by Brussel, 1968, p. 62). This response betrayed his grudge against his former employer, Consolidated Edison, leading to a frantic search through its personnel records, but the records for the 1930s were quite disorganized.

Finally, on January 18, 1957, the search through the Consolidated Edison records produced a breakthrough. A long-forgotten employee named George Metesky (age 28 at the time) had been injured and felt the company owed him more money than it had agreed to pay. The injury dated back to 1931, and it really didn't differ from a lot of other cases—except for one detail. In one of the vituperative letters written by the employee to the company appeared the words "dastardly deeds."

Metesky had been knocked down by a back draft of hot gases from a boiler. Doctors had identified no injuries, but Metesky complained of headaches and other symptoms. For several months, the company had given him sick pay while he stayed home. Because follow-up medical examinations by Consolidated Edison staff found no tangible injuries, he was dropped from the payroll. Two and a half years later he filed a claim for permanent-disability pay with the Workmen's Compensation Board, arguing that the boiler accident had given him tuberculosis, but it was denied. Other, equally bitter letters followed for three years, until 1937, and then he disappeared from view.

Metesky was located, living in Waterbury, Connecticut, about 80 miles (128 kilometres) from New York City. He was 54 years old (slightly older than Brussel envisioned), unemployed, and living with two older sisters, also unmarried. He weighed 170 pounds (77 kilograms), stood 5 feet 9 inches (1.75 m) tall, and was well proportioned. After he prepared to accompany the police to the police station, he was neatly dressed in a blue double-breasted suit. It was buttoned.

He was eventually judged to be mentally ill and was committed to a state institution for mentally ill criminals, where he remained until his release in 1973. He died in 1994, at the age of 90.

Two aspects of the Mad Bomber case are particularly noteworthy:

1. Brussel was remarkably accurate on both major and minor aspects of the case, but he did make an error in predicting what kind of chronic illness Metesky claimed. He said:

There are hundreds of chronic conditions, and if we wanted to we could go through a medical textbook and come up with a list a yard long. But let's stick to the usual. Let's place our bets on chronic conditions that are statistically the commonest. This means heart disease, cancer, and tuberculosis. (Brussel, 1968, p. 43)

He chose heart disease. Brussel later acknowledged his "unpardonable error"; he wrote: "I failed to make every possible allowance for the known facts" (1968, p. 42).

2. It is important to note that Metesky was identified not because of the profile per se but because of information in the Consolidated Edison personnel files. It did not require a psychiatrist to propose that the Mad Bomber was possibly a former employee; the very first bomb was wrapped in a note that said, "Con Edison crooks, this is for you."

We should always remember that the goal of criminal profiling is not to pinpoint a specific person, but to identify the type of individual who would perpetrate such crimes.

Procedures

The Mad Bomber example provides some insight into the procedures used in criminal profiling. **Crime scene analysis** is an important part. Detailed analysis generates many specific questions. Dealing with a case in which a 67-year-old woman was found tied up in her bathroom and beaten to death, an FBI agent asked his associates: "Why so many loops in the rope? You don't need that many to control an old woman … Why is she in the bathroom? It's a closed-in space—is he after security, or is he secretive? … Were the cuts on the body made before or after she died?" (quoted by Toufexis, 1991, p. 68).

Crime Scene Analysis

The profiling in the Mad Bomber case reflects an emphasis on the psychological versus the practical. Another approach to criminal profiling places somewhat greater emphasis on the dynamics of the crime scene. The goals of the two are the same, and in both approaches the profilers make hypothetical formulations, or educated guesses, based on their past experience. Douglas, Ressler, Burgess, and Hartman defined a formulation as "a concept that organizes, explains, or makes investigative sense out of information, and that influences the profile hypotheses" (1986, p. 405).

For example, in a rape and murder of a woman, the manner in which the assailant has positioned the body will lead the profiler to make certain inferences. If he made no attempt to conceal the victim, he may have felt no respect for her and desired to shock whomever found her. Placing objects inside her mouth and vagina is interpreted as a way of humiliating his victim, but insertion of these after her death would mean he was not motivated by sadism. If no money or possessions were taken, the conclusion might be that the attacker had a stable income (Toufexis, 1991). The fact that the victim was female would suggest to the profiler that the perpetrator was male and about the same age as the victim (Douglas & Olshaker, 1995). However, this capacity to determine the offender's age based on the age of the victim may be moderated by situational factors such as the amount of planning that went into the attack as well as the level of aggressiveness (Goodwill & Alison, 2007). As an example, if little planning went into the attack then it is possible that it was a crime of opportunity and that the offender chose an available victim as opposed to his or her usual victim of choice.

The pattern of blood can be highly revealing; for example, the force of a gun bullet sprays blood farther than the swing of a blunt instrument. As Detective Dusty Hesskew observed, with the blood pattern, "We can say, 'Okay, the victim started out here, ran to this point, fell down, and tried to get back up.' We can even determine whether the killer was left-handed or right-handed and where he stood when he did it" (quoted by Dingus, 1994, p. 84). Another example of a link between forensic science and criminal profiling is using shoe impressions left behind at a crime scene to determine the physical and social characteristics of the offender, including his or her employment status, age, and living situation (Tonkin, Woodhams, Bond, & Loe, 2009). This particular study, conducted using foot impressions recovered at domestic burglary crime scenes, revealed that individuals who wore expensive footwear when committing a crime were more likely to be unemployed and live in a deprived area (Tonkin, Bond, & Woodhams, 2009).

GENERATING THE CRIMINAL PROFILE

Despite Brussel's success, the use of criminal profiles was infrequent until the FBI established a psychological profiling program within its Behavioral Science Unit in Quantico, Virginia. Since then, investigators at this facility have developed a criminal-profile generating process with five main stages; apprehension of a suspect is the goal and the final step in the process. This **criminal-profile generating process** involves the following steps:

1. A comprehensive study of the nature of the criminal act and the types of persons who have committed like offences in the past
2. A detailed analysis of the crime scene
3. An in-depth examination of the background and activities of the victim or victims
4. A formulation of possible motivating factors for all parties involved
5. The development of a description of the perpetrator based on overt characteristics from the crime scene and past criminals' behaviour (Pinizzotto, 1984, p. 33).

Initially, the profiler would acquire evidence from the crime scene, knowledge of the victim, and specific forensic evidence about the crime (cause of death, nature of wounds, autopsy report, etc.) and compare the crime scene behaviour to other offenders who have committed similar crimes. Photographs of the victim and crime scene are included. This evidence then is used to conduct a thorough analysis of the crime scene itself. In particular, efforts are made to understand why this person, in particular, was the victim. Information about possible suspects is not included, so as not to subconsciously prejudice the profilers (Douglas, Ressler, Burgess, & Hartman, 1986).

The next step involves decision making, by organizing and arranging inputs into meaningful patterns. The crime is classified. For example, is the crime a **mass murder** (defined as anything more than three victims in one location and within a single criminal event)? Family murders are distinguished from so-called classic murders. Richard Smith killed his entire family (his wife and two sons aged 9 years and 1 year) before killing

himself on December 11, 2011, in Pudsey, England. In contrast are the "classic" murders of Charles Whitman, the man who barricaded himself at the top of the University of Texas tower and killed 16 people, wounding 30 others. There are two other classifications: **spree murder** (killings at two or more locations with no emotional cooling-off period between homicides) and serial murder (three or more separate events with a cooling-off period between homicides) (Douglas et al., 1986). The type of crime perpetrated may also give an investigator insight into the offender's reason for committing the crime (i.e., the offender's motive).

The next procedure is to reconstruct the sequence of events and the behaviour of both the perpetrator and the victim. One important distinction is that between **organized** (or nonsocial) and **disorganized** (or asocial) **criminals**. This classification was first applied by Hazelwood and Douglas (1980) to murders motivated by lust, but since then has been expanded to other types of crimes. In their book *Sexual Homicide* (1988), Ressler, Burgess, and Douglas extended the classification but deleted the terms *asocial* and *nonsocial*. Finally, all of this information is used to create a detailed description or "profile" of the person who was most likely to have committed the crime.

Organized murderers are those who plan their murders, target their victims (who usually do not know the perpetrator), show self-control at the crime scene by leaving few clues, and possibly act out a violent fantasy against the victim, including dismemberment or torture (Douglas et al., 1986; Jackson & Bekerian, 1997a; Koscis, 2007). The majority of such offenders are psychopathic and often motivated by thrill seeking and curiosity, as established by Porter et al. (2003, 2010).

Ted Bundy was a clear example of the organized rapist-murderer; he planned his abductions, usually using a ruse such as feigning a broken arm in order to get assistance. He selected victims who were young and attractive women, similar in appearance. He used verbal manipulation and then physical force. He sexually abused them after he killed them. In the Canadian context, Paul Bernardo was an organized offender who, along with his sadistic wife Karla Homolka, carefully planned his rapes and murders of teenage girls.

The disorganized murderer does not plan his crime in such detail and typically obtains his victims by chance, and behaves haphazardly during the crime (Douglas et al., 1986). Herbert Mullin was an example of the disorganized murderer. Between October 1972 and February 1973, Herbert Mullin killed 13 persons in or near Santa Cruz, California. No clear pattern existed in his selection of victims, who included a homeless person, a hitchhiker, a priest in a church, and four teenage campers (Lunde & Morgan, 1980). On one occasion, he was "instructed by voices" to kill a man he had never seen before.

Ressler, Burgess, Douglas, Hartman, and D'Agostino (1986) analyzed the crime scene characteristics in cases involving 36 convicted serial murderers. After providing consent, each was interviewed extensively by FBI agents. Two-thirds were classified by the FBI agents as organized offenders and 12 were placed in the disorganized group. In looking at aspects of the crime scene, the agents found that organized offenders were more apt to:

- Plan
- Use restraints
- Commit sexual acts with live victims
- Emphasize control over the victim by using manipulative or threatening techniques
- Use a car or truck.

Disorganized offenders were more likely to:

- Leave a weapon at the crime scene
- Reposition the dead body
- Perform sexual acts with a dead body
- Keep the dead body
- Try to depersonalize the body
- Not use a vehicle (Ressler et al., 1986, p. 293).

While the inclusion of "did not use a vehicle" sounds like an unusual manifestation of the disorganized personality, Holmes and Holmes (1996) described one murderer whom they profiled as travelling by city bus because he lacked both a car and a driver's licence:

He killed and assaulted within the immediate area of his home, and his range of travel was restricted to within his own neighborhood. The hunting area was immediate to his personal activities and was determined not only by his daily actions, but also by his personality. He was a disorganized personality who saw visions and heard voices. His restricted comfort zone was defined by his daily activities, limited by the range and mode of his travels and by his own personal inadequacies. (p. 150)

There has been much debate as to the validity of using a dichotomous organized/disorganized typology for profiling. To assess the utility of this method, Canter and colleagues (2004) attempted to dichotomize 100 cases of serial murder as organized versus disorganized. The results of their study revealed that this dichotomy is not valid in that most serial killings appear to be mixed, with both organized and disorganized features. They also noted that purely disorganized serial killings are very rare. This pattern corroborates the one identified by Woodworth and Porter (2002), who found that the majority of Canadian homicides contained features of both premeditation and impulsivity/opportunistic features.

The outcome of the criminal-profile generating process is usually a profile that follows a standard format, including hypotheses about the perpetrator's age, sex, race, educational level, marital status, habits, family characteristics, type of vehicle, and indications of psychopathology.

This step-by-step method is characteristic of the "deductive inference" method of criminal profiling. As discussed, the deductive method of inference involves developing the profile of the offender based on the evidence that he leaves behind at the crime scene. Deductive methods of profiling are used to infer the background characteristics of an offender. An example of the deductive method is using the presence of a weapon at the crime scene to assign a "disorganized" status to the offender. But there also exists an "inductive inference" method of criminal profiling. The inductive method of inference involves developing the profile based on what is known about other similar crimes that have been solved. Inductive methods of profiling are most commonly used when attempting to assign a specific typology to the offender and his or her crime. An example of the inductive method is inferring personality characteristics commonly found in sadistic serial killers to an offender based on the sadistic nature of his or her crime. In an attempt to compare the effectiveness of inductive versus deductive methods of profiling, Yonge and Jacquin (2010) trained 100 undergraduate students in the deductive method of profiling and another 100 undergraduate students in the inductive method of profiling. All of the participants then were asked to review a double sexual homicide case and create a profile. The results of this study support the inductive method of profiling; the participants trained in this method had a higher overall profile accuracy. Additionally, the participants trained in the inductive method of profiling were significantly better at identifying the physical characteristics of the offender. While each profiler may go about developing a criminal profile differently, all profilers using the deductive strategy must use the available physical evidence in a particular case. It is imperative that investigators wishing to build a profile understand the concept of behavioural salience, the relevant behavioural features of a crime that may help to build a profile, as well as the salience of physical evidence, the importance of the physical evidence left behind at a crime scene (Canter & Wentink, 2004). To begin, it is important to define "crime scene." There can be a number of crime scenes for one specific offence, depending on whether the perpetrator transported the body. The *primary* crime scene is where the offence took place, and the *disposal site* is the location where the body was left (Hicks & Sales, 2006). Secondary and tertiary crime scenes may exist if the offender transported the body to a second site, after the offence was committed, but before the body was disposed of (Hicks & Sales, 2006). If the body is left where the offence took place then that location is both the primary crime scene and the disposal site. If there are numerous crime scenes, it is important to collect evidence from each to develop a complete profile.

There are a number of different types of evidence left at every crime scene. The primary type of evidence left at each crime scene is physical evidence, such as patterns of evidence (e.g., blood spatter and methods of restraint), the position of the body, and the presence or absence of weapons (Douglas et al., 1986). It is at this time that the investigators should also note the location of the crime scene itself; factors such as the ease of access to the site, as well as the traffic patterns, can provide helpful clues about the individual who committed the crime. Another important type of evidence at a crime scene is the victim him- or herself (Douglas et al., 1986). Conducting **victimology** is to collect relevant information about the deceased such as age, physical characteristics, personality, reputation, potential criminal history, habits, hobbies, family structure, romantic relationships, location of residence, and occupation (Hicks & Sales, 2006). It is possible that by understanding the victim, aspects of the offender's personality can be revealed. A third type of evidence that can be gleaned from the crime scene is **forensic evidence** such as cause of death, the type of weapon used, the timeline of wounds/death, and whether or not sexual acts were performed

both pre- and postmortem (Douglas et al., 1986). Other possible sources of evidence may come from witnesses, and the time of day that the act was committed (Douglas et al., 1986).

It is important to note that all of these types of evidence would be salient when using an inductive approach to profiling as well. The more details available to investigators about the crime and the victim, the better able they will be to match the type of crime to a similar incident, leading to a more accurate profile. An issue that often arises when attempting to match serial crimes to similar incidents is commonly called "missing linkages." Missing linkages between crimes occur when offences are committed across different jurisdictions, and the investigators who are responsible for solving the crimes are not aware that similar crimes have been committed (called "linkage blindness"; Egger, 1984). This lack of communication between policing agencies and/or separate detachments of the same police force can result in the offender not being apprehended because the police are unaware that there is an offender committing serial crimes. In an attempt to prevent "missing linkages" from occurring, the RCMP

Snapshots

"It's a ransom note from the intruder -- and look, he drew a cute little Snoopy cartoon."

Relative to organized offenders, disorganized offenders are less circumspect in committing their crimes and typically leave a wealth of evidence at the crime scene.

created a computer program to link crimes across the country (discussed later in this chapter).

Typologies are a group of personality and background characteristics associated with specific types of crime (Canter & Wentink, 2004). Specific crime characteristics such as motivation, crime scene evidence, spatial behaviour, type of victim, and method used to commit the offence can be used as grouping variables for typologies. There have been a number of proposed typologies for serial homicide, serial rape, and serial arson (Hicks & Sales, 2006). As an example, Holmes and Holmes (1998) proposed a five-typology model for serial murder. Within serial killers, they argued that there were *visionary* killers, those who were experiencing a break from reality and voices were instructing them to kill, *mission* killers, who were focused on the act of murder itself because they were trying to rid the world of a certain group of people, and *power/control* killers, murderers who are motivated by a need for dominance over another individual. The fourth typology is the *hedonistic* killer, which is divided into two subcategories: the lust killer and the thrill killer. The lust killer murders because he or she derives sexual pleasure from the act, while thrill killers murder because the act of murder itself provides them with pleasure (see Porter et al., 2010). Although typologies appear to provide a clear-cut breakdown of serial killers, research on the validity of typologies has demonstrated that many serial killers fall into more than one of these categories (Canter, 2010; Canter & Wentink, 2004a, 2004b). This study also revealed that the motivation for killing may change over time. Further, typologies often are based on the offender's motivation for the crime and it is difficult to determine motive from crime scene evidence (Canter & Wentink, 2004b). It also is important when using typologies to not pigeonhole the offender as one being one type without considering others. The purpose of the criminal profile is to equip investigators with a tool that provides a different perspective on the offender, and being close-minded about the typologies available may blind the investigator to other possible typologies or motivations.

RESEARCH ON CONVICTED OFFENDERS

In 1981, the FBI established the Violent Criminal Apprehension Program, or **ViCAP**. The success of this program and that of the Psychological Profiling Program generated U.S. legislation that established a National Center for the Analysis of Violent Crime in 1984. It is based at the FBI Academy as a subdivision of what was originally called the Behavioral Science Unit. The profiling procedures used in other countries, including Canada (ViCLAS), Great Britain, and the Netherlands, have reflected the FBI's approach (Jackson & Bekerian, 1997a). Also, advances in computer technology permitted each of these countries to develop databases on characteristics of specific crimes and procedures for the sharing of information between agencies (Stevens, 1997).

One activity of the FBI centre was to interview incarcerated offenders, leading to classifications that might aid in future profiling. For example, with regard to child molesters, FBI agent Kenneth Lanning has concluded that "about 90 percent are what we call situational molesters; they have no real sexual preference for children and have relatively few victims a piece. They may turn to a youngster because an adult woman isn't available" (quoted by Toufexis, 1991, p. 68). Only the remaining 10 percent have a true sexual preference for children, but each may have victimized hundreds of young people. The two types have different patterns of behaviour (Douglas & Olshaker, 1997).

Canadian researchers have examined the relevance of psychopathy in correlating personality and behaviour in incarcerated sex offenders. Porter, Fairweather, and colleagues (2000) found that psychopathic sex offenders were more likely to engage in diverse types of sexually deviant behaviour. For example, they were more likely to rape women and molest children of both genders than were nonpsychopathic offenders, who usually targeted a single victim type. Recently, some of the first research to examine the relation between psychopathy and sexual homicide was conducted by a team of Canadian academic researchers and Correctional Service of Canada psychologists. Porter, Woodworth, Earle, Drugge, and Boer (2003) looked at the types of violent actions used by murderers in the context of the murder and as a function of psychopathy. The main source of information was the detailed file description of the crime known as the criminal profile report, based on police, forensic/autopsy, and court information. Of greatest interest was the level of gratuitous and sadistic violence that the killer had perpetrated on the victim. Evidence for gratuitous violence included torture, beating, mutilation, and the use of multiple weapons at the crime scene. Evidence that the offender obtained enjoyment or pleasure from the violent acts was coded as sadistic violence. It turned out that almost all offenders scored in the moderate to high range on the Psychopathy Checklist-Revised (Hare, 2002). Murders by psychopaths were more gratuitous and sadistic than those by other offenders. In fact, most psychopaths (82.4 percent) had committed sadistic acts on their victims, compared to 52.6 percent of the nonpsychopaths. This type of empirical research correlating specific crime scene behaviours with personality pathology in the offender could give profiling a stronger foundation in the future.

Other recent research by collaborators from Dalhousie University and UBC examined the characteristics of incarcerated murderers whose murder(s) had been perpetrated with an accomplice (Juodis, Starzomski, Porter, & Woodworth, 2010). This study examined the crime, victim, and perpetrator characteristics of individual homicides ($n = 84$) versus multiperpetrator homicides ($n = 40$), according to official file information from two Canadian federal penitentiaries. Compared to multiple perpetrators, individual perpetrators were more likely to be older and to target female victims, and their homicides were more likely to contain reactive, sexual, and sadistic elements. Multiperpetrator homicides tended to involve younger offenders, male victims, and instrumental motives. Psychopathic offenders were likely to act alone in committing sexual homicides and to involve an accomplice in other types of murders, but they typically committed gratuitous violence against women regardless of whether they acted alone or with a coperpetrator.

HOW EFFECTIVE IS CRIMINAL PROFILING?

It is a mistake to assume that the solution of a crime is the only indication of the usefulness of criminal profiling. A survey (Gudjonsson & Copson, 1997) in Great Britain of 184 cases indicated that in only five (or 2.7 percent) did profiling lead to identification of the offender, but police frequently reported other benefits—that it "furthered understanding of the case or the offender" (61 percent of cases), "reassured their own conclusions" (52 percent), and "offered a structure for interviewing" (5 percent). In 32 of these cases, or 17 percent, the police concluded that the profiling information was not useful. In a

study of 200 serial killers, White, Lester, Gentile, and Rosenbleeth (2011) developed 12 categories that describe how serial killers come to the attention of the police. They found that most serial killers are captured as a result of citizens and surviving victims providing information that resulted in police investigations that led to an arrest. Criminal profiling and forensic science in general appear to be important in convicting rather than identifying the perpetrator.

A profile may lead police in a new direction in their investigation. For example, in the winter of 1981, Atlanta was beset by the acts of a killer of a series of black children. Some commentators believed the crimes had been perpetrated by the Ku Klux Klan, but the FBI's John Douglas, on the basis of a crime-scene analysis, announced that they were the acts of a lone black man, between the ages of 25 and 29, a police buff who drove a police-type vehicle. "He would have a police-type dog, either a German shepherd or a Doberman" (Douglas & Olshaker, 1995, p. 204). When Wayne Williams was taken into custody (and later convicted of two of the murders), he:

---

fit our profile in every respect [actually he was 23 years old], including his ownership of a German shepherd. He was a police buff who had been arrested some years earlier for impersonating a law officer. After that, he had driven a surplus police vehicle and used police scanners to get to crime scenes to take pictures. (Douglas & Olshaker, 1995, p. 213)

Profiling generates hypotheses but its conclusions should not be treated as final. One problem is that sometimes police "lock in" on certain characteristics and prematurely apprehend an innocent person because he or she fits the profile. On other occasions, the profile may be misguided, as in the Boston Strangler case described in Box 4.4.

When Can Profiling Be Productive?

As noted earlier, not all murders are alike. As mentioned, there are two basic behaviours of murderers: (a) premeditated, intentional, planned and rational murder and (b) killing in the heat of passion or slaying with an intent to harm, but without a deliberate intent to kill. Criminal personality profiling is more likely to be productive in cases in which the offenders plan their crimes (and repeat them) or in which some psychopathology is present (Geberth, 1990; Koscis, 2007). A homicide that results from a sudden barroom fight is not as good a candidate for profiling as a homicide that includes sadistic torture or an idiosyncratic signature behaviour. According to the FBI analyses, a person with abnormal behaviour patterns becomes more ritualized, displaying a distinct pattern in his or her behaviour (Geberth, 1990). The personality and behaviour scene thus produce much more in the way of idiosyncratic and useful cues. For profiling efforts to succeed, it is almost essential that the offender's personality or signature be revealed.

Implicit in the above statements are two fundamental assumptions that profilers make about the nature of the criminal's behaviour:

1. The signature of the perpetrator (the unique way in which he or she commits the crimes) will remain the same. For example, in his writings, former FBI agent John Douglas (see Douglas & Olshaker, 1995, 1997) states that such actions do not change.
2. The offender's personality will not change (Holmes & Holmes, 1996, pp. 41–43).

The Dangers of Exaggerating the Benefits of Profiling

We already have seen that it is dangerously inaccurate to use the MMPI or other personality tests to claim that offenders' personalities are homogeneous. The distinction between organized and disorganized offenders was presented above; the following is Geberth's evaluation of the general characteristics of the organized offender:

- *Age.* This offender is approximately the same age as the victim.
- *Marital status.* The offender is married or living with a partner. This type of offender is sexually competent and usually is in a significant relationship with a woman. (Most serial murderers are men, and most of the victims are women.)
- *Automobile.* The offender drives a middle-class vehicle, maybe a sedan or possibly a station wagon. The auto may be dark in colour and may resemble local police cars. This vehicle will be clean and well maintained (1990, pp. 504–505).

Geberth went on to list 40 "general behaviour characteristics" of organized offenders, including

---

BOX 4.4   **A PROFILE GONE AWRY—THE BOSTON STRANGLER CASE**

For a period of a year and a half, from June 1962 through January 1964, the city of Boston was paralyzed by the murders of 13 women—in all cases by strangulation. Most of the first victims were elderly (from age 55 to 75) but most of the later ones were in their 20s or younger. The various crime scenes reflected hate and chaos—and enough general similarities to justify the construction of a criminal profile. For example, 19-year-old Mary Sullivan, the last victim, was found nude in her bed with a broom handle inserted in her vagina. Both breasts were exposed, the murderer had ejaculated on her face, and a card reading "Happy New Year" had been placed next to her left foot.

A profiling committee, composed of a psychiatrist with knowledge about sex crimes, a physician with experience in anthropology, a gynecologist, and others, was established. James Brussel of "Mad Bomber" fame was also a member. The psychiatric profile that they developed suggested that there were two different perpetrators for different strangulations. According to the majority opinion, one killer was raised by a domineering and seductive mother; he was unable to express hatred toward his mother and thus directed anger toward other women, especially older women. It was predicted that he lived alone. The committee report proposed that the younger victims had been killed by a homosexual man who knew his victims. (Dr. Brussel filed a minority view, that one killer committed all the murders.)

Albert DeSalvo was eventually arrested and convicted, after he confessed to the crimes. Married and living with his wife, DeSalvo had an insatiable sexual appetite, demanding sex from his wife five or six times a day. He was sentenced to life in prison.

He showed no signs of the detailed predictions in the profile—no consuming rage toward his mother, no lack of sexual potency, no Oedipus complex.

(From Frank, 1966; Holmes & Holmes, 1996.)

"high birth order status, may be first born son," "methodical and cunning," "travels frequently," and (if unmarried) "dates frequently" (pp. 506–507). Other traits that have been associated with organized offenders include average to high intelligence, social competence, and employment in a skilled trade (Petherick, 2009). A danger exists in giving too much weight to these classifications. For example, police may limit their search to suspects who fit all or most of the characteristics.

Another trap of profiling is to assume that if a person possesses several characteristics of a criminal profile, he or she is necessarily guilty. For example, the profile of drug couriers used by the U.S. Drug Enforcement Administration, smacking of racial profiling, includes the description of them as dark-skinned; hence, innocent members of minority groups are frequently stopped, searched, and harassed by the police. At the Buffalo, New York, airport in 1989, U.S. federal agents detained 600 people as potential couriers; only 10 were arrested (Bovard, 1994). Yet drug courier profiling—which has been approved by the U.S. Supreme Court—allows police to search almost anyone they please.

In Canada, however, the situation is different. In an Ontario Court of Appeal decision, the judge ruled that police are not able to detain an individual or search his or her vehicle simply because there is evidence to suggest that the person may be a drug courier (*R. v. Calderon,* 2004). In the case of *R. v. Calderon,* two members of the Ontario Provincial Police observed a vehicle that was exceeding the speed limit and, after determining that the car was a rental, decided to pull it over. This conclusion was based on a course that one of the police officers had completed. After the vehicle was pulled over, the two officers observed two cellular phones, a pager, road maps, fast-food wrappers, and luggage in the back seat instead of the trunk, further confirming their belief that the individuals were drug couriers. After initially consenting to allow the police to search the car, one of the suspects withdrew his consent, but the police officers continued the search, finding 10 kilograms of marijuana. During the trial, the police officer testified that he had continued the search because there were reasonable grounds to suspect that there were drugs in the vehicle. Although the suspects were originally convicted, on appeal the judge ruled that the Charter rights of the individuals were violated and, as such, an acquittal should be admitted for the appellants (*R. v. Calderon,* 2004).

FBI agents themselves sometimes downplay the powers of profiling (Toufexis, 1991). "It's a myth that a profile always solves the case," stated Robert Ressler, former FBI agent and now an author and consultant; "It's not the magic bullet of investigations; it's simply another tool" (quoted by Toufexis, 1991, p. 69). And sometimes police can be misled when they rely too heavily on the conclusions from FBI profiling. In 1993 police on Long Island, New York, searching for the missing ten-year-old Katie Beers, complained that they had been distracted by an FBI profile that said that pedophiles didn't usually hide their victims in their homes (Rosenbaum, 1993).

Are Professional Profilers Better?

Another way to assess the effectiveness of profiling is to determine whether professional profilers do better in a controlled test than do those less experienced in this task. Pinizzotto and Finkel (1990) sought to determine whether the process used by professional profilers and their success rate differs from those of nonprofessionals. They submitted the same materials to 28 persons divided into five categories:

1. Group A, Experts/Teachers ($n = 4$), profiling experts who had trained police detectives in profiling at the FBI Academy in Quantico, Virginia. Each was or had been an FBI agent; they possessed from 4 to 17 years' profiling experience.
2. Group B, Profilers ($n = 6$), police detectives from different police agencies across the United States who had been specially trained in personality profiling, through a one-year program at the FBI headquarters. These six profilers had from 7 to 15 years' experience as police detectives and from one to six years in profiling.
3. Group C, Detectives ($n = 6$), detectives from a large metropolitan police department who were experienced investigators but had no training in criminal profiling. Individual experience in criminal investigation ranged from 6 to 15 years.
4. Group D, Psychologists ($n = 6$), practising clinical psychologists naïve to both criminal profiling and criminal investigations.
5. Group E, Students ($n = 6$), undergraduate students from a large metropolitan university, naïve to both criminal profiling and criminal investigations. Their average age was 19 years.

Two actual cases were used, one a homicide and one a sex offence; both cases were "closed" at the time, meaning that an individual had been arrested and convicted of the crime. The materials for the homicide case included 14 black-and-white crime scene photographs, information about the victim, autopsy and toxicology reports, and crime scene reports. For the sex offence, the material included a detailed statement by the victim-survivor, crime scene reports by the first officer on the scene and the detectives, and a victimology report.

The researchers collected a variety of responses from the subjects after the subjects had reviewed the two case materials. Each subject was asked to write a profile of the offender in each case. For both cases, the profiles written by the professional profilers were richer than those of the nonprofiler groups of detectives, psychologists, and students. Measures with significant differences between groups included the time spent writing the report, the length of the report, and the number of predictions made. The number of accurate predictions made by the professional profilers was twice as high as that of the detectives, three times greater than that of the psychologists, and almost five times greater than that of the students. However, the sex offence case accounted for the majority of the differences; the accuracy of the predictions and the correctness of lineup identifications did not differ much between groups with respect to the homicide case materials. In fact, with regard to the homicide case, students on the average got 6.5 line-up questions correct out of 15, whereas the profilers got only 5.3 correct (a nonsignificant difference).

The superiority the profilers demonstrated in this study may have their expertise, and/or their level of motivation to do well on the task. It is hard to specify just how differently the groups would respond to an actual case because the case materials had been sanitized to protect the identities of the parties involved and the police agencies. Some material ordinarily available to profilers (such as maps of the geographical area and the neighbourhood) therefore was not included. (All of the profilers spontaneously mentioned that some of the usual types of information were missing; no other subjects did.)

The profilers did not appear to process the material in qualitatively different ways from the nonprofilers (Pinizzotto & Finkel, 1990, p. 229) but they did recall more information. The authors concluded that the profilers' greater ability to extract and designate more details is what made the difference in predictive accuracy.

A systematic study of detectives and profilers done in the Netherlands (Jackson, van den Eshof, & de Kleuver, 1997) led to a different conclusion—one that surprised the investigators, who assumed that the profiling processes of profilers and detectives were similar. They concluded:

One of the main characteristics of offender profiling is that it is based on inferences drawn from considerable experiences both of and with similar types of case. This experience is achieved by extensively studying the main characteristics of a large number of solved crimes. Solved crimes produce data which can then function as statistical probabilities or testable hypotheses rather than facts. This probabilistic way of thinking is virtually unknown in everyday police practice. For detectives, facts are all-important. (1997, p. 118)

Currently, a heated debate about the accuracy of criminal profilers rages on in the field of forensic psychology. In particular, Australian researcher Richard Kocsis stands firm that criminal profiling is a valid and important investigative tool, and that trained profilers are better able to predict offender characteristics from crime scenes than nonprofilers (Kocsis, 2010; Kocsis, Middledorp, & Karpin, 2008). Brent Snook (see Canadian Researcher Profile) staunchly believes that profiling lacks empirical support, and that criminal profilers are no better than laypersons at creating criminal profiles (Snook, Cullen, Bennell, Taylor, & Gendreau, 2008). Further, Snook and colleagues (2008) claim that criminal profilers use an outdated theory of personality, that they do not keep up to date on relevant scientific literature, and that normal cognitive tendencies often lead to an illusion of skilled profiling. Snook et al. (2007) conducted a systematic review of 130 studies on criminal profiling and concluded that in some respects profiling relies on common sense rather than deep investigative insights. In addition, they concluded that profilers often were little—if at all—better than nonexperts and laypersons in inferring perpetrator characteristics from crime scenes. While other researchers may support criminal profiling, mostly everyone can agree that at this time there are methodological issues with profiling that need to be overcome before it is supported as an effective investigative tool that should be used by police (Bennell, Jones, Taylor, & Snook, 2006; Crabbé et al., 2008; Devery, 2010; Salfati, 2010; Trojan & Salfati, 2011).

An Evaluation of Profiling

As noted earlier, profiling is an art; Holmes and Holmes (1996) concluded that a good profiler develops a "feel" for certain types of crimes, thus reflecting the intuitive quality of an art. Often, when profilers perceive patterns in behaviour, they cannot describe how their processes work, "they just do." No two profilers will necessarily produce the same profile (Bekerian & Jackson, 1997; Stevens, 1997). But deductions that are drawn from a crime scene analysis qualify as legitimate scientific pursuits, albeit in need of much more research.

The introduction of a profile can result in more (or sometimes less!) efficient use of the detective's time. Cases sometimes overwhelm the detectives with details to be investigated. In the case of the Green River Killer in Washington State in which 49 prostitutes were murdered, police had 18 000 names in their suspect files, and a single television program generated 3500 tips (Rossmo, 1997). The killings seemed to stop in 1984, after Marie Malvar's boyfriend viewed her getting into Gary Ridgway's truck, and Ridgway became a suspect. He was questioned by detectives that year but passed a polygraph (despite the fact that he was lying). When Ridgway was finally apprehended (and convicted based on DNA evidence) in 2003, many observers noted that he had some characteristics that were typical of most serial killers (e.g., age, ethnicity, personality), and others that were

CANADIAN RESEARCHER PROFILE

Brent Snook

Dr. Brent Snook is an associate professor of psychology and director of the Bounded Rationality and Law Laboratory at Memorial University of Newfoundland. He holds a Ph.D. in experimental psychology from the University of Liverpool in the United Kingdom, where he conducted research on the spatial behaviour of serial offenders and simple strategies for making accurate geographic profiling predictions.

Dr. Snook's overarching research goal is to improve the criminal justice system, with an emphasis on the professionalization of policing. His specific research interests pertain to the study of the simple cognitive strategies (heuristics) that offenders, police officers, lawyers, and judges use to make judgments and decisions (and when and why they work); the enhancement of investigative interviewing practices for investigators and front-line police officers; ways to improve the delivery and comprehension of legal information; and the identification and eradication of pseudoscientific practices in the criminal justice system (e.g., criminal profiling).

His most recent program of research is aimed at improving the comprehension of legal information

that police officers provide to interviewees. In one recent study published in *Law and Human Behavior*, Dr. Snook and his doctoral student Dr. Joseph Eastwood were able to dramatically improve the comprehension Charter-based police caution regarding the right to legal counsel by modifying it according to the theory of listenability (Eastwood & Snook, 2012). His current research is attempting to explore how well those findings hold up under more realistic interrogation settings. He is also examining how well youths are able to understand the rights that are presented to them via youth waiver forms.

In 2008, Dr. Snook introduced the PEACE model of interviewing to Canada. He has since trained over 200 members of the Royal Newfoundland Constabulary on the UK–based method of interviewing and has trained numerous other investigators across Canada on the model. Dr. Snook is hopeful that this ethical and scientific-based method of interviewing will soon replace the highly questionable Reid Model of Interrogation as the interviewing style of choice in North America. He is also advocating for all Canadian police officers to be given training on the cognitive interview.

In his spare time, Dr. Snook enjoys playing basketball in a local old fogies league where he is chuffed when he is still able to hit an uncontested layup. His greatest pleasure in life, however, is spending time with his wife Brenda and their new twin girls, Mila and Freya.

atypical. He held a job painting trucks for 32 years and was married. Such stability is rare in serial killers, although not unheard of; Jeffrey Dahmer held a job at a chocolate factory, and Robert Yates of Spokane, Washington, who also preyed on prostitutes, had five children and a wife.

But profiling (and polygraphy) is not a panacea; rather, it should be viewed as an instrument to facilitate the work of the investigators and detectives, by evaluating suspects and providing useful advice on investigation and interviewing (Jackson, van den Eshof, & de Kleuver, 1997; Stevens, 1997).

PSYCHOLOGICAL AUTOPSIES IN UNEXPECTED OR EQUIVOCAL DEATHS

Profiling can be used in other arenas besides crime detection. Often the cause of a person's death is a matter of forensic concern even if no criminal act is assumed to be involved. Even when the cause of death is certain, issues related to the mental state of the person prior to his or her death may require the application of psychological analysis. Canadian researcher James Ogloff and his colleague Randy Otto (1993) suggested several types of relevant situations:

- It may be necessary to determine whether the person was competent to draw up a will (called the decedent's **testamentary capacity**).
- In workers' compensation cases, claims may be made that stressful working conditions contributed to the person's premature death.
- In a criminal case, the defendant, on trial for murder, may claim that his victim was a violent person who instilled such fear in the defendant that his act was truly one of self-defence.

However, probably the most frequent situation in which profiling is applied is to determine whether a death was a suicide or homicide. On July 20, 1993, the body of Vincent Foster, deputy White House counsel and a former law partner of Hillary Rodham Clinton, was found in a Virginia park across the Potomac River from Washington, DC. Law enforcement officials, including the Park Police, concluded that the death from a gunshot wound was suicide. But speculation about the death persisted, not only about why Foster died but even about where he died. "Who killed Vincent Foster?" the *Washington Times* asked in a front-page story (Ruddy, 1997). Probably the most persistent of the speculations was that the White House aide had been murdered (Isikoff, 1994). Supporters of this view described Foster's body as lying gently on an incline with a .38-caliber revolver in one hand. They claimed that contrary to the usual mess from a suicide by gunshot, only a "thin trickle of blood" came from the corner of Foster's mouth (Ruddy, 1997). Actions by the White House staff immediately after the discovery of Foster's body—such as controlling and curtailing the search of Foster's office and the discovery several days later of a shredded suicide note—doubtless contributed to the conspiracy theories, despite the fact that a Park Police investigator stated that Foster's shirt was still wet, there was blood on the ground, and black powder burns were found on his hand and mouth.

In early 1995 Kenneth Starr, the special prosecutor handling the investigation of President Clinton's Whitewater land deals, announced that he was reopening some aspects of the investigation of Foster's death, and it was not until July 1997 that Starr announced a reaffirmed conclusion that suicide was the mode of death. This saga only verifies the need to carry out a thorough and competent initial investigation of any suspicious death, including an inquiry into the psychological state of the person before his or her death.

The term **psychological autopsy** refers to the investigative method used by psychologists or other social scientists to help determine the mode of death in equivocal cases (La Fon, 2008; Ogloff & Otto, 1993; Selkin & Loya, 1979; Zhang et al., 2010). For example, as Shneidman (1981) noted, asphyxiation as a result of drowning in a swimming pool does not tell us whether the victim struggled and drowned (accident), entered the pool with the intention of drowning himself or herself (suicide), or was held under water until he or she drowned (homicide). The cause of death—water in the lungs—is quite clear, but the **mode of death** is not.

As noted above, the range of such cases is broad; for example, an insurance company handling a claim of death wants to know if the cause was an accident or suicide. Was an on-the-job accidental death a result of operator error or equipment malfunction? When a man's car plunges off a bridge and he dies, was it a result of a heart attack, a failure in the steering mechanism, or a desire to kill himself? It is estimated that between 5 percent and 20 percent of all deaths that need to be certified are equivocal deaths.

Selkin (1987) concluded that the most common inquiry in a psychological autopsy questions whether the death was an accident or suicide. A central task of medical examiners is to certify whether a death could reliably be classified as natural, accidental, suicidal, or homicidal (Jobes, Berman, & Josselson, 1986); this classification—the so-called **NASH classification** (Shneidman, 1981)—reflects the four traditional modes in which death is currently reported.

The addition of a psychological autopsy to the standard examination by a coroner or medical examiner may uncover new facts about the case, information that had not been used by the medical examiner. An empirical study (Jobes et al., 1986) demonstrated this. The researchers used as subjects 195 medical examiners drawn from the population of 400 practising examiners in the United States. All were MDs and members of the National Association of Medical Examiners. The examiners were given two kinds of cases, one in which the death was "typical" (i.e., one in which the manner of death was not difficult to certify), and one in which the death was an "equivocal" case (i.e., the mode of death was less clear).

To determine generalizability of results, five different pairs of cases were used, ranging from a single-car accident to the death of a child to a Russian roulette death. For half of the cases, psychological autopsies were provided to the medical examiner in addition to the standard information. These psychological autopsies included information about the dead person's lifestyle, personality, and demographics, as well as a psychological interpretation of the death.

As expected, the availability of the psychological-autopsy information did not influence the manner of death certification in most of the typical cases, but it did influence reactions to two of these typical cases (psychotic and Russian roulette cases). But in regard to the equivocal cases, the psychological information had a statistically significant impact on the determination of the manner of death in four of the five types of cases, with a trend toward significance in the fifth (the Russian roulette case).

Consider, for example, the single-car death. In the typical case, examiners were told that a woman had lost control of her car on a mountain road and her blood alcohol content was 0.21 percent. All but one examiner agreed that the case should be certified as an accidental death, and the inclusion of psychological-autopsy information had no effect on these decisions. But, in great contrast were the results in the equivocal single-car death. Here, a man's car collided head-on with a truck. The incident occurred late at night on a winding road, and the victim's car swerved into the path of the oncoming truck. A few short skid marks were left by the car. The examiners who received no additional information were about equally divided as to cause of death between accident, suicide, and undetermined (with slightly more favouring suicide). The psychological autopsy added that the victim was depressed, had anxiety attacks, and recently suffered a significant loss. Examiners given this added information almost unanimously (90 percent) ruled that suicide was the cause of death.

Perhaps such results are not surprising. Given the extra information—and especially in the context that these were not real-life cases for these examiners—the outcome may be inevitable. More research is needed to determine the extent of receptiveness by medical examiners to psychological evidence in cases for which they are responsible for the certification. Although the use of psychological autopsies has not been adopted widely in Canada, this situation may change as the science progresses.

Psychological autopsies also can be used as an extension to another criminal profiling technique, victimology (La Fon, 2008). This is done by examining the psychosocial aspects of the victim's life, as well as his or her mental state before and at the time of death (La Fon, 2008). La Fon (2008) suggests that psychologists and other mental health practitioners are best suited to conduct these autopsies because they are based on psychological theory. While this investigative tool has not been empirically validated and cannot be used to draw strong conclusions, it may provide insight or a new perspective on the case.

RECENT PROFILING ADVANCEMENTS IN CANADA

In recent years, we have witnessed some significant developments in innovative, nontraditional approaches by both law enforcement and psychological researchers. Inspired by the FBI's ViCAP approach, the RCMP has developed a profiling technique called ViCLAS using computer technology. Geographic profiling, also relying upon computer technology, attempts to profile where the offender may be located.

Violent Crime Linkage Analysis System (ViCLAS)

In 2000, the first author of this textbook conducted a psychological assessment on a serial rapist for the National Parole Board. The offender, now incarcerated at Mountain Institution in Agassiz, BC, had been first arrested after perpetrating a brutal sexual assault on a teenage girl in British Columbia. A year into his three-year sentence, he was connected to the rapes of other women in Alberta and Saskatchewan over a period of several years. Although he had not been a suspect during the original investigations of these offences, his unique behaviours during his current offence were matched to the others using the ViCLAS profiling system (including cutting a lock of hair from his victims and taking their driver's licence).

Using ViCLAS (with each database linked to a main server in Ottawa), police in every province record the information for all solved and unsolved homicides, sexual assaults, and unidentified bodies of known or suspected homicide. After a number of cases of serial crime, including that of Clifford Olson, the RCMP and other Canadian police forces recognized the need for a system that would help them to quickly identify and link serial crimes. The RCMP originally looked to the FBI for a linkage system, but realized that the FBI's ViCAP system was flawed in a number of ways. The creators of ViCLAS realized that they would need to create their own system and studied a number of other linkage programs including ViCAP, and the systems used in Iowa, Minnesota, Washington, and New York among others, for ideas on how to create the best system. ViCLAS is now the top linkage system in the world and has been implemented across the world (to be discussed later). To add a case to the ViCLAS system, the investigator must complete a booklet covering more than 200 details of the incident including victimology, forensic information, behavioural information, and MO. The questions in the ViCLAS booklet cover all aspects of the crime, and it has been said that if an investigator can answer all 262 questions in the ViCLAS booklet that he or she has done a thorough investigation. The booklet then is sent to ViCLAS headquarters where the information is entered into the database. With the advent of technology, ViCLAS booklets can now be filled out using a computer program and the information can be imported directly into the ViCLAS system. Once the data have been entered, ViCLAS specialists use structured queries and special analyses to look for potential linkages with other crimes in Canada. The RCMP has been reluctant to open its ViCLAS files for psychological research for a number of reasons including security and not wanting to educate other criminals about the information used to connect cases. However, the RCMP recently created a board of advisory consultants, which includes forensic psychologists and psychiatrists, to advise them on the types of research that could most benefit their investigations.

As of 2007, over 300 000 cases had been entered into the ViCLAS system and 3200 linkages between crimes had been made (RCMP, 2011b). After a linkage between two crimes has been made, the ViCLAS specialists enter this link into a "series," which connects all of these crimes committed by the same offender. As of 2007, there were 88 000 series on the ViCLAS system. These numbers are expected to increase as the use of ViCLAS becomes mandatory for all police departments across the country.

Although ViCLAS was developed for use in Canada, other countries such as Belgium, France, Germany, Ireland, and the United Kingdom have adopted this crime linkage system. The RCMP works with these other countries to help them to use ViCLAS to its full extent, and currently Canada is working with police departments in Germany and the United Kingdom to revise the ViCLAS booklets to better represent the types of crimes committed in those two countries (RCMP, 2011b).

Geographic Profiling

Another Canadian development in the field of profiling is geographic profiling, a computer-based system developed by Dr. Kim Rossmo for his Ph.D. in criminology at Simon Fraser University. This approach considers the pattern of documented crime scene locations to provide a statistical estimate of the probable residence or base of operations of a serial offender (Rossmo, 1997). Offenders commit crimes, or do not commit crimes, in specific areas (Canter & Youngs, 2009). As an example, an offender may avoid committing a crime in a location where he or she would be recognized. The computer program produces a three-dimensional "map" to highlight the most probable locations of the offender's residence. The main purpose of geographic profiling is to allow law enforcement to focus its investigative efforts in certain regions (Rossmo, 1996). The results of

Rossmo's initial research project, based on a large sample of solved serial murder cases, revealed that geographic profiling had considerable validity (Rossmo, 1997, 2010).

Geographic profiling can be used with serial homicide and sexual assault, as well as burglary, vandalism, and arson. The geographic profile most often is used to rank order suspects based on the proximity of the crime scenes to their permanent residence. Those suspects who live closest to the crime scenes are ranked highest, based on the previously discussed assumption that offenders are likely to commit their crimes in close proximity to their residence.

The type of crime committed may play a role in the location of the crime in relation to where the perpetrator resides. Rhodes and Conly (1981) stated that offenders are more likely to travel further from their place of residence to commit property crimes, whereas offenders who commit crimes against a person are more likely to do so near their place of residence. Motivation also may have an influence on the location of a crime; Canter and Youngs (2009) suggest that crimes of revenge are more likely to occur close to the perpetrator's residence than crimes that are motivated by other reasons.

There has been considerable research done on geographical profiling within the last few years. This research added to the generation of knowledge about geographic profiling in a number of areas. As an example, Kent and Leitner (2007) discovered that not only does the type of crime and the type of offender contribute to the location of a crime, but that the physical and cultural landscape in the city where the crimes are committed are relevant to narrowing the possible locations of residence. A study conducted by Ebberline (2008) revealed that geographic profiling can be used to locate the perpetrator of obscene phone calls. Recent research by Lundrigan, Czarnomski, and Wilson (2010) provided support for the use of geographic profiling by demonstrating that offenders have spatial consistency in relation to the distance that they travel to commit their crimes. The researchers also provided support for environmental consistencies in crime scenes, including physical, temporal and contextual similarities. A final example is a study by Beauregard, Rossmo, and Proulx (2007) with a Canadian sample of offenders. This study revealed that behavioural elements including victim selection and hunting method can be used to improve the accuracy of geographic profiling.

Similar to ViCLAS, there have been computer-based systems created to aid in the development of geographic profiles. These geographic profiling systems use mathematical models of a specific offender's crime scenes to predict where the offender is likely to reside (Rossmo, 1997). An example of a geographic profiling system is "Rigel," the program created by Rossmo (1997). While computerized geographic profiling systems increase the rate at which investigators can create geographic profiles, research has demonstrated that using heuristics, (general rules of thumb that can be used to make decisions) are just as effective as the geographic profiling computer programs (Paulsen, 2006). There are advantages to both the heuristic methods and geographic profiling systems. The ability to use simple heuristics is cost effective in that it eliminates the need for expensive computerized programs, whereas the geographical profiling systems can quickly produce the most likely location of the perpetrator's residence. Similar to criminal and offender profiling, geographic profiling should not be used as the sole method of investigation, but in conjunction with other investigative tools. Although it is clear that this technology requires further scientific validation, Rossmo's approach is gaining much attention from law enforcement agencies around the world.

In Canada, geographic profiling is used by the RCMP not only to narrow down the possible location of the offender's residence, employment, social venues, and travel routes, but also to identify the offender's cachement area and mode of transportation (based on the speed at which he or she leaves the crime scene), and produce detailed maps of the crime scenes. To become a geographical profiling specialist in Canada, one must be a police officer with many years of experience with violent crime (RCMP, 2011b). Further, geographical profiling is conducted only by the RCMP in Canada, and if the service is required, other police forces must request the aid of the RCMP early in an investigation and only for serial crimes.

SUMMARY

Criminal profiling is an educated attempt to provide specific information about a certain type of suspect. Several types of activities fall under the general label. For example, attempts to determine the psychological makeup of a specific person posing a threat of national security, such as

Adolf Hitler in the 1940s or Saddam Hussein more recently, reflect one approach to profiling. Other activities include determining whether people who commit a particular type of crime reflect a common set of characteristics, and extracting characteristics from a particular crime or set of crimes in order to identify the criminal. The latter approach is typical of the criminal profiling procedures used by the FBI. Profilers carry out a thorough analysis of the crime scene in search of a signature left by the criminal. They have created the categories of organized and disorganized offenders to help them develop more accurate profiles of perpetrators. In the Canadian context, innovative new profiling techniques such as the computer-based ViCLAS and geographic profiling have extended the definition and scope of profiling and offer potentially more objective approaches.

The effectiveness of criminal profiling has yet to be firmly established. Some cases reflect remarkable accuracy in predicting specific characteristics of the offender but in other cases, such as that of the Unabomber, much of the FBI's profile was inaccurate. An empirical study of its effectiveness found only weak support for a conclusion that experienced profilers generated more information and more accurate information about the perpetrator from an examination of the files than did other types of law enforcement officials, clinical psychologists, and students. As discussed, the Ontario Court of Appeal ruled that criminal profiling should not be allowed as expert opinion evidence (*R. v. Ranger*, 2003). As such, the scientific foundations of profiling must be strengthened if this type of evidence is to move beyond the criminal investigation and into the courtroom.

KEY TERMS

crime scene analysis, p. 93

criminal profile, p. 78

criminal profiling, p. 75

criminal-profile generating process, p. 94

disorganized criminals, p. 94

forensic evidence, p. 96

geographic profiling, p. 78

mass murder, p. 94

mode of death, p. 103

modus operandi, p. 88

NASH classification, p. 104

organized criminals, p. 94

physical evidence, p. 78

psychological autopsy, p. 103

psychological profile, p. 78

serial murder, p. 77

signature of a criminal, p. 88

sociopsychological profile, p. 78

spree murder, p. 94

testamentary capacity, p. 103

ViCAP, p. 97

ViCLAS, p. 78

victimology, p. 96

SUGGESTED READINGS

Brussel, J. A. (1968). *Casebook of a crime psychiatrist*. New York: Bernard Geis Associates.
This work includes a readable description of the Mad Bomber case plus others by an early forensic psychiatrist.

Douglas, J. E., & Olshaker, M. (1995). *Mindhunter: Inside the FBI's elite serial crime unit*. New York: Scribner.
The first of several books describing some of John Douglas's classic cases of criminal profiling, this one is especially valuable because it also serves as an autobiography that describes how Douglas became a highly regarded profiler.

Fowler, R. D. (1986, May). Howard Hughes: A psychological autopsy. *Psychology Today*, pp. 22–33.
After the death of Howard Hughes, the flamboyant millionaire-turned-recluse, numerous persons claimed to be inheritors of his estate. Raymond Fowler, the chief executive officer of the American Psychological Association, was asked to complete a psychological autopsy of Hughes, especially focusing on his testamentary capacity.

Harris, T. (1981). *The red dragon*. New York: G. P. Putnam's Sons.
This novel's hero, a criminal profiler, is based on famed profiler John Douglas.

Jackson, J. L., & Bekerian, D. A. (Eds.). (1997). *Offender profiling: Theory, research and practice*. New York: John Wiley.
This thorough, critical evaluation of criminal profiling includes chapters written by experts from

the United Kingdom, the Netherlands, and Canada. Chapter 2 provides a classification of crime motives, with case histories; the final chapter describes criticisms of profiling. Highly recommended.

Kocsis, R. (Ed.). (2007). *Criminal profiling: International theory, research, and practice.* Totowa, NJ: Humana Press.

This book amalgamates evidence from researchers of criminal profiling and practising profilers to provide support for the use of criminal profiling as an investigative tool. Kocsis includes a detailed examination of the research and theory behind the practice of profiling as well as a detailed summary of the issues facing the field of criminal profiling today. This is a great read for anyone interested in criminology, policing, and especially the resolution of serial crimes using criminal profiling.

Meloy, J. R. (Ed.). (1998). *The psychology of stalking: Clinical and forensic perspectives.* San Diego: Academic Press.

Research psychologists, clinicians, and other experts in the field contributed the 15 chapters of this work dealing with classifications of stalkers, victims, explicit and implicit threats, and other related topics.

Michaud, S. G., with Hazelwood, R. (1998). *The evil that men do: FBI profiler Roy Hazelwood's journey into the minds of sexual predators.* New York: St. Martin's Press.

This very readable description of many of the cases investigated by former FBI profiler Roy Hazelwood, who developed the organized/disorganized crime classification, includes descriptions of the fatal explosion on the USS *Iowa* and the Atlanta child murders. The book also includes some controversial conclusions, not shared by all psychologists, about the effects of pornography.

Ressler, R. K., & Shachtman, T. (1992). *Whoever fights monsters.* New York: St. Martin's Press.

This book offers a vivid description of how Robert Ressler used interviews with convicted serial killers to develop the procedure now known as criminal profiling.

Snook, B., Cullen, R. M., Bennell, C., Taylor, P. J., & Gendreau, P. (2008). The criminal profiling illusion: What's behind the smoke and mirrors? *Criminal Justice and Behavior, 35,* 1257–1276.

This article, which was quite controversial upon its release, provides a critical look at the field of criminal profiling. The authors suggest that criminal profiling may be an illusion as there is no empirical evidence to support its use. The authors conclude that criminal profiling should not be used as an investigative technique because there is no evidence that it is effective.

Snook, B., Eastwood, J., Gendreau, P., Goggin, C., & Cullen, R. M. (2007). Taking stock of criminal profiling: A narrative review and meta-analysis. *Criminal Justice and Behavior, 34*(4), 437–453.

This article includes a comprehensive review and meta-analysis of the criminal profiling literature. The results of this article reveal that criminal profilers rely mainly on common sense judgment and that criminal profilers may not be better at determining offender characteristics than laypersons.

Deception Detection in the Legal System

> *Both Mr. Corkum and Mr. Jabarianha were less than believable as they gave much of their evidence. ... Each was evasive at times or his eyes shifted around. Thus in certain points of the story each by the story and his demeanour, displayed signs of untruthfulness.*
>
> —Honourable Madam Justice M. Koenigsberg (*R. v. Jabarianha,* 1997).

> *He had killed my daughter and was able to fool us all.*
>
> —Murder victim Liana White's mother Maureen Kelly, referring to her son-in-law killer Michael White's pleas to the public for Liana's safe return (CBC News, 2006).

In 2005, Michael White gave an emotional public appeal to the Canadian media, pleading for the safe return of his missing pregnant wife Liana. This public appeal gathered widespread support from the community and drew sympathy from viewers across Canada. After overwhelming evidence surfaced linking him to Liana's murder, her mother commented that the plea had "fooled us all"' (CBC News, 2006).

During a 1938 meeting in Munich, Adolf Hitler swore that he would not invade Czechoslovakia. After scrutinizing Hitler's face, Chamberlain concluded "I got the impression that here was a man who could be relied upon when he had given his word" (see Ekman, 1992), a deception detection failure that contributed to a global catastrophe. In the infamous example of a politician's deceit, Bill Clinton adamantly denied having an affair with Monica Lewinsky, as he waved his finger several times, stating he "did not have sexual relations with that woman." Bernie Madoff successfully deceived his investors for years and subsequently pulled off the largest fraud in history (Creswell & Thomas, 2009; Porter, ten Brinke, Baker, & Wallace, 2011; see Canadian Researcher Profile on page 119 for more information about Leanne ten Brinke). These all are examples of lies that initially were not detected, resulting in powerful negative consequences of various types. But missing deception is not the only problem; honest people have been labelled as liars on numerous occasions, leading to major injustices. Traditionally, courts of law have assumed that judges and juries are able to determine whether someone is telling the truth on the stand. However, several notorious wrongful convictions (the best known ones—interestingly, all male— include Truscott, Morin, Milgaard, Mullins-Johnson, Driskell) in Canada have challenged this assumption (and recall that Karla Homolka convinced the court—falsely—that she was coerced into murder by her spouse Paul Bernardo). In fact, many injustices have resulted directly from the inability of legal decision makers to recognize whether witnesses or defendants are being honest. The judge quoted at the beginning of this chapter believed that she could determine honesty by paying attention to someone's demeanour and mannerisms on the stand. But was she right? In this chapter, we critique many of the long-standing approaches to assessing honesty in the courtroom and describe newer, empirically validated approaches.

But long before the trial, police must apprehend suspects and, in the process, generate evidence that may be used to convict the person. Further, they may question victims and other witnesses in order to determine what they know about the crime and the suspect. In gathering their evidence, police use a variety of techniques to determine the honesty of these individuals. (We critically evaluate commonly used police interrogation techniques in Chapter 7.) The Reid Technique, including its largely discredited list of recommendations for spotting deceptive behaviour (e.g., Kassin & Fong, 1999; Vrij, Granhag, & Porter, 2011), typically is used in Canadian police interviews (see Snook et al., 2010). The Reid Technique seems to be a sacred cow in many police circles. The Newfoundland Constabulary is an exception; reportedly, it has largely abandoned the technique for more scientifically validated approaches (Snook et al., 2010).

However, other investigative techniques that are supposed to unearth the truth, particularly forensic hypnosis and polygraphy, have been heavily criticized by psychological researchers. When witnesses or victims of crime have trouble recalling aspects of the event (for example, relating to the perpetrator's appearance or a vehicle), the police may suggest hypnosis as a way of improving their recall (see Wagstaff, 2008). Sometimes, even people suspected of extreme violence are assumed by police to be experiencing dissociative amnesia (or repression) for their actions (Porter, Birt, Yuille, & Herve, 2001). While there have been cases in which hypnosis apparently has facilitated the generation of valid evidence (e.g., Reiser, 1985), in Chapter 7 we explore the potential sad outcome of using hypnosis to "refresh" a suspect's memory in the Paul Ingram case (after hypnosis Ingram came to falsely recall brutal crimes against his daughters; see Kassin, 1997a; Meissner et al., 2009).

But are the police really able to enhance someone's memory or determine whether someone is telling the truth? While the RCMP is still publicly stating that the organization relies on forensic hypnosis (RCMP, 2011a), the Canadian courts are increasingly reluctant to admit "hypnotically refreshed" testimony. In 2007, the Supreme Court of Canada issued its ruling in *R. v. Trochym* (2007), a case that addressed the admissibility of posthypnosis witness testimony. As described by Patry, Stinson, and Smith (2009) (Patry and Smith are both profiled in this textbook in Chapter 7), the decision of a majority of five justices established a presumption of inadmissibility for such evidence that is very unlikely to be overcome in future cases.

When suspects are questioned by the police, they may be asked to complete a polygraph examination if they maintain their innocence. Polygraph examiners assume that changes in physiological reactions in response to incriminating questions are indications that the suspect is lying. Police believe in the accuracy of the polygraph, but are their assumptions verified by empirical research findings? The polygraph is the most widely used technological tool for discriminating liars and truth tellers. While it is not without merit (for example, it can elicit valid confessions from some perpetrators), laboratory and field studies suggest that it suffers from a high false positive rate, often classifying honest suspects as being deceptive (Elaad, Ginton, & Ben-Shakhar, 1994; Iacono, 2008; MacLaren, 2001; Vrij, 2008). As noted by Porter and ten Brinke (2010):

---

the weak theoretical basis of common polygraph techniques, tenuous relationship between nervousness and deception, lack of test and scoring standardization, use of approximate measures of ground truth and successful countermeasures have, with some exceptions (e.g., Honts, 2004), led to a general skepticism of polygraphy in the field of psychology and law (e.g., Ben-Shakhar, 2008; Iacono, 2008; Vrij, 2008).

Both hypnosis and polygraphy have their advocates (among not only the police but also some psychologists) and are widely used in some jurisdictions, but they have major limitations. As such, in this chapter, we focus on research that highlights better approaches and the biases that plague deception detection, both of which investigators need to be aware.

DEFINITION

The detection of deception is a critical concern in forensic contexts, and has been the target of forensic psychological research for over a century (e.g., Munsterberg, 1908). While there are differing definitions of "deception," Vrij (2008) defines deception as "a successful or unsuccessful deliberate attempt, without forewarning, to create in another a belief which the communicator considers to be untrue" (pp. 15). We agree with Vrij Granhag, and Porter (2011a) that this definition is the most valid because it addresses the inherent limitations of alternatives. For example, some definitions propose that deception should include unconsciously or mistakenly misleading another individual, while others conclude that a lie must be intending to misinform the receiver (Burgoon & Buller, 1994; Mitchell, 1986). Vrij's definition not only addresses this issue, but also suggests that deception is possible during nonhuman interactions as well. For example, animals use deception during camouflage, mimicry, and intimidation, and some have argued that this serves a fundamental evolutionary function (e.g., Bond, Kahler, & Paolicelli, 1985; Livingstone Smith, 2004; Trivers, 2011).

FREQUENCY OF LYING IN HUMAN INTERACTION

Deception is a fundamental element of human communication that has evolved to promote both social cohesion and the exploitation of others (e.g., O'Sullivan, 2003; ten Brinke, Porter, & Baker, 2012; Trivers, 2011). How often do people lie to one another? As discussed by Vrij (2008), this question can be difficult to answer because many people underreport the number of lies that they tell. People may be hesitant to provide reliable reports of deception because of the negative societal attitudes towards lying. Despite this challenge, studies typically find that people admit to lying on average twice a day (DePaulo, Kashy, Kirkendol, Wyer, & Epstein, 1996), while other research finds that there is tremendous variation in how often individuals lie (Serota, Levine, & Boster, 2010). In daily life, lies occur at different rates according to the type of communication media used. For example, people admit to lying in 14 percent of emails, 27 percent of face-to-face interactions, and 37 percent of phone calls (Hancock, 2007), or about 22 to 25 percent of all social interactions (George & Robb, 2008). Tyler et al. (2006) found that during a 10-minute conversation, participants lied on average 2.2 times and often lied to enhance others' perception of themselves (e.g., achievements) or to portray themselves in a more positive light.

TYPES OF LIES AND REASONS FOR LYING

Why do people lie so often to one another? Most lies clearly are minor in nature (DePaulo et al., 1996); low-stakes, "white lies" are the most common in everyday life. Consider, for example, the husband who quickly assures his wife that she looks great in her new dress, despite the visual reality. Because these lies are associated with low motivation and minor negative consequences, and are less difficult stories to create, white lies usually go undetected (e.g., Porter & ten Brinke, 2010). While some lies can be detrimental, they also can contribute to a more smooth social interaction or can serve a psychological function for the deceiver. For example, DePaulo et al. (1996) found three main reasons for lying: (1) for the benefit of others; (2) to gain advantage or to avoid costs; or (3) for materialistic or psychological reasons (Vrij, 2007). The researchers found that the most common white lie was self-oriented, including lies told to protect or enhance the interests of the liar. This concept further ties into the promotion of one's "idealized self," that individuals often present to others in a manner that is consistent with their idealized persona (e.g., DePaulo et al., 2003; van Dongen, 2002), reminiscent of Jung's persona concept (see Goffman, 1959). In other words, the idealized self or persona is the way we want to be seen by others, and people often resort to deception in order to maintain this self.

High-Stakes Lies

While common, everyday lies are trivial in nature, **high-stakes deception** is more relevant in forensic contexts. Consider, for example, Penny Boudreau, who, in 2008 in Nova Scotia, made an emotional public appeal for the safe return of her 12-year-old missing daughter, Karissa, after brutally killing her and making it appear to have been a sexual assault. Despite the enormous importance of catching these high-stakes lies, research in the area of high-stakes lies is considered embryonic in comparison to the study of low-stakes lies (Porter & ten Brinke, 2010). It can be very difficult to study high-stakes lies relative to the ease of studying low-stakes lies in the psychological laboratory in which the researcher has control over things like "ground truth" (for example, controlling whether someone is telling the truth or lying by instructing a participant to lie about a videotaped crime he or she has watched). As Porter and ten Brinke (2010) observed, it is hard to study forensically relevant lies for many reasons. For example, factors such as getting access to material depicting high-stakes lies (e.g., police interviews), determining the truth in this material (ground truth), and finding pairs of truthful and deceptive accounts that are comparable have contributed to the difficulty of studying the features of high-stakes lies (Porter & ten Brinke, 2010; Vrij, 2004). Nonetheless, if we are to understand the nature of deceptive behaviour in high-stakes contexts, we must study the behaviour.

Arguably, high-stakes, emotional lies should be more easily detected than white lies because of the major detrimental potential consequence for the liar. As such, it is likely that these more difficult lies, requiring excellent multitasking skills, are associated with more salient behavioural cues (e.g., Ekman & Friesen, 1969; Porter & ten Brinke, 2010; Vrij, 2001; Warren, Scherer, & Bull, 2008). This often is referred to as the **motivational impairment effect** (DePaulo & Kirkendol, 1989), whereby individuals most motivated to escape detection should be less likely to be successful in doing so. Not surprisingly, attempts to go undetected while telling a lie with profound consequences can be daunting. For example, the mother (like Penny Boudreau; see Box 5.1) who is publicly pleading for information on the whereabouts of her missing daughter (but in reality knows exactly where her body is) must ensure that she keeps her details consistent, falsify emotions that she may not actually be feeling, suppress her genuine emotions, attempt to appear credible to her audience, and monitor her

---

BOX 5.1 CROCODILE TEARS

It was snowing in the sleepy Nova Scotia town of Bridge-water the evening that 12-year-old Karissa Boudreau disappeared. It was reported that she had run away, out of the family vehicle, as her mother shopped at the local grocery store. Reported missing on January 27, 2008, the community at large feared the worst as time passed and temperatures dropped. Karissa's mother, Penny, made a tearful appeal to her daughter and the small Nova Scotia town gathered to support Penny in the search for her daughter. The community was shocked to learn, months later, that Penny harboured a terrible secret. She confessed to strangling the 12-year-old and staging it as a sexually motivated crime by pulling down her own daughter's pants after she was confronted with incriminating wiretap evidence, making her the first murderer Bridgewater had seen in over a decade. Penny currently is serving a life sentence (CBC News, 2009). How could so many people have been fooled by Penny's performance? Research suggests that even professional lie catchers often are fooled by such crocodile tears; police officers perform no better than chance in discriminating deceptive murderers from genuinely distressed pleaders (Vrij & Mann, 2001). However, Penny's appeal included several signals of deception detectable to the trained eye. Failed attempts to appear sad, leakage of happiness, and peculiar aspects of her verbal (i.e., minimization [discussed later in this chapter]) and body language (i.e., use of facial manipulators (touching the face with one's hands)) behaviour suggested that she held covert knowledge of her daughter's demise.

In another Canadian case, Michael White, made a televised appeal for the safe return of his pregnant wife Liana. His emotional appeal even garnered the support of Liana's mother (quoted at the outset of this chapter); however, White was subsequently found to be in possession of Liana's bloody clothes and was seen on surveillance video running from the scene of the crime. He was convicted of her murder on December 7, 2006 (CTV News, 2006). To the trained observer, signals of his duplicity were evident in his televised plea: White failed in his simulation of a facial expression of sadness, leaked signs of disgust and anger, and covered his face with his hand when his emotional masks began to fail (i.e., used facial manipulators). Further, White used tentative words to (unconsciously) avoid commitment in his words or subtly communicate his guilty knowledge. He stated, "*If* whoever has her, *or if* she's out there and you see me, and you see this, just stay there, we'll find you. We will, I'll find you." White tells his (deceased) wife that *if* she sees this message (which he knows she will not) she should stay where she is and he will find her. Interestingly, White indeed led a search party to his wife's body several days later (CTV News, 2006). Thus, while White played the role of a distressed husband and father, his statements betrayed his knowledge of Liana's fate (see ten Brinke & Porter, 2011).

Collecting a large number of videos of pleaders such as Penny Boudreau and Michael White, ten Brinke and Porter (2011) recently set out on the largest study of high-stakes deception to date. In a novel paradigm, televised footage of a large international sample of individuals ($n = 78$) emotionally pleading to the public for the return of a missing relative was meticulously coded for verbal, body language, and emotional facial cues to deception (ten Brinke & Porter, 2011; ten Brinke, Porter, & Baker, 2011). About half of the pleaders eventually were convicted of killing the missing person based on overwhelming evidence and, as such, were deceiving the public as they played the part of the distressed relative. Analyses revealed that deceptive murderers were more likely to fail in simulating sadness, leak signals of disgust and happiness, provide shorter pleas, and use more tentative language relative to genuinely distressed pleaders. While it remains to be replicated, the combination of these variables could classify the veracity of 90 percent of pleaders correctly. This research is an important step forward in our understanding of high-stakes, emotional deception, and makes the responsible application of behavioural deception detection in applied settings a realistic possibility.

body language. The combination of high motivation and significant cognitive load characteristic of high-stakes lies suggests that they should be easier to detect than everyday, trivial lies. However, many of these lies still go undetected, even by experienced police investigators (Vrij & Mann, 2001a).

DETECTING LIES

While more salient indicators of deceit may accompany high-stakes lies, this does not seem to translate into greater detection rates, likely because most individuals (including professional detectors) are not adequately educated in valid cues to deception. However, the Supreme Court of Canada apparently believes that only common sense is required for jurors to identify a deceptive witness (*R. v. Maquard*, 1993), so long as the individual's face and demeanor are visible to be scrutinized (*R. v. B. (K.G.),* 1993; see Porter & ten Brinke, 2010). Despite the suggestion that common sense will lead to successful deception detection, research has found that most professional lie detectors rely on inaccurate indicators of deceit and have poor detection rates.

Accuracy Rate of Detecting Lies

Despite the ubiquity of deception within society, numerous findings have established that people's ability to detect deceit is at the level of chance (e.g., Vrij, Granhag, & Porter, 2011). For example, a meta-analysis by Bond and DePaulo (2006) found that the average accuracy in discriminating liars from truth tellers was 54 percent. However, this accuracy rate is not limited to laypersons but also is found with professional lie detectors, such as judges and police officers (e.g., Vrij & Mann, 2001a).

Common Pitfalls

Empirical research has identified numerous pitfalls that may lead the detector astray (Porter & ten Brinke, 2010; Vrij, Granhag, & Porter, 2011). It widely is accepted that human decision making is subject to a host of biases that are often irrational (e.g., Kahneman & Tversky, 1982). Subsequently, credibility assessments and evaluations of truthfulness may be impaired by these biases, which can have a significant impact in forensic settings (Berry & Zebrowitz-McArthur, 1988; Dumas & Teste, 2006; Macrae & Shepherd, 1989; Shoemaker,

South, & Lowe, 1973). Dangerous decisions theory (DDT; Porter & ten Brinke, 2009) posits that individuals make instantaneous (and frequently inaccurate) decisions about an individual's credibility upon seeing that person and that this initial assessment often leads to mistaken evaluations of honesty. DDT describes the path of psychological processes leading to mistaken evaluations of honesty and ultimately leading to wrongful judicial outcomes. According to DDT, the reading of a suspect's, witness', or defendant's face and emotional expressions plays a powerful and enduring role in initiating a series of "dangerous" decisions concerning honesty (see Chapter 8 for a detailed discussion of DDT). To take a courtroom example: potent but often inaccurate intuitive judgments by jurors of a defendant's general trustworthiness occur rapidly upon seeing his or her face for the first time, with a substantial influence on the manner in which the credibility of subsequent information from and about the individual is interpreted (Bar, Neta, & Linz, 2006; Willis & Todorov, 2006). Despite the lack of validity associated with such intuitive assessments of trustworthiness (Porter, England, Juodis, & ten Brinke, 2008), they are encouraged by Canadian judges (see *R. v. Lifchus*, 1997; *R. v. Mervyn*, 2003; *R. v. Roble*, 2004; *R. v. S. (R.D.)*, 1997; see Porter & ten Brinke, 2009). Based on this immediate evaluation, ensuing inferences about his or her honesty will become progressively irrational, but seem subjectively rational according to the decision maker's deception schemas and heuristics (including false notions such as the gaze aversion hypothesis). Such false ideas about liars' behaviour can (subconsciously) buttress the initial impression of the subject's perceived trustworthiness.

Further leading detectors astray is reliance on stereotypical indicators of deceit, such as signs of nervousness, gaze aversion, or fidgeting (Stromwall, Granhag, & Hartwig, 2004; Vrij, 2008; Vrij, Granhag, & Porter, 2011). Despite the widespread acceptance that these cues are indicative of deceit, numerous empirical findings have suggested that these are not reliable indicators (e.g., DePaulo et al., 2003). In addition, despite the popular notion of the existence of a "Pinocchio's nose," no single channel is reliable in revealing deceptive behaviour (Vrij, 2008). As such, it is imperative that lie catchers consider a multicue approach (see Porter & ten Brinke, 2010). Later in this chapter we will discuss the reliable cues to deceit that recent research has identified.

An additional factor that contributes to poor deception detection is overconfidence. Not only do laypersons overestimate their detection abilities, but an even more powerful trend is evident with professional lie catchers. For example, Kassin, Meissner, and Norwick (2005) asked students and police investigators to judge the veracity of inmate confessions. Their results indicated that students had higher accuracy rates than police officers but police officers had much greater confidence in their decisions. Further, Porter, Woodworth, and Birt (2000) found that confidence grew as professional lie detectors' experience increased. However, numerous studies have highlighted a negative relationship between accuracy and confidence (DePaulo et al., 1997; Porter, Woodworth, & Birt, 2000; Vrij, Granhag, & Porter, 2011). More specifically, high confidence can lead the detector astray when it is based on an instantaneous evaluation of the supposed liar or inaccurate cues to deceit, leading the deceiver to develop tunnel vision. This tunnel vision causes the individual to discount contradictory evidence to his or her initial assessment and overvalue supporting evidence, resulting in an even more inflated confidence.

Leading the lie catcher further astray are commonly held truth and deception biases. Research has revealed that most individuals hold a truth bias—the tendency of observers to perceive others as being truthful more often than not—leading to low accuracy rates (e.g., Bond & DePaulo, 2006; Peace, Porter, & Almon, 2011; Vrij, 2008; Vrij & Baxter, 1999). On the other hand, some research has shown that professional lie detectors seem to exhibit a lie bias. For example, Meissner and Kassin (2002) examined the existing literature of detection studies that examined the accuracy rates between a control group and either trained detectors or professional lie catchers and found evidence for an **investigator bias** or deception bias. Arguably, this lie bias may result from the overwhelming suspiciousness stemming from their job experience. Levine and McCornack (1992) found that people who are most circumspect during interpersonal communication are more likely to consider others to be deceptive.

Individual Differences

While the majority of studies have suggested that laypersons and professionals alike generally detect deceit at chance levels, some researchers have proposed that individual differences contribute to people's abilities (e.g., O'Sullivan & Ekman, 2004; Fiori, 2009). This proposal has stimulated a controversial debate between various scholars with some suggesting detection **wizards** exist (O'Sullivan & Ekman, 2004), while others argue that the limited evidence suggesting the existence of wizards is plagued with methodological and statistical issues (Bond & Uysal, 2007). Further, Bond and DePaulo (2008) conducted psychometric analyses of 247 samples in their recent meta-analysis and found that individual differences in detection were tiny; standard deviations in judgment ability were less than 1 percent, ranging no more widely than would be expected by chance. Similarly, various research consistently finds that observers simply perform at the level of chance, regardless of gender or job experience, for example (DePaulo et al., 1997).

On the other hand, some research has identified individual differences that may play an important role in deception detection (e.g., Bond & DePaulo, 2006; Etcoffe, Ekman, Magee, & Frank, 2000). For example, during their investigation of detection ability between various groups, Ekman and O'Sullivan (1991) found that Secret Service agents performed significantly better than chance. Further, O'Sullivan (2005) speculated that those high in emotional intelligence would be better detectors of deceit because of their superior knowledge of emotions and their ability to use emotional information to enhance thought. However, in the first empirical investigation of this proposition, Baker, ten Brinke, and Porter (2011) found that individuals high in emotional intelligence actually had diminished skills in detecting lies. Further, the authors speculated that these poor detection abilities resulted from their excessive confidence and greater self-reported sympathetic responses to deceptive individuals as found in the study.

HISTORICAL METHODS

Throughout history, the act of lying always has been seen as having a negative impact on society, and has been punished with an intended deterrent effect. In order to identify these deceivers, various methods of detecting lies have been used.

Methods of Ordeals

Historically, the first major way of detecting deception was the reliance on the "**ordeal**" to prove an individual's guilt. The concept of the ordeal did not have any scientific or empirical basis but, rather, was based on superstition and religious beliefs (Trovillo, 1939). However, not surprisingly, most informed modern assessors would never consider implementing such detection procedures. The various types of ordeals include the following (Trovillo, 1939):

- First, the *red-hot iron ordeal*, used in tribes in Bengal, required individuals to prove their innocence by applying a red hot iron nine times to their tongue. If the rod burnt their tongue, the individual would be deemed guilty and put to death. This method was used throughout various societies dating back 1000 years.
- Second, the *ordeal of the balance* required accused individuals to originally stand on a balance with a counterbalance on the other side. Next, the individual was instructed to get off of the balance and back on following words from the judge. The individual was deemed to be guilty if he or she were found to be heavier on the second weighing.
- Third, the *boiling water ordeal,* used in Africa, required citizens to plunge their hand in cold water followed by boiling water. Subsequently, those presenting blisters and peeling skin during a public examination were deemed thieves.
- Fourth, variations of the *ordeal of rice chewing* have been identified in various times of history. For example, in India, individuals accused of lying were asked to eat a particular kind of rice (prepared with chanting/spells) and then were required to spit it on a peepul leaf. If any sort of weakness was identified following this procedure, such as blood in the saliva, swollen lip corners, the person was deemed a liar.
- Fifth, the *ordeal of red water*, used in Western Africa, required individuals to fast for 12 hours, ingest rice, and then ingest red, bark-coloured water. If the individual's stomach could not handle this process and rejected the contents, the individual was deemed to be innocent.

Blood Pressure and Pulse

Following this era in which deceit was determined by superstition and religious beliefs, society moved toward more objective measures, such as examining blood pressure and pulse. In the early 1700s, a popular physician's belief jumpstarted the focus on blood pressure and pulse as indicators of one's inner state (and emotions). The physician, Lancisi, believed that emotions stemmed from varying strengths of the heart (Trovillo, 1939). Stemming from this idea, later physicians created preliminary versions of a blood pressure test that Munsterberg (1908) suggested should be used in the courtroom to discriminate genuine and deceptive testimony. Further, Munsterberg (1908) argued for the use of objective, empirical measures within the courtroom to determine veracity. After subsequent advances in blood pressure measures, such as the plethysmograph and hydrosphygmograph in the 19th century, elements of the modern-day polygraph began to develop (including more advanced blood pressure measures, heart rate monitors, and breathing rate monitors) (Trovillo, 1939). An in-depth discussion of the polygraph is presented later in this chapter.

THEORIES OF DECEPTIVE BEHAVIOUR

Several theories have been proposed to predict differential behaviour exhibited by genuine and truthful individuals. In general, it is expected that the presentation of liars and truth tellers will differ because of the elevated arousal, cognitive load, and/or required behavioural control associated with lying (Porter & ten Brinke, 2010; Vrij, 2008; Vrij et al., 2011b). The liar must avoid betraying his or her false story by controlling or suppressing feelings of guilt or excitement. Further, the liar must monitor his or her words to provide a coherent and logical tale that is consistent with information known to the observer. In this way, the liar must present enough detail to appear credible, but might avoid giving excessive information, which may lead to problems recalling and maintaining the falsified information. While describing the false tale to a potentially skeptical observer, the liar also must try to control facial expressions and monitor body language. Clearly, the liar has a demanding scenario, requiring multitasking to successfully deceive the observer. However, this distribution of attentional resources across verbal, body language, and facial channels reduces the level of conscious control over each, and increases the amount of relative "leakage" from that which is receiving the least degree of effort (e.g., ten Brinke & Porter, 2011). In general, because liars are hypothesized to be more emotionally aroused, are more likely to control their behaviour, and are

Savage Chickens

by Doug Savage

www.savagechickens.com

© Doug Savage

Research shows that knowledge of the universal emotional expressions can help an observer determine whether a target such as a suspect is concealing his or her true emotional state.

engaging in a more cognitively demanding task than truth tellers, opportunities arise for the subtle and unintentional behavioural communication of the deception.

Emotional Arousal

Emotional arousal is likely to be elevated during deception for a variety of reasons. For example, the deceiver may feel nervous or guilty about telling the lie (Vrij, 2008). And while some deceivers may be immune from feelings of guilt (e.g., psychopathic criminals; see Porter & Woodworth, 2007), they may experience **duping delight**, enjoying the act of "pulling the wool over the eyes" of the deceived (Ekman, 1992). Regardless of the type of emotion experienced, the emotional arousal hypothesis posits that the deceiver will experience heightened arousal, relative to the truth teller. Indeed, this hypothesis forms the foundation of the polygraph; the contentious lie detection method popular in law enforcement settings (Ben-Shakhar, 2008).

POLYGRAPH

The measurement of heart rate first was proposed as an indicator of fear relating to the possibility of being caught in a web of one's lies by the "father of criminology," Italian psychiatrist Césare Lombroso in the late 19th century. Following this presumption, Lombroso assisted the police in identifying deceptive criminal suspects by monitoring both heart rate and blood pressure during interrogations, a method he described in his *L'Homme Criminel* (1895). By 1908, Munsterburg was advocating the use of these methods for the detection of deception in the courts. These methods—precursors of the modern polygraph—remain a topic of contention today.

As introduced early in this chapter, the modern polygraph is an investigative tool often used by police investigators that measures the manner in which a suspect responds physiologically to questions that are relevant and irrelevant to the crime in question. Typically, the **polygraph** measures changes in electrodermal activity (such as sweating of the hands), blood pressure, heart rate, and respiration. These physiological measures are tracked over the interview and changes across questions are subjectively scored by a polygrapher to inform a veracity decision (Ben-Shakar & Furedy, 1990). A primary assumption of the polygraph is that the suspect will experience increased arousal—reflected by physiological measures—during questions to which he or she responds deceptively, relative to genuine replies (Ben-Shakar & Furedy, 1990).

Question Techniques

Scoring of a polygraph exam requires that the polygrapher has a baseline of physiological reaction to *known* truthful or deceptive responses to which key question responses can be compared. The most popular method, and that most frequently used in law enforcement, is the **control question technique (CQT)**. Specifically, in this method, the polygraph records changes in arousal when asked neutral (e.g., Do you go to university?), relevant (e.g., Were you involved in the crime?), and probable lie (e.g., Have you ever taken something that didn't belong to you?) questions. The CQT rests upon the assumption that there will be a difference in arousal response between the neutral question and the lies that are relevant; arousal will increase when lies are told. Thus, the investigator attempts to elicit known deceptive responses, to which crime-relevant questions can be compared; if responses to each appear similar, the investigator may assume the suspect is being deceptive about his or her involvement in the crime. A concern of the CQT is the number of false positives (i.e., genuine individuals labelled as liars) associated with this method (Ben-Shakar & Furedy,

1990; Porter & ten Brinke, 2010; Saxe et al., 1985). A person who is innocent could be nervous during the interview—particularly during questions about the crime of which he or she has been wrongfully accused—and thus may appear to be guilty due to increases in the physiological measures related to stress. In laboratory studies, the CQT has correctly classified between 74 and 82 percent of guilty examinees correctly, but falsely accuses between 12 and 16 percent of innocent suspects as being deceptive (Vrij, 2008). In general, field test studies report similar hit rates (correct identification of deceptive suspects) and somewhat higher **false positive** rates (e.g., Ben-Shakar & Furedy, 1990; Iacono & Patrick, 1997).

Alternatively, the **guilty knowledge test (GKT)** has been proposed as a more accurate and theoretically grounded question technique. Indeed, Vrij (2008) and others (e.g., Ben-Shakhar, Bar-Hillel, & Kremnitzer, 2002; Iacono, 2008) recommend the use of GKT over CQT. The GKT method of polygraph questioning relies on orientation reflexes that occur when a stimulus is relevant to the individual being questioned. Questions are presented with several response choices and one relevant choice is expected to result in an orienting response (e.g., increased physiological arousal) in the subject harbouring but denying this knowledge. For example, a question (e.g., "What colour was the car?") is asked and the suspect is instructed to respond "No" to each answer provided (e.g., "Black?," "White?," "Blue?," "Red?"), despite his or her knowledge that the getaway car was blue. The reasoning behind this line of questioning is that only a person with intimate knowledge of the crime would have a physiological reaction to the mention of the word "blue." Research on the effectiveness of this questioning method suggests that it can accurately classify innocent suspects (94–99 percent) and the majority of guilty suspects (76–88 percent) (Honts, 1995; Lykken, 1998; MacLaren, 2001; Vrij, 2008).

Criticisms

Despite its popularity in police settings, the polygraph is often criticized by the scientific community (e.g., Porter & ten Brinke, 2010; Vrij et al., 2011). Although the GKT has a relatively strong theoretical basis, the CQT lacks the same. Indeed, there are several reasons to believe that the innocent suspect may exhibit a larger physiological response to the relevant question relative to the probable-lie question. For example, the innocent individual, knowing that the police have already made a mistake in their investigation by suspecting the wrong person, may be particularly wary of relevant questions as he or she worries of being further indicted for a crime that he or she did not commit (Ekman, 1992; Porter & Yuille, 1995). Indeed, the innocent individual is likely to be nervous when responding to crime-related questions and may experience physiological arousal that is interpreted as a sign of deception, leading to a "false positive" outcome. In other words, theoretical and empirical evidence does not support the CQT assumption that innocent individuals will not experience arousal in response to relevant questions (Vrij, 2008).

The formulation of questions in the CQT also is a difficult task that lacks standardization. In theory, the examiner should create probable-lie questions that will elicit stronger physiological arousal than relevant questions for the innocent suspect, while also ensuring that pattern of arousal will be the opposite for guilty suspects. If questions are not created in a manner that is consistent with this assumption, responses will be incorrectly interpreted, potentially leading to false-negative or false-positive outcomes (Vrij, 2008; Lykken, 1998). Another problem with the formulation of a CQT interview is that of the probable-lie questions. Although the examiner believes that anyone who answers "No" to the query, "Have you ever stolen anything in your life?," is lying, this is an assumption and cannot be certain in a particular case. As such, probable-lie responses may actually be truthful, and provide the examiner with an inaccurate perception of the suspect's physiological reaction during deception.

In addition to issues with physiological arousal assumptions, there is a lack of standardization about how physiological output should be scored. In general, scoring is highly subjective and outside information, such as the suspect's previous criminal record, demeanour, and other evidence in the case, may factor into the examiner's decision. Indeed, research suggests that the original examiner, who has access to more than simply the physiological output, is more accurate in his or her conclusions of veracity than independent evaluators of the physiological output (Patrick & Iacono, 1991). While independent examiners achieved only 55 percent accuracy, original evaluators, with access to case reports and the opportunity to assess suspect demeanour, classified 90 percent accuracy.

While the GKT is built upon a stronger theoretical base, it too suffers from several limitations. One of the largest criticisms is that of applicability. If the suspect is not denying knowledge of the crime, the GKT may not be applied. For example, if the suspect contends that he or she was present at the crime, but that it was perpetrated by an accomplice, one would expect that he or she would show physiological responses to key question responses; however, harbouring such knowledge would not be inconsistent with his or her alibi. Further, in situations in which the technique is applicable, questions and responses must concern information that only the perpetrator would know. If the nature of the murder weapon has been publicized in the media, a physiological response to the key response option associated with this information would not indicate guilt, but rather perhaps that the suspect watched the evening news the evening before! The GKT also assumes that the suspect noticed and currently remembers the details in question; if the victim's shirt colour was unnoticed by the guilty perpetrator, he or she is unlikely to show a physiological response to this key response, thereby appearing innocent (Nakayama, 2002; Vrij, 2008).

Both the CQT and GKT are susceptible to **countermeasures.** In other words, examinees may engage in deliberate tactics to manipulate their physiological arousal, distort the polygraph output, and mislead the examiner. Specifically, physical (e.g., biting one's tongue, pressing one's foot into the floor, constricting one's anal sphincter muscle) or mental (e.g., counting backward, recalling an emotional experience) countermeasures during probable-lie questions (CQT) or control response choices (GKT) will increase physiological arousal such that arousal during deceptive responses does not appear out of ordinary (Vrij, 2008). These techniques, particularly the mental tasks, can be difficult for the examiner to detect and as such, the examiner is likely to be unaware that the responses are unreliable. Further, such countermeasures seem to be highly effective; after 30 minutes of

Leanne ten Brinke

Dr. Leanne ten Brinke received a Bachelor of Science with Honours in Psychology, and a Certificate in Forensic Psychology, from Dalhousie University in 2007. Having realized her love of psychological science and eager to continue the unique line of investigation that she had established during her undergraduate degree—examining emotional facial cues to deception—she relocated to the University of British Columbia to pursue her Ph.D. under the tutelage of Dr. Stephen Porter. This work represents the most comprehensive study to date of extremely high stakes, real-life deception, comprising examination of televised footage of a large international sample of individuals emotionally pleading to the public for the return of a missing relative. About half of the pleaders eventually were convicted of killing the missing person based on overwhelming physical evidence. Having been entranced by the writing of Charles Darwin, Leanne largely derived her hypotheses about pleaders' emotional expression from his work and found that—as expected—emotional facial expressions could differentiate genuine and deceptive individuals; genuine pleaders showed genuine expressions of sadness while deceptive murderers failed in this regard and leaked smiles. Leanne complements her study of deception with investigations of interpersonal intuition and human decision making, publishing her work in leading academic journals. In general, her work reflects her fascination with the human face—the information that we can accurately draw from detailed analysis of its morphology and movement, as well as the (in)accuracy of our natural first impressions and ensuing decisions. Future research plans are diverse and the list of studies to do seems to grow daily. However, Leanne is most excited about testing environmental manipulations (i.e., interview settings) that may increase the "leakage" of behavioural cues to deception and make lies easier to detect. She hopes that such techniques, combined with empirically based training, can help people detect the "big lies" before their negative consequences are realized. She proudly hails from Antigonish, Nova Scotia, where she once held the title of provincial champion in the ultra-Canadian sport of curling.

instruction on how to employ these techniques, 50 percent of participants were able to "beat" the polygraph (Honts et al., 1994). In an earlier study, 100 percent of guilty participants instructed to bite their tongue during a polygraph were either classified as innocent or their physiological patterns were "inconclusive," meaning that all examinees employing countermeasures "beat" the polygraph (Honts et al., 1987). As such, it appears that with relative ease, individuals can learn to undermine any ability that polygraphic measures have to discriminate veracity (Ben-Shakar, 2002), and more generally, scientific conclusions about the polygraph do not encourage its use as a reliable means of detecting deception.

Admission to Court

The pivotal Canadian court decision pertaining to polygraph evidence occurred in the case *R. v. Bèland* (1987). In that case, the Supreme Court of Canada ruled that polygraph evidence related to a crime would not be allowed into the court under any circumstances. The court stated that "the results of a polygraph examination are not admissible as evidence. The polygraph has no place in the judicial process where it is employed as a tool to determine or test the credibility of witnesses" (*R. v. Bèland*, 1987, para. 5). More recently, the Supreme Court of Canada reviewed the legal status of the polygraph and concluded that "As many sources have demonstrated, polygraphs are far from infallible. … Similarly, the court recognized in *Bèland* that the results of the polygraph are sufficiently unreliable that they cannot be admitted in court" (*R. v. Oickle*, 2000, para. 95). Thus, at present, the use of the polygraph in Canada must be limited to the police investigation stage in formulating suspects; evidence generated through a polygraph examination is not admissible in Canadian courts.

EMOTIONAL FACIAL EXPRESSION

Measures of generalized physiological arousal provide less information than can be derived from facial expression, which often is manipulated by the liar to be consistent with his or her message, and provides indicators of both emotional arousal and valence. The face is a dynamic canvas on which we express our emotional states and infer states and traits of those around us (Martelli, Majib, & Pelli, 2005; Porter & ten Brinke, 2008). Reading emotional expressions can inform our approach/avoidance decisions. For example, faced with a man glaring at you through narrowed eyes, breathing through flared nostrils and baring his teeth, you might wisely make your escape (ten Brinke & Porter, 2011). Alternatively, the bachelor quickly realizes that his night will be more successful if he approaches smiling women (Guéguen, 2008). While reading the emotional expression of others sometimes can facilitate social interaction, the genuine expression of emotional state is not always in the best interest of the bearer, particularly when his or her genuine emotion (or lack thereof) is inconsistent with the content of his or her lies. As such, humans (and other primates; e.g., Trivers, 2011) have learned to manipulate their facial expressions in a manner that facilitates deception (O'Sullivan, 2003). Emotional expression may be *simulated* (a facial expression is adopted in the absence of any affective experience), *masked* (expression of the felt emotion is inhibited and replaced with a different, falsified expression) or *neutralized* (the felt emotion is inhibited and facial expression remains emotionally neutral) (Ekman, 2003).

Emotional facial expression long has been a topic of scholarly interest; scientific research on the subject was first documented by the French neurologist Duchenne de Boulogne in 1862. In particular, he was interested in the muscles involved in a genuine smile, and used the recent advent of photography to document the product of electrical stimulation of selected facial muscles. He found that when stimulating the muscles of the lower face that raise the lip corners (*zygomatic major* muscles), the smile did not appear genuine. Indeed, the *zygomatic major* muscle requires the simultaneous stimulation of the *orbicularis oculi*, the muscles surrounding the eye and creating crows' feet in the eye corners, to express genuine happiness (e.g., Ekman, Davidson, & Friesen, 1990). These observations influenced Charles Darwin (1872) in writing *The Expression of Emotion in Man and Animals*. Darwin (1872) posited that, "A man when moderately angry, or even when enraged, may command the movements of his body, but … those muscles of the face which are least obedient to the will, will sometimes alone betray a slight and passing emotion" (p. 79). He hypothesized that some muscles, associated with true emotion, are difficult to control and, particularly when the felt emotion is strong, the facial expression will be particularly difficult to conceal. He further proposed that certain muscles could not be actively engaged when the associated emotion is not present. Together, these two proposals form the **inhibition hypothesis** (Ekman, 2003, 2009), with many potential practical applications. However, until recently, it had not been tested empirically. A related hypothesis is Ekman's (1992) **microexpression**—a brief leakage of genuine emotions that manifest in the form of full-face emotional expressions for 1/25th–1/5th of a second—which has been afforded similarly positive attention in applied and academic settings without sufficient empirical testing.

In the first direct examination of the inhibition hypothesis, and with attention to the potential utility of microexpressions as a cue to deception, Porter and ten Brinke (2008) examined facial behaviour during genuine, simulated, masked, and neutralized expressions of happiness, sadness, fear, and disgust. Participants viewed strong emotional images while attempting to express convincing facial expressions, either genuine or deceptive. The expression conditions were genuine (facial expression consistent with felt emotion), simulated (facial expression with no felt emotion), masked (facial expression opposite to felt emotion), and neutralized (no facial expression with felt emotion). In line with the inhibition hypothesis, masked emotions were associated with greater **emotional leakage** (e.g., a smirk when trying to appear sad) compared to genuine conditions. Such leakage was ubiquitous; no one was able to falsify all emotions without leakage during at least one of his or her deceptive expressions. Further, participants were less successful at expressing false displays of negative emotions (sadness, disgust, fear) than happiness—an important finding when applied to the forensic context. Despite the common presence of leakage as a cue to deceit, judges performed at the level of chance in discriminating genuine and deceptive emotions. However, microexpressions occurred only rarely, did not manifest as full-face expressions (appearing in the upper or lower face only), and sometimes occurred in genuine expressions, bringing their utility as a reliable indicator of deception into question. In a follow-up study, Porter, ten Brinke, and Wallace (2011) replicated previous findings on the impact of felt emotional intensity on the leakage of facial cues to deceit. As expected, high-intensity emotions were more difficult to mask relative to low-intensity emotions. Further, high-intensity emotions were more difficult to neutralize than low-intensity affective experiences. Similarly, microexpressions were a rare phenomenon that were not exclusive

to deceptive emotions. They sometimes appeared during genuine expressions! If you think of a muscle "tick" you may have had in your eyelid, arm, or leg perhaps it will seem intuitive that this can occur in facial muscles as well, representing not a deep underlying emotion but rather a random muscle activation.

The importance of attention to emotional facial cues in detecting deception also is highlighted in laboratory studies by several other research groups. For example, Ekman, Friesen, and O'Sullivan (1988) established that smiles masking feelings of disgust were more likely to include subtle leakage of discordant emotions. Similarly, Hess and Kleck (1990) examined deliberate (masked) versus spontaneous (genuine) facial expressions of happiness and disgust, finding that emotional masks were shorter and more turbulent—with more phases and/or irregularities—than genuine expressions. Deceptive mock interrogations have been found to include leakage of fear and disgust (Frank & Ekman, 1997), and recently it was found that despite instructions to suppress eyebrow raises or smiles during similar interrogations, participants are often unsuccessful (Hurley & Frank, 2011).

While research mounts supporting the effectiveness of emotional facial expression as a cue to deception in controlled, laboratory environments, empirical research in real-life scenarios remains scarce (Porter & ten Brinke, 2010). In the first field study to examine facial cues to emotional, high-stakes deception, ten Brinke and Porter (2011) collected media from news agencies around the world in which a (seemingly) distressed individual made a desperate appeal to the public for assistance in the safe return of a missing relative. In approximately half of the 78 cases collected, the pleader was actually involved in the disappearance and murder of the missing person, and was engaged in a dramatic on-camera lie, playing the part of a distressed relative while harbouring knowledge of the missing person's whereabouts and demise. Comprehensive behavioural analysis revealed that deceptive pleaders both failed to replicate a genuine-looking expression of sadness, and "leaked" signs of the true feelings in the form of lower-face expressions of disgust and brief smiles. Detailed coding further revealed that these expressions were related to the failure of specific facial muscles, presumed to be less under cortical control and likely to reveal one's true feelings (ten Brinke, Porter, & Baker, 2011). In general, these studies suggest that the face can be of great assistance to the educated lie catcher. In particular, an understanding of facial muscles involved in emotional expressions as well as those that are least under willful control can allow the lie catcher to direct his or her attention to particular muscles or facial regions of interest, in search of failed simulations or genuine leakages of emotion.

BLINK RATE

While analysis of facial expression requires considerable training, recent research suggests that attention to blink rate may be a simple and noninvasive proxy measure of arousal related to emotional deception. In Porter and ten Brinke's (2008) study of emotional facial expressive cues to deception, blink rate was found to discriminate genuine versus deceptive expressions. Specifically, masked emotional expressions (i.e., covering one's genuine feelings of happiness with a false veneer of sadness) were associated with increases in blink rate, while emotional neutralization (i.e., a "poker face") was accompanied by decreases in blink rate relative to genuine expressions. This differential change in blink rate across deception types may explain why DePaulo et al. (2003) did not find blink rate to be a significant indicator of deceit in their meta-analysis. Rather, expected changes in blink rate may require some understanding of the liar's deceptive strategy (i.e., masking vs. neutralizing emotional expression).

An understanding of how blink rate changes in emotionally deceptive situations may be combined with the aforementioned GKT to reveal the deceptive suspect without invasive physiological measures. Leal and Vrij (2010) measured the blink rate of participants in a mock theft paradigm where half of all participants (i.e., the guilty suspects) were told to steal a copy of an upcoming exam from a professor's office. All participants were read the same questions (e.g., From what floor was the exam stolen?) and were instructed to respond "No" to each of the seven (six control and one key) possible responses. Guilty suspects blinked significantly less during the key question responses, compared to the innocent participants and this difference in blink rate correctly classified 75 percent of guilty participants and 77 percent of innocent participants. In line with the findings of Porter and ten Brinke (2008), this decrease in blink rate likely is associated with emotional neutralization that accompanies the denial of guilty knowledge.

COGNITIVE LOAD

In 1879, Sir Francis Galton suggested that "[Word association tasks] lay bare the foundations of a man's thoughts with curious distinctiveness, and exhibit his mental anatomy with more vividness and truth than he would probably care to publish to the world" (p. 60). He reasoned that when confronted with words associated with guilty knowledge, deceptive suspects would experience mental conflict related to blocking their genuine response and the creation of a nonincriminating answer. As such, their responses would be characterized by delayed reaction times, repeated responses, and uncoordinated movements. These hypotheses and early word association experiments by Langfeld (1920) were the first formal investigations of what we now refer to as the **cognitive load theory** of deceptive behaviour.

The cognitive load theory rests upon the assumption that telling a lie is more mentally taxing than relaying truthful information. This is likely to be the case for several reasons. The preparation of the lie itself may be a demanding task. For example, the guilty individual must construct a plausible-sounding alibi that does not contradict facts known to the police. Further, the liar is likely to attempt to modify his or her behaviour to appear more credible; the distribution of attentional resources to aspects of speech, body language, and facial expression reduces the cognitive resources available for other aspects of the deceptive task (Vrij, 2008). In line with this assumption, functional Magnetic Resonance Imaging (fMRI) research has found that deception is related to increased activity in the "executive" centres of the brain, located in the prefrontal and anterior cingulate cortices (Spence et al., 2004).

When cognitive load is experienced, the liar may exhibit a slowed speech rate, longer pauses, and increased speech hesitations. These verbal cues reflect the decreased processing speed associated with limited cognitive resources, and allow the liar more time to construct a plausible story (Porter & ten Brinke, 2010; Vrij, 2008). The difficulty of deceiving also may result in increased speech errors (i.e., verbal corrections). In contrast, the honest speaker simply must relate his or her memory for the event in question, and without the added demands of fabricating a lie, is less likely to exhibit these behavioural markers. In addition to verbal cues of cognitive load, changes in body language may occur if the liar's attentional resources

Knowledge of scientific findings relating to body language cues associated with high-stakes deception can help investigators figure out whether a suspect is being honest or concealing information.

a mental record of this presentation for replication while being deceptive. Third, the liar may be overzealous in his or her attempts to inhibit colloquial cues to deception. For example, knowing that others interpret gaze aversion as a signal of deception, the liar may attempt to avoid this behaviour but work too hard in this regard, effectively staring too long and hard at the receiver of the lie (Mann et al., 2011). Similarly, the liar, attempting to inhibit his or her fidgeting behaviour, may appear overcontrolled and rigid (Porter & ten Brinke, 2010).

A decrease in the use of controllable hand and arm gestures, used to illustrate one's verbal message (i.e., illustrators), is among the most reliable effects found for body language cues to deception (DePaulo et al., 2003). Although this finding is reliably found among student participants in low-stakes situations, it does not appear to extend to high-stakes lies, criminal populations, or other skilled deceivers. Some sophisticated liars display the opposite pattern, increasing their use of illustrators during lies relative to truthful statements, in an attempt to enhance their credibility and/or distract attention from their false message. For example, Bill Clinton literally pointed a finger at the American public as he vehemently denied having a sexual relationship with Monica Lewinsky; he subsequently admitted that the allegations were indeed true (Porter & ten Brinke, 2010). Nazi Adolf Eichmann showed a similar behavioural pattern, using dramatic illustrators during deceitful statements during his interrogations (see Porter & Yuille, 1996). This behavioural strategy also may be related to personality factors; studies with criminal populations scoring high on psychopathic and antisocial personality traits suggest that these skilled deceivers also may use more movements (e.g., illustrators, self-manipulators) to distract the receiver from inadequacies of the false message (DePaulo et al., 2003; Klaver, Lee, & Hart, 2007; Porter et al., 2008). Thus, while the laboratory-based literature on low-stakes deception suggests that a reduction in illustrators is indicative of deceit, high-stakes lies and those told by skilled deceivers may show the opposite pattern. Certainly, behaviours that are under conscious control pose a problem to the lie catcher in that they are subject to behavioural control strategies by the liar that may not be consistent across situations and personalities. However, despite potential changes in direction and magnitude of behavioural changes, it is clear that deviations from comparable baseline behaviour—in either direction—should arouse suspicion in the observer.

are consumed with other tasks. For example, the liar may neglect his or her body language, and use fewer hand/arm movements that naturally accompany and illustrate speech, while preoccupied with the challenges of deception (at least this has been found in low-stakes laboratory situations with student participants; DePaulo et al., 2003).

ATTEMPTED BEHAVIOURAL CONTROL

Liars also are likely to attempt to consciously control their behaviour in an attempt to appear more credible (Vrij, 2008). However, they are likely to fail for several reasons. First, some behaviours—such as facial expression and blink rate—are very difficult to voluntarily control and deception is likely to be revealed in subtle ways despite one's best efforts. Second, the liar may not have an accurate understanding of how he or she acts when being truthful. Given that truthful individuals often take their perceived credibility for granted (i.e., **belief in a just world, illusion of transparency**), they are less likely to monitor their behaviour and have

In line with this conclusion, Porter and ten Brinke (2010) advocated the use of the baseline approach as a means of detecting deception. Referred to as the comparable truth technique by Vrij and colleagues (2011), this form of analysis proved successful in a case study of a real-life deceptive murderer. Vrij and Mann (2001b) examined a murder suspect's behaviour as he described his activities on the day of the homicide in question. Relative to his description of his morning (went to work), his demeanour changed dramatically as he described visiting a market and his neighbour in the afternoon and evening. As he described his mid-day activities, he showed less gaze aversion, and spoke more slowly, with more pauses and speech hesitations (e.g., "um," "ah," "er"). Police investigators later unearthed evidence that confirmed his story had been deceptive; he had met the victim that afternoon and killed her later that day. While demeanour may certainly change for reasons other than deceit, the comparable truth technique may be beneficial to professional lie catchers.

MULTIPLE CUE APPROACH

It is clear that there is no Pinocchio's nose—no single behavioural cue that will infallibly indicate the veracity of a statement (DePaulo et al., 2003; Vrij, 2008). As such, the lie detector would be wise to consider a wide variety of potential behavioural cues, and allow for evidence to build in favour of the suspect's credibility (or lack thereof). Leal and Vrij (2001) were able to achieve 76 percent accuracy in the discrimination of genuine and deceptive individuals in a guilty knowledge testing paradigm, using blink rate alone as a predictor of veracity. Ekman and colleagues (1991) found that a combination of genuine and deceptive smile presence and voice pitch could classify 86 percent of nurses motivated to lie about their emotional reactions to a pleasant or disgusting video. And in ten Brinke and Porter's (2011) study of emotional, high-stakes pleas to the public, a combination of four cues (failed expressions of sadness, leakage of happiness, decreased word count, and proportion of tentative words) classified the veracity of 90 percent of pleaders accurately. As such, empirical evidence is mounting that supports the **multiple cue method**; the assessment of credibility is an uncertain task that requires the evaluation of a large body of behavioural evidence prior to coming to a conclusion. However, as verbal,

Savage Chickens by Doug Savage

BUT I'VE GOT THESE SPECIAL TRUTH-HANDLING GLOVES!

MY MISTAKE... YOU CAN HANDLE THE TRUTH

www.savagechickens.com

© Doug Savage

How do judges and juries determine the truth in "he said/she said" cases?

body language, and facial evidence converge on the possibility that the suspect is being deceptive (or genuine), the lie detector can gain justified confidence in his or her decision.

CURRENT RESEARCH IN DECEPTION DETECTION

Interviewing Strategies

Recently, there has been a surge of interest in interviewing to detect deception; that is, asking questions in a manner that will exacerbate cues to deception in liars, but not truth tellers. In this way, the interviewer takes some control over the cues to deception that he or she expects to appear, allowing the interviewer to focus attention on specific theoretically relevant cues to deception rather than examining a broad range of potentially subtle and varied behavioural cues. In general, information-gathering interview styles are preferred over accusatory styles, as advocated by the PEACE approach described in Chapter 7 (e.g., Snook et al., 2010; Vrij et al., 2011b). Information-gathering approaches result in longer responses than accusatory questions that often yield short denials. During these longer responses, there is greater opportunity for verbal and nonverbal cues to deception to appear (Vrij, 2006).

Eliciting information in a manner that may incriminate the deceptive suspect also has been advocated. While some police are traditionally inclined to bombard the suspect with all the evidence against him or her at the outset of the interview, evidence can be used strategically to catch the liar in a web of his or her deceit (Hartwig et al., 2006). For example, let's suppose that the police have in custody a man who is suspected of stealing a wallet from under a briefcase in the university library. This suspect's fingerprint has been found on the briefcase, which makes him a suspect but does not necessarily incriminate him as the culprit (i.e., he may have touched the briefcase for some other reason). Using the **strategic use of evidence (SUE) technique**, the interviewer first asks the suspect to describe his or her activities in the library. In the second, questioning, phase, the suspect is asked questions regarding the briefcase, without revealing the fingerprint evidence. Given that deceptive suspects are likely to adopt an avoidance/denial strategy in their interview, it is likely that the suspect will deny having touched the briefcase—a statement that would contradict the physical evidence (Granhag & Hartwig, 2008). Following this contradictory message, the third phase of the SUE technique is to reveal the evidence and ask the suspect to explain the apparent contradiction. Using a similar mock-theft scenario, Hartwig et al. (2006) found that Swedish police trainees using the SUE technique were able to discriminate genuine and deceptive participants at a rate of 85.4 percent, while traditional interviewing methods led to only 56.1 percent accuracy. Indeed, it appears that eliciting information in a strategic manner can provide credibility assessors with valuable and empirically validated information in their pursuit to unmask liars.

In addition to eliciting information, Vrij and colleagues (2011b) have advocated that interviews of suspected deceptive suspects capitalize on the cognitive load experienced by liars. This cognitive load makes liars vulnerable, and less able to rise to additional challenges without leaking some indication of their mental taxation. For example, interviews imposing cognitive load may ask the suspect to tell his or her alibi in reverse order. This request increases the mental resources necessary to lie because relating a story backward runs counter to the natural sequence of events, and disrupts the liar's ability to use schemas as a skeleton for the deceptive tale (Geiselman & Callot, 1990; Gilbert & Fisher, 2006). In a recent study, half of the liars

and truth tellers were asked to relate their story in reverse order, while the other half were given no instruction (and recalled the event in forward order) (Vrij et al., 2008). As expected, many indices of deception, including indicators of cognitive load (i.e., changes in details, speech rate, speech hesitations, speech errors, blink rate) were leaked by deceptive individuals in the reverse-order condition relative to truth tellers in the same order condition. In contrast, liars and truth tellers in the forward order condition behaved largely the same. Importantly, naïve observers were able to detect reverse-order lies at a level greater than chance (60 percent), while forward-order lies were correctly classified only 42 percent of the time. Cognitive load also has been imposed by instructing the interviewee to maintain eye contact with the interviewer, yielding similar results (Vrij, Mann, Leal, & Fisher, 2010). Further, it has been suggested that lying while engaging in a secondary task, such as driving, may also increase the ease of detecting deception by exacerbating behavioural cues (Vrij, Fisher, Mann, & Leal, 2008). In general, it appears that increasing the theoretical antecedents (e.g., cognitive load, emotional arousal) can exacerbate related indices of deception, to the great benefit of deception detectors.

New Technologies

Following the 9/11 terrorist attacks, there has been a surge of interest in the application of new technologies in security settings; particularly in airports, for the screening of suspicious passengers (see Porter & ten Brinke, 2010). For example, transport security officials were trained in the detection of microexpressions of emotion, presumed to unmask passengers attempting to conceal plans of attack or other illegal activities (e.g., drug trafficking). While this program, dubbed "SPOT," was originally heralded as a great advance in passenger security (Adelson, 2004; Duenwald, 2005), it eventually was met with scrutiny based on its weak theoretical and empirical foundations (Porter & ten Brinke, 2008). Enthusiasm for the program has reduced as results suggested that it identifies many suspicious passengers, as many as 99 000 in 2008 alone, while less than 1 percent of those individuals were arrested for any illegal activity (Segura, 2009). Similarly, mass screening by means of thermal imaging has been proposed as a means of identifying suspicious individuals in airport settings (Pavlidis, Eberhardt, & Levine,

2002). However, subsequent research by Warmelink and colleagues (2011) suggests that the measurement of this arousal response is useful only during interviews and that passengers who intended to lie could not be differentiated prior to the interview. Further, while thermal imaging data could correctly classify 64 percent of truth tellers and 69 percent of liars correctly, naïve interviewers outperformed this technique without access to the thermal imaging data (classifying 72 percent of truth tellers and 77 percent of liars correctly). As such, the use of thermal imaging does not appear to be effective for mass screening in security settings and does not confer a significant advantage over observer judgments.

As with many topics in psychology, the advent of brain imaging technology has led to an interest in neuroscience and deception. In particular, there recently has been a surge in interest in the use of functional Magnetic Resonance Imaging (fMRI) as a means of detecting lies (see Iacono, 2008; Vrij, 2008; and Box 5.2). In general, it appears that the prefrontal cortex is an important structure for the complex task of inhibiting the truth and developing a cogent lie (Abe, 2011). Specifically, the dorsolateral prefrontal cortex, ventrolateral prefrontal cortex, anterior prefrontal cortex, and anterior cingulate cortex have been consistently reported as correlates of deception in functional neuroimaging studies (Abe, 2009; Spence, 2008). While this research is promising in its contribution to our understanding of deception processes, it is clear that there is no Pinocchio's nose within the brain; no structure that reliably indicates deception specifically (Spence, 2008). While functional neuroimaging of deception remains in its infancy, several companies have inevitably begun to offer fMRI deception detection services; at least two companies—Cephos in Massachusetts and No Lie MRI in California—claim to determine with at least 90 percent accuracy whether a subject is telling the truth (Stix, 2008). However, the small number of research studies on the topic have prompted scientists to send justifiable warnings to the legal system concerning the premature application of neuroimaging technology in this context (Greely & Illes, 2007; Wolpe et al., 2005). Specifically, Spence (2008) points to problems with replication, large individual brain differences, and no clear brain regions associated with truth telling. Further, covert countermeasures (such as moving the toe or finger) may be employed in the scanner, disrupting deception detection via functional

neuroimaging (Ganis et al., 2011). Heeding these concerns, a federal magistrate judge in the United States ruled that fMRI lie detection evidence cannot be accepted in court given that it remains unreliable and unaccepted by the scientific community (Abe, 2011). Nonetheless, there is a high demand for accurate and objective lie-detection methods; with the rapid development of neuroimaging technology, this may become a future reality. Indeed, if differences in the brain function of truth tellers and liars can be reliably detected by neuroimaging, it will become a major weapon in the deception detection arsenal. However, at present, the lie detector is best advised to combine strategic interviewing techniques with an understanding of behavioural consequences of deception.

In addition to interest in physiological measures, related to emerging technologies, the verbal content of the lie continues to be of interest to deception researchers. While previous research has generally focused on "big picture" characteristics of potentially deceptive statements, such as the amount of detail provided, the extent to which it is embedded in time and space, and the structure of the account (i.e., Criteria Based Content Analysis; Undeutsch, 1967; Vrij, 2005), new interest in verbal cues to deception focuses on the linguistic characteristics of liar's chosen words. One advantage of this approach to verbal lie detection is that analysis is not limited to lengthy stories; computerized linguistic software (e.g., Linguistic Inquiry and Word Count (LIWC); Pennebaker, Francis, & Booth, 2001) can be used to examine even short utterances. Specifically, deceptive speech tends to include fewer first-person pronouns (possibly to avoid accepting responsibility) and more negative

Many of the signs of lying traditionally seen as important by investigators have been invalidated by science.

emotion words such as "hate" and "sad" (possibly due to feelings of guilt). Consideration of linguistic cues in narratives where participants wrote about their (genuine or deceptive) views on personally significant topics (e.g., abortion) indicated that veracity could be discriminated correctly in 67 percent of cases (Newman, Pennebaker, Berry, & Richards, 2003). Similar results were obtained when genuine and deceptive statements of incarcerated offenders were examined for linguistic markers of deception (Bond & Lee, 2005). While both of these studies were of laboratory-based low-stakes lies, ten Brinke and Porter's (2011) analysis of high-stakes emotional lies revealed that deceptive pleaders were likely to use deceptive speech, avoiding commitment to their false role as

a distressed individual seeking the safe return of a missing relative.

Lying about Intentions

A new line of research in deception detection has focused on the issue of *preventing* criminal attacks and, as such, detecting deceptive intentions. In this context, intentions have been defined as mental representations of planned future actions and are based on some reasoning, planning, and commitment to carry out the actions (Malle, Moses, & Baldwin, 2001). Participants advised to collect a package from a specified location and deliver it somewhere else were advised either to lie or tell the truth to interviewers along the way. Prior to

---

BOX 5.2 **BRAIN-BASED LIE DETECTION**

In recent years, neuroimaging technology has advanced greatly, allowing psychologists to peer into the brains of their subjects and watch psychological processes unfold in real-time. Among those psychological processes that have been of interest is deception. What occurs in the brain when we lie? And can we use neuroimaging technology to detect deception? In this chapter, we have briefly reviewed some of the cortical areas associated with deception and outlined the follies of brain-based lie detection: unreliable findings across studies, issues of generalization to real-life situations, and effects of simple countermeasures. Certainly, the scientific community appears to agree that—at least at the present time—brain-based lie detection is an imperfect technology and application in real-world scenarios would be irresponsible (for a detailed discussion of fMRI as a lie detection tool, see the invited Langleben, 2008 vs. Spence, 2008 debate in *Legal and Criminological Psychology*). Based on the present issues related to fMRI lie detection and the opinion of the scientific community, a federal magistrate judge in the United States recently ruled that fMRI evidence should not be permitted in the courtroom as an indicator of credibility (Abe, 2011). This ruling, however, has not stopped private enterprises from offering such services. Two companies in the United States—Cephos in Massachusetts and No Lie MRI in California—claim to determine with at least 90 percent accuracy whether a subject is telling the truth on the basis of fMRI scans (Stix, 2008).

While credibility reports offered by such companies are unlikely to end up in an American courtroom, other jurisdictions appear to be more receptive to brain-based technologies in the assessment of veracity. India recently became the first country to convict someone of a crime based on neuroscientific evidence. The defendant, Aditi Sharma, was accused of killing her former fiancé, Udit Bharati, by poisoning his food. Using a guilty knowledge approach, investigators placed 32 electrodes on her head and read aloud their version of events, making first-person statements such as "I bought arsenic" and "I met Udit at McDonald's," along with neutral (control) statements such as "The sky is blue." Apparently, Sharma's P300 brain waves (which occur in response to concealed autobiographical and incidentally acquired information) revealed that she harboured guilty knowledge of the murder (Giridharadas, 2008). The judge believed that this test proved "experiential knowledge" of committing the murder, corroborating other evidence, and leading him to believe that Sharma was guilty of the crime.

Given the alarming emergence of this type of evidence in the courtroom, there is an urgent need for further research on the responsible use of brain-based technologies in credibility assessment, for an objective assessment of these technologies, and regulation of their use (Abe, 2011; Greely & Illes, 2007; Rosenfeld, 2005). In the meantime, researchers should caution legal decision makers about the pitfalls of neuroscientific evidence in the courtroom to prevent potential miscarriages of justice.

---

carrying out the mission, participants were interviewed about their intentions; deceptive individuals provided less plausible descriptions of their plans, relative to genuine participants (Vrij, Leal, Mann, & Granhag, 2011). Similarly, using an ecologically valid paradigm—having passengers in an airport departure hall lie or tell the truth about their upcoming trip—deceptive intentions were found to include more contradictions, fewer spontaneous corrections, and were rated as less plausible than genuine intentions (Vrij, Granhag, Mann, & Leal, 2011). Certainly, these theoretically based efforts to *prevent* consequential antisocial behaviour represent an exciting new endeavour in deception research, and one with considerable potential for applied impact.

SUMMARY

Deception is a ubiquitous aspect of human communication. Often used to facilitate social interaction, the consequences of lies can sometimes be catastrophic, for example in legal, security, or business settings. While humans tend to be better natural liars than lie detectors, behavioural cues to deception do exist and training can lead to more accurate discrimination of liars and truth tellers (Porter et al., 2010). Indeed, behavioural cues that may arouse suspicion of the trained lie detector include verbal, body-language, and facial indices of emotional arousal, cognitive load, and attempted behavioural control (Vrij, 2008). While popular approaches such as forensic hypnosis and polygraphy suffer from several theoretical and empirical shortcomings, attention to behavioural deviations from the suspected liar's genuine baseline demeanour and accumulating evidence from various behavioural channels can increase the lie detector's confidence that the suspect is being deceptive (ten Brinke & Porter, 2011). Further, the credibility assessor may utilize interviewing techniques aimed at exacerbating cues to deception and increase the ease of detecting falsehoods by using an information-gathering approach, presenting evidence strategically, and/or increasing cognitive load (Vrij et al., 2011). In general, the psychological study of deception has much to offer lie detectors; despite the lack of a single, reliable cue to deceit, empirical research—including that focused on new technologies and challenges associated with detecting false intent—can enhance the accuracy of credibility assessments for the safety of society.

KEY TERMS

belief in a just world, p. 123

cognitive load theory, p. 122

control question technique (CQT), p. 117

countermeasures, p. 119

duping delight, p. 117

emotional arousal, p. 117

emotional leakage, p. 121

false positive, p. 118

guilty knowledge test (GKT), p. 118

high-stakes deception, p. 112

illusion of transparency, p. 123

inhibition hypothesis, p. 121

investigator bias, p. 115

microexpression, p. 121

motivational impairment effect, p. 112

multiple cue method, p. 124

ordeal, p. 115

polygraph, p. 117

strategic use of evidence (SUE) technique, p. 125

wizards, p. 115

SUGGESTED READINGS

Abe, N. (2011). How the brain shapes deception: An integrated review of the literature. *The Neuroscientist.* Published online first. http://nro.sagepub.com/content/early/2011/03/29/1073858410393359.abstract

A succinct review of what is currently known about how brain structure and function facilitates deception, this paper is an interesting summary of a hot topic in the study of deception detection.

Ekman, P. (1992). *Telling lies: Clues to deceit in the marketplace, politics, and marriage.* New York: W. W. Norton.

Written by Dr. Paul Ekman, this text focuses on emotional lies and how they may be revealed, largely by emotional facial expressions.

Porter, S., & ten Brinke, L. (2010). The truth about lies: What works in detecting high-stakes deception? *Legal and Criminological Psychology, 15,* 57–75.

This paper reviews the literature on the behavioural consequences of high-stakes deception, provides recommendations for lie catchers and future research in the area.

Vrij, A. (2008). *Detecting lies and deceit: Pitfalls and opportunities.* Chichester, England: Wiley.

This book is the most comprehensive summary of empirical research on deception to date, written by Prof. Aldert Vrij, the world's foremost expert in deceptive behaviour.

Vrij, A., Granhag, P. A., & Porter, S. (2011). Pitfalls and opportunities in nonverbal and verbal lie detection. *Psychological Science in the Public Interest, 11,* 89–121.

A recent review of the literature to date, this paper provides a concise review of our knowledge about deceptive behaviour and makes several practical recommendations for lie catchers.

Remembering Crime

> *The Trial Judge should stress that tragedies have occurred as a result of mistakes made by honest, right-thinking eyewitnesses. It should be explained that the vast majority of the wrongful convictions of innocent persons have arisen as a result of faulty eyewitness identification.*
>
> —Justice Peter de C. Cory (*Sophonow Inquiry Report*, 2001)

On a return to my [S.P.] hometown, my sense of reality was undermined during a discussion of a personally traumatic event with a close friend. In the course of the chat, a bizarre and highly memorable incident that had occurred 12 years before came up. The way I was telling it, the friend and I had been strolling down a street in a little Nova Scotian town when a shot rang out. I vividly remembered my friend a few steps ahead of me and who, on hearing the shot, immediately turned to see if I was okay. Seeing my chest, her face paled, which prompted me to look down at my T-shirt, a sight I will never forget. Over the emaciated bodies of Jagger and Richards, meandering tributaries were flowing from three great pools of crimson. Realizing that I had been struck by a shotgun blast, I keeled over in shock while she shouted at the top of her lungs for help. As she frantically tried to beckon a car, she noticed something on the ground near the crime scene and then eyed my wounds more closely. As I reflected on my life, pining its brevity, and preparing to meet my maker, her tears flowed not to existential cries but rather to the tune of hearty laughter. She held up the remnants of the most unusual weapon—a packet labelled Heinz Ketchup. On this sweltering summer day, she had stepped on the expanded packet with a heel and the contents had sprayed back on yours truly. A humbling experience indeed.

After recounting this version to my friend, she declared that I had the whole story backward. Rather, it was she who had been the recipient of the ketchup attack and I the heavy-heeled perpetrator. As I had told this traumatic tale on numerous occasions, I could claim the accurate version with a high degree of certainty. However, a second friend intervened at this point to inform us that I had related her story to him shortly after the event happened 12 years before. I trust my inaccuracy was not the result of vacillating sanity or early-onset Alzheimer's. Instead, it demonstrates the reconstruction and fallibility memory for past life events, even potentially traumatic ones.

PSYCHOLOGY OF THE WITNESS

The Canadian court's reliance on witness testimony puts enormous importance on memory evidence (Brewer & Wells, 2011). Witness testimony and identification are given considerable weight during the decision-making process of jurors, despite their difficulty with discriminating accurate and inaccurate testimonies and their often novice understanding of the fallibility of memory (e.g., Benton et al., 2006; Kassin & Barnadollar, 1992; Lindsay, Wells, & O'Connor, 1989). Even law enforcement officers are naïve about witness memory; Wise, Safer, and Maro (2011) surveyed two samples of 532 law enforcement officers about witness factors and how they conduct witness interviews and identification procedures. Officers from both samples had limited knowledge of witness factors. As such, understanding law professionals' knowledge about the process of generating witness information, avoiding witness memory errors, and representing witness information in the courtroom is critical. In a recent investigation, Sharps, Janigian, and Hess (2009) aimed to create a taxonomy of witness error by specifying the type of errors witnesses make and the subsequent error prevalence. They grouped the errors identified in their study into the following categories that have been identified in the literature (e.g., Meissner et al., 2007; Wells et al., 2006):

1. Errors in clothing or physical attributes of perpetrator
2. Errors in environmental detail
3. Errors in perpetrator race or sex
4. Weapon errors
5. Inferential, extrapolative, or imaginative errors.

The researchers found that the most common errors were the perpetrator's clothing or physical attributes, surrounding environmental characteristics, and inferential, extrapolative or imaginative errors (Sharps, Janigian, & Hess, 2009). Evidently, gathering accurate information and avoiding biasing a witness's memory is of great importance.

Gathering Useful Information from Witnesses

Information provided by witnesses plays a critical role in the identification process and aids in the solving of a criminal investigation. For example, Fisher (1995, 2000) cited a 1975 Rand Corporation study of the process of crime investigation that concluded that the major factor determining whether a case would be solved was the completeness and accuracy of the witness's account. In fact, the crimes most likely to be cleared were those in which the offenders were captured within minutes or those in which a witness provided a *specific* relevant piece of information—a licence plate number, a name, an address, or a unique identification. If one of these was not present, the chance that the crime would be solved was less than 10 percent (Greenwood & Petersilia, 1976). As such, the role of the witness is invaluable within the courtroom and a strong predictor of solving a crime (Berresheim & Weber, 2003; Kebbell & Milne, 1998).

But the importance of the witness accurately remembering events from the past does not end with the arrest of a suspect. At a trial, the testimony of a witness who incriminates the defendant is—along with the presence of a confession—usually the most influential evidence. If a jury or a judge believes witnesses who have testified in good faith, it easily can lead to a conclusion of guilt. Alibis, circumstantial evidence, even masses of physical evidence favouring the defendant's innocence wither away in light of a witness's identification. The powerful influence of witness courtroom identification is understandable. Consider, for example, a witness approaching the stand, swearing to be completely honest, and when asked who he or she saw commit the crime, points directly to the defendant across the room. This proves to be a compelling process; however, if jurors are aware of the fallibility of human memory, they may take this identification with a critical eye.

Unfortunately, as we mentioned in Chapter 5, judges and juries have a difficult time determining whether a witness is giving accurate testimony. In the 2001 inquiry into Thomas Sophonow's wrongful murder conviction in Manitoba, Justice Cory observed that injustices in Canada often have resulted directly from mistakes by "honest, right-thinking eyewitnesses." Nowhere is the problem and significance of accurate witness testimony more clear than in the increasingly common "he said, she said" historical cases. As highlighted by researchers at Simon Fraser University and Dalhousie University, in such cases, allegations often go back years or decades with little evidence other than contradictory reports (Connolly & Read, 2003; Porter, Campbell, Birt, & Woodworth, 2003a). Take, for example, the case involving the former premier of Nova Scotia, Gerald Regan (*R. v. Regan*, 1999, 2002). In 1995, Regan was charged with 18 sexual offences (from sexual touching to rape) against 13 women, dating as far back as the 1950s. The complainants were 14 to 24 years of age when the incidents were alleged to have occurred. Regan denied all wrongdoing. After he was acquitted on several of the original charges, the Crown prosecutor decided not to pursue prosecution on any of the remaining counts. In this type of case, a determination of guilt or innocence hinges on the accuracy of the complainants' recollections and the perceived credibility of both the witnesses and the accused. In light of the difficulties in assessing the credibility of witnesses in historical cases, some legal experts have called for a statute of limitations in Canada for sexual assault cases (we will explore this issue later in the chapter).

As pointed out by Justice Cory, witnesses clearly are not infallible. Wells (1993) concluded that witnesses' errors provide the single most frequent cause of wrongful convictions; an examination of the first 40 persons in the United States who were convicted of crimes but later exonerated on the basis of DNA testing found that in 36 of these cases (or 90 percent), one or more witnesses falsely identified the innocent person (Wells et al., 1998). In Canada, one wrongful conviction association, the Innocence Network, overturned 21 wrongful convictions in 2011 alone (The Innocence Network, 2012). The rise of DNA testing has shed light on the magnitude of issues surrounding witness testimony. The Innocence Project in the United States has overturned 254 wrongful conviction cases and estimates that over 75 percent of convictions overturned through DNA relied on witness identification (The Innocence Project, 2010). An estimated 4500 people are convicted each year in the United States as a result of mistaken witness identifications (Cutler & Penrod, 1995). As noted by Yarmey (2003), although corresponding estimates have not been made for Canada, numerous well-known wrongful convictions here have established that mistaken witnesses pose a major problem in our legal system. Various law schools at Canadian universities (e.g., York University, McGill University) have followed the work of the Innocence Project and made wrongful conviction occurring in Canada their focus. For example, the University of British Columbia Law Innocence Project has established a variety of programs, initiating collaborations between students and professors, to examine cases involving claims of wrongful convictions (UBC Law Innocence Project, 2012).

Can forensic psychology contribute to reducing the error rate? As Chapter 1 described, the field of experimental psychology has a long history of studying memory and especially errors in memory, as far back as the work by Ebbinghaus and Münsterberg more than a century ago. But in the last 40 years there has been an explosion of research on forensic aspects of memory. The first scholarly conference devoted to witness testimony took place in Edmonton in 1980, organized by Gary Wells (see Yarmey, 2003). A group of witness researchers from Canada and the United States came together to discuss their work, and the result was the first special issue of a scientific journal (*Law and Human Behavior,* 1980) focused on the psychology of witness testimony. As a result of literally hundreds of studies, psychologists now possess extensive information on how the accuracy of memory can be improved in real-world cases. Some implications of a century's worth of memory research are described in this chapter.

The act of a witness describing or identifying a suspect involves more than memory alone; included are reasoning processes, suggestibility and social influence, self-confidence, authoritarian submission, and conformity. Wells (1995) has pointed out that "*memory testimony* and *memory* are not identical twins. **Memory testimony** is the witness's statement of what he or she recalls of a prior event. These statements can be influenced by more than just memory processes" (p. 727, italics in original, boldface added).

The examples of questionable police interrogation procedures—to be described later in the chapter—illustrate the distinction between memory and memory testimony and some of the determinants of problematic witness evidence. A goal of forensic psychology is to make a witness's identification a product of his or her memory rather than a product of the identification procedures used by the police or other confounding factors. Numerous studies in the psychological laboratory or controlled field studies that simulate a crime and then determine the degree of accuracy of witnesses legitimize the fear that false identifications by bystanders occur with considerable frequency (Brigham, Maass, Snyder, & Spaulding, 1982; Buckhout, 1974; Cutler, Penrod, & Martens, 1987; Ellis, Shepherd, & Davies, 1980; Leippe, Wells, & Ostrom, 1978; McAllister, Baiamonte, Ory, & Sherer, 2011; Wells, 1984b; Wells, Lindsay, & Ferguson, 1979; Wells & Olson, 2003). In crime simulations in which participants believed the crime was real and their identification would have consequences for the accused, high rates of false identification still occurred (Malpass & Devine, 1980; Murray & Wells, 1982). How high a rate of inaccuracy? In some studies, as many as 90 percent of responses were false identifications; in others, only a few participants erred. The extreme variation exemplifies a central theme of this chapter: the degree of accuracy of witness identification can be determined partially by the specific procedures used in the criminal investigation.

System Variables versus Estimator Variables

In fact, a point emphasized by Gary Wells and his colleagues who study witness identification is that rather than being satisfied simply to point out that the reports of witnesses often are inaccurate, we should recognize that the degree of accuracy often is influenced by the procedures used by the police and other criminal justice professionals (Brewer & Wells, 2011; Wells & Seelau, 1995). Wells (1978; Wells & Olson, 2003), originally at the University of Alberta, referred to these as **system variables**; they include the type of questioning done by the police, the nature of the lineup or photo arrays, and the presence or absence of videotaping of procedures. Although these variables contribute to witness inaccuracy, they prove to be *preventable* errors (Wells, 1993; Wells & Olson, 2003); in fact, psychologists can aid in the construction of lineups and the development of interviewing procedures that reduce inaccuracy.

The other factor contributing to the accuracy of a witness—what Wells called **estimator variables**—is not controllable by the criminal justice system and thus not reviewed in detail in this chapter. Estimator variables include environmental factors (e.g., the amount of lighting at the crime scene, length of exposure of the criminal to the witness) and within-the-person variables (the witness's psychological state, physical condition, etc.). Estimator variables are influential before the police respond. For example, the presence of a weapon or degree of violence associated with a crime may affect the witness's ability to recall the event (e.g., Fawcett, Russell, Peace, & Christie, 2011). In addition, research has suggested that particular emotions felt by victims and bystanders can influence memory (e.g., Clifford & Hollin, 1981; Clifford & Scott, 1978; Wessel, van der Kooy, & Merckelbach, 2000; Woodworth et al., 2009). Further, an archival study examined witnesses' ability to remember particular aspects of a perpetrator (e.g., hair colour, hair style, build, height, age) as a function of crime; however, the only effect identified was that hair colour was most accurately described in high violence cases (Wagstaff et al., 2003).

Hairstyle and hair colour also have been identified as being most accurately recalled in other studies (e.g., Wagstaff et al., 2003). On the other hand, Pozzulo and Siobhan (2006) found that correct identifications were negatively impacted by a simple change of hairstyle. Evidently, the relation between violence and memory accuracy is complex. Some research in real-life settings suggests that witnesses to violence can hold accurate memories for the event. In addition, other factors such as cognitive load, divided attention, and exposure duration can influence identification accuracy (e.g., Palmer, Brewer, & Weber, 2010). While estimator variables are those that cannot be changed or prevented (Wells, 1978; Wells & Olson, 2003), acknowledging these confounding factors and understanding their impact on witness memory is important.

In a landmark field study, John Yuille and Judith Cutshall (now Judith Daylen) (1986) of the University of British Columbia examined the recollections of 13 witnesses several months after they

CANADIAN RESEARCHER PROFILE

Kristine Peace

Being a police officer's daughter, Dr. Kristine Peace (KP) always had been concerned with forensic issues, but began to fine-tune her interest in forensic psychology (and research on memory and credibility) upon studying with Dr. Don Read during her undergraduate degree at the University of Lethbridge. From there, she commenced her graduate studies at Dalhousie University under the guidance of Dr. Stephen Porter. Together, they conducted several influential studies on how traumatic events were retained in memory over time (e.g., Peace & Porter, 2004; Porter & Peace, 2007). Her Ph.D. dissertation focused on how true and false allegations of trauma differ and how content-based techniques can be used in credibility assessments (e.g., Peace & Porter, 2011; Porter, Peace, & Emmett, 2007).

Upon completion of her doctorate in 2006, Dr. Peace joined the Department of Psychology at Grant MacEwan University, where she has continued her research on a range of forensic psychological issues: credibility and

deception detection (e.g., Peace & Bouvier, 2008; Peace, Brower, & Shudra, 2012; Peace, Porter, & Almon, 2011); memory for trauma and criminal events (e.g., Fawcett, Russell, Peace, & Christie, in press; Peace, Porter, & ten Brinke, 2008; Porter, Peace, Douglas, & Doucette, in press); PTSD and malingering (e.g., Peace & Harder, 2011; Peace & Masliuk, 2011; Peace, Porter, & Cook, 2010); and psychopathy and emotional processing (e.g., Peace & Sinclair, 2012; Peace & Wells, 2011). She has worked extensively with honours and independent study students, and has coauthored presentations with students at conferences such as SARMAC, AP-LS, BBCS, and BASICS. Her future goals involve further research in the areas above, as well as planned studies on victim impact statements and the role of arousal on deception content and detection.

Besides research, she recently has taken over the role of Psychology Honours Adviser, which keeps her busy along with teaching, writing a social psychology text, supervising her own honours students' projects, as well as consulting on criminal cases involving credibility assessment of memory. In her spare time, she loves inventing new culinary delights, shooting, travelling, collecting sarcastic comical magnets, and avoiding spiders and robots.

off the mark.com   by Mark Parisi

THAT'S HIM...THIRD FROM THE LEFT...

Cartoon @ Mark Parisi, Permission Granted for use. www.offthemark.com

In a valid lineup, the "foils" must look similar to the description of the perpetrator initially given to police by the witness.

had witnessed a murder and an attempted murder in Burnaby, British Columbia. Results indicated that the witnesses' memories generally remained accurate, detailed, and resistant to the effect of misinformation. Although there was no "nonviolent" control condition, the researchers' results suggested that under some circumstances memory for violence can be enduring. But the occurrence of violence during a crime is an estimator variable, and there is nothing the police can do to change the characteristics of the criminal incident to increase or decrease the accuracy of this aspect. Thus the distinction of these two types of variables suggests that system variables can sometimes be controlled. We can do nothing about poor lighting conditions or the brevity of exposure to the criminal, but police can eliminate practices that lead to further inaccuracies in reports.

POLICE PROCEDURES

Improper Police Procedures

Gary Wells (1995; Brewer & Wells, 2011) has observed that although police use caution and care when collecting physical evidence at the crime scene, they do not necessarily apply the same caution to the concept of memory, despite its susceptibility to confounding sources. Yarmey (2003) traced the development of guidelines for use by police in witness identification. A major development occurred in the early 1980s when the Law Reform Commission of Canada commissioned Osgoode Hall law professor Neil Brooks to prepare

a paper entitled "Police Guidelines: Pretrial Eyewitness Identification Procedures." For the first time, several psychologists from Canada (Tony Doob at the University of Toronto, Don Read at the University of Lethbridge, Gary Wells at the University of Alberta, and Yarmey himself) and the United States (Elizabeth Loftus then at the University of Seattle) were asked to act as consultants. Many of their recommendations echoed a 1929 Royal English Commission Report, intended to instruct police officers in optimal lineup procedures. One of the report's recommendations was that lineup "foils," or fillers in a lineup, should be matched to the suspect on the basis of their physical characteristics.

Yet police in Canada often have ignored such recommendations. Yarmey brings up the 1959 case of *R. v. Armstrong*, in which child witnesses were shown a live lineup containing the Asian suspect and a group of Caucasian foils. In more recent years, there have been numerous cases (such as the Thomas Sophonow case earlier in the chapter) in which police practices have deviated greatly from accepted standards. In the Court of Queen's Bench of Alberta case, *R. v. Redbreast* (2004), the judge observed that the police detectives had shown a "rather unique" photograph of the defendant in the photo array, strongly distinguishable from all of the other photographs in the group of 15 in the lineup. One witness testified that the defendant's photograph with long, untied hair "jumped out" at the viewer from the group (para. 109). Obviously, the recommendations by the Royal English Commission Report from nearly 80 years ago still are not being consistently followed in Canada.

Variations from acceptable procedures in questioning witnesses identified by Wells and colleagues (1995, 2009) are still relevant today and include the following:

1. Asking witnesses poorly constructed questions immediately upon discovering the crime.
2. Allowing one witness to overhear the responses of other witnesses (see also Paterson, Kemp, & Ng, 2011; Wright, Memon, Skagerberg, & Gabbert, 2009).
3. Taking "spotty" notes of witnesses' answers (and not recording the actual questions asked).
4. Failing to use any theory of a proper memory interview.
5. Using investigators who have little training in interviewing or the psychology of memory.

Further compounding the problem is the fact that, as Fisher (1995) noted, many interviews with witnesses are conducted under the worst conditions imaginable: witnesses who are agitated and/or injured, time pressures that demand rapid-fire questioning, and background conditions characterized by distractions, confusion, and noise. On top of this, police officers often are pressured by their supervisors to file their reports quickly.

An even broader concern is the motivation of police in questioning witnesses. A temptation of police investigators is to act prematurely in forming a conclusion about the likely perpetrator; this too-early hunch then guides the investigator toward questions and procedures that validate the belief (Fisher, 1995; Porter & ten Brinke, 2010). For example, in the 2004 Cecilia Zhang murder investigation in Ontario, Peel Region Police Chief Noel Catney was widely criticized for this description of suspect Min Chen at a press conference: "Ladies and gentlemen, this is not just a murderer. This is the most despicable of criminals. This is a child murderer" (CBC Online News, 2004). Obviously, Catney did not hold a presumption of innocence for Chen, having already come to his own conclusion about guilt. So, in interviewing witnesses, police may be tempted to ask leading questions or offer subtle confirmation of their hunches; they may construct biased **lineups** or **photo arrays** (six-packs) to aid in identifying whom they consider the "correct" suspect, as observed by leading lineup researcher Rod Lindsay at Queens University (Lindsay, 1994). Clark (2005) conducted a meta-analysis and found that particular types of police instruction may impair the identification procedure (see also Greathouse & Kovera, 2009).

In the case of *R. v. Samuel* (2004), Justice Brown thoroughly considered the frailties of identification evidence and frequently referenced important findings from the *Sophonow Inquiry Report*. In coming to her decision, she expressed concern regarding the construction of the lineup and the manner in which it was presented. For example, Justice Brown stated that "photos should resemble as closely as possible the witnesses' description, and if that is not possible, they should be as close as possible to the suspect"—a rule that was not followed by the police officers. Further, she urged that "an officer who does not know the suspect and who is not involved in the investigation should conduct the lineup" (*R. v. Samuel*, 2004, para 20).

But, in several important cases before the Canadian Supreme Court with regard to witness identification, the court decided—rather than reject police practices as improper—to try to deal with the problem by considering and warning the jury about the possible frailties of the witness evidence. For example, in *Mezzo v. the Queen* (1986), the court ruled that in determining whether to convict in cases hinging on witness testimony, the trial judge should first consider the factors that have affected the quality of the identification evidence (such as police procedures). Then, it was argued, the frailties in the evidence can be "remedied" by a caution to the jury, and the judge should leave the matter in their hands.

In other words, rather than ruling against the use of improper police procedures, the court concluded that judges and juries could make up their own minds about whether testimony is tainted. But why not try to prevent those practices from occurring at all, as well as attempting to protect defendants' rights if damage still occurs? The following are three cases where errors by the police have been documented; the cases provide raw material for guidelines advocated by forensic psychologists.

The Thomas Sophonow Case

Barbara Stoppel was a vivacious 16-year-old who was murdered on December 23, 1981, in Winnipeg. Thomas Sophonow was charged with her murder and eventually went through three trials. The first was declared a mistrial, as the jury was unable to reach a unanimous verdict, while in the second and third trials he was convicted. The Court of Appeal finally acquitted him. The case largely hinged on the witness testimony of John Doerksen.

In the **Sophonow Inquiry** (*Sophonow Inquiry Report*, 2001, [Online]), the problems with the main witness in the case were outlined by Justice Cory:

Sometime after 8:15 p.m. on December 23rd, John Doerksen went to the Ideal Donut Shop to get a coffee. The door was locked and he saw a person inside the shop. He saw that person at the cash register take a cardboard box. He saw the murderer leave the shop with a box, unlock the door, close it behind him and then move rapidly towards the Norwood Bridge. ... Later that evening, he gave a description of the man he followed to the police.

Sometime later, Mr. Doerksen agreed to a session with a hypnotist at the University of Manitoba where he again described the murderer with some variations from his first description. The questionable nature of Mr. Doerksen's identification became readily apparent in the following weeks. On the 6th of January 1982, Mr. Doerksen called the police from the Norwood Hotel. He reported that the killer was in the hotel at that moment. He said that, if he was not the killer, he was certainly his twin brother. This was an identification of Mr. Dubé [an innocent bystander] as the killer and he was quickly exonerated by the police. Shortly thereafter, Mr. Doerksen identified a *Sun* reporter as the killer and he too was speedily exonerated.

He reported that he was seeing the killer everywhere and that every tall man resembled the killer. Most significantly, he attended a line-up on March 13th, which included Thomas Sophonow. The line-up was conducted by Sergeant Biener. Although Thomas Sophonow stood out as the tallest person in that line-up, Mr. Doerksen was unable to identify anyone as the man he had seen leaving the Ideal Donut Shop on the 23rd of December. ... Mr. Doerksen testified that Sergeant Shipman was in the room with him while the identification parade was held. He stated that Sergeant Shipman suggested that he should consider number seven, which was the number that Thomas Sophonow had been given for this parade. He also stated that Sergeant Shipman told him that those in the line-up could change articles of clothing with any other member of the line-up. Sergeant Shipman vehemently denied these suggestions.

The evidence relating to Mr. Doerksen becomes even more troublesome. At approximately 9:30 a.m. on Monday the 15th, Constable Foster saw John Doerksen on the street and picked him up for a spot check. Constable Foster was unable to tell the Commission why he picked up Mr. Doerksen. In any event, he found that there was a warrant for Mr. Doerksen for unpaid fines. He took him to the Public Safety Building. While he was waiting for his father to pay the fines, Mr. Doerksen came face to face with Thomas Sophonow. He had with him a copy of a Winnipeg newspaper, which contained a picture of Thomas Sophonow. He spoke to Mr. Henley, a custodial officer at the Remand Centre, and asked if he could see Thomas Sophonow. He was directed by Mr. Henley to the area of Thomas Sophonow's cell. There, he again saw Thomas Sophonow. I wonder how many people would have been directed to Thomas Sophonow simply because they had a picture of him published in a recent edition of a Winnipeg newspaper. In any event, as strange and disturbing as this apparent chance meeting may be, there is no evidence of any arrangement or conspiracy on the part of the Winnipeg police to have Mr. Doerksen meet Thomas Sophonow. Mr. Doerksen explained that his ability to identify Thomas Sophonow when he saw him in a cell at the Remand Centre was because he was clean-shaven whereas he had not been at the time that he viewed the line-up on the 13th. However, Exhibits 52 and 53 are photos of the line-ups of the 13th and 15th of March[;] in both of which Thomas Sophonow appears to be clean-shaven. His appearance was just the same on the 13th as it was on the 15th, when he was seen and purportedly identified by Mr. Doerksen. There really is no basis for the statement that there was any difference in Thomas Sophonow's appearance from the time that he was seen in the line-up on March 13th and the time that he was seen in the Remand Centre on the 15th of March.

On the 24th of March at the Public Safety Building, Mr. Doerksen met Sergeants Wawryk and Paulishyn and advised them that he had seen Thomas Sophonow in court that day and he was now "90% sure" that Thomas Sophonow was the man even though he had not been able to pick him out at the line-up. Prior to the preliminary hearing, Sergeant Biener prepared a "can say" report which indicated that, although Mr. Doerksen was unable to identify Thomas Sophonow at the time of the line-up on March 13th, after seeing him at the Provincial Remand Centre he was now 90% sure that Thomas Sophonow was the killer. (Inquiry, Exhibit 149E Police Supplemental Report, Vol. 16B, page 812). It is, indeed, strange that by the time he testified at the preliminary hearing, he was certain of the identity of Thomas Sophonow and he had no reservations whatsoever. He testified with the same certainty that Thomas Sophonow was the killer at each of the three trials.

This situation becomes even more troublesome. Mr. Doerksen advised the Winnipeg Police, when they were reinvestigating the case, that in 1982 he required glasses and he had trouble with his eyes at night and in poor lighting conditions (Inquiry, Vol. 22, page 2254). Further, Mr. Doerksen had developed a friendship with the Stoppel family, particularly Mr. Fred Stoppel. He met with him on numerous occasions and it may be that the friendship that he developed affected his opinion with regard to the identification of Thomas Sophonow.

Lastly, Sergeant Biener noted that Mr. Doerksen came to court during the first and second trials on the days that he was to testify with "quite a shine on" [drunk] (Inquiry, Exhibit 149 Police Supplemental Report, Vol. 16B, page 924). In light of all these circumstances, it is apparent that little, if any, weight can be attached to the evidence of Mr. Doerksen.*

Sophonow Inquiry Report (2001). Retrieved August 20, 2004 from Government of Manitoba website: http://www.gov.mb.ca/justice/sophonow/.

It should be apparent to the reader that this witness and the use of ill-advised police practices created a nightmare for the legal system and for Mr. Sophonow. From Justice Cory's report, three major problems with the police evidence-gathering procedures with Doerksen become apparent:

- The use of hypnosis to "refresh" Doerksen's memory for the perpetrator
- The use of foils who differed on an important physical attribute from the main suspect: during the original lineup, Mr. Sophonow was taller than the foils
- Leading a witness to choose a particular person in the lineup as the perpetrator: Doerksen reportedly was led by police to choose Mr. Sophonow from the lineup.

Ivan Henry reunited with his daughters after being released from prison.

The Ivan Henry Case

In the 1980s a series of sexual offences plagued Vancouver, British Columbia, and in 1983 Ivan Henry was charged in connection with these offences. While Ivan claimed he was innocent from the beginning of the trial, he later was convicted based mainly on witness identification and voice identification. However, numerous improper procedures surrounded Henry's trial and initial identification. For example, during his trial the jury was improperly instructed and his defence counsel was denied access to important documents relevant to the case. Further, police used biased lineup procedures. For example, the lineup portrayed a series of ten individuals, only one of whom was being restrained by three officers in uniform—Ivan Henry. Henry served 27 years in prison in British Columbia before being acquitted in October 2010.

The John Demjanjuk Case

In the 1980s John Demjanjuk was a retired automobile worker living in Cleveland, Ohio, but he was accused of having been "Ivan the Terrible," a Nazi collaborator who was a guard at a concentration camp where thousands of German and Polish Jews were annihilated during World War II. With the cooperation of the U.S. government, he was deported to Israel, where he was put on trial as a war criminal in February 1987.

Incredibly, several survivors of the concentration camp at Treblinka identified him after examining his 1951 visa photo; note that these identifications reflect the assumption of accurate memories of interactions that occurred more than 30 years before. For example, Yossef Czarny survived the Treblinka camp and later was freed from the camp at Bergen Belsen; when he examined a photo album of Ukrainian suspects, he immediately pointed to Demjanjuk's photo and exclaimed:

This is Ivan, yes. It is Ivan, the notorious Ivan. Thirty years have gone by, but I recognize him at first sight with complete certainty. I would know him, I believe, even in the dark. He was very tall, of sturdy frame, his face at the time was not as full and fat from gorging himself with food, as in the picture. However, it is the same face construction, the same nose, the same eyes and forehead, as he had at that time. A mistake is out of the question. (quoted by Wagenaar, 1988, pp. 110–111)

Czarny and other survivors testified at Demjanjuk's trial, but cross-examination of the Israeli police investigator, Miriam Radiwker, revealed that she did not think it was wrong to direct the survivors' attention to one particular photo during the questioning. She admitted having used this very suggestive procedure. Furthermore, the photos of **foils** (persons who are not suspects in the crime at hand) presented to the survivors did not fit the description of "Ivan the Terrible"; his picture was the only one that could be described as balding, with a round face and short neck (Wagenaar, 1988,

p. 133). Also, in their report to the court, investigators failed to mention that some survivors did not recognize Demjanjuk. Even though Demjanjuk was convicted of war crimes in April 1988, the Supreme Court of Israel five years later overturned the conviction, basing its conclusion on the inconsistency of evidence that created a reasonable doubt as to the identity of Demjanjuk as "Ivan the Terrible."

Whereas most witness studies have focused on memory for relatively benign events, researchers are now paying more attention to emotional or traumatic events (e.g., McNally, 2003; Read & Lindsay, 1997). The use of improper police procedures in cases such as Demjanjuk's is particularly problematic when one considers the body of research showing that traumatic memory can be very accurate over long periods under the right circumstances (as we saw in the Yuille & Cutshall, 1986, study of murder witnesses earlier in the chapter). Wagenaar and Groenewed (1990) compared the memory reports of 78 World War II concentration camp survivors from the trial of Marinus De Rijke in the 1980s with statements given to Nuremberg investigators shortly after the war. The witness accounts were accurate and detailed despite the passage of time. For example, the accounts of the camp, camp registration numbers, malicious treatment, daily activities, labour, housing, and main guards were "remarkably consistent" over four decades. Dalhousie University doctoral student Kristine Peace now a professor (profiled in this chapter) examined the reliability of the traumatic memories in 52 people who had recently gone through a violent or nonviolent experience (Peace & Porter, 2004; Porter & Peace, 2007). After three months, the details of the traumatic experiences remained highly consistent and had changed far less than memories for positive experiences by the same participants.

Clearly, it is possible for memories of crime to be reliable. Also, it is evident that the interviewing approach that many law enforcement officials take can be problematic (see Fisher & Schreiber, 2007 for review). The onus is on investigators to ensure that they do not taint witness evidence through their own evidence-gathering practices.

QUESTIONING WITNESSES (INFORMATION GENERATION)

Police engage in a variety of activities as part of a criminal investigation. This section focuses on the task of eliciting descriptions from bystander witnesses (versus victim witnesses). Although some of these concepts may apply to victims as well, we will discuss witness memory of victims more in depth later in the chapter. As in Fisher's (1995) useful article, the goal of the following section is to propose methods that improve the quality of the methods police use to interview witnesses. In doing so, it is necessary to assess the current state of police interviewing techniques. Unfortunately, the picture is a rather bleak one.

The Role of the Police in Interviewing

First, police receive surprisingly little instruction on how to interview cooperative witnesses (Fisher, 1995; Fisher, Milne, & Bull, 2011). Only the larger departments and major training centres offer what we consider adequate training. Further, the handbooks and textbooks used in police training "either omit the issue of effective interviewing techniques or provide only superficial coverage" (Fisher, 1995, p. 733). More recently, Snook, Eastwood, Stinson, Tedeschini, and House (2010) concluded that Canadian police officers receive minimal training on how to properly interview witnesses. Further, research has found that current interviewers from Canadian police forces most frequently use closed-ended and probing questions and least frequently use open-ended questions (Snook & Keating, 2011). Although it has been recommended that interviewees talk for 80 percent of the interview, interviews conducted by Atlantic Canadian police forces violated this rule 89 percent of the time (Snook & Keating, 2011). These researchers, among many others, hope that studies such as these encourage Canadian police organizations to integrate empirically supported techniques into their witness interview training. Despite this lack of training, the interviews carried out by different police officers have some similarities (Fisher, Geiselman, & Raymond, 1987; Fisher, Milne, & Bull, 2011). For example, the typical interview begins with a standard open-ended question, followed by a focused closed-ended question, and ends with a general open-ended question asking if there is anything else to be reported (Fisher et al., 2011).

In their observations over the years, Fisher and colleagues have identified three types of errors that occur almost universally: interrupting the witness, asking too many short-answer questions, and an inappropriate sequencing of questions (Fisher,

Geiselman, & Raymond, 1987; Fisher et al., 2011). Further, they found that the average interview had three open-ended questions and 26 direct ones; the latter were asked in a staccato, rapid-fire style, usually a second or less after the witness's answer to the previous question.

In addition, police appear to be insensitive to the dynamics of the situation when a witness is being interviewed. The witness often is seeking confirmation or justification from the interviewer. The **demand characteristics** (cues that suggest what response is expected from the witness) of the situation may elicit pressures to give a "right answer" to an authority figure, or at least to avoid appearing ignorant when asked a specific relevant question. Thus, when asked, "Was he wearing jeans?" a victim may be reluctant to acknowledge not noticing. (Even more serious is the failure by the police to evaluate whether a victim-witness might be lying.) For example, Roper and Shewan (2002) conducted a study that labelled participants as "good" or "poor" witnesses to examine the impact of receiving a negative label on suggestibility. They found that those labelled as a poor witness were more likely to alter their initial accounts according to leading questions. In conclusion, it is evident that the police play an important role in extracting information from witnesses and the interview style is imperative (Fischer & Geiselman, 2010).

Psychologists probably are more aware of the dangers of postevent suggestion (e.g., asking "What colour was his coat?" instead of "Was he wearing a coat?") than are police investigators (see discussion below). Less clear is the frequency with which police ask **leading questions** or make subtle suggestions during the questioning of witnesses. Fisher (1995) acknowledged that the empirical evidence about actual use of leading questions "is meager and, at best, difficult to interpret" (p. 740). A laboratory study (Geiselman, Fisher, MacKinnon, & Holland, 1985) found that few leading questions were offered, but a field study that tape-recorded the actual interviews by British police officers concluded that one of every six questions was leading (George & Clifford, 1992). Snook and Keating (2011) examined the interviewing techniques used by Canadian police officers. The researchers found that problematic types of questions—including close-ended and probing questions—were used the most, while better questioning approaches advocated in the literature (e.g., open-ended questions) rarely were used. Fisher concludes that we must be cautious and assume that leading questions occur fairly frequently, acknowledge the detrimental effects, and safeguard against them (Fisher, 1995; Fisher & Gieselman, 2010).

Police also seem to be unaware that a witness's previous exposure to the photograph of a suspect can increase the witness's likelihood—when shown the photograph again at a later time—to identify the suspect as the culprit. Research suggests that repeated identification procedures actually are commonplace during police investigations when they are attempting to identify a culprit (Behrman & Davey, 2001) and have been shown to inflate confidence in the witness (Odinot, Wolters, & Lavender, 2009). Brown, Deffenbacher, and Sturgill (1977) carried out an experiment that manipulated this experience, using a one-week time interval between viewings. Approximately 20 percent of subjects who had been shown an earlier photograph wrongly identified a suspect. That is, people may remember a face but forget where they saw it—an example of the phenomenon called **unconscious transference** (see also Buckhout, 1974; Deffenbacher, Bornstein, & Penrod, 2006; Loftus, 1976). Recent research has examined these effects and found that prior exposure to those suspected not only decreases accuracy rates but also increases false-alarm identification rates (see Deffenbacher, Bornstein, & Penrod, 2006 for a meta-analysis on this topic).

Also, police officers seem to be insensitive to types of errors in their own interviews. Although many recognized that it was a poor interviewing technique to interrupt a witness repeatedly and denied that they do so in their own interviews, many of these same officers made this error at an alarmingly high rate (Fisher, Geiselman, & Amador, 1989). Fisher (1995) observed: "I have witnessed countless times in training workshops detectives who claim at the outset that they already know the principles of effective interviewing from earlier training programs, only to make the same interviewing mistakes as those who have never had any formal training" (p. 757).

Another interviewing technique fraught with potential danger is to ask the same question several times during the same interview (Fisher, 1995). If the witness failed to answer the question the first time, the repeated questioning may create a demand characteristic to respond *in some way* (as discussed earlier), even if it means that the witness lowers his or her standard of confidence (Chan & LaPaglia, 2011; Krahenbuhl, Blades &

Elser, 2009; Roper & Schwan, 2002). If the witness did answer the first time questioned, the repetition may communicate that the answer was not satisfactory to the police/authority figure, creating social pressure to substitute another response (Fisher, 1995). The latter result is especially likely with witnesses who are young children (Fivish & Schwarzmueller, 1995; Geiselman & Padilla, 1988; Memon & Vartoukin, 1996). Memorial University researcher Carole Peterson and her colleagues interviewed children four times about an injury that required hospital emergency room treatment, namely at one week, six months, one year, and two years after the incident. Although new details that were introduced after six months were more likely to be accurate than inaccurate, new information introduced at one or two years following the injury was as likely to be wrong as right (except for 12- and 13-year-olds, the oldest group studied) (Peterson, Moores, & White, 2001). Although we do not know how often police use repeated questions, laboratory research concludes that such a procedure increases a witness's mistakes in recollection (Poole & White, 1991).

Similarly, the use of multiple-choice questions may encourage guessing. Unless witnesses are clearly told that they shouldn't respond unless they are sure—an admonition rarely offered by the police—such a procedure may lead to an increase in information apparently uncovered, but at a reduction in accuracy (Lipton, 1977; see also Fisher, 1995, pp. 748–749, for a discussion of the difficulty in comparing the accuracy levels of open-ended and forced-choice questions).

Children as Witnesses

Because of beliefs and research findings about their heightened suggestibility, children as witnesses pose particular challenges to investigators who seek information from them about the nature of perpetrators (Bruck & Ceci, 1999; Ceci & Bruck, 1993; Ceci, Toglia, & Ross, 1987; Crossman, Schullin, & Melnyk, 2004; Fisher, Milne, & Bull, 2011; Lindsay, Pozzulo, Craig, Lee, & Corber, 1997; Melinder et al., 2010; Melnyk, Crossman, & Schullin, 2007; Yuille et al., 1993). The recommendations noted above in questioning adult witnesses would, of course, apply to the questioning of children also. Special problems with respect to the questioning of children and procedures for reducing suggestibility are covered in Chapter 12, which deals with forensic responses to the sexual abuse of children.

IMPROVING POLICE PROCEDURES

As highlighted in the previous section, numerous factors can contribute to witness error. For example, Wright, Memon, Skagerberg, and Gabbert (2009) suggest three main reasons for the presence of witness errors. First, a witness's memory may be influenced by social influences, such as wanting to agree with investigators. Second, through the recall process and investigation, the witness may hear alternative stories or theories that he or she considers to be more probable or accurate and subsequently internalizes that account as his or her own memory. Finally, being asked misleading questions or being exposed to misinformation could contaminate a witness's memory. Fisher's (1995) thorough review details a number of procedures specific to the questioning process that can either increase the memory retrieval of a witness or improve the witness's conversion of a conscious recollection into a statement to the interviewer. Many of these suggestions are quite straightforward; for example:

- *Slow down the rate of questioning.* When asked a specific question, witnesses may need time to retrieve the memory; police should not impatiently interrupt the search with another question.
- *Re-create the original context.* A staple of the **cognitive interview** (for brief discussion see Fisher et al., 2011; Fisher, Ross, & Cahill, 2010), this principle proposes that, before answering any questions about the crime, witnesses should be told to re-create, in their own minds, the environment that existed when the crime happened. They should focus on how things looked and sounded and smelled, what they were doing, how they felt, and what was happening around them.
- *Tailor questions to the individual witness.* Many police routinely plod through a standardized checklist of questions (Fisher, Geiselman, & Raymond, 1987). Instead, Fisher encourages the investigation to be sensitive to each witness's unique perspective.
- *Make the interview witness-centred, not interviewer-centred.* Too often, the interview is structured so that the witness sits passively waiting for the police officer to ask question after question (Fisher, Geiselman, & Raymond, 1987). Investigators even apply their aggressive, controlling, intimidating style for questioning

suspects to the interviewing of cooperative witnesses. For the latter, police should use more open-ended questions and tell the subject that he or she should do most of the talking. Similarly, police officers need to convey what they need from the witnesses more explicitly than the typical "Tell me what happened," because the detailed, extensive responses wanted from witnesses go beyond the level of precision typical of ordinary discourse. For example, witnesses should be told not to edit their thoughts, but rather to pour forth all of them no matter how trivial they may seem.

- *Be sensitive to the distinction between correct and incorrect responses.* How do we know when someone is giving us false information? Common sense suggests that when a witness is slow to respond, is less confident in his or her answers, or is inconsistent in answering from one situation to another, the response is less likely to be an accurate one. Psychological research has confirmed that subjects who take longer to respond make incorrect responses (Sporer, 1993).

- *Be sensitive to temptations to form premature conclusions.* At the beginning of the chapter it was noted that one problem with police interviewing techniques is the bias of the police interviewer who has already formed a conclusion about the identity of the perpetrator. Several ways of dealing with this bias have been suggested; these will be described in detail later in the chapter. For example, Wells (see Fisher, 1995, p. 754) proposed that police interviewers be given only general knowledge about the crime (e.g., that a bank was robbed) before doing their witness interviews. A second suggestion is to videotape interviews and provide them to both the prosecution and the defence (Fisher, 1995; Kassin, 1998b).

Laura Melnyk

Dr. Laura Melnyk is an Associate Professor in the Department of Psychology at King's University College at Western University, previously known as the University of Western Ontario, in London, Ontario.

Laura was raised in Hamilton, Ontario. She completed her B.A. in psychology at McMaster University in Hamilton in 1995. She completed her Ph.D. in experimental psychology at McGill University in Montréal, Québec, under the supervision of Dr. Maggie Bruck, studying children's memory and suggestibility.

Laura's research focus is forensic developmental psychology. Her primary interest is child witnesses; she studies factors related to the accuracy and completeness of children's event reports. Her published work examines how the timing of suggestive interviews affects children's memory suggestibility, the duration of misinformation effects, individual differences in children's suggestibility, the use of drawing as an interviewing technique, and meta-suggestibility. Her current work has broadened to include developmental studies of young children's lineup performance and adults' abilities to describe the basic physical characteristics of strangers. Laura has recently become increasingly engaged in working directly with the legal system; she has given talks on child witnesses and lineups to the local police department and consults on cases involving child witnesses.

King's University College is a liberal arts university with a focus on undergraduate education; Laura loves her academic role at King's because it allows her to balance her commitment to research with her enthusiasm for teaching and mentoring undergraduates. With her background in children's memory development, she teaches courses in forensic psychology, psychology and law, developmental psychology, and cognition. Laura is a passionate and dedicated teacher; she was awarded the Bank of Nova Scotia, Western University Alumni Association, and University Students' Council Award for Excellence in Undergraduate Teaching in her first year of university teaching, and was awarded the King's University College Award for Excellence in Teaching in 2010. Laura's greatest joy is her young family. She is an avid cyclist (in part because the London area boasts many flat country roads); she also loves travelling, and has an extensive and diverse music collection.

The most basic suggestion is to provide proper training for police interviewers (Yuille, Marxsen, & Cooper, 1999). Although it is true that some police officers have better interviewing skills than others, psychologists have been able to improve the skills of both recruits and experienced detectives (Fisher, Geiselman, & Amador, 1989; George & Clifford, 1992).

University of British Columbia forensic psychologist Dr. John Yuille and his colleagues developed one of the most highly regarded forensic interviewing approaches for use with victims and witnesses, known as the Step-Wise Interview (Yuille, Hunter, Joffe, & Zaparniuk, 1993). The Step-Wise Interview attempts to minimize any trauma the witness may experience during the interview, maximize the amount and quality of the information obtained from the witness, minimize any contamination of the reported information, and maintain the integrity of the investigative process for the agencies involved. Following rapport building, the steps in this approach begin with the most open, least leading, least suggestive form of questioning (free narrative) and, if necessary, proceed to more specific questioning. For more than 15 years, Yuille has been active in training police, prosecutors, defence lawyers, and child protection staff in Canada and other countries in this approach. The Step-Wise Interview has been adopted as the standard for child abuse interviews in many jurisdictions. Such training not only acts as a highly effective bridge between forensic psychology and policing, but also may contribute to better legal decision making.

PSYCHOLOGY OF THE VICTIM

Although the impact of traumatic experiences on memory has received enormous empirical study over the years, the manner in which traumatic memories are processed and retained is controversial. Further, much research has been dedicated to the investigation of bystander witness memory but has failed to examine the difference in memory for a victim, despite it being clear that victims and bystanders sometimes recall the same event quite differently (e.g., Yuille, Davies, Gibling, Marxsen, & Porter, 1994).

Two main views exist regarding memory for stressful or traumatic events. The first, the *traumatic-memory argument,* posits that trauma impairs memory and leads to defences aimed at reducing anxiety associated with the event, such as repression (Kihlstrom, 1996; Nadel & Jacobs, 1998; Porter & Peace, 2007; Sotgiu, 2008; van der Kolk & Fisler, 1995; Woodworth et al., 2009). However, some have suggested that previous research supporting this notion is limited and often has concerning methodological considerations (Briere & Conte, 1993; McNally, 2003; Williams, 1994). Alternatively, others have suggested that traumatic memories follow a similar pattern as any other type of memory—progressive deterioration over time. This view suggests that traumatic memories are not unique as others have speculated and indeed are malleable and fallible like other types of memories (e.g., Loftus, 2003a; Porter & Peace, 2007). For example, lending support to the fallibility of traumatic memories, studies have found that these memories are particularly vulnerable when associated with strong negative emotion (e.g., Nourkova, Bernstein, & Loftus, 2004; Porter, Spencer, & Birt, 2003) and others have found that through misleading interviews people can mistakenly recall entire experiences (e.g., Cabeza & St. Jazques, 2007; Otgaar, Candel, Merckelbach, & Wade, 2009; Wade, Garry, Read, & Lindsay, 2002).

However, as mentioned, most studies have failed to examine the consistency of victim's memory for personally traumatic events. Preliminary findings of this relationship suggest that memory for traumatic events may actually be unimpaired, and in some cases, enhanced (e.g., Peterson & Parsons, 2005; Wagenaar & Groeneweg, 1990). For example, Alexander et al. (2005) investigated child sexual abuse victims' memory accuracy for the event and found that victims' memory was fairly reliable over time.

But do memories of personal significant events differ as a function of emotion (i.e., positive vs. negative)? The first author and Dr. Kristine Peace (see Canadian Research Profile earlier) looked into this relationship in a longitudinal study examining the memory for highly traumatic and highly positive emotionally experiences (Porter & Peace, 2007). Reassessing participants who described their experiences five years earlier, the researchers examined participants' consistency, vividness, overall quality, and sensory components for the highly traumatic event and the positively emotional event after the approximate five-year delay. They found that traumatic events were highly consistent in comparison to positive experiences and that the delay had an insignificant impact on the vividness, overall quality, and sensory components of the event. However, a slow deterioration of these components was characteristic of positive memories. As such, it seems as though memories for traumatic events may actually be more enduring than other experiences.

THE FRAGILITY OF MEMORY AND FALSE MEMORIES

Before we examine some ways in which the accuracy of witnesses' memory can be improved, it is important to give a brief background concerning various factors that influence our memory and that can subsequently distort those memories. Distortion in witness memory has become a major focus of research in cognitive psychology and neuroscience, and has significant implications in forensic settings. Consistent with a constructive memory framework, research findings show that memory is greatly affected by the conditions of **encoding** and **retrieval** (e.g., Loftus, 2003a). In the case of a crime, encoding would refer to how the witness or victim experienced the event, and retrieval would refer to the act of recalling the event privately or to another person such as a police officer. Although **false memories** have been studied for more than 80 years (Bartlett, 1932), the catalyst for the enormous level of interest in the phenomenon at present was Elizabeth Loftus's **postevent misinformation paradigm**, developed in the 1970s. In the original paradigm, participants were shown a slide presentation of a crime or accident (e.g., Loftus, Miller, & Burns, 1978). Some witnesses then received misinformation after which they answered questions about the event. For example, in studies using a slide sequence depicting a car accident, experimental witnesses were provided misinformation such as "Did the car stop at the stop sign?" when, in fact, there had been a yield sign. On a recognition test, misled witnesses chose a stop sign far more often than did control witnesses. Since the initial investigation of this paradigm by Loftus and colleagues, numerous studies have supported the malleability of memory and the misinformation effect (Frenda, Nichols, & Loftus, 2011). Further, it seems that postevent information is enduring; London, Bruck, and Melnyk (2008) found that both true and false suggestions about experiences have an impact on children's memory after a year has passed.

While the misinformation paradigm has stimulated research of the fallibility of memory, Chan, Thomas, and Bulevich (2009) suggest that this paradigm fails to measure memory following the event but prior to the misinformation. As such, this process fails to adequately re-enact the process of a real criminal event because witnesses typically are tested for recall following the event. While Chan et al. suspected that the recall process immediately following an event would cause the misinformation to have a lessened effect on memory, their findings suggested that immediate recall actually aggravated the effect of misinformation. In other words, recall tests following the event seemed to prime the memory to be more susceptible to future misinformation.

Another advance in the area was the Deese-Roediger-McDermott (DRM) paradigm (e.g., Roediger & McDermott, 1995), inspiring numerous false memory studies since the 1990s to the present (Brainerd, Rayna, & Zember, 2011). This work established that after participants encode related words (e.g., "rest", "bed," "awake"), many later misremember a related word (e.g., "sleep") that was not presented. The premise of the DRM is that memory is associative; when items are associated semantically, processing one tends to activate the other in recall.

Building upon these experiments, studies have established that it is not only minor details that can be altered in memory. With misleading questions and other suggestive techniques sometimes used by police, false memories are possible for major details in a scene or even entire personal experiences. By enlisting the aid of participants' family members, Loftus and Pickrell (1995) attempted to convince adults that at the age of five they had been lost in a shopping mall and later rescued. Participants were given brief descriptions of three real events and a false event of being lost in a shopping mall. In later interviews, a quarter of participants came to generate false memories. Using a similar approach, Hyman, Husband, and Billings (1995) found that 20 percent of their participants experienced false memories for other childhood experiences, such as an eventful birthday or the loss of a pet. To further examine the durability of false memories, Sharman and Scoboria (2009) examined the influence of imagination on people's confidence of particular events/

memories (i.e., imagination inflation; e.g., Garry et al., 2001; Sharman, Garry, & Hunt, 2005). The researchers found that imagining particular events leads to greater confidence that the events were genuine and subsequently resulted in clearer and more complete reports of the memory.

Further, not only has research highlighted that memories can be created for significant past events, but also researchers have suggested that false memories can influence future behaviour and attitudes (see Mazzoni & Scoboria, 2007, for review; Smeets, Merckelback, Horselenberg, & Jelec, 2005). For example, Scoboria, Mazzonie, and Jarry (2008) found that participants who had received suggesting information about a childhood reaction to food later showed a decreased preference for that particular food.

Porter, Yuille, and Lehman (1999) investigated whether false memories were possible for more stressful, potentially traumatic events. Parents of the participants were asked to provide information about several negative events (e.g., medical procedure, animal attack) that may have happened to their child. Participants then were questioned about a real and false event in three suggestive interviews over two weeks. Results indicated that 26 percent of participants came to fully recall the false event, while another 30 percent recalled something about it. Such findings have been used to challenge the validity of many "recovered" memories of alleged crimes, as discussed in Chapter 1. Evidence suggests that many such "recollections" were false memories generated during questionable police interviews or psychotherapy (e.g., Loftus, 2003a).

Increasingly sophisticated techniques are being developed for use information-gathering in criminal investigations.

In a more recent study, Porter, Demetrioff, McDougall, ten Brinke, and Wilson (2010) investigated whether the vulnerability of memory accuracy and susceptibility to misinformation was affected by the emotional content of visual scenes. Participants viewed an extremely positive or extremely negative scene and were then provided with misinformation pertaining to what they viewed. After a time delay (one week or one month), they were presented with a surprise memory test regarding the images they had seen, which highlighted two important trends. First, the memory of participants receiving misleading information was significantly less accurate. Further, relative to positive scenes, negative scenes were particularly impacted by the misleading information, suggesting a heightened susceptibility of misinformation effects (Frenda, Nichols, & Loftus, 2011).

Some have argued that in order to adequately study the factors influencing witness memory, studies must induce an activation mode of attention control (inducing increased heart rate, breathing, and blood pressure), which would best parallel the state of the bystander witness victim's physiological state (Deffenbacher, Bornstein, Penrod, & McGorty, 2004). Using this suggestion, Valentine and Mesout (2009) examined the effect of stress on participants' witness memory ability and the identification process after completing the Horror Labyrinth in the London Dungeon. As predicted, results indicated that high state of anxiety was associated with poorer accuracy at identifying the individual they witnessed within the labyrinth. Clearly, witness memory is highly malleable in the face of stress, trauma, misleading questions, and social pressure. As such, investigations in which such system variables are present can lead to questionable evidence and, ultimately, equivocal legal decisions.

Technology may play an increasingly important role in investigations in the upcoming decades as developments continue. For example, technologies available to identify the location of suspects during the criminal activity or other geoforensic methods may aid in assessing witness evidence. More specifically, by using technology that identifies a person's location through his or her cell phone at a particular time, for example, suspects misidentified as the perpetrator by a witness may be quickly dismissed. The rates of misidentifications through the use of locating devices further will highlight the fallibility of human memory.

IDENTIFICATION PROCEDURES

Lineups and Photo Arrays

When the police have a suspect, they usually ask any victim or other witnesses to identify him or her through the use of a lineup (called a **parade** in Great Britain) or a photo array (also called a photo spread). The use of photo arrays is now more frequent than the use of live lineups, perhaps because the suspect has no right to counsel when witnesses look through a "mug book" (in contrast to suspects' rights to have a lawyer present when they are placed in a lineup). Then, too, it is easier for the police to assemble a photo spread than arranging for a live lineup including four to seven innocent persons who bear some resemblance to the suspect. Despite an assumption that live lineups should be more effective than photo arrays, research findings have not indicated any consistent differences between the two methods (Brewer & Palmer, 2010; Cutler, Berman, Penrod, & Fisher, 1994), and the conclusion of prominent researchers is that the principles governing the responses of the witness are the same (Wells, Seelau, Rydell, & Luus, 1994). Box 6.1 presents a comparison of lineups and photo arrays.

As discussed by Lindsay et al. (2009), sequential lineups serve as an alternative to simultaneous presentation of suspects. By presenting suspects one at a time, the procedure disallows witnesses to compare suspects in relation to their memory (i.e., make "relative" judgments). While a concern of simultaneous lineups is high false-positive rates, research suggests that sequential lineups seem to significantly reduce these rates (17 percent) when compared to simultaneous lineups (43 percent; Lindsay & Wells, 1985). However, the superiority of sequential lineups still remains controversial because of the inconsistent findings with different populations (e.g., Brigham, Bennet, Meissner, & Mitchell, 2007; Malpass, Tredoux & McQuiston-Surrett, 2009). For example, a meta-analysis found that sequential lineups result in a smaller likelihood that a suspect is identified and is more indicative of guilt in comparison with simultaneous lineups (Steblay, Dysart, Fulero, & Lindsay, 2003).

Show-Ups

A special mention should be made of a procedure called the **show-up**—essentially a lineup composed of only one person (see Brewer & Palmer, 2010). Both psychologists, and the courts when considering the procedure have assumed that show-ups are inherently more suggestive than lineups that include four, five, or six foils (*Stovall v. Denno*, 1967, p. 302); these views are amplified later in the chapter. In fact, experimental psychologists who study the accuracy of memory are quite strong in their belief that the procedure is prejudicial (Malpass & Devine, 1983; Wells, Leippe, & Ostrom, 1979; Wells & Quinlivan, 2009; Yarmey, 1979). However, in a meta-analysis, Steblay, Dysart, Fulero, and Lindsay (2003) examined the differences between show-ups and lineups. First, the correct rejection rate was significantly higher in culprit-absent show-ups (85 percent) than lineups (57 percent). Second, overall witness accuracy was higher for show-ups (69 percent) than lineups (51 percent). Further, a set of studies by Gonzalez and his colleagues (Davis & Gonzalez, 1996; Gonzalez, Ellsworth, & Pembroke, 1993) found that show-ups resulted in a no greater number of mistaken identifications than did lineups and that show-up witnesses were more likely to say that the perpetrator was "not there" than were lineup witnesses. Gonzalez and his colleagues concluded on the basis of their research that the show-up is *not* the equivalent of a lineup with a functional size of one; instead, the witness uses a different mode of processing information when viewing a show-up. Witnesses appear to make more absolute judgments in show-up procedures as opposed to the relative judgments characteristic of lineups (Brewer & Palmer, 2010; Gonzalez et al., 1993). In fact, in a replication of the original study, Davis and Gonzalez (1996) found that 82 percent of the participants were willing to identify one of the persons in the lineup as the perpetrator, but in the show-up only 48 percent were willing to do so. Further, Steblay, Dysart, Fulero, and Lindsay (2003) conducted a meta-analysis that included over 3013 participants across the studies, yielding the following results:

1. In target-present conditions, show-ups (47 percent) and lineups (45 percent) yield approximately equal hit rates.
2. In target-absent conditions, show-ups produce higher level of correct rejections (85 percent) than lineups (57 percent).
3. False identifications were more likely during show-ups when the innocent suspect resembles the target perpetrator.

Evidently the relationship between accuracy rates and false identifications of show-ups and lineups is complex, and a debate remains.

However, the above results may not be as applicable in real-world settings; there, the implementation of a show-up reflects other differences from that of a lineup besides the sheer number of persons involved. The show-up is more likely to be carried out immediately following the apprehension of a suspect filling the witness's description; it may even occur at the crime scene. If the latter is the case, the suspect's clothes (are they the same as the perpetrator's?) and other qualities contribute to the decision by the witness, and would suggest a guilt presumption by the police. In contrast, lineups usually come later when the police have a definite suspect. In which situation is the danger of suggestion the strongest? Gonzalez and his colleagues argue that contrary to popular belief, the pressures on the witness to make an identification may actually be greater in a lineup procedure. The important point for police is to be aware that in each of these situations there are pressures on the witness to "help the police" and so specific instructions are necessary to try to mitigate the effects of suggestion.

The conclusion that show-ups produce fewer inaccurate identifications than lineups has not gone unchallenged. A University of Guelph study by Yarmey, Yarmey, and Yarmey (1996) drew the opposite conclusion, finding that six-person lineups were superior to show-ups over a 24-hour retention period; innocent lineup members were significantly less likely to be identified in the six-person lineup. The latter study differed from those by Gonzalez and his colleagues in several respects. The Yarmeys' study tested witnesses individually and used a successive lineup procedure. In Gonzalez's laboratory experiments, a staged crime before a class and a videotaped staged crime before groups of subjects served as stimulus materials.

The majority of psychologists who are experts on witness memory remain dubious that the

---

BOX 6.1   LINEUPS VERSUS PHOTO ARRAYS

The greatest threats to the accuracy of identifications—regardless of which procedure is used—may come from the actions of the police questioner. Cutler, Berman, Penrod, and Fisher (1994) have noted that an inherent distinction between a lineup and a photo array is image quality: "Common sense tells us that live lineups produce the clearest image" (p. 163). Further, photo arrays do not provide information about the behaviour of the offender, including his or her voice and gait. But the other side of the picture is that many advantages exist for the photo array or photo spread approach (Cutler et al., 1994):

1. Its immediate availability and selection of foils.
2. Its portability.
3. The control over the behaviour of lineup members. (In a live lineup a possibility always exists that a suspect will act in some way to draw the witness's attention. This can invalidate the lineup.)
4. The opportunity to examine a photo array repeatedly and over extended lengths of time.
5. Anxiety of witnesses is probably lessened when they use a mug book, in contrast to viewing their attacker through a one-way glass.

The careful analysis by Cutler and his colleagues of studies using different procedures concluded that "given the apparent comparability of lineups and photo arrays, it is not worth the trouble and expense to use live lineups" (Cutler et al., 1994, p. 180). However, a newer development may offer promise. Videotaping lineups is increasingly popular in police departments. Cutler and his colleagues noted that the use of videotaped lineups has advantages not present in either live lineups or photo arrays:

> With the use of large monitors, faces can be blown up larger than life. With the use of jog-and-roll dials, lineup members can be shown moving in slow motion, even on a frame-by-frame basis. Videotaped lineups can be paused on a specific frame, showing a lineup member in a specific body position. In addition, videotaped lineups can be shown repeatedly and for an unlimited amount of time. The equipment is simple enough to use that witnesses can be placed in control of some of the features, such as the jog-and-roll dial. (Cutler et al., 1994, p. 179)

---

show-up's convenience can overcome its potential for error, as Box 6.2 illustrates (see page 154).

On the basis of their research, Yarmey and his colleagues recommend that show-up encounters generally should not be used. Further research is needed to determine whether, as Gonzalez and his colleagues have proposed, the show-up procedure does not create as much suggestibility as its critics believe.

Common Errors

Ellison and Buckhout (1981), psychologists who have testified frequently about witness-identification issues, reported that the most biased lineup they ever encountered:

---

was composed of five white men and one Black man in an actual murder investigation in which a black suspect had been arrested. The excuse given was that the police wanted to make the lineup representative of the town's population, which had few Black people! Another "justification" was that there were no other people in the building. (p. 115)

Certainly, improper procedures used by the police can have the same effect on witnesses' reactions, regardless of whether the witness is viewing a lineup or scanning a mug book (Lindsay, 1994). We can summarize the frequent kinds of errors as follows:

1. Implying that the criminal is definitely one of the stimulus persons (as apparently occurred in the Sophonow case)
2. Pressuring the witness to make a choice (i.e., creating a demand characteristic)
3. Asking the witness specifically about the suspect while not asking those same questions about the foils (or what Wells and Seelau [1995] call a **confirmation bias**)
4. Encouraging a loose recognition threshold in the witness
5. Leaking the police officer's hunch, by making it obvious to the witness who is the suspect (Wells & Seelau, 1995, pp. 767–768)
6. After a witness's selection, telling the witness that his or her choice is the "right" one (Roper & Schwan, 2002); this increases witnesses' confidence that they are accurate when they later testify.

The fact that witnesses are highly susceptible to the powers of suggestion from police is demonstrated in a study by Wells and Bradfield (1998), who showed undergraduate-student participants a grainy videotape made by a department store surveillance camera; it portrayed a man entering the store. Participants were told to notice the man as they would be asked questions about him later. After viewing the tape, they were informed that the man had engaged in a robbery that went wrong and that a store security guard had been killed. Each participant was then shown a five-person photo spread, which did not contain the photograph of the man who had been seen in the surveillance tape. Each participant selected someone from the photo spread as the person in the video. Upon making this response, the participant was either told, "Good, you identified the actual suspect" (called confirming feedback), or "Actually, the suspect is No.___" (disconfirming feedback); one third of the subjects were given no feedback. Immediately thereafter, each participant answered a long set of questions, some of which assessed the effect of the feedback. Those who had been told, "Good, you identified the actual suspect" were far more confident in their choices than were those who were told the suspect was someone else; the latter feedback had a moderate detrimental effect on the subject's confidence. The mean confidence ratings were Confirming feedback, 5.4; No feedback, 4.0; Disconfirming feedback, 3.5 (on a seven-point Likert scale). This confidence-feedback relationship also has been found in other studies (e.g., Leippe, Eisenstadt, & Rauch, 2008). In addition, those given positive feedback felt they had a better view of the perpetrator, reported paying greater attention to the videotape, had an easier time making the identification, and were more willing to testify about their identification. The nature of feedback from an authority distorts the witness's reports, across a wide variety of phenomena.

The use of such responses by police questioners is particularly disturbing, given the emerging conclusion from psychological research that the act of lineup identification is largely governed by a **relative judgment process** (Wells, 1984b, 1993); that is, the witness selects the stimulus person who most resembles, in the witness's memory, the perpetrator of the crime. If the real culprit is present, this procedure is effective, but if the lineup contains only foils, an innocent person who resembles the perpetrator is likely to be chosen. For example, Malpass and Devine (1981) conducted a study in which they staged a crime and then asked witnesses to pick out the culprit from a lineup. When the actual culprit was *not* in the lineup and when witnesses were *not* warned of this, 78 percent of the subjects chose one of the innocent persons. When warned about the possibility of the perpetrator's absence, only 33 percent chose someone from the culprit-absent lineup. Brewer and Wells (2006) also found support for this trend. The latter figure (33 percent) is important. In fact, other research (Wells, 1993) confirmed that about one-third of witnesses or more select an innocent person in a culprit-absent photo spread or lineup, even when told that the culprit might not be present. As such, a commonly held view is that relative judgments are most problematic in target-absent lineups as opposed to target-present lineups (e.g., Pozzulo, Crescini, & Lemieux, 2008).

Operational Rules to Improve Identifications

It is clear that the procedures used by some police have the potential of increasing the rate of false identifications (Loftus, 1993a; Yarmey, 2003). As research and case studies emerge highlighting the startling number of false witness identifications that have occurred (The Innocence Project, 2010), many researchers and research groups have focused their attention on reducing the harmful effects of false witness identifications. For example, the American Psychology/Law Society (division 41 of the American Psychological Association) gathered a committee of experts to examine the current state of literature and identify problematic areas. Resulting from this collaboration, Wells and colleagues (1998) published an article that addressed the concerning aspects of identification procedures in both Canada and the United States and suggested the application of four straightforward rules can reduce such errors (see also Wells & Seelau, 1995).

Rule 1. "The person who conducts the lineup or photo spread should not be aware of which member of the lineup or photo spread is the suspect" (Wells et al., 1998, p. 627). Customarily, the detective

who has handled the case administers the lineup. The problem is that this officer, knowing the identity of the suspect, may communicate this knowledge, *even without intending to do so*. A variation in eye contact with the witness, or a subtle shift in body position or facial expression, may be enough to communicate feedback to the witness (who often is unsure and hence seeks guidance and confirmation from the detective). And, as we know, some detectives are not reluctant to tell witnesses when their choices identified the suspect or even explicitly draw attention to the suspect. But if a **double-blind procedure** is used, in which the lineup administrator is unaware of the "correct" answer, neither subtle nor overt communication would be made, and a purer estimate of the witness's confidence level could be determined.

Rule 2. "Eyewitnesses should be told explicitly that the perpetrator might not be in the lineup or photo spread and therefore eyewitnesses should not feel that they must make an identification. They also should be told that the person administering the lineup does not know which person is the suspect in the case" (Wells et al., 1998, p. 629). Consider the reaction of a witness when he or she is shown a lineup; it probably is something like this: "They wouldn't have gone to this trouble unless they have a suspect. So one of these guys must have done it." (Given a book containing several hundred mug shots, the witness is less likely to have this reaction, but in contrast, the witness faced with a mug book usually assumes that *everyone* in it is a previous offender.) Empirical studies, analyzed by Steblay (1997), find that an explicit warning reduces the rate of incorrect identifications when the offender is not in the lineup.

Rule 3. "The suspect should not stand out in the lineup or photo array as being different from the distractors based on the eyewitness's previous description of the culprit or based on other factors that would draw extra attention to the suspect" (Wells et al., 1998, p. 630). In previous lineups the ways that the suspect stood out included:

1. He or she was the only one who fit the verbal description that the witness had given to the police earlier (Lindsay & Wells, 1980).
2. He or she was the only one dressed in the type of clothes worn by the perpetrator (Lindsay, Wallbridge, & Drennan, 1987).

3. The suspect's photo was taken from a different angle than the foils' photos (Buckhout & Friere, 1975, as cited by Wells & Seelau, 1995).

Wells and his colleagues emphasize that distractors should not necessarily be selected to look like the police detectives' prime suspect; instead, they should be chosen to match the description of the criminal given by the witness. Note that this recommendation goes against the common police procedure: Police choose foils to resemble the suspect, rather than resembling the witness's description of the offender.

Rule 4. "A clear statement should be taken from the eyewitness at the time of the identification and prior to any feedback as to his or her confidence that the identified person is the actual culprit" (Wells et al., 1998, p. 635). Repeated questioning by authorities (police, investigators, prosecutors) may increase the confidence of the witness's answers (Shaw, 1996; Shaw & McClure, 1996), reduce their accuracy (Krahenbuhl, Blades, & Elser, 2009), or increase suggestibility (Chan & LaPaglia, 2011). More specifically, repeated interviewing or questioning (in both misleading and unbiased manners) can create more opportunities for the recall of misleading information (Melnyk & Bruck, 2004; Roediger et al., 1996). By the time witnesses reach the witness box at the trial, their behaviour may be quite different from their initial response. The initial levels of confidence should be recorded.

To summarize, the committee provided the following recommendations:

1. Double-blind lineup testing should be utilized.
2. Instructions should be given to the witness that the lineup may not contain the culprit.
3. Foils should be selected based on the witness' provided verbal description.
4. Confidence should be taken into consideration during the identification (and should be recorded).

Fortunately, the legal system has acknowledged the issues raised and recommendations provided by this committee of experts and has used this valuable information to improve legislation, interviewing processes, and training. In response to the above guidelines (and especially Rule 4), Saul Kassin (1998b) has suggested one more rule: that the identification process (especially the lineup and the interaction between the detective and the witness) be videotaped, so that lawyers, the judge, and the jury can later assess for themselves whether the results of the procedure by police are accurate.

The **evaluation research** role of psychologists is relevant in terms of other approaches that police use to generate information from witnesses. Victims and witnesses may be asked to describe the perpetrator, after which a sketch artist will draw the criminal based on this description. Traditionally, police have used the **Identikit**, a collection of various facial characteristics from which witnesses can choose to put together the lips, eyes, and hair of the criminal. More recently, computer-generated faces have replaced the Identikit.

The problem with these procedures is that it is much harder than we think to recall individual facial features of a person, especially after only a limited opportunity to observe them. Further, features interact; when using the Identikit, a nose will look different when the witness changes the eyes. In reviewing the literature on this issue, Wells (1993) concluded that the identification of faces by a witness is a **holistic process** rather than an analysis of component features, meaning that face recognition is an act in which the relationship of features and the general appearance serve as determinants so that piecemeal analyses are not productive (e.g., Frowd, Bruce, Smith, & Hancock, 2008; Wells & Hasel, 2007). Psychologists should continue to evaluate such procedures and advise police departments and the courts on their effectiveness.

PUBLIC POLICY ISSUES

In Chapter 1 it was noted that psychology and the law often are in conflict and that psychology's attempts to have an impact on the legal system sometimes have failed. Despite the various evidence suggesting the fallibility of witness memory, some have argued that neither the police nor the courts at present have been very responsive to input from psychological research, as psychologists have trying to inform the legal system for over a century now (Doyle, 2005; Wells & Quinlivan, 2009). Wells concluded: "To date, the scientific literature on witness memory has not been a driving force behind the legal system's assumptions, procedures, and decisions regarding witness memory" (1995, p. 730). On the other hand, as mentioned in Chapter 1, influential agencies such as the National Judicial Institute based in Ottawa have been

inviting psychological researchers (such as lineup researcher R. C. L. Lindsay of Queen's University) to train members of the judiciary in recent years. Further, training in forensic interviewing by people such as John Yuille is being welcomed by some police forces. Hence the situation may be changing for the better. Two ways to continue to influence this situation are to change legislation and to educate jurists. This section discusses three approaches to changes in public policy: recent statute-of-limitation laws, trial judges' decisions on admitting psychologists as expert witnesses, and relevant Supreme Court decisions.

Statute-of-Limitation Laws

Traditionally, crimes such as sexual violence were "hidden" in that most victims chose not to report their experiences for years (if ever), because of embarrassment, fear of the offender, fear of being disbelieved, or fear of being blamed for the incident (Porter et al., 2003a). In fact, most victims of sexual assault still do not report a recent sexual assault experience (e.g., Kennedy & Yuille, 1999; Statistics Canada, 2009). It is only recently that Canadian courts began to recognize that many crime victims remain silent about the incident for a lengthy period of time, if they report it at all (as noted by the Supreme Court of Canada in *R. v. W. [R.],* 1992). As such, Canada has no **statute of limitations** to forestall the prosecution of historical offences. This perspective encouraged people to report historical crimes and brought many guilty perpetrators to justice. On the other hand, in the United States, legislative decisions concerning the statute of limitations in child sexual abuse cases have disregarded the complexity of psychological viewpoints on recovered memories. As discussed earlier in this text, some alleged victims of abuse as children do not recall the abuse until much later in life; previously, such claims had to be brought forward within a specific period of time after the act in order to be responded to by the criminal justice system. Legislators and judges have accepted the concept of "**delayed discovery**" (Boland & Quirk, 1994; Bulkley & Horwitz, 1994). The goal of this liberalization of the statutes of limitation was to provide opportunities for the delayed but legitimate claims of child abuse to be reported. But in light of the recent heightened concern about such cases (e.g., Loftus, 2003b), the legal changes may encourage false reports to be brought forward. Some psychologists (Bulkley & Horwitz,

1994; Ernsdorff & Loftus, 1993) have proposed several changes, ranging from complete exclusion of cases based on claims of recovered memory to an imposition of a higher burden of proof in civil cases.

Thus, an absence of a statute of limitations in Canada and some jurisdictions within the United States allows victims to report crimes long after their occurrence.

Judges' Decisions on the Admissibility of Expert Testimony

Chapter 1 recounted the efforts of Hugo Münsterberg more than 100 years ago to educate trial judges about the relevance of psychological expertise when fact finders evaluated witness accuracy. But consider that Münsterberg also arrogantly wrote, "It seems indeed astonishing that the work of justice is ever carried out in the courts without ever consulting the psychologist and asking him for all the aid which the modern study of suggestion can offer" (1908, p. 194). It is not surprising that the legal community (e.g., Wigmore, 1909) treated such advocacy with disdain then, and—if not disdain—at least ambivalence now. Despite these conflicts, expert witnesses do have something to offer with respect to witness interview system variables and how witness interviews can be conducted to reduce bias (Seelau & Wells, 1995).

Expert testimony about the determinants of witness accuracy is an example of what Monahan and Walker (1988) have called **social framework testimony**; that is, it presents "general conclusions from social science research" in order to assist the fact finder (whether that is judge or jury) "in determining factual issues in a specific case" (Monahan & Walker, 1988, p. 470). As noted in Chapter 2, a judge's decision to admit or exclude scientific testimony in Canada is usually based on a combination of four criteria: the relevance of the evidence, the necessity of the evidence (and the extent to which the expert might unduly influence the jury), the absence of any exclusionary rule, and qualification of the expert. But in real life, matters are not so straightforward:

From a legal and public policy perspective ... there is a problem to the extent that the variation in admissibility decisions is attributable more to ambiguity in the criteria for admissibility, the idiosyncratic views of the trial judge, or the characteristics of the jurisdiction than it is to the specific characteristics or needs of the case. (Wells, 1995, p. 729)

Also noted in Chapter 2, the Canadian courts have been reluctant to allow expert testimony on witness testimony (recall that Dr. Yarmey's evidence was excluded in *R. v. McIntosh and McCarthy*, 1997). How can psychologists convince trial judges of the importance of their findings? Two relevant issues are reviewed here: the tendency for fact finders not to be adequately informed on the topic and the high level of consistency in conclusions among experts.

How Accurate Is the Knowledge of Jurors?

Until the mid-1970s, expert testimony in cases involving the testimony of witnesses was rarely admitted; among reasons given by judges were that "jurors already know all this" and that experts would "waste the court's time" (Leippe, 1995, p. 912). But jurors often are in error in two respects: They overestimate the level of accuracy of witnesses and they do not appreciate the impact of environmental factors on reducing accuracy. They fail to consider the impact of system variables such as those described in this chapter. People usually begin with the assumption that the memory of an adult witness is accurate (Leippe, 1995) and hence they expect a far greater percentage of witnesses to be accurate than are found in the studies that create a mock crime and determine levels of witness accuracy (Brigham & Bothwell, 1983; Lindsay, Wells, & Rumpel, 1981; Lindsay, Wells, & O'Connor, 1989; Wells, 1984a; Wells & Leippe, 1981). Further, research has suggested that observers are actually poor at detecting truthful and fabricated accounts of crime (e.g., Peace, Porter, & Almon, 2011; see Vrij, Granhag, & Porter, 2011).

An assumption that "jurors already know all of this" clearly is unwarranted. Four different surveys came to the same conclusion: "that much of what is known about eyewitness memory—that eyewitness experts might talk about in court—is not common sense" (Leippe, 1995, p. 921). Specific findings of these surveys documented this conclusion, as follows:

1. Deffenbacher and Loftus (1982) gave a set of multiple-choice questions on variables associated with witness accuracy to university students and nonstudents with and without jury experience. At least half the respondents chose

the wrong answer (i.e., an answer in conflict with the direction of empirical findings) on questions about the confidence-accuracy relationship, cross-racial bias in identification, and weapon focus (the victim's tendency to pay attention to the gun pointed at him or her and to ignore every other stimulus).

2. Using law students, legal professionals, undergraduate students, and adults as participants, Yarmey and Jones (1983) found that respondents did not recognize the empirically derived relationships between level of accuracy and factors such as a witness's confidence, the presence of a weapon, and the status of the witness (i.e., that police are no better at identification than are other witnesses).

3. Using the 13 empirical findings deemed by experts to be reliable enough to testify about, Kassin and Barndollar (1992) found that significantly fewer students and adults than experts considered the findings as reliable. In 4 of the 13 reliable findings, the majority of the students and adults disagreed with the experts.

4. Brigham and Wolfskeil (1983) surveyed trial lawyers and found, not surprisingly, that prosecutors were much more likely to believe that witnesses were accurate than were criminal defence lawyers.

Recent research has revealed that jurors, judges, and the general public continue to remain

©Alamy Creative/Alamy

Psychological research shows that the presence of a weapon and degree of violence associated with a crime may affect the witness's ability to recall the event.

unknowledgeable about witness (in)accuracy and (un)reliability. For example, researchers have examined the amount of knowledge of U.S. and Norwegian judges on a series of topics critical to criminal trials regarding witness memory and found that both samples had limited knowledge on important factors surrounding witness memory (Magnussen et al., 2008; Magnussen, Melinder, Stridebeck, & Raja, 2010; Wise & Safer, 2004).

Further, when examining the similarities between juror, judge, and law enforcement professionals' knowledge of witness memory, Benton et al. (2006) found that these individuals had conflicting ideas in comparison to witness experts. For example, jurors deviated from witness experts' opinions on 87 percent of the issues, suggesting the use of witness experts may be important within the courtroom. An additional factor that significantly impacts the juror's decision making is credibility assessment (for further discussion see Chapter 5). It widely is recognized that human decision making is subject to a host of biases that often are irrational (e.g., Kahneman & Tversky, 1982). For example, with estimated error rates of 45 percent, credibility assessments prove to be much more fallible than the judiciary assume (Bond & DePaulo, 2006). Willis and Todorov (2006) demonstrated that judgments made in as little as 100 milliseconds are often retained for longer periods of time during which confidence increases (see also Porter & ten Brinke, 2009). Credibility assessments in the modern context can be biased depending on the presence of particular facial characteristics. For example, characteristic facial features associated with trustworthiness include "babyfacedness," symmetry, and attractiveness (Bull, 2006; Bull & Vine, 2003; Zebrowitz, Voinescu, & Collins, 1996). Specifically, Todorov et al. (2008) found that facial characteristics, such as higher eyebrows, more pronounced cheekbones, shallow nose sellion, and wider chins, were associated with high trustworthiness ratings. Similarly, certain (presumably untrustworthy) faces are perceived to be congruent with the faces of certain criminal types such as a rapist or murderer (Bull & McAlpine, 1998; Dumas & Testé, 2006). As a result, the types of credibility assessments jurors make likely influence the way in which subsequent decisions are made within the courtroom.

But this wealth of empirical findings is not enough. As Leippe (1995) has pointed out, even though the empirical relationships may not fit "common sense" when they are presented to jurors, the reaction of the jurors often is that "we knew these things all along." This **hindsight bias** (Slovic & Fischhoff, 1977) may create problems for the admissibility of expert testimony, and Leippe (1995) wisely suggests that requests to admit expert testimony must speak explicitly about the possibility of hindsight bias in trial fact finders.

A second argument to be used in trying to persuade judges to admit psychological testimony is the consistency of agreement among experts on the phenomenon. A survey by Kassin, Ellsworth, and Smith (1989, 1994) of 63 active psychological researchers determined just which specific phenomena, in their opinion, were reliable enough to testify about in court. Box 6.2 describes those findings that at least 70 percent of this sample felt were reliable.

These are not idle speculations; they are based, for most of the findings, on a multitude of studies using a variety of methods and types of subjects. As Leippe observed:

In matters of reliability, a number of witness research findings score highly. They are replicable, the opposite findings (as opposed to simply null findings) are seldom reported, the research has high internal validity, and the settings and measures often have high mundane realism in terms of approximating certain witness situations. A strong argument can be made for reliability and validity. (Leippe, 1995, p. 918)

However, some psychologists have questioned this statement because of a lack of consistency they consider necessary for use in the courtroom (Egeth, 1993; Elliot, 1993; Konecni & Ebbesen, 1986).

BOX 6.2   WHAT IS RELIABLE ENOUGH TO TESTIFY ABOUT?

The following are the findings advocated by at least 70 percent of the researcher-experts surveyed by Kassin, Ellsworth, and Smith (1989), that are rated as reliable enough to include in courtroom testimony. These findings were replicated in a follow-up study by Kassin et al. in 2001 (Note: percentages of experts rating the statement as "reliable enough" in 1989 and 2001 are given in parentheses beside each statement.)

1. Wording of questions: A witness's testimony about an event can be affected by how the questions put to that witness are worded. (97 percent; 98 percent)
2. Lineup instructions: Police instructions can affect a witness's willingness to make an identification and/or the likelihood that he or she will identify a particular person. (95 percent; 98 percent)
3. Postevent information: Witness testimony about an event often reflects not only what the person actually saw but information the person obtained later on. (87 percent; 94 percent)
4. Accuracy-confidence: A witness's confidence is not a good predictor of his or her identification accuracy. (87 percent; 87 percent)
5. Attitudes and expectations: A witness's perception and memory for an event may be affected by his or her attitudes and expectations. (87 percent; 92 percent)
6. Exposure time: The less time a witness has to observe an event, the less well he or she will remember it. (85 percent; 81 percent)

7. Unconscious transference: Witnesses sometimes identify as a culprit someone they have seen in another situation or context. (85 percent; 81 percent)
8. Show-ups: The use of a one-person show-up instead of a full lineup increases the risk of misidentification. (83 percent; 74 percent)
9. Forgetting curve: The rate of memory loss for an event is greatest right after the event, and then levels off over time. (83 percent; 83 percent)
10. Cross-racial/white: White witnesses are better at identifying other white people than they are at identifying black people. (79 percent; 90 percent)
11. Lineup fairness: The more the members of a lineup resemble the suspect, the higher is the likelihood that identification of the suspect is accurate. (77 percent; 70 percent)
12. Time estimation: Witnesses tend to overestimate the duration of events. (75 percent; not asked)
13. Stress: Very high levels of stress impair the accuracy of witness testimony. (71 percent; 60 percent)

Court Decisions and Recommendations

In Canada, the 2001 Sophonow Inquiry should be considered the major milestone in the court's agreement with and advocacy of research-based practices by police with witnesses. Justice Cory's recommendations concerning lineup procedures, for example, virtually mirror the major conclusions of psychologists in the area. Further, Justice Cory recommended that trial judges must emphasize the potential frailties of witness testimony. A critical development in the United States was a 1999 report to the Department of Justice commission by the Office of the Attorney General. This report, authored by a group of police officers, witness researchers, defence lawyers, and prosecutors, provides national guidelines concerning the gathering of witness evidence at all stages of criminal investigation (see Wells, Malpass, Lindsay, Fisher, Turtle, & Fulero, 2000, for a description of the psychological foundations of the report).

But the Sophonow Inquiry and U.S. Department of Justice reports were a long time coming. Traditionally, many of the major legal decisions of the higher courts completely contradict the empirical findings of psychologists . One dealt with the question of when suggestion becomes so strong that it intrudes on the right of defendants to fair treatment. In attempts of identifying the perpetrator of a series of sexual assault charges, Ivan Henry was shown to witnesses in a lineup procedure while being restrained by three police officers in uniform. After spending 27 years in jail, Ivan was acquitted for wrongful conviction. Further, in the case of *Stovall v. Denno* (1967), a man named Paul Behrendt was stabbed to death in the presence of his wife; she was so severely wounded that her survival was questionable. Stovall, a suspect, was brought to Ms. Behrendt's hospital room in handcuffs, two days after the crime, and in this show-up circumstance, the victim identified him as the perpetrator. This procedure was justified by the authorities because it was uncertain whether the victim would survive, and, under such conditions, the victim could not come to the police station. Stovall appealed his conviction, but the U.S. Supreme Court ruled that the procedure was not a violation of due process because—although the procedure was suggestive—it was not "unnecessarily" suggestive. That is, a show-up procedure would be excluded if it were "unnecessary"—if the circumstances had permitted the use of a lineup as a viable alternative.

Although we may be able to agree about the justification in this case, the Court has not taken a position on how suggestive procedures can be reduced or avoided; in fact, as Wells and Seelau (1995) observed: "The Court has not articulated some simple and effective minimal requirements for lineups and photospreads for the vast majority of cases for which there is no necessity for suggestive procedures" (p. 785).

The second difference between the U.S. Supreme Court and experimental psychology deals with the relationship of witnesses' accuracy levels and their levels of confidence. In *Neil v. Biggers* (1972), the Court concluded that even the pressure of unnecessarily suggestive procedures by the police didn't mean that the testimony of the witness had to be excluded from the trial *if* the procedure did not reflect a substantial possibility of a mistaken identification. (In this case, a rape victim identified her attacker in a show-up seven months after the crime occurred.) The criteria that the Court, in the above decision and in *Manson v. Braithwaite* (1977), felt increased the likelihood of an accurate identification were the following:

1. The opportunity for witnesses to view the criminal at the time of the crime
2. The length of time between the crime and the later identification
3. The level of certainty shown by the witnesses at the identification
4. The witness's degree of attention during the crime
5. The accuracy of the witness's prior description of the criminal.

For example, if little time had passed since the crime, even a suggestive procedure should not have had an impact and it could be assumed that the witness was on target. Most of these reflect plausible assumptions, but they are questionable, for several reasons. Leading questions (e.g., "You had a pretty long time to look at him, didn't you?") can alter the witnesses' responses about their degree of attention and opportunity to view the criminal—and, indirectly, can then alter their level of confidence. Second, the initial relationship between different witnesses' levels of accuracy and their levels of confidence about their own accuracy usually is quite low (Brewer, Keast, & Rishworth, 2002; Bothwell, Deffenbacher, & Brigham, 1987; Cutler & Penrod, 1989; Penrod & Cutler, 1995; see Brewer & Wells, 2011 for review).

A third reason for concern about the U.S. Supreme Court's criteria is that—contrary to the assumptions of most jurors—the confidence of a witness is malleable; that is, events that happen after the initial identification can cause the witness to become more or less confident (Wells et al., 1998). Studies by Luus and Wells (1994) and Wells and Bradfield (1998) that certain suggestive procedures used by police found can increase the confidence of witnesses without changing their accuracy (Wells, Rydell, & Seelau, 1993). If a police officer tells a witness that her choice from the lineup is "the guy we think did it," such a reaction quite likely increases her confidence, without affecting her accuracy. And once the confidence of the witness is heightened by the feedback, the witness's assessments of some of the other criteria are endangered; recall that the Wells and Bradfield (1998) subjects who received positive feedback reported that they had paid more attention to the video; such feedback could colour witnesses' self-reports about several of the *Neil v. Biggers* criteria.

Thus, witness confidence should be considered a system variable (i.e., police questioning procedures can affect it) as well as being an estimator variable. But jurors are ordinarily not aware of this; in fact, "jurors appear to overestimate the accuracy of identifications, fail to differentiate accurate from inaccurate witnesses—because they rely so heavily on witness confidence, which is relatively nondiagnostic—and are generally insensitive to other factors that influence identification accuracy" (Wells et al., 1998, p. 624).

SUMMARY

This chapter attempts to demonstrate that the field of psychology has much to offer police officials who wish to reduce bias in witness interviews. Some of the suggestions in this chapter stem from the conclusions of empirical research; others are common sense principles derived from the observation of police investigations. Some police detectives will object to representatives from another discipline "telling them how to run their business," and psychologists always need to remember the pressures and constraints on police in conducting crime investigations. In fact, the field of psychology needs to do feasibility studies to determine what factors affect the level of receptivity of police to suggestions from psychologists.

Psychologists must remember that the goals for the forensic application of their findings may differ from the goals of testing a theory in the laboratory. The results of laboratory studies may not generalize to the real world of crime victims and witnesses, who may have high levels of stress and concerns about the impact of their testimony (Kebbell & Wagstaff, 1997; Wells, Memon, & Penrod, 2006; Yuille, 1989, 1993; Yuille, Ternes, & Cooper, 2010). Criticisms by some experimental psychologists that high levels of stress inhibit accuracy of memory may conflict with the experience of police officers, who find that real witnesses often have good recall for many of the details of armed robberies, such as the weapons used and statements made by the criminals (Christianson & Hubinette, 1993) (not to mention conflicting with the finding of field studies by Yuille and others that stress does not necessarily impair memory). Although stress may have an adverse effect on overall performance, it may improve the recall for specific relevant information (Kebbell & Wagstaff, 1997; Porter & Peace, 2007).

Further, the often repeated conclusion that a witness's high degree of confidence may not reflect an equivalent level of accuracy fails to account for various other confounding factors (Behrman & Richards, 2005; Lindsay, Read, & Sharma, 1998; Robert & Higham, 2002). For example, Robert and Higham (2002) found that the relationship between witnesses' confidence and accuracy was high for relevant information as opposed to peripheral information. In addition, Lindsay, Read, and Sharma (1998) found that the confidence-accuracy relationship depended on particular conditions.

The research findings described in this chapter are only a beginning to the task of helping police improve their investigative procedures with witnesses. For example, the effects of police officers' provision of feedback to witnesses about the "correctness" of their identifications, as illustrated in the study by Wells and Bradfield (1998) described earlier, needs to be extended to other types of subjects in other types of situations, and particularly to actual crime victims who are given disconfirming feedback by the police investigator.

KEY TERMS

cognitive interview, p. 141

confirmation bias, p. 148

delayed discovery, p. 151

demand characteristics, p. 140

double-blind procedure, p. 150

encoding, p. 144

estimator variables, p. 133

evaluation research, p. 151

false memories, p. 144

foils, p. 138

hindsight bias, p. 154

holistic process, p. 151

Identikit, p. 151

leading questions, p. 140

lineup, p. 136

memory testimony, p. 133

parade, p. 146

photo array, p. 136

postevent misinformation paradigm, p. 144

relative judgment process, p. 148

retrieval, p. 144

show-up, p. 146

social framework testimony, p. 152

Sophonow Inquiry, p. 136

statute of limitations, p. 151

system variables, p. 133

unconscious transference, p. 140

SUGGESTED READINGS

Brewer, N., & Wells, G. L. (2011). Eyewitness identification. *Current Directions in Psychological Science, 20*, 24–27.

This comprehensive, up-to-date review provides a thorough discussion on the various variables influencing eyewitness identifications and the effect of postidentification indicators.

Cutler, B. L., & Penrod, S. D. (1995). *Mistaken identification: The eyewitness, psychology, and the law*. New York: Cambridge University Press.

This comprehensive account presents psychological research on eyewitness accuracy, and a good description of errors in estimator variables (not covered in this chapter) as well as system variables.

Devenport, J. L., Penrod, S. D., & Cutler, B. L. (1997). Eyewitness identification evidence: Evaluating common sense evaluations. *Psychology, Public Policy, and Law, 3*, 338–361.

This useful review evaluates the safeguards developed by the legal system to protect defendants from being convicted falsely on the basis of mistaken identifications. The article concludes that many of these safeguards are not as effective as the legal system assumes them to be.

Fisher, R. P. (1995). Interviewing victims and witnesses of crime. *Psychology, Public Policy, and Law, 1*, 732–764.

The definitive article on the ways that psychologists can assist the police to improve the quality of their interviews with crime witnesses.

Fisher, R. P., & Schreiber, N. (2007). Interviewing protocols to improve eyewitness memory. In M. Toglia, J. Reed, D. Ross, & R. Lindsay (Eds.) *The handbook of eyewitness psychology: Memory for events*, (pp. 53–80). Mahwah, NJ: Erlbaum Associates.

This is an important chapter highlighting valuable interviewing approaches that can improve eyewitness memory and reduce misidentification.

Loftus, E. F., & Ketcham, K. (1991). *Witness for the defense: The accused, the eyewitness, and the expert who puts memory on trial*. New York: St. Martin's Press.

This immensely readable work recounts some of the cases (including those of Steve Titus, Ted Bundy, and Ivan the Terrible) for which Elizabeth Loftus, premiere researcher–expert witness, was asked to testify for the defence regarding the inaccuracy of eyewitnesses' testimony.

Sporer, S. L. (1993). Eyewitness identification accuracy, confidence, and decision times in simultaneous and sequential lineups. *Journal of Applied Psychology, 78*, 22–33.

In contrast to the standard lineup procedure, a sequential lineup procedure has the witness view only one person at a time, deciding whether that person is the offender before seeing the remaining members of the lineup. This article is one of several that find that sensitivity to the presence or absence of the culprit in the lineup is greater when the sequential procedure is used rather than the traditional simultaneous procedure.

Steblay, N. M. (1997). Social influence in eyewitness recall: A meta-analytic review of lineup instruction effects. *Law and Human Behavior, 21*, 283–297.

This review and analysis of 18 studies assesses the impact of biased police lineup instructions; it contains a useful bibliography.

Wells, G. L., & Olson, E. (2003). Eyewitness testimony. *Annual Reviews of Psychology, 54,* 277–295.

This article is a thorough review of the psychological research on eyewitness identification and provides an exhaustive discussion on the various dynamics influencing eyewitness identification.

Wells, G. L., & Quinlivan, D. S. (2009). Suggestive eyewitness identification procedures and the Supreme Court's reliability test in light of eyewitness science: 30 years later. *Law and Human Behavior,* 33, 1–24.

A discussion of previous legal cases accentuating the fallibility of memory and the courts' response to the accumulating evidence emphasizing the weaknesses of eyewitness identifications.

Wells, G. L., & Seelau, E. (1995). Eyewitness identification: Psychological research and legal policy on lineups. *Psychology, Public Policy, and the Law, 1,* 765–791.

Among the many authoritative articles by Gary Wells, this one applies what forensic psychologists know to the recent court decisions and legislative acts.

Wells, G. L., Small, M., Penrod, S., Malpass, R. S., Fulero, S. M., & Brimacombe, C. A. E. (1998). Eyewitness identification procedures: Recommendations for lineups and photospreads. *Law and Human Behavior, 22,* 603–647.

The first scientific review paper of the American Psychology-Law Society, this article provides a detailed rationale for its four recommendations for improving the construction and administration of lineups and photo arrays. In October 1999, the U.S. Department of Justice published a manual for police and prosecutors, titled *Eyewitness Evidence: A Guide for Law Enforcement,* that supported most of the recommendations of this review paper.

WEBSITES

The Association in the Defence of the Wrongfully Convicted: **http://www.aidwyc.org/public_html/index.html**

Innocence McGill: **http://www.mcgill.ca/innocence/history**

The Innocence Project (US): **http://www.innocenceproject.org**

UBC Law Innocence Project: **http://www.innocenceproject.law.ubc.ca**

York University Innocence Project: **http://www.osgoode.yorku.ca/clinics-experiential/clinical-education/innocence-project**

Police Interrogations and Confessions

> *The voluntary Confession of the Party in Interest is reckoned the best Evidence.*
>
> —Lord Chief Baron Gilbert (1754)

THE IMPORTANCE OF A CONFESSION

A **confession** by a suspect—an admission of guilt—is among the most powerful evidence that can be presented at the defendant's trial (Kassin, 1997a; Kassin et al., 2010a), as acknowledged by the Supreme Court of Canada in *R. v. Hodgson* (1998, para. 14). Because of its great impact in legal decision making, the courts need to be wary about the circumstances under which a confession was obtained and ensure its reliability. In the ground-breaking case ***R. v. Oickle*** (2000), the Canadian Supreme Court stated: "In sum, because of the criminal justice system's overriding concern not to convict the innocent, a confession will not be admissible if it is made under circumstances that raise a reasonable doubt as to voluntariness."

In the *Oickle* case, the police interrogators misled Richard Oickle during an investigation of eight fires around Waterville, Nova Scotia, by telling him that he had "failed" a polygraph examination and that it was an infallible technique. Before the polygraph examination, Oickle was informed of his rights to silence, to legal counsel, and to leave the interview at any time. He also was told that while the interpretation of the polygraph results was not admissible in court, anything he said during the examination was admissible. At the end of the examination, the polygrapher informed Oickle that he had "failed" the exam and, after nine hours of further questioning, he confessed to setting most of the fires. While the trial judge in Nova Scotia ruled that his statements were admissible and convicted him on all counts, the Court of Appeal excluded the confessions and entered an acquittal. Finally, the Supreme Court of Canada restored the conviction. Six of the seven Supreme Court justices ruled that the confession by Oickle was acceptable:

The police conducted a proper interrogation. The accused was fully apprised of his rights at all times.

The police questioning, while persistent and often accusatorial, was never hostile, aggressive, or intimidating. In this context, the alleged inducements offered by the police do not raise a reasonable doubt as to the confession's voluntariness. (*R. v. Oickle*, 2000, summary para. 6)

Apparently, the Court was not fazed by the police trickery in relation to its influence on Oikle's decision to confess. Nonetheless, the dissenting judge, Madame Justice Louise Arbour, strongly disagreed with her colleagues. She seemed shocked by what she viewed as the unfair deception, threats, and inducements by the police. In her dissenting opinion, she wrote that a "failed" polygraph test is likely to be perceived as simply a confession by another name: "Given the unparalleled weight attributed to confessions, I believe that the prejudicial effect that flows from an accused's reference to his 'failed' polygraph test is overwhelming" (*R. v. Oickle*, para. 146). Clearly, she felt that the confession should have been ruled inadmissible.

The quest for a confession from a suspect by police and prosecutors can be fierce. In their zeal to obtain an admission of guilt, police may intimidate not only guilty suspects but also innocent ones. Not all confessions represent the truth, and one of the tasks of the forensic psychologist—among the most difficult ones—is to try to convince law enforcement authorities to re-examine their interrogation procedures, and as a result, perhaps reduce their clearance rate (Snook et al., 2010). In fact, the Supreme Court of Canada has described situations in which "police trickery … is so appalling as to shock the community" and confessions obtained in this fashion should be excluded (*R. v. Oickle*, 2000, para. 67). Although the word "shock" may seem highly subjective, it is clear that the police can never act in a way that contravenes the Canadian Charter of Rights and Freedoms (1982), requiring that suspects be informed of their right to retain and instruct counsel, and the common-law right to remain silent and not make incriminating statements. The Newfoundland Provincial Court case *R. v. McLean* (2003) exemplifies this point. On September 19, 2002, a dog was found hanging with a chain around its neck from a tree on a path in Corner Brook. Raymond McLean was charged with unlawfully killing the dog, contrary to section 445 of the Criminal Code. McLean gave two separate confession statements to detectives with the Royal Newfoundland Constabulary. The Crown planned to introduce the two statements as evidence at trial. However, the defence argued that his statements should be considered inadmissible because they were false confessions resulting from false promises by police (that he would not get jail time) and in violation of his right to contact counsel in accordance with section 10 of the Charter. Judge Gorman agreed with the defence, concluding that both statements made by McLean were induced by the two factors above.

This chapter deals with one of the most controversial topics that can divide psychologists and police officers. We examine how police use interrogations in order to obtain confessions, what the courts permit police to do and prohibit them from doing, and what psychology has to contribute to ensure that the confessions obtained from suspects are valid.

The Darrelle Exner and Paul Ingram Cases

When people confess to crimes, sometimes questions persist about the accuracy of the confession; false confessions occur for a number of reasons, as this chapter illustrates. Perhaps the suspect was overly suggestible, or simply too fatigued or anxious. Perhaps excessive pressure was placed on the suspect to confess. We also must realize that it is not always easy to separate false confessions from authentic ones; some confessions are proven to be false whereas others are equivocal. Two notorious cases, a murder case and a ritual abuse case, will highlight the complexities of evaluating confession evidence.

The Darrelle Exner Murder

On October 25, 1996, 14-year-old Darrelle Exner left a restaurant in Regina and started walking home. Tragically, she ended up being raped, beaten, and murdered before her body was found by Kenneth Patton. After several weeks, the police still had no suspect and they began to canvas the neighbourhood. They finally encountered a 17-year-old male (who cannot be named) who said that he knew Darrelle and that he had started walking her home that night, along with his two friends, 23-year-old Douglas Firemoon and 20-year-old Joel Labadie. The police proceeded to interview the suspects and each, independently, confessed to the girl's murder. It turned out, however, that all three confessions were completely false; DNA evidence established that Kenneth Patton had raped and killed Darrelle and he pled guilty to her murder.

As documented in the CBC documentary series *Disclosure* (2003, January 28a), during the interrogations Firemoon and the 17-year-old had produced different versions of how Darrelle had been killed. Whereas Firemoon reported that they had stabbed her, the 17-year-old confessed to having struck her over the head. However, the police knew that Darrelle had been strangled. Regarding Labadie, the police had convinced him that he must have "blacked out," so he was unable to remember committing the murder but still confessed. Interrogation approaches taken from the "Reid technique" (described in detail later in this chapter) were implicated in the false confessions. The three suspects spent nearly four and a half months in jail following their confessions. Although the Crown prosecutor in the case later acknowledged that the three original suspects were innocent, according to the documentary (*Disclosure,* 2003, January 28b), some of the officers from the investigation still believe that the three men were involved in the murder (in accordance with the predictions of dangerous decisions theory and 'tunnel vision" (Porter & ten Brinke, 2009), described in Chapters 5 and 8, respectively.

Interviewed for the CBC documentary (*Disclosure,* 2003, January 28b), Joel Labadie later stated, "I'm not even sure how to explain it, 'cause I'm not sure how it happened to me. All I know is for hours on end I said, 'No, I had nothing to do with it.' Next thing you know I'm sitting here going 'Sure, why not? I did it.' More or less it's like they kill your spirit or something."

The Paul Ingram Case

In 1988 Paul Ingram was serving as a deputy sheriff in the state of Washington, a position he had held for almost 17 years (see Meissner, Horgan, & Albrechtsen, 2009). He was married, the father of five, and a central member of a local church. Apparently the paragon of mainstream American values, he even was the chair of the Thurston County Republican Party. He spent many of his working hours in schools, warning children of the dangers of drug use (Wright, 1994). But suddenly his life changed, as he was charged with a number of heinous crimes: sexual abuse, the rape of his own daughters, and participation in hundreds of satanic cult rituals that included the slaughter of some 25 babies. Incredibly, these charges stemmed from allegations by his eldest daughter Ericka, age 22 at that time, who claimed that her father had repeatedly molested not only her but also her sister. The abuse had ended in 1979, Ericka said, when she was nine and her sister Julie was five. But Julie later reported that she had been molested as recently as five years before, when she was 13.

Ericka first made the charges public in the summer of 1988 at a church camp where she served as a counsellor. As she talked to police later, the allegations grew in detail and bizarreness: she had caught a disease from her father; he had led satanic rituals in which live babies were sacrificed; a fetus had been forcibly removed from her body when it was almost full term. Contrary to her first revelations, Ericka now told the police that the last incidents of abuse had happened just two weeks earlier.

After Ericka came forward with these claims, Julie provided further allegations; the police acquired two letters that Julie had written a teacher five or six weeks before. One stated:

I can remember when I was 4 yr. old he would have poker game [sic] at our house and a lot of men would come over and play poker w/my dad, and they would all get drunk and one or two at a time would come into my room and have sex with me they would be in and out all night laughing and cursing. I was so scared I didn't know what to say or who to talk to. (quoted by Wright, 1994, p. 36)

Even though he was a law enforcement officer, Paul Ingram had no experience with interrogations (Kassin, 1997a; Ofshe & Watters, 1994). After his arrest, he was kept in jail for five months and interrogated 23 times during that period. At first, he denied any knowledge of the claims. He was hypnotized and given graphic crime details; mystified by his inability to remember any details of these acts, he was told by a Tacoma forensic psychologist Richard Peterson that sex offenders often repress memories of their offences because they

were too horrible to acknowledge. His pastor—who urged him to own up to the claims—told him the charges were probably true, because children did not make up such things. Even while Ingram's response was that he could not remember having ever molested his daughters, he added, "If this did happen, we need to take care of it" (Wright, 1994, pp. 6–7).

Leading questions by the police and the psychologist were used to cause Ingram to visualize images of scenes involving group rapes and satanic cult activities. His response began to change from "I didn't do it" to "I don't remember doing it" (Ofshe & Watters, 1994, p. 167). After further questioning, he told the police:

I really believe that the allegations did occur and that I did violate them and abuse them and probably for a long period of time. I've repressed it, probably very successfully from myself, and now I'm trying to bring it all out. I know from what they're saying that the incidents had to occur, that I had to have done these things ... my girls know me. They wouldn't lie about something like this. (Ofshe & Watters, 1994, p. 167)

Yet, at that point he could not recall any specific incidents of abuse.

Eventually, Ingram came to visualize scenes suggested by the detectives, and he did confess in detail, but in a rather detached and almost remorseless manner. For example, he would describe events by saying "I would have …" rather than "I did …" The admissions—given after relaxation exercises by the psychologist—were horrific; they included having sex with each of his daughters many times (beginning when Ericka was five years old) and having taken Julie for an abortion of a fetus he had fathered, when Julie was 15 years old. For a time, he came to believe the validity of the allegations. He "recalled" the crime scenes in detail and admitted guilt; for example, he reported seeing people in robes kneeling around a fire and cutting out a beating heart from a live cat, as well as watching another of the sheriff's deputies having sexual intercourse with Ingram's own daughter (Kassin, 1997a).

A social scientist played a unique role in this case, as an expert witness. Richard Ofshe is a social psychologist and professor of sociology at the University of California at Berkeley. Even though he was called as a witness by the prosecution, he came to conclude—after interviewing Ingram—that through hypnosis and "trance logic" Ingram had been "brainwashed" into believing that he had been part of a satanic cult. Ofshe decided to try a daring experiment with Ingram. He suggested that Ingram had forced one of his sons and one of his daughters to have sex with each other and watched them while they did. (No one had ever brought that accusation against Ingram before.) After repeated questions and suggestions by Ofshe, Ingram began to "remember" and acknowledged that he had done that, too, and even embellished details of the act. He prepared a three-page, excessively detailed description of the incestuous act. Thus Ofshe (1992) began to have serious doubts "that Ingram was guilty of anything, except of being a highly suggestible individual with a tendency to float in and out of trance states and a … rather dangerous eagerness to please authority" (Wright, 1994, p. 146); Professor Ofshe became an advocate of Ingram's innocence (see Meissner et al., 2009). But it was too late. Ingram had not only pleaded guilty but also plea-bargained to six counts of third-degree rape. There was no trial. He began serving a 20-year term in prison, with the possibility of parole after 12 years.

Yet no physical evidence exists that he was a Satanist or a child abuser. Ingram no longer believes that he was, and his lawyers have appealed, unsuccessfully, to withdraw his guilty plea. The Washington State Supreme Court rejected his appeal in September 1992. Ingram was finally released from prison on April 8, 2003.

THE FORENSIC PSYCHOLOGIST AND POLICE INTERROGATIONS

What is the appropriate role of the forensic psychologist when asked to evaluate the procedures or outcome of a police interrogation? The short answer is that there are many appropriate roles. First asked to be an expert witness by one side, Richard Ofshe came to play an active role for the other. This chapter examines possible roles by considering the clients to whom the psychologist might be responsible. For example, acting as a consultant or employee of a police department, a psychologist might seek to educate police investigators about the possibility of false confessions. If the client is a lawyer or the judiciary, the psychologist could serve as an expert witness or author of a consultation report about how the use of coercion and trickery by the police contributes to false confessions. And

Police have devised interrogation techniques borrowed from social psychology that maximize the likelihood that suspects will confess.

last, the forensic psychologist may feel that his or her ultimate responsibility is to society in general and attempt to educate the public about the dangers of misleading interrogations. This chapter considers each of these roles, but first we examine why false confessions occur in the first place.

The Psychology of False Confessions

People assume that most confessions are spontaneous and that almost all are truthful. In reality, many confessions are negotiated, and 20 percent are **recanted**; that is, the suspect who has made an incriminating statement to the police later states that it was false. Among the reasons that people confess is the desire to escape further interrogation. They may say to themselves at some level: "I'll tell the police whatever they want, to avoid this terrible situation and deny it later." Sometimes they may come to believe what the police have told them, as some observers concluded had temporarily occurred with Paul Ingram.

Three Types of False Confessions

Recanted or disputed confessions are not necessarily false confessions. With regard to those that are, Kassin and Wrightsman (1985; Wrightsman & Kassin, 1993; also see Gudjonsson & Pearse, 2011; Kassin, 2008; Perillo & Kassin, 2011) have identified three types of false confessions: voluntary, coerced-compliant, and coerced-internalized.

Voluntary. **Voluntary false confessions** are offered willingly, without elicitation. They may be prompted by a desire for publicity or by generalized guilt, or they may reflect some form of psychotic behaviour. Oddly, most highly publicized crimes inspire certain individuals to come forward and claim to have committed the crime. When the baby son of the famed pilot Charles Lindbergh was kidnapped in 1932, more than 200 people falsely confessed (Note, 1953).

Kassin (1997b) described a case in which he was contacted as a possible expert witness by the defence lawyer; a young woman had falsely implicated herself and a group of bikers in a murder case. She later told the police that she had lied about participating in the murder because she craved the notoriety and attention.

Coerced-compliant. **Coerced-compliant false confessions** are those in which the suspect confesses, while knowing that he or she is innocent. Coerced-compliant confessions may be given to escape further interrogation, to gain a promised benefit, or to avoid a threatened punishment. For example, Raymond McLean in the Newfoundland case described above may have given a coerced-compliant confession because of the falsely promised police inducements. In such cases, the person does not privately believe that he or she has committed the criminal act. In general, **compliance** refers to an inconsistency between one's public behaviour and one's private opinion, a phenomenon reflected in Asch's (1956) classic study of the impact of others' false estimates in a line-judging task (in his study a high proportion of participants matched a line with a comparison line differing in size after witnessing other "participants" (confederates) indicate they were the same length).

In the fall of 1974, the Irish Republican Army (IRA) placed bombs in two pubs in Guildford (in the county of Surrey) and Birmingham, England. In one bombing five people were killed; 21 were killed in the other, and more than 150 were injured in total. Under great pressure to make arrests, police questioned four Irishmen about one bombing and six others about the other. After intense questioning, the four men questioned in the Guildford bombing and four of the six men interrogated about the other bombing made written confessions, although they all recanted their confessions at trial. They said that their confessions had been beaten out of them (Mullin, 1986). One, Paddy Hill, claimed that he had been kicked, punched in the side of the head, and kneed in the thigh. "We're going to get a statement out of you or kick you to death," was the threat that he later reported (Mullin, 1986, p. 100). Those claims were rejected by the jury, which found the Irishmen guilty and they were sentenced to life in prison.

One of the men convicted in the Guildford bombing (who came to be known as the Guildford Four), Gerry Conlon, was the subject of the 1993 movie *In the Name of the Father.* Both sets of defendants spent close to 15 years in prison before their convictions were overturned when the English courts acknowledged that the police had coerced the defendants to confess by subjecting them to psychological and physical pressure (Gudjonsson, 2003).

Psychologist Gisli Gudjonsson (1992, 2003) was able to later interview and administer suggestibility scales to one member of the Guildford Four and each of the Birmingham Six. The most dramatic finding from the responses of the Birmingham Six was the difference in personality test scores between the two defendants who did not confess versus the four who did. Thirteen years after their interrogations, the two who did not make written confessions "scored exceptionally low on tests of suggestibility and compliance" (Gudjonsson, 1992, p. 273). Gudjonsson concluded that all eight of the defendants who made self-incriminating written statements reflected the coerced-compliant type.

Certainly the **third-degree tactics** that were commonplace all over the world a century ago—such as extreme deprivation, brutality, and torture—led to many coerced-compliant confessions (see *Brown v. Mississippi*, 1936, for an example). But do they still occur today? The 2004 revelations of widespread physical and sexual abuse of incarcerated detainees in Iraq by American and British soldiers establish that they certainly occur in modern wartime. What about in more commonplace, everyday interrogations in the North American context? In at least some jurisdictions and at least with selected suspects, they may still take place. In the mid-1980s, four New York City police officers were arrested and accused of extracting confessions from suspects by jolting them with a stun gun; one of the victims was found to have 40 burn marks on his body (Huff, Rattner, & Sagarin, 1996). Lawyers for Barry Lee Fairchild, a black man with an IQ of 62, have claimed that he confessed to the murder of a white nurse only after Pulaski County (Arkansas) sheriff's deputies "put telephone books on the top of his head and slammed downward repeatedly with blackjacks" (Lacayo, 1991, p. 27). Such actions cause excruciating pain but leave no marks as evidence of coercion. The sheriff of Pulaski County denied Fairchild's claims, but 11 other black men brought in for questioning about that time reported almost equally intimidating procedures. Three said that pistols were placed in their mouths, with officers pulling the triggers of the unloaded guns (Lacayo, 1991). A former sheriff's deputy even came forward and testified that he had seen the sheriff and some deputies abuse various suspects (Annin, 1990).

More common are procedures that more subtly influence suspects to confess. Now popular among police interrogation procedures are psychologically oriented ploys, such as apparent solicitousness and sympathy, the use of informants, and even lying to suspects (Hasel & Kassin, 2012; Leo, 1992). When a bomb exploded during the 1996 Summer Olympics in Atlanta, the FBI brought in a man named Richard Jewell for questioning because he fit their criminal profile of someone intrigued with law enforcement. Although Jewell clearly was a suspect, the FBI got his initial cooperation by telling him that they needed his help in preparing a training film. While he willingly came in for an interview, the next thing he knew, FBI agents, with a search warrant, were going through his apartment and plucking hair from his head (Brenner, 1997).

When the two sons of Susan Smith were found in the family car, drowned in a South Carolina lake, Smith first told the sheriff that a black man had hijacked her car and kidnapped her children. The Union County sheriff, Howard Wells, noted inconsistencies in her story and her behaviour, doubted her story, and—after extensive questioning—tricked Smith by telling her that his deputies had been working a drug stakeout at the very same crossroads at the time Susan Smith claimed the abduction had occurred. "This could not have happened as you said," he told her, upon which she broke down in tears and confessed to driving the car into the lake (Bragg, 1995, p. A1).

Richard Jewell was innocent and did not falsely confess; Susan Smith was guilty and did eventually confess, truthfully, to the murder of her two children. In fairness, it must be acknowledged that in both of these cases "the system worked," but the willingness on the part of law enforcement authorities to mislead suspects in the hopes of eliciting a confession still creates problems for a society in which many members of the community distrust and fear the police.

In the 2000 *Oickle* case, the Supreme Court of Canada confirmed that police deception is justifiable. Specifically, the Court concluded that a confession should be excluded only if the police deception "shocks the community" or, even if not rising to that level, the use of deception is a relevant factor in whether the confession was voluntary. Many legal experts disagreed (as with Madame Justice Arbour) or expressed outrage. Noted Toronto defence lawyer Clayton Ruby wrote in an October 17, 2000, *Globe and Mail* article:

Such treatment sets Canada's standards at the lowest common denominator of civilized behaviour. Our values are revealed. They are these: Lie, cheat, mislead if you must. Ignore tears and repeated protestations of innocence. But get a confession from whomever you have in your hands. That's the message the Supreme Court has just sent to police forces across our land. We're playing with fire.

Can questioning by the police lead to false confessions, even if intimidation is absent? Sometimes suspects believe in the transparency of their innocence and that it will easily be established after an uncomfortable interrogation is completed. Unfortunately, we consistently underestimate the rate at which we would falsely confess to something, regardless of the level of coercion. Research to this effect, indicating a general disbelief in the possibility of false confessions, is relevant to jury decisions in trials involving contested confession evidence. As Wakefield and Underwager wrote: "Widespread overconfidence in personal ability to resist coercion may lead jurors to give undue and erroneous weight to a coerced confession" (1998, p. 424).

Coerced-internalized. In the **coerced-internalized false confession**, the innocent suspect confesses and comes to believe that he or/she is guilty. Interrogation by the police is a highly stressful experience that can create a number of reactions, including a state of heightened suggestibility in which truth and falsehood become hopelessly confused in the suspect's mind. When this type of false confession occurs, Gudjonsson concluded that "after confessing for instrumental gain, the persistent questioning continues and the accused becomes increasingly confused and puzzled by the interrogator's apparent confidence in the accused's guilt" (1992, p. 273). In such cases, the suspect may even come to "remember" committing the crime, a type of false memory discussed in Chapter 6 (e.g., Loftus, 2010; Porter et al., 1999). Ofshe and some other observers of his

Steven Smith

Dr. Steven Smith is the Dean of Science and a Professor of Psychology at Saint Mary's University in Halifax. He completed his B.A. at Bishop's University and his M.A. and Ph.D. in Social Psychology at Queen's University.

While at Queen's, Dr. Smith met and took a class from Dr. Rod Lindsay, a world-renowned eyewitness identification researcher. This class, the research they conducted together afterward, and Dr. Smith's own interactions with the law in the distant past, led to a career-long interest in all things forensic.

Most recently, Dr. Smith and his colleagues Drs. Marc Patry and Veronica Stinson have been looking into the ramifications of police use of the "Mr. Big" technique. The Mr. Big technique—originating in Kelowna, British Columbia— is a complex and often very expensive sting operation during which criminal suspects are slowly entangled in a "criminal organization" that is really an elaborate hoax put on by police. After the police gain the trust of the suspect, he or she is are offered the chance to move up in the organization after successfully completing an interview with "Mr. Big"—the big boss. Mr. Big tells the suspect that in order to move up, he or she has to confess to a crime he or she has committed—the one the police are actually investigating. The suspect is offered substantial inducements: money, a job, friendship; and is often told that failing to confess will result in being kicked out of the gang. Not surprisingly, the suspect almost always confesses (see Box 7.2 on page 175 for more information on the Mr. Big technique).

For guilty suspects, this is very effective, but for potential innocent suspects, the pressure to falsely confess is immense. The Mr. Big technique is almost uniquely Canadian—it has been used only a few times in other jurisdictions. We know from case studies that false confessions do happen with the Mr. Big scenario; however, the *likelihood* of obtaining a false confession has never been assessed.

In addition to the Mr. Big research described above, Dr. Smith has conducted and published research on the evaluation of the effectiveness of police eyewitness identification procedures (particularly simultaneous and sequential lineups); understanding the causes and consequences of eyewitness errors (with a particular interest in cross-race IDs); and the role of media in legal decision making (focusing on the so-called "CSI" effect).

case concluded that Paul Ingram—reflecting an extreme state of **suggestibility**—should be placed in this category (Wright, 1994), and case reports exist of other coerced-internalized false confessions (Gudjonsson & Lebegue, 1989; Kassin, 2007). It appears that suspects who cannot recall their actions at the time of the crime of which they have been accused (due to a drinking binge, for example) may be especially susceptible to such false memories (Porter, Birt, Yuille, & Hervé, 2001). Joel Labadie in the Darrelle Exner murder case in Regina may have provided this type of confession. Another notorious case in Canada seemingly involved this type of false confession. In 1997, Simon Marshall was convicted of 15 counts of rape, based primarily on his confession (see Smith et al., 2010b). Marshall, a mentally challenged man from Ste-Foy, Quebec, was imprisoned until 2003, when he was cleared based on DNA evidence. Marshall had convinced even his lawyer that he had committed the crimes. An inquiry concluded that the police investigation was deeply flawed and that untested DNA evidence would have exonerated him much earlier.

At times, it is difficult to classify a specific person's response as compliant or internalized. This is especially true of the responses of children to interrogations. They may later say things like, "I was so confused; I couldn't separate what happened from what they told me happened." In Chicago in 1998, two boys—ages seven and eight years—were arrested and charged with the sex-related murder of a young girl. They had confessed to the murder during an intensive interrogation. Later, however, the authorities concluded that the boys were not physically mature enough to produce the semen found on the victim's body, and they were released. Although no recording was made of the questioning, it appears that the boys simply had repeated what the detectives had told them (Kotlowitz, 1999). The validity of the responses of children to questioning by authorities—whether the children are suspects, as in the Chicago case, or victims—is a matter of great concern.

FROM FALSE CONFESSION TO WRONGFUL CONVICTION

Clearly, in at least a few isolated cases, false confessions may occur. But how extensive is the problem? It is not possible to determine conclusively how many people confess falsely. In fact, estimates of the number of convictions that are a result of a false confession vary widely (e.g., Cassell, 1996a; Huff, Rattner, & Sagarin, 1996; Kassin et al., 2010). As Kassin observed, determining the number is difficult for two reasons: (1) even if it was coerced and the accused retracts it, a confession may be true and; (2) "a confession may be false even if the defendant is convicted, imprisoned, and never heard from again" (Kassin, 1997b, p. 224). But overwhelming evidence exists that some confessions are false.

Numerous convictions have been caused by a false confession (Bedau & Radelet, 1987; Borchard, 1932; Kassin, 2008; Rattner, 1988; Smith et al., 2010b). For example, Rattner (1988; Huff, Rattner, & Sagarin, 1996) analyzed 205 cases of known wrongful convictions and concluded that 16, or 8 percent, were the result of coerced confessions. Risinger (2007) analyzed 2235 American capital rape-murder sentences from the 1980s and established a minimum empirically justified wrongful conviction rate of 5 percent, many of which resulted from false confessions. One of the largest organizations dealing with wrongful convictions, the Innocence Project, has exonerated over 280 incarcerated individuals through DNA evidence alone (Innocence Project, 2011). Of these, 25 percent made incriminating statements, delivered outright confessions, or pleaded guilty.

Although these percentages are relatively low, false confessions more often occur in highly publicized cases dealing with extremely serious crimes because police devote more effort—in part through extensive interrogations—to solving them. According to Kassin et al. (2010), in 1989, Gary Dotson was the first wrongfully convicted individual to be proven innocent through the then-new science of DNA testing. While we cannot know how often false confessions occur across the spectrum of criminal investigations, in 15–20 percent of established wrongful conviction cases in the United States since that time, police-induced false confessions were involved (Garrett, 2008; http://www.innocence project .org, 2011).

Seven Psychological Processes

We have discussed at length the literature on the specific mechanisms operating behind false confessions, but the processes through which false confessions may lead to an actual wrongful conviction also are of interest to forensic psychologists. After the police have obtained a false confession, what happens? If it is later identified as a false confession, can it truly be dismissed in the minds of decision makers? How is this information dealt with by the criminal justice system? Leo and Davis (2010) have summarized the path to wrongful conviction as relating to seven psychological processes.

1. *Misleading specialized knowledge.* Confessions are exceptionally persuasive, and bias the interpretation of any further information, especially when they include information that "only the perpetrator would know." Misleading specialized knowledge occurs when a suspect is provided unique, nonpublic facts about the crime at hand (often referred to as "guilty knowledge") during the course of police procedures, and the police insist that the information originated with the suspect (Gudjonsson, 2003; Leo, 2008). While the police may have inadvertently provided this information, they relentlessly launch the false confession into a vicious cycle. In this cycle, police rely on this information to convince prosecutors of the confession's accuracy, prosecutors use it to convince jurors of the defendant's guilt, and judges base their evaluations of the confession's admissibility on it.

2. *Tunnel vision and confirmation biases.* Strong beliefs can lead investigators to focus on the guilt of a particular suspect (tunnel vision), and lead to a selective search for, and interpretation of, information that confirms this initial presumption of guilt (confirmation biases) (Kassin, 2010; Kassin & Fong, 1999; Kassin, Goldstein & Savitsky, 2003; Meissner & Kassin, 2002). Because these processes exclude the search for information that may suggest a suspect's innocence, they lead to a series of biases in further levels of the correctional system. Much of the original information relevant to the suspect's innocence is slowly filtered out, as each correctional source limits its focus to the information it deems relevant. The final false confession is then interpreted without the necessary exculpating information to prevent a wrongful conviction. This process

has been described as a series of increasingly "dangerous decisions" about a defendant (see Chapter 8). Evidence that is consistent with the initial impressions—which can be informed by confession evidence—is prominent in the juror's mind while evidence that is counter to the initial impression is discounted. For example, Porter et al. (2010) found that mock jurors maintained their belief in the guilt of a highly untrustworthy-looking defendant, even when DNA evidence completely exonerating the defendant was offered.

3. *Motivational biases.* The understandably high motivation to solve crimes—especially serious crimes—quickly and efficiently can promote rushed judgments and increase the risk of misclassifying innocent individuals as perpetrators (Findley & Scott, 2006; Porter & ten Brinke, 2009). In addition to the pressures contributed by police supervisors, victims, and society at large, self-justifying motivations also are at work. These self-protective motivations are likely the major contributing factor to the reluctance of prosecutors and investigators to acknowledge exculpatory evidence when it indicates they may have generated a false confession and/or convicted the wrong individual (Medwed, 2004; Tavris & Aronson, 2007). In general, the motivation of the correctional system to process cases quickly can lead to a failure to use appropriate safeguards to prevent (or find ways of dealing with) false confessions.

4. *Emotion.* Powerful emotions often accompany crime, particularly violent crimes such as sexual assault or murder. Anger, in particular, typically is associated with the goals of punishing or removing the source of the anger (Levine & Pizzarro, 2004). In the criminal justice context, this means punishing and incarcerating the perpetrator of the crime. Unfortunately, this emotion can cloud the decision-making capacity of the legal community and can lead to the tunnel-vision process explored earlier. Emotional accounts of crimes can thus lead investigators, jurors, and judges to be heavily swayed toward a guilty verdict, as emotions may lead them to discount evidence suggesting that the suspect may be innocent. For example, Kaufmann et al. (2002) found that the emotional expression of the alleged rape victim was more influential on the perception of credibility than the actual content of the story.

5. *Institutional influences.* Institutions within the criminal justice system affect the resources to which police, lawyers, and judges have access. Limitations on time or money, in particular, affect the manner in which evidence is collected (e.g., an officer with a high caseload will have limited time to look for evidence in a specific case). Such financially motivated and time-limited decisions lead to systemic problems that can lead to false confessions slipping through the cracks and becoming wrongful convictions.

6. *Lack of knowledge.* In order to prevent false confessions, and identify them when they occur, professionals first must understand/concede their existence and the ways in which they occur. Legal professionals with a lack of knowledge regarding false confessions will not take steps to prevent them (such as not avoiding problematic interrogation techniques), and are likely to not even consider the possibility that a confession is false (thereby not seeking evidence to discredit the confession). Unfortunately, police often not only fail to understand the causes of police-induced false confessions, but often they are ill advised during training to use methods that actually generate them (e.g., Davis & O'Donohue, 2004). Unfortunately, a general lack of knowledge about false confessions prevails in the correctional system, contributing to wrongful convictions.

7. *Progressive constriction of relevant evidence.* Judging the validity of a confession becomes increasingly difficult over time because the available evidence becomes progressively more filtered as it moves through the system. While tunnel-vision and other mechanisms can bias evidence—or the perception of evidence—from the very beginning of an investigation, evidence necessarily becomes more limited as a case proceeds through the legal system. Although investigators will have access to most or all relevant evidence in the investigation phase of a case, by the time it reaches the judge or jury, only some of this information will be presented in court. Information regarding contact with the suspect and other potential suspects is limited, as memory and notes cannot possibly capture all the nuances of an investigation. This becomes increasingly more limited as police documents become a lawyer's case notes, which become trial proceedings, and finally become a judge's or jurors' evidence.

Sometimes the information that is lost along the way could have prevented a false confession from becoming a wrongful conviction.

As you can discern, there are many factors contributing to false confessions and they can remain unnoticed or not considered by the legal system. While it is possible that some of these cannot be changed systemically, safeguards that prevent false confessions and help decision makers to identify them when they do happen can be successfully implemented. The most important preventive safeguard involves training police to use empirically based interview techniques that facilitate noncoerced true confessions while minimizing the rate of false confessions. The best way of identifying police-induced false confessions and preventing wrongful convictions is to videotape all police interviews, and to evaluate each interview for coercion and other adverse psychological pressures (Gudjonsson & Pearse, 2011). Overall, understanding false confessions and how they can slip through the criminal justice system is critical and allows us to address this problem most effectively.

False Confessions in the Laboratory

If we proceed with the assumption that on occasion a confession can result from suggestibility and pseudo-memories and that the suspect did not

Savage Chickens   by Doug Savage

YOU'RE GONNA GO TO PRISON FOR A LONG TIME, PUNK!

YOUR MOTHER MUST BE DEEPLY DISAPPOINTED IN YOU

BAD COP / GUILT COP

© Doug Savage

www.savagechickens.com

Real or false confessions can result from the psychological dynamics created in police interrogations that play upon the vulnerabilities of a particular suspect.

commit an alleged crime, the question remains: Is this an isolated case? Is there any evidence that under controlled conditions, in the psychological laboratory, people can be convinced that they committed undesirable acts that, in fact, they did not commit?

To study such a question under controlled conditions, and still protect participants' rights and to act in an ethical manner, is a challenge for research psychologists. Ethical guidelines prevent most researchers from placing research participants in a situation in which they may succumb to a belief that they committed a criminal act. The solution to the challenge, described here, may strike some as contrived and not generalizable to real crime-related interrogations. Similarly, we might consider the classic and infamous Milgram shock experiments (in which participants were led to punish their supposed fellow participants via shock in spite of their screams and seemingly to their deaths) and decide that the findings are not generalizable to "real life." However, collectively research seems to substantiate the plausibility of induced false confessions.

Kassin (1997b; Kassin & Kiechel, 1996) developed the following paradigm to test the proposal that people can be convinced that they had perpetrated false undesirable acts. He and Kiechel had pairs of students (one participant and one confederate) participate in a reaction-time task on a computer, with the participant typing the letters on a keyboard. Before beginning the session, the participants were instructed in the manner in which to use the computer and were specifically told not to press the ALT key near the space bar. If they did, the program would crash and the data would be lost. But during the experiment, the computer "crashed" and the seemingly distressed experimenter accused the participant of hitting the forbidden key.

Although when this happened, all 75 of the participants denied the experimenter's charge, in half of the cases the confederate sheepishly "admitted" that she saw the participant accidentally strike the ALT key. (This procedure was designed to reflect the use by police of false incriminating evidence, a topic described later in this chapter.) At this point, participants were given a chance to sign a confession of wrongdoing prepared by the experimenter. A refusal to sign the confession would cause a confrontation with the professor supervising the study. Perhaps not surprisingly, all participants in the crucial condition (that is, the case in which the confederate informed on the participant) agreed to sign the confession. But as each was leaving the experimental area, a waiting "participant" (actually another confederate of the experimenter) asked the participant what had happened. Two-thirds of the participants in the crucial condition indicated that they had erred and hit the wrong button; they didn't say, "He said I hit the wrong button" but rather things like "I hit the wrong button and ruined the program."

Since the ALT key experiment, other researchers have tried to create other situations that elicit false confessions. Most recently, Nash and Wade (2008) created a paradigm involving fake video evidence. In this scenario, participants completed a gambling task and, after a delay, were accused of cheating on the task. Half of the participants then were informed that video evidence of their cheating existed and the other half were exposed to doctored video evidence. Those who watched the doctored videos of themselves cheating were more likely to confess, internalize, and fabricate details for the confession than those who were simply told about a video. Only 13 percent of participants who were told about a video, but a whopping 93 percent of those exposed to the doctored videos, internalized the false confessions. In an age in which Photoshop is ubiquitous, we cannot help but wonder how many false confessions and false memories have been elicited through doctored videos and images.

Thus, even under laboratory conditions, not just compliance but **internalization** occurs, and people can come to believe that they committed acts that they, in fact, did not commit, reminiscent of the false memory studies described in Chapter 6 (e.g., Frenda, Nichols, & Loftus, 2011; Porter et al., 2001). Further, some participants even manufactured explanations for how they had made the "mistake." These results are consistent with those of Milgram's (1974) classic obedience studies (in which some adult participants were willing to administer painful electric shocks to other subjects) in that—despite their protestations beforehand—many people conform to an authority figure when in a coercive environment.

THE ROLE OF POLICE INTERROGATIONS IN GENERATING CONFESSIONS

Throughout history, every society has been concerned with violations of its laws, customs, and social expectations. Those who were suspected of such violations often were subjected to interrogations in the hopes that they would confess to various transgressions. In fact, many did so during centuries-old investigations, through the trials by ordeal in Europe, by the torture of "witches," and in modern-day interrogations around the globe. The first pictures ever drawn of police—found in 12th-dynasty Egyptian tombs of about 2000 B.C. — show them torturing a suspect. In light of the videotape of the manner in which Rodney King was treated by the Los Angeles police, it is provocative to note that in one of the ancient drawings, "a man is being beaten with a stick by one of the policemen, while his legs and arms are being held by three others; a fifth officer looks on, supervising the proceedings" (Franklin, 1970, p. 15).

Most police officers recognize that intimidating and coercive actions with a suspect are illegal and often counterproductive; "confessions" created by such coercion will usually not stand the scrutiny of a judge in a preliminary hearing. Police and legal experts differ about whether the warnings that inform suspects of their rights to a lawyer and to remain silent (in accordance with the Charter of Rights and Freedoms in Canada and the Miranda warning in the United States) are a good idea. It is claimed that the requirement that police use such warnings has decreased the conviction rate and that more criminals remain on the street (Cassell, 1996a, 1996b; Cassell & Hayman, 1996). However, Leo (1996a) has argued that the requirements that police use such warnings has had a civilizing effect on police practices and has increased the public's awareness of defendants' rights. But some police officers may ignore such rules, viewing themselves as members of a profession with an agreed-upon set of practices deriving partly from the law, partly from common sense, and partly from tradition. This culture is so strong that a study on police opinions regarding informing individuals of their right to remain silent suggested that nearly 40 percent of police chiefs agreed that the Supreme Court should overturn the Miranda decision (thus *not* mandating police to read these rights to suspects). The main reasoning was that "offenders already know their rights," and that reading the Miranda rights "prevents voluntary confessions" (Payne & Gustaferro, 2009). Neither of these lines of reasoning is supported by the academic literature. In fact, researchers advocate the utmost importance of informing suspects of their rights and recommend that suspects utilize them (e.g., Gudjonsson & Pearse, 2011).

Police recognize that suspects confess for a variety of reasons, some of which may be unreliable. The greatest value of obtaining a confession may be that it leads to other incriminating evidence. But even false statements are useful, because "the subject who lies is then committed to the psychological defense of a fantasy" (Royal & Schutt, 1976, p. 25). If the goal of the forensic psychologist is to improve the accuracy rate of confessions, it is appropriate to examine the nature of the procedures that the police use in questioning suspects.

The Goals of Interrogation

Police question suspects for two reasons: to get more information about the case and to induce suspects to confess. Contrary to the stereotype held by some, police handbooks state that the main goal for the **interrogation** of suspects by the police is to gain information that furthers the investigation, and "is not simply a means of inducing an admission of guilt," wrote O'Hara and O'Hara (1980, p. 111). According to the current law enforcement practices in Canada and the United States:

Interrogation is an *evidence-gathering* activity that is supposed to occur after detectives have conducted an initial investigation and determined, to a reasonable degree of certainty, that the suspect to be questioned committed the crime ... The purpose of interrogation is therefore not to discern the truth, determine if the suspect committed the crime, or evaluate his or her denials. (Kassin et al., 2010, p. 38; emphasis added)

The decision of whether an individual is guilty is made by a judge or jury, not by the police. The police are supposed to simply provide evidence to these triers of fact so that they can make the most informed sentencing decisions. In an effort to provide the best evidence, police are often provided interrogation manuals. The most commonly used interrogation manual internationally, written by Inbau, Reid, Buckley, and Jayne (2001), advises: "Avoid creating the impression that the investigator is seeking a confession or conviction. It is far better to fulfill the role of one who is merely seeking the truth ..." (p. 81). However, sometimes a police manual conflicts with itself about the primary goal of interrogation. Inbau and colleagues (2001), after asserting that "the purpose of an interrogation is

to learn the truth" (p. 8) go on to elaborate how the final step of an interrogation should be gaining a written confession. They appear to assume that confessions are reliable, which, as the previous sections of this chapter already have shown, unfortunately, is not the case. The originators of the Reid Technique came from law enforcement circles; polygrapher John E. Reid and renowned Chicago interrogator Fred Inbau joined forces in the 1940s and 1950s.

Sometimes, investigators have advocated keeping the pressure on suspects who, close to the point of deciding to confess, begin to fidget and show confusion. But on other occasions, investigators have proposed a more promising approach to dealing with the suspect's conflict over making a decision; in these situations, they have suggested that the interrogator lead the suspect away from the ultimate choice and thus take the pressure off, so that the suspect is not faced with making the critical choice until the optimal point in the questioning.

What Police Can and Cannot Do to Elicit Confessions

Police handbooks emphasize the need to be professional in conducting investigations and interrogations. Beyond the previously described reasons for restraint, too much pressure may induce such a vulnerable emotional state in the suspect that his or her capacity for rational judgment is impaired. Some manuals suggest opening with a positive statement: "We're investigating an armed robbery and we think you can help us" (Macdonald & Michaud, 1987, p. 19). But the question remains: What other kinds of tactics do police use in questioning suspects? What are the limits?

The public has limited knowledge about the broad powers given to Canadian police during interrogations. We will return to this point later when we consider the forensic psychologist's role in working with society in general as a client. Police can use trickery; they can lie to suspects, and can otherwise mislead them. Box 7.1 outlines the rules on using confessions as evidence.

Methods of Interrogation

The term "interrogation" traditionally was used to describe all questioning by police, regardless of whether it was conducted in custody or in the field, or before or after the laying of a charge. The term

| BOX 7.1 | CONFESSION EVIDENCE IN THE CANADIAN LEGAL SYSTEM |

As mentioned earlier, in Canada the Charter of Rights and Freedoms describes what police must do prior to attempting to elicit a confession. However, courts long have relied on a higher-level "confessions rule," which states that "no statement made out of court by an accused to a person in authority can be admitted into evidence against him [or her] unless the prosecution shows, to the satisfaction of the trial judge, that the statement was made freely and voluntarily" (*Erven v. The Queen*, 1979, para. 931). The court must consider two main factors in deciding whether to admit a confession:

1. *The voluntariness of the statement.* A statement is said to be voluntary when it is made "without fear of prejudice or hope of advantage" (*Boudreau v. The King*, 1949) and must be the product of an "operating mind" (*Ward v. The Queen*, 1979). This principle assumes that when people freely incriminate themselves, the statement is probably true. However, when a confession follows threats or promises by an authority figure, the truthfulness of the statement can no longer be presumed.

2. *Whether the recipient of the statement was a person in authority.* This requires the recipient to be a person involved in "the arrest, detention, examination, or prosecution of the accused" (*Horvath v. The Queen*, 1979).

was preferred over "interviewing" because it implies a much more active and accusatory role by the police detective (Macdonald & Michaud, 1987). On the other hand, many police officers now prefer the more general term "interviewing" because of the powerful, negative connotations of the term "interrogation." Here, we use the term "interrogation" simply to refer to an interview with a suspect. Despite the persistence of controversy surrounding this aspect of criminal investigation, surprisingly little exists in the way of empirical documentation of interrogation practices.

In 1931, the U.S. National Commission on Law Observance and Enforcement published a report of its findings and confirmed the worst fears about police abuse, noting that the use of severe third-degree tactics to extract confessions was at that time "widespread" (p. 153). As examples, the commission cited as commonplace the use of physical violence, methods of intimidation that capitalized on the youth or mental abilities of the accused, refusals to give access to counsel, fraudulent promises that could not be fulfilled, and prolonged illegal detention. In an effort to find out whether and the manner in which the interrogation process had changed, the U.S. Supreme Court in its *Miranda v. Arizona* (1966) decision—lacking direct observational or interview data—turned for information to reported cases involving coerced confessions and to reviews of the most popular manuals then available for advising law enforcement officials about successful tactics for eliciting confessions (see Aubry & Caputo, 1965; Inbau & Reid, 1962;

O'Hara & O'Hara, 1956). Essentially, the Court concluded from its inquiry that "the modern practice of in-custody interrogation is [now] psychologically rather than physically oriented" (p. 448), but that the degree of coerciveness inherent in the situation had not diminished. The Court's opinion in *Miranda v. Arizona* (1966) noted that "the use of physical brutality and violence is not, unfortunately, relegated to the past" (p. 446). The well-known case of Iraqi detainees being systematically abused by American soldiers during the Iraq war gives extreme evidence that they still remain. But what about questionable psychological tactics?

Manipulative Tactics

When their still highly popular manual was first published, Inbau and Reid (1962) described in considerable detail 16 overlapping strategies by which confessions could be elicited from initially reluctant suspects. From these, three major themes emerge (see Kassin et al., 2010):

1. *Minimization.* The tactic of **minimization** is reflected in "soft sell" techniques in which the interrogator offers sympathy, face-saving excuses, or moral justification (Kassin, Appleby, & Perillo, 2010; Kassin & McNall, 1991). Thus the detective reconceptualizes for the suspect the attributional implications of his or her crime by seemingly belittling its seriousness (e.g., "It's not all that unusual" or "I've seen thousands of others in the same situation"), or by providing a face-saving external attribution

of blame (e.g., "on the spur of the moment you did this"). The interrogator, for example, might suggest to the suspect that there were extenuating circumstances in his or her particular case, providing excusing conditions such as self-defence, passion, or simple negligence. Or the blame might be shifted onto a specific person such as the victim or an accomplice. Often the suspect is asked whether the act was instigated by the victim. Sometimes, as in the *McLean* case in Newfoundland discussed earlier, the officer might tell the suspect that there is "no chance" he or she will receive jail time, in return for a confession.

Inbau and Reid (1962) offered the following example of how such attributional manipulation has been used successfully as bait: A middle-aged man, accused of having attempted sexual intercourse with a 10-year-old girl, was told that "this girl is well-developed for her age. She probably learned a lot about sex from boys ... she may have deliberately tried to excite you to see what you would do." In another documented instance, a detective told a break-and-enter suspect that "the guy should never have left all that liquor in the window to tempt honest guys like you and me" (Wald et al., 1967, p. 1544).

2. *Maximization*. The opposite strategy is to use "scare tactics" to frighten the suspect into confessing (Kassin et al., 2010; Kassin & McNall, 1991). One way to accomplish **maximization** is by exaggerating the gravity of the offence and the magnitude of the charges. For example, in theft or fraud cases, the reported loss—and the consequences for a convicted defendant—might be exaggerated. Another variation of the scare tactic is for the interrogator to presume to have a firm belief about the suspect's culpability, based on independent, supposedly factual evidence. A variation of this procedure, advocated by Inbau and Reid (1962), is to falsify the magnitude of the crime in the hopes of obtaining a denial that would implicate the suspect—for example, accusing the suspect of stealing $80 000 when only $20 000 was taken.

Police manuals are replete with specific suggestions about how to use what is referred to as the **knowledge-bluff trick**. The interrogator could pretend to have strong evidence, such as the suspect's fingerprints at the crime scene or DNA. The interrogator might even have a police officer pose as an eyewitness and identify the suspect in a rigged lineup. Another technique is to focus the suspect on his or her physiological and nonverbal indicators of an apparent guilty conscience, such as dryness of the mouth, sweating, fidgety bodily movements, or downcast eyes.

In the Alberta case *Dix v. Canada (A.G.)* (2002), it was established that police had lied about nonexistent evidence in numerous other ways. The use of outright deception with suspects and witnesses by the RCMP came under intense scrutiny. Ultimately, Jason Dix was awarded $764 863 in damages in a malicious prosecution lawsuit brought against police officers and prosecutors. Dix had spent 22 months in jail before the charges against him for an execution-style double murder were dismissed. The Court of Queen's Bench Justice Keith Ritter slammed police tactics in the investigation as "reprehensible," including police lies to Dix and his ex-wife that he had "failed" a polygraph examination. In the lawsuit, Dix gave 23 allegations of the RCMP lying to witnesses during the investigation. These included that Dix had failed the polygraph, that he had a "dual personality," that he often picked up prostitutes, that he may have killed before, that "medical evidence" existed that he was a homosexual, and that the police "would not lie to you" (para. 287). The judge agreed with Dix, concluding that, in fact, "many of them were lies" (para. 288).

Baiting questions sometimes are used if this approach is employed. These are not necessarily accusatory in nature but still convey to suspects that some (false) evidence exists that links them to the crime. For example, the detective may ask: "Jim, is there any reason you can think of why one of Mary's neighbours would say that your car was seen parked in front of her home that night?" Without waiting for an answer, the interrogator would then say: "Now, I'm not accusing you of anything; maybe you just stopped by to see if Mary was at home" (Inbau, Reid, & Buckley, 1986, p. 69). Sometimes baiting questions carry the strong implication that the answer is already known to the police, when in fact it is not.

3. *Building rapport*. The third type of approach is based on the development of a personal rapport with the suspect. Referring to **rapport building** as the emotional appeal, police

manuals advise the interrogator to show sympathy, understanding, and respect through flattery and gestures such as the offer of a drink. Having then establish an amicable relationship, the interrogator might try to persuade the suspect that confessing is in his or her own best interests. In a more elaborate version of this strategy, two detectives use the **Mutt-and-Jeff tactic** (also called playing "good cop, bad cop"), in which one comes across as hostile and relentless, while the other gains the suspect's confidence by being protective and supportive. This tactic used to be quite common in the United States (Zimbardo, 1967), but today it is used infrequently in the United States (Culhane, Hosch, & Heck, 2008) and in only about 1 percent of Canadian interrogations (King & Snook, 2009).

Police investigators also often emphasize the need to maintain pressure on the suspect:

You put your suspect on a rail. ... You push him forward, then back up a little. But once you get any kind of statement, he is committed to that statement. You back off a little, but stay on the rail. If your suspect feels he's losing control, he'll back off. You let that aspect go for a while, go on to something else, then come back. And ask another question that will incriminate him. He'll finally put the pieces together and realize you've nailed him. (p. 183, Rachlin, 1995)

CURIOUSLY, OFFICERS OWENS AND IRBY NEVER HAD MUCH SUCCESS WITH THEIR GOOD COP/ BAD COP ROUTINE

Observational Data on Interrogation Methods

Are such examples an accurate depiction of the everyday interrogation process or do they portray only the most atypical and extreme forms of coercion? David Simon's year-long observations of Baltimore detectives led him to characterize such tactics as routine, "limited only by a detective's imagination and his ability to sustain the fraud" (1991, p. 217). In a U.S. study of 127 law enforcement officers, officers endorsed 12 out of 23 Reid Technique tactics on average, including high endorsement rates for lying to a suspect about evidence, attempting to confuse the suspect, and minimizing the moral seriousness of the offence (Culhane, Hosch, & Heck, 2008). But what about real interrogation settings? Leo (1996b) observed 182 interrogations, either live or videotaped, in three police departments, all in California. Typically, five or more different tactics were used in an interrogation; detectives would note contradictions in the suspect's statements and confront the suspect with incriminating evidence (some of it faked), but they also used minimization and positive incentives such as praising the suspect. Leo's observations led him to characterize the interrogation as a **confidence game** that involved the well-developed use of deception and manipulation, and thus the betrayal of trust (Leo, 1996c). While officers clearly prefer passive over aggressive techniques, this suggests that even today the use of coercive and manipulative tactics is common.

Does this also apply to Canada? In 2009, King and Snook examined the use of interrogation tactics in Canada and found that most of the interrogations examined followed the recommendations made by the Reid Technique of interrogations (as elaborated by Inbau, Reid, Buckley, & Jayne, 2001). Minimization tactics were observed slightly more than maximization techniques, and about 27 percent of the interrogations were deemed coercive. The most commonly observed core Reid model tactics observed in interrogations were as follows:

- Appeal to the suspect's pride with flattery (57 percent)
- Play one offender against the other (43 percent)
- Minimize the moral seriousness of the offence (36 percent)
- Sympathize with suspect by condemning others (25 percent)

Infrequently observed tactics include suggesting that anyone else under similar circumstances might have done the same (9 percent) and that the victim is probably exaggerating (7 percent). The tactics recommended by Inbau and Reid (1962) appear to be gaining popularity in all of North America over time, despite being contrary to evidence-based recommendations and contributing to miscarriages of justice.

What Is Allowed?

The discussion above reveals that the police have much greater leeway in the interrogation of suspects than most people assume. As confirmed in the *R. v. Oickle* (2000) case, police are allowed to misrepresent certain facts of the case, use techniques that take advantage of the emotions or beliefs of the suspect, and fail to inform the suspect of some important fact or circumstance that might make the suspect less likely to confess. One of the most common forms of acceptable deception used is making false claims about evidence pointing to the accused, such as a "failed" polygraph test, as in the Jason Dix case. As established in *Oickle*, the court determined that police deception is unacceptable only when it is "so appalling as to shock the community."

The Canadian Supreme Court has decided that imminent physical threats by a police officer are sufficiently "shocking," and bans confession evidence obtained in this manner. The types of tactics that are illegal include physical force, abuse, and torture; explicit threats of harm or punishment; prolonged isolation or deprivation of food or sleep; promises of leniency; and failure to notify the suspect of his or her right to counsel (e.g., Kassin, 1997). However, surprisingly, the Canadian Supreme Court has argued that the use of "veiled threats" requires close examination. While the police are allowed to offer certain inducements to obtain a confession, they are not allowed to offer "quid pro quo" offers, regardless of whether they are in the form of threats or promises. Trial judges have been instructed to assess whether a suspect was questioned aggressively for a long period and/ or was confronted with fabricated evidence and police trickery. Whereas either of these practices on its own may be acceptable in some forms, the judge must decide whether, collectively, they may have contributed to false self-incriminating statements (*R. v. Oickle*, 2000).

Why Isn't Police Trickery Uniformly Prohibited?

Two reasons lie behind a court's decision that a confession is inadmissible because it was coerced: As described by Judge Gorman (cited above in

---

BOX 7.2 — **THE "MR. BIG" INVESTIGATIVE TECHNIQUE**

In recent years, a controversial investigative method called the "Mr. Big" technique (originally devised by police in Kelowna, British Columbia) has been revived in Canada (see Smith, Stinson, & Patry, 2009). Police use this noncustodial (i.e., suspects are not taken into police custody) technique when they have a suspect in a serious crime but do not have enough evidence against the suspect. The basic method of the Mr. Big scenario involves undercover police officers posing as organized crime (e.g., a gang) figures who befriend the suspect and suggest that he or she join their organization. In order to join the organization, the suspect must demonstrate that he or she is capable of committing serious crimes required by the organization and that he or she can be trusted. In order to do so, the suspect is persuaded to admit to a serious crime to demonstrate loyalty to the organization and that he or she can be counted on to carry out the criminal orders of the leader (i.e., Mr. Big). At this point the undercover officers elicit a confession, which then serves as a pivotal piece of evidence against the defendant and usually results in a conviction. As of 2008, the Royal Canadian Mounted Police has used the Mr. Big technique over 350 times, with 95 percent of prosecuted cases resulting in convictions (Royal Canadian Mounted Police, 2010). The Mr. Big technique is considered controversial because it utilizes techniques known to elicit false confessions, including high pressure and enticement to confess. While it has been found to be an effective and admissible way to obtain confessions from reluctant suspects, the pressures exerted upon suspects are extreme and go far beyond what a suspect might experience during a typical (in-custody) interrogation (Smith, Stinson, & Patry, 2010a).

R. v. McLean, 2003), such confessions violate the Charter of Rights and Freedoms and they may be unreliable because of the possibility of false confessions. When the police lie to a suspect, the courts apparently assume that such lying would be counterproductive with truly innocent suspects. That is, if suspects are told that they were seen at the crime location, and the suspects know that they have never been there, the suspects would recognize that the police are lying to them and refuse to confess. But human behaviour clearly is not that simple, and forensic psychologists can try to educate the police about the power of the interrogation process to convince innocent suspects that the false information they received is true. Further, false evidence presented to suspects by the police might cause them to doubt the likelihood of their receiving a fair trial and lead them to plea-bargain.

WHAT CAN PSYCHOLOGISTS CONTRIBUTE?

The responsibilities of the forensic psychologist with respect to the use of police interrogations are diverse and often conflicting.

The Police as Client

Police and psychologists have a complex relationship, as the previous two chapters have illustrated. Psychologists want to assist police in improving their interrogation procedures when they lead to authentic confessions, but at the same time, many psychologists are appalled by the coercive procedures often used and are concerned that the use of manipulation and falsehoods leads to false confessions. How may the two professions work together to achieve common goals? Some of the ways suggested in this section, such as psychologically strengthening the interrogation process, reflect an effort to better achieve police goals; others, such as videotaping of interrogations, reflect psychologists' concern about the validity of confessions.

The Role of Interrogative Suggestibility

Police tend to believe that almost all suspects are guilty and that they confess only if they are guilty. Thus, interrogators may extract confessions that are false without realizing it. Psychologists need to educate the police in the concepts of coerced-internalized and coerced-compliant false confessions. The forensic psychologist also must help police understand that some suspects are subject to **interrogative suggestibility**; that is, the idea that because suspects are anxious or lack a strong self-concept, or for other reasons, they actually come to believe what the police are telling them. Gisli Gudjonsson (1984, 1989, 1992, 1997, 2003) developed a procedure to identify subjects high in interrogative suggestibility. The subject first is read a narrative paragraph; then he or she is asked to provide a free recall of the story and to answer 20 memory questions, 15 of which are misleading. After being told—in a firm voice— that he or she made several errors, the subject is then retested, and shifts in the subject's answers are studied. A distinction is made between the number of shifts in memory and the number of responses that reflect a yielding to the misleading questions. Subjects who score high on interrogative suggestibility also tend to have high levels of anxiety, low self-esteem, poor memories, and a lack of assertiveness (Gudjonsson, 2003). Among criminal suspects, those who confessed to the police but later retracted their statements scored higher than the general population (Gudjonsson, 1991). While in the above description interrogative suggestibility is portrayed as a trait, it also may be a temporary state; for example, sleep deprivation increases scores on interrogative suggestibility (Blagrove, 1996).

The way in which to make police aware of such problems is a challenge. First, police do not consider these to be "problems," and police detectives do not routinely solicit advice from psychologists to improve the accuracy of their interrogation techniques. Police detectives do not necessarily see the use of false evidence during the interrogation as unfair (Culhane, Hosch, & Heck, 2008; Skolnick & Leo, 1992), because most of them believe that if the suspect is innocent, he or she won't "bite" on the false information. Such techniques, for Inbau, Reid, Buckley, and Jayne, are not "apt to make an innocent person confess" (2001, p. 212). And as noted earlier in the chapter, the actual number of innocent persons who confess under such an inducement remains controversial (Cassell, 1998; Ofshe & Leo, 1997; Rinsinger, 2007; Slobogin, 1997).

Prior Planning of Interrogations

Police are always interested in ways to improve their ability to get suspects to cooperate and reveal information. Part of the prevalent stereotype of police interrogation is the belief that the criminal usually is driven to confessing after having been trapped by the piercing brilliance of the police interrogator (Deeley, 1971). "In reality," states a Scotland Yard detective:

---

there is no sudden blinding shaft of light. You pick a villain [the British word for a suspect] up on something he said yesterday ... Usually it's a matter of wearing a person down. You may consider that a form of duress, but that's what it amounts to— wearing them down by persistence, like water dripping on a stone. Not brilliance. (quoted by Deeley, 1971, p. 139)

Prior planning is one facilitator of a successful crime investigation. Psychologists can aid by encouraging investigators to ask themselves whether the questioning of a suspect potentially is the most valuable means of getting the desired information under the existing circumstances (Royal & Schutt, 1976). If a decision is made to question suspects, the police officer should first read all the investigation reports and statements already taken, as well as visiting the scene of the crime, checking out suspects' alibis, examining any previous criminal records of suspects, and making inquiries of other people who may have relevant information (Macdonald & Michaud, 1987; Royal & Schutt, 1976). One detective commented:

The more you know about the man you are going to interrogate the better position you are in to know his weak points. I had a case where I could have talked till hell froze over and this guy wouldn't have confessed. But another policeman had supplied me with a tiny scrap of information beforehand which opened him up. (quoted by Deeley, 1971, p. 142)

The Physical Setting of the Interrogation

Whether police like it or not, social psychologists have a number of concepts and research findings that are helpful to them as they seek to generate confessions. Consider, for example, what we know about the effects of the physical setting on behaviour. Police manuals agree with social psychologists in urging officials to employ a room

that is specifically constructed such that the subject is psychologically removed from the sights and sounds of everyday existence and to maintain rigid control over the space. The novelty of this facility serves the function of promoting a sense of lack of control and social isolation and hence gives the suspect the illusion that the outside world is withdrawing further and further away (Aubry & Caputo, 1980). Inbau, Reid, Buckley, and Jayne (2001) go so far as to conclude that privacy— being alone with the suspect—is "the principal psychological factor contributing to a successful interrogation" (p. 57).

To further minimize sensory stimulation and remove all extraneous sources of distraction, social support, and relief from tension, the manuals recommend that the interrogation room be acoustically soundproofed and bare, without furniture or ornaments—only two chairs and perhaps a desk (see, for example, Macdonald & Michaud, 1987, p. 15). Also critical, of course, is that the accused be denied communicative access to friends and family. Finally, the interrogator is advised to sit as close as possible to the subject, in armless, straight-backed chairs, and at equal eye level. Such advice reflects the psychological hypothesis that invading the suspect's personal space will increase his or her level of anxiety, from which one means of escape is confession.

Establishing Authority During the Interrogation

In keeping with the above constraints, psychological principles would advise police interviewers to avoid letting the suspect establish the ground rules. The most common procedure is the **stipulation**, in which the detectives attempt to stifle attempts by the suspect to set down ground rules for the questioning. A suspect may say, "I will answer any questions about 'X' or 'Y' or 'Z' but not others" (Royal & Schutt, 1976, p. 67). Some suspects may use seductive behaviours or may cry in order to try to control the situation. In response, the interviewer must display firmness and authority without reflecting arrogance.

Emphasis in the police manuals on establishing authority is consistent with the findings of psychological research. As Lloyd-Bostock (1989) observed, the relationship between an individual and someone in authority can generate quite dramatic psychological effects. As mentioned earlier, Milgram's (1974) series of studies showed the appalling degree to which ordinary people would obey instructions to administer painful shocks—instructions that came from an experimenter who had established a position of authority. Many subjects in Milgram's studies were willing to follow instructions to administer painful and dangerous shocks to other participants. Lloyd-Bostock (1989) concluded that subjects being interrogated can become, like Milgram's subjects, as acquiescent to the demands of the interrogator who has carefully established control over the situation.

The Police's Ability to Detect Deception

Psychologists have carried out extensive research on the accuracy of persons in detecting deception in others and in the cues that indicate deception. These research findings can be applied to the task of the police detective in assessing the truth telling of a suspect.

Police Assumptions about Their Own Accuracy

Police believe they can spot the liar in the interrogation room. Inbau and his colleagues (2001) claimed that it is possible, using a variety of cues from the suspect, to distinguish between guilt and innocence. For example, they proposed that the guilty suspect will be afraid to speak because "of a fear of being trapped" (p. 158) and be "overly friendly and polite to the investigator" (p. 129). In contrast, innocent suspects will "maintain direct eye contact and perhaps even lean forward in the chair" (p. 625).

Rachlin (1995) was given permission by the New York City Police Department to observe police detectives at work. He has provided information about how these detectives formed impressions of suspects immediately:

Detectives often wanted to appraise how compliant their subject would be, and there was one simple method that gave them a good clue right from the start. When the detective shook hands with the subject at the time of introduction, in grasping the subject's hand, the detective pivoted his own around clockwise. If the subject's hand followed [quite] easily, it could be interpreted to mean he would be tractable and forthcoming; if not, it was an indication he might be resistant. ... (1995, p. 180)

Interrogators also had their strategies for detecting deception:

The so-called **scan technique** involved asking the subject to describe his activities the day of the crime, covering a period from several hours before to several hours after. The detective would listen to the entire recital without interrupting, paying attention to the degree of denial. If the person provided explicit particulars of events up until the time of the actual crime, then glossed over what he was doing at the time of the crime and concluded with a detailed post-crime accounting of events, it was a signal to the detective that the subject was trying to conceal the criminal behaviour that was the focus of the interview. (Rachlin, 1995, p. 181, boldface added)

Research on the Ability to Detect Deception

Much research in Canada, the United States, and the United Kingdom suggests that law enforcement and other legal professionals cannot generally tell whether someone is lying, even though they are confident in their abilities (see Vrij, Granhag, & Porter, 2011). In a classic study by Ekman and O'Sullivan (1991), customs officials, police officers, judges, FBI agents, forensic psychiatrists, and other groups were no better than chance at judging the honesty of videotaped speakers. More recently, in response to correctional officers stating that they would know a false confession if they saw one, Kassin, Meisner, and Norwick (2005) videotaped prisoners providing true or false accounts of their crimes and gave these to students and law enforcement officers. Again, both groups were unable to differentiate true and false confessions beyond chance, and law enforcement training did not improve performance. These findings, including the notion that confidence does not translate into accuracy in deception detection, have been replicated multiple times around the world. For example, Dalhousie-based researchers Porter, Woodworth, and Birt (2000) found that parole officers performed significantly below chance at detecting deception prior to participating in a deception-detection training workshop, a finding of mediocrity that was replicated in a group of health care professionals including psychologists (Porter et al., 2010).

Videotaping Interrogations

Given that police often use manipulation and trickery in interrogations and that some suspects are susceptible to making false confessions, it is essential that an independent record of the proceeding be made available to the judge and jury (Cassell, 1996b; Gudjonsson, 2003; Kassin, 1997b; Kassin et al., 2010; Leo, 1996a). In Great Britain the Police and Criminal Evidence Act requires that all interrogations be taped. In the United States, approximately one third of states currently require recording of interrogations at least in some instances (Lassiter, 2010). According to Sullivan (2010), many more states are taping interrogations on a voluntary basis, mainly because it eliminates the need for officers to take notes and can reveal important information missed in person. However, often what is shown to jurors is only the defendant's final confession. In Canada, although there is no formal legal requirement that interrogations be videotaped, in many municipalities, such as Toronto, police agencies expect their detectives to record interrogations whenever possible (we do not know how often this occurs!).

Further, the manner in which the interrogation is videotaped can affect jurors' reactions to it. While common sense may suggest that the video camera should be focused on the suspect during the interrogation, this actually takes the individual out of context and does not provide adequate information on what the interviewer is doing. This biases observers' evaluations of the situation, and can lead to the viewer missing important coercive tactics and attributing too much voluntariness to statements made by the suspect. Known as the camera perspective bias (Lassiter, Ware, Lindberg, & Ratcliff, 2010), videos in which observers' visual attention is on the suspect tend to produce a bias that is detrimental for the suspect. So detrimental, in fact, that because statements are assessed as more voluntary, these suspects are also more likely to be judged guilty and to receive more severe sentences. The research results are consistent with social-psychological tests of **correspondent inference theory** (Jones & Davis, 1965; Jones & Harris, 1967), which deals with the decision to infer whether a person's actions reflect (or "correspond to") an internal characteristic. A camera focused on the suspect increases the attribution by observers that the suspect's response was determined by his or her internal predispositions rather than by any coercive nature of the situation. Based on this, an equal-focus camera perspective, showing the interaction of both individuals clearly, is recommended by the academic literature (Snyder, Lassiter, Lindberg, & Pinegar, 2009).

Education

Psychologists also can help to minimize the prevalence of poor interrogations and false confessions through education. By training investigators to use evidenced-based practices and informing them about psychological processes, we may be able to reduce their risk of engaging in avoidable errors. The ability of educating police has been demonstrated in the success of training investigators to use the cognitive interview (a nonaccusatory investigative technique) around the world. For example, Canadian interviewers who have completed intensive, empirically based training program are much more likely to use open-ended prompts and to elicit more information from children with open-ended prompts following training (Price, Roberts, & Collins, 2011). This kind of research suggests the importance of explicit training for police in scientifically validated approaches to interrogations and an overall need for more educated police officers.

In addition to educating police recruits, psychologists can also help inform witnesses. Most importantly, psychologists can help educate witnesses on how memory works. For example, child witnesses benefit from training in source monitoring, which increases their ability to distinguish between events they recently witnessed and events they only heard described (Poole & Lindsey, 2001). While this type of witness training is rare, it presents many avenues for future research and a way for witnesses to actively deal with their own potential biases independently of those introduced by interrogators.

THE COURTS AS CLIENT

On the matter of suspects' confessions, the forensic psychologist can play a role in advising trial judges as well as the police. Courts have, over the years, made a number of decisions relevant to the admissibility of confession evidence; these are reviewed in this section.

What Do the Courts Want to Know?

In determining whether to admit a confession into evidence, the fundamental question asked by judges is whether it was voluntary. Involuntary confessions, usually generated by coercion, are seen as false by the courts and hence are inadmissible. But where do we draw the line between involuntary and voluntary? We may agree that physical brutality or torture contribute to an involuntary confession, but often the police and the defendant will disagree as to whether such actions by the police occurred. With increased recording of interrogations, this situation undoubtedly will improve. But what about more subtle "psychological" coercion? In general, judges rarely conclude that the police trickery (e.g., fabricating evidence) was so severe that it undermined voluntariness (Young, 1996). To date, no legal rulings have prohibited the use of police trickery in Canada, thereby sustaining it as a widely used interrogation tactic (Smith, Stinson, & Patry, 2010a—see the Canadian Researcher Profiles in this chapter for more information about Drs. Smith and Patry).

When told that a suspect confessed, mock jurors do not always consider the circumstances or give much weight to the possibility that coercion caused the confession; rather, they tend to reflect an application of the **fundamental attribution error**, accepting a dispositional attribution of a person's actions without fully accounting for the effects of situational factors (e.g., Jones, 1990).

Forensic psychologists can serve the court by pointing out how judicial assumptions about juries are sometimes in conflict with the findings of psychological research. For example, the conclusion of the exhaustive literature review (or white paper) conducted by Kassin and his colleagues (2011) is that confession evidence is "inherently prejudicial and highly damaging to a defendant, even if it is the product of coercive interrogation, even if it is supported by no other evidence, and even if it is ultimately proven false beyond any reasonable doubt (p. 24)" (Drizin & Leo, 2004 as cited by Kassin et al., 2010).

When a defence lawyer attempts to introduce the testimony of a psychologist regarding the circumstances that lead to involuntary confessions, the trial judge may not admit such testimony. But the effort needs to continue, if for no other reason than it establishes grounds for an appeal, and sometimes such appeals have been successful. For example, in *United States v. Hall* (1996), the court reversed a trial judge's decision not to admit the testimony of Dr. Richard Ofshe. The court ruled that:

Once the trial judge decided that Hall's confession was voluntary, the jury was entitled to hear the relevant evidence on the issue of voluntariness. ... This ruling [by the trial judge] overlooked the utility

CANADIAN RESEARCHER PROFILE

Marc Patry

Dr. Marc Patry is an associate professor of Psychology at Saint Mary's University in Halifax, Nova Scotia. He is originally from outside Boston, Massachusetts. In 1997 he received a Bachelor of Arts from Castleton State College in Vermont: Honours Psychology with a concentration in Forensic Psychology. He went on to doctoral work in the Law-Psychology Program at the University of Nebraska–Lincoln, which he completed in 2001 with a Master of Legal Studies and a Ph.D. in Social Psychology. His dissertation research was an exploration of jury decision making at the sentencing phase of capital cases. After graduate school, he worked for four years as an assistant professor at his alma mater in Vermont. In 2005, he joined the Psychology Department at Saint Mary's University. When he is not working, he enjoys spending time outdoors, especially in his sea kayak.

Dr. Patry has an avid interest in the social psychology of police procedures, including interrogations and confessions. His current research includes work on law and public policy, correctional psychology, and teaching and learning. More specifically, his recent work includes publications on the infamous "Mr. Big" investigation technique employed by the RCMP, the influence of popular television crime dramas such as *CSI* on the legal system, the utility of the Personality Assessment Inventory (PAI) with inmates, workforce trends in correctional psychology, and recent Supreme Court of Canada rulings on forensic hypnosis and civil liability for negligence in police investigations. He is a regular research consultant to the U.S. Federal Bureau of Prisons. He also is interested in the scholarship of teaching and learning. In addition to continued work in these areas, his plans for the future include a new program of research on eyewitness characteristics during lineup identifications.

of valid social science. Even though the jury may have had beliefs about the subject, the question is whether those beliefs were correct. Properly conducted social science research often shows that commonly held beliefs are in error. Dr. Ofshe's testimony, assuming its scientific validity, would have let the jury know that a phenomenon known as false confessions exists, how to recognize it, and how to decide whether it fits the facts of the case being tried. (*United States v. Hall,* 1996, pp. 1344–1345)

Judges also need to be exposed to the psychological perspective that has concluded, in the words of Kassin (1997b), that "for all intents and purposes, [techniques of minimization and rapport building] circumvent laws designed to prohibit the use of coerced confessions" (p. 224).

SOCIETY AS CLIENT

The typical layperson does not think much about confessions of suspects until a highly publicized case brings a claimed confession into question. But people have expectations and standards for how the police should behave when interrogating suspects, and some are concerned when judges permit the admission of evidence that unfairly convicts a defendant.

Lying to Suspects by the Police

Deceit is generally viewed negatively in our society. Police manuals differ about its acceptability during interrogations. Macdonald and Michaud (1987) advise police:

Do not make any false statements. Do not tell him his fingerprints were found at the scene if they were not found at the scene. Do not tell him he was identified by an eyewitness if he was not identified by an eyewitness. If he catches you in a false statement, he will no longer trust you, he will assume that you do not have sufficient evidence to prove his guilt, and his self-confidence will go up. (p. 23)

But, as we have seen, *many police interrogators disregard such admonitions.* Further, some police manuals conclude that without the use of some trickery—leading the suspect to believe that the police have some tangible or specific evidence of guilt—many interrogations would be totally ineffective. Documented cases exist of police telling the kinds of lies admonished by Macdonald and Michaud; such behaviour may even be the norm (Aronson, 1990; King & Snook, 2009).

Do people subscribe to such tactics? Research has indicated that while jurors can accurately identify coercive manoeuvres, they often do not believe that these can generate false confessions (Blandón-Gitlin, Sperry, & Leo, 2011). Additionally, Kassin and Sukel (1997) have conducted research substantiating the overwhelming influence of any kind of confession evidence. Mock jurors were presented with one of three versions of a murder trial transcription, with varying degrees of pressure and coercion exerted by the police during the interrogation. Although jurors successfully identified the coercive tactics as inadmissible and illegal, those exposed to a false confession were significantly more likely to reach a guilty verdict. This increase occurred even when participants were explicitly told to disregard the evidence. Related results have been found in research involving juveniles or children who are interrogated by police; Redlich, Quas, and Ghetti (2008) found that participants reading transcripts of police interviews perceived young suspects as being less credible and less suggestible than victims who were the same age. Clearly, jurors often fail to account for the problem of suggestibility and false confessions among suspects and underappreciate the consequences of lying to suspects in interrogations.

At a broader level, betrayal in the interrogation room not only taints the police but also our society in general, a society built on relationships of trust (Paris, 1996; Slobogin, 1997). A general distrust of police interrogators creates an unwillingness on the part of innocent law-abiding citizens to cooperate with law enforcement authorities. Perhaps a better strategy would be for the police to devise and rely on nondeceptive but effective interviewing strategies. Recently, Canadian researchers in collaboration with police investigators have advocated a move away from deceptive or other "third degree" tactics and instead have begun to rely on productive, empirically supported interview approaches. Snook and colleagues (2010) made four broad recommendations for improving police interviewing in Canada. First, they advocated the development of a standardized tier-based training program for interviewing victims, witnesses, and suspects, noting that current training is inadequate and misleading (based largely on the Reid technique). Second, they recommended that each police organization dedicate an entire unit to investigative interview training and supervision. Third, they argued that professional bodies such as the Canadian Association of Chiefs of Police (CACP) and the Canadian Police Association (CPA) should advocate for the implementation of standardized practices. Finally, they noted that there needs to be better communication and collaboration between criminal justice researchers and police organizations. This would allow police to be aware of empirically based training developments, and allow researchers to develop a greater understanding of the conditions under which interviews are conducted. The researchers describe the PEACE (Preparation and Planning, Engage and Explain, Account, Closure, Evaluation) model of interviewing—which was developed in Great Britain—as a much more effective interviewing approach than the Reid model (see Milne & Bull, 1999; Snook et al., 2010). According to PEACE, investigators first learn as much as possible about the interviewee and then prepare the opening question and subsequent questions based on an analysis of existing evidence. During the interview, the interviewer engages the interviewee (suspect, witness, or victim) in conversation/rapport building and then explains what will occur during the interview. Second, the interviewer elicits the interviewee's account of the incident in question (using various noncoercive techniques depending on the interviewee and his or her response style; see Snook et al., 2010). Next, the interviewer closes the interview by restating the main points and allowing the interviewee to correct or change any information. Following the interview, the interviewers evaluate the interview and their performance to develop their skills and facilitate positive changes in future interviews. The PEACE model has a solid foundation of empirical support. Gudjonsson and Pearse (2011) observed that despite its widespread use in Britain there are no known cases of false confession involving the PEACE model, but this has not been empirically investigated (Bull & Soukara, 2010). It is important to note that the PEACE model is still producing a high rate of valid confessions (Gudjonsson, 2003).

SUMMARY

The goals for police when interrogating suspects are the elicitation of information about the crime and a confession of wrongdoing by the suspect. Confessions, as evidence at trial, are extremely influential; however, an uncertain number of confessions are false. These can be of three types: voluntary, coerced-compliant, and coerced-internalized. Of these, the coerced-compliant type is probably the most frequent; suspects confess—perhaps to get relief from the persistent questioning—even though they know they are innocent.

Police use a number of techniques during interrogations that reflect psychological principles; these include maximization and minimization, "baiting questions," and rapport building. Courts have been reluctant to prohibit the use of lying and trickery by the police, apparently on the assumption that innocent suspects would not succumb to such ruses and confess falsely.

One contribution that can be made by forensic psychologists is to emphasize to police that their procedures can produce false confessions and that some suspects are susceptible to what has been called interrogative suggestibility, in which suspects will sometimes come to believe false information about their role in the crime. It is recommended that police videotape the entire interrogation, so that judges and jurors can observe the procedures used by the interrogators and the style and content of the suspect's responses.

Psychologists can be called by defence lawyers to testify as expert witnesses with regard to the coercive effects of certain interrogation techniques. Forensic psychologists also serve society as a client by evaluating the public's reaction to the use of trickery in interrogations. General distrust of police interrogators erodes the willingness of innocent citizens to cooperate in investigations.

KEY TERMS

baiting questions, p. 173

coerced-compliant false
    confession, p. 164

coerced-internalized false
    confession, p. 165

compliance, p. 164

confession, p. 160

confidence game, p. 174

SUGGESTED READINGS

Ekman, P. (1985). *Telling lies: Clues to deceit in the marketplace, politics, and marriage.* New York: Norton.
Can people tell when someone else is lying? Most cannot, using customary procedures. But psychologist Paul Ekman has developed a system that analyzes brief, specific muscle movement such as a fleeting grimace that may momentarily precede a liar's smile; these are quite difficult to fake.

Gudjonsson, G. (2003). *The psychology of interrogations and confessions: A handbook.* London: Wiley.
This updated comprehensive review of the interrogation process was written by one of the world's leading authorities.

Inbau, F. E., Reid, J. E., Buckley, J. P. & Jayne, B. C. (2001). *Criminal interrogation and confessions* (4th ed.). Sudbury, MA: Jones and Bartlett Publishers.
This guide is the most frequently used police manual. It is available in print or online through http://www.google.ca/books .

Kassin, S. M., Appleby, S. C., & Perillo, J. (2010). Interviewing suspects: Practice, science, and future directions. *Legal and Criminological Psychology, 15,* 39–55.
This article covers extensive recommendations regarding how we should properly interview suspects in ways that minimize false confessions and maximize the amount of correct information obtained.

Kassin, S. M., Drizin, S. A., Grisso, T., Gudjonsson, G. H., Leo, R. A., & Redlich, A. D. (2010). Police-induced confessions: Risk factors and recommendations. *Law and Human Behavior, 34,* 3–38.
Many of the issues introduced in this chapter are discussed in this outstanding article.

Kotlowitz, A. (1999, February 8). The unprotected. *New Yorker,* pp. 42–53.
A disturbing account of the threats to validity when children are interrogated as crime suspects.

McCann, J. T. (1998). A conceptual framework for identifying various types of confessions. *Behavioral Sciences and the Law, 16,* 441–453.
This article proposes a fourth type of false confession, called the coercive-reactive type, that reflects coercion from sources other than the police; for example, a teenager who is threatened with death by his gang members unless he admits responsibility for a crime actually committed by the gang leader.

Shuy, R. W. (1998). *The language of confession, interrogation, and deception.* Thousand Oaks, CA: Sage.
Many examples from actual cases are provided in this examination of criminal confessions through the use of linguistic analysis. Highly recommended.

Smith, S. M., Stinson, V., & Patry, M. W. (2009). Using the "Mr. Big" technique to elicit confessions: Successful innovation or dangerous development in the Canadian legal system? *Psychology, Public Policy, and Law, 15*(3), 168–193.
A great review of the "Mr. Big" technique, including legal cases and an in-depth examination of this controversial noncustodial method.

Wakefield, H., & Underwager, R. (1998). Coerced or nonvoluntary confessions. *Behavioral Sciences and the Law, 16,* 423–440.
This article covers a number of topics from this chapter, including types of false confessions, police interrogation procedures, and the admissibility of psychologists as expert witnesses. Specific cases are described in detail.

Young, D. (1996). Unnecessary evil: Police lying in interrogations. *Connecticut Law Review, 28,* 425–477.
This law review article documents how courts have had shifting standards over the years regarding the admissibility of confessions elicited in interrogations that involved questionable police tactics.

The Psychology of the Jury

Like many aspects of the Canadian legal system, our jury system is founded in English traditions and practices from the United States. However, the process of jury selection in Canada is very different from that of the United States. In Canada, the kind of litigation consulting and jury "manipulation" that is witnessed to our south does not occur. In the first section of this chapter, the basis of and process of selecting juries in Canada is described. Next, we introduce the important role of forensic psychologists in conducting research on and making observations about jury decision-making (see Bornstein & Greene, 2011) As you will see, our current laws offer particular challenges to conducting research on Canadian juries that do not exist in some other countries.

As we have observed (Porter & ten Brinke, 2009), one of the pillars of society is a legal system—and juries—that make fair and reliable decisions concerning guilt and innocence of defendants. Although this assumption has prevailed for more than a thousand years in the English common-law system on which the current Canadian legal system is based, there are good reasons to question its accuracy:

1. It is not possible to assess the accuracy of trial outcomes.
2. Like science, the courts acknowledge that their decisions are infallible. As psychological researchers, we accept an error rate of 5 percent (the commonly accepted rate of statistical error we use in significance testing). The courts continue to use the "beyond a reasonable doubt" criterion for establishing guilt, one that would never be accepted by scientists because of its ambiguity, but certainly one that acknowledges some error rate.
3. One doesn't need to dig too deeply into the psychology literature to find that in numerous contexts human decision making is highly irrational (e.g., Englich, Mussweiler, & Strack, 2006; Kahneman & Tversky, 1982).

Therefore, to accept the assumption that the decisions of juries are sound, one must also assume that it is untestable, that the reasonable-doubt standard ensures that only a few errors occur, and that jurors have the knowledge and capacity to overcome normal biases to make rational decisions. What do you think? If you were an innocent defendant in a criminal trial, would you have faith that this is an acceptable set of assumptions to predict that you would be found innocent?

JURY SELECTION IN CANADA: THE "RANDOM" IDEAL

In Canada, the Charter of Rights and Freedoms (1982) provides the overriding principles according to which juries are to be selected. The Supreme Court interprets these principles and directs lower

Do you think jurors are able to make objective decisions about witness credibility and whether a defendant is guilty?

courts in their application. Section 11(d) of the Charter requires that an accused person receive a fair trial by an independent and impartial judge or jury. The selection of a jury is based on the idea that an accused person should have his or her charge judged by a random, unbiased sample of his or her peers. When it is established that a jury was not impartial, the Charter rights of the accused have been violated.

In line with this principle, the Supreme Court of Canada has been careful to try to ensure that juries judging the guilt of accused persons are always unbiased (e.g., Schuller & Vidmar, 2011). However, as the Supreme Court outlined in *R. v. Bain* (1992, para. 93), the court takes a conservative approach in deciding whether a person's Charter rights have been violated in this way. So, interestingly, in order for an infringement of the Charter to occur, a jury does not actually have to be biased. The test for whether a jury is biased is whether it may be "reasonably perceived" as such by the courts. For example, if, for some reason, either the defence or Crown has too much influence on the selection of jurors, the judge needs only to have a reasonable perception or suspicion of a biased jury.

Based on a long history of English common law, the Supreme Court has decided that the best way to create an impartial jury is by taking a **random sample of jurors** from citizens in society (see Schuller & Vidmar, 2011). As such, the information about potential jurors during the selection process generally is limited to name, gender, age, and occupation. Despite this ideal, jury selection in our country is not purely random. A proper jury also must be *competent* to make a decision of guilt or innocence. Similar in some ways to the criteria for judging whether an accused person is competent to stand trial (discussed in Chapter 9), all jurors must have a basic understanding of the trial, their role in the process, and the evidence that is offered. As noted in *R. v. Bain* (1992), "Some trials are more complex and complicated, however, and a tampering with randomness may be appropriate to achieve a minimal ability to understand the evidence and issues" (para. 96). The Crown in particular must work toward the "random" ideal, while sometimes "tampering" to ensure that jurors are unbiased, representative, and competent. As such, the Crown is expected to exclude jurors who do not meet any of these criteria. For example, numerous members of motorcycle gangs in Quebec have been tried and convicted of various serious

offences in the past two decades. If a potential juror in such a case enters the court wearing a Hell's Angels jacket, the wise Crown prosecutor would probably make a challenge. However, unlike jury selection in the United States, no fishing expeditions are allowed in Canadian courts.

Thus, the Supreme Court recognizes that randomness is not a "panacea" and the Criminal Code offers both sides a means of challenging prospective jurors. Specifically, section 634 of the Criminal Code states that the Crown prosecutor and the accused each are entitled to 20 challenges if the charge is high treason (not exactly one of our more common crimes) or first-degree murder, 12 challenges if the charge is another offence for which the accused may be sentenced to a term of over five years, or four challenges if the charge involves any other offence.

The challenges can be based on any of the following:

1. The identity of the potential juror is not the name stated on the list.
2. The juror has already formed an opinion about guilt.
3. The juror has been convicted of an offence for which he or she was sentenced to a term of imprisonment exceeding 12 months.
4. The juror is an alien (i.e., not a Canadian citizen).
5. The juror, even with the aid of technical, personal, interpretative, or other support services is physically unable to perform properly the duties of a juror.
6. The juror does not speak an official language of Canada or the language in which the accused can best give testimony.

In practice, it is common for neither side to oppose the first 12 jurors whose names have been randomly generated from the voters' list. However, often a judge may decide that a juror can be excused from jury service, even if neither side has offered a challenge. Jurors can be excluded from duty if they have any personal involvement in the case or any relationship with the defendant, the judge, the prosecutor, the defence lawyer, or any potential witness in the case. They also can be excluded if serving on a jury is likely to cause any personal hardship, such as losing their job or experiencing health problems. Further, although the court seeks to maintain "12 good men and women and true" on each jury, occasionally a juror will die or be dismissed during the course of a trial. As such, as long as there are at least ten jurors remaining, the trial shall proceed and the remaining jurors will decide on a verdict.

One reason that a juror might be dismissed during a trial or that a trial verdict might be challenged is a revelation of a **conflict of interest** or outright unethical behaviour. Shakespeare observed the fallibility of individual jurors in *Measure for Measure*: "I not deny, The jury, passing on the prisoner's life, May in the sworn twelve have a thief or two Guiltier than him they try."

A notorious example of a conflict of interest that was not identified until after the verdict occurred in the 1995 Vancouver murder case involving Peter Gill (who was on bail during the trial). The jury in the case acquitted Gill and five other men accused of the first-degree murder of Ron and Jimmy Dosanjh, who had been gunned down execution-style during a drug war in Vancouver. However, the decision was later appealed after one of the jurors, a 40-year-old single mother named Gillian Guess, was convicted of willfully attempting to obstruct the course of justice. It was revealed that Guess was having sex with the accused during the time of his trial. At Guess's own 1998 trial, evidence was presented that she had flirted with Gill early in his trial, and, ultimately, they began a secret sexual relationship during his six-month trial. For the first time in the history of North America or the British Commonwealth, a juror was charged with having an affair with an accused killer during a trial. Guess was sentenced to 18 months in jail (but served only three). Gill himself was eventually convicted of obstruction of justice and received a 70-month sentence. Since then, similar incidents have occurred in British Columbia. In the 1994 case of Mindy Tran, the 8-year-old young girl went missing near her house in Kelowna, and later was found buried in a shallow grave near her parent's home with evidence of having being beaten and sexually assaulted (CBC News, 2000a). The defendant, Newfoundlander Shannon Murrin, was acquitted in 2000 after a gruelling several-month trial as a result of questionable mitochondrial DNA evidence, but soon after the trial was found to be in a romantic relationship with one of the original jurors (Kathy Macdonald) who had evaluated his culpability. Although both Murrin and Macdonald advised that there was nothing romantic between them during the trial, they ended up starting a relationship and cohabiting in Newfoundland soon after (CBC News, 2000b; RCMP Watch, 2009).

Jury selection occurs in a very different way in the United States. There, lawyers have been given broad powers to generate a group of jurors with particular characteristics. Potential jurors typically undergo extensive questioning before trial to allow the two sides to gain sufficient information for their challenges. These questions can address the potential jurors' attitudes toward the accused and criminals in general, and their views on certain issues such as the death penalty. In addition, the types of reasons for which a juror can be excluded are almost limitless. Often, psychologists or other consultants are hired to form the right jury. In fact, there is now an entire cottage industry or subspecialty of psychologists who perform as "litigation consultants" in American cases.

JURY RESEARCH IN CANADA: NOT SO IDEAL

A considerable amount of research on jury decision making has been conducted in Canada. One prominent group, Regina Schuller and her colleagues at York University, has conducted many important studies of various influences on juror decisions, including knowledge of a complainant's sexual history (Klippenstein, Schuller, & Wall, 2007; Schuller & Hastings, 2002; Schuller & Klippenstein, 2004) and the victim's self-defence behaviour in battered-spouse cases (e.g., Schuller & Rzepa, 2002). For example, Schuller has found that jurors view battered women who have fought back or behaved aggressively toward their abusers' violence more negatively than more passive victims.

However, existing laws in Canada offer a limitation on the type of research that can be conducted. Generally, researchers such as Schuller use a **mock jury approach** in which people (usually undergraduates) are asked to pretend they are jurors and are presented with fictitious or real case materials to come up with an appropriate verdict or sentence. At present, it is not possible for researchers to observe jury decision making in real cases or interview jurors about their decisions after the trial. In fact, section 649 of the Criminal Code states that if a juror discloses any information relating to the proceedings of the jury during its deliberations (that was not subsequently disclosed in open court), he or she is guilty of a criminal offence. This rule does not apply in the United States; in fact, although judges may "recommend" to jurors that they refrain from discussing their deliberations publicly, jurors often choose to share their experiences with the media.

Because of differences between actual and mock juror decision making (such as the consequences of the decisions), the generalizability of mock jury studies can always be questioned. James Ogloff, previously a psychology professor at Simon Fraser University (now at Monash University in Australia) and past president of the Canadian Psychological Association, has published widely on the psychology of juries (e.g., Chopra & Ogloff, 2000; Ogloff & Vidmar, 1994; Nikonova & Ogloff, 2005). He has outlined his concerns with the current legislation that does not permit researchers to discuss jury decisions with actual jurors (Ogloff, 2001). In addition to this prohibition making research on juries impossible, he describes the problem of **juror stress** in cases involving violent, heinous crimes. The current law does not permit jurors to discuss their deliberations with anyone (including their spouse, a researcher, or a psychologist), which can lead to long-term psychological difficulties such as posttraumatic stress disorder (PTSD). (This will be discussed later in the "Implications of Jury Duty" section of the chapter.) He felt that the state of affairs was so problematic that he and a CPA Board known as the Committee on Legal Affairs in 2000 (unsuccessfully) attempted to intervene in two Supreme Court cases. In these cases, former jurors revealed that the juries had engaged in serious misconducts during their deliberations (such as coercing one juror into agreeing with the majority). However, the Supreme Court continues to insist that the confidentiality of what happens in the jury room is paramount and there are no exceptions.

Thus, at present, we must continue to rely largely on mock jury research or research from other countries to understand how juries make their decisions. Hopefully, the Canadian courts will revise the laws on juries in the coming years. For example, the laws could be changed to become more flexible in allowing jurors to discuss their experiences with certain others, such as mental health professionals and researchers in a confidential interview setting.

IMPLICATIONS OF JURY DUTY

Serving on a jury has many implications including negative health affects like posttraumatic stress disorder (PTSD) (Anand & Manweiller, 2005),

traumatic experiences from exposure to disturbing criminal evidence (e.g., videotaped assault or images of gruesome crimes) (Robertson, Davies, & Nettleingham, 2009), and harassment from family and friends of the victim/complainant after a not-guilty finding (e.g., see Mellili, 2009).

Juror Trauma and Stress

As mentioned above, jurors are subject to viewing gruesome evidence and make legal decisions that will alter someone else's life, which may cause moderate to severe stress, and even PTSD. One example of this occurred in the well-known Canadian case of Robert Pickton, who is now serving a 25-year sentence for the murder of eight women, and is the alleged killer of twenty other women in British Columbia. After the gruelling 11-month trial, one anonymous juror came forward and divulged his regrets for taking part in the trial (CBC News, 2010). He stated that aside from losing his job because of the length of the trial, he was subject to viewing horrible and gruesome evidence/photographs, and even developed marital problems because he could not discuss the content of what he was feeling or going through. Similarly, in the infamous Canadian case of Paul Bernardo, jurors were exposed to videotaped live footage of the accused and his wife sexually assaulting two teenage girls; even the Chief Justice, Patrick LeSage, admitted to continually waking up in the middle of the night in the months and years following the trial because of the exposure to the horrific evidence (Bowman, 2007). Miller, Flores, and Dolezilek (2007) suggest that high levels of stress can influence the decision-making process and have negative effects on the justice system. Further, they suggest that stress interventions can help educate jurors (and judges) about prevention of juror stress and advising on coping strategies. In the Bernardo case, the trial judge Patrick LeSage became one of the first jurists in Canada to hire psychologists to provide counselling to the jurors following the trial (e.g., see Anand & Manweiller, 2005). The stressful and traumatic nature of this particular case led the judge to believe the jurors would benefit from post-trial counselling. Although by law, jurors are not permitted to discuss anything that occurred in the jury room, a sympathetic judge is well aware that he or she could never be privy to what occurs in the therapy room between a mental health professional and former juror. Psychologists are bound to maintain confidentiality with clients and we (society) would never know what a juror disclosed in therapy (unless one of the three conditions for violating confidentiality with a client was met, described in Chapter 2).

Juror stress commonly occurs. In a study from the National Center for the State Courts (2002) assessing juror stress during each stage of trial, the percentage of jurors experiencing stress was highest when having to determine guilt (44 percent of jurors) or reach a unanimous verdict (49 percent of jurors), as well as the general disruption of a juror's schedule (45 percent of jurors). In particular, high-profile and serious crimes (e.g., the Robert Pickton case) elicit more trauma and posttrial stress in jurors (Anand & Manweiller, 2005; Miller et al., 2007). Antonio (2008) also found that both male and female jurors reported signs and symptoms of posttrial stress after serving on capital murder trials, but female jurors discussed these issues of juror stress more often than men.

How Can We Alleviate Juror Stress?

Because of the severe negative effects that jury duty can have on a juror, several researchers have suggested ways of alleviating courtroom stress (e.g., see Miller et al., 2007). One of the suggestions to alleviate juror stress is by adding posttrial debriefings. This is the most commonly used intervention and it involves talking with a professional about the trial experience and conclusions of the trial. The juror discusses his or her emotions, concerns, and thoughts about the experience, which is thought to alleviate stress and minimize the negative posttrial effects. Robertson et al. (2009) discuss the implications that jury duty can have on a person, and suggest that jurors should have similar options as vulnerable witnesses, who can attend specialized Crown Court counselling offices and discuss their experiences in confidence.

Publication Bans

In addition to developing psychological problems from the time spent during jury duty, jurors also can endure problems after the trial, especially when there is no court-ordered **publication ban**. Publication bans often are issued when the safety of the jurors, victim, or witness is at stake, or when the judge feels that the scrutiny and criticism from society will influence the jury's decision (Burritt, 2012). However, publication bans are not always

issued, and rarely occur in the United States because they violate freedom of speech (Shade, 1994). In the recent case of Casey Anthony, who was found innocent after being accused of killing her two-year-old daughter, jurors have been receiving death threats upon release of their names (Hightower & Lush, 2011). As demonstrated by this case, there still is controversy regarding whether juror names should be released to the public, especially in high-profile cases. Melilli (2009) suggests that jurors should be given the option of having their names and addresses withheld from the press in highly publicized cases, in order to prevent harassment. Willis (2004) explains that jurors worry about how their friends, coworkers, and other peers might perceive them, and are even afraid to leave their homes after deliberations because of the potential for psychological and physical harassment. Therefore, he questions whether the disclosure of names in high-profile cases should be allowed because of the costs it could cause citizens for carrying out a civic obligation. However, other researchers suggest that lack of anonymity for jurors places more accountability on jurors for their decisions. Therefore, the jurors are pressured to make a decision based on the "doing the right thing" phenomenon (e.g., see Keleher, 2010). Jurors also may be more likely to convict when they feel less accountable, and thus accountability may have adverse effects for the defendant. Another repercussion of jurors feeling accountable for their decisions could be that jurors might rationalize their verdicts under pressure from the media.

Jurors make a commitment to assisting with determinations of justice that can require an enormous personal and professional toll.

JUROR BIAS AND TOOLS OF MEASUREMENT

Broad Attitudes and Traits

A fundamental principle of social psychology is that each of us perceives the world in an idiosyncratic way. Two different jurors will interpret the same evidence differently, based on their past experiences with the justice system, developmental background, and education (not to mention their intelligence and personality features). The phenomenon of **juror bias** refers to the assumption that each of us makes interpretations based on past experience and that these interpretations can colour our verdicts. An example of potential juror bias recently was highlighted by a group of Simon Fraser University researchers (Connolly, Price, & Gordon, 2010). They analyzed judicial assessments of complainants' credibility in 52 "timely" (child complainants who reported the alleged crime soon after it happened) and 49 delayed (adult complainant) criminal prosecutions of child sexual abuse. They found that judges viewed adult complainants more positively than children, despite that all complainants were children when the alleged offence occurred. On the other hand, Pozzulo and Demsey (2009) found (using a mock jury approach) that child victims were perceived as being as credible as adult victims, but a child as a bystander/witness was perceived as less credible than an adult as a bystander. Another salient issue is the race of the defendant; for example, disturbing evidence from the United States indicates that the racial attributes of the accused person can powerfully influence legal decision making; Eberhardt, Davies, Purdie-Vaughns, and Johnson (2006) found in a study of capital cases in the United States that the more stereotypically black a defendant is perceived to be, the more likely that person is to be sentenced to death, controlling for case/evidentiary factors.

In criminal trials, juror biases can be classified as favouring the prosecution or the defence. That is, some prospective jurors—without knowing anything about the evidence—may assume, for example, that the defendant is guilty. Pro-prosecution bias reflects, in some jurors, the aforementioned trust of authority figures; in others, a belief in a just world; in others, perhaps an acquiescent response set (i.e., a tendency to agree with what has been said), regardless of its content. In contrast, a pro-defence bias often stems from an intrinsic sympathy with the underprivileged or an opposition to or suspicion of those in power.

In general, civil cases are rarely decided by juries in Canada. In fact, some provinces never allow juries to decide such cases. Nova Scotia, on the other hand, has liberal rules regarding the participation of juries in civil trials; there, they are allowed in any civil case. When juries make decisions in civil cases, biases also can occur. Here the biases are more varied, and it may not be possible to identify a single dimension of bias that applies to every civil suit. Some complainants who sue resemble defendants in criminal trials, in that they are (sometimes powerless) individuals in opposition to a powerful organization. Consider, for example, a parent whose child was injured in a car wreck who claims that the child seat in the car was defective. A suit by an individual against a major corporation with seemingly limitless resources evokes from some jurors a sympathy bias that resembles a pro-defence bias in criminal trials, but here, in civil trials, it reflects a **pro-plaintiff bias**. But other jurors may manifest a **pro-defendant bias** (or at least **antiplaintiff biases**); for example, some jurors feel strongly that society is too litigious and that many lawsuits are without merit. By identifying with powerful corporations, some pro-defendant jurors in civil cases may possess some of the authoritarian orientations that pro-prosecution jurors show in a criminal case.

Several instruments have been developed to attempt to measure the basic biases. A later section reviews and evaluates these instruments. But recall that some trial consultants prefer to relate jury selection to specific issues in the case at hand, rather than trying to assess general biases.

The general attitudes that may be related to jurors' verdicts in criminal trials differ from the attitudes relevant to responses in civil trials; thus different instruments have been developed to assess each type of attitude.

Criminal Trials

Two concepts have provided the structure for the measure of criminal juror bias—**authoritarianism** (the favouring of obedience to authority) and the distinction between a pro-prosecution and a pro-defence orientation. Attitude scales have been developed to measure each.

The Revised Legal Attitudes Questionnaire

The Revised Legal Attitudes Questionnaire (RLAQ) was constructed by Kravitz, Cutler, and Brock (1993), who created 30 items with statements from the original Legal Attitudes Questionnaire (LAQ). (The items on the RLAQ may be found in Box 8.1.)

The statements in the Revised Legal Attitudes Questionnaire are the following:

1. Unfair treatment of underprivileged groups and classes is the chief cause of crime. (AA, R, F)
2. Too many obviously guilty persons escape punishment because of legal technicalities. (A, F)
3. The Supreme Court is, by and large, an effective guardian of the Constitution. (E)
4. Evidence illegally obtained should be admissible in court if such evidence is the only way of obtaining a conviction. (A, F)
5. Most prosecuting attorneys have a strong sadistic streak. (AA, R)
6. Search warrants should clearly specify the person or things to be seized. (E, R, F)
7. No one should be convicted of a crime on the basis of circumstantial evidence, no matter how strong such evidence is. (AA, R, F)
8. There is no need in a criminal case for the accused to prove his innocence beyond a reasonable doubt. (E, R, F)
9. Any person who resists arrest commits a crime. (A, F)
10. When determining a person's guilt or innocence, the existence of a prior arrest record should not be considered. (E, R, F)
11. Wiretapping by anyone or for any reason should be completely illegal. (AA, R, F)
12. A lot of recent Supreme Court decisions sound suspiciously Communistic. (A)
13. Treachery and deceit are common tools of prosecutors. (AA, R)
14. Defendants in a criminal case should be required to take the witness stand. (A, F)
15. All too often, minority group members do not get fair trials. (E, R, F)
16. Because of the oppression and persecution minority group members suffer, they deserve leniency and special treatment in the courts. (AA, R, F)
17. Citizens need to be protected against excess police power as well as against criminals. (E, R, F)
18. Persons who testify in court against underworld characters should be allowed to do so anonymously to protect themselves from retaliation. (A)
19. It is better for society that several guilty men be freed than one innocent one wrongfully imprisoned. (E, R, F)
20. Accused persons should be required to take lie-detector tests. (A, F)
21. It is moral and ethical for a lawyer to represent a defendant in a criminal case even when he believes his client is guilty. (E, R, F)
22. A society with true freedom and equality for all would have very little crime. (AA, R, F)
23. When there is a "hung" jury in a criminal case, the defendant should always be freed and the indictment dismissed. (AA, R, F)
24. Police should be allowed to arrest and question suspicious-looking persons to determine whether they have been up to something illegal. (A, F)
25. The law coddles criminals to the detriment of society. (A, F)
26. A lot of judges have connections with the underworld. (AA, R)
27. The freedom of society is endangered as much by zealous law enforcement as by the acts of individual criminals. (E, R, F)
28. There is just about no such thing as an honest cop. (AA, R)
29. In the long run, liberty is more important than order. (E, R, F)
30. Upstanding citizens have nothing to fear from the police. (A, F)

Note: Identification of subscales (A = authoritarian, AA = anti-authoritarian, E = equalitarian) is given immediately following each item. Items that were reverse-coded (scored in the opposite direction) on the overall RLAQ scale are indicated with an R following the subscale identification. Items included in the final RLAQ23 scale are indicated with an F.

Further item analyses reduced the number of scored items to 23. (In Box 8.1 items that were included in the final 23 are marked with an F.) This version can be administered with the usual Likert-scale response options (that is, strongly agree, agree somewhat, etc.).

Several types of evidence for the general validity of this revised scale are available:

- Several studies converted the format of the original LAQ to that of the RLAQ, dropped some items, and related scale responses to verdicts. Using 24 of the items, Moran and Comfort (1982) administered the scale to 319 persons who had served as jurors in felony trials; the researchers found that legal authoritarianism scores were significantly related to verdicts in female jurors but not male jurors. Moran and Cutler (1989) dropped three more items and compared responses to mock juror verdicts in another sample of persons with jury experience; again, those with higher scores on the attitude scale were more likely to convict.
- In their second study, Cutler, Moran, and Narby (1992) used all 30 items in a Likert-type response format with 61 undergraduate respondents, who also watched a videotaped simulation of a murder trial in which the defendant claimed he was not guilty by reason of insanity. Again, high scorers (i.e., relatively authoritarian subjects) on this revised LAQ were significantly more likely to vote guilty than were low scorers. This version of the LAQ had greater predictive validity than the Juror Bias Scale (described below).
- Construct validity of the RLAQ was assessed by comparing respondents of different ethnic groups (black versus Hispanic versus white) and political parties. As expected, lower legal authoritarianism scores were found among blacks and among Democrats (those supporting the more left wing of the two major U.S. political parties).*

Since the validation of the RLAQ, several studies have used the scale to assess legal attitudes. Butler (2010) used the RLAQ to survey 250 residents in Florida on legal authoritarianism. The author found that legal authoritarianism was positively related to attitudes toward punishment of the elderly and the physically disabled. Butler (2007) also found—by administering the RLAQ—that participants in support of the death penalty were more likely to recommend the death sentence for a juvenile defendant over an adult defendant.

The Juror Bias Scale

In seeking to uncover attitudes that would predict jurors' verdicts, Kassin and Wrightsman (1983) chose another dimension, the bias to favour the prosecution or the defence. They noted that virtually all models of juror decision making (cf., Pennington & Hastie, 1981) assumed that jurors make decisions in criminal cases that reflect the implicit operation of two judgments. The first of these is an estimate of the **probability of commission**; specifically, how likely is it that the defendant was the person who committed the crime? Though jurors will base their estimates of this probability mainly on the strength of the evidence, their previous experiences will influence their interpretation of the evidence. For example, if a police officer testifies that she found a bag of heroin on the person of the defendant, some jurors, trusting police, would use this to increase their estimate that the defendant did commit a crime, but other jurors, given the same testimony, would discount or reject it based on their prior experiences and beliefs that police witnesses are dishonest. A second judgment by the juror concerns his or her use of the concept of **reasonable doubt**, or the threshold of certainty deemed necessary for conviction. Judges always instruct jurors in criminal trials that they should bring back a verdict of not guilty if they have a reasonable doubt about the defendant's guilt. But the legal system has great reluctance to operationally "define" reasonable doubt; when juries, during their deliberations, ask the judge for a definition, the judge usually falls back on the prior instruction, or tells them that it is a doubt in one's head that the person can explain/give a reason for to another person/juror. Left to their own devices, different jurors apply their own standards for how close they must be to certainty in order to vote guilty. Some jurors may interpret "beyond a reasonable doubt" to mean "beyond any doubt," or 100 percent certainty. Others may interpret it quite loosely (Dane, 1985; Kagehiro & Stanton, 1985; Tenney, Cleary, & Spellman, 2009), and Heffer (2006) specifically suggested that there is no legal consensus that the concept of reasonable doubt should be fixed.

Kassin and Wrightsman (1983) proposed that judgments of guilt arise when a juror's probability-of-commission estimate exceeds his or her reasonable-doubt criterion; thus they used these two factors to classify jurors as having a pro-prosecution or pro-defence bias. To determine whether bias affected one's verdicts, they constructed a 17-statement Juror Bias Scale (JBS). (The statements, and filler items, are reprinted in Box 8.2.) The JBS gives scores on each of the two factors of probability of commission and reasonable doubt.

Two methods of validation of the Juror Bias Scale have been used:

1. Kassin and Wrightsman (1983) had university students and jury-eligible respondents complete the JBS scale and later watch videotapes of re-enacted actual trials or read transcripts of simulated trials. Four types of criminal trials were used, dealing with offences ranging from auto theft to conspiracy to assault and rape. After being exposed to the trial, each mock juror was asked to render an individual verdict about the defendant's guilt or innocence. These verdicts then were related to the respondents' scores on the JBS. On three of the four cases, mock jurors with a pro-prosecution bias more often voted to convict the defendant than did mock jurors with a pro-defence bias. The differences were large; the average rate of conviction for prosecution-biased jurors was 81 percent, compared to 52 percent for defence-biased ones. Thus, in most cases, scores on the JBS have predictive validity.

BOX 8.2   ITEMS OF THE JUROR BIAS SCALE

The second measure of general juror attitudes is the Juror Bias Scale. The instructions and scale items are listed here. (Note: On the version of the scale administered to respondents, each statement is followed by five choices: 1. Strongly agree; 2. Mildly agree; 3. Agree and disagree equally; 4. Mildly disagree; and 5. Strongly disagree. In order to conserve space these are deleted here.)

Instructions: This is a questionnaire to determine people's attitudes and beliefs on a variety of general legal issues. Please answer each statement by giving as true a picture of your position as possible.

1. Appointed judges are more competent than elected judges.
2. A suspect who runs from the police most probably committed the crime.
3. A defendant should be found guilty if only 11 out of 12 jurors vote guilty.
4. Most politicians are really as honest as humanly possible.
5. Too often jurors hesitate to convict someone who is guilty out of pure sympathy.
6. In most cases where the accused presents a strong defence, it is only because of a good lawyer.
7. In general, children should be excused for their misbehaviour.
8. The death penalty is cruel and inhumane.
9. Out of every 100 people brought to trial, at least 75 are guilty of the crime with which they are charged.
10. For serious crimes like murder, a defendant should be found guilty if there is a 90 percent chance that he or she committed the crime.
11. Defence lawyers don't really care about guilt or innocence, they are just in business to make money.

12. Generally, the police make an arrest only when they are sure about who committed the crime.
13. Circumstantial evidence is too weak to use in court.
14. Many accident claims filed against insurance companies are phony.
15. The defendant is often a victim of his or her own bad reputation.
16. If the grand jury recommends that a person be brought to trial, then he or she probably committed the crime.
17. Extenuating circumstances should not be considered— if a person commits a crime, then that person should be punished.
18. Hypocrisy is on the increase in society.
19. Too many innocent people are wrongfully imprisoned.
20. If a majority of the evidence—but not all of it— suggests that the defendant committed the crime, the jury should vote not guilty.
21. If the defendant committed a victimless crime like gambling or possession of marijuana, he should never be convicted.
22. Some laws are made to be broken.

Scoring procedures: The following are filler items and are not scored: Items 1, 4, 7, 18, and 22.

The following nine items are part of the Probability of Commission subscale: Items 2, 6, 9, 11, 12, 13 (reversed scoring), 14, 15 (reversed scoring), and 16.

These eight items are part of the Reasonable Doubt subscale: Items 3, 5, 8 (reversed scoring), 10, 17, 19 (reversed scoring), 20 (reversed scoring), and 21 (reversed scoring).

Kassin, S.M., "The construction and validation of a juror bias scale", *Journal of Research in Personality*, 17(4) Dec. 1983.

But with regard to the trial for rape, mock jurors generally predisposed to favour the defence were just as likely to find the defendant guilty as were jurors who favoured the prosecution. It is possible that pro-defence jurors, who are relatively liberal in their political views, are especially sympathetic with the victim when the crime involves a sexual assault; that is, their usual bias is balanced by a concern for the victim.

2. Lecci and Myers (1996; Myers & Lecci, 1998) sought, through the use of factor analysis, to determine whether the two theoretical dimensions, reasonable doubt and probability of commission, were verified empirically. Two samples, each consisting of 301 university students, completed the JBS, and several factor analyses were done. (A **factor analysis** is a statistical procedure that examines relationships between responses to different items and thus identifies which items are related to each other; factors are theoretical labels for what is common to the item statements that cluster together.) The reasonable-doubt concept survived the empirical analysis fairly intact; results produced a six-item empirically driven reasonable-doubt factor, but the original eight items also achieved a reasonable fit with the data in a cross-validation (Lecci & Myers, 1996, p. 6). Lecci and Myers recommend the six-item empirically based scale; the items from Box 8.2 on this scale are items 3, 5, 10, 17, 20 (reverse scored), and 21 (reverse scored).

The dimension of probability of commission was not supported empirically as one factor. Three items—numbers 2, 12, and 16—formed one factor, which could keep the "probability of commission" label. Three other items from this scale—items 6, 11, and 14—emerged on another factor, which seems to reflect cynicism about the legal system.

To determine the predictive validity of the empirically derived scales, Myers and Lecci (1998) administered the JBS scale to 406 university students and had them watch a videotape of a simulated rape and murder trial; the videotape included opening and closing statements by the prosecution and defence, direct and cross-examination of eight witnesses, and the judge's instructions, which included an explanation of reasonable doubt. The tape lasted 60 minutes. Participants were classified as either prosecution-biased or defence-biased, on the basis of their responses to the original 17 items on the JBS. Consistent with previous results, prosecution-biased respondents were more likely to find the defendant guilty than were defence-biased ones. Although the difference was statistically significant, it was not as large as in the previous validation: 54 percent of the prosecution-biased respondents voted guilty, compared to 46 percent of the defence-biased respondents. A similar analysis was done with the empirically based scales—essentially 12 of the original 17 items—and similar results were found: 52 percent of the prosecution-biased respondents convicted the defendant, compared to 47 percent of the defence-biased respondents, a difference that was also statistically significant. The reasonable-doubt items accounted for the bulk of the predictive validity, as was the case in the original validation.

Several studies have demonstrated effects on decision making after administering the Juror Bias Scale. Keller and Wiener (2011) found that the JBS was a significant predictor of confidence in sexual assault guilty verdicts as well as how convincing the state's case was in sexual assault cases. Warling and Peterson-Badali (2003) found that prosecution bias was positively associated with guilty verdicts. Similarly, Walker and Woody (2011) found that pro-defence or pro-prosecution biases are strongly associated with juror verdicts.

Of what use are the Revised Legal Attitudes Questionnaire and the Juror Bias Questionnaire to the trial consultant faced with aiding a lawyer in jury selection in the United States for a criminal trial? Individual items can serve as the basis for questions to individual prospective jurors during the **voir dire** (or jury-selection phase), or if there is an opportunity to administer a supplemental juror questionnaire (to be described subsequently), prospective jurors can be asked to respond to all the statements. But the trial consultant should always remember that general traits, as measured here, have a very limited relationship to verdicts in specific cases. They are better than nothing, and they are probably better than most people's intuitions, but their predictive accuracy is low when it comes to verdicts by individual jurors. Because there is no equivalent of jury selection in Canada, questionnaires such as the Juror Bias Scale and the Revised Legal Attitudes Questionnaire (and other similar questionnaires/surveys) are used for research purposes on the topic of legal decision making and individual attitudes/differences toward the legal system. The theoretical approaches to biased decision making that have evolved from such research are described below.

Biased Decision Making

As reviewed earlier, the first author of this textbook and his colleagues proposed the Dangerous Decisions Theory, which—in general—suggests that credibility assessments are the key contributor to courtroom biased decision making. The Dangerous Decisions Theory and theory behind credibility assessments are discussed in detail below.

CREDIBILITY ASSESSMENTS IN THE COURTROOM

Willis and Todorov (2006) suggest that initial impressions of trustworthiness are made instantaneously after seeing a face. The face acts as a canvas of emotional display, which allow for observers to infer certain trait characteristics, such as trustworthiness (Martelli, Majib, & Pelli, 2005). Unfortunately, this initial evaluation often generates biased opinions that affect decisions made upon further interactions with the individual, such as the evaluation of evidence against him or her. These evaluations also could affect decisions made in more pertinent circumstances such as the evaluation of guilt or innocence in the courtroom. More specifically, judges and jurors often are presented with the difficult task of evaluating the trustworthiness of witnesses and defendants. Many judges and jurors often are in situations in which they must weigh the word of the defendant against contradicting testimony or evidence, and thus must come to a verdict based on the trustworthiness of the defendant's testimony. Biased opinions, whether positive or negative, have tremendous influence on these trustworthiness evaluations and can dramatically alter the interpretation of evidence. With this in mind, it is important for judges and jurors to make sentencing decisions objectively, as biases can lead to flawed reasoning and incorrect assessments of evidence.

As reviewed in Chapter 5, it has been argued that legal decision making is guided in a significant way by credibility assessments (Porter & ten Brinke, 2009). For example, in *R. v. Malik & Bagri* (2005), the judge declared that the Air India mass murder was reduced to a "credibility contest." However, the decisions of judges regarding defendants also are informed by their previous experiences with similar defendants or cases (Greenberg & Ruback, 1982; Konecni & Ebbesen, 1982). In support of this contention, when a group of 16 Canadian judges were asked how they assess credibility, the judges' responses were highly variable (Porter & ten Brinke, 2009). Further, nearly half of the judges believed that it was more difficult to assess credibility and detect deception based on a transcript rather than on a defendant's live testimony.

In *R. v. B. (K.G.)* (1993), the Supreme Court of Canada concluded that judges and jurors must be able to clearly view a witness to be able to make adequate judgments and evaluations of body language, facial expressions, and other indicators of credibility. It decided that these indicators of credibility are not apparent when referring only to a written transcript. Previous research has suggested that observers generally associate lying with various nervous behaviours such as speech disturbances, gaze aversion, body movement, and fidgeting (Porter & ten Brinke, 2010; Vrij, 2008). In *Morales v. Artuz* (2002), the court noted that "seeing a witness's eyes has sometimes been explicitly mentioned as of value in assessing credibility." The Supreme Court of Canada (in *R. v. B. (K. G.)*, 1993) concluded that judges and jurors must view a witness to "adequately evaluate body language, facial expressions and other indicators of credibility" and that credibility assessment is "common sense." In a recent landmark, Canadian case *R v. N.S.* (2010), the Ontario Court of Appeal—in deciding whether to permit a Muslim complainant to wear her face-covering niqab during testimony—concluded that:

Covering the face of a witness may impede cross-examination in two ways. First, it limits the trier of fact's ability to assess the demeanour of the witness. Demeanour is relevant to the assessment of the witness's credibility and the reliability of the evidence given by that witness. Second, witnesses do not respond to questions by words alone. Non-verbal communication can provide the cross-examiner with valuable insights. (p. 54)

(See Porter, ten Brinke, Baker, & Wallace, 2011.)

However, such judgments of "nervous behaviours" are nonvalid cues when making these assessments (Vrij, Granhag, & Porter, 2011). For example, many Aboriginal people avert their gaze as a sign of respect when interacting with other individuals (see Porter & ten Brinke, 2009). This already puts Aboriginal people at an unfair disadvantage because avoidance of eye contact is concluded to be the number-one sign of lying to which professionals attend (Bond & Atoum, 2000; Porter & ten Brinke, 2007).

Previous research also indicated that observers rely on facial characteristics such as attractiveness, facial symmetry, and baby-facedness when first interacting with others to make predictions about trustworthiness and assess credibility (Bull, 2006; Bull & Vine, 2003; Porter & ten Brinke, 2010). For example, research suggests that large, round eyes, high eyebrows, and a small chin are considered "baby-face" facial characteristics, and often are associated with kindness, warmth, and honesty (Berry & McArthur, 1986; Berry & Zebrowitz-McArthur, 1988; Zebrowitz, Voinescu, & Collins, 1996). Berry et al. (1988) found that these particular baby-face features are associated with childlike qualities, and are seen as weak and naïve. Not surprisingly, individuals with perceived baby-faced qualities are more likely to receive leniency when being assessed in court (e.g., Flowe & Humphries, 2011). Similar to this phenomenon, attractive defendants are perceived to be more honest (Zebrowitz et al., 1996), and are less likely to be seen as guilty compared to their unattractive counterparts (Kulka & Kessler, 1978). Physical attractiveness of a person is a key characteristic that influences the perception of positive traits, and reflects the "what is beautiful is good" stereotype (Dion, Berscheid, & Walster, 1972). Also, people who are "socially attractive" are seen as less culpable than others (e.g., Alicke & Zell, 2009). Similarly, certain faces are viewed as being congruent with particular crimes. Thus, there are some faces that people would agree look like the face of a rapist, an armed robber, or a murderer (Bull & McAlpine, 1998; Dumas & Testé, 2006). Defendants whose faces are congruent with the offence label are more likely to be found guilty regardless of weak evidence (Dumas & Testé, 2006). There is no evidence that particular facial features are accurate predictors of individuals' trait characteristics. Porter, England, Juodis, ten Brinke, and Wilson (2008) presented participants with faces of both America's Most Wanted criminals, and recipients of humanitarian awards (e.g., Nobel Peace Prize). The participants were given the simple task to evaluate the faces on trustworthiness and then to estimate group membership (criminal or award recipient). Porter, England, Juodis, ten Brinke, and Wilson (2008) found that judgment accuracy was only slightly above chance, suggesting that one cannot assess credibility and trustworthiness based on the face alone. Relying on first impressions may lead to flawed decision making and could ultimately lead to wrongful convictions.

Judges and jurors can be influenced by the language and demeanour of the defendant in ways that have nothing to do with actual credibility.

The Dangerous Decisions Theory

The **Dangerous Decisions Theory** (DDT; Porter & ten Brinke, 2009, 2010) provides a framework to conceptualize the impact that first impressions can make on legal decision making. DDT suggests that instantaneous impressions of trustworthiness based on facial appearance may play a major role in the assessment of credibility and decisions about the target, such as a witness or defendant. (See Figure 8.1.) Adolphs (2002) suggested that the process of judging an individual's trustworthiness is associated with increased activity in the primitive brain areas such as the amygdala. Untrustworthiness is perceived as a "threat" in the environment, and the corresponding brain areas react (Adolphs, 2002).

It is well recognized that human decision making is subject to biases that can often be irrational (Kahneman & Tversky, 1982). Although both judges and jurors strive to maintain objectivity when making legal decisions, neither can escape the normal human biases that may influence their ultimate decisions (Kaufmann et al., 2003). As reviewed in Chapter 5, research has shown that judges, police officers, and professionals alike perform around the level of chance when judging the credibility of videotaped speakers (e.g., Ekman & O'Sullivan, 1991; see Porter & ten Brinke, 2010). Professionals are more confident in their decisions based on their past experiences and line of work; however, Ask and Granhag (2007) found that criminal investigators are more skeptical around evidence that contradicts their original perceptions. Decision

Figure 8.1

DDT: A Framework for Understanding How Flawed Decisions about Witness Credibility Occur in the Courtroom

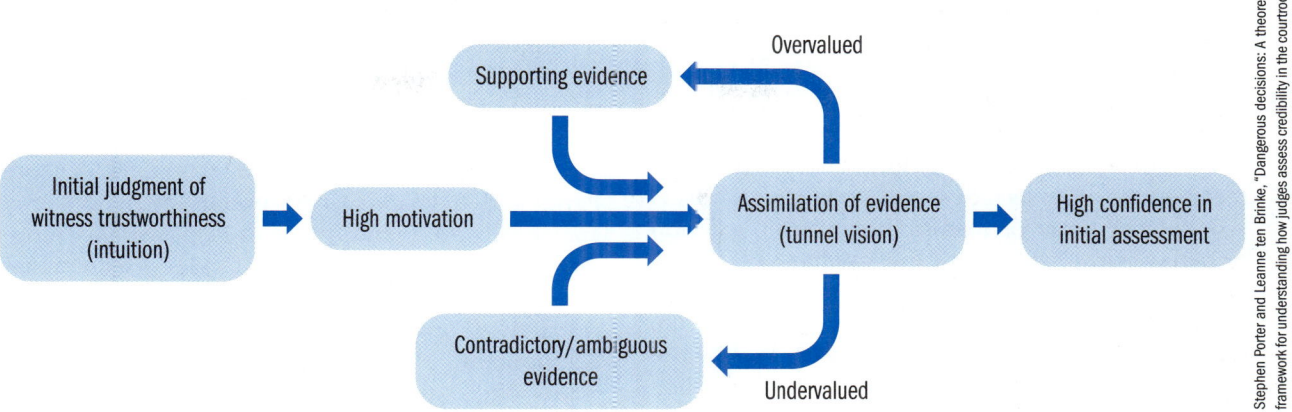

Stephen Porter and Leanne ten Brinke, "Dangerous decisions: A theoretical framework for understanding how judges assess credibility in the courtroom", *Legal and Criminological Psychology* (February 2009), 14(1), p. 119–134.

makers and other professionals are likely to seek out evidence to support initial impressions of the defendant's trustworthiness, generating a tunnel vision and failing to give weight to evidence that contradicts initial opinions. This tunnel vision may artificially inflate confidence in legal decision making (e.g., Vrij, 2008), and it becomes significantly more difficult for exonerating evidence (i.e., DNA) to influence a verdict.

Preliminary research has supported the DDT. Porter, Gustaw, and ten Brinke (2010) provided participants with a case description, corresponding evidence, and a photo of a defendant that had been previously rated in several characteristics including trustworthiness. They found that participants were more likely to render a verdict of guilt for untrustworthy-looking defendants when they had been accused of a severe crime, confirming that facial appearance plays an important role in assessments of credibility in court. In a follow-up study, Korva, Porter, O'Connor, Shaw, and ten Brinke (2012, in press) replicated Porter, Gustaw, and ten Brinke's (2010) study, but examined the effects of the particular attitudes and biases on legal decision making. As expected, they found that individuals with negative biases toward the legal system were less likely to exonerate perceived untrustworthy defendants.

CIVIL TRIALS

Most of the published work on assessment of jurors' pretrial biases has dealt with criminal trials. But it can be argued that the issue of civil law is most susceptible to the effects of bias by individual jurors. Traditionally, criminal cases come to trial because the prosecution believes there is a chance for conviction. The defendant may feel there is little chance of acquittal but, having refused to plea-bargain, he or she is faced with only one last resort. In civil cases, however, it is necessary that *both* the plaintiff and the defendant be reasonably assured of a favourable decision. A litigant who is not so assured will, most likely, settle the issue out of court. Given this aspect of civil jury trials, in many cases the amount of evidence favouring each side will be nearly equal. But what are the basic dimensions or qualities of a pretrial bias in a juror in a civil trial? Several factors, including juror demographics (Underwood, Boudreaux, & Rao, 2009), have been suggested to influence juror decisions in civil trials. Although such trials can differ in the nature of the claim, the types of parties involved, and other specifics, it may be useful to examine some general attitudes.

General Attitudes

Biases in civil trials may not be as easily verbalized as those in criminal cases, but they can include several possible attitudes, which together can be collapsed into a distinction between pro-plaintiff and pro-defendant jurors. These differing attitudes are outlined below.

Attitudes about the "Litigation Explosion"

Whether there truly has been an increase in the amount of civil litigation in recent years, there has been ample publicity in the media to bolster such a claim. Some prospective jurors—believing media claims of a **litigation explosion**—may have adopted beliefs that too many lawsuits are frivolous and that people are too quick to sue, thus reflecting an anticomplainant bias.

Attitudes about Risk Taking

Risk, as a concept, is central to Anglo-American jurisprudence (Carson, 1988), but it has not received the analysis it deserves. In law, **risk** means a danger of harm or loss from a plaintiff's action or behaviour. Traditionally, the law has said that "a plaintiff who voluntarily encounters a known risk cannot recover" (Cox, 1991, p. 24). But in real life things are not that simple, as demonstrated by the attempts to classify the allocation of blame implicit in contributory negligence. For example, in one case a man sued Sears and Roebuck because he had a heart attack while trying to get his Sears lawnmower started (Cox, 1992), and everyone is familiar with the elderly woman's lawsuit against McDonald's for the too-hot cup of coffee.

Jurors can differ in their attitudes toward the **assumption of risk**. Assumption of risk can be thought of as a continuum ranging from no risk to 100 percent risk. Particular actions by plaintiffs can be assigned values along this continuum. For example, a person who buys a package of Tylenol and takes several tablets assumes very little risk; a patient undergoing double-bypass heart surgery assumes some risk; a person who mixes drugs whose interactive effects are unknown takes a higher risk. But the same action may be rated differently by different jurors.

Attitudes about Standard of Care

How stringent a standard do jurors hold with regard to the manufacture of products or the provision of services? Should a drug be 100 percent free of serious side effects before it is approved for sale? The availability of Viagra made its use instantly popular, but it apparently contributed to the sudden death of several men. How much should a new car be tested to determine whether its design is faulty before it is placed on the market? How risk-free should a surgical procedure be before a doctor uses it?

Attitudes about Personal Responsibility

The public has stereotyped civil juries as proplaintiff that is, sympathetic to claims of misfortune and willing to tap into the **deep pockets** of rich defendants. However, the empirical evidence challenges this view (see Vidmar, 1995) and even leads to a conclusion that an anticomplainant bias often emerges in jury decisions. Several causes for this doubtless exist. When talking to jurors after civil trials, the second author of this textbook got the impression that they had a strong belief in personal responsibility; these jurors lack sympathy for people with unhappy outcomes and (sometimes justified) grievances against a manufacturer, physician, or governmental organization. Feigenson, Park, and Salovey (1997) noted "evidence of a specifically antiplaintiff bias in responsibility judgments" (p. 600) and refer to interviews with actual jurors (Hans & Lofquist, 1992) and experimental research (Lupfer, Cohen, Bernard, Smalley, & Schippmann, 1985) supporting a conclusion that jurors often attribute the behaviour of complainants to undesirable motives, such as greed, rather than to legitimate grievances. In addition, Bright and Goodman-Delahunty (2010) found that mock jurors were more biased and sympathetic toward an injured plaintiff after reading about the severely injured plaintiff. However, jurors exposed to gruesome photographs of the injured plaintiff rated the defendant as being more negligent compared to those exposed to neutral photographs. These findings suggest that evidence presented in civil trials relating to personal responsibility of the plaintiff biases jurors in their decisions.

CORPORATE RESPONSIBILITY

Attitudes toward corporations are related to some of the general attitudes detailed above, but they deserve special concern (Hans, 1990). Some potential jurors are antibusiness, standing up for the powerless individual against the monolithic corporation. But others believe that businesses are hampered too much by government regulations. Should we hold corporations to higher standards of responsibility than individuals? Who deserved the blame when the Exxon tanker *Valdez* ran aground off the coast of Alaska, the captain or the oil company?

Hans and Lofquist (1992) constructed an attitude scale to measure potential jurors' attitudes toward business regulation. The 16 items on this scale tap attitudes about civil litigation, the benefits and costs of government regulation of business, and standards for worker safety and product safety. After reviewing this work, Wrightsman and Heili (1992) formulated additional items that might reflect jurors' biases in civil trials. These items, called the Civil Trial Bias Scale, were administered along with Hans and Lofquist's items, to 204 undergraduate students, and the responses were factor-analyzed to determine what constructs underlay the responses. The first factor that emerged in this analysis was to favour business and the easing of stringent requirements for safety. For example, the highest loading item (the one that correlated the highest with the factor), number 16 from the Hans and Lofquist set, states: "Requiring that products be 100 percent safe before they're sold to the public is just too expensive." The other factors emerging from this analysis also covered a variety of attitudes.

A separate analysis of the Hans and Lofquist items produced clearer results than the factor analysis of the two scales together. What emerges is one set of attitudes opposed to government regulation and another dealing with what are "proper safety standards." But other dimensions also may be present; the separate factor analysis of the Civil Trial Bias Scale, not detailed here, found that jurors differed on assigning responsibility for bad outcomes, the inexplicability of bad events, and the value of risk taking.

A recent instrument that shows promise here is the Attitudes Toward Corporations (ATC) scale (Robinette, 1999). It contains five subscales that measure product safety, government regulation, treatment of employees by corporations, and anti-plaintiff and anticorporation attitudes. The original pool of items from which the ATC emerged capitalized on the items developed by Hans and Lofquist (1992), described above, but other items were constructed, and then the early versions of the scale were subjected to item analyses so that a 15-item scale resulted.

PSYCHOLOGICAL CONSULTANTS IN JURY SELECTION OUTSIDE CANADA

In some jurisdictions, the role of psychological consultants in jury selection is a major one. In some cases, there is disagreement between the lawyer and the consultant concerning the "best" jury composition for the case. In one famous case, it was the lawyer who won—but only in the short run. This refers to the decision about who would be "ideal jurors" for the prosecution in the first O. J. Simpson trial. Were certain types of individuals more likely to find the defendant guilty? Donald Vinson, founder of the large trial-consulting firm

Litigation Sciences, offered his services pro bono to the prosecution for the Simpson trial, and for a while Los Angeles County Deputy District Attorney Marcia Clark accepted them. Litigation consultants on both sides, on the basis of their surveys and focus groups, concluded that black women, as a group, were sympathetic to the defence, so Vinson strongly urged the prosecution lawyers to use some of their **peremptory challenges** to dismiss them from the jury pool. But Marcia Clark firmly believed that she could convince these women; she had a gut feeling that black women, if on the jury, would commiserate with the victim and accept the prosecution's contention that the murder of Nicole Brown Simpson was related to the pattern of domestic violence she had experienced while married to O. J. Simpson. As the lead lawyer, Clark prevailed; in fact, the prosecution did not even use all 20 of its peremptory challenges (Toobin, 1996a). Vinson came to have "zero credibility" in Clark's eyes (Clark, 1997, p. 118), and so she summarily dismissed him after only a day and a half of jury selection (Toobin, 1996b). The 12-person jury that found Simpson not guilty included eight black women and one black man.

Conflicts in Styles and Values

A theme of this book is that forensic psychologists—whatever their duties—must ask: "Am I acting ethically?" and "Who is the client?" Although psychologists serving as jury consultants outside Canada must be responsive to the ethics code of their national psychological association, they also must be aware that they are advocates, hired by lawyers, and conflicts between the two professions and perspectives may occur. Sometimes the only resolution of such clashes is for the trial consultant to disengage from the relationship.

In her book about the O. J. Simpson trial, Marcia Clark (1997) was candid that she did not like Donald Vinson from their first meeting. She had been urged by her supervisor to accept Vinson's **pro bono** offer (i.e., that he would assist the prosecution free of charge). However, it is clear that Marcia Clark does not like trial consultants: "As far as I'm concerned they are creatures of the defense. They charge a lot, so the only people who can afford them are wealthy defendants in a criminal trial or fat-cat corporations defending against class-action suits" (p. 138). (This, despite the fact that Vinson had offered his services free to the *prosecution.*) She agreed to the trial consultant's participation only against her better judgment and in deference to her boss's insistence. Additionally, Clark was opposed to many of the staples of trial consultants' practices: "I don't feel that the government should be in the position of market-testing its arguments" (1997, p. 138).

In many ways, the above example is not typical of the relationship between litigation consultants and lawyers. Few lawyers turn down an offer of free professional help. The example also is unusual in that consultants are much more likely to be hired by the defence than by the prosecution. But conflict can occur in even the most congenial of relationships between a psychologist-consultant and a lawyer, and nowhere can the conflict between the law and psychology become more intense than in the task of **jury selection**. (Actually, *deselection* would be a better term, as lawyers cannot select jurors; they can only prevent some from being chosen. Nevertheless, the common expression will be used here.) Most psychologists are committed to procedures that reflect an empirical approach; whether litigation consultants use

community surveys, focus groups, or mock juries, they are exemplifying a belief that it is not enough "to fly by the seat of one's pants" or to rely on intuitions or "gut feelings." As a group, trial lawyers are harder to characterize. A few are not particularly concerned with which individuals are on the jury; some of these lawyers are so self-assured that they believe they can persuade anybody, while others may be convinced that their side will prevail, regardless of the obstacles. Some lawyers, such as Marcia Clark (mentioned above) are so confident that they fail to exercise all their opportunities to dismiss prospective jurors.

Other trial lawyers in the United States increasingly rely on consultants and empirical methods to advise them in making jury selection decisions. These procedures are a main focus of the remainder of this chapter. But most lawyers have their own ingrained assumptions about who makes a good or bad juror (Fulero & Penrod, 1990). If they cannot hire the expertise of a trial consultant, these lawyers will employ their assumptions and stereotypes in their choices. Thus it can be

argued that the goals of trial consultants, despite their negative reputation in the eyes of the public, aren't any different from those of trial lawyers—they both seek a jury composed of persons who will be open-minded about (or, better, sympathetic to) their side's set of facts and arguments. The difference is that litigation consultants use what is called systematic jury selection, or scientific procedures, rather than rely on intuition, as do many lawyers.

Examples of Lawyers' Stereotypes

Examples of trial lawyers' stereotyped beliefs about jurors are the stuff of legend. Jeffrey Toobin recounted, "Early in my career as a prosecutor, when I first began selecting juries, a senior colleague warned me about men with beards. 'Guys with beards are independent and iconoclastic,' my mentor said. 'They resist authority. Get rid of them'" (Toobin, 1994, p. 42). The master lawyer Clarence Darrow believed that, as a defence lawyer, he was better off with jurors of an Irish background; he avoided Scandinavians, who—he presumed—had too much respect for the law. The celebrated contemporary lawyer Gerry Spence has said: "Women are more punitive than men by a score of about five to one" (quoted by Franklin, 1994, p. A25). And the lawyer Keith Mossman (1973) has reported that "a nationally known trial lawyer once told me he would not accept any left-handed jurors" (p. 78). The first author of this textbook was once told by an Ontario lawyer at a judges' conference that the lawyer distrusted the judgment of any juror of Guyanese descent because he felt that that culture encouraged manipulation and lying (which the juror apparently would use on other jurors).

Such stereotypes may be specific to the individual lawyer. But the problem is more pervasive than that; general stereotypes are taught in law school trial advocacy courses, as well as passed down to neophyte lawyers on the job. Toobin described how, as a new member of the staff of federal prosecutors, he learned that "[W]e preferred jurors who were old rather than young; married rather than single; employed rather than jobless. ... We sought jurors smart enough to understand the evidence but not so clever that they would over-analyze it; educated, but not to excess" (1994, p. 42). Stereotypes also abound for the defence for whom the ideal juror is a member of the helping professions—a teacher, a social worker, a psychologist—because such people had sympathy for the underdog. Despite the lawyer mentioned

above, members of racial minorities also were seen as pro-defence jurors in criminal trials, because of their more frequent conflicts with police and other authorities in the legal system.

Should such stereotypes be dismissed as lame folklore? Or is there some basis for their evolution? Early in the psychological study of racial stereotypes, a position was advanced, which came to be called the **kernel-of-truth hypothesis**, that group stereotypes may be unwisely generalized, but that some basic distinctions exist between groups. A review by Brigham (1971) concluded that ethnic and racial stereotypes could have such a "kernel of truth" in the sense that different groups of respondents agreed on which traits were associated with a particular object group; for example, respondents may all associate Newfoundlanders with being down-to-earth, light-hearted, and forgiving. (But we often lack the information to know whether the object group actually possesses the traits.) Even if the kernel-of-truth proposal is accepted as a general proposition, do these stereotypes have enough predictability to be used in selecting or rejecting individual jurors? Usually not.

The Psychologist's Role in Jury Selection

Psychologists have sought to determine whether **group differences** (including racial and ethnic classifications as well as broad personality characteristics and attitudes) are predictive of verdicts (see Lieberman, 2011). Their conclusion is not a simple one, for the verdict of an individual juror is the product of a wealth of factors, not only that juror's gender and race, attitudes and personality, but also the weight of the evidence in the case, the responses to the pressures on the juror to vote one way or another, and other factors specific to the situation. At the broadest level, we can say that jurors' verdicts can be affected by their biases, but how their biases are manifested may depend on specific aspects of the trial. For example, jurors who are relatively authoritarian *tend* to go along with the prosecution, but what if the defendant is an authority figure, such as a police officer or a physician? Then, the relationship may shift, and the authoritarian juror may side with the defence.

Case-Specific Approaches

Some litigation consultants seek to determine the criteria for jury selection by "working from the inside out" rather than beginning with hypothetical determinants. The goal is to determine characteristics of the **ideal juror** or, if that is not possible, the ideal juror to avoid. Two examples of trials illustrating this approach are described. But recall that the procedure does not permit one to compose an "ideal jury" without restrictions. First, the procedure is to remove the supposedly undesirable jurors rather than to select the desirable ones; second, there is no way to prevent the other side from dismissing those whom your side considers most desirable. As we will see, this often happens.

The Harrisburg Seven Trial

The trial of the "Harrisburg Seven," in 1972, was the first highly publicized application of social-science techniques, or scientific jury selection. Despite the case having transpired more than four decades ago, it remains an illustrative standard for several reasons, including the comprehensiveness of the procedures and the availability of a detailed account of what the trial consultants did (Schulman, Shaver, Colman, Emrich, & Christie, 1973).

The "Harrisburg Seven" actually is something of a misnomer; the trial took place in Harrisburg, Pennsylvania, but otherwise the defendants had nothing to do with that city. Catholic priests and nuns who had protested against the Vietnam War by pouring blood over draft-board records were charged by the U.S. government with a conspiratorial plan to carry out a number of other anti-war activities, including blowing up the heating tunnels under Washington, D.C., and kidnapping Henry Kissinger, then U.S. secretary of state. The government persuaded the presiding judge to move the trial to Harrisburg because it was considered the most conservative area in that judicial district.

Capitalizing on a number of volunteer participants who were opposed to the war, Jay Schulman and the other social scientists carried out a number of studies prior to the trial:

1. Suspecting that the original jury pool was not representative of the population, they compared the demographic characteristics of those drawn in the jury pool with a random sample of voters and found that the average age of the jury pool members was somewhat older. This caused the judge to order the drawing of a second, more representative jury pool.
2. Schulman and his colleagues (1973) sought to discover what background and demographic characteristics were related to potential jurors'

biases in favour or against the defendants. They surveyed 250 people from the Harrisburg area (not members of the jury pool) to assess their degrees of tolerance toward dissidents and war protesters. These attitudes were related to a number of demographic characteristics, including age, education, religion, and gender, and some surprises emerged. For example, contrary to their expectation, the more educated members of the community were less sympathetic to the defendants. These results permitted the social scientists to develop a profile of the ideal juror—a female Democrat with no religious preferences who held a skilled-labour or white-collar job.

3. Armed with this information, the social scientists and the defence lawyers rated each of the 46 prospective jurors who survived the earlier winnowing process. On the basis of their demographic characteristics, the way they responded to questions during voir dire, and their nonverbal behaviour, these jurors were classified on a five-point scale, with 5 = Very good for the defence, 4 = A good defence juror, 3 = Neither good nor bad, 2 = Undesirable, and 1 = Very undesirable. Of the 46, only eight were rated as very good, and the prosecution used its six peremptory challenges to remove six of these eight. So the defence team was left with two "very good" jurors, five "good" ones, and five whom they had rated as neither desirable nor undesirable. (The defence had been given 28 peremptory strikes, compared to the prosecution's six.)

Did the strategy work? Yes and no. The jury ended up deadlocked, with 10 jurors voting to acquit and only two to convict. The judge declared a mistrial, and the U.S. government decided not to retry the defendants. In that sense, the jury selection was successful. But the social scientists missed completely on the two jurors who voted to convict; each of these two had been rated rather positively by the trial consultants.

The de la Beckwith Retrial

Late one summer evening in 1963, at the height of the civil rights protest in the southern United States, Medgar Evers was shot and killed as he returned to his home in Jackson, Mississippi. Evers had been leading the drive to register black Americans to vote in Mississippi. It was a particularly heinous crime—someone, crouched in a honeysuckle bush

60 metres away, fired a shot into Evers's back as his wife and children watched from the front porch. A gun was abandoned at the crime scene; it was later traced to Byron de la Beckwith.

De la Beckwith was a white supremacist, active in the Ku Klux Klan and other pro-segregation organizations. He was known for his intense hostility to Jews and blacks. In addition to his fingerprints on the gun, there was some other evidence that linked de la Beckwith to the crime; several cabdrivers came forward to report that some days earlier he had been inquiring as to where Evers lived. De la Beckwith denied committing the crime and claimed that the rifle had been stolen from him two days before the killing; yet, at the same time he seemed to revel in his sudden celebrity as a prime suspect (Morris, 1998; Vollers, 1991).

De la Beckwith was put on trial for murder in January 1964; the jury was all white and all male. The prosecution presented strong circumstantial evidence pointing to de la Beckwith; in his defence, his lawyers produced several white police officers who testified that he had been seen in his hometown, 230 kilometres away, at the time of the murder. The jury could not reach a unanimous verdict. After deliberating 11 hours, the jurors were deadlocked, six to six.

A second trial was held three months later, still in 1964, with a similar outcome—again deadlocked (the vote was eight to four for acquittal). De la Beckwith was released and allowed to return to his home in Greenwood, Mississippi.

But reports persisted that de la Beckwith had committed the crime; people even came forward describing how he had bragged about doing it. Meanwhile, in 1973, de la Beckwith was suspected of planning the bombing of an office of the Anti-Defamation League, a Jewish organization, in New Orleans. He served five years in prison in Louisiana for illegal possession of dynamite.

Early in the 1990s, the district attorney in Jackson, Mississippi, decided to reactivate the case. (There is no statute of limitations for murder.) At this point, several psychologists at the University of Kansas offered their services pro bono to the prosecution, to aid that side in its jury selection. Professor C. K. Rowland spearheaded the effort; he knew the district attorney and had worked with him on earlier cases. Rowland, then a doctoral student in psychology, was assisted by Amy Posey, Andrew Sheldon, and Lawrence Wrightsman in the preparation of a jury questionnaire that included questions about due process, racial attitudes, and items from the Juror Bias Scale.

This case presented unique challenges in the selection of jurors. It is true that racial relationships had dramatically changed in Mississippi in 30 years; blacks and whites went to school together, worked side by side, and ate in the same restaurants. But were racist attitudes still below the surface in some prospective jurors? And what was the reaction of the jury pool to the decision to retry de la Beckwith *30 years* after the murder had taken place; he was now 73 years old, frail, and not in good health. Would that affect some jurors? In considering who would be the "ideal juror" for the prosecution, the obvious choice would seem to be a black person, but preliminary surveys indicated that not all blacks thought alike. Members of some black fundamentalist churches believed "judge not, that ye are not judged"—that it was God's job to determine guilt and punishment; they were reluctant to play the role of jurors deciding the fate of another community member.

The trial judge permitted a change of venue; jurors for the third trial were from Panola County (county seat: Batesville), a rural county about 240 kilometres from Jackson. The social scientists assisting the prosecution learned several things about residents of this county that were helpful in identifying potential jurors who might be racist and hence likely to sympathize with de la Beckwith; these included:

- In Batesville, there were two softball leagues; one was racially integrated while the other was all white.
- In the wake of public school desegregation, a number of private (translation: all white) "academies" had been established. These were a haven for parents who didn't want their children mingling with children of other races.
- Political party identification was potentially diagnostic; if a person was Republican and financially well-off, that was of little use as an indicator, but poor Republicans were likely to be racist (Rowland, 1994).

The judge did not permit the administration of the 80-item questionnaire developed by the social scientists; the court clerk had said it would be too much trouble to copy and collate them. But the judge did institute a **sequestered voir dire**, in which each of the potential jurors was questioned individually in the judge's chambers. This questioning facilitated a sometimes-frank revelation of racial attitudes, and prosecutors found the younger whites to be candid; some straightforwardly said, "I don't like integration." But it was harder to pin down the racial attitudes of older middle-class whites. The second issue of concern by the prosecutors was potential sympathy for the defendant. On the advice of the social scientists, the lawyers asked: "What was your first thought when you heard that Byron de la Beckwith was to be retried?" Again, many prospective jurors were open about their feeling that it was hard to accept the idea of a retrial. Some were even **challenged for cause** because their answers reflected that they had already formed an opinion, or because they knew trial participants, and they were dismissed by the judge.

The social scientists were not permitted in the judge's chambers while individual jurors were questioned, but they were able to provide questions to the lawyers. One of the contributions was to urge the prosecution lawyers to move away from their usual style (similar to cross-examination) of asking closed-ended, yes-or-no questions to the prospective jurors and instead use open-ended ones like the question above. The answers to these are much more informative.

The successful challenges for cause shifted the racial composition, from an original pool that was composed about equally of the two races to a jury of eight blacks and four whites. A 70-year-old black minister was chosen as foreperson.

Exactly 30 years after his first trial, de la Beckwith's third trial began, in late January 1994. Testimony lasted only six days; de la Beckwith did not testify. The jury deliberated six hours before unanimously finding the defendant guilty. Byron de la Beckwith was sentenced to life in prison; his appeal of his conviction was rejected by the Mississippi Supreme Court late in 1997 and he died in 2001 at the age of 80.

Juror Investigation

Citizens clearly have their privacy invaded to some extent when they become prospective jurors. The courts have accepted certain procedures because they subscribe to the principle that a voir dire can identify prospective jurors whose biases impair their critical thinking skills. But how far can the inquiry go into one's personal life or views?

Trial consultants do, on occasion, use out-of-court investigations to determine the attitudes and values of prospective jurors. Public records, such as house appraisals, may be consulted; the trial consultants' team may drive by the prospective juror's house, note its condition and the quality of its neighbourhood, and search for any "diagnostic" bumper stickers on the juror's car. Friends and neighbours may be interviewed.

There are limits to such activities. Clearly, prospective jurors cannot be contacted outside the courtroom; **jury tampering** is illegal, and the courts have held persons to be in contempt of court for communicating with jurors even though it was not clear that they sought to influence the jurors. But would such rules apply to investigation of *prospective* jurors? Herbsleb, Sales, and Berman thought not; they have written that "it seems unlikely that [such jury tampering laws as the above] will be applied today to hold social scientists in contempt for gathering jury information, unless some communication with the sworn jurors has occurred in or near the courtroom" (1979, p. 206).

But the dangers of out-of-court investigations remain. As Herbsleb and colleagues (1979) suggested:

Suppose that as social scientists are establishing their network, one of the people contacted becomes suspicious of the investigators' motives and of the propriety of their actions. ... [H]e may contact the prospective juror to inform him that persons of questionable character and motives are conducting an investigation into his personal affairs. The prospective juror in turn may well feel threatened or intimidated by the knowledge that someone is "checking up" on him. (pp. 207–208)

What is the solution to this problem? To seek court approval for such inquiries? To inform prospective jurors that such information will be used only to exercise challenges? Although the above have been suggested as remedies, they fail to recognize that out-of-court investigations by psychologists may violate ethical guidelines about participants' rights to decline or withdraw from research participation. Herbsleb and colleagues (1979) offered one solution: "Have the court announce the presence of the social scientists and ask jurors if they object. If objections are voiced, the judge orders the social scientists to discontinue their research; if no objections are voiced, it is assumed that the jurors are participating voluntarily" (p. 211). But the "compliance" in this situation may be a rather coerced one, not well thought out. And invasions of privacy, whether "voluntary" or not, are still invasions of privacy.

SUMMARY

In Canada, the way in which juries are selected is governed by the Charter of Rights and Freedoms, which says that everyone accused of a crime is entitled to a fair trial by an impartial jury. Canadian courts attempt to ensure a jury that is "as random as possible," while requiring jurors to be unbiased and competent to do their job. We do not see the type of jury manipulation that is witnessed in other countries, particularly the United States. Psychologists in Canada have conducted important work on jury decision making, while working within the constraints of laws preventing jurors from speaking about their deliberations after trials. As such, much of the research on juries has used a mock jury approach in which people are asked to act as if they are jurors in an actual case.

The use of broad traits or general attitudes reflects an assumption that certain predispositions of jurors may predict their verdicts in a wide variety of trials, thus biasing their decisions. With regard to criminal trials, two attitude scales have some limited general utility in predicting juror verdicts: the Revised Legal Attitudes Questionnaire Scale, which measures authoritarianism, and the Juror Bias Scale, which measures biases regarding probability of commission and reasonable doubt.

Much theoretical and empirical evidence suggests that jury decision making can be substantially biased. For example, the Dangerous Decisions Theory proposes that individuals—or jurors—develop instantaneous impressions upon seeing a defendant's face, and thus their assessments of credibility and ultimate verdicts may be biased.

With regard to general characteristics that may predict verdicts in civil suits, measures of risk taking, beliefs in personal responsibility and corporate responsibility, and attitudes toward the "litigation explosion" are promising.

Some American lawyers believe that trials can be won or lost on the basis of the specific jury "selected" for the trial. In actuality, jury "selection" is a misnomer, because lawyers on each side can dismiss prospective jurors but cannot ensure that any one juror is chosen, as the other side also has the opportunity to "strike" or dismiss jurors through the use of peremptory challenges. Trial lawyers are increasingly relying on psychologists as trial consultants. In jurisdictions that allow this type of activity, in advising the lawyer about jury selection, the psychologist uses information based on mock trials, focus groups, community attitude surveys, and sometimes out-of-court investigations.

Psychologists disagree about whether scientific jury selection in the United States is appropriate or useful. One laboratory study found that it was more effective than the traditional method in some trials, but not all trials. A conservative conclusion is that the use of such procedures may account for a small degree of variance in jurors' verdicts—perhaps 10 percent, thus not enough to conclude that trial consultants can "rig" juries, but enough of an edge to make them useful to some trial lawyers.

Identifying specific aspects of a particular case and then assessing prospective jurors on those characteristics (such as racial attitudes or attitudes toward protesters) is described in two examples of jury selection: the Harrisburg Seven trial and Byron de la Beckwith's retrial.

A number of ethical issues surface when forensic psychologists assist in jury selection. Investigations of prospective jurors may violate their right to give consent and to privacy. Another concern is the inequality between prosecution and defence of the utilization of trial consultants. Use of a **supplemental juror questionnaire** (which may expose juror biases) may lessen this concern.

In Canada, we have a unique and diverse society. Research examining actual jury decision making in this context is essential. It remains to be seen whether Canadian laws will advance to become more flexible in allowing jurors to discuss their experiences with mental health professionals and researchers.

KEY TERMS

SUGGESTED READINGS

Bornstein, B. H. & Greene, E. (2011). Jury decision making: Implications for and from psychology. *Psychological Science, 20*(1), 63–67.
    This comprehensive review discusses the implications of jury decision making.

Daftary-Kapur, T., Dumas, R., & Penrod, S. (2011). Jury decision-making biases and methods to counter them. *Legal and Criminological Psychology, 15*(1), 133–154.
    This review gives a broad overview of various biases that are associated with jury decision making.

Instructions related to the jury selection process. (2012). Retrieved from http://www.cjc-ccm .gc.ca
    This webpage outlines in detail the process of selecting jurors in Canada.

Korva, N., Porter, S., O'Connor, B., Shaw J., & ten Brinke, L. (2012, in press). Dangerous decisions: Influence of juror attitude and defendant appearance on legal decision-making. *Psychiatry, Psychology, and Law*.
    Based on Porter and ten Brinke's (2009) dangerous decisions theory, this study investigates the influence that juror attitudes and biases may have on legal decisions.

Lieberman, J. D. (2011). The utility of scientific jury selection: Still murky after 30 years. *Psychological Science, 20*(1), 48–52.
    This article discusses the methodological flaws associated with previous research on jury selection.

Porter, S., & ten Brinke, L. (2009). Dangerous decisions: A theoretical framework for understanding how judges assess credibility in the courtroom. *Legal and Criminological Psychology, 14*, 119–134.
    This comprehensive review on jury decision-making proposes a new theory to understand biased decision making in court. The authors discuss the implications of credibility assessments, and the effect that they can have on verdicts made in court.

Criminal Responsibility and Competency to Stand Trial

> *He stated that The Holy Father has punished his mother, a local Anglican priest and an RCMP officer, all of whom he believes to be involved in the reported conspiracy against him, by giving his mother, the priest's wife and the officer's mother cancer and that "maybe they'll see the light." He also believes that crows warn him of danger by cawing.*
>
> —Justice P. C. Gorman in the Provincial Court of Newfoundland and Labrador (*R. v. Normore*, 2002, para. 13)

- A mother drowns her infant son in the bathtub to save him from an imagined threat of physical and sexual abuse.
- A man who believes that he has an electronic device implanted in his neck kills his elderly mother with an axe in their home.
- A woman stabs her husband 200 times because she thinks he plans to steal her money and run off with another woman.

These are all cases in Nova Scotia in which a person was ultimately found to be not criminally responsible by the courts (*Chronicle Herald*, April 28, 1999). From 1987 to 1997, eight homicides in Nova Scotia were perpetrated by people with mental illnesses who were found by the courts to be either insane, or after the Criminal Code of Canada was revised, **not criminally responsible by reason of a mental disorder (NCRMD)**. In all cases, the killer and victim knew or were related to one another. Psychiatrists and psychologists who assessed the defendants found that five of the eight had experienced delusions or hallucinations that led them to kill. Two specifically heard voices telling them to kill the victim.

One of the most notorious episodes of violence in Canadian history occurred on July 30, 2008, when 22-year-old Tim McLean was stabbed, decapitated, and cannibalized while riding a Greyhound bus near Portage La Prairie, Manitoba (see CBC Fifth Estate Timeline). McLean's killer was 40-year-old Vince Li. According to the horrified witnesses, McLean was asleep when Li, who was sitting next to him, pulled out a large knife and proceeded to stab McLean in the neck and chest. Eventually, he decapitated McLean and waved the head around menacingly to other passengers. After waving his weapon at would-be rescuers, Li returned to the body and started eating

McLean's flesh. Li, a diagnosed schizophrenic, was found to be NCRMD for the murder and was remanded to a high-security forensic psychiatric facility. According to published reports, the psychiatrist who examined Li stated that Li's motive for the attack was that God's voice told him McLean was an evil force and was about to kill Li (CTV News, 2012b). According to a CBC report (CBC News, May 30, 2011), as of May 30, 2011, Li was responding well to psychiatric treatment and his doctor has recommended that he'll receive more freedoms (such as outdoor walks) phased in gradually (see Box 9.5 on page 226 for more Canadian cases of NCRMD).

When someone like Li is found to be NCRMD in Canada it can incense the public (CTV News, May 21, 2011), who may see such a determination as the defendant "getting off" (e.g., Acorn, 2011; Chappell, 2010). Often those close to the victim feel that justice was not served, and find it difficult to understand why no one was held accountable for the crime committed. Melton, Petrila, Poythress, and Slobogin (1997) have highlighted some of the major public misperceptions of the insanity defence: (1) that it is used by a large number of defendants; (2) that when used it is often successful; (3) that those acquitted with this defence are usually released; and (4) that such individuals are extremely dangerous. A recent study reveals that the general public continues to support myths about the insanity defence (Daftary-Kapur, Groscup, O'Connor, Coffaro, & Galietta, 2011). In fact, whereas the public estimates that the defence is used in 33 percent to 42.7 percent of cases, it is actually used about nine times in 1000 cases (0.009 percent). Whereas the public estimates that the "success" of the defence is between 36 percent and 45 percent when it's used, in reality the success rate is less than 20 percent. Daftary-Kapur et al. (2011) found that the laypersons falsely believe that the insanity defence is more likely to be raised in cases that involve violent crimes, that insanity acquittees are quickly released from custody, and that defendants who plead insanity are usually faking.

Criminal defendants who are found to be not criminally responsible are usually committed to a psychiatric hospital and remain there as long as they—in the judgment of the psychiatric staff—fit the criteria for having serious psychiatric disorders, although technically they have to be a risk to themselves or others for continued incarceration. Most spend extended periods of time in confinement, sometimes longer than if they had been found guilty and sentenced to prison (Borum & Fulero, 1999; Rodriguez, LeWinn, & Perlin, 1983).

As we will see, a key issue concerning whether a defendant is NCRMD is whether he or she had a mental illness at the time that caused his or her criminal actions. This is an extremely complicated matter. In fact, the determination of a person's psychological state at the time of an offence is one of the most challenging tasks given to the forensic psychologist. As indicated above, the NCRMD and insanity defence are rare. However, the presence of a mental illness among those who have committed offences is not. For example, according to a 2000 report, 32 percent of all inmates in British Columbia have a mental disorder (Hall, 2000). The Correctional Service of Canada regularly collects data on admission to prison on the mental health of incarcerated inmates. According to the "Corrections and Conditional Release Statistical Overview," 10 percent of the federal inmates in 2006/2007 were diagnosed with a mental illness on admission (Public Safety Canada Portfolio Corrections Statistics Committee, 2007), and more than double the proportion were prescribed medication for psychological issues compared to 1997/1998. How do we decide whether some offenders' illnesses caused them to commit crimes while others did not? It is clear that psychosis, typically schizophrenia, is implicated in finding someone not criminally responsible or not fit to stand trial; for example, Pirelli and Zapf (2011) found that defendants diagnosed with a psychotic disorder (associated with delusions and/or hallucinations) were approximately eight times more likely to be found incompetent than defendants without such a diagnosis.

In addition to advising the court and lawyers as to whether a defendant has the features of someone who is NCRMD, the forensic psychologist is frequently asked to make competency assessments. Does the defendant understand what it means to be on trial and is he or she competent to stand trial? The issue of predicting the dangerousness of offenders who have been hospitalized because of mental illness, now called risk assessment, exemplifies a more specialized task for the psychologist, but still a vital one. And throughout the above assessments underlies the question: Is the person malingering? That is, is the defendant simulating a serious mental disorder in order to avoid a guilty verdict or a prison sentence?

DETERMINING CRIMINAL RESPONSIBILITY/SANITY

One of the most important tasks facing forensic psychologists is assisting the courts in making a determination of criminal responsibility (see Ferguson & Ogloff, 2011). And some might argue that it is the most difficult or even impossible. In this chapter, we will examine the process of evaluating criminal responsibility/insanity by considering some recent cases and matching the behaviour of defendants with the definitions of NCRMD used in the courts.

Why Is Evaluating Criminal Responsibility Difficult?

The sources of difficulty when evaluating NCRMD are many. First, criminal responsibility is a legal concept, to be decided by the triers of fact, and not a psychological or medical one decided by psychologists or psychiatrists. A person may demonstrate psychotic behaviour and still not fulfill the legal definition of NCRMD (e.g., Torry & Billick, 2010). Additionally, the forensic psychiatrist or psychologist faced with the task of assessing criminal responsibility must make a retrospective assessment of the person's psychological state at the time of the offence, several months or years before. Often, this can be done only on the basis of the person's present status in a comprehensive examination of his or her psychological functioning, via testing and interviews. The judge ultimately must make a decision about the defendant's ability to have the required mental capacity before and during the criminal action based largely on the psychiatric/psychological evidence presented in court.

A Brief History of the Insanity Defence

Part of Western moral and legal tradition is that a person who is unaware of the meaning of his or her acts should not be held criminally responsible for them. For thousands of years, the presence of **mens rea**, or "guilty mind" (in addition to the **actus reus** or "criminal action"), has been essential to the classification of an illegal act, according to many societies. A determination of guilt and an appropriate punishment, as evaluations and responses, should ensue only if there is free will and intent to do harm. **Guilt** requires not only the commission of an illegal act but also a state of mind reflecting awareness of its implications. The Canadian Supreme Court reasoned in *R. v. Chaulk* (1990) that the insanity defence is based on the principle that an accused person has no capacity for criminal intention because his or her psychological condition has created a skewed frame of reference. As such there is no capacity for mens rea.

As outlined by Quen (1981), Aristotle reasoned that free will was essential in evaluating blameworthiness, a capacity lacking in animals, children, and insane individuals. The first legal milestone concerning insanity in the British court system occurred in 1724. Edward Arnold, known locally as "Crazy Ned," had shot and wounded Lord Onslow. The evidence indicated that Arnold believed that Onslow had "bewitched" him and entered his body to torment him. Justice Tracey instructed the jury that in order for a man to be acquitted on the grounds of insanity he could not have known what he was doing any more than an infant, brute, or wild beast. (Interestingly, Arnold was found guilty and sentenced to death but Lord Onslow intervened and the sentence was reduced to life imprisonment.) This came to be known as the "Wild Beast Test," the first formal legal definition of insanity.

The next landmark in the history of the insanity plea occurred in an 1834 trial in England. The accused in this case was Daniel McNaughton (also spelled M'Naghten and a multitude of other ways), who was found not guilty by reason of insanity after making an assassination attempt on British Prime Minister Robert Peel. The **McNaughton Rules** established by the judge in that case have been the foundation for the insanity criteria in many jurisdictions around the world. This definition contains three elements. According to the definition, a person should be judged insane if:

1. The defendant was suffering from "a defect of reason, from a disease of the mind."

2. As a result, the defendant did not "know" the "nature and quality of the act he was doing."
3. An inquiry has been carried out to determine whether the defendant knew "what he was doing was wrong" (Ogloff, Roberts, & Roesch, 1993).

The McNaughton test is called a **cognitive test of insanity** because it emphasizes the quality of the person's thought processes and perceptions of reality at the time of the crime (Low, Jeffries, & Bonnie, 1986).

The Irresistible Impulse Standard

Criticism of the McNaughton standard for its narrow focus on the defendant's cognitive knowledge led to its being supplemented—temporarily—by what was called the **irresistible impulse exception**. If a defendant demonstrated cognitive knowledge of right or wrong, he or she could still be found not guilty by reason of insanity if his or her free will was so destroyed or overruled that the person had lost the power to choose between right and wrong (Ogloff, Roberts, & Roesch, 1993). When referring to this loss of ability to control one's behaviour, the courts sometimes refer to the **volitional aspect of insanity**.

The Durham Test

Continued criticism of the McNaughton standard's cognitive focus caused the courts to abandon reliance on the irresistible impulse exception and to seek broader definitions. In the case of *Durham v. United States* (1954), Judge David Bazelon developed a new definition, which came to be called the Durham rule; it stated that the accused was not criminally responsible if his or her unlawful act was a product of mental disease or defect. First seen as a progressive step because it moved the legal definitions closer to psychiatric concepts, the Durham rule soon became a problem. Mental health experts, who increasingly were testifying in trials involving the insanity plea, interpreted the term "mental disease" to mean any familiar clinical-diagnostic label found in the DSM (Ogloff et al., 1993). However, as we will see shortly, many DSM disorders are not appropriate as the basis for an insanity plea (for example, many of the personality disorders rarely, if ever, would apply). The Durham standard is currently used in only one U.S. state, New Hampshire.

The ALI Standard, or Brawner Rule

Further development stemmed from criticisms of the Durham rule. The American Law Institute developed a new definition that received acceptance in the case of *United States v. Brawner* in 1972; this innovation, now called the **ALI standard**, sought comprehensiveness. It stated: "A person is not responsible for criminal conduct if at the time of the action, as a result of mental disease or defect, he [or she] lacks substantial capacity either to appreciate the criminality (wrongfulness) of his [or her] conduct or to conform his or her conduct to the requirements of the law" (American Law Institute, 1962, p. 401). As used in this statement, the term "mental disease or defect" does not include an abnormality manifested only by repeated criminal or otherwise antisocial conduct.

There are several aspects worth noting in this attempt at a comprehensive definition. First, note it states "substantial" rather than total incapacity. For example, a five-year-old can know that it is wrong to kill someone but not fully appreciate the wrongfulness of it. Second, the use of "appreciate" wrongfulness rather than to "know" it connotes volitional or affective as well as cognitive understanding and fits better with modern psychiatric perspectives (Ogloff et al., 1993). Thus, the ALI standard includes two aspects, or prongs, one cognitive ("can't appreciate the wrongfulness") and one volitional ("can't conform his conduct"). Currently, 21 U.S. states use the ALI standard. Wisconsin, the site of Jeffrey Dahmer's trial, has a unique procedure that combines elements of the McNaughton and ALI standards.

Another development in the history of the insanity defence is the "guilty but mentally ill" (GMBI) verdict. This decision combines a recognition of mental illness in defendants while still holding them guilty. Thirteen U.S. states provide for this type of verdict (Borum & Fulero, 1999). After such verdicts, the defendant is provided treatment at a state psychiatric hospital until he or she is declared to be sane. Then, he or she is sent to prison, to complete an equivalent term as offenders without mental illnesses who have been convicted of similar offences. Some jurisdictions (such as Idaho, Montana, Nevada, Kansas, and Utah) do not have a provision for an insanity defence, although the defence lawyer can introduce evidence of the defendant's psychological status to try to disprove the mens rea element of the charged offence (Borum & Fulero, 1999). In the United States, the jury's verdict that John Hinckley—charged with the attempted assassination of President Reagan—was not guilty by reason of insanity not only incensed the public but also motivated Congress to radically overhaul the federal laws regarding the determination of insanity (Caplan, 1984). The U.S. Congress passed the Insanity Defense Reform Act of 1984, removing the volitional prong of the ALI rule and leaving it substantially like the McNaughton rule, with focus on the accused's cognitive "appreciation." Congress also removed "substantial" as a modifier, so that the U.S. federal insanity test now instructs the fact finder to decide whether or not the defendant "lacks capacity to appreciate the wrongfulness of his conduct."

THE CANADIAN APPROACH: NCRMD

In Canada we have a unifying set of guidelines concerning mental disorder and criminal responsibility that have been incorporated in the Criminal Code. Section 16 of the Criminal Code used to describe the "not guilty by reason of insanity" (NGRI) defence, reformulated to reflect the concept of NCRMD. The Criminal Code legislation was revised on February 4, 1992, following the introduction of Bill C-30. The changes were initiated by the Supreme Court of Canada in the *R. v. Swain* (1991) case. The Court decided that the existing Criminal Code law requiring that a person found NGRI be automatically detained violated the Charter of Rights and Freedoms. At present, if the judge or jury decides that the accused committed the offence but it was caused by a mental disorder, he or she will be found NCRMD and will not go to prison.

The Criminal Code dictates that all accused persons are presumed *not* to suffer from a mental disorder and allows an NCRMD defence only when the mental disorder is proved on the "balance of probabilities." In Canada, unlike many American states, the burden of proof in establishing NCRMD is on whomever raises the issue, either the defence or Crown prosecutor.

Section 16 of the Code now states that "no person is criminally responsible for an act committed or an omission made while suffering from a mental disorder that rendered the person incapable of appreciating the nature and quality of the act or omission or of knowing that it was wrong." The elements of this definition suggest that the accused person must have had a mental disorder that prevented him or her from understanding the criminal action or knowing that it was wrong; that is, the mental disorder had to justify the action. The courts have often had to grapple with what "knowing that it was wrong" means. Does this mean knowing that the criminal action was legally wrong, morally wrong, or both? In *R. v. Chaulk* (1990), the Supreme Court of Canada established that knowing that something is legally wrong does not result in a finding of NCRMD (or "insanity" at the time). The Crown must show that the accused person knew that what he or she was doing was morally wrong: "A person may well be aware that an act is contrary to the law but by reason of disease of the mind is at the same time incapable of knowing that the act is morally wrong in the circumstances according to the moral standards of society" (*R. v. Chaulk*, 1990, summary para. 10).

Take, for example, the Provincial Court of Newfoundland and Labrador case *R. v. Normore* (2002), which is cited at the start of the chapter. In this case, evidence indicated that on May 29, 2001, Alex Normore had threatened to burn down a pigpen that was being constructed close to his mother's residence. On that day, he approached an RCMP officer with a loaded, unlicensed 30-30 rifle on the front seat of his vehicle and live rounds in his pocket. He told police that the pigpen constituted a health hazard, and that he was in possession of the gun to protect himself from oil companies that meant to kill him. Other evidence indicated that he had long believed the RCMP were conspiring against him, stemming from a 2001 incident in Deer Lake in which he thought they had attempted to drown him in a bathtub. Justice Gorman concluded that Mr. Normore had a profound delusion. He noted that Mr. Normore had appreciated that his actions with the weapon were illegal. However, he decided that Mr. Normore was not capable of understanding that his actions would have been viewed as morally condemned by reasonable members of society. As such, he found the accused to be NCRMD on the weapons offences (but guilty on others).

There is a specific type of defence in the Criminal Code, known as **automatism**, that can lead to a finding of NCRMD. In the British Columbia case *R. v. Stone* (1999), the Supreme Court of Canada defined this defence, noting that there are two distinct forms of the defence, noninsane and insane automatism. Noninsane automatism refers to an involuntary action that is not caused by mental disorder and will lead to a verdict of complete acquittal. For example, if a person was struck on the head or had an adverse reaction to medication immediately prior to committing a criminal action, the defence might argue noninsane automatism. Another example is someone who commits a criminal action while sleepwalking. In an infamous Ontario case, Kenneth Parks from Toronto was sleepwalking when he killed his mother-in-law and tried to kill his father-in-law. He had been suffering from severe insomnia before the attack. According to the evidence, early in the morning on May 23, 1987, while he was sleeping, he drove 23 kilometres to the victims' home where he proceeded to stab them (he killed the mother-in-law but the father-in-law survived). The jury accepted expert evidence that his actions were involuntary and he was acquitted, a finding upheld by the Ontario Court of Appeal and Supreme Court of Canada (*R. v. Parks*, 1992).

The second type of this defence is insane automatism, used if an involuntary action was caused by a disease of the mind. If the court agrees with this defence, the accused person is found to be NCRMD. This disease of the mind can be in the form of mental disorder caused by a "psychological blow" in which the person experiences psychiatric symptoms following an extremely stressful experience (Samuels, O'Driscoll, & Allnut, 2007). For example, in the Halifax case *R. v. Lomax* (2002), the judge rejected the insane automatism claim made by the defence that Lomax had robbed a gas station following a psychological blow. The psychological blow described by the defence was the accused being told by his wife that "the neighbour was fucking me with a dildo and we had a good time." In many cases, however, courts have accepted similar arguments and found the accused to be NCRMD (see Porter, Birt, Yuille, & Herve, 2001).

Characteristics of NCRMD Individuals

In a study entitled "A Follow-up Study of Persons Found Not Criminally Responsible on Account of Mental Disorder in British Columbia," Livingston, Wilson, Tien, and Bond (2003) examined the characteristics of people found NCRMD between 1992 (when Bill C-30 was introduced) and 1998. Some of their key findings were the following:

- In the six years after the Criminal Code changes, a much higher number of people were found NCRMD in British Columbia, compared with those found NGRI in the years before the change. The difference was apparently due to a much higher frequency of minor charges leading to a finding of NCRMD after 1992.
- The average length of hospitalization for the NCRMD group was only 9.8 months, much

shorter than the average for the NGRI group (49.9 months).

- Very few NCRMD individuals were convicted of new criminal charges following their discharge into the community, but most required rehospitalization.
- Of the 276 NCRMD individuals in British Columbia, 85.5 percent were male and 14.5 percent were female.
- Prior to committing their offence, 76.5 percent of the NCRMD group had been treated in a psychiatric inpatient facility. Further, 51.8 percent of the patients had been admitted to a psychiatric facility on at least four occasions previously.

The authors concluded that the "Bill C-30 provisions have made the NCRMD defence an attractive option for defendants and legal counsel" (Livingston et al., 2003, p. 408). Overall, the effects of the legal changes seemed to be positive in that they reduced the length of time that a person is initially detained in custody. Unfortunately (but perhaps not surprisingly), a high proportion of those who were found NCRMD but later conditionally discharged required lengthy rehospitalizations.

A finding of NCRMD typically follows expert testimony from psychiatrists and psychologists concerning the accused. Often, within the context of

"Dont worry, you're a politician. You'll have no trouble pleading insanity."

While the public may believe that the insanity (NCRMD) defence may be a "get out of jail free" card, psychological science suggests that it is infrequently used and when used it typically leads to severe restriction of freedoms (such as a lengthy period of hospitalization).

www.CartoonStock.com

the same assessment, the mental health professionals will consider whether the accused is competent to stand trial and whether the accused was, at the time of the commission of the alleged offence, suffering from a mental disorder so as to be NCRMD.

PSYCHOLOGISTS' ROLES IN NCRMD/INSANITY CASES

The forensic psychologist may play several roles when NCRMD is used by a defendant as a legal defence. Prior to trial, the psychologist may be asked to assess the defendant; then at the trial, the psychologist may testify about his or her findings.

Assessment of Criminal Responsibility

As mentioned earlier, assessing criminal responsibility is a difficult task. The first thing the psychologist requires is a sound understanding of the Criminal Code definition of the NCRMD defence. Historically, a common problem in this context was a failure to understand that the mere presence of a mental disorder is not enough for NCRMD. It is certainly possible for someone with a mental disorder to commit a crime and be fully responsible for his or her actions.

In deciding whether offenders were aware of the implications of their actions, psychologists have traditionally used interviews. However, such interviews were unstandardized and unstructured. A more reliable procedure was needed. Developed for this purpose, the Rogers Criminal Responsibility Assessment Scales (R-CRAS) have as their goal the application of the logic of diagnostic structured interviews to the forensic assessment of criminal responsibility (Rogers, 1984, 1986; Rogers & Cavanaugh, 1981; Rogers & Ewing, 1992; Rogers, Wasyliw, & Cavanaugh, 1984). They attempt to transfer the ALI definition of insanity into 25 quantifiable variables, grouped into five topics of psycho-legal relevance: organicity, psychopathology, cognitive control, behavioural control, and the reliability of the report. Each R-CRAS item requires the examiner to rate a specific psychological or situational variable on the delineated criteria; Box 9.1 gives examples of these items.

The authors reported high interjudge reliabilities (the degree of agreement between raters) for assignment of scores to the five topics and for a final judgment of insanity; the mean rate of agreement was more than 90 percent (Nicholson, 1999;

Two of the 25 items from the Rogers Criminal Responsibility Assessment Scales are the following:

Item 10. Amnesia about the alleged crime.
Item 11. Delusions at the time of the alleged crime.

(This refers to the examiner's assessment of amnesia, not necessarily the patient's reported amnesia.)

(0) No information.
(0) No information.
(1) None. Remembers the entire event in considerable detail.
(1) Absent.
(2) Slight; of doubtful significance. The patient forgets a few minor details.
(2) Suspected delusions (e.g., supported only by questionable self-report).
(3) Mild. Patient remembers the substance of what happened, but is forgetful of many minor details.

(3) Definite delusions, but not actually associated with the commission of the alleged crime.
(4) Moderate. The patient has forgotten a major portion of the alleged crime but remembers enough details to believe it happened.
(4) Definite delusions, which contributed to, but were not the predominant force in the commission of the alleged crime.
(5) Severe. The patient is amnesic to most of the alleged crime, but remembers enough details to believe it happened.
(5) Definite controlling delusions, on the basis of which the alleged crime was committed.
(6) Extreme. Patient is completely amnesic to the whole alleged crime.

Rogers, Dolmetsch, Wasyliw, & Cavanaugh, 1982). Also there is a high correspondence between the examiners' ratings and the final legal adjudications (Rogers, Cavanaugh, Seman, & Harris, 1984; Rogers & Sewell, 1999), although these data are derived from examiners who "work closely with one another in specialized forensic evaluation centres, and whose reports and testimony are well known to and influential in local courts" (Ogloff et al., 1993, p. 171).

The review of the R-CRAS by Canadian researcher James Ogloff and his colleagues (1993) concluded that it is a useful tool. These reviewers saw one of its benefits as the requirement that forensic psychologists be comprehensive and explicit about the contributing factors in their judgments regarding the presence of insanity/ NCRMD. Other reviewers have not been as accepting of the R-CRAS; Golding and Roesch (1987) were quite critical and questioned whether the interjudge reliabilities of the R-CRAS were any higher than those resulting from unstructured interviews. In evaluating various reviews of the R-CRAS, Robert Nicholson (1999) noted that its variable rate of acceptance may partly reflect differences of opinion about the goal of forensic

assessment; specifically, does it seek to provide an *ultimate opinion* regarding the criminal responsibility of the individual?

A second instrument for assessing criminal responsibility, the Mental Screening Evaluation, or MSE (Slobogin, Melton, & Showalter, 1984), has a more modest goal: to "screen out" defendants whose law-breaking actions clearly were not caused by a mental disorder. The MSE includes questions about the defendant's general psychological history, questions about the alleged offence, and an evaluation of his or her present mental state. For example, in the first section, the psychologist is asked, "Does the defendant have a history of prolonged bizarre behaviour (i.e., delusions, hallucinations, looseness of association of ideas … [or] distur-bances of affect?" (p. 319).

A purpose of the MSE is to sensitize psychological examiners to the kinds of information required when addressing the legal question of the defendant's mental state at the time of the law-breaking behaviour. But there is neither a standardized administration nor a formal scoring procedure for the test's use, and empirical evidence on its validity is limited (Grisso, 1986; Nicholson, 1999).

A third measure has been used to assess criminal responsibility in recent years: neuroimaging technology (Batts, 2009). Neuroimaging technologies such as MRIs, fMRIs, CT scans, and PET scans are used to determine the structure and function of different areas of the brain (Batts, 2009; Greenfield, 2009; Shuman & Gold, 2008). It has been proposed that these neuroimaging scans are able to identify mental disorder in the brain, and thus provide evidence for (or against) an NCRMD defence (Batts, 2009). While biological evidence of mental disorder appears to be a promising solution to the criminal responsibility issue, there are many problems with the use of neuroimaging technology, including that (1) not all mental disorders are represented physically, (2) lesions and abnormalities that are visible in the brain do not necessarily indicate a mental disorder, and (3) there is no "moral area" in the brain, so it is impossible to determine an area in the brain that, if damaged, guarantees an impairment in moral reasoning (Batts, 2009; Greenfield, 2009).

Although no solid evidence supports the use of neuroimaging in criminal responsibility cases, this method is becoming increasingly popular. A fear of some researchers is that jurors are more likely to trust biological evidence over other evaluations. A recent study by Gurley and Marcus (2008) had mock jurors deliver verdicts on insanity defence cases. The results revealed that the mock jurors were more likely to deliver a "not guilty by reason of insanity" verdict if the defendant had a history of brain injury, had been diagnosed with a psychotic disorder, or had a brain lesion shown by an MRI. While neuroimaging technologies may be able to provide some evidence for diminished capacity in insanity cases, it is imperative to keep in mind that biological evidence in the form of neuroimaging scans is not a guarantee.

Testifying as an Expert Witness

In making decisions on issues beyond their knowledge, jurors often pay attention to the testimony of expert witnesses. But the forensic psychologist who testifies for the defence that the defendant meets the definition of NCRMD faces several challenges. First, the Crown is likely to have an expert witness of its own, with conflicting conclusions. Second, any expert witness is likely to face a withering cross-examination. On this last point, the volumes prepared by the late forensic psychologist Jay Ziskin (1995) and a highly publicized article in *Science* by Faust and Ziskin

(1988) provide a compendium of material that challenges the claim that the assessments done by clinical psychologists and other mental health professionals possess adequate levels of validity and reliability for use in court (see Nicholson, 1999, pp. 125–131, for a critique of Ziskin's efforts). Many recent trials illustrate the concerns about expert witness testimony, especially the differing assessments by defence and prosecution experts of the defendant's psychological state. Two familiar murder cases from the United States will be used to exemplify the "battle of the experts" problem.

The Hinckley Trial

The trial of John W. Hinckley, Jr. included expert psychiatrists on each side. When Hinckley went on trial 15 months after shooting President Reagan, his lawyers didn't dispute the evidence that he had planned the attack, bought special bullets, tracked the president, and fired from a shooter's crouch. But he couldn't help it, they claimed, for he was only responding to the "driving forces" of a diseased mind. Their claims were supported by the testimony of psychiatrist William Carpenter, that Hinckley did not "appreciate" the consequences of his act: he had lost the ability to control himself and was suffering from process schizophrenia. The defence also tried to introduce the results of a CAT scan of Hinckley's brain to support its contention that he was schizophrenic.

The psychiatrists testifying for the prosecution conceded that Hinckley had strange fantasies but argued that he did not have schizophrenia, only relatively mild and commonplace mental disorders. They stated that he had no delusions or psychoses and that he was always in touch with reality, including the reality that Jodie Foster would never feel affection for him. The real motives, they said, had been to win fame and to give Ms. Foster and his parents a jolt (Caplan, 1984).

A prominent forensic psychiatrist testifying for the prosecution, Park Dietz, diagnosed Hinckley as having a borderline personality disorder with depressive neurosis. He concluded that Hinckley's goal of making an impression on Jodie Foster was indeed reasonable, because he accomplished it (Caplan, 1984). Even though his were not the reasonable acts of a completely rational individual, no evidence existed that he was so impaired that he could not appreciate the wrongfulness of his conduct or conform his conduct to the requirements of the law.

The decision by the jury that found Hinckley not guilty by reason of insanity appears to have been strongly influenced by the judge's instruction that the burden of proof was on the prosecution to prove that Hinckley was sane.

The Dahmer Trial

The 1992 trial of Jeffrey Dahmer is unusual for more than the fact that he had admitted killing and dismembering 17 young men over a 10-year period. Some bodies he cannibalized. Others he tried to turn into "zombies" who could remain with him for companionship (Berlin, 1994). The purpose of the trial was to determine whether Dahmer could be absolved of responsibility by reason of insanity rather than to determine guilt, as he had already conceded that he had committed the acts. Hence, the jury was given two different characterizations of the defendant. His lawyer told the jury: "This is not an evil man; this is a sick man." The prosecuting lawyer disagreed, claiming that Dahmer "knew at all times that what he was doing was wrong."

The trial also was unusual in that in addition to the expert witnesses introduced by each side, the presiding judge asked two experts to testify, one psychiatrist and one psychologist. The defence experts, who testified first (in Wisconsin the defence had the burden of proof to prove that Dahmer was insane), included the following:

- Dr. Fred S. Berlin, a psychiatrist from Johns Hopkins University School of Medicine, who

The Jeffrey Dahmer trial showed that expert psychologists can have very diverse opinions about a defendant's mental state and culpability.

diagnosed Dahmer's psychiatric disorder as **necrophilia** (a type of paraphilia or abnormal sexual behaviour), reflecting sexual urges that caused him to kill young men and then preserve their body parts, in an effort to maintain sexual intimacy. Dahmer used terms such as "overpowering" in describing the strength of his cravings; hence Berlin felt that he lacked "substantial capacity" to control his actions. In a subsequent article (1994), Berlin concluded that Dahmer came to believe it was his destiny to kill, even though he often felt miserable, alone, and despairing. Berlin also testified that Dahmer would become erotically aroused by thoughts of having sex with dead male bodies. He was frequently impotent and unable to sustain an erection when relating to those who were still alive (Berlin, 1994).

In his article on the case, Berlin stated: "I did not feel uncomfortable defending the position that an individual who recurrently experiences much more powerful urges to have sex with a corpse than with a living human being is an individual who is afflicted with a mental disease or defect" (1994, p. 14). Of all the expert witnesses, he came closest to the layperson's view when he said, "If this isn't mental illness I don't know what is."

- Dr. Judith Becker, a clinical psychologist and professor at the University of Arizona, who offered a sexual history of Dahmer and described Dahmer's fantasies about capturing young men and building a kind of "temple" in his apartment from the body parts, skulls, and skeletons of his victims (Norris, 1992). She, too, felt that Dahmer suffered from a sexual disorder of necrophilia and that he lacked control of his urges. She did not diagnose him as psychotic, although she felt that some of his behaviour was "psychotic-like."

- Dr. Carl Wahlstrom, a psychiatrist who, on cross-examination, acknowledged that he had not yet passed his board certification and that this was his first defence testimony (Norris, 1992). He proposed that Dahmer killed in order to avoid abandonment; Wahlstrom was the only defence witness to conclude that Dahmer had a borderline personality and was psychotic, even though he lacked hallucinations.

The prosecution countered with two experts:

- Dr. Frederick Fosdal, a forensic psychiatrist from the University of Wisconsin Medical School, who noted that Dahmer's were not brutal, sadistic acts and, further, that Dahmer was able to control himself and had some control as to when he followed through on his sexual desires.

- Dr. Park Dietz (who had testified in the Hinckley trial also), formerly of the faculty at the University of Virginia but now a full-time forensic psychiatrist. (Box 9.2 elaborates on Dietz's background.) Perhaps the most effective of the expert witnesses, Dietz pointed to Dahmer's capacity to exert methodical control as an indicator of his sanity and premeditation (Norris, 1992). Further, "the mere fact that Dahmer disposed of his bodies efficiently, planned different methods of disposal, was able to control his murderous urges for years between crimes, and was able to fool his probation officer and policemen on different occasions proved that the man knew exactly what he was doing" (quoted by Norris, 1992, p. 281). He offered two diagnoses: alcohol dependence, of a mild to moderate nature, and paraphilia (sexual deviation). These two interacted; Dahmer would drink to overcome his inhibitions against killing and dismemberment. Thus Dietz concluded that Dahmer did not meet the Wisconsin standard of insanity.

The two court-appointed expert witnesses were the following:

- Dr. George Palermo, a psychiatrist, who read his report to the jury. He concluded that Dahmer was not insane, that he had a serious personality disorder and was driven by obsessive fantasies, but that he knew what he was doing.
- Dr. Thomas Friedman, a psychologist in independent practice, who, in response to a question, waxed philosophical about the nature of mental illness. Friedman agreed with Dietz and Palermo that Dahmer had a personality disorder and that he was not psychotic. In that respect, his testimony aided the prosecution, but he probably was not very effective because of his self-deprecatory manner ("My understanding of the literature is not the most sophisticated" [Court TV, 1992]).

In Wisconsin, a unique version of the ALI rule is used to define insanity; consequently, to have found Dahmer insane, the jury first would have had to conclude that he had suffered from a mental disorder or defect that made him unable to know right from wrong and, second, whether, as a consequence of that, he lacked substantial capacity to control his conduct, as required by the law. In a

---

BOX 9.2   PARK DIETZ—EXPERT WITNESS FOR THE PROSECUTION

Among forensic psychiatrists who testify in murder cases in which the defence is a claim of insanity, Park Dietz is clearly the most consistently effective as an expert witness for the prosecution. Always meticulously prepared, he is able to provide jurors with plausible explanations of defendants' behaviour that do not involve insanity or psychosis. In both the Hinckley and the Dahmer trials, Dietz effectively related the specifics of the defendant's behaviour to show qualities in conflict with the local definition of insanity.

Dietz characteristically testifies for the prosecution. He holds little sympathy for defence lawyers—in discussing his own experience with them, he wrote: "Criminal defence lawyers routinely withheld evidence of their clients' guilt, at least until confident that the government has the evidence" (1996, p. 159). In contrast, he noted, "I have known the prosecution to withhold important evidence on only one occasion, and it was in the context of a court-ordered evaluation" (Dietz, 1996, p. 159).

To what extent is Dr. Dietz's interpretation of behaviour related to his political ideology? While an undergraduate at Cornell University he was president of the Conservative Club (Johnson, 1994). He has no clinical caseload. Defence lawyers, not surprisingly, believe that he sees things through the eyes of the prosecutor. When he agrees to take a case, Dietz warns the prosecutor that he might well end up forming an opinion that would prevent him from testifying against the defendant. But in the cases of John W. Hinckley, Jr.; Jeffrey Dahmer; Betty Broderick; Arthur Shawcross; Joel Rifkin, and others, he has always concluded that the behaviour did not meet the definition of insanity. In the opinion of one observer, "[I]n his view, when criminal charges are heavy, truth is rarely to be found on the side of a defence [lawyer's] client. Dietz's predilection for the prosecutor's side does not seem unconnected to his conservative politics or to his profound alienation from the physician's role in traditional psychiatry" (Johnson, 1994, p. 48).

---

split decision, acceptable by Wisconsin rules, the jury concluded that Dahmer was not an individual who suffered from mental disease, perhaps because of the evidence that Dahmer was careful to kill his victims in a manner that minimized his chances of getting caught—such a degree of cautiousness suggested that he appreciated the wrongfulness of his behaviour *and* could control this behaviour when it was to his advantage to do so. Thus, Dahmer was sentenced to 999 years in prison, where he was bludgeoned to death by another inmate in 1994.

Ultimate-Issue Testimony

As noted earlier, one of the roles of the expert is "to explore carefully, and to explain to the court, how psychopathological processes at the time of the crime might have influenced the defendant's then-existing perceptions, motivations, cognitions, intentions, and behaviours" (Ogloff et al., 1993, p. 172). This retrospective evaluation has to be expressed in terms of likelihood rather than finality, and it is subject to several sources of error, including examiner bias, possible malingering, and undetected defensive covering of genuine paranoid pathology, among other factors (Ogloff et al., 1993).

How far should a psychologist or psychiatrist be allowed to go when testifying in a case involving an NCRMD defence? Is it appropriate for an expert to express an opinion about whether the defendant was criminally responsible at the time of the offence? Psychologists are divided on this issue; some strenuously oppose the court's questioning of mental health experts about the status of the specific defendant, while others do not (Bonnie & Slobogin, 1980; Morse, 1978). Some of the concerns stem from a belief that it is the role of the jury, not the psychiatric expert, to determine the criminal responsibility of the defendant. In keeping with the issues that introduced this chapter, we need to remember that the judgment of responsibility is a legal one, not a psychological one, and that psychologists, as experts, should stop at the limits of their expertise. But some psychologists have gone further in their criticisms, questioning whether psychology and psychiatry have any valid viewpoints on such issues, and have challenged their colleagues to provide supporting evidence for their claims of accuracy in forensic opinions (Dawes, Faust, & Meehl, 1989; Hagen, 1997; Ziskin, 1995; Ziskin & Faust, 1988).

One resolution to this conflict is to prevent the expert from expressing an opinion on the ultimate issue of legal criminal responsibility/insanity itself. In Canada, **ultimate-issue testimony** by experts was once not allowed in the court. While current rules of evidence are more liberal, the *Mohan* case (see Chapter 1) determined that if an expert's testimony speaks to the ultimate issue, "the criteria of relevance and necessity are applied strictly, on occasion, to exclude expert evidence as to the ultimate issue" (*R. v. Mohan*, para. 24). In the United States, ultimate-issue or ultimate-opinion testimony was one of the targets of the Insanity Defense Reform Act of 1984, passed by Congress after John Hinckley's trial. It modified U.S. federal law specifically to prohibit mental health experts from testifying about ultimate legal issues. As amended, Federal Rule of Evidence 704(b), which allows ultimate-issue testimony in other types of cases, now states:

To expert witness testifying with respect to the mental state or condition of the defendant in a criminal case may state an opinion or inference as to whether the defendant did or did not have the mental state or condition constituting an element of the crime charged or of the defense thereto. Such ultimate issues are matters for the trier of fact alone.

Note that this proscription applies to U.S. federal cases only; Jeffrey Dahmer's trial, as is the vast majority of trials using the insanity plea, was a state matter. Some state courts have permitted experts to testify as to the ultimate issue of insanity but have instructed jurors that they may give such testimony as much or as little weight as they wish. Similar to Canada, some other countries (including the United Kingdom and South Africa) permit ultimate-opinion testimony, at least in some types of cases (Allan & Louw, 1997).

This ruling has led to consternation and confusion in the U.S. federal courts. Supposedly, the expert could describe a defendant's psychological condition and the effects it could have had on his or her thinking and behavioural control, but could not state conclusions about whether the defendant was sane or insane. But some commentators have speculated that this exclusion may lead to the omission at the trial of clinical information quite relevant to the case (Braswell, 1987; Goldstein, 1989; Rogers & Ewing, 1989, as cited by Ogloff et al., 1993). For example, Canadians Ogloff and colleagues have observed:

> If the revised rule were applied strictly, an expert could not testify as to whether a given defendant was legally sane or insane *and* whether he or she had a "mental disease," "intended" to do great bodily harm, "knew" the probable consequences of his or her act, "knew" what he or she was doing, "appreciated" the criminality of his or her conduct, and so forth. Yet the same expert is literally being asked by the courts to give testimony that bears directly on such psychological constructs. (1993, p. 172, italics in original)

Further, forensic psychologists, whose expertise includes in evaluating policy changes, need to ask whether this prohibition solves any problems, or whether it is, in the words of Rogers and Ewing (1989), merely a "cosmetic fix" that has few effects.

(Similarly, Fulero, 1998, sees it as a "semantic" issue, only.) A study by Fulero and Finkel (1991) was designed to answer this question. Mock jurors read one of several versions of a murder trial in which the defendant claimed that he was insane at the time of the offence. Some mock jurors were told that expert witnesses had testified, but only that they had given diagnostic testimony, specifically that the defendant suffered a mental disorder at the time of the offence; other jurors were told about the effects of this disorder on the degree to which the defendant understood the wrongfulness of his act; and a third group of jurors heard ultimate-opinion testimony about whether the defendant was sane or insane at the time of the act. In this study, the type of information the mock jurors heard from the expert witness did *not* affect whether they found the defendant guilty or not guilty by reason of insanity. Does this mean the prohibition is unnecessary? Further research is needed. Let us say that a psychologist testifies that the defendant did not know the difference between right and wrong and was not able to appreciate the wrongfulness of

CANADIAN RESEARCHER PROFILE

Jodi Viljoen

Jodi Viljoen completed her Honours degree in Psychology from the University of Alberta, and graduated with her Master's and Ph.D. in Clinical Forensic Psychology from Simon Fraser University. After completing her clinical internship at the University of Massachusetts Medical School, she took her first academic job at the University of Nebraska—Lincoln. Currently, she is an associate professor at Simon Fraser University. During her summer jobs as an undergraduate student, she worked with youth at risk and adolescent offenders. While she found these jobs rewarding, they also raised a lot of questions for her about whether the services that are provided to adolescents are effective. These questions drew her to this field and led her to pursue graduate school.

In her dissertation, she examined adolescents' legal rights and competencies (e.g., fitness to stand trial). Her research showed that while adolescents who commit crimes are often presumed to be mature and adult-like, they are still developing in important ways that affect their legal capacities and decision making. In her recent work, she has focused primarily on adolescents' risk of violence and tools to assess violence risk. Although many adolescents engage in some illegal behaviour, most do not become career criminals. Therefore, her current research focuses on how adolescent offenders change, what protects them from ongoing involvement in crime, and how risk assessment tools might be able to help guide treatment. In her work with adolescent offenders, she has been struck by the resiliency and strengths that they show, often in the face of significant adversity. As such, her future plans focus heavily on protective factors and treatment.

Most of her research is applied in nature, and she particularly enjoys working with youth justice agencies and mental health clinics to implement empirically supported practices. Also, a favourite part of her job as a professor is working with graduate and undergraduate students in her research lab. They constantly amaze her with their energy, enthusiasm, and ideas. In her free time, she enjoys playing at the playground (with her two young kids!) and anything that involves being outside (hiking, snowboarding, skiing, rock-climbing, mountain biking, and sea kayaking).

his or her actions. If the expert is allowed to testify thus (and stops there), the jury probably has a good idea of the expert's opinion on the ultimate question (i.e., that there should be a finding of insanity).

ASSESSING COMPETENCY

A fundamental principle of the criminal justice system in Canada is that criminal proceedings should not continue against any person who is not able to understand their nature or purpose. To have a fair trial, criminal defendants must be able to understand the nature of the proceedings and assist counsel, as noted by Patricia Zapf, Ronald Roesch, and Jodi Viljoen (2001; see the Canadian Researcher Profile for more information on Dr. Viljoen). If an accused person is unable to contribute to the defence due to a mental disorder, he or she may be found unfit to stand trial, and proceedings will be delayed until fitness is regained. It is estimated that at least 5000 criminal defendants are referred for evaluation of their competency to participate in legal proceedings annually in Canada (Roesch, Webster, & Eaves, 1984). The criterion in the determination of competency is the present level of ability of the defendant, not his or her state at the time of the offence; thus the focus drastically differs from the evaluation of the defendant's criminal responsibility (Pirelli, Gottdiener, & Zapf, 2011). Nonetheless, the typical presence of a mental disorder is the strongest commonality of NCRMD and "not competent to stand trial" findings.

Traditionally, the disposition for a defendant found incompetent or "not fit" to stand trial was committal to a psychiatric facility for an indeterminate period until fitness was regained. However, with revisions to the Criminal Code of Canada in 1992, the definition of fitness and the dispositions following such a finding changed (e.g., Zapf et al., 2001). The Criminal Code now defines "unfit to stand trial" as:

Unable on account of mental disorder to conduct a defence at any stage of the proceedings before a verdict is rendered or to instruct counsel to do so, and, in particular, unable on account of mental disorder to (a) understand the nature or object of the proceedings, (b) understand the possible consequences of the proceedings, or (c) communicate with counsel.

Forensic psychologists and psychiatrists assist in assessing competency of defendants who come before the court. In general, **competency** (or "competence") refers to the person's ability to understand the nature and purpose of court proceedings, and it is applicable at every stage of the criminal justice process, from interrogations and pretrial hearings to trials and sentencing hearings (Pirelli et al., 2011). Competency or fitness is especially an issue when a defendant goes to trial or when he or she plea-bargains a guilty plea.

Although the subsequent emphasis in this section is on assessing competency of defendants facing criminal charges, competency also is a relevant question in some types of civil suits. For example, in a civil case it may be necessary to evaluate the testamentary capacity of a person when he or she makes out a will. Also, when issues of guardianship are raised, the courts want to know whether the individual possesses the necessary mental ability to make decisions regarding his or her health care, living conditions, and finances. These and other types of civil cases provide expanding demands for competency assessments by forensic psychologists and other mental health professionals.

Defence lawyers express concerns about their clients' fitness to stand trial in about 10 to 15 percent of their cases (Hoge, Bonnie, Poythress, & Monahan, 1992; Poythress, Bonnie, Hoge, Monahan, & Oberlander, 1994). If, as in the case of competency to plead, a question is raised about the defendant's fitness to stand trial, the judge will order an evaluation of the defendant. While early reviews (Melton, Weithorn, & Slobogin, 1997) estimated that in 10 to 30 percent of these referrals, the defendant was found to be incompetent, more recent studies suggest a much higher rate of positive findings. For example, Stafford and Wygant (2005) found that judges decided the defendant was incompetent in 77.5 percent of cases in which the issue was raised. Most evaluations are completed on an inpatient basis, although some psychologists have questioned the necessity of this costly procedure and have recommended that it be done on an outpatient basis (Melton, Weithorn, & Slobogin, 1985; Roesch & Golding, 1987).

The judge, of course, makes the decision of whether the defendant is fit to stand trial. But studies consistently find that judges often defer to the opinion of the examining psychologist or psychiatrist, with judge-examiner rates of agreement at 90 percent or higher (Hart & Hare, 1992; Reich & Tookey, 1986; Williams & Miller, 1981, reviewed by Skeem, Golding, Cohn, & Berge, 1998).

The basic question to be answered in such an evaluation is: If the defendant has an impairment, does it affect his or her ability to participate knowingly and meaningfully in the trial and to cooperate with the defence lawyer? The procedure in the competency evaluation is subject to the usual problems of subjectivity of clinical examinations. Thus psychiatrists and psychologists have designed competency assessment instruments that seek greater objectivity. Five of these are described below; though some call themselves "tests," they serve as semistructured interviews.

The Fitness Interview Test-Revised (FIT-R)

The Fitness Interview Test-Revised (originally named the Interdisciplinary Fitness Interview), now one of the most widely used fitness assessment tools in Canada, was developed by Ron Roesch and Steven Golding (1980; Golding, Roesch, & Schreiber, 1984). The revised version includes questions on three main topics adhering to the Criminal Code criteria: understanding of the proceedings, understanding of the consequences of the proceedings, and the defendant's ability to communicate with counsel (Roesch, Webster, & Eaves, 1994; Roesch, Zapf, Eaves, & Webster, 1998; Zapf & Roesch, 1997; Zapf, Roesch, & Viljoen, 2001). The FIT involves a semistructured interview, which takes about 30 minutes to administer to the accused person. Each of the 16 items is rated on a three-point scale (0–2), with 0 indicating no impairment on the criterion and 2 indicating definite or serious impairment. The revised version responded to criticisms of the earlier version and reflected the 1992 changes made to the Criminal Code (Roesch, Zapf, & Eaves, 2006). It appears to work very well as a screening device to assess fitness to stand trial in Canada (Nicholson, 1999). Zapf and colleagues (2001) compared decisions about fitness to stand trial based on FIT results with the findings of institution-based decision makers on the same male patients. They found that the FIT had excellent utility as a screening instrument that can reduce the number of remands to an inpatient facility.

The Competency Screening Test (CST)

This 22-item sentence-completion task, developed by Lipsitt, Lelos, and McGarry (1971), serves as an initial screening test for competency. The CST is reproduced in Box 9.3.

Each answer by the defendant is scored as a 2 (a competent answer), a 1 (a marginally competent answer), or a 0 (an incompetent answer); thus the range is from 0 to 66. A score of 20 or below indicates that the respondent should be given a more comprehensive evaluation.

This procedure is an improvement over the traditional, rather unstructured interview that led to subjective conclusions and a global, unquantified indication of competency (Golding, 1990). But the CST still has some subjectivity, especially in the scoring of responses (Roesch & Golding, 1987). For example, for the statement "Jack felt that the judge …," a response of "was unjust" receives 0 points. The CST had the lowest predictive validity index of the instruments reviewed by Melton, Petrila, Poythress, and Slobogin (1997). Even though the interrater reliability coefficients on the CST appear to be high—generally .85 or better—these are apparently derived from raters who have had extensive training and have used the instrument frequently (Melton et al., 1987). Studies that seek to identify a factor structure (the structure of the variables) have found inconsistent results (Ustad, Rogers, Sewell, & Guarnaccia, 1996). Of greater concern is the outcome of a study (Felchlia, 1992) that sought to determine whether there was a relationship between the constructs that the CST claimed to assess and measures of parallel psychological constructs. The results were disappointing. For example, assessments of the defendant's ability to cope with events in the trial, as indicated by CST responses, were not significantly related to psychological measures of adaptive and coping potential.

The Competency Assessment Instrument (CAI)

The Competency Assessment Instrument (CAI) is a structured interview, lasting about one hour, that seeks to explore 13 aspects of competent functioning (Laboratory of Community Psychiatry, 1974). The defendant's response is rated with a score from 1 (total incapacity) to 5 (no incapacity). In the CAI, the mental health worker is asked to appraise where the defendant stands on a number of qualities, including how he or she relates to the lawyer, the defendant's ability to testify relevantly, his or her appreciation of the charges and the possible penalties, and his or her ability to

BOX 9.3   **COMPETENCY SCREENING TEST**

1. The lawyer told Bill that _____
   _____
   _____
   _____

2. When I go to court, the lawyer will _____
   _____
   _____
   _____

3. Jack felt that the judge _____
   _____
   _____
   _____

4. When Phil was accused of the crime, he _____
   _____
   _____
   _____

5. When I prepare to go to court with my lawyer _____
   _____
   _____
   _____

6. If the jury finds me guilty, I _____
   _____
   _____
   _____

7. The way a court trial is decided _____
   _____
   _____
   _____

8. When the evidence in George's case was presented
   to the jury _____
   _____
   _____
   _____

9. When the lawyer questioned his client in court, the
   client said _____
   _____
   _____

10. If Jack had to try his own case, he _____
   _____
   _____
   _____

11. Each time the DA asked me a question, I _____
   _____
   _____
   _____

12. While listening to the witnesses testify against me, I
   _____

13. When the witness testifying against Harry gave
   incorrect evidence, he _____
   _____
   _____

14. When Bob disagreed with his lawyer on his defence, he
   _____
   _____
   _____

15. When I was formally accused of the crime, I thought
   to myself _____
   _____
   _____

16. If Ed's lawyer suggests that he plead guilty, he ____
   _____
   _____
   _____

17. What concerns Fred most about his lawyer is _____
   _____
   _____
   _____

18. When they say a man is innocent until proven guilty
   _____
   _____
   _____

19. When I think of being sent to prison, I _____
   _____
   _____
   _____

20. When Phil thinks of what he is accused of, he ____
   _____
   _____
   _____

21. When the jury hears my case, they will _____
   _____
   _____

22. If I had a chance to speak to the judge, I _____
   _____
   _____
   _____

Lipsitt, Paul D.; Lelos, David; McGarry, A. Louis, "Competency for Trial: A Screening Instrument", *The American Journal of Psychiatry*, Vol. 128(1), Jul 1971, p. 105–109. Reprinted with permission from the American Journal of Psychiatry, (Copyright © 1971). American Psychiatric Association.

realistically assess the outcome of the trial. Many of these characteristics are, of course, similar to those in the CST.

Little research exists on the reliability of this system; in a review of research done between 1991 and 1995, Cooper and Grisso (1997) reported no published articles on the CAI. The administration and scoring are not standardized. A revision of the CAI has been developed by John A. Riley (1998), along with colleagues Craig Nelson and John Gannon, at Atascadero State Hospital, in California. It assesses 14 aspects of functioning and takes about 30 to 45 minutes to administer. These aspects include understanding of the charges against the accused, appreciation of the penalties, ability to cooperate with counsel, and capacity to cope with incarceration while awaiting trial. The subject's responses are evaluated for their adequacy on a 1-to-4 scale.

Georgia Court Competency Test (GCCT)

The Georgia Court Competency Test or GCCT (Wildman et al., 1978) consists of 21 questions. Although it is more limited in coverage, its reliability appears to be acceptable (Bagby, Nicholson, Rogers, & Nussbaum, 1992). It has demonstrated the same factor structure in two samples (Nicholson, Briggs, & Robertson, 1988)—specifically, general legal knowledge, courtroom layout, and specific legal knowledge. However, another study suggested that the two legal knowledge factors can be combined into one (Ustad, Rogers, Sewell, & Guarnaccia, 1996).

The original form of the GCCT was modified by psychologists at Mississippi State Hospital by adding four questions, changing the weighting of some answers, and making scoring criteria more explicit (Johnson & Mullett, 1987). Studies using this revision, the GCCT-MSH, have found significant correlations with independent criteria of competency (Nicholson, 1999). One of these validity studies concluded that performance on the GCCT-MSH "made a significant, independent contribution to prediction of competence status beyond that based on diagnosis, intellectual functioning, offence type, and background characteristics" (Nicholson & Johnson, 1991, quoted in Nicholson, 1999, p. 139).

The MacArthur Competence Assessment Tool-Criminal Adjudication (MacCAT-CA)

The most recently developed competency-assessment device is the MacArthur Competence Assessment Tool-Criminal Adjudication, abbreviated MacCAT-CA (Hoge et al., 1997). Its purpose is to measure the person's competence to proceed to adjudication; that is, his or her ability to plead guilty as well as the ability to go to trial (Rogers & Johansson-Love, 2009). It is a more structured measure than the CAI and uses an objective, theory-based scoring system. In keeping with four kinds of abilities seen as relevant to the competency evaluation, questions are grouped into four categories:

- Understanding of charges and trials (including understanding of general trial issues, competence to assist counsel, understanding whether to plead guilty, and understanding whether to waive a jury and request a bench trial)
- Appreciation of the relevance of information for a defence
- Reasoning with information during decision making, or an assessment of logical problem-solving abilities
- Making a choice

Most of the MacCAT-CA contains hypothetical situations about which the defendant is questioned. (See Box 9.4.) Administration time is from 25 to 55 minutes. The instrument effectively discriminates adult defendants the court has judged to be incompetent from those for whom competence was never an issue (Hoge et al., 1997), and it possesses construct validity in that it shows the expected patterns of relationships with cognitive ability, psychopathology, and judgments by clinicians of the degree of impaired competency (Otto, Edens, Poythress, & Nicholson, 1998). Its results show strong agreement with those of the FIT-R (Zapf, 1998). A Canadian study conducted by Viljoen, Slaney, and Grisso reveals that while the MacCAT-CA is an effective competency measure for adults, it may not be as accurate a measure for adolescents because a large number of the questions show an age bias (2009).

The MacCAT-CA clearly reflects a "new generation" of instruments. Melton et al. (1997) were quite positive about its promise:

It taps legal domains related to both the general capacity to assist counsel and competence for discrete legal decisions, simultaneously examining multiple competence-related abilities such as understanding, reasoning, and appreciation, both before and after competency instruction. It retains the relative efficiency of existing measures, yet it

The MacArthur instrument uses hypothetical situations and asks the defendant questions about them. For example: "Two men, Fred and Reggie, are playing pool at a bar and get into a fight. Fred hits Reggie with a pool stick. Reggie falls and hits his head on the floor so hard that he nearly dies" (quoted by Melton, Petrila, Poythress, & Slobogin, 1997, p. 146).

Defendants are asked a number of specific questions; for example, to measure understanding, the subject is told the following: Fred may plead not guilty and go to trial, or Fred may plead guilty. Now, if Fred pleads guilty to attempted murder, he would give up some legal rights and protections. What are they? (quoted by Melton et al., 1997, p. 146).

To measure the defendant's ability to identify relevant information, the defendant is asked to decide which of the following is relevant:

A. At the bar, there was a country and western band playing in the room next to the pool room.
B. Fred himself called the ambulance because he could see that Reggie was hurt very badly.

Thus the MacArthur instrument strives to provide an objective assessment of competency.

offers standardized administration and, for most of its submeasures, objective, criterion-based scoring that should minimize the subjectivity that plagues existing comprehensive measures. (pp. 149–150)

Much work needs to be done by forensic psychologists to improve the process in judging competency to stand trial. Research indicates that many lawyers do not follow through when they have fears about their clients' passivity and failure to understand (Hoge, Bonnie, Poythress, & Monahan, 1992; Poythress, Bonnie, Hoge, Monahan, & Oberlander, 1994). We grant that lawyers often face a dilemma; if they raise the question of their client's competency, they may sacrifice their client's trust (Gould, 1995).

RISK ASSESSMENT

Persons are committed to psychiatric hospitals because they are judged to be in danger of harming themselves or others. Sexual offenders are sentenced to a period in a correctional institution but eventually come before a parole board or release review board. Can forensic psychologists predict which individuals within these groups will engage in violence against others or predict which will attempt suicide?

Predicting Suicide

Answers to such questions have been put within the context of the accuracy of clinical prediction.

The term **clinical prediction** usually refers to the process by which the psychologist reviews all the information about an individual and, combining this information in an intuitive—or at least, an unspecified—way, then makes a prediction about the individual's actions or outcome, such as, "If released, this person will become violent toward others." Traditionally, such clinical predictions have not fared well when compared with what are called **actuarial predictions**, or those that combine information based on prespecified, empirically established decision rules (see Chapter 11 for a more in-depth discussion of actuarial predictions; Dawes, 1994; Grove & Meehl, 1996; Meehl, 1954). One cause of the difference in accuracy, according to critics of clinical prediction, is that clinicians fail to consider **base rates** fully. For example, a clinician may predict that a higher percentage of schizophrenic patients will commit violence than the actual rate in the population, which is exceedingly low. Another example concerns depression and risk for suicide. It is expected that any mental health professional working with psychiatric inpatients will assess and monitor suicidal risk. But how difficult is this task? Pokorny (1983) studied the progress of 4800 psychiatric inpatients in U.S. Veterans Administration hospitals. During a five-year period, 67 of the 4800 persons committed suicide, a base rate of 1.4 percent. Given this base rate, the predictive task for the clinician would be nearly impossible: Which one out of every one hundred patients being assessed is the most likely to commit suicide? A review of the literature (Garb, 1998) concluded that predictions of suicide risk generally have not been reliable (Janofsky, Spears, & Neubauer, 1988; Large, 2010).

Predicting Danger to Others

Is there a relationship between mental disorder and a tendency to be violent toward others? Certainly the public believes that there is. Psychologists have been more skeptical, although prominent psychologists (see, for example, Monahan, 1992) now believe that a consistent but small relationship may be present. However, in a longitudinal study of more than 34 000 American citizens, Elbogen and Johnson (2009) found that severe mental illness did not predict violent behaviour (also see Douglas, Guy, & Hart, 2009).

If such a relationship exists, can forensic psychologists specify which persons are at risk of harming others? Monahan (1992) has concluded that only people who are experiencing psychotic symptoms are at an increased risk of violence; he wrote: "Being a former patient in a mental hospital—that is, having experienced psychotic symptoms *in the past*—bears no direct relationship to violence" (p. 519, italics in original).

Second, the vast majority of persons who have mental disorders to a significant degree are not violent. With a low probability that any one individual in a population will commit a violent act against another, it becomes very difficult to assess risk, because of the base rate problem described above. In fact, the validity of such assessments has been described by reviewers as "modest." One review concluded that the validity of these assessments was only slightly above chance (Steadman et al., 1996). Another (Garb, 1998) concluded that clinical psychologists make "moderately valid" short-term and long-term predictions of violence; a third review (Mossman, 1994) asserted that the accuracy rates of psychologists' predictions remain below those using statistical prediction.

Rejuvenated interest in risk assessment, spurred by the MacArthur Foundation's financing of a massive study, has allowed **dangerousness** to be divided into component parts (Heilbrun & Heilbrun, 1995), specifically, risk factors (or the variables used to predict violence), **harm** (the amount and type of violence being predicted), and **risk level** (or the probability that harm will occur). Further, better methodologies in more recent studies have increased the rate of accuracy. For example, older research studies often used only limited resources for assessing violence (e.g., only arrest records), while more recent research relies also on self-reports and other outcome variables. The increased use of actuarial methods also has improved the accuracy of predictions (Monahan & Steadman, 1994; Skeem & Monahan, 2011). An example of contemporary risk assessment reflecting this approach is the program of work by Ontario researchers Vernon Quinsey, Grant Harris, Marnie Rice, and their colleagues (Quinsey, Harris, Rice, & Cormier, 1998; Rice & Harris, 1995). For example, Harris, Rice, and Quinsey (1993) used 12 variables coded from institutional files of 618 men at a maximum-security forensic hospital in Canada. These variables included scores on the Hare Psychopathy Checklist (Hare, 1991), separation from parents before the age of 16 years, never having been married, early reports of maladjustment, presence of alcohol abuse, injuries to victims, and DSM classifications. The criterion for subsequent violence was any new criminal charge for a violent offence or return to the institution for such acts, with the typical follow-up period being seven years. The actuarial combination of predictor variables led to a correlation of .46 with violent recidivism. The use of actuarial procedures is improving prediction, but current estimates are that predictions may still be inaccurate as much as 40 percent to 50 percent of the time (Slobogin, 1996). Skeem and Monahan (2011) argue that empirically based actuarial approaches to risk assessment may improve decision making, but that there is little evidence for the superiority of one measure over another. They emphasize the importance of studying factors that contribute to violence in the first place versus predicting its occurrence.

PSYCHOPATHY

As we describe in Chapter 13, psychopaths are manipulative, callous, remorseless, impulsive, irresponsible individuals (e.g., Hare, 2003; Shaw & Porter, 2012), as defined by the well-validated Psychopathy Checklist-Revised (PCL-R; Hare, 1991, 2003). So defined, psychopathy is one of the best predictors of future violence, and must be a consideration when a psychologist is conducting a risk assessment. As reviewed by Porter and Woodworth (2006), research has established a strong link between psychopathic traits and future aggressive behaviour in adult offenders, antisocial

BOX 9.5   SUCCESSFUL NCRMD DEFENCES IN CANADA

Jeffrey Arenburg

Jeffrey Arenburg is known for shooting the popular Canadian sportscaster, Brian Smith, in a parking lot in Ottawa in 1995. Arenburg, diagnosed with paranoid schizophrenia at the time, believed that the news station that Smith worked for was broadcasting messages into his head. In an attempt to stop the "brainwashing," Arenburg went to the station and waited in the parking lot for the first person he could confront. Unfortunately for Smith, he was the first person to leave the station. After Arenburg's arrest, in his apartment police found a list of other media personalities that Arenburg planned to confront. It was also revealed that Arenburg had attempted to gain access to government officials at the Parliament buildings but was turned away each time. Arenburg was found to be NCRMD and was committed to the Oak Ridge Division of the Mental Health Centre at Penetanguishene for treatment. Arenburg was released from the facility in 2006, but was arrested again in 2007 after becoming violent with a U.S. Customs Officer when he was denied entrance to the United States due to his criminal record. He was found guilty and jailed for the assault against the Customs Officer, but was released again in 2009. Today, Arenburg is a free man (CBC News, 2006, 2008).

Allan Schoenborn

Allan Schoenborn was found to be guilty of first-degree murder but not criminally responsible for the murders of his three children, Kaitlynne (10 years), Max (8 years), and Cordon (5 years) in April 2008. After a three-month trial, and testimony from two expert witnesses about Schoenborn's mental state at the time of the murders, B.C. Supreme Court Justice Robert Powers ruled that Schoenborn's killings were deliberate and planned but that he was not sane at the time of the slayings. Schoenborn, a man with a long history of untreated mental illness, suffered a psychotic break and became convinced that his three children were being molested. Further, Schoenborn became convinced that nothing could be done to help his children and that the only way to save them from the abuse was to kill them. Schoenborn remains incarcerated in the B.C. Forensic Psychiatric Institute in Port Coquitlam, British Columbia (CBC.ca, 2010; Huffington Post, 2012).

Dr. Guy Turcotte

On July 5, 2009, Dr. Guy Turcotte, a prominent cardiologist at the time, was found NCRMD for the deaths of his two children Olivier (5 years) and Anne-Sophie (3 years). On the day of the murders, Turcotte discovered that his wife had been having an affair. After reading about the intimate details of the infidelity through his wife's e-mails, Turcotte suffered a psychotic break. Turcotte became so upset that he attempted suicide by drinking five litres of windshield wiper fluid. After consuming the fluid, Turcotte felt that he could not leave his children behind with their mother, so he stabbed them each multiple times. At trial, Turcotte admitted that he had committed the murders but claimed that he could remember only parts of the murder and that he did not possess the required intent, or mens rea, to be convicted of the crime. Turcotte was committed to Montreal's Pinel Institute and, in 2012, a psychiatrist from the Institute recommended him for release, stating that he shows no signs of mental illness (CTV News, 2009, 2012a). As of June 2012, he was determined to be too dangerous to be released, but was granted supervised day leaves.

---

children and adolescents, and civil (noncriminal) psychiatric patients. Some findings were as follows:

- *Adult offenders.* Numerous studies have demonstrated that the presence of psychopathy is associated with violent behaviour in adults. In one of the first studies of this relationship, Hare and Jutai (1983) found that incarcerated adult psychopaths had been charged with violent crimes about twice as often as nonpsychopathic counterparts in prison. And virtually all of the adult psychopaths had committed at least one violent crime compared to about half of the nonpsychopaths. Within a large sample of Canadian offenders, Porter, Birt, and Boer (2001) found that psychopaths had been convicted of an average of 7.32 violent crimes, compared to 4.52 violent crimes for other offenders. Knowledge of the psychopathy–violence link greatly aids in the prediction of future violent behaviour in adult offenders (e.g., Harris, Rice, & Quinsey,

1993; Hemphill, Hare, & Wong, 1998; Rice & Harris, 1997; Salekin, Rogers, & Sewell, 1996). For example, Serin and Amos (1995) found that psychopaths were about five times more likely than nonpsychopaths to engage in violent recidivism within five years of their release. Recent meta-analyses show that PCL-R scores show an overall correlation of $r = .27$ to .37 in predicting violence (e.g., Hemphill, Templeman, Wong, & Hare, 1998; Salekin et al., 1996; Shaw & Porter, 2012). In a study of patients in a forensic psychiatric unit, 78 percent of individuals scoring high on the PCL-Screening version were reconvicted and 53 percent were reconvicted for a violent crime (Pedersen, Kunz, Rasmussen, & Elsass, 2010). Additionally, psychopathic patients were four times more likely to reoffend than nonpsychopathic patients. For violent recidivism specifically, there was a sevenfold risk of reoffending for psychopathic patients.

- *Young people with conduct problems.* Porter and Woodworth (2006) note that growing evidence suggests that psychopathy is related to aggression early in life. It appears that precursors to psychopathy emerge in early childhood in the form of "callous/unemotional" traits (e.g., Frick, Bodin, & Barry, 2000; Frick & Ellis, 1999; Lynam, 2002; Porter, 1996), which seem to map onto adult psychopathy. These features can signal a pattern of persistent antisocial and violent behaviour (e.g., Dodge, 1991; Frick, 1998; Frick, O'Brien, Wooton, & McBurnett, 1994; Lynam, 2002; Waschbusch et al., 2004). Additionally, during adolescence, psychopathic traits are associated with convictions for violent offences (e.g., Campbell, Porter, & Santor, 2004; Forth & Mailloux, 2000), a high level of institutional aggression (Edens, Poythress, & Lilienfeld, 1999; Murdock, Hicks, Rogers, & Cashel, 2000; Rogers, Johansen, Chang, & Salekin, 1997), and a high level of violent reoffending (Brandt, Kennedy, Patrick, Curtain, 1997; Gretton et al., 2001). In a study tracking 182 male adolescent offenders after their release, Corrado et al. (2004) found that psychopathic youth reoffended violently faster (an average of 14 months) than other nonpsychopathic young offenders (average of 19 months). For general offences, psychopathic youth were charged on average after seven months compared to 12 months for nonpsychopathic youth (also see Falkenbach, Poythress, & Heide, 2003). In a recent study by Salekin (2008), psychopathy was independently predictive of both general and violent recidivism from midadolescence to young adulthood.

- *Psychiatric patients.* Very few civil psychiatric patients are psychopathic, relative to the proportion within the criminal offender population (e.g., Douglas, Ogloff, Nicholls, & Grant, 1999). Yet, psychopathy can still help predict future violence in this population. In a study of 1136 psychiatric patients, Skeem and Mulvey (2001) found that psychopathy scores predicted future serious violence, despite a psychopathy base rate of only 8 percent. During a one-year follow-up, 50 percent of psychopaths and 22 percent of nonpsychopaths had committed violence. In addition, there was a 73 percent chance that a patient who became violent had scored higher on psychopathy than one who did not become violent (see also Douglas et al., 1999).

Although antisocial personality disorder, and some elements of psychopathy, can be found in the *DSM-IV-TR*, this disorder cannot be used as a NCRMD defence in Canada (Felthous, 2010). Currently this is a hot topic in the field of forensic psychology with some arguing for psychopathy to be considered a disease of the mind that reduces culpability for a crime. Others insist that psychopaths understand the difference between right and wrong and do not meet the criteria for a NCRMD defence (Felthous, 2010). Those who support the use of psychopathy as a defence argue that emotion plays a major role in moral judgments and subsequent behaviour. Further, they report that there is scientific evidence to support that the brain regions responsible for emotion and moral reasoning are impaired in psychopaths (Yang & Raine, 2009). Thus, these individuals cognitively understand the concept of right and wrong but are unable to understand the emotion involved (Glenn, Raine, & Laufer, 2011). Morse (2008) takes a strong stance on the matter by arguing that individuals with elevated scores on the PCL-R should not be held criminally responsible for their crimes and are not deserving of punishment. Others take a much different approach to the issue of psychopathy as a legal defence, arguing that while psychopaths may be morally deficient, they can comprehend that they are breaking the law and committing a crime and so should be held responsible for their actions.

A recent study evaluated mock jurors' beliefs about psychopathy as a legal defence and discovered that even when presented with information about psychopathy, people are still much more likely to convict psychopaths of a crime than those with other mental illnesses (Rendell, Huss, & Jensen, 2010). There is no clear-cut solution to this issue, and it is likely that this debate will rage on between psychologists for years to come.

MALINGERING

A special problem in assessing the mental state of individuals is to determine whether their statements are truthful or are the result of **malingering**. In the DSM-IV-TR malingering is defined as the conscious fabrication or gross exaggeration of physical and/or psychological symptoms, done in order to achieve external goals such as avoiding prison or receiving monetary compensation (see Kramer & Gagliardi, 2009).

Richard Rogers and his colleagues (Rogers, 1990; Rogers, Sewell, & Goldstein, 1994) have distinguished three types of malingerers:

1. *The pathogenic*. Persons who are motivated by underlying pathology. These people are genuinely disturbed, and Rogers and his associates assume that "the voluntary production of bogus symptoms will eventually erode and be replaced by a genuine disorder" (Roger et al., 1994, pp. 543–544).
2. *The criminological*. Persons with an antisocial or oppositional motivation; they may feign mental disorders in order to obtain outcomes they do not deserve. That is, individuals who have antisocial personalities are more likely to malinger than other offenders.
3. *The adaptational*. The type of person who makes "a constructive attempt, at least from the feigner's perspective, to succeed in highly adversarial circumstances" (Rogers et al., 1994, p. 544). This type can be characterized as an individual who feigns symptoms when his or her personal life is at stake (e.g., the individual will go to prison) and he or she do not believe that there is any choice but to malinger.

Individuals may be tempted to fake mental illness at several points in the criminal justice process, including determining competency to stand trial, pleading NCRMD, and attempting to influence the sentence (Iverson, Franzen, &

Hammond, 1993; Kramer & Gagliardi, 2009). But detection of malingering also is central in a variety of other forensic psychological contexts. Claims of injuries and disabilities, such as lower back pain, head injury, or posttraumatic stress disorder, may require a check for malingering. Claims of amnesia or other kinds of memory impairment have increasingly involved the assessment by neuropsychologists of malingering (Arnett, Hammeke, & Schwartz, 1993; Bernard & Fowler, 1990; Lee, Loring, & Martin, 1992; Wiggins & Brandt, 1988).

There are indications that psychologists are poor at detecting malingering during forensic evaluations. Silverton, Gruber, and Bindman (1993) cite the classic study done by David Rosenhan (1973) as an example. Rosenhan and seven other persons free of mental abnormalities gained admission to various mental hospitals by complaining that they heard voices repeating the word "one." No other complaints were reported. Seven of the eight were diagnosed as schizophrenic, the other as manic-depressive. Immediately after being admitted, the pseudo-patients stopped saying they heard voices. None of the pseudo-patients were detected as malingerers by the hospital staff; in fact, the only persons who sometimes recognized the pseudopatients as normal were the other patients. Several of the pseudopatients were confined for several months despite their proclamations of being fine.

As a result of dissatisfaction with traditional procedures, psychologists have begun to use scales and other assessment procedures to try to effectively detect malingering. Two strategies have been used: applying existing measures and developing new ones.

As a traditional measure, the Minnesota Multiphasic Personality Inventory (MMPI) has an L scale of 15 items measuring social desirability, but this is a rather unsophisticated measure of malingering. Further, the person who "fakes" on these items is attempting to communicate an unduly *favourable* impression, whereas the malingering of concern to the courts is often of the opposite type. The original MMPI also included an F scale, designed to assess inconsistent or deviant answering. On the newer MMPI-2, the Fb scale seeks to detect malingering or a "fake bad" response style. This procedure seems promising in differentiating between persons instructed (by an experimenter) to malinger and actual psychiatric patients (Iverson, Franzen, & Hammond, 1993), but research needs to move beyond such designs with questionable ecological validity.

A second approach is to construct assessment instruments. A number of these have been developed in the last 20 years. Some, including the Malingering Probability Scale, by Silverton and Gruber (1998), are available only through commercial publishers. Frequently used is the Structured Interview of Reported Symptoms, or SIRS (Rogers, 1988), a 16-page structured interview covering signs of malingering. Although this procedure has produced some encouraging results (Rogers, Gillis, Bagby, & Monteiro, 1991), it requires an extended administration time and the need for a trained examiner (Smith & Burger, 1993).

A self-report measure, the M test (Beaber, Marston, Michelli, & Mills, 1985) is a 33-item inventory composed of three separate scales: the Confusion Scale, the Schizophrenia Scale, and the Malingering Scale. The last of these is composed of 15 items tapping unusual or rare symptoms that would be expected to be endorsed only by malingerers (e.g., atypical hallucinations and delusions or extremely severe symptoms).

Another type of assessment device is the Malingering Scale (MS) (Schretlen, 1986). It is lengthy (150 items) and requires judgment calls on the part of the test administrator (Smith & Burger, 1993). A replication is needed to confirm the high detection rates reported in the initial study.

COMMUNITY TREATMENT

After an individual is found to be NCRMD he or she most often is placed directly into a psychiatric hospital for an extended period of time. Here the individual receives ongoing evaluation and treatment for his or her mental illness. Eventually, after the illness has been brought under control with the use of medication and psychotherapy, the patient is discharged back into the community. Many cities have Forensic Community Programs (FCP) in place to monitor individuals who have been found NCRMD, once they are released from the institution. Woodworth, Peace, O'Donnell, and Porter (2003) were asked by a hospital in Nova Scotia to review the effectiveness of the current FCP in Dartmouth, and to make a number of recommendations to improve the operations of the FCP with relation to client management, treatment, and risk reduction. Woodworth et al. (2003) made the following suggestions:

1. *Necessity of community treatment programs for NCRMD individuals*. It is important to gauge the level of need for a Forensic Community Program before it is established. This is not a simple task but can be done by evaluating recidivism rates as well as the rate of rearrest or rehospitalization for NCRMD patients in the community.

2. *Community awareness of Forensic Community Programs*. Considering that the basis of a FCP is releasing individuals who have been found NCRMD into the public, it is important to provide the public with factual information about these individuals. An example of this is debunking the myth that all individuals with mental illnesses are dangerous by creating awareness that the majority of NCRMD patients commit nonviolent crimes. A second example is debunking the myth that many individuals found NCRMD are faking it by creating awareness that the majority of NCRMD patients have a long history of serious mental illness.

3. *Level of monitoring*. It is critical that the individual found NCRMD have close and regular contact with his or her supervisors at the FCP.

4. *Assessment of psychopathy*. Psychopathy is a mental disorder that is strongly correlated to both criminal behaviour and violent recidivism. This should be assessed using the PCL-R before an NCRMD individual is accepted into an FCP as psychopathy may have a direct relation to the likelihood of the individual found NCRMD succeeding in the program.

5. *Actuarial risk assessment tools*. In addition to the PCL-R, other actuarial assessments of risk, such as the Violence Risk Appraisal Guide (VRAG) and the Historical Clinical Risk Management-20 (HCR-20), should be used to predict the NCRMD patient's risk of reoffence once released. If the patient continues to be at a high risk to violently reoffend, he or she is not an ideal candidate for an FCP.

6. *Combining clinical and actuarial tools*. Professionals should combine both actuarial risk assessments and clinical judgments when attempting to predict the likelihood of future violence of the NCRMD individual applying for community supervision.

7. *Effective communication and understanding of risk*. A key component of assessing the risk for future violence is being able to effectively communicate this risk to the individuals who make the decisions about release, such as parole review boards.

8. *Incorporating elements of other community programs.* When establishing a Forensic Community Program it is important to rely on FCP models that are already in place in other cities, and that effectively monitor NCRMD patients in the community.*

Forensic Community Programs are important, not only to monitor individuals found NCRMD, but also as a resource for individuals with a mental illness.

SUMMARY

One of the most important tasks of the forensic psychologist is to aid the court in its determination of the mental state of defendants. This chapter reviews four relevant concepts: the legal term "criminal responsibility," competency, risk assessment, and malingering.

Although criminal responsibility is a legal concept and not a psychiatric one, forensic psychologists and psychiatrists may be called on to make judgments related to the NCRMD (or insanity) defence. The difficulty in achieving consistent diagnoses is illustrated by the trial of Jeffrey Dahmer, in which seven psychiatrists and psychologists gave conflicting judgments about whether Dahmer's state of mind met the definition of insanity. The horrific 2009 murder of Tim McLean by Vince Li, who suffers from paranoid schizophrenia, was a more clear-cut case in which there was no disagreement that auditory hallucinations (in which Li heard God say that McLean was about to execute Li) prompted the violent act. However, the case also highlights the disbelief and outrage that the public and families of victims, in particular, often experience in response to an NCRMD finding.

A related activity of the forensic psychologist is assessing the fitness or competency of those who come before the court. In general, "competency" or "fitness" refers to the person's ability to understand the nature and purpose of court proceedings. Competency is relevant to the decision to stand trial and the decision whether to plead guilty. Several tools are available for assessing competency, including the Fitness Interview Test-Revised and the recent MacArthur assessment procedure.

Predictions of dangerousness long have been a challenge to forensic psychologists. Predictions of suicide are not always accurate, partially because of the base-rate problem, (that is, the small percentage of mentally ill or depressed persons who actually commit suicide). The prediction of dangerousness to others, now called risk assessment, has had a rejuvenated research interest; here, predictions of individuals' behaviour are often closer to accuracy than in suicide prediction, but such forensic estimates are far from perfect. One thing, however, is clear: psychopathy should be a critical consideration in evaluating an offender's or patient's risk for future violence.

When assessing the mental state of persons appearing before the court, the possibility of malingering is always a concern. Several instruments are available for the assessment of malingering.

KEY TERMS

actuarial prediction, p. 224

actus reus, p. 210

ALI standard, p. 211

automatism, p. 212

base rate, p. 224

clinical prediction, p. 224

cognitive test of insanity, p. 210

competency, p. 220

dangerousness, p. 225

guilt, p. 210

harm, p. 225

irresistible impulse exception, p. 210

malingering, p. 228

McNaughton Rules, p. 210

mens rea, p. 210

necrophilia, p. 216

not criminally responsible by reason of a mental disorder (NCRMD), p. 208

risk level, p. 225

ultimate-issue testimony, p. 218

volitional aspect of insanity, p. 210

SUGGESTED READINGS

Borum, R., & Fulero, S. M. (1999). Empirical research on the insanity defence and attempted reforms: Evidence toward informed policy. *Law and Human Behaviour, 23*, 117–135.

This very useful article examines many of the myths and current misconceptions about the use of the insanity defence. Various reforms, including the authors' proposal of carefully developed, intensively monitored release programs for defendants found NGRI, are described and evaluated.

Douglas, K. S., Guy, L. S., & Hart, S. D. (2009). Psychosis as a risk factor for violence to others: A meta-analysis. *Psychological Bulletin, 135,* 679–706.

This article confirms that numerous studies have reported a correlation between experiencing psychosis and acting violently. This is a great read to learn more about the relationship between psychosis and violence, as well as the role of psychosis in risk assessment.

Lilienfeld, S. O. & Arkowitz, H. (2011, January 10). The insanity verdict on trial: The insanity defense, widely used, is misunderstood. *Scientific American.* Retrieved from http://www.scientificamerican.com/article.cfm?id=the-insanity-verdict-on-trial

This two-page magazine article gives a brief overview of the history of the insanity plea, its current use in the United States, and the always-fascinating Andrea Yates case.

Zapf, P. A., Zottoli, T. M., & Pirelli, G. (2009). Insanity in the courtroom: Issues of criminal responsibility and competency to stand trial. In D. A. Kraus & J. D. Lieberman (Eds.), *Psychological expertise in court: Psychology in the courtroom Volume II* (pp. 79–102). Surrey, England: Ashgate Publishing.

A chapter on the insanity plea and competency to stand trial. This chapter, written according to law in the United States, discusses different areas of these broad topics than the current chapter, including the procedures followed to declare someone insane or not competent to stand trial.

Intimate Partner Violence, Homicide and Stalking

I'll be watching you day and night. If I can't have you, then no one will.

—intimate partner homicide offender in an interview for Juodis, Woodworth, Porter, & ten Brinke (2009)

THE EXTENT OF DOMESTIC VIOLENCE IN CANADA

In Canada, domestic violence and its most severe outcome—domestic homicide—represent a major societal concern. Sometimes, when we hear about a domestic murder, we discover that the perpetrator already was known as a domestic violence perpetrator and the public wants to know why the family member was not protected and the homicide not prevented (Hilton et al., 2004; Jaffe & Juodis, 2006). In this chapter, we explore the findings of psychological research relating to domestic violence perpetrators, myths about perpetrators and victims, and how forensic psychologists can contribute to the policy and practice leading to the increased prevention and prosecution of this crime. Our focus will be on **intimate partner violence (IPV)**, in which a current or former intimate partner commits violence or homicide against an individual. Further, we examine a specific form of psychological and emotional abuse, criminal harassment or stalking which is a codified crime in Canada. When perpetrated by current or former intimate partners or other family members, criminal harassment is a form of domestic violence. This crime occurs when persistent unwanted attention from a perpetrator causes a victim to fear for his or her safety or that of someone known to them.

Self- and Official Reports of Incidence Rates

Whereas domestic violence long was a largely hidden crime, seen as a "family matter," it now is widely recognized to be a major societal problem. But just how large is the scope of the problem of IPV in Canada and elsewhere? The financial costs of domestic violence, encompassing health care for victims, criminal justice, social services, and lost job productivity, are estimated in the billions of dollars (Statistics Canada, 2006). While some groups and advocates offer alarming statistics concerning the frequency of domestic violence, often their conclusions about incidence rates are generalized from small and unrepresentative samples. Nonetheless, if we examine the self-report and official statistics collectively, it is clear that domestic violence is a pressing social issue in terms of its frequency.

Evidence documenting the severity of the domestic violence problem includes the following (Department of Justice Canada, 2009):

1. An estimated 7 percent of Canadian women (a total of 653 000 victims) and 6 percent of men (a total of 546 000 victims) who were in a current or previous, marital or common-law relationship, experienced some form of spousal violence in the five years prior to a national 2004 survey (Statistics Canada, 2005).

2. Most incidents of domestic partner violence are not reported to the police. According to a 2004 national survey, less than one third (28 percent) of victims reported the violence to the police and, before they did, almost two thirds (61 percent) had experienced more than one violent incident (Statistics Canada, 2005).

3. The same survey indicated that Aboriginal people were three times more likely than were non-Aboriginal people to be victims of spousal violence. Overall, 21 percent of Aboriginal people (24 percent of Aboriginal women and 18 percent of Aboriginal men) reported that they had suffered violence from a current or previous partner. Further, it appears that Aboriginal women suffer extreme brutalization (up to 30 to 40 assaults) before calling the police (McIvor & Nahanee, 1998).

4. More than 2.3 million adult Canadians had been stalked in the five years prior to the same 2004 national survey; 17 percent reported being stalked by current or former intimate partners (Statistics Canada, 2005).

These statistics reflect self-reports by victims, via the General Social Survey (GSS) in particular, which is conducted periodically by the Canadian government. Staff with the GSS program, established in 1985, conduct telephone surveys with samples across the provinces, and, of course, must assume truthful, accurate answers from respondents. Other statistics derive from official police/crime reports, which, not surprisingly, reflect only a "drop in the bucket" of actual domestic violence incidents. For example, in Canada, nearly 40 200 incidents of spousal violence were reported to police in 2007 (Statistics Canada, 2009a). Although this represents about 12 percent of all police-reported violent crime in Canada, it is only a fraction of the more than one million instances of spousal violence that are estimated to occur on an annual basis, according to self-report statistics. Other findings according to police-reported incidents include that spousal violence steadily declined by 15 percent between 1998 and 2007, that the majority (83 percent) of victims of spousal violence continue to be females, and that common assault comprised nearly two thirds of offences, followed by major assault, uttering threats, and criminal harassment or stalking (Statistics Canada, 2009a). According to 2008 police-reported data, dating relationships accounted for more than 25 percent of all violent incidents in Canada (Mahoney, 2008).

THE OFFICIAL RESPONSE TO THE PROBLEM OF DOMESTIC VIOLENCE

There is no question that there has been remarkable progress over the past several decades in the response to domestic violence from the public and from social services, health care, and criminal justice systems (Campbell, 2004). Because of its recognition as a major societal concern, the reduction of domestic violence, in particular, intimate partner violence (IPV), has been identified as a national priority (Government of Canada, 2002). Accordingly, there has been an explosion of research by psychologists and other social scientists that contributes to our understanding of this widespread crime.

In the Canadian context, what has been done to deal with the problem of domestic violence? Here, there are reasons for optimism in the response against domestic violence. In 1983, Solicitor General Robert Kaplan urged police chiefs across Canada to implement aggressive charging policies in spousal

assault cases. Thus, domestic violence, which before that year had been considered a social issue, now was considered to be a serious crime. Since then, the Canadian legal system has introduced several pieces of legislation that validate the gravity of spousal assault (described in the section "Domestic Violence Law in Canada" on page 244). For example, Bill C-41 amended the Criminal Code of Canada to require the courts to consider the abuse of a spouse or a child to be an aggravating factor (making the crime more serious) for sentencing purposes. Additionally, spouses and children now can seek monetary restitution from the offender for expenses incurred because they had to leave home to avoid being harmed. Based on Solicitor Kaplan's recommendation, one strategy has been to implement a "pro-charge" policy for domestic violence, adopted by most police departments across Canada. The policy usually states that if there are reasonable and probable grounds to believe that abuse has occurred, police must lay charges regardless of the wishes of the complainant. For example, in Canada in 2006 charges were laid in 77 percent of all reported incidents of spousal assault. In addition to police pro-charge policies, Crown prosecutors in Canada have a pro-prosecution policy, under which the prosecution proceeds regardless of the wishes of the victim (e.g., Henning & Feder, 2005). The wisdom of pro-charge and pro-prosecution policies has been debated, with advocates arguing that such approaches may deter future abuse (Buzawa, Austin, & Buzawa, 1996; Dutton, Hart, Kennedy, Williams, 1992), and others arguing that it may have the opposite effect and/or violate the rights of individuals who are presumed innocent until proven guilty. Despite this debate, in general, the Canadian response has been aggressive and positive in trying to address domestic violence.

However, in some ways the response to IPV in Canada has been problematic, particularly in terms of resources available for abused family members. For example, in a research "snapshot" taken in 2001, 89 Canadian shelters had to turn away 476 people (254 women and 222 children). The majority (71 percent) of these shelters turned away abuse victims because the facility was at capacity (Locke & Code, 2001). In 2008, the Alberta Council of Women's Shelters (2008) made the alarming report that 27 000 clients had been turned away from women's shelters in the province in 2006—about half of whom were children. Further, the mass media sometimes glosses over or minimizes the violence. Victims of IPV sometimes often are perceived as uncooperative, combative, and hard to deal with (Beichner & Spohn, 2005; Buzawa & Buzawa, 2003; Dawson & Dinovitzer, 2001; Gillis et al., 2006; Hartman & Belknap, 2003).

Some advertisers have been criticized for "glamourizing" IPV in their ads, or even finding humour in female-to-male domestic violence. An example of glamourizing IPV is an advertisement used by Edmonton-based hair salon Fluid Hair that shows a woman with a black eye and coiffed hair sitting in front of a menacing man with a tagline which reads "Look good in all you do."

Misleading images may influence societal views; a study evaluating the public's beliefs about IPV reveal that both university students and RCMP officers reported that the abuse perpetrated in female-to-male IPV is less severe than male-to-female abuse. Further, both the students and the police officers reported male-to-male and female-to-female IPV to be less severe than male-to-female (Cormier & Woodworth, 2008—see the Canadian Researcher Profile on page 250 for more information about Dr. Michael Woodworth).

THE NATURE OF INTIMATE PARTNER VIOLENCE

Domestic violence can take many forms, including adolescent-to-parent, sibling-to-sibling, parent-to-child, or spouse-to-spouse. The focus of this chapter is on intimate partner violence (IPV), including couples who are dating, living common law, or married.

What Characterizes an Abuser?

Who are the men and women who physically abuse their partners? While the stereotype may suggest an extremely violent man who abuses, intimidates, and controls his partner (as in Box 10.1), the body of research suggests this pattern is relatively rare, and that there is a diversity of violence profiles, including female-to-male violence (e.g., Hines, 2007). However, the vast majority of studies on IPV have been conducted on male offenders and suggest that there are several patterns of violence associated with the personality features of males (Dutton, 1995b). In an early study of IPV, using a sample of 182 wife assaulters referred for treatment because of their severe violence, Saunders (1992) administered a number of personality, behaviour, and attitude measures and then completed a statistical analysis to determine whether distinct subgroups of abusers existed. This procedure led to the recognition of three groups of abusers:

1. The *generally violent* men, who were described as antisocial and impulsive; Donald Dutton (1995a) at UBC calls them **psychopathic abusers**. As implied by the label, they were assaultive both inside and outside the home. They used alcohol frequently.

| BOX 10.1 | AN EXAMPLE OF ABUSE IN A RELATIONSHIP AND ITS AFTERMATH |

The case of Jane Stafford (later Jane Whynot) in Nova Scotia was detailed in the 1986 book by Brian Vallee and the 1993 film *Life with Billy*, produced by Salter Street Films in Halifax. It stands as one of the most disturbing cases of domestic violence and its aftermath in recent Canadian history.

Jane's husband, Billy Stafford, terrorized her and her son throughout their marriage, inflicting severe beatings upon them, and constantly humiliating and degrading her. For example, on at least one occasion, he forced her into sexual relations with the family dog. Billy threatened to kill all of the members of her family, one by one, if she tried to leave him (in fact, he was widely suspected of having murdered a coworker by throwing him from a boat) When Jane spoke with police officers, they belittled the danger she was in and considered her abuse to be a "family matter." On the night of his death, Billy had made threats about killing Jane's son. After Billy passed out in his pickup truck from drinking, Jane obtained one of his many shotguns and killed him by shooting him in the head as he slept.

Although she pleaded self-defence and was acquitted at her trial (*R. v. Whynot*, 1983), the Crown appealed, arguing that the self-defence plea should not have been considered since Jane was not being assaulted and was in no immediate danger before she killed him. Jane ultimately pleaded guilty to manslaughter and served six months in prison. Several years later she committed suicide.

2. The *overcontrolled* men, who could not express feelings, including anger, and whose reaction to conflict was to suddenly explode.

3. The *emotionally volatile* men, who were characterized as being angry, jealous, or depressed. They were violent only toward their wives and showed a buildup of tension leading to battering. Dutton's (1995a) analysis of abusers focused on this group. He described them as Jekyll-and-Hyde types, men whose abusive personality stemmed from a childhood characterized by an ambivalent attachment to the mother, experiencing abuse in the home, and being shamed by the father.

Other typologies of IPV are described below.

Controversies over Gender and Intimate Partner Violence

One interesting observation from the above statistics concerns gender. The stereotype, as per the horrific Jane Stafford case, suggests that there is a substantial subset of males who persistently terrorize and abuse their partners. While this can occur, it appears to be rare and the more widespread reality of IPV seems to be one of both genders and diverse abusive actions. While domestic violence is much more likely to be reported to police by female victims, the self-reported victimization rates of men and women in the general population are similar. Related findings are witnessed in specific geographical regions and among specific groups of people. For example, Kwong, Bartholomew, and Dutton (1999), a group of researchers at Simon Fraser University and the University of British Columbia, examined gender differences in patterns of relationship violence in a representative sample of 356 men and 351 women from Alberta. The respondents reported on whether they had been the victim and/or perpetrator of violent acts in the year before the survey. The results indicated that men and women, respectively, reported similar rates of husband-to-wife violence (12.9 percent and 9.6 percent) and wife-to-husband violence (12.3 percent and 12.5 percent). However, there were some gender differences. On average, men reported that they and their female partners were equally likely to engage in and initiate violent acts. Women, however, surprisingly, reported lower levels of victimization than perpetration of violence, and they reported less male-only and male-initiated violence than did men. While we must keep in mind the limitations of self-report in this context, the majority of respondents in violent relationships reported a pattern of violence that was bi-directional or "went both ways."

Other research indicates that the prevalence of female-perpetrated aggression is equal to, or greater than, that of their male counterparts (Archer, 2000; Cunradi, 2007). Brown (2004) found major discrepancies in arrest and prosecution of spousal assault as a function of gender; women were four times more likely to report partner violence to police (81 percent vs. 19 percent). Stets & Straus (1992a) found that women were 10 times more likely to call police in response to partner assault. The higher arrest rate of men occurs despite injuries to male victims; when men are injured, female perpetrators are arrested only 60.2 percent of the time, compared to 91.1 percent of cases involving the reverse situation (Brown, 2004, p. 34). Dutton and Nicholls (2005) concluded that a combination of men's unwillingness to report and the police being unwilling to arrest female perpetrators means that only 2 percent of female perpetrators are arrested (Brown, 2004).

In a study of more than 800 couples in which one partner was in the construction industry, Cunradi, Todd, Duke, and Ames (2009) found that similar numbers of men and women reported abusing their partners (20 percent and 24 percent, respectively). Men are less likely to report being victims of spousal violence, and there seem to be different responses of the criminal justice system as a function of gender of the complainant. Male spouses (20 percent) are almost three times as likely as female spouses (7 percent) to be sentenced to jail or prison on conviction for IPV (Brzozowski, 2004). UBC researchers Dutton, Nicholls, and Spidel (2005) concluded that "females are as abusive as males in intimate relationships according to survey and epidemiological studies. This is especially so for younger 'cohort community samples' followed longitudinally. Predictors of intimate violence with women appear to be similar to those of men; including antisocial criminal records, alcohol abuse, and personality disorders" (p. 1). Straus (2010) reports that the percentage of women and men who assault partners is similar across a range of 32 nations. Straus (2010) also concluded that the effects of being a victim of partner violence are greater for women than men (both physically and psychologically).

Thus, although both men and women engage in, and are victimized, by IPV (Archer, 2000), it appears that much of the most severe violence is male to female. For example, in one large-scale study, of the participants who reported being the victim of spousal violence, 3 percent of the women, and only 0.4 percent of the men, required medical care for resulting injuries (Stets & Straus, 1990). In Canada in 2002, females accounted for 85 percent of all victims of spousal assaults reported to police. Further, between 1993 and 2002, women were far more at risk than men of being killed by their spouse (eight homicides per million couples versus two homicides per million couples, respectively) (Canadian Centre for Justice Statistics, 2004). Henning, Renauer, and Holdford (2006) examined self-report and official records of 485 women convicted of IPV. Only 8 percent of women were identified as primary aggressors, and men were 8 times more likely to be the primary aggressor. Thus, although both men and women use violence in relationships, the consequences appear to be more severe for women.

This may or may not be simply a result of differential size and strength of the partners versus some gender moral/character difference. As a result, research has focused on male perpetrators and female victims, and the characteristics of IPV have not been extensively explored across gender. Why is the stereotype of the "evil husband abusing his wife" so prominent in society (see Hines, 2007)? According to Canadian researchers Donald Dutton and Tonia Nicholls (2005), it results from a highly biased feminist perspective in which the following historical data are ignored:

1. Unidirectional "severe" female-to-male intimate violence was more common than male-to-female unidirectional intimate violence (Stets & Straus, 1992b).
2. Lesbian abuse rates were higher than heterosexual male–female abuse rates (Lie et al., 1991).
3. Only a small percentage of males were violent over the life course of a marriage (Straus et al., 1980).
4. As many females as males were violent over the course of a marriage (Straus et al., 1980).
5. Very few males find spousal abuse to be acceptable (Stark & McEvoy, 1970).
6. Only 9.6 percent of abusive males were the "dominant" partner in their marriage (Coleman & Straus, 1986).
7. Male violence was not linearly related to cultural indicators of patriarchy (not related to cultures in which there is an established patriarchy) across U.S. states (Yllo & Straus, 1990).

TYPOLOGIES OF INTIMATE PARTNER VIOLENCE

The data described above suggest—despite a long-standing view—that gender may not be the most relevant factor in understanding IPV (e.g., Dutton, 2007, concluded that personality [not gender] is the best predictor of the perpetration of IPV). Perhaps personality or other psychological features may be more important? One of the most substantial developments in the past two decades of IPV research involves the identification of distinct subtypes of IPV perpetrators, based on personality and behaviour (Cavanaugh & Gelles, 2005). Despite this conclusion, the main body of research on IPV has focused on male abusers and has highlighted the importance of considering perpetrator heterogeneity for understanding, assessing, and treating male IPV perpetrators (Cavanaugh & Gelles, 2005). Based on his research on more than 400 male abusers, Dutton (2007) concluded that many abusers exhibit high levels of trauma symptoms, linked to elements of childhood experience including witnessing of violence, the use of shaming techniques by parents, and insecure attachment.

Based on a synthesis of research on males, Holtzworth-Munroe and Stuart (1994) proposed a (now classic) typology comprising a *generally violent/antisocial* (AS) group characterized by violence and antisociality, a *borderline/dysphoric* (BD) group characterized by features related to borderline personality disorder and negative affect, and a *family only/low psychopathology* (LP) group characterized by low levels of nonpartner violence and psychopathology. The AS group (representing about 30 percent of abusers) displayed high levels of marital violence and violence outside the home, had characteristics of Antisocial Personality Disorder (substance use, history of criminal behaviour, and disregard for social norms), and experienced high levels of family violence as children. They had impulsive personalities, hostility toward women, and reported a general acceptance of violence as a normal way of interacting with others (Holtzworth-Monroe et al., 2000). The BD group (representing about 20 percent of abusers) committed moderate to severe domestic violence that was usually confined to their female partners and experienced high levels of psychological distress in the form of mood disorders (depression/anxiety), and personality disorders. Such individuals often had traumatic childhoods that resulted in attachment problems, insecurity, anger, and borderline personality characteristics. These men also had difficulty de-escalating and initiated violence toward their attachment figure (Holtzworth-Monroe et al., 2000). The LP group (representing about 50 percent of abusers) inflicted the lowest levels of marital abuse, sexual abuse, and psychological abuse, were not usually violent outside the home, and rarely experienced psychopathology. Further, they were generally better able to cope and de-escalate themselves without causing serious injury to a partner (Holtzworth-Monroe et al., 2000). Subsequent studies of male abusers have identified clusters that resemble AS, BD, and LP and, in some cases, also have identified a fourth low-level antisocial (LA) subtype characterized by intermediate levels of antisociality (Dixon & Browne, 2003; Hamberger, et al., 1996; Holtzworth-Munroe et al., 2000; Huss & Langhinrichsen-Rohling, 2006). A key study in this area was published in 2010 in the *Journal of Abnormal Psychology*, indicating that the AS, BD, and LP subtypes generalized across gender (Walsh et al., 2010). The researchers examined 567 patients drawn from the MacArthur Violence Risk Assessment Study (Monahan et al., 2001), comparing 138 women and 93 men with histories of IPV versus a large sample of men and women with no histories of IPV. Their findings were consistent with reports from studies of male perpetrators in forensic and community settings in that generally AS, BD, and LP subtypes of perpetrators were identified in both men and women.

An alternative approach to conceptualizing IPV heterogeneity was proposed by Johnson (1995, 2006). It focuses on *configurations of violence in relationships*, and posits four categories of IPV; *situational couple violence, mutual violent control, intimate terrorism*, and *violent resistance*. Efforts to synthesize this typology with the Holtzworth-Munroe typology note the correspondence between situational couple violence and LP perpetrators, and between intimate terrorism and AS and BD (Cavanaugh & Gelles, 2005; Johnson, 2006). The Johnson typology includes specific predictions regarding gender; situational couple violence and mutual violent control are proposed to be relatively symmetrical across gender, whereas intimate terrorism is predominantly male, and violent resistance predominantly female (Johnson, 2006). These asymmetries are supported by findings that females are overrepresented among primary victims (i.e., violent resistors) and underrepresented among primary aggressors (i.e., intimate terrorists) (Graham-Kevan & Archer, 2003; Henning et al., 2006; Swan & Snow, 2002). However, although studies of gender symmetry in types of IPV perpetration provide some evidence for similarities and differences between male and female perpetrator typologies, the extent to which prominent typologies of male perpetrators describe female perpetrators has not been well established.

Another approach to understanding IPV is to *categorize various groups of victims*. Roberts and Roberts (2005) developed abused women typologies. They argued that there are five categories of female victims of IPF:

Level 1—*Short term*. These women experienced violence in short dating relationships that they left shortly after the violence began.

Level 2—*Intermediate*. These women experienced violence in the context of relatively short marriages or cohabiting relationships that lasted a few months to two years. These women experienced 3 to 15 incidents that sometimes escalated to more serious violence, and may have resulted in serious injuries. Women often left their abusive marriages shortly after a severe assault.

Level 3—*Intermittent long term*. Such women experienced severe violence over the course of a marriage that lasted many years. Violence was unpredictable and would occur after months without violence. Women were middle or upper class, well educated, and often stayed in marriages for the sake of young children.

Level 4—*Chronic and predictable*. These women experienced severe violence on a regular basis over the course of a long marriage. Many of the abusers had serious alcohol problems that exacerbated the violence.

Level 5—*Homicidal subtype*. These women were in long-term marriages or divorces with lethal levels of violence. Many of these women had low levels of education. Prior to the murder of the IPV perpetrator, many of these women had received lethal death threats, and often restraining orders had been violated. The violence had escalated to the point that the women killed the abuser (as with Jane Stafford above). These women suffered from high rates of PTSD, insomnia, nightmares, and suicidality.

Not surprisingly, anger is related to IPV perpetration. Shorey, Brasfield, Febres, and Stuart (2011) looked at the association between trait anger and impulsivity, and the perpetration of physical and psychological IPV and general aggression among women arrested for domestic violence in 80 women. They found that both trait anger and impulsivity were significantly associated with aggression perpetration. Other research has examined factors that are associated with risk for IPV among women. Abramsky et al. (2011) surveyed women of many cultures and found that high socioeconomic status (SES), secondary education, and formal marriage offered protection against IPV, while alcohol abuse, cohabitation, young age, attitudes supportive of spousal violence, having outside sexual partners, experience of childhood abuse, growing up with domestic violence, and experiencing or perpetrating other forms of violence in adulthood all increased risk of IPV.

We need to consider also the psychological effects of IPV on the most common witnesses of such violence: children. DeBoard-Lucas and Grych (2011) employed semistructured interviews to assess the thoughts and feelings of 34 children (ages 7–12) whose mothers were receiving services at domestic violence agencies. They found that children generally viewed their mother's partner as responsible for violence, although a significant number viewed both parental figures as playing a role; often experienced sadness and anger versus anxiety; thought family violence occurred because of perpetrators' lack of control of anger; and often (one third of children) felt that the victims had provoked the aggression.

THE ROLE OF SUBSTANCE ABUSE IN IPV PERPETRATION AND ARREST

It seems intuitive that there is a relation between substance abuse and IPV. Generally, we assume that IPV is an alcohol-fuelled event. Indeed, for couples who enter treatment for drug and alcohol abuse, rates of partner aggression are extremely high, with 53 percent to 63 percent of couples reporting one or more episodes of partner violence in the year prior to program entry (Klostermann et al., 2010; Murphy & O'Farrell, 1994; Murphy, O'Farrell, Fals-Stewart, & Feeham, 2001; Stuart et al., 2003). Further, Friend, Langhinrichsen-Rohling, and Eichold (2011) analyzed archival data of 196 closed domestic violence files from a large southern U.S. city from 1999 to 2006 and found that 141 of 196 cases were associated with documented drug or alcohol involvement: 67.4 percent of the cases confirmed that there was drug or alcohol use on the day of the incident. Male perpetrators were more likely to have had alcohol and/or drugs the day of a violent episode compared to female perpetrators. Simmons, Lehmann, and Cobb (2008) studied northern Texas intimate partner violence arrestees enrolled in a domestic violence diversion program, and found that women had a lower occurrence of substance abuse at the time of arrest than did male arrestees. Further, the study showed that men were three times more likely to have used alcohol at the time of arrest.

However, there also is evidence to suggest that victim intoxication relates to victimization. A recent American study by the Centers for Disease Control and Prevention (2008) looked at 42 566 women, and found that women who had lifetime experience of IPV had a significantly higher likelihood of being heavy or binge drinkers than women who had not experienced such violence. Further, the relation between substance use and IPV does not appear to be a direct one (i.e., the idea that drunkenness promotes IPV). Kantor and Straus (1990) found that men who were heavy drinkers—but believed it wrong to hit a woman—had much lower rates of violence than light drinkers who believed the opposite. Lipsey, Wilson, Cohen, and Derzon (2002) suggested that if alcohol has causal effects on violence, it occurs only for some persons/circumstances, and the relation is not straightforward.

Other research indicates that substance use not only influences IPV perpetration but also the likelihood of making a call to police and arrest by investigating officers. Some studies have suggested that there is a general consensus that male alcohol use increases the likelihood that the police are called (Brookoff, O'Brien, Cook, Thompson, & Williams, 1997; Hutchison, 2003; Johnson, 1990; Jones and Belknap, 1996; Kantor & Straus, 1990; Hutchison, 2003). From this perspective, the perception of male drunkenness influences the decision of a victim to call the police, rather than the actual amount of alcohol consumed (cf. Hirschel, Hutschison, & Shaw 2010).

THE NATURE OF DOMESTIC HOMICIDE

All too often in the media we hear about a spouse murdering his or her partner. A quick Google News search finds several recent Canadian cases.

For example, the *Edmonton Journal* reported that on December 7, 2011, Christopher Daniel McCallum, a 41-year-old man from Bonnyville, Alberta, was charged with second-degree murder in the death of his common-law wife (who is not being identified by RCMP at the request of her family) and that alcohol is believed to have been a factor in the death. While it can be difficult to estimate the true incidence of domestic violence in Canada because of the limitations of self- and official reports of the crime (as described above), we can be much more certain about the true incidence of domestic homicide. Of the 554 homicides that were committed in Canada in 2010 (the lowest rate in 40 years) (Statistics Canada, 2011), 89 (16.1 percent) were committed against an intimate partner. While this represents a horrendous societal problem, the rate of intimate partner homicide in Canada has been on the decline for three decades (a 32 percent decline from 1980 to 2010), with the largest declines in British Columbia and Ontario. The reason for the decline has been debated, with some suggesting that it is attributable to improvements in women's socioeconomic status and the increased availability of resources for victims of violence in Canada (e.g., Dawson et al., 2009). Nonetheless, the *proportion* of all homicides perpetrated by intimate partners has remained stable over time; between 2000 and 2009 in Canada, there were 738 spousal homicides, representing 16 percent of all solved homicides. Women continue to be more likely than men to be victims of spousal homicide; in 2009, the rate was three times higher for women than men. Further, female victims were more likely than males to be killed by a partner from whom they were separated (26 percent versus 11 percent). Stabbing was the most common method to commit spousal homicide, particularly against male victims (Statistics Canada, 2010).

Despite the obvious societal concern around this type of crime, intimate partner homicide (IPH) has been subjected to little empirical research (Eke et al., 2011). A common response of the media and the average person is to view IPH as "inexplicable." As Juodis et al. (2012) observed, when describing perpetrators, shocked and confused neighbours make statements such as "They seemed to be nice" (Ryan, Anastario, & DaCunha, 2006, p. 215). Other community residents may be quoted as describing the perpetrator as a kind, hard-working, or devoted parent who had a strong sense of family, loved life, or always helped the neighbours (Taylor, 2009). But research indicates that many IPH offenders

display predictable patterns and precursors, and many IPV experts believe these homicides are potentially preventable (de Becker, 1997; Websdale, 2003). Whether the victim is a male or female, research has shown that the number-one risk factor for IPH is a history of IPV against the woman (Campbell et al., 2007; Juodis et al., 2012). Recent Canadian research by Angela Eke and colleagues examined the characteristics of 146 men who committed an actual or attempted incident of IPH. They found that 42 percent had prior criminal charges, 15 percent had a psychiatric history, and 18 percent had both, leading the researchers to conclude that these murders could have been predicted. However, very few studies have examined the psychological features of IPH perpetrators. For example (see Juodis et al., 2012), a review of 35 major IPH studies conducted over nearly 50 years indicated that only two studies sampled interview data from male perpetrators and only one of these two studies included interviews (Campbell, Glass, Sharps, Laughon, & Bloom, 2007).

As suggested by the Eke study mentioned above, some researchers believe that IPHs are potentially predictable and preventable. Often, IPHs are portrayed as "random," unpredictable acts (Ryan et al., 2006) or murders that seem to come "out of the blue" when the perpetrators appear to have no known history of violence or criminality (Dobash, Dobash, & Cavanagh, 2009). Yet, as reviewed by Canadian researchers Juodis and colleagues, a dominant theme evidenced prior to such a murder is male control/proprietary attitude, with jealousy, the woman leaving, and the woman having a new relationship identified as major triggers (e.g., Campbell et al., 2003; Wilson & Daly, 1993). Formal or informal child custody/access disputes also have been identified as a major contributing variable in this regard (Ontario DVDRC, 2005).

Dalhousie University Ph.D. candidate Marcus Juodis, who has a background in working with IPV offenders, set out to facilitate a deeper understanding of IPH by examining the criminal profile and psychological assessment reports in the institutional files of 37 male IPH perpetrators from two Canadian federal prisons compared to 78 other murderers (Juodis, Starzomski, Porter, & Woodworth, 2012). He and colleagues found that IPH perpetrators were quite different from other offenders. In particular, they showed a predominant drive to inflict suffering on their victims out of revenge for perceived wrongdoings. Contrary to popular views, most IPHs did not occur "out of the blue," as 82.9 percent of cases showed elements of planning, and 86.5 percent were identified as a homicide risk according to a well-established risk assessment tool for IPV. Further, psychopathy played a role; IPH perpetrators with psychopathic traits were less likely to act suicidal prior to homicides, and were more likely to kill in an unemotional, premeditated, and gratuitously violent manner. The researchers concluded that IPHs were potentially predictable in light of the relation between the crime and salient behavioural and psychological features of the perpetrators.

MYTHS ABOUT THE ABUSED SPOUSE

Despite some grounds for optimism, experts continue to emphasize the prevalence of invidious *myths about the abused spouse* (see Ehrensaft, 2008). Diane Follingstad (1994b) listed the following false assumptions:

1. Abused women are masochists.
2. IPV victims provoke the assaults inflicted on them.

3. IPV victims get the treatment they deserve.
4. IPV victims are free to leave these violent relationships at any time they want to.
5. IPV victimization is not at all common.
6. Men who are personable and nonviolent in their dealings with outsiders must be the same in their dealings with their intimates.
7. Middle-class and upper-class men do not abuse, and middle-class and upper-class women are not abused.
8. IPV is a lower-class, ethnic-minority phenomenon, and such women don't mind because it is part of their culture.
9. "Good" abused women are passive and never try to defend themselves.

Walker (1979) has provided an even more extensive list, summarized in Box 10.2. How widely are these ideas held by the public? Are jurors' beliefs and verdicts influenced by such myths?

Although Walker concluded that such myths are extensively held by the public, other psychologists (cf. Acker & Toch, 1985) have questioned this

---

BOX 10.2 — SOME MYTHS ABOUT THE ABUSE VICTIM

In introducing her study of abused women more than 30 years ago, Walker (1979) described 21 myths about these women, their abusers, and the relationship among them.

Myth No. 1: The "battered woman syndrome" affects only a small percentage of the population.

Myth No. 2: Abused women are masochistic. The prevailing belief has always been that only women who "liked it and deserved it" were beaten ... (p. 20).

Myth No. 3: Abused women are crazy. This myth is related to the masochism myth in that it places the blame for the battering on the woman's negative personality characteristics (p. 21).

Myth No. 4: Middle-class women do not get abused as frequently or as violently as do poorer women.

Myth No. 5: Minority-group women are abused more frequently.

Myth No. 6: Religious beliefs will prevent abuse.

Myth No. 7: Abused women are uneducated and have few job skills.

Myth No. 8: Abusers are violent in all their relationships.

Myth No. 9: Abusers are unsuccessful and lack resources to cope with the world.

Myth No. 10: Drinking causes abusive behaviour.

Myth No. 11: Abusive partners are psychopathic personalities.

Myth No. 12: Police can readily protect the abused spouse.

Myth No. 13: The abuser is not a loving partner.

Myth No. 14: An abuser also beats his children.

Myth No. 15: Once an abused woman, always an abused woman.

Myth No. 16: Once an abuser, always an abuser.

Myth No. 17: Long-standing abusive relationships can change for the better.

Myth No. 18: Abused women deserve to get beaten. The myth that abused women provoke their beatings by pushing their men beyond the breaking point is a popular one ... (p. 29).

Myth No. 19: Abused women can always leave home ... (p. 29).

Myth No. 20: Abusers will cease their violence "when we get married."

Myth No. 21: Children need their father even if he is violent—or, "I'm only staying for the sake of the children."

(Adapted from Walker, 1979, pp. 19–30.)

---

assumption. For example, Acker and Toch then argued that Walker may well have been wrong with regard to the prevalence of these myths about abused women:

Absent evidence to the contrary, the most reasonable and charitable assumption is that the public (and members of juries) may have more awareness, more open-mindedness and less prejudice than the court (or Walker) implies. (p. 140)

Several studies sought to determine the pervasiveness of these myths. Relying on responses to a hypothetical scenario that they developed, Ewing and his colleagues (Ewing & Aubrey, 1987; Ewing, Aubrey, & Jamison, 1986) found that a clear majority of their adult-age participants subscribed to some of the myths and about one third of the participants subscribed to most of them. These authors concluded that their results supported recommendations that expert testimony be admitted at trial because many of the facts were "beyond the ken" of respondents. On the other hand (also see Westbrook, 2009), Gover, Paul, and Dodge (2011) found that police officers are well versed in handling domestic violence, but are concerned about their limited amount of discretion.

Another study (Greene, Raitz, & Lindblad, 1989) indicated that not everyone subscribed to these myths. This study also exposed subjects, acting as mock jurors, to scenarios about spousal violence. Dutton and McGregor (1992) commented on this study's results:

Jurors seemed to understand that once violence was used in a relationship the potential for its use again constitutes an ever-present threat, and that women so threatened suffer anxiety and depression, feel helpless, believe their spouses might kill them, and believe that leaving will result in further harm. (p. 334)

In summary, some people hold such myths but perhaps not to the degree that Walker assumed. But we would expect that as publicity about family violence has increased, so too has a more accurate understanding of the phenomenon by the public.

Two trends in the criminal justice system may contribute to the acceptance of these myths by some people. Akin to the "blame the victim" phenomenon identified in social psychology (e.g., Basow & Minieri, 2011; van den Bos & Maas, 2009), Jones (1994b) proposed that a deep uneasiness and even hostility exists toward victims. People have a desire to believe "I'm okay, we're okay," and if some women have problems, it is because they are pathological doormats or obsessive delusional people crying "wolf."

The Correctional Service of Canada studied 181 women who had been convicted of a homicide offence. Of these women, 26 percent had killed their spouse (Hoffman, Lavigne, Dickie, & Women Offender Sector, 1998). The following is the breakdown of the sentence lengths of the spousal murderers: two to six years less a day, 22.1 percent; six to ten years less a day, 6.6 percent; ten to 20 years, 15.5 percent; life in prison 55.6 percent. The numbers were not dissimilar from those for homicide during a theft or child homicide. However, women convicted of spousal homicide were more likely to have received a conviction for first-degree murder than women who were convicted for "defence against a sexual assault" homicide. However, it was unclear how previous abuse from the victim had contributed to sentencing.

We cannot say from these figures whether women are treated more harshly than men. What is most striking is the variability both in judgments of guilt and in the punishments given to those found guilty. More basic than severity may be a pervasive ideology about gender roles, which in some cases may lead to leniency or paternalism and in others to harsher dispositions of cases—"all reflecting an intrinsic gender inequality within the criminal justice system" (Jenkins & Davidson, 1990, p. 162).

RESEARCH AND LEGAL FINDINGS ON BATTERED WOMAN SYNDROME

The most controversial aspect of the defence of battered women who kill their abusers is the use of the **battered woman syndrome (BWS)**. Although the claimed presence of this syndrome is not a legal defence in and of itself, it can be used as a justification for arguing, as a defence, either self-defence or being not criminally responsible (reviewed in Chapter 9).

Components of BWS

Despite the conclusions that victims may show heterogeneity in their symptoms, some psychologists have proposed the existence of a common set of components to BWS. These include (Walker, 1984b):

1. **Learned helplessness**, or a response to having been exposed to painful stimuli over which one has no control and finding that no avenue readily exists for escape.
2. Lowered self-esteem or an acceptance of continued feedback from the abuser about one's worthlessness.
3. Impaired functioning, including an inability to engage in playful behaviour.
4. Loss of the assumption of invulnerability and safety. Previous beliefs that "things would turn out all right" or "this wouldn't happen to me" dissipate in the onslaught of abuse and violence.
5. Fear and terror, as reactions to the abuser, based on past experiences.
6. Anger/rage.
7. Diminished alternatives. Of 400 battered women interviewed by Walker (1993), 85 percent felt they could or would be killed at some point. Also, as a part of the diminished-alternatives reaction, battered women focus their energies on survival within the relationship rather than exploring options outside (Blackman, 1986).
8. The **cycle of abuse** or cycle of violence. The Jekyll-and-Hyde nature of abusers has been proposed as a contribution to the BWS. Men may be loving, nurturing, giving, and attentive to the woman's needs during courtship and perhaps early in the marriage. But then there is a **tension-building phase**—more criticism, verbal bickering, increased strain, and perhaps minor physical abuse. This is followed by the violent step in the cycle: an **acute battering incident**, in which the abuser explodes into an uncontrollable rage, leading to injuries to the woman.

   When this dark side appears, the woman may be too involved with the man to break off the relationship. Also she may remember the good times and believe if she can find the right thing to do, he will revert to his earlier behaviour; thus, she often blames herself for his actions. As reflected in her list of myths (see Box 10.2), Walker (1992) proposed that "Research has demonstrated that this is a **contrite phase** in which the abuser's use of promises and gifts increases the battered woman's hope that violence occurred for the last time." The abuser expresses regret and apologizes, perhaps promising never to lose control again. But eventually the cycle starts all over once more (Walker, 1984b).

   According to the theory of the cycle of violence, the woman feels growing tension during phase one, develops a fear of death or serious bodily harm during phase two, and, anticipating another attack, defends herself by retaliating during a lull in the violence (Walker, 1984b). Not all battering follows this cycle (M. A. Dutton, 1993); in fact, of the 400 women interviewed by Walker (1979), involving 1600 battering incidents, only two thirds reflected this cycle.

9. Hypervigilance to cues of danger. Other components of the BWS are less obvious; **hypervigilance** is one of the more important. As a result of being abused, women notice subtle things—things that others don't recognize as dangerous. The woman may notice her husband's words come faster, or she might claim that his eyes get darker. She may make a pre-emptive strike before the abuser has actually inflicted much damage.
10. High tolerance for **cognitive inconsistency** (Blackman, 1986). Abused women often express two ideas that appear to be logically inconsistent with each other:

For example, a battered woman might say, 'My husband only hit me when he was drunk,' but later describes an episode during which he was not drunk and yet abusive. I believe this tolerance for inconsistency grows out of the fundamental inconsistency of a battered woman's life: that the man who supposedly loves her a so hurts her. (Blackman, 1986, pp. 228–229)

THE ROLE OF THE FORENSIC PSYCHOLOGIST IN THE ASSESSMENT OF IPV

An important role for clinical forensic psychologists is the careful assessment of the responses of an individual who has killed his or her spouse. What symptoms does he or she report, and is there corroborating evidence? Follingstad (1994b) has identified several procedures to be followed by forensic psychologists who assess the status of a spouse charged with homicide who reports previous abuse by the victim. First, there should be a thorough psychological examination that explores the history of the relationship, the history of abuse, the attempts to leave the relationship, and the spouse's feelings about the deceased. The examination needs to be carried out in a nonjudgmental manner.

The psychologist should seek verification/corroboration of self-reports through medical records and interviews with others. He or she may use a survey instrument to systemize the nature of the abuse. One possible measure is Mary Ann Dutton's (1992) Abusive Behaviour Observation Checklist. It is an interviewer-administered listing of specific physical, sexual, and psychological actions that incorporates psychological abusive items from the Power and Control Wheel (Pence & Paymor, 1985) and physical violence items from the Conflict Tactics Scale (Straus, 1979).

The **Power and Control Wheel** lists eight categories of psychological abuse:

1. Coercion and threats (threat to kill, to injure spouse or children, to burn the house down, or to steal the car).
2. Intimidation (displaying weapons, giving a look that instills fear).
3. Emotional abuse (humiliating name calling, insults, restriction from personal hygiene [bath, toilet], forced nudity).
4. Isolation (restricting access to mail, TV, phone, friends, family; demanding an account of wife's whereabouts).
5. Minimization, denial, and blaming (denying that abuse happened, blaming victim for abuse).
6. Use of children to control the woman (threatening to kidnap or abuse, relaying of threatening messages through the children).
7. Use of "male privilege," that is, that the man always gets what he wants, that his preferences overrule those of the woman, that his demands cannot be questioned.
8. Economic/resource abuse (requiring that the partner "beg" for money, stealing money from partner, destroying credit cards, controlling access to transportation).

POSSIBLE DEFENCES OF A SPOUSE WHO HAS KILLED THE ABUSER

The next section of this chapter describes the use of BWS as part of a defence. In other words, the focus is now solely on women who have killed their abuser.

Abused Women Who Kill Their Abusers

The first known case of a battered woman killing her spouse in Canada occurred in Sault Ste. Marie, Ontario. On April 16, 1911, Angelina Napolitano, a 28-year-old immigrant mother of four, killed her husband with an axe while he slept. Although she was found guilty of murder, an international clemency case on her behalf later was successful as a result of the years of severe spousal abuse she had experienced (Regehr & Glancy, 1995).

According to Statistics Canada (2001b), the number of men accused of killing their current wife or ex-wife rose from 52 in 2000 to 69 in 2001, with virtually all of this increase occurring in Ontario. The number of women accused of killing their husbands (16) was unchanged from 2000. One homicide was committed by a same-sex common-law spouse. About 4 percent of the homicides in Canada are committed by women (Motiuk & Belcourt, 1995), and a significant percentage of such women have killed an abusive partner (Browne & Williams, 1989; Jones, 1981). Most of the women in prison for murder convictions report that they were abuse victims prior to the murder. For example, of 181 Canadian women convicted of murder, 82.3 percent of them reported experiencing some form of IPV, either physical (beatings and assault), sexual (sexual assault and molestation), or emotional abuse (verbal attacks and neglect) (Hoffman et al., 1998).

Domestic Violence Law in Canada

The pivotal Supreme Court of Canada case to deal with the issue of BWS was **R. v. Lavallee** (1990). Twenty-two-year-old Angelique Lyn Lavallee shot and killed her partner, Kevin Rust, with whom she had been living for three or four years and who had a history of assaulting her. On August 30, 1986, their home was the scene of a party. After most guests had departed, Lavallee and Rust had a loud argument in the upstairs bedroom during which Rust had threatened to kill her after all the guests had departed. After he told her that if she did not kill him, he would kill her, she shot him in the back of the head as he was walking away from her.

Although she did not testify in her trial, her statement to the police read:

Me and Wendy argued as usual and I ran in the house after Kevin pushed me. I was scared, I was really scared. I locked the door. Herb was downstairs with Joanne and I called for Herb but I was crying when I called him. I said, "Herb come up here please." Herb came up to the top of the stairs and I told him that Kevin was going to hit me, actually beat on me again. Herb said he knew and that if I was his old lady things would be different, he gave me a hug. OK, we're friends, there's nothing between us. He said "Yeah, I know" and he went outside to talk to Kevin leaving the door unlocked. I went upstairs and hid in my closet from Kevin. I was so scared. ... My window was open and I could hear Kevin asking questions about what I was doing and what I was saying. Next thing I know he was coming up the stairs for me. He came into my bedroom and said "Wench, where are you?" And he turned on my light and he said "Your purse is on the floor" and he kicked it. OK then he turned and he saw me in the closet. He wanted me to come out but I didn't want to come out because I was scared. I was so scared. [The officer who took the statement then testified that the appellant started to cry at this point and stopped after a minute or two.] He grabbed me by the arm right there. There's a bruise on my face also where he slapped me. He didn't slap me right then, first he yelled at me then he pushed me and I pushed him back and he hit me twice on the right hand side of my head. I was scared. All I thought about was all the other times he used to beat me, I was scared, I was shaking as usual. The rest is a blank, all I remember is he gave me the gun and a shot was fired through my screen. This is all so fast. And then the guns were in another room and he loaded it the second shot and gave it to me. And I was going to shoot myself. I pointed it to myself, I was so upset. OK and then he went and I was sitting on the bed and he started going like this with his finger [the appellant made a shaking motion with an index finger] and said something like "You're my old lady and you do as you're told" or something like that. He said "wait till everybody leaves, you'll get it then" and he said something to the effect of "either you kill me or I'll get you" that was what it was. He kind of smiled and then he turned around. I shot him but I aimed out. I thought I aimed above him and a piece of his head went that way. (R v. Lavallee, 1990)

An expert witness, Dr. Fred Shane, was hired by the defence to testify regarding Angelique Lavallee's state of mind at the time of the killing. Using Walker's "battered woman syndrome" description, Dr. Shane gave the opinion that because of her continuing abuse, Lavallee had reasonably believed that Rust was going to kill her later that night. He testified:

I think she felt, she felt in the final tragic moment that her life was on the line, that unless she defended herself, unless she reacted in a violent way that she would die. I mean he made it very explicit to her, from what she told me and from the information I have from the material that you forwarded to me, that she had, I think, to defend herself against his violence. (R v. Lavallee, 1990)

At her original trial, Lavallee was acquitted. However, the Manitoba Court of Appeal overturned the acquittal. Ultimately, the Supreme Court restored the acquittal; its recognition of the **battered woman defence** widely was viewed as a significant victory for women.

Since the *Lavallee* decision, there have been several important reforms in the Canadian legal system in dealing with the problem of spousal violence. Examples of recent legislative reforms include the following:

- Bill C-15, reintroduced on March 14, 2001 (previously Bill C-36), proposed to change the Criminal Code to increase the maximum penalty for criminal harassment from five to ten years in prison.
- Bill C-79 (December 1, 1999) changed the Criminal Code to facilitate the participation of victims and witnesses in the criminal justice process, and to prevent their revictimization by the system. For example, bail decisions must take the safety of victims into account, and publication bans are now permitted to protect the identity of any victim or witness.
- Bill C-27 (May 26, 1997) amended the Criminal Code to strengthen the criminal harassment (stalking) provisions. The bill also requires the courts to consider a breach of a no-contact order to be an aggravating factor in sentencing for criminal harassment.
- Bill C-41 (introduced on September 3, 1996) led to Criminal Code changes requiring the courts to take into account the abuse of a spouse or a child as an aggravating factor in sentencing.
- Bill C-42 (introduced on February 1, 1995) changed the Criminal Code to make it easier to obtain peace bonds (no-contact orders). Police

and others can now apply for a peace bond on behalf of a person at risk of harm. The maximum penalty for violation of a peace bond was increased from six months to two years.

- Bill C-126 (introduced on August 1, 1993) created the new antistalking offence of criminal harassment.

It is important to recall that BWS is not a legal defence (Aron, 1993). As the Supreme Court of Canada has stated in *R. v. Malott* (1998):

"Battered woman syndrome" is not a legal defense in itself, but rather is a psychiatric explanation of the mental state of an abused woman which can be relevant to understanding a battered woman's state of mind. The utility of such evidence is not limited to self-defense situations, but is potentially relevant to other situations where the reasonableness of a battered woman's actions or perceptions is at issue. (summary para. 5)

In Canada, in cases in which the abused woman kills her spouse or partner, she must show the need for self-defence or at least provocation.

Self-Defence

The battered woman defence, as it is called, rests on the justification of the act as necessary to protect the woman or someone else (usually the children) from further harm or death (Walker, 1992). **Self-defence** is defined in Canada and in most U.S. states as the use of equal force or the least amount of force necessary to repel danger when the person reasonably perceives that she or he is in **imminent danger** of serious bodily harm or death. Its key items include a reasonable perception of imminent danger and a justified use of lethal force.

One of the Supreme Court of Canada's most recent considerations of BWS is found in *R. v. Malott* (1998) and is relevant to understanding its stance on self-defence in this context. In this case, Margaret Ann Malott was charged with the murder and attempted murder of her common-law husband Paul Malott and his girlfriend Carrie Sherwood, respectively. Her husband had abused her physically, sexually, psychologically, and emotionally, but then he left Margaret to live with Sherwood. Several months after the separation, Malott shot her husband after he drove her to a

medical centre to assist him in his illegal drug trade. After shooting him, she took a cab to his girlfriend's home where Malott shot her and stabbed her with a knife (this victim survived).

At the trial, Malott testified about her extensive abuse at the hands of her husband, a fact with which the Crown had no disagreement. Expert evidence was admitted to demonstrate that Malott had experienced BWS. However, she was found guilty by the jury of both second-degree murder and attempted murder, but they recommended that she receive the minimum sentence in light of BWS. These convictions were upheld by the Ontario Appeal Court in 1996. Malott finally appealed her conviction for second-degree murder to the Supreme Court of Canada, which also dismissed her appeal, finding that the imminence of danger requiring self-defence was not present.

Justification of the Self-Defence Defence

In order to justify a self-defence defence and therefore acquit the abused spouse, the laws of Canada and most U.S. states require that the judge or jury be convinced that at the time of the incident he or she had a reasonable apprehension of imminent life-threatening danger. Although such a defence is the primary one chosen by such defendants, it faces several obstacles. The first is the "masculine" nature of the defence.

The legal concept of self-defence developed in response to two basic kinds of situations in which men found themselves: a sudden assault by a murderous stranger (e.g., a robbery attempt with a threat to kill) or a fistfight or brawl between two equals that gets out of hand and turns deadly. Thus, "classic" self-defence action is stranger-to-stranger assault between two males (Blackman, 1986).

But self-defence cases certainly vary from this scenario, and research findings have led some researchers (Finkel, Meister, & Lightfoot, 1991) to conclude that more community support exists for the self-defence defence by abused women than the above would imply. Consider the following case: In the mid-1970s Inez Garcia was raped by two neighbourhood men who told her they were going to come back and rape her again. She went home, got a gun, and after several hours had passed, she found one of the men and shot him dead. She was acquitted at her second trial, a trial in which the court permitted evidence of self-defence even though the actual rape had taken place several hours earlier and there was an intervening time between the act and her responses. The court decided that the threat of further abuse was sufficient to raise her perception of danger to the imminence standard (Bochnak, 1981; Schneider, 1986).

The most fundamental element of the self-defence claim is that at the time of the killing, the defendant honestly and reasonably feared unlawful bodily harm at the hands of her assailant:

> In this regard, proof of violent acts previously committed by the victim against the defendant as well as any evidence that the defendant was aware of specific prior violent acts by the victim upon third parties is admissible as bearing upon the reasonableness of defendant's apprehension of danger at the time of the encounter. (*People v. Torres*, 1985, p. 360)

Psychological Self-Defence

As we have seen, many abused women who kill their abusers are convicted, even though they use the self-defence defence, because the requirements of the current self-defence law equate "self" with only the *physical* aspects of personhood (i.e., there is a threat to the *physical* self; Ewing, 1990, p. 580). That is, most do not kill at the moment they are being abused or directly threatened. Ewing's survey of well-documented homicides by abused women found only about one third took place during an act of violence. Thus, he has proposed a new concept, the **psychological self-defence**. He has written:

> In brief, my position is that failure to meet these narrow legal requirements does not mean that a battered woman did not kill in defense of self. I argue that many, perhaps most, battered women who kill their abusers do so in *psychological* self-defense—that is, to protect themselves from being destroyed *psychologically*—and that under certain circumstances the law should recognize psychological self-defense as a justification for the use of deadly force. (Ewing, 1990, p. 581, italics in original)

Ewing, a psychologist, lawyer, and law professor, wrote further:

Should a battered woman—or anyone else—who uses deadly force to prevent that result, to avert what reasonably appears to be the threat of psychological destruction, be branded a criminal and sent to prison? I think not, but that is precisely what is happening in many cases under current self-defense law. Contrary to current law, I suggest that the use of deadly force to avoid such a dire fate is a legitimate form of self-defense and should be recognized as such by the criminal law. In short, I believe that, under certain circumstances, psychological self-defense should be a legal justification for homicide.

> The legal doctrine I am proposing is not a battered woman defense. Such a defense would not only arguably violate constitutional guarantees of equal protection, but would be unsound as a matter of public policy. Attaining the status of battered woman or even battered person is not and should not by itself be justification for homicide. Stated most simply, the proposed doctrine of psychological self-defense would justify the use of deadly force where such force appeared reasonably necessary to prevent the infliction of extremely serious psychological injury. *Extremely serious psychological injury* would be defined as gross and enduring impairment of one's psychological functioning that significantly limits the meaning and value of one's physical existence. (1990, p. 587, italics in original)

The major criticism of the use of psychological self-defence as a defence comes from Morse (1990). His major objections are the following:

> The proposal to justify homicide by psychological self-defense rests on an insecure scientific foundation and would be legally mischievous. The core concepts are unacceptably vague and lack rigorous empirical support. The proposed defense is better characterized as an excuse than as a justification because rational victims of purely psychological abuse do have socially preferable alternatives to homicide, and the proposal is inconsistent with modern criminal law that limits justifications for homicide. The defense would create substantial administrative problems and would facilitate adoption or expansion of related undesirable doctrines. The best response to abhorrent physical and psychological abuse is not unnecessary further violence, but the creation of adequate deterrents and alternative solutions for victims. (1990, p. 595)

The psychological self-defence defence remains untested in Canadian courts.

USING A PSYCHOLOGIST AS AN EXPERT WITNESS ON BWS

Testimony by an expert witness on BWS was first introduced in U.S. courts in 1979 (*Ibn-Tamas v. United States*). Walker (1993) estimated that witness experts on BWS had been allowed to testify in at least 500 trials in the United States. She wrote:

My own work as an expert witness in almost 300 of these trials in the United States began in 1977 when I was asked to evaluate Miriam Griegg, a Billings, Montana[,] woman who had been seriously assaulted during most of her marriage. One night she shot and killed her husband with six hollow point bullets from his own Magnum .357 gun. During an argument, he threw the gun at her and ordered her to shoot him or else, he threatened, he would shoot and kill her. When the police arrived, Miriam Griegg warned them to be careful as she knew her husband would be very angry. Obviously, her emotional state caused her to be unaware that he was dead; any one of the six bullets would have killed him instantly. She made it perfectly clear, however, that she shot him because she believed that he would have killed her otherwise, a straightforward self-defense argument. After listening to her testimony and mine—I explained the context of the relationship and how Miriam Griegg knew in her own mind that she would die if she did not do what he ordered her to do—the jury agreed that she was not guilty. (1993, pp. 233–234)

But, as described in detail later in this chapter, the empirical research on the effect of an expert witness does not lead to a solid conclusion about overall effectiveness of psychologists who testify for the defence.

Basically, the purpose of the expert witness is to provide fact finders with another perspective, or a "social framework" (Walker & Monahan, 1987) for interpreting the woman's actions. Mary Ann Dutton (1993) described different purposes for testimony by a psychologist:

Typically, expert testimony concerning the battered woman's psychological reactions to violence has been used to address a number of different issues. Within a criminal context, the testimony is used to bolster a standard defense, (e.g., self-defense or duress) not provide a separate defense, *per se*. Issues toward which the psychological testimony is applied include, for example, whether the victim's perception of danger was reasonable (e.g., self-defense), the psychological damage resulting from domestic violence (e.g., civil tort), the basis for sole custody or restriction of child visitation (e.g., child custody), and why the battered woman engaged in seemingly puzzling behaviours (e.g., remained with or returned to the battering partner, expressed anger toward the abuser in public, left children alone with abuser, recanted testimony regarding occurrence of past violence).

It is, of course, necessary to establish that the particular aspects of a battered woman's experience of violence (and its aftermath) toward which the testimony is addressed are directly relevant to specific legal issues at hand in order for its application to be both helpful and admissible. It is essential that this link be made explicit to the factfinder, otherwise the relevance of the expert witness testimony may not be clearly understood or missed altogether. (p. 1216)

The expert witness can describe three types of reaction to trauma (described further in Chapter 11):

- Psychological distress or dysfunction
- Cognitive reactions
- Relational disturbances.

One of the most important contributions is to confront questions that jurors might be asking themselves. For example, jurors want to know "Why didn't she leave?" This question, one frequently asked, assumes that there are viable options; that is, it assumes that leaving will stop the violence. The law is explicit: You have no obligation to rearrange your life in order to avoid a situation in which the need to act in self-defence might arise. The expert witness needs to deflect the assumption that the victim she didn't leave after the abuse, she wasn't bothered by it. The expert witness can bring out strategies the woman has used to stop the violence (Follingstad, 1994b). These form three types:

1. Personal strategies
   - Compliance with the abuser's demands in order to "keep the peace"
   - Attempting to talk with abuser about stopping the violence

- Temporarily escaping
- Hiding
- Physical resistance

2. Informal help-seeking efforts
   - Soliciting help from neighbours and others in escaping from the abuser
   - Asking others to intervene in an attempt to get him to stop

3. Formal help-seeking efforts
   - Legal strategies—calling the police, prosecuting, getting a lawyer, going to a shelter.

The expert can point out that, in some cases, the lack of the victim's economic resources can make it difficult for her to leave. But the expert also needs to alert the jury to the fact that different victims use different strategies and to *why* any one option is not frequently used. A second question jurors ponder is "Why did she attack when he was asleep?" The expert witness can inform the jury of the reasonableness of the battered woman's perception of danger. Walker has argued:

Many women know that their abusive partner is still dangerous even while he is asleep, frequently forcing his sexual demands upon waking and immediately beginning another attack. Often these men do not sleep for long periods of time, waking early, especially if she is not right by his side as he frequently orders. (1992, p. 325)

In further support of this position, Crocker (1985) suggested:

The battered woman perceived an imminent danger of physical injury even though there was no overt act of violence. Defendants offer battered woman syndrome expert testimony to explain why their perception of danger was reasonable—why they acted in self-defense after a "reasonable man" would have cooled off or before he would have acted. The testimony may demonstrate how repeated physical abuse can so heighten a battered woman's fear and her awareness of her husband's physical capabilities that she considers him as dangerous asleep as awake, as dangerous before an attack as during one. (p. 141)

A 2004 study by York University researchers Regina Schuller, Elisabeth Wells, Sara Rzepa, and Marc Klippenstine, entitled "Re-thinking Battered Woman Syndrome Evidence," suggested that lawyers should consider dropping the terminology of BWS and focus on the woman's situation and lack of options, because of jurors' misconceptions about abused women. The authors found that when the woman's homicide had been committed outside a direct confrontation (as her husband was asleep), mock jurors were less likely to believe her claim of self-defence and more likely to render a verdict of guilty. Further, expert evidence concerning BWS was beneficial to jurors only in the confrontational condition; expert testimony in the nonconfrontational condition was ineffective in influencing juror verdicts.

PROCEDURAL AND ETHICAL ISSUES REGARDING THE USE OF EXPERT WITNESSES

The use of a psychologist as an expert witness in cases in which BWS is introduced is fraught with both procedural and ethical questions.

Admissibility of Expert Testimony

The rationale for many court decisions to admit expert testimony is that it bears upon a crucial issue of fact that is beyond the knowledge of the average layperson or jury member (Ewing, Aubrey, & Jamieson, 1986).

A decision by the Supreme Court of Canada is illustrative. In *R. v. Malott* (1998), the court wrote:

To the extent that expert evidence respecting battered woman syndrome may assist a jury in assessing the reasonableness of an accused's perceptions, it is relevant to the issue of unlawful assault ... The Court accepted the need for expert evidence in order to dispel the myths and stereotypes inherent in our understanding of a battered woman's experiences. (para. 18 and summary para. 6)

Jurors' Reactions to BWS as Defence Evidence

But what is the effect of expert testimony? Does it change jurors' verdicts? If so, how? Several jury-simulation studies are relevant (e.g., Blackman &

Michael Woodworth, Ph.D., is an associate professor at UBC Okanagan. Dr. Woodworth travelled by horse and carriage across the country in 1999 to work under the fast up-and-coming professor at Dalhousie University— Dr. Stephen Porter. Until that time, Dr. Woodworth had been planning to be a lawyer. He received his Ph.D. in 2004 and began working at UBC Okanagan. He is very excited he and his colleagues, Dr. Porter, and Dr. Zach Walsh, have just opened the CFI-funded Centre for the Advancement of Psychological Science and Law (CAPSL). Dr. Woodworth's primary areas of research include psychopathy, criminal behaviour, and deception detection; he has published in journals such as *Law and Human Behaviour, Criminal Justice and Behaviour,* and *Journal of Abnormal Psychology.*

Dr. Woodworth has collaborated on research projects with the RCMP (Royal Canadian Mounted Police) and CSC (Correctional Services of Canada), consulted with the FBI, and regularly presents at national and international psychology conferences, including a recent conference in Berlin where afterward he travelled to the small town of Bad Schandau and was terrorized by a chimera. Dr. Woodworth has also been qualified as an expert in the Canadian courts in the general area of forensic psychology and in more specific areas such as detecting deceit. In addition to his work at the university, Dr. Woodworth is a registered psychologist in the Okanagan valley who has been providing general clinical services to the community since 2004.

Some of his favourite published texts include a 2002 paper examining psychopathy and motivation in homicide offenders, a 2009 paper considering the nature of emotional deficits in youth with high levels of callous and unemotional traits, a 2010 paper exploring the impact of motivation on ability to deceive specifically in online environments, and a just recently published paper investigating the linguistic differences of psychopathic and nonpsychopathic homicide offenders. Dr. Woodworth recently received SSHRC funding (2012–2105) to continue to explore the language and nonverbal behaviour of individuals with a high number of psychopathic traits.

Dr. Woodworth loves to teach and was recently the recipient of the UBC Teaching Excellence and Innovation Award. He often rewards his students for answering questions by having his Mexican marionette sidekick, "Pico," do a boisterous dance for the class. Dr. Woodworth is currently teaching a Forensic Psychology course (3rd year) and an Introduction to Clinical Psychology (4th year). Dr. Woodworth also regularly teaches specialized upper-level courses on topics related to psychology and law, such as a recent one considering the nature of evil (Will the real horror of horrors please stand up, please stand up, please stand up: A quest for a true delineation of evil).

Dr. Woodworth is a squash (the invigorating sporting event, not the ho-hum vegetable) enthusiast and a music promoter and fanatic. For example, he has over 200 official recordings of Ennio Morricone and Peter Brötzmann alone. In fact, Dr. Woodworth and Dr. Walsh have formed a band called "Tonight We Hunt Buffalo" and recently premiered their first (and only) single, "So Sincere and Smiley faces" at the Western Front Art Gallery in Vancouver, B.C. Another interesting secret about Dr. Woodworth is that he once built a giant pyramid comprising over 500 000 pennies. He has also kept his hand on a car continuously for nearly 40 hours to raise money for brain injury research. For more information about Dr. Woodworth see http://www.MichaelWoodworth.ca

---

Brickman, 1984), keeping in mind the limitations to this approach described in Chapter 8. Regina Schuller and her colleagues have conducted several such studies (Schuller, 1992; Schuller, Smith, & Olson, 1994). In the first, 108 mock jurors (Canadian university students) read about a homicide trial in which a battered woman had killed her husband. The transcript, based on an actual case, was 50 pages in length. Three versions of the trial were used. In one, an expert witness presented only general research findings on BWS. In the second version, the expert went further and was more specific, concluding that the defendant's behavioural and emotional characteristics fit the syndrome. In the third version, no expert testimony was presented. Compared to the control condition, jurors exposed to the transcript with the specific expert gave interpretations that were more consistent with the woman's account of what occurred, and more lenient verdicts.

Schuller's (1992) second study—which substituted an hour-long audiotape for the transcript—had the jurors deliberate. (A total of 131 participants were divided into 30 juries.) In this study, compared to the control condition, each expert-witness condition led to a moderate shift in verdicts from murder to manslaughter. If they had heard the testimony of an expert witness, the jurors—during deliberations—discussed the defendant and her actions in a more favourable light.

A third study in Schuller's program of research (Schuller, Smith, & Olson, 1994) collected participants' beliefs about sexual abuse two months prior to their participation as mock jurors in a study that used the same audiotape as the prior study. The presence of testimony by an expert witness again influenced verdicts but especially for the mock jurors whose earlier responses had reflected more informed attitudes about domestic abuse. These jurors attributed less responsibility to the defendant and more responsibility to the alleged abuser, compared to control subjects.

A jury simulation by Greenwald, Tomkins, Kenning, and Zavodny (1990) sought to evaluate Ewing's "psychological self-defence" defence. A total of 196 undergraduate participants read two trial vignettes. The instructions given to the jury were varied: psychological self-defence only, physical self-defence only, psychological and physical self-defence, or none of these. Instructions were given after the vignettes, so that elements of self-defence were the last thing given to the jurors. Only the psychological self-defence instructions significantly influenced verdict patterns, primarily by shifting would-be voluntary manslaughter convictions to acquittals.

However, not all studies have concluded that testimony by a psychologist expert is that effective. A study by Follingstad and her colleagues (Follingstad et al., 1989) varied the level of force directed by the husband prior to his wife's killing him, as well as the presence or absence of an expert witness (who testified about the relationship of the defendant's actions to abusive relationships in general). The presence of the expert witness had no direct influence on the jurors' verdicts, although 80 percent of the jurors in the expert-witness condition reported that it was influential. The factor that had the greatest impact was the level of force used by the abuser; that is, jurors were more sympathetic with the defendant in the condition in which the abuser used the most force (where the husband was described as advancing toward the woman with a weapon).

Similarly, a study by Finkel, Meister, and Lightfoot (1991) manipulated the degree of threat posed by the husband, as well as the presence or absence of expert testimony. As in Schuller's first study, two types of expert testimony were offered; either the expert diagnosed the defendant as having BWS and described the symptoms of the syndrome, or the expert supplemented the diagnosis with an opinion about the woman's perceptions at the time of the killing. As in the study by Follingstad and her colleagues, the only variable that influenced the mock jurors' verdicts was the level of force used by the husband; that is, verdicts of guilt were rendered more often when the woman acted without direct provocation from the man.

Hodell, Dunlap, Wasarhaley, and Golding (2011) had 187 community participants give judgments about a case of an abused woman who killed her abuser allegedly in self-defence. The researchers found that a delay between abuse and the killing affected conviction rates only for women; men were convicted at high rates regardless of delay, whereas women were convicted at higher rates when the killing occurred following a long delay versus a short delay. Regardless of participant gender, sleeping status significantly predicted verdicts: conviction rates were higher when the victim was asleep than when he was awake.

Thus, the research results give no consistent answer to the question of effectiveness of expert testimony. Methodological differences among the studies described above may account for the differences in results. Schuller (1994) has suggested that it may be necessary for the woman's account of what happened to be challenged (as it is in a real-life trial) for the expert witness to have any impact.

RISK ASSESSMENTS IN IPV CASES

A critical issue in IPV cases is the manner in which to evaluate the risk an abusive partner presents to the victim. Work is under way that seeks to predict violence perpetration and victimization among spouses who are at risk. This research focuses on both individual factors that predict recidivism and tools that examine a collection of statistically related items and its relation to IPV. IPV history has been the most consistently studied risk factor, with physical abuse, emotional abuse, threats, stalking, controlling behaviour, and jealous behaviour typically associated with victims reporting a high risk for future violence (Bennett Cattaneo, 2007; Bennett Cattaneo, & Goodman, 2003; Gondolf & Heckert, 2003; Harding & Helweg-Larse, 2009; Helweg-Larsen et al., 2008; Weisz et al., 2000), and several empirically derived instruments have been developed to assess IPV risk. The most commonly used risk assessment tools include the **Spousal Assault Risk Assessment** (SARA; Kropp, Hart, Webster, & Eaves, 1995), the **Domestic Violence Screening Instrument—Reviews** (DVSI-R; Williams & Grant, 2006), the *Ontario Domestic Assault Risk Assessment* (ODARA; Hilton et al., 2004), and the related **Domestic Violence Risk Appraisal Guide** (DVRAG; Hilton, Harris, Rice, Houghton, & Eke, 2008). Further, the **Danger Assessment** (DA; Campbell, Webster, & Glass, 2009) was designed to predict risk for lethal IPV violence. Research shows that all of these tools are useful in identifying men at risk of perpetrating IPV in the future (e.g., Hanson, Helmus, & Bourgon, 2007).

Randall Kropp, Stephen Hart, Christopher Webster, and Derek Eaves—a collaborative team of academic and government researchers in British Columbia—have developed the SARA instrument. The SARA is a 20-item set of empirically based risk factors for use in the assessment of risk for spousal assault. The SARA seeks to determine the extent to which assaulters are likely to commit violent acts in the future (Kropp & Hart, 1997; Kropp, Hart, Webster, & Eaves, 1998). Kropp and Hart (2000) examined the usefulness of the SARA in assessing risk for violence in 2681 male offenders. The SARA ratings were significantly different in offenders with and without a history of spousal violence in one subsample, and between reoffending and nonreoffending spousal assaulters in another. More recently, Belfrage and colleagues (2012) found that the SARA, when employed by police officers, had significant predictive validity for future contact with police. Although more research is needed, the SARA is a promising tool with some research validation and is becoming widely used in practice.

A newer tool was created by a group of Ontario researchers; an actuarial tool, the Ontario Domestic Assault Risk Assessment (ODARA), predicts recidivism using only variables readily obtained by frontline police officers. Correctional settings permit more comprehensive assessments. In a subset of ODARA construction and cross-validation cases,

303 men with a police record for domestic assault and a correctional system file, the VRAG, SARA, Danger Assessment, and DVSI also predicted recidivism, but the Hare Psychopathy Checklist (PCL-R; Hare, 2003) best improved prediction of recidivism, occurrence, frequency, severity, injury, and charges. In 346 new cases, ODARA and PCL-R independently predicted recidivism. Hilton et al. (2010) tested the ODARA with 150 incarcerated male IPV offenders followed for an average of eight years. The base rate of post-release charges for IPV was 27 percent, and the mean ODARA score was 5.81. The ODARA predicted IPV recidivism significantly better than a general risk assessment, the Level of Service Inventory, and in follow-ups as short as six months. The ODARA also predicted recidivism severity and survival. Thus, it is critical that psychologists consider such empirically validated tools in conducting their risk assessments.

Of course, one recommendation in a psychologist's assessment report regarding an IPV perpetrator is that he or she receives treatment to reduce future risk. In North America, most IPV treatment programs are in a group format that can be described as either having a primary feminist psychoeducational model (sometimes called the "Duluth model") or a cognitive behavioural perpective (e.g., Babcock, Greene, & Robie, 2004). The former emphasizes challenging the presumed dominant, patriarchal view of the male offender and replacing it with a more enlightened egalitarian view. The latter programs are diverse but emphasize changing of the offender's problematic cognitions about men and women, relationships, and violent behaviour through reward and punishment, restructuring thoughts, and relapse prevention. The CBT approach tackles things like denial, victim blaming, and rationalizations. What does the literature have to say about the effectiveness of such programs? It should be noted that evaluating the effectiveness of offender treatment programs is extremely difficult, for many reasons, but in particular because of the difficulty (practically and ethically) of creating an untreated control group. For example, some program evaluators compare the recidivism rate of treatment completers versus those who drop out midprogram. It is quite apparent that these two groups typically differ before treatment commences, so differences in recidivism cannot be attributed to treatment effects. Olver, Stockdale, and Wormith (2011) conducted a major meta-analysis of existing IPV program evaluations and found that attrition (drop-out rate) in such programs was 27.1 percent! Further, these drop-outs had considerably higher needs, were higher risk, and had higher recidivism rates than treatment completers.

When considering studies that are the "best" in terms of randomization, control groups, defining and measuring treatment success, and having sufficient follow-up periods, the literature suggests that programs have a modest impact on reducing IPV recidivism. Babcock et al. (2004) conducted a meta-analysis of 22 treatment studies and found "small" positive treatment effects. Specifically, on average the recidivism rate of treated offenders was reduced about one third of a standard deviation compared to untreated offenders. One might question whether the massive resources that are directed at such programs are worth such modest gains. Looking at it the other way, however, even modest gains over the huge number of offenders who have been treated would have reduced the victimization of a large number of people, probably even saving lives. While IPV treatment may have little or no effect for many offenders, many individual offenders turn their lives around completely as a result of treatment and never reoffend. Further, there is virtually no research on the effectiveness of (much more costly and less frequently used) individual or one-on-one therapy of offenders with a psychologist. It is quite possible that this approach may be more effective than group approaches and that certain therapists may be much more effective than others in eliciting positive change in offenders.

What is clear in reviewing the literature on IPV is that risk assessment is increasingly sophisticated and accurate (to the extent that arguably some domestic homicides can be prevented) and that treatment is certainly not a panacea for ending this problem. We need to develop new treatment approaches and more carefully address individual versus group therapy, and identify not only characteristics of offenders that are associated with the likelihood of treatment success but also those of the mental health professionals delivering the treatment. Also, as noted on several occasions in this textbook, we need to devise better strategies for evaluating the sincerity/remorse/changes of offenders during and following treatment to make more effective management decisions.

LEGAL AND PSYCHOLOGICAL PERSPECTIVES ON INTER-PARTNER STALKING

There has been a great increase in the recognition of the problem and crime of **stalking** behaviour in Canada. Stalking, or **criminal harassment**, according to the Criminal Code of Canada (2011), can be defined as repeated unwanted, harassing, or threatening behaviours directed toward the victim over a period of time (Meloy, 1998). In this chapter, we are concerned with intimate partner (i.e., current or past) stalking. There are varying definitions in terms of victim perception, such that some require that the victim experiences fear, while others do not (Fox, Nobles, & Akers, 2011). The behaviours themselves can include following the individual at home or the workplace, making unwanted calls/texts, and repeatedly making romantic requests, despite consistent denials (e.g., Meloy, 1998). According to the Department of Justice (2003), the following are examples of stalking behaviour:

- Calling a former partner over and over again, and perhaps hanging up whenever the person answers the phone
- Contacting a former partner on the Internet or through constant e-mail messages
- Following a former partner, or his or her family or friends
- Leaving threatening voice messages
- Sending a former partner gifts he or she does not want
- Watching a former partner or tracking where he or she goes
- Threatening a former partner, his or her children, family, pets, or friends

Stalking is a highly damaging behaviour affecting the lives of at least 8 percent of women and 2 percent of men at some stage of their lives (Tjaden & Thoennes, 1998) with some estimates being considerably higher (Dressing, Kuehner, & Gass, 2005; Purcell, Pathe, & Mullen, 2002). In Canada, the five-year prevalence rates (the frequency of this behaviour in a five-year period) for stalking are 11 percent in women and 7 percent in men (Statistics Canada, 2005). A major review by Spitzberg and Cupach (2007) of 175 studies of stalking found that 25 percent of respondents reported being stalked, and for an average of almost two years. Women were more likely to report being victims. The researchers found that more than half of stalking cases indicated the use of physical threat, and 32 percent of stalking cases involved physical violence, whereas 12 percent involved sexual violence. The majority of stalking cases involved former romantic relationships, the focus of this chapter. In another review, Spitzberg, Cupach, and Ciceraro (2010) reviewed a large group of studies of almost 7000 university students and found that women are more likely to experience persistent unwanted pursuit, more likely to view such pursuit as threatening, and two to three times as likely as men to be victims of stalking, but that men report longer durations of unwanted pursuit.

Who engages in such stalking behaviour? Storey, Hart, Meloy, and Reavis (2009) predicted that psychopathic traits would be associated with such behaviour. They examined 61 men convicted of stalking-related offences, finding that psychopathic features were, in fact, rare. However, when psychopathic features were present, they were associated with victimization of casual acquaintances and with several known risk factors of crime in general. It seems that most stalking behaviour is not perpetrated by evil psychopaths but rather by otherwise seemingly normal individuals. Or is it? A fascinating study by Davis, Ace, and Andra (2000) involving university students found that about 40 percent of men and women reported having engaged in at least one stalking behaviour following a breakup. The researchers found that stalking often was related to psychological maltreatment/abuse by the partner/victim prior to the breakup. Interestingly, being "broken up with" was associated with feelings of anger, jealousy and obsessiveness and with higher levels of "courtship persistence," and stalking. In general, there was a relation between anger and jealousy and stalking behaviours.

Two studies by Spitzberg and colleagues examined the relation between gender and stalking behaviour. In a major study of more than 6000 university students and a total of more than 300 000 people, Spitzberg and Cupach (2007) found across 82 studies that 32 percent of stalking cases involved physical violence, whereas 12 percent involved sexual violence. They also found that the vast majority (79 percent) of victims were acquainted with their pursuer.

SUMMARY

In recent years, the extent and seriousness of IPV in Canada has been increasingly publicized. Useful typologies of individuals who abuse have been developed. Further, there is accumulating research to suggest that risk prediction tools such as the SARA (Kropp & Hart, 2000) can help us predict whether an abuser is likely to reoffend. Some psychologists have proposed that the responses of women who have been continually abused by their partners are consistent enough to qualify as a syndrome, called battered woman syndrome (BWS). Among these reactions are learned helplessness, lowered self-esteem, loss of a feeling of invulnerability, a sense of diminished alternatives, and hypervigilance. Walker proposed that the interaction between the abuser and his or her partner goes through a set of observable phases—a tension-building phase, an acute battering incident, and then a contrite phase; she called this the cycle of abuse or cycle of violence. Others have argued that gender is largely irrelevant and that we ought to focus on personality factors in IPV instead of gender.

Future research needs to examine in a more refined way the "bi-directionality" argument, suggesting that male and females are equally likely to be violent in romantic relationships, and the means to reducing this major societal problem. Further, we need more research on stalking behaviour and its prevention.

KEY TERMS

acute battering incident, p. 243

battered woman defence, p. 245

battered woman syndrome (BWS), p. 242

cognitive inconsistency, p. 243

contrite phase, p. 243

criminal harassment, p. 253

cycle of abuse, p. 243

SUGGESTED READINGS

Browne, A. (1987). *When battered women kill*. New York: Free Press.

This text analyzes the causes for the actions of 42 women charged with killing or seriously injuring their partners. Case studies are sensitively presented.

Dutton, D. G. (1995). *The domestic assault of women: Psychological and criminal justice perspectives* (Rev. ed.). Vancouver: UBC Press.

This comprehensive examination of the causes and effects of spousal assault includes a detailed classification of types of violent men and an analysis of the dynamics of the victim–abuser relationship.

Dutton, D. (2006). *Rethinking domestic violence*. Vancouver: UBC Press.

This text critically reviews research in the area of IPV through several perspectives (social and clinical psychology, sociology, psychiatry, etc.).

Hilton, N., Harris, G. T., Popham, S., & Lang, C. (2010). Risk assessment among incarcerated male domestic violence offenders. *Criminal Justice and Behavior*, 37(8), 815–832.

This article describes the examination of risk assessment (using the ODARA) in a group of incarcerated domestic violence offenders; the results are discussed.

Torpy, J. M., Lynm, C., & Class, R. M. (2010). Intimate partner violence. *The Journal of the American Medical Association, 304*(5), 596.

This short article describes the signs of relationship abuse, and advises ways of seeking help.

Walker, L. E. A. (1979). *The battered woman*. New York: Harper & Row.

This detailed analysis of the components of the battered woman syndrome and the cycle of violence includes examples from the author's interviews and case studies.

Walsh, Z., Swogger, M. T., O'Connor, B. P., Chatav Schonbrun, Y., Shea, M., & Stuart, G. L. (2010). Subtypes of partner violence perpetrators among male and female psychiatric patients. *Journal of Abnormal Psychology*, 119(3), 563–574.

This study examined heterogeneity among female and male psychiatric patients with a history of IPV. Results of the study are discussed, along with suggestions for future investigation of female IPV perpetration.

CHAPTER

Sex Offenders

> *I'm concerned that they're tearing apart my wife's brand new house.*
> *This place, it's been my wife's dream.*
>
> —Colonel Russell Williams during the 10-hour interrogation that eventually led to his confession. Williams admitted to confessing to his heinous sexual crimes to make his wife's life easier (*Toronto Star*, 2010b).

Picture the following. A car pulls into a dark driveway and an older male exits the vehicle and proceeds to the front door. A 14-year-old girl answers the door and invites the man in, letting him know that there are cookies in the kitchen and that he can make himself at home while she leaves the room to answer the phone. The man excitedly enters the house and reveals that he has brought a case of beer with him. He recently has met the young girl in an online chat room and has come to her house to engage in sexual activity with the minor while her parents supposedly are out of town. Suddenly, he hears a noise from behind him and turns to see a middle-aged man holding a microphone enter the kitchen followed by a cameraman. The man asks "Why did you come to this house tonight?" and then announces "My name is Chris Hansen, and I am a *Dateline NBC* correspondent." This scene has played out numerous times on the *Dateline NBC* specials "To Catch a Predator." Partnering with the U.S. watchdog group Perverted Justice, Chris Hansen goes undercover as a 14-year-old girl in online chat rooms to catch sex offenders who use the Internet to find victims. While this show has caught a number of online sex offenders, there still are a huge number of individuals who continue to use the Internet as a hunting ground for potential targets. Luring on the Internet is only one type of sexual offence; as we will discuss throughout the chapter, there are a number of different types of sex offenders and illegal sexual acts.

THE SCOPE OF SEXUAL OFFENDING

With the tremendous increase in self- and official reports of sexual crimes in Canada over the past several decades, the problem of sexual violence never has been so clear. Early epidemiological surveys indicated that about one in eight males and one in four females have been sexually assaulted in childhood (Finkelhor, Hotaling, Lewis, & Smith, 1990). A meta-analysis of 22 American-based studies suggested that 30–40 percent of girls and 13 percent of boys experience sexual abuse during childhood (Bolan & Scannapieco, 1999). An international meta-analysis of 169 studies found that lifetime prevalence rates of sexual abuse for females around the world is 25 percent and for males is 8 percent. This same study found that rates for North America range from 15 to 22 percent for both males and females (World Health Organization, 2001). These self-report numbers are, not surprisingly, far higher than the number of sexual assaults reported to police. In 2009, almost 21 000 sex crimes were reported in Canada. Canadian police also reported about 2600 sex offences against children (sexual interference, invitation to sexual touching, sexual exploitation, and luring a child via a computer). In addition, almost 1600 incidents of child pornography were reported by police, a 13 percent increase from 2008 (Dauvergne & Turner, 2010). This pattern has highlighted the need to better our understanding of sexual violence and try to develop treatment programs that can reduce recidivism. The focus of this chapter is to examine who are sexual offenders and what can be done to deal with this important societal problem. Sadly, recent Canadian statistics suggest that the official incidence of sexual violence remains high (Johnson, 2006). In fact, the self-report data suggest a societal problem of staggering proportions. The most detailed self-report information available on Canadian rates of sexual violence comes from a 1993 Violence Against Women Survey (VAWS) in which 39 percent of adult women reported at least one experience of sexual assault during adulthood.

To begin, the definition of **sexual assault** in Canada is any nonconsensual sexual act committed by a male or a female against either a male or a female, regardless of the relationship between the individuals involved. There are three levels of sexual assault: (1) simple sexual assault; (2) sexual assault with a weapon or causing bodily harm; and (3) aggravated sexual assault (Criminal Code of Canada, 2011). The severity of the crime and the length of the maximum sentence are the basis for the division of these offence categories. Although these three categories define the types of physical actions that sex offenders can use to perpetrate sexual crimes, they do not take into account the psychological trauma that sex offenders are likely to induce by committing their crimes (in fact, psychological research indicates that sexual assault is one of the most traumatic kinds of events one can experience: Leserman, 2005; Liang, Williams, & Siegel, 2006). Further, these categories do not account for the sexual offences that do not involve direct contact with the victim (e.g., voyeurism, exhibitionism, and viewing child pornography).

Further, it is important to address the issue of "**consent**." Obviously, if a person is forced into sexual activity against his or her will, a sexual offence has occurred. However, in some cases, there may be no salient element of force or coercion. In Canada, all people younger than 16 years old (or 18 if the older individual is in a position of authority, such as a teacher–student relationship) are presumed to be unable to give full informed consent and thus, any adult engaging in sexual behaviour with these individuals is guilty of an indictable offence (Criminal Code of Canada, 2011), regardless of whether the victim had given verbal consent. The issue of the appropriate age of consent is controversial and its resolution differs across time and cultures. For example, the age of consent in Canada changed from 14 to 16 years only in 2008 (and it had been 12 years until 1890). The age of consent varies around the world. In the United States, the age of consent is decided at the state level, and all states have set the age of consent between 16 and 18 years. Currently, the lowest age of consent internationally is 12 years (in Angola, Zimbabwe, and some parts of Mexico) and the highest is 21 years (in Cameroon). It also is noteworthy that some places such as Iran and Pakistan do not have an age of consent because females are not allowed to engage in intercourse before they are married. Full consent must be given for all sexual activity between all participating individuals over the age of 16 years. Consent is defined as the voluntary agreement of both parties to engage in sexual activity (Criminal Code of Canada, 2011).

There are a number of offences in Canada that do not fall under the stereotypical "sexual offences" category. An example of this is the act of incest, characterized by engaging in sexual intercourse with a consenting adult blood relative, that is a parent, grandparent, sibling, child, or cousin. While this is not necessarily one of the more physically threatening or severe sexual offences, individuals found to have engaged in an incestual relationship potentially are guilty of an indictable offence and are subject to a prison term of no longer than 14 years. Another example of illegal sexual behaviour in Canada is the act of bestiality, characterized by engaging in a sexual act with an animal. Any individual who commits bestiality is considered guilty of an indictable offence and is subject to a prison sentence of up to 10 years.

THE SCOPE OF SEXUAL OFFENDERS

Who are the people committing sexual offences in Canada? While it might be tempting for the citizen or politician to categorize sex offenders as a homogeneous group of "deviants," there is growing recognition that they are a diverse group in terms of their behavioural profiles, criminal diversity, treatment needs, personalities, and risk for reoffending. Regarding the latter, for example, Canadian researchers Michael Seto and Yolanda Fernandez (2011) studied 419 male sex offenders in Ontario and identified four distinct risk groups based on their scores on the Stable-2000 (Hanson, Harris, Scott, & Helmus, 2007), a measure that helps to identify when we should be most concerned about a particular offender. The groups included *low-needs*; *typical* group; a *sexually deviant* group who scored relatively high on deviant sexual interests, sexual preoccupation, emotional identification with children, and child molester attitudes; and a *pervasive high-needs* group who had numerous problems relating to both general and sexual self-regulation.

Sex offenders often are differentiated by the type of sexually deviant behaviour in which they engage, the age of their typical victim, and their relationship with the victim. The different classifications of sexual offender include voyeurs, exhibitionists, child pornographers, offenders who lure children over the Internet, frotteurs, child molesters, and rapists. Some of the categories also break down the offender type into further typologies, usually based on the type of victim they offend against or the motivation for their offending. Each of the offender types will be discussed in some detail below.

Voyeurs

Voyeurism (derived from the word "**voyeur**," French for "one who looks") is a *DSM-IV-TR* **paraphilia** characterized by becoming sexually aroused from secretly spying on others as they disrobe or engage in sexual behaviour. This paraphilia is characterized by two criteria: (1) that the individual experiences overwhelming fantasies, urges, thoughts, and behaviours about observing another individual naked, while disrobing, or while engaging in sexual behaviour without the individual being aware of being watched for a period longer than six months; and (2) that these fantasies, thoughts, urges, and behaviours cause the voyeur personal distress and interfere with his or her ability to function normally or that he or she acts on these urges (APA, 2000). It is important to note that an individual cannot be diagnosed with voyeurism simply by becoming aroused at the sight of a naked person he or she happens to view. A recent review of voyeurism revealed that being a voyeur is linked to being male, increased psychological problems, increased issues with drugs and alcohol, and a heightened overall level of sexual arousability (Långström & Seto, 2006).

Voyeurism is the most common illegal action relating to sexual acts (Långström, 2010). A study conducted with the general population in Sweden revealed that 8 percent of the sample reported previous acts of voyeurism (Långström & Seto, 2006; see the first Canadian Researcher Profile in this chapter on page 268 for more information about Dr. Seto). This apparently popular interest in viewing other people without their consent recently was explored in a study by Rye and Meaney (2009). They offered their university student participants the opportunity to watch an attractive person undress, and manipulated whether the participant was told that he or she would have a 0, 10, or 25 percent chance of being caught. They discovered that many of their participants (more males than females) were willing to engage in voyeurism if there was no chance of being caught in the act.

While most people envision voyeurs as individuals lurking outside others' bedroom windows at night, the advent of technology has increased the means of voyeurs to secretly observe other individuals. Specifically, there has been an increase in the popularity of installing microscopic cameras in public areas to capture footage of others (Bell, Hemmens, & Steiner, 2007; Metzl, 2004). An example of this is attaching a camera to one's shoe to capture video or pictures up women's skirts in public places. Another example is hiding cameras in public washroom stalls to watch women as they use the bathroom. It was only in 2005 that voyeurism was included in the Criminal Code of Canada. The criteria in the Code encompass the act of direct voyeurism as well as the recording (whether it be video or photographs) of individuals for a sexual purpose.

The research on voyeurs is limited. It is recognized that most voyeurs begin their activities before the age of 15 years (Abel & Rouleau, 1990). Although most voyeurs are not violent, some do go on to perpetrate "hands-on" sex crimes (from about one in three to one in five; Abel & Rouleau, 1990; Freund, 1990) and some have co-morbid (co-occurring) paraphilias.

A highly publicized case of stalking for the purposes of voyeurism was that of ESPN sportscaster and TV personality Erin Andrews. Andrews, currently the host of College Gameday and a correspondent for *Good Morning America*, caught the attention of Michael David Barrett. Barrett became obsessed with Andrews and admitted to stalking her for 18 months across three states. In 2008, Barrett followed Andrews to Tennessee where he removed the peephole from her hotel room door and recorded her undressing. He also captured footage of Andrews in Wisconsin, and then posted both of the videos online. These videos have since gone viral and provide any individual with access to the Internet the opportunity to peep on a naked Andrews. Barrett was arrested by the FBI soon after for interstate stalking and was given a two and a half year sentence.

Exhibitionists

Exhibitionism is characterized by becoming sexually aroused upon exposing one's genitals to a stranger (Långström, 2010). Like voyeurism, exhibitionism is a paraphilia that is included in the *DSM-IV-TR* with two criteria that need to be fulfilled for diagnosis: (1) that the **exhibitionist** experiences overwhelming thoughts, fantasies, urges, and behaviours about him- or herself to strangers for a period longer than six months; and (2) that these fantasies, thoughts, urges, and behaviours cause him or her personal distress and interferes with his or her ability to function normally or that he or she act on these urges (APA, 2000). There are many types of exhibitionism including "flashing" (the baring of breasts or genitals), mooning (the baring of the buttocks), streaking (running through a public place completely nude), and masturbating in public. Some consider telephone scatalogia (using foul or sexual language during a telephone call to an unknown individual or a known unwilling individual) a form of exhibitionism. Exhibitionism is strongly linked to a number of characteristics including being male, having more psychological problems, having a lower level of life satisfaction, having an increased degree of alcohol and drug use, and an increased level of masturbation and pornography viewing (Bader, Schoeneman-Morris, Scalora, & Casady, 2008; Långström & Seto, 2006). Individuals who engage in exhibitionism also are likely to engage in other unusual behaviours (Långström & Seto, 2006). Exhibitionism is the second most common law-breaking sexual behaviour. In the same study of the prevalence of paraphilias in the general Swedish population previously discussed, 3.1 percent of the sample reported exhibitionist acts. A study conducted by Canadian researchers with a sample of psychiatric inpatients revealed that 5.4 percent of the patients met the criteria for exhibitionism; the prevalence of this paraphilia was second only to voyeurism (8 percent) (Marsh et al., 2010). Exhibitionists have the highest rate of reoffending among sex offenders, with up to 57 percent of Canadian exhibitionists being arrested again after the original conviction (Marshall, Eccles, & Barbaree, 1991). Further, Canadian researchers have found that a substantial proportion of exhibitionists go on to perpetrate "hands-on" sex crimes (Firestone, Kingston, Wexler, & Bradford, 2006). As such, exhibitionism can be a "red flag" for future sexual violence.

Child Pornographers

While **child pornography** has been created and consumed for centuries, the advent of the Internet has helped the child pornography industry to expand exponentially (Cumming & McGrath, 2005). According to the Criminal Code of Canada, child pornography is defined as any visual representation—whether it be a photograph or video, audio recording, or written description—that depicts a person who is, or is made to appear,

under the age of 18 years old engaged in explicit sexual activity. There are many levels of offenders within the child pornography domain including those who only consume the pornography, those who create and consume child pornography, and those who consume pornography and molest children but do not abuse children to produce child pornography (Cumming & McGrath, 2005). Often these offenders will force their child victims to view images of child pornography during the offence (Langevin & Curnoe, 2004). Consumers of child pornography often masturbate while viewing the sexually explicit images of children.

A proportion of child pornographers are sexually attracted to children; that is, they are pedophiles (Seto, 2006). **Pedophilia**, a *DSM-IV-TR* paraphilia, is characterized by persistent fantasies, urges, thoughts, behaviours, and sexual desire for prepubescent children and a lack of sexual interest in other adults. Similar to the other paraphilias, to warrant a diagnosis of pedophilia the fantasies, thoughts, urges, and behaviours must cause the individual significant personal distress and interfere with his or her ability to function normally or he or she must act on these urges (APA, 2000; Seto & Hanson, 2011). There has been controversy about these latter requirements; O'Donohue (2010) suggested that attraction to children alone is diagnostic and that "subjective distress" is irrelevant. Canadian researchers Barbaree and Seto (1997) recommended that sexual behaviours involving children should suffice in the absence of the "distress" requirement. Pedophilia should not be confused with hebephilia, which is sexual interest in adolescents—youths who have not reached adulthood but do show signs of secondary sexual development (Seto, 2006).

Men are more likely to be pedophiles than women, and often do not have a sexual interest in other adults. Not surprisingly, pedophilia has been empirically linked to offending against children, and child molesters and child pornographers are often but not always pedophiles (Seto, 2006). A study by Seto, Cantor, and Blanchard (2006) with a Canadian sample revealed that child pornographers demonstrated greater sexual arousal to children than to other adults, and that consuming child pornography was more indicative of pedophilia than actually offending against a child.

A recent study in the United States revealed that the number of arrests made for child pornography doubled between the years 2000 and 2006 (Wolak et al., 2011). The majority of child pornographers arrested were white males, with a diverse socioeconomic background, and full-time employment (Wolak et al., 2011). Only a small number of the arrested child pornographers had been convicted of previous sexual offences. During the six-year period study there had been a shift in the type of pornography being consumed and the methods used to trade child porn. Specifically, the children in the videos were significantly younger in 2006 than those in the year 2000. Also, child pornographers were using more peer-to-peer networks to trade their child pornography collections (Wolak et al., 2011). The use of peer-to-peer networks makes the sharing of child pornography more covert and more difficult to track.

As with exhibitionists, a major concern is that child pornography users may go on to (or concurrently) commit "hands-on" offences against children. Seto and colleagues (2011) conducted meta-analyses and found that one in eight online offenders has an official contact sexual offence history prior to the time of his or her index offence. The researchers also found that about half of online offenders admit (self-report) that they have perpetrated contact (in-person) sexual offences. Additionally, even for those offenders who solely view child pornography, the images promote an increased need to meet the demand for novel sexual images. This demand causes an increase in the sexual abuse necessary to create new images of child pornography.

Internet Lurers

The Internet provides new opportunities for the sexual exploitation of both children and adults. As previously discussed, children may be abused in order to create images of child pornography, but there is another way that sexual offenders victimize children on the Internet, the act of "luring" (Babchisin, Hanson, & Hermann, 2010). **Internet lurers** contact children or adolescents online and **groom** them; that is, over time gain their trust, build a relationship with them, and sometimes introduce sexual content such as child pornography over the Internet, and then meet in person with the intent of engaging in sexual activity (Briggs, Simon, & Simonsen, 2010). A recent study revealed that online sex offenders follow the same basic stages of grooming as face-to-face sex offenders (Black, Woodworth, Hancock, & Wollis, 2012). There are two types of Internet lurers; a group that is driven to engage in sexual activity with the child or adolescent offline and those who are driven solely by fantasy and do not make plans

to physically victimize the target but attempt to engage in cybersex with him or her (Briggs et al., 2010). Within those that are driven to engage in real-life sexual activity with the child or adolescent, there is another typology: the traveller. Travellers are individuals who meet children or adolescents online, groom them, and then travel some distance to sexually abuse them.

As the prevalence of sex crimes perpetrated using the Internet increases exponentially (Wolak et al., 2011), more becomes known about these types of offenders. A number of characteristics of online sex offenders have been identified and they differ significantly from the common characteristics of other sex offenders. Child lurers often are white males, are less likely to be members of a racial minority, are younger, experienced less physical abuse as a child, and express higher rates of victim empathy than sex offenders who do not find their victims online (Babchisin et al., 2010). These offenders often have an increased level of sexual deviancy, but fewer cognitive distortions (Babchisin et al., 2010). Finally, these offenders may possess fewer and less severe criminogenic factors than offline-only offenders and are more likely to emotionally identify with children (Babchisin et al., 2010; Briggs et al., 2010). It is important to understand that these offenders have significantly different characteristics from offline offenders; it could be that the most commonly used risk assessments and sex offender treatment programs will not be effective with online offenders.

Frotteurs

Frotteurism is derived from the French word "frotter" meaning "to rub" (Guterman, Martin, & Rudes, 2011). This is descriptive of the behaviour involved in this sexual offence; a **frotteur** becomes sexually aroused by touching or rubbing against a nonconsenting individual (Långström, 2010). This behaviour also is considered to be a paraphilia and is included in the *DSM-IV-TR*, requiring that (1) the individual experiences overwhelming recurring thoughts, fantasies, urges, or behaviours about touching or rubbing up against a nonconsenting person for a period longer than six months; and (2) these fantasies, thoughts, urges, and behaviours cause them personal distress and interferes with his or her ability to function normally or that he or she acts on these urges. Frotteurism can involve groping, but simply groping another individual is not grounds for a diagnosis of this paraphilia.

Frotteurism often begins during adolescence and is much more common among males than females (Guterman et al., 2011; Långström, 2010). Like the other paraphilias, frotteurism often is comorbid with other paraphilias and psychological issues (Hydes & DeLamater, 2003). It is difficult to garner accurate prevalence rates of acts of frotteurism because victims often are too embarrassed to come forward and because it is common for the victims to not even know that they are being "frotteured". This is because frotteurs often seek out crowded public places, such as malls, to commit their sexually deviant acts. Another popular location for frotteurism is on public transportation in highly populated cities. Recently, the problem with frotteurism has become so serious that public transportation boards in Japan, Rio de Janeiro, and Mexico City have implemented female-only passenger cars so that female passengers can avoid being groped during their ride (Guterman et al., 2011). Closer to home, one of the first author's graduate student (Pamela Black, who helped prepare this chapter) recently was the victim of frotteurism in Paris. She was standing on the Champs D'Élysées watching a parade on France's national holiday, Bastille Day, when she felt what she thought was another bystander's camera rub up against her leg. This brushing of her leg lasted for a couple of minutes before she turned to ask the tourist to take a step back or move the camera. However, when she turned around she realized it was, in fact, not a camera brushing her leg but a man rubbing his body against her. Before she was able to react, the man walked off, leaving her with an unsettling feeling to say the least.

Child Molesters

Child molesting, or sexual abuse against a child, includes an array of sexual activities ranging from fondling of the genitals to oral, vaginal, or anal penetration (Christiansen & Thyer, 2003; Deering & Mellor, 2007; Wijkman et al., 2010). There are a number of ways to categorize **child molesters**, the most common being by victim type (familial versus nonfamilial) or sexual interests (situational versus preferential). The first way to categorize child molesters is quite intuitive, one intrafamilial group offends against child family members (children, nieces/nephews/cousins, etc.), while the other group offends against children outside the family (extrafamilial). The second type of classification focuses more on the sexual interests of the offender (Cumming & McGrath, 2005). Child molesters who are exclusively sexually interested in children would be considered preferential offenders, while those who are sexually interested in adults but offend against children because the opportunity presents itself are considered to be situational or opportunistic offenders (Porter et al., 2000).

Preferential offenders, those solely interested in sexual activity with children, versus adults are likely to prefer a specific gender, age, and body type. Situational offenders, those who are not specifically interested in children, may also take advantage of opportunities to offend against other vulnerable populations, including elderly or disabled people (Cumming & McGrath, 2005). Often, such offenders are psycho-pathic and their offending relates to thrill seeking or simple access to victims (Porter et al., 2000). The characteristics most often associated with child molesters will be discussed throughout the remainder of the chapter.

There are some known differences between child molesters and rapists (discussed next). For example, in general, child molesters generally are more interested in sexual aspects of the offence (e.g., Malcolm, Andrews, & Quinsey, 1993), whereas rapists are more motivated by anger and the violence itself (e.g., Barbaree et al., 1994). Molesters generally are more socially inept and less assertive than rapists (e.g., Prentky & Knight, 1991). Rapists have more severe antisocial histories and are at a higher rate of violent recidivism than molesters (e.g., Quinsey, Rice, & Harris, 1995).

Rapists

Rape is the penetrative sexual assault (most often specified to be vaginal penetration but any kind of penetrative offence) of nonconsenting victims at least 16 years of age (individuals under the age of 16 years can be raped, but it is considered to be "child rape," which is often studied separately from the rape of adults). Rape typically is a severe and violent type of sexual assault and the maximum sentence for aggravated sexual assault is life imprisonment (Criminal Code of Canada, 2011). As with most of the sexual offender types discussed, there also are a number of rapist typologies that have been created because not all rapists commit this sexual offence in the same way or for the same reason. There are differing views as to the number of categories there should be and the names used to describe the typologies. We will discuss the most common of **rapist** typologies, those of Hazelwood (1995) and rooted in the motivation for the assault, including power-reassurance rapists, power-assertive rapists, anger-retaliatory rapists, anger-excitement rapists, and opportunistic rapists. *Power-assurance rapists* often feel unsure of their own adequacy and masculinity, and use rape to reassure themselves that they are powerful. Power-assurance rapists use rape as a way to feel masculine and powerful. Sometimes they will apologize to the victim after the rape is over. The *power-assertive rapist* does not lack in confidence or feelings of inadequacy but instead sexually assaults women to feel dominant and powerful. He is likely to be quite macho in his attitude and often tears the clothing of the victim. *Anger-retaliatory rapists* dislike women in general and use sexual assault as a means to degrade and punish women for their perceived wrongdoings. Anger-retaliatory rapists are unlikely to plan their offences; they simply attack women when feeling angry. These offenders often use more force than necessary during the assault but leave after they have vented their anger. *The anger-excitement rapists* are similar to sadists in that they derive pleasure and sexual arousal from inflicting pain on their victims. Anger-excitement rapists become sexually excited by the fear demonstrated by the victim and often are extremely cruel to their victims. Finally, *opportunistic rapists* are individuals who sexually assault a victim during the execution of other crimes. These crimes are not premeditated and occur only because of opportunity. An example of this is an offender breaking into a home with the intent to burglarize and finding a woman alone, and then sexually assaulting her (Cumming & McGrath, 2005). (For a different set of rape typologies, see Beauregard, Proulx, Rossmo, Leclerc, & Allaire, 2007; and Beauregard, Rebocho, & Rossmo, 2010.)

The etiology of rape is controversial, although as you will learn later in the chapter, sexual offenders, and rapists in particular, often have a number of characteristics in common. It is possible that the combination of these risk factors predispose an individual to commit acts of sexual assault. But before we address these characteristics, it is important to examine the characteristics of a few more sex offender types.

FEMALE SEX OFFENDERS

While the majority of known perpetrators of childhood sexual abuse are male, females are known to sexually abuse children as well (Miccio-Fonseca, 2000; Vandiver & Teske, 2006; Wijkman, Bijleveld, & Hendriks, 2010). It is a widely held societal belief that females do not or rarely sexually offend against children (Bunting, 2007; Denov, 2003a, 2003b). Due to recent mounting evidence, it is known that this is false and one that may be harmful to the victims of female sexual abusers (Denov, 2003a). The true prevalence of female sexual offending is unknown for a number of reasons. One of the most pervasive reasons is that male victims of female perpetrators are less likely to report sexual offences in general, and it appears that children are even less likely to report being the victim of a sexually abusive female than a sexually abusive male (Denov, 2004). The individual may feel like he or she will not be taken seriously or not be believed (Bunting, 2007). A Canadian study revealed that claims of female-perpetrated sexual abuse are treated more ambivalently than claims about male-perpetrated sexual abuse (Denov, 2003a). Further, when claims are made by children against their female sexual abusers, these investigations rarely end in arrest (Denov, 2003a). Another possible explanation for the low rates of reporting female sexual abuse is that close to half of the victims of this type of abuse are the children of the perpetrators (Turner, 2008). These children may fear that they will lose their bond with their caregiver and cause problems within the family (a fear that sometimes is encouraged by the abuser). A final reason that an individual would be less likely to report being the victim of a female-perpetrated sex crime is because research has shown that when an adult woman sexually abuses an adolescent male, it is likely that the male will be blamed for the crime and the offending female will be considered to be a victim (Johansson-Love & Fremouw, 2006; Knoll, 2010). The explanation for this phenomenon is that the authorities and the public may believe that the young male is fortunate to have had a sexual experience with an experienced adult female (Bunting, 2007; Knoll, 2010).

As an example of the lack of knowledge available about female-perpetrated sex offences, Denov (2001) interviewed Canadian police officers and psychiatrists to examine their concept of the female sex offender. Both professional groups reacted with skepticism about the reality of a female sex offender. Further, both of these professional groups received minimal, if any, training about female sex offenders during their own extensive training process. A final result of the study was that both groups reinforced the belief that female sex offenders were not a threat, did not have malicious intent, and actually denied the claim that female sex offenders exist. They also blamed the victim for the abuse. It is obvious that Canadian professionals need more training in dealing with this type of offender, as well as with the victims of these offenders.

One of the biggest problems with the detection of female sex offending is the widespread cultural belief that females are by nature nurturing and caring individuals (Denov, 2003a, 2004; Frei, 2008; Kaplan & Green, 1995). This allows females to be more overtly affectionate with children, including behaviours such as touching and caressing. Females also are expected to take care of children, including dressing and bathing them (Denov, 2003a, 2004). Female sexual abuse situations often occur in a babysitting situation, mostly because this caring and nurturing role provides females with many opportunities to sexually abuse children (Vandiver, Dial, & Worley, 2008; Wijkman et al., 2010). In general, the public is much less suspicious of a female providing a child with obvious physical affection than a male displaying the same level of affection (Kaplan & Green, 1995). This creates an environment that allows females to perpetrate sexual abuse under the guise of being affectionate and reduces the ability for others to detect the inappropriate behaviour (Tewksbury, 2004). A second issue in relation to the detection of female sex offending is that female sex offenders appear to be highly heterogeneous, making it difficult to determine a female sex offender from her salient characteristics alone.

Although the literature on the typical age of the female sex offender varies, most agree that the average female sex offender is in her 20s or 30s (Denov, 2004; Kaplan & Green, 1995; Miccio-Fonseca, 2000; Vandiver et al., 2008; Wijkman et al., 2010). Although most convicted female sex offenders are between 20 years and 40 years of age, studies report a wide range of perpetrator ages, with the youngest being in her early teens and the oldest being in her late 70s (Johansson-Love & Fremouw, 2009). In relation to ethnicity, most studies reported a higher rate of Caucasian women than other ethnicities (Ferguson & Meehan, 2005), although African American women and other ethnicities were represented within the samples (Ferguson & Meehan, 2005). Although there was some variation in the results of the studies, most female sex offenders are married and more likely to have children than other offenders (Kaplan & Green, 1995).

Female sex offenders also share a number of other characteristics, including problems with mental illness, substance abuse, and being the victim of abuse themselves. The rates of mental illness among female sex offender vary by study (Davis, 2006; Hendriks & Bijleveld, 2006; Johansson-Love & Fremouw, 2009; Miccio-Fonseca, 2000; Turner, 2008). One of the most commonly reported psychological issues is alcohol and drug abuse (Denov, 2004; Hendriks & Bijleveld, 2006; Johansson-Love & Fremouw, 2009). Along with substance abuse, a number of studies also report that psychotic symptoms are present in a subset of female sex offenders (Johansson-Love & Fremouw, 2009). Wijkman and colleagues (2010) found that only 25 percent of their sample of female sex offenders from the Netherlands reported no problems with mental disorders, addictions, or abusive relationships. Similarly, a study conducted by Fazel et al. (2010) reported that female sex offenders were more likely than the general public to be diagnosed with psychosis and substance abuse disorders and more likely to be hospitalized for psychiatric issues. Female sex offenders may suffer from a number of undiagnosed mental issues as well, including low self-esteem, distorted cognitions, depression, and anxiety (Elliott et al., 2010). These mental issues may stem from being a victim of abuse themselves.

The most common characteristic reported by female sex offenders across studies is a self-reported history of being a victim of sexual, physical, and emotional abuse (Elliott et al., 2010; Johansson-Love & Fremouw, 2009). Elliott et al. (2010) reported that 67 percent of their female sex offender sample reported being the victim of some type of abuse. Similarly, Turner (2008) reported that 68 percent of her all-female sex offender sample reported being the victim of either sexual or physical abuse. One of the most prominent characteristics that differentiates female and male sex offenders is the inclusion of a co-offender during the commission of the abuse (Bunting, 2007; Lewis & Stanley, 2000; Nathan & Ward, 2002; Wijkman et al., 2010). Wijkman and colleagues (2010) reported that 63 percent of the female sex offenders in their sample reported committing the sexual abuse with another individual. This individual most often is male, and 75 percent of this subset of individuals who offend with a partner revealed that the partner was either their husband or someone with whom they were in a relationship. When the victims are not related to the female offender, it is common for the children to possess vulnerable personality traits such as low self-esteem and low assertiveness (Knoll, 2010). While there have been a number of proposed typologies (e.g., Vandiver and Kercher, 2004), the typology most often cited is that of Matthews, Matthews, and Speltz from 1989 (Elliott et al., 2010; Ferguson & Meehan, 2005; Hendriks & Bijleveld, 2006; Knoll, 2010; Wijkman, et al., 2010). They proposed three typologies of female sex offenders: the teacher-lover type, the intergenerational predisposed type, and the male-coerced type. They also proposed two sub-types: the exploration/exploitation subtype and the psychologically disturbed subtype (Matthews et al., 1989).

The **teacher-lover type** of female sex offender prototypically is a female teacher who offends against a male student (or a female student, depending on the sexual orientation of the female teacher) (Matthews et al., 1989). This offender believes that she and the student are in love, and that the abuse is a positive and educational experience for the child. She does not believe that she is committing a criminal act by engaging in sexual behaviours with her student. The females who fit the characteristics of this typology often were not sexually abused as children, but were emotionally and physically abused. It also is likely that the emotional and physical abuse continued into her adult relationships. The female teacher often feels that the younger male student is more understanding and more loving than adult males. She may also believe that she and the student are at the same emotional level, making the younger male more attractive and safer than adult

males. Females who fit the teacher-lover typology typically do not have a co-perpetrator (Matthews et al., 1989).

Recently, female teachers who have engaged in a sexual relationship with a student have garnered increased media attention (Knoll, 2010). In the 1990s, Mary Kay Letourneau, a 34-year-old school teacher who engaged in sexual behaviour with her then-13-year-old male student, Vili Fualaau, was convicted of sexually assaulting a child (see Box 11.1 for more information about Letourneau; Knoll, 2010). This particular case was followed by the media for years, and popularized the idea of the female teacher-lover typology. There have been numerous cases of such scenarios in Canada in recent years. For example, the BC College of Teachers barred a woman convicted of sexual exploitation involving a St. Thomas More Collegiate student from ever teaching again. The St. Thomas More teacher, who cannot be named due to a publication ban, pleaded guilty to one count of sexual exploitation and was sentenced in August 2009 to six months in jail and two years probation.

The second type of female sex offender, the **intergenerationally predisposed type**, is characterized as a woman who suffered extensive sexual, physical, and/or emotional abuse as a child (Matthews et al., 1989). This type of offender often works without a co-perpetrator and targets children opportunistically. Due to the opportunistic nature of these offences, the intergenerationally predisposed offender abuses both male and female children. This type of offender perpetuates the cycle of abuse.

BOX 11.1   **A CASE STUDY OF A FEMALE SEX OFFENDER: MARY KAY LETOURNEAU**

Mary Kay Letourneau was a 34-year-old mother of four when she became romantically involved with one of the students in her Grade 6 class. Letourneau and Vili Fualaau, her 13-year-old victim, were caught having sex by Letourneau's then husband, who reported them to the authorities. Letourneau pleaded guilty to two counts of child rape and was sentenced to six months in a county jail followed by three years of sex offender treatment as well as being prohibited from contacting Fualaau. During her six months in jail, Letourneau gave birth to Fualaau's daughter and not long after her release she and Fualaau were caught

engaging in intercourse in her car. Police searched the car upon her arrest, and discovered a large sum of money, baby clothes, and her passport. Letourneau was then sentenced to 7 and a half years in state prison for violating the terms of her probation. While in prison, she gave birth to her and Fualaau's second daughter. Letourneau was released at the end of her sentence in 2004 and was required to register as a Level 2 sex offender. Upon Letourneau's release from prison, Fualaau reversed the "no-contact order" that prohibited the two of them from seeing each other, and on May 20, 2005, they married.

The third typology of the female sex offender is the **male-coerced type** (Matthews et al., 1989). This female sex offender does not offend against children on her own, but partakes in the sexual abuse of children in the presence of a male co-offender. The male-coerced type is characterized as a co-dependent woman who often experienced sexual abuse herself during childhood and is now in a dysfunctional relationship with a male who abuses her. The female who is characteristic of this type holds strong traditional gender roles and believes that she must do what her partner wishes. She also fears abandonment and often partakes in the abuse to ensure that her partner does not leave her (Wijkman et al., 2010). Finally, with this type of female sexual offender, the male co-offender initiates the sexual abuse.

Since the original delineation of the three categories by Matthews and colleagues in 1989, research has revealed that there are a number of different circumstances that may be characteristic of the male-coerced type (Johansson-Love & Fremouw, 2006). As an example, the female who has a co-offender when sexually abusing children may not always be coerced (Johansson-Love & Fremouw, 2006). The female sex offender may willingly take part in the abuse, and even initiate the abuse herself (Nathan & Ward, 2002). Further, Johansson-Love and Fremouw (2006) propose that females who were originally forced to take part in the abuse may begin to willingly participate in the sexual abuse, and may even begin to offend on their own. A notorious Canadian example is Karla Homolka (described in Chapter 2), who was thought to have been coerced into raping and murdering two teenage girls by her husband Paul Bernardo, but who, in reality, engaged in her crimes in an active, independent manner, even in the absence of Bernardo. Thus, it is important to recognize that female offenders can be every bit as predatory as male offenders. A final form of the male-coerced type of female sex offending does not involve the female physically performing sexual acts with a child, but being aware that the male was abusing a child and not reporting the abuse to the authorities. The females may be coerced into watching the abuse or keeping the abuse a secret (Vandiver, 2003).

Matthews and colleagues (1989) also detailed two subtypes of female sex offenders: the exploration/exploitation subtype and the psychologically disturbed subtype. The exploration/exploitation subtype is characterized as a young female who does not have a history of sexual, physical, or emotional abuse. Further, this young female has experienced little or no sexual activity and may be curious about sex. This type of offence often occurs in babysitting situations. The psychologically disturbed subtype is characterized as a female who is severely psychologically disturbed at the time of the offence, and who has a long history of psychological problems. These women may be unaware of the consequences of their actions.

Although these three types and the two subtypes were developed in the early days of female sex offender research, they still are commonly used in the field (Johannson-Love & Fremouw, 2006). A study conducted by Ferguson and Meehan (2005) with 279 female sex offenders in Florida supported the use of the three sex offender types as well as the two subtypes. There are a wide range of treatment programs and methods for male sex offenders, but the same attention is not given to creating programs to rehabilitate female sex offenders (Nathan & Ward, 2001). A study conducted by Nathan and Ward (2001) revealed the most pertinent risk factors of recidivism for female sex offenders. They found that a history of self-harm prior to the abuse, the inability to properly express emotions, and experiencing feelings of rejection, rage, and despair were most likely to lead to sexual reoffending for all female sex offenders, regardless of typology. It is important to address these risks for recidivism during any female sex offender treatment program.

JUVENILE SEX OFFENDERS

Adolescents not only are often the victims of sexual offences, but also perpetrate these crimes, as the Kimberly Proctor case discussed more thoroughly in Chapter 13 demonstrates. Adolescence is the time when people begin to develop sexual interests. It also is at this time that deviant sexual interests may become apparent. While some may believe that teens are simply exploring their sexuality, recent reports reveal that juveniles actually commit a surprisingly high number of sexual offences, as high as 20 percent of all reported rapes and 50 percent of all reported sexual abuse in the United States (Sickmund, Snyder, & Poe-Yamagata, 1997). Juvenile offenders are most likely to offend against young females (Ryan, Miyoshi, Metzner, Krugman, & Fryer, 1996), but can offend in the same diverse ways as adult offenders.

A recent meta-analysis examining antisociality and sexual deviance among adolescents came to a number of interesting conclusions (McCann & Lussier, 2008). First, 53 percent of the juvenile sex offenders in the sample reoffended within five years following their release. It should be noted that of the juveniles who reoffended, most of them reoffended with nonsexual acts. Second, juvenile sex offenders are similar to adult sex offenders on a number of risk factors including criminal history and antisocial attitudes. Third, juvenile offenders share with adult offenders the risk factor that they themselves were likely the victims of sexual abuse (Ryan et al., 1996). *However, it is important to note that most victims of sexual abuse do not become offenders themselves.* Fortunately, recent research has revealed that juvenile sex offenders respond well to sex offender treatment programs, and cognitive-behavioural therapy (CBT)-based programs reduce the rate of reoffence among juvenile offenders (Walker, McGovern, Poey, & Otis, 2004).

SEXUAL MURDERERS

A **sexual homicide** is one that includes sexual activity before, during, or after the commission of the murder (e.g., Porter, Campbell, Birt, & Woodworth, 2003; Porter, Demetrioff, & ten Brinke, 2010). For example, in the Russell Williams case introduced at the beginning of this chapter, the former colonel and commander of CFB Trenton sexually assaulted, tortured, and murdered two women before being caught (see Box 11.2 for more information on the Williams case).

For more than a century, sexual homicide has been addressed in the psychiatric literature. Its first major study was undertaken by Krafft-Ebing (1898/1965) in his classic *Psychopathia Sexualis*, which discussed fatal and nonfatal sadism and referred to a sadistic homicide as "lust murder." He considered sadism to be the combination of lust and cruelty, during which the perpetrator achieved sexual pleasure from another person's physical suffering. According to Krafft-Ebing,

---

| BOX 11.2 | THE CASE OF COLONEL RUSSELL WILLIAMS |

Metroland Durham Region Media Group

On October 21, 2010, David Russell Williams was sentenced to two life sentences for first degree murder, two 10-year sentences for his other two sexual assaults, two more 10- year sentences for the forcible confinement convictions and 82 one-year sentences for his fetish-related paraphilia-related burglary to be served concurrently at Kingston Penitentiary (before it was announced in 2012 that it would be closing). These convictions stemmed from Williams' sexual crime spree

across southern Ontario that began with over 40 break and enters for the sole purpose of stealing women of all ages' underwear and lingerie (all of the stolen undergarments were later found neatly organized and catalogued in Williams' home). Williams progressed to sexual assault without penetration before raping and murdering Marie-France Comeau and Jessica Lloyd in their respective homes before being caught.

Williams, a colonel in the Canadian Forces and a decorated military pilot who had piloted flights for the likes of Queen Elizabeth II and the prime minister, confessed to all of his crimes after a 10-hour interrogation. Jim Smyth, a former member of the OPP's behavioural science unit, who conducted the interrogation, was praised for his outstanding work with Williams. The interrogation was recorded and aired on Canada's *The Fifth Estate* under the title "The Confession." Interested students can find the episode online using the following link http://www.cbc.ca/fifth/2010-2011/theconfession. Since his conviction, Williams has been discharged from the Forces and his uniform and medals destroyed (CBC News, 2010b; *Toronto Star*, 2010a, 2010b).

many individuals who had sadistic fantasies (even homicidal fantasies) refrained from acting upon such thoughts because of their moral beliefs, while others (whom we might refer to as "psychopathic") had no such ethical inhibitions. Despite the high level of clinical and investigative interest surrounding sexual homicide (e.g., Firestone, Bradford, Greenberg, & Larose, 1998; Meloy, 2000), there has been little empirical research on the crime. Because most official crime databases do not document the specific manner in which homicides are committed (e.g., Arrigo & Purcell, 2001), even the prevalence of sexual homicide is not clear. Estimates range from 1 percent of all homicides in the United States (Meloy, 2000) to 4 percent of homicides in Canada (Roberts & Grossman, 1993). However, because few researchers have had access to detailed descriptions of homicides, such estimates are likely to be conservative. For example, in a detailed examination of Canadian homicides, Porter et al. (2003) found that 30.4 percent had a sexual component.

The limited research on sexual homicide suggests that the crime is associated with factors that are unique from other sex crimes. A study conducted by Langevin (2003) at the University of Toronto compared sexual murderers to aggressive sex offenders, general sex offenders, and sadists, finding that sexual murderers were more likely to engage in criminal acts at a younger age, were disturbed as children, attended reform school, were more likely to be part of a gang, and their murders occurred when they were younger (30 percent before the age of 20 years). Sexual murderers also were more likely to exhibit antisocial behaviour during childhood such as fire setting, being cruel to animals, theft, and vandalism. Finally, this study revealed that sexual murderers were more likely to be diagnosed with paraphilias, and have a history of sexual offences including voyeurism, fetishism, transvestism, and gender identity issues. It is important to note that just because sexual murderers were more likely to exhibit paraphilias, not all individuals who engage in voyeurism, fetishism, or transvestism, or struggle with gender issues, will become sexual murderers. In a study of 38 Canadian sexual homicides, Porter et al. (2003) found that 84.7 percent of the

sexual murderers scored in the moderate to high range on the PCL-R (described in Chapter 13). Two thirds of victims were female strangers. Homicides by psychopathic offenders contained a much higher level of both gratuitous and sadistic violence than nonpsychopathic offenders. Most (82.4 percent) of the psychopaths exhibited some degree of sadistic behaviour in their homicides compared to 52.6 percent of the nonpsychopaths. This suggests that sexual homicides typically are committed by psychopathic offenders who engage in sadistic behaviour during the offences, likely a result of their thrill-seeking motivation (e.g., Porter, Demetrioff, & ten Brinke, 2010; Shaw & Porter, 2011).

PREDICTORS/CAUSES OF SEX OFFENDING

Now that we have discussed the various different types of sexual offenders, it is time to discuss the factors that contribute to an offender's decision to sexually offend. Please note that we used the word "decision" to emphasize that it is always the offender's choice to sexually offend. Regardless of the presence of any or all of the following factors, it is always the offender chooses to sexually victimize another human. This is despite an argument that some sexual offenders are fundamentally "impulsive"; we believe that everyone has the choice to commit or not commit a particular sexually motivated offence, or any kind of violent offence (see Woodworth & Porter, 2002). However, it should be noted that many sex offenders do possess similar traits that may "predispose" them to sexual offending, including cognitive distortions about their victims and crimes, deficits in empathy, antisocial attitudes, experiencing abuse themselves, and brain abnormalities.

Sexual offenders often have a profound lack of empathy for their victims (Buschman et al., 2008). A lack of empathy is characteristic of psychopathic traits, but Buschman and colleagues (2008) specify that most of these offenders do not actually have pervasive empathy deficits, but rather that this deficit specifically relates to their sexual abuse victims. A potential explanation is that these offenders possess cognitive distortions that prevent them from feeling empathy for their victims, not that the offenders have affective disturbances. Similar results were found in a meta-analysis to determine whether "cognitive and affective" empathy was related to sex offending (Jolliffe & Farrington, 2004). This study revealed that low cognitive empathy was much more strongly related to sexual offending than low affective empathy. This means that individuals with high affective empathy are much less likely to commit sex offences (Jolliffe & Farrington, 2004). In addition to a lack of empathy for the victim, sex offenders often use victim blaming in order to feel less guilty. **Victim blaming** occurs when the offender justifies his or her actions by believing that the victim acted or dressed seductively and was asking to be offended against (Muchoki, 2011).

Another type of cognitive distortion that often is employed by sex offenders is denial or minimization. This distortion is used to deny that the offender committed a crime or did anything wrong, and minimization may be used if the offender acknowl-edges that he or she committed a crime, but believes that the crime caused no harm to the victim. As will be discussed, denial and minimi-zation often are directly addressed in sex offender treatment programs (Langton et al., 2008). Research has revealed that few sex offenders who have completed sex offender treatment programs continue to completely deny that they committed a sexual offence, but that the majority of offenders continue to minimize the consequences of their actions to some degree (Langton et al., 2008).

Further, sex offenders may experience sexual problems or deviancy. This can be represented in a number of different ways, including paraphilias, intimacy deficits, emotional identification with children, and conflicts in interpersonal rela-tionships (Hanson & Morton-Bourgon, 2005). We earlier discussed a number of the paraphilias associated with sex offending including voyeurism, exhibitionism, frotteurism, and sadism. In relation to intimacy deficits and emotional identification with children, research has shown that many sex offenders lack heterosocial competence; that is, they lack the necessary skills to engage socially with the opposite sex, which in turn impairs their ability to function with peers (Dreznick, 2003). A meta-analysis evaluating the prevalence of heterosocial competence in sex offenders revealed that rapists had lower competence than non–sex offenders, and that child molesters has lower heterosocial competence than rapists, incarcerated non–sex offenders, and non–sex offenders (Dreznick, 2003). This lack of heterosocial competence may explain why these offenders have issues with intimacy, and why they feel more comfortable identifying emotionally with children. Further, it has been speculated that sex offenders suffer from "sexual addiction." Although still controversial, sexual addiction is the inability to control sexual desire and the persistence of sexual behaviours regardless of the consequences (Marshall & Marshall, 2006). Marshall and Marshall (2006) studied a Canadian sample of 80 incarcerated offenders (40 sex offenders and 40 non–sex offenders) to investigate whether sex offenders were more likely to be sex addicts. They found that sex offenders were three times more likely to be classified as sex addicts than their non–sex offender counterparts. Sex offenders were also more likely to report a preoccupation with sex and having been the victim of child sexual abuse (Marshall & Marshall, 2006).

Further, by no means an excuse (given that the vast majority of sexual abuse victims do not offend against others), it appears that many sexual offenders also have been the victim of abuse. A recent meta-analysis revealed that sex offenders were more likely to have experienced sexual abuse than non–sex offenders but there were no differences in rates of physical and emotional abuse (Jesperson, Lalumiere, & Seto, 2009). There also were some inter–sex offender differences. The first difference was that sex offenders who offended against other adults were less likely to have experienced sex abuse than sex offenders who offended against children and more likely to have been the victim of physical abuse (Jesperson et al., 2009). While these data support the cycle of abuse theory, it is important to understand that *most victims of abuse do not become sex offenders themselves.*

A meta-analysis revealed that the following risk factors are related to sex offending: a history of sexual abuse, possessing antisocial personality traits, difficulty with intimate relationships, experiencing harsh discipline as a child, and loneliness (Whitaker et al., 2008). This is supported by Marshall (2010), who reported that sex offenders suffer from attachment problems, intimacy deficits, and loneliness. Further, a number of studies reveal that rapists often are found to be more antisocial in general that child molesters (Looman & Marshall, 2001; Mills, Anderson, & Kroner, 2004).

There also is some support for the contention that sex offenders' brains may differ from those of non–sex offenders. In 2008, Langevin and Curnoe studied the brains of sex offenders to investigate whether such individuals have brain damage or abnormalities. Their study revealed that one third of their sample showed cognitive impairments, but that these impairments were not significantly different from the general population. They discovered that sex offenders in general were more likely to have learning disorders, low IQ, and endocrine abnormalities. Specifically, they discovered that sex offenders who had targeted adults had more alcohol issues and that those who had targeted children had more overall cognitive impairments. The search for the neuroscientific underpinnings of sexual violence will continue.

Sadism is a *DSM-IV-TR* paraphilia that is characteristic of people who become sexually aroused from the infliction of pain or humiliation on another human being (APA, 2000), as was diagnosed in the perpetrators of the Kimberly Proctor murder (see Chapter 13). Sadism can be diagnosed using the DSM criteria or phallometric measures (Kingston, Seto, Firestone, & Bradford, 2010). While sadism is a rare paraphilia, it is important to note that sadists often become sex offenders due to their compulsion to commit behaviour that is characteristic of sexual assault. Psychopathy also is related to committing sexual offences (see Chapter 13 for a more detailed discussion of psychopathy and sex crimes); Doren & Yates, 2007; Gretton, McBride, Hare, O'Shaughnessy, & Kumka, 2001). It is important to note that in relation to the commission of sex crimes, sadism and psychopathy are related but statistically different constructs (Mokros, Osterheider, Husker, & Nitschke, 2011).

RECIDIVISM

The determination of accurate rates of recidivism for sex offenders is difficult, perhaps even impossible, (Correctional Service Canada, 2009a). Nonetheless, while our society may value the principles of offender rehabilitation and conditional release over punishment, the problem of sexual violence is not easily resolved with treatment. Despite a debate over the actual rate of sexual offender recidivism, recent research suggests that sexual offenders in Canada—most of whom will receive some form of treatment—are at a high risk of reoffending upon release. For example, a recent study found that over a quarter (27 percent) of federally sentenced sexual offenders were convicted of a new sexual offence and the majority (59 percent) were convicted of a new nonsexual conviction) within 10 years of release (Olver & Wong, 2006). A well-cited meta-analysis by Hanson and Bussière (1998), comprising 61 samples, found that the recidivism rate of sex offenders within 4 to 5 years after release into the community was 13 percent for sexual offences and 36 percent for non-sexual offences. A meta-analysis conducted by McCann and Lussier (2008) reports that across 18 studies, the average rate of reoffence is 53 percent. Of this 53 percent, 60.9 percent reoffended nonviolently, 28.5 percent reoffended violently, and only 12.2 percent reoffended sex-ually. Similarly, a meta-analysis conducted a few years earlier revealed that the rate of sexual reof-fence for that sample of sexual offenders was 13.7 percent, and that the general rate of reoffence was 36.2 percent (Hanson & Morton-Bourgon, 2005). A third study comprised of a Canadian sample of male sex offenders (Lussier, Deslauriers-Varin, & Ratel, 2008). These men were all living in British Columbia when they were served with a recognizance order to stay away from children because they were considered to be high-risk sex offenders. These offenders were mostly Caucasian, although a substantial portion of offenders were Aboriginal people, and were close to their mid-40s. Of this sample, 30 percent of the men reoffended within nine months of release (Lussier et al., 2008).

There appear to be a number of factors associated with elevated risk for re-offending. A meta-analysis analyzing the characteristics of persistent offenders across 82 studies revealed that offenders who are likely to recidivate possess deviant sexual interests, an antisocial orientation (personality traits such as impulsivity, substance abuse, and a history of rule violation), intimacy deficits, negative family backgrounds, and internalization of psychological problems (Hanson & Morton-Bourgon, 2005). McCann and Lussier (2008) expanded on this list by including a history of criminal behaviour, having a male victim, offending against a stranger, and offending against a child or adult victim (as opposed to a peer). Many of these characteristics are similar to the factors that may predispose individuals to initiate sexual offending.

Some research suggests that a combination of psychopathic traits and sexual deviance may suggest a particularly dangerous kind of sex offender (see Porter et al., 2010). Olver and Wong (2006) found that offenders who scored high on a measure of sexual deviance had a higher rate of sexual recidivism than those who scored low. Although sexual deviance was a stronger predictor of sexual recidivism than psychopathy, the authors proposed that the presence of psychopathic traits (e.g., lack of empathy, callousness) interacted with sexual deviance to facilitate sexual reoffending. Other studies also have found that the combination of psychopathy and sexual deviance predicts sexual and/or violent recidivism (Harris et al., 2003; Rice & Harris, 1997) and to a lesser extent, general recidivism (Serin, Mailloux, & Malcolm, 2001); individuals with both of these characteristics are more likely to reoffend sooner and more often. Similar results have been found with adolescent sex offenders (e.g., Gretton, McBride, Hare, O'Shaughnessy, & Kumka, 2001), suggesting that the combination of psychopathy and deviant sexual preferences increases recidivism rates across the lifespan. With this understanding of the risk factors that lead to reoffending among sex offenders, it is possible to create risk assessments to determine a particular offender's risk for reoffence.

RISK ASSESSMENT

Risk assessments are conducted to determine the likelihood of an offender committing new offences, or "recidivating". Risk assessments are conducted at various times throughout the offender's contact with the justice system to help inform decisions about sentencing, the level of supervision required, institutional and program placement, treatment planning, recommendations for parole, restrictiveness of conditions once released into the community, and the length of time the offender should be supervised (Barbaree, Seto, Langton, & Peacock, 2001; Douglas & Reeves, 2010; Douglas & Skeem, 2005; see the Canadian Researcher Profile in Chapter 15 to learn more about Kevin Douglas).

Risk assessments are actuarial scales used to measure an offender's risk factors (see Skeem & Monohan, 2011). Risk factors are personal factors that put an individual at risk for reoffending. Hanson (1998) breaks down risk factors into three categories; (1) stable risk factors, (2) stable dynamic risk factors, and (3) acute dynamic risk factors. **Stable risk factors** are those factors that are historical and cannot change. An example is a history of childhood behavioural problems. The fact that the offender exhibited behavioural problems as a child cannot be changed. **Stable dynamic risk factors** are behavioural and personality traits that are constant over time but are able to be changed or readjusted. An example of a stable dynamic risk factor is an offender's sexual preference for victims; these preferences are stable over time but are amenable to change. **Acute dynamic risk factors** are factors that are able to change rapidly and are easily readjusted with intervention and treatment. An example of an acute dynamic risk factor is an offender's current mental state (e.g., his or her mood and emotional stability); this state can change rapidly.

The accuracy and reliability of risk assessments have greatly improved over the last 20 years (Abracen & Looman, 2005). One of the biggest shifts in risk assessment practices has been to the implementation and use of **actuarial risk assessments** vs. **clinical opinion.** Actuarial risk assessments are based on statistical models that determine an offender's risk of reoffence via how similar the offender is to other offenders for whom the risk of reoffence is known (Cumming & McGrath, 2005). Actuarial risk assessments commonly comprise both static and dynamic risk factors. The evaluator obtains data on several characteristics (the necessary characteristics vary depending on the risk assessment used). which are then weighted depending on their importance for prediction, and added together to get a total risk score. This risk score often is translated into a percentage for risk to reoffend, or is used to place the offender in a category of risk (low to high), and the risk to reoffend is determined based on the risk attributed to that category. Actuarial risk assessments are the most commonly used risk assessments for calculating a sex offender's risk of recidivism (Kingston, Yates, Firestone, Babchisin, & Bradford, 2008). There are four commonly used risk assessments to predict risk for recidivism among sex offenders: the Violence Risk Appraisal Guide, the Sex Offender Risk Appraisal Guide, the Rapid Risk Assessment for Sex Offence Recidivism, and the STATIC-99.

The Violence Risk Appraisal Guide (VRAG)

This is a 12-item actuarial risk assessment that assesses violent (both sexual and nonsexual behaviour) among adult men using static risk factors. Examples of the items included in the VRAG are the individual's history of alcohol problems, the age at which he committed the offence, his Psychopathy Checklist Score, and whether or not he victimized a female (Quinsey et al., 1998). Items are scored based on the answer provided, and each question is weighted for its predictive validity.

The Sex Offender Risk Appraisal Guide (SORAG)

The SORAG (see Box 11.3) is a 14-item actuarial risk assessment that is very similar to the VRAG. It assesses risk for violent recidivism (sexual and nonsexual) but should be used only with individuals who have a history of committing sexual crimes (Quinsey et al., 1998). The risk assessments are identical except for the addition of two items. The additional two items address the number of sexual offences committed by the offender in question, as well as his phallometric test results (Quinsey et al., 1998) (phallometric tests will be discussed later in this chapter). The SORAG and the VRAG are scored in the same manner.

The Rapid Risk Assessment for Sex Offence Recidivism (RRASOR)

This risk assessment comprises only four static items; prior sexual arrests, age, whether the offender has ever targeted male victims, and whether the victims were unrelated to the offender (Hanson, 1997). This risk assessment is valid only for predicting recidivism risk for adult males. The scores for this assessment are tabulated and fall into one of six categories. These categories represent the likelihood to reoffend within 5 to 10 years (Cumming & McGrath, 2005).

The STATIC-99

This assessment comprises 10 static items: the four items used in the RRASOR, and six additional items (Hanson & Thornton, 1999). Some of the additional items include whether the offender ever lived with an intimate partner, whether the offender had committed any previous contact sexual offences, and whether the offender had ever committed non-contact sexual offences (Hanson & Thornton, 1999). The STATIC-99 is scored in the same manner as the RRASOR; however, the tabulated scores can fall in to one of seven categories of risk

BOX 11.3   SCORING THE SORAG

1. Lived with both biological parents to age 16 (except for death of parent)
   (a) Score *no* if offender did not live continuously with both biological parents until age 16, except if one or both parents died. In case of parent death, score as for *yes*.
   (b) Yes = −2, No = +3

2. Elementary school maladjustment (up to and including Grade 8)
   (a) No problems = −1
   (b) Slight or moderate discipline or attendance problems = +2
   (c) Severe (i.e., frequent or serious) behavior or attendance problems (e.g., truancy or disruptive behavior that persisted over several years or resulted in expulsion) = +5

3. History of alcohol problems
   (a) Allot one point for each of the following: alcohol abuse in biological parent, teenage alcohol problem, adult alcohol problem, alcohol involved in a prior offense, alcohol involved in the index offense.
   (b) 0 points = −1, 1 or 2 points = 0, 3 points = +1, 4 or 5 points = +2

4. Marital status (at time of index offense)
   (a) Ever married (or lived common law in the same home for at least 6 months) = −2
   (b) Never married = +1

5. Criminal history score for convictions and charges for non-violent offenses prior to the index offense (from the Cormier-Lang system shown in Table A.1)
   (a) Score of 0 = −2
   (b) Score of 1 or 2 = 0
   (c) Score of 3 or above = +3

6. Criminal history score for convictions and charges for violent offenses prior to the index offense (from the Cormier-Lang system shown in Table B.1)
   (a) Score of 0 = −1
   (b) Score of 1 or 2 = 0
   (c) Score of 3 or above = +6

7. Number of convictions for previous sexual offenses (pertains to convictions for sexual offenses that occurred prior to the index offense)
   Count any offenses known to be sexual, including, for example, indecent exposure.
   (a) 0 = −1
   (b) 1 or 2 = +1
   (c) ≥ 3 = +5

8. History of sex offenses against girls under age 14 *only* (includes index offense; if offender was less than 5 years older than victim, always score +4)
   (a) Yes = 0, No = +4

9. Failure on prior conditional release (includes parole violation or revocation; breach of or failure to comply with recognizance or probation; bail violation; and any new charges, including the index offense, while on a conditional release)
   (a) No = 0, Yes = +3

10. Age at index offense (at most recent birthday)
    (a) ≥ 39 = −5
    (b) 34−38 = −2
    (c) 28−33 = -5
    (d) 27 = 0
    (e) ≤26 = +2

11. Meets DSM-III criteria for any personality disorder
    (a) No = −2, Yes = +3

12. Meets DSM-III criteria for schizophrenia
    (a) Yes = −3, No = +1

13. Phallometric test results
    (a) *All* indicate nondeviant sexual preferences = −1
    (b) *Any test* indicates deviant sexual preferences = +1

14. Hare Psychopathy Checklist – Revised score (PCL-R; Hare, 1991)
    (a) ≤4 = −5
    (b) 5−9 = −3
    (c) 10−14 = −1
    (d) 15−24 = 0
    (e) 25−34 = +4
    (f) ≥35 = +12

Note: Variables are listed in the order in which they are addressed in the final report. DSM-III — *Diagnostic and Statistical Manual of Mental Disorders* (3rd ed.; American Psychiatric Association, 1980).

(as opposed to the six available categories with the RRASOR). These categories are used to predict the risk of recidivism at 5-, 10-, and 15-year intervals.

The validity and reliability of all of these actuarial risk assessments have been thoroughly investigated. Results of these studies reveal that all these risk assessment tools have some validity with a sex offender sample (see Abracen & Looman, 2005; Kingston et al., 2008; Looman, 2006). A comparison of four risk assessments revealed that the VRAG, SORAG, STATIC-99, and RRASOR all reliably predicted general, violent, and sexual recidivism. The MnSOST-R (the Minnesota Sex Offender Screening Tool—Revised; another risk assessment used with sexual offenders) was shown to accurately predict violent recidivism but did not reliably predict sexual recidivism (Barbaree et al., 2001; Hanson & Morton-Bourgon, 2007; Rettenberger, Matthes, Boer, & Eher, 2010).

As has been previously discussed, actuarial risk assessment tools are the most common approach to predict risk for reoffence among sex offenders. They are popular because they are objectively scored and they produce probabilistic estimates of risk based on a statistical model (Barbaree et al., 2001; Kingston et al., 2008). However, it should be noted that evaluators use numerous other methods to determine the likelihood of the offender reoffending. Specifically, evaluators may use clinical prediction, intuition (Cumming & McGrath, 2005), or penile phallometry. Clinical prediction often is based on professional wisdom, training, and experience. The clinician will conduct a lengthy interview with the offender and, using the information gleaned from the interview, will subjectively determine whether the offender is at risk to reoffend after release from custody. Intuition, the evaluator's feeling or hunch, is also sometimes used to determine risk to reoffend. The issues with these methods are that they are completely subjective, they cannot be empirically tested, and they are unreliable (Barbaree et al., 2001; Skeem & Monahan, 2011; ten Brinke & Porter, 2010).

Penile phallometry measures blood flow to the penis with the use of a penile plethysmograph, which is" placed around the base of the penis placed around the base of the penis and detects erections and physical sexual arousal. Plethysmographs are used for both research and risk assessment (Clift, Rajlic, & Gretton, 2009; Tong, 2007). This method involves attaching the penile plethysmograph to the offender and then showing him various images, depending on what the evaluator is trying to measure. As an example, if the purpose of the assessment is to determine whether the offender is sexually aroused by children, pictures of nude children will be shown to the offender. The measure of tumescence, or the degree to which the penis is engorged with blood, will then be used to determine whether the offender is sexually aroused by the images. The plethysmograph also has been used to measure other deviant sexual interests. A study conducted by Lalumiere and Quinsey (1994) to investigate the response of rapists to "consent" cues used the penile plethysmograph to detect arousal. Participants, including rapists and non–sex offenders, had the penile plethysmograph attached and then were asked to view graphic violent and sexual images. The results of this study revealed that rapists responded with sexual arousal to the rape images and non–sex offenders responded more to the images of consensual sex. Although this study was correlational, it demonstrates the deviant sexual interests of rapists, as well as the utility of the penile plethysmograph. Interestingly, until recently, all juvenile sex offenders in British Columbia were required to undergo a plethysmograph exam upon arrest (CBC News, 2010a). The BC Minister of Children and Family Development abolished this intrusive practice in 2010 (CBC News, 2010a).

TREATMENTS

Most offenders in Canada have the opportunity to participate in sex offender treatment programs (Correctional Service Canada, 2009b). Such treatment programs are offered during incarceration as well as after release back into the community (Cumming & McGrath, 2005). The purpose of sex offender sex offender treatment programs is to prevent or reduce the likelihood of future sex crimes (Olver, Stockdale, & Wormith, 2011; see the second Canadian Researcher Profile in this chapter for more information about Olver). There are a number of different treatment programs for sex offenders including cognitive behavioural strategies, psychodynamic therapy, and medical/physical treatments.

Cognitive-Behavioural Therapy (CBT)

Cognitive-behavioural therapy (CBT) is the most commonly used form of treatment with sex

Mark Olver

Mark Olver was born and raised in Vancouver, British Columbia. He completed his B.A. (Honors) at Simon Fraser University in 1997 (supervisor, Dr. Stephen Hart), and continued his training in the clinical psychology program at the University of Saskatchewan (U of S), obtaining his Ph.D. in 2003 (supervisor, Dr. Stephen Wong). As part of his graduate training, Mark completed his predoctoral residency at the Department of Clinical Health Psychology, University of Manitoba, Faculty of Medicine. Mark subsequently completed his registration with the Saskatchewan College of Psychologists and worked as a full-time clinician in various forensic settings including the Saskatoon Health Region (Young Offender Team) and the Correctional Service of Canada (Regional Psychiatric Centre, Saskatoon, Saskatchewan, and Stony Mountain Institution, Winnipeg, Manitoba). In 2007, Mark was hired on as full-time faculty at the U of S, and is currently an associate professor in the clinical psychology program where he is active in research and clinical training.

Mark's research interests are varied and broadly encompass many topics germane to the assessment and treatment of offenders including therapeutic change in offenders, sexual deviance, psychopathy, young offenders, risk assessment and recidivism prediction, treatment attrition, treatment outcome evaluation, criminal attitudes, and training issues in clinical forensic psychology. A particularly prominent research focus has been the assessment and treatment of sexual offenders. Mark is a co-developer of the Violence Risk Scale-Sexual Offender version (VRS-SO; Wong, Olver, Nicholaichuk, & Gordon, 2003), a sex offender risk assessment and treatment planning tool designed to appraise risk for sexual violence, identify criminogenic needs to be targeted for sex offender treatment, and evaluate changes in risk on identified treatment needs (Olver, Wong, Nicholaichuk, & Gordon, 2007).

Mark's current research involves examining dynamic sexual violence risk with the VRS-SO; that is, specifically the measurement and evaluation of risk-related change among sex offenders as a function of treatment and the extent to which such changes are linked to reductions in sexual and violent recidivism. He is particularly interested in the implications this has for Andrews and Bonta's (2010) risk, need, and responsivity principles (defined later in the chapter) specifically that risk changes have the most substantive implications for reductions in postrelease recidivism among higher-risk (as opposed to lower-risk) offenders, even those who may have substantial psychopathic traits (see Olver & Wong, 2009, 2011).

During graduate school, Mark competed in varsity cross-country and track and field with the U of S Huskies. He continues to run (albeit a fair bit slower) and is an avid guitar player, with his favourite genres being classical guitar and heavy metal.

---

offenders (Cumming & McGrath, 2005). CBT is a talk-based psychotherapy that addresses cognitive distortions and beliefs as well as dysfunctional behaviour. During CBT, the sex offender is encouraged to confront the offence that he or she committed and the deleterious consequences for the victim(s) (Walker et al., 2004). Specifically, CBT with sex offenders addresses cognitive distortions, empathy, and the expe-rience of the victim of the sexual offence (Grady, Broderson, & Abramson, 2011; Langton et al., 2008). Traditionally, empathy was addressed by having the offender imagine him- or herself as the victim of the crime, to be able to understand the experience of victimization. There have been criticisms of this component of treatment, including that it is not possible to "induce" empathy in certain offenders such as psychopaths (Rice, Harris, & Cormier, 1992). Offenders undergoing CBT are provided with anger and stress management training, social skills training, problem-solving strategies, moral judgment training, and treatment for any substance abuse issues they may have (Walker et al., 2004). Finally, offenders are provided with relapse prevention training. During this training, the offender is taught the multiple factors that often lead to reoffending, and strategies to avoid reoffending. Finally, psychoeducation, education provided to the offender about his/her mental state and treatment options, may be included. A number of studies have investigated the effectiveness of CBT with sex offenders and discovered that CBT appears to be the most effective sex offender treatment program with both adult and juvenile offenders (Abracen & Looman, 2004; Grady et al., 2011; Walker et al., 2004).

In addition to general CBT practices, a study by Abracen and Looman (2005) revealed that delivering CBT in accordance with Andrews and Bonta's risk, needs, and responsivity principle (an assessment and treatment model for offenders that requires treatment providers to first assess the offender's risk for recidivism, followed by his or her criminogenic needs, and then target the specific issues using cognitive behavioural treatment specifically tailored to the offender) reduced the risk of reoffending relative to those who did not complete treatment. Further, a recent analysis of the National Sex Offender Program implemented across Canada reveals that a significant portion of the sex offenders who completed the program demonstrated reliable change and increased social functioning upon completion of the program (Nunes, Babchisin, & Cortoni, 2011). The National Sex Offender program, created by clinicians at Correctional Services Canada, is CBT based and addresses seven specific components including cognitive distortions, self-management, and deviant sexual fantasies (Nunes et al., 2011).

Biological Treatment

A number of different biological treatments are currently used to treat sexual offenders. One of the more extreme methods is chemical castration, the administration of pharmacological medication to reduce libido, sexual urges, and sexual arousal. Chemical castration should not be confused with physical castration, which is the removal of the testicles through a small incision in the skin. Chemical castration is achieved using medications such as cyproterone acetate and medroxyprogesterone acetate (Walker et al., 2004). Another chemical treatment is androgen deprivation therapy, a treatment often used for prostate cancer. Androgen deprivation therapy, or hormone therapy, reduces the levels of male hormones in the body, specifically testosterone (Rice & Harris, 2011). It is believed that reducing the hormones associated with sexual arousal will result in a significant reduction in sexually deviant thoughts and behaviors. At this time, there is a dearth of information about the use of androgen deprivation therapy with male sex offenders, and the long-term effects are not known (Rice & Harris, 2011). The use of chemical castration is legal in Canada, but this treatment can be implemented only if the offender voluntarily agrees to undergo this drastic intervention (Harrison, 2008). Another biological treatment is the use of stereotaxic neurosurgery, a procedure that makes a small lesion on the brain to reduce libido and sexual arousal. Although these treatment methods are used, results show that CBT is the most effective sex offender treatment method (Grady et al., 2011), and clinicians generally should use CBT as opposed to biological treatments

Evaluating Treatment Effects

"How effect are treatments with sex offenders?" It appears that the completion of a sex offender treatment program reduces the offender's risk to reoffend to some extent (Hanson et al., 2002; Larochelle, Diguer, Laverdiere, & Greenman, 2010). Results of a meta-analysis revealed that successful completion of a sex offender treatment program can reduce the rate of sexual reoffence by 40 percent (Hanson et al., 2002, an impressive number). A second meta-analysis obtained similar results; reporting that sex offender treatment programs reduced recidivism by 37 percent (Lösel & Schmucker, 2005). Unfortunately, many sex offenders do not complete their sex offender treatment programs; a recent meta-analysis revealed that between 15 to 86 percent of sex offenders did not complete their programs (Larochelle et al., 2010). Those individuals who did not complete the sex offender treatment programs are likely to possess a negative treatment attitude, have a lower level of education, have committed previous offences, and be at a high actuarial risk to reoffend before entering the program (Olver et al., 2011). Another study of the causes of attrition from sex offender treatment programs in Canada revealed that being single (never being married) and an elevated Factor 1 score (the emotional facet) on the PCL-R were related to noncompletion of sex offender treatment programs (Olver & Wong, 2011). A study focusing on the recidivism rates of individuals who refuse treatment altogether revealed that their risk for future crime is similar to that of individuals who drop out after beginning treatment (Hanson et al., 2002). This is a matter of public safety, as those sex offenders who do not complete treatment are at a higher risk to reoffend (Olver et al., 2011).

SEX OFFENDER REGISTRIES

A sex offender registry is a database that contains information about people convicted of sexual offences (Murphy, Federoff, & Martineau, 2009). The list is made up of adult offenders and juvenile offenders who were tried and convicted as adults, and those who were found NCRMD. Canada currently has two sex offender registries, the **Ontario Sex Offender Registry** (OSOR) and the **National Sex Offender Registry** (NSOR). The following section will take you through a brief history of the development and the reason for the two separate sex offender registries.

Unfortunately, this story begins quite tragically, as is often the case in the stories of newly created policies for offenders. In 1988, at the age of 11, Christopher Stephenson was abducted from a shopping mall in Brampton, Ontario (Murphy et al., 2009). His body was discovered a few days later badly beaten and sexually abused, and it was soon discovered that the crime was committed by a sex offender on parole at the time. Christopher's murder led to a series of events including a coroner's inquest and a recommendation from the coroner that Canada needed to find a more effective way to manage sex offenders. After it became apparent that the federal government was not going to implement a sex offender registry, the government of Ontario took matters into its own hands and developed "Christopher's Law," a law that required all sex offenders in Ontario to register with the OSOR (Murphy et al., 2009). The OSOR was launched on April 1, 2001.

Profiles on the OSOR database include a photograph of the offender's face; physical descriptors such as height, weight, and hair and eye colour; date of birth; known aliases; information about the offence itself; and the addresses for the offender's home, place of work, and any other place he or she frequents, such as a volunteer opportunity. Upon release from prison, sex offenders have 15 days to report to the police station to register on the OSOR. After their initial registration, they must return to the police station annually to update their sex offender profile. Those who do not comply with these demands are subject to a fine or being reincarcerated. The length of time that an individual will spend on the list depends on the length of his or her jail sentence (Murphy et al., 2009). The minimum length of time an individual can be on the list is 10 years, and the maximum amount of time is for the remainder of his or her life. If the offender commits more than one offence or receives a maximum prison sentence, he or she is required to remain on the list for life (Murphy et al., 2009).

The NSOR was established three and a half years later, and was launched on December 15, 2004 (www.rcmp-grc.ca, 2011). Sex offenders must register on the NSOR in accordance with the Sex Offender Information Registration Act (SOIRA). There are some differences between the NSOR and the OSOR. The NSOR is the responsibility of the RCMP, whereas the OSOR is the responsibility of the Ontario Provincial Police (OPP). Another difference is that all sex offenders residing in Ontario must register on the OSOR, whereas only those sex offenders ordered to by the judge must register on the NSOR (the prosecutor must fill out a form to request the offender be placed on the NSOR). Unlike the OSOR, individuals convicted of voyeurism or bestiality are eligible to be included in the NSOR, and the NSOR profiles include additional information including distinguishable marks such as scars or tattoos. Finally, the length of time that an individual can be on the NSOR differs from the OSOR; individuals can be placed on the list for 10 years, 20 years, or for the remainder of their lifetime, also based on sentence length.

Sex offender registries provide quick and easy access for police officers investigating sex crimes (Murphy et al., 2009), allowing police to effectively eliminate suspects or narrow the list of possible suspects. Officers are able to search the database using the offender's name, a geographic region where the crime took place, and characteristics of the crime itself (Murphy et al., 2009). Now, before you go to your smart phone to download the app that alerts you to the location of individuals registered on the sex offender registry, it is important to note that contrary to the model of sex offender registries in the United States, *the sex offender registry is not made available to the Canadian public.* This may be one of the reasons for the high level of compliance with registry rules that is seen among Canadian sex offenders (Cole & Petrunik, 2007).

SUMMARY

Sexual assault takes many forms, including contact and noncontact crimes. There also are many types of sexual offenders. Offenders are commonly classified by the type of sexual offence that they commit, and there are often a number of typologies (based on motivation and victim choice) within each sex offender type. The major sex offender types discussed in this chapter include voyeurs, exhibitionists, frotteurs, child pornographers, internet lurers, child molesters, and rapists. In addition to the sex offender types, female sex offenders and juvenile sex offenders also were examined Many female offenders are able to go mostly unnoticed for a number of reasons including low rates of victim reporting and cultural stereotypes that support the misguided belief that female sex offenders are simply loving mothers/guardians.

There has been much speculation about the possible causes of sexual offending. Research reveals that a combination of cognitive distortions, deficits in empathy, antisocial attitudes, and biological factors contribute to sexual offending. Further, there are factors that contribute to the likelihood of reoffending. These recidivism risk factors include a high score on the psychopathy checklist, having offended against male victims, and possessing deviant sexual interests. Based on these factors, risk assessments were created to measure the likelihood of sexual reoffending. Sexual reoffending is often predicted using actuarial risk assessments. There are a number of actuarial risk assessments for sexual recidivism available including the VRAG, the SORAG, the STATIC-99, and the RRASOR.

In addition to the advances in predicting recidivism, researchers have also developed more effective treatment programs for sexual offenders. The most common form of treatment for sexual offending is a cognitive behavioural therapy–based intervention, often focusing on helping the offender to feel empathy for his or her victims. Pharmacological treatments also have been used with sexual offenders in an attempt to reduce testosterone levels, and subsequently high levels of aggression and sexual arousal. Finally, to monitor sex offenders after treatment, Canada has two official sex offender registries, one solely for Ontario and the other nationwide. These registries are used to monitor the activities of sex offenders, as well as to help police narrow down a list of suspects as they investigate sex crimes.

KEY TERMS

actuarial risk assessment, p. 272

acute dynamic risk factors, p. 272

child molesters, p. 262

child pornography, p. 260

clinical opinion, p. 272

consent, p. 258

exhibitionist, p. 259

frotteurs, p. 261

grooming, p. 261

intergenerationally predisposed type, p. 265

Internet lurers, p. 261

male-coerced type, p. 266

National Sex Offender Registry (NSOR), p. 277

Ontario Sex Offender Registry (OSOR), p. 277

paraphilia, p. 259

pedophilia, p. 260

rapists, p. 262

sadism, p. 270

sexual assault, p. 257

sexual homicide, p. 267

stable dynamic risk factors, p. 272

stable risk factors, p. 271

teacher-lover type, p. 265

victim blaming, p. 269

voyeur, p. 259

SUGGESTED READINGS

Babchishin, K. M., Hanson, R., & Hermann, C. A. (2011). The characteristics of online sex offenders: A meta-analysis. *Sexual Abuse: Journal of Research and Treatment, 23(1),* 92–123.

This review article compares online sex offenders to offline sex offenders on a number of demographic and psychological variables. You will have to read this interesting article to learn about the differences between online and offline sex offenders.

Mokros, A., Osterheider, M., Hucker, S. J., & Nitschke, J. (2011). Psychopathy and sexual sadism. *Law and Human Behavior, 35(3),* 188–199.

In this fascinating study, Mokros et al. attempt to determine whether psychopathy and sexual sadism are two separate constructs by studying psychopathic and sadistic forensic patients. This is a great read for anyone interested in the difference between psychopathy and sexual sadism.

Saleh, F. M., Grudzinskas, A. J., Bradford, J. M., & Brodsky, D. J. (Eds.). (2009). *Sex offenders: Identification, risk assessment, treatment, and legal issues.* New York: Oxford University Press.

This book, written by experts in the field of sexual offending, discusses a number of relevant topics such as risk assessment and treatment. This book also touches on the assessment and treatment of special offenders, such as female sex offenders and juvenile sex offenders. This is a great read for both students and clinicians.

Seto, M. C. (2007). *Pedophilia and sexual offending against children: Theory, assessment, and intervention.* Washington, DC: American Psychological Association.

This book addresses a number of key concerns about sexual offending against children including how it can be detected and what can be done to stop it. The author goes on to discuss how research can be used to inform sex offender treatment practices. An interesting read for anyone interested in the etiology and treatment of child sex offenders.

WEBSITE

Female sex offender from Burnaby: **http://www.theprovince.com/news/Burnaby+teacher+convicted+offence+handed+lifetime+teaching/3734806/story.html**

The Psychology of Child and Adult Sexual Assault Victims

> *I remember his hands as he was choking me. I thought he was going to kill me. The whole event is just ingrained in my brain, I can remember it all so clearly.*
>
> —Research participant/sexual assault victim (cited in Porter and Peace, 2007, p. 440)

A "TYPICAL" SEXUAL ASSAULT CASE

A young woman—a Canadian university student—leaves a bar with a man whom she had met an hour and a half and two drinks earlier. After accompanying him to his apartment, the woman is forced to engage in oral and vaginal intercourse. Because she resists, she is threatened with violence unless she complies. After returning to her home, she finds it difficult to know whether she should call the police. (In a study of female undergraduate sexual assault victims, the most frequently reported barriers to reporting were "I handled it myself" and "I didn't think it was serious enough," as well as the shame associated with the victimization; Zinzow & Thompson, 2011.) She decides to call the police, and she is taken to a hospital. A laceration is found near the opening of her vagina, but no other bruises or marks are noted.

How likely is it that charges will result in this case? It seems to depend on a variety of factors. For example, the gender of the investigator seems to make a difference. While one might assume that female investigators would be more sympathetic to the complainant, Alderden and Ullman (2012) found that female detectives are considerably less likely than male detectives to arrest suspects in sexual assault cases even after controlling for the influence of other factors shown to predict arrest. Consider this hypothetical scenario: After the woman chooses to report her victimization to the police, they press charges against her alleged attacker (which are to be approved by the Crown prosecutor), and he refuses to plead guilty. A jury trial is held and he is found not guilty of aggravated sexual assault. Often, in such "he said, she said" cases the prosecution does not even occur, or, if it does, it results in a jury conclusion that there is insufficient evidence to convict the defendant (Porter, Campbell, Birt, & Woodworth, 2003a). In some cases (Bristow, 1984), a successful prosecution results from the testimony of an expert witness, showing, for example, that the complainant suffered from rape trauma syndrome. Another factor related to charge and guilt decisions is the emotion expressed by the complainant during testimony (see Ask & Landström, 2010; Bollingmo, Wessel, Eilertson, & Magnussen, 2008; Dahl et al., 2007). Klippenstine and Schuller (2012) gave participants one of four trial summaries in which the victim's emotional response was varied. They found that the victim's claim was given more credibility when she was portrayed as tearful/upset as opposed to calm/controlled. How accurate are jurors in evaluating the credibility of such sexual assault allegations? Peace, Porter, and Almon (2012) showed observers four truthful (substantiated) and four deceptive written allegations of sexual assault and found that observers essentially "flipped a coin" in deciding which were truthful. Other research shows that being highly motivated to decide on the sincerity of such allegations can, paradoxically, induce tunnel vision and impair credibility assessment.

The purpose of this chapter is to examine the relevant research and the different roles of the forensic psychologist in cases involving the charges of sexual assault of children and adults. The emphasis in this chapter is on two separate topics: first, the psychology of child sexual abuse victims and, second, the psychology of adult sexual abuse victims, including testimony about the effects of sexual assault, especially with regard to the admissibility of expert testimony by psychologists and the cross-examination of these witnesses. The nature of "rape trauma syndrome" is controversial, and forensic psychologists called to testify for the prosecution may be tempted to conclude on the basis of limited evidence that the complainant shows signs of the syndrome.

THE PSYCHOLOGY OF CHILD SEXUAL ASSAULT VICTIMS

The Emergence of Concern about Sexual Child Abuse

As reviewed in Chapter 11, the sexual abuse of children is a major problem in Canada and internationally (Amstadter et al., 2011). Definitive work in the 1990s by David Finkelhor and his colleagues established that approximately one in eight males and one in four females reports having been sexually victimized in childhood (e.g., Finkelhor, Hotaling, Lewis, & Smith, 1990). The 2001 *Canadian Incidence Study of Reported Child Abuse and Neglect* (Trocme et al., 2001) made the following conclusions about child abuse in Canada:

- Approximately 135 600 (22 per 1000 children) child maltreatment investigations were conducted in 1998. Forty-five percent of the reports were substantiated.
- Approximately 10 percent (more than 13 000) of these investigations involved sexual abuse allegations.
- Touching and fondling of the genitals were the most common form of substantiated child sexual abuse (68 percent). Attempted and completed intercourse together accounted for 35 percent of the cases.
- Overall, 93 percent of the alleged perpetrators were related to the children (usually parents).

Theo Fleury is an ex-NHL player who wrote a book about his experiences of sexual abuse at the hands of a former hockey coach.

More recent data reveals that, in 2009, there were close to 21 000 sexual assaults reported in Canada (Statistics Canada, 2009). The large majority of these assaults were "level 1" sexual assaults, defined as the least serious form of sexual assault in Canada. Further, in 2009, 26 000 cases of child sexual abuse were reported to Canadian police (Statistics Canada, 2009). While these numbers may seem high, it is important to note that only around *1 out of 10* sexual assaults is reported to police. Indeed, the recent exposure of systematic coverup of child sexual abuse in institutions such as Scouts Canada and the Catholic Church leaves little doubt that this crime is often unreported (CBC News, 2011a, 2011b). However, it should also be noted that the number of sexual assaults reported to police has been steadily declining since 1993 (when it peaked after 15 years of steady incline) (Finkelhor & Jones, 2006; Statistics Canada, 2009; Trocmé & Bala, 2005).

For the past few decades, society has been most concerned about non–family strangers sexually assaulting and/or killing their children, such as the 2003 murders of 10-year-old Holly Jones and 9-year-old Cecilia Zhang in Ontario. But such cases are very rare. The possibility that children may be sexually abused by their parents or caretakers was largely ignored and even denied in our society. Slowly, awareness of the problem has increased; first, as a result of parental claims of abuse by daycare providers and, soon thereafter, as a result of claims of victims and alleged victims. Sometimes these reports were made only when the alleged victim reached adulthood. Because of these reports, public concern has increased, motivating forensic psychologists to develop methods for evaluating abuse claims from children and for facilitating the adjustment of children who have been abused.

The Martensville and McMartin Cases

In the past 20 years, allegations have arisen about the sexual abuse of children while being cared for in daycare centres in Canada, the United States, and Europe. The Martensville case in Saskatchewan and the McMartin case in California serve to illustrate the complexities that can arise in evaluating such allegations.

The Martensville Case

In 1992 in Martensville, Saskatchewan, members of the Sterling family (Ron, Linda, and their 25-year-old son Travis, along with an unidentified female minor), and five other men were charged with 190 counts of physical and sexual abuse against two dozen children at their babysitting service. Several of the male defendants were police officers, and one was a prison deputy director. After a report of an infant's diaper rash, suspicions of child abuse arose, and interviews with more children at the service were conducted. Some of the allegations included oral and anal sex, a child being locked in a cage, and anal penetration with an axe handle. One child testified that he had witnessed Mrs. Sterling cut off a boy's nipple and eat it. During the interviews, children reported that they had been taken to "the devil's church" where they were forced to drink urine, consume feces, and submit to abuse. During and after the investigation, rumours of Satanism circulated throughout the community. All charges were dismissed but one.

The interview techniques used by investigators with the child complainants came under great criticism. The Saskatchewan Court of Appeal (*R. v. Sterling*, 1995, para. 277) noted that "the use of coercive or highly suggestive interrogation techniques can create a serious and significant risk that the interrogation will distort the child's recollection of events, thereby undermining the reliability of the statements and subsequent testimony concerning such events." In 1994, one of the accused police officers, John Popowich, launched a lawsuit against the government for malicious prosecution. The province fought back tenaciously with countersuits, but Popowich eventually received a $1.3 million settlement from the Saskatchewan government.

Another Saskatchewan case, remarkably similar to the Martensville case in many ways, surfaced around the same time. In 1991, 16 adults (several members of the Klassen family and others) were arrested and charged with over 70 counts of sexual assault, incest, and gross indecency. The reports made by three foster children against these adults included child–adult orgies, baby sacrifices, ritual abuse, and bestiality. Eventually, the children who made most of the allegations of sexual and physical abuse recanted all of their allegations (saying that they made up the stories in response to interviewers' demands) and these recantations were publicized in the media.

The McMartin Case

On August 12, 1983, the mother of a two-and-half-year-old boy called the local police to tell them that she believed that her child had been molested by a teacher, Raymond Buckey. (Buckey also was the grandson of the school's 82-year-old founder, Virginia McMartin.) According to the child's mother, the child reported that he was forced to drink blood, he witnessed the head of a live baby being chopped off, and that "Mr. Ray" was able to fly.

Shortly thereafter, the Manhattan Beach, California, police sent a letter to 200 parents, asking whether their children had reported any incidents of molestation at the school. The letter indicated that the police investigation had discovered possible criminal acts including oral sex, sodomy, and fondling of genitals. Raymond Buckey was even named in the letter as a prime suspect.

As you would expect, the receipt of the letter created panic in many of the parents; many sent their children for assessment to a social service agency under contract with the prosecutor's office, the Children's Institute International (CII). Of the 400 children interviewed by CII staff, at least 350 were judged to have been abused. A grand jury subsequently indicted Raymond Buckey, his mother (Peggy McMartin Buckey), and five other teachers on charges of sexually abusing children. In June 1984 (almost a year after the initial charges) a preliminary hearing was initiated; it lasted an incredible 17 months. After another year-long delay, charges against five of the teachers were dropped, but in April 1987 jury selection was begun for the trial of Raymond Buckey and his mother (*People v. Raymond Buckey et al.*, 1990).

The jury reached its verdicts in January 1990, after the longest criminal trial in U.S. history. The Buckeys were acquitted on 52 of the counts, and the jury was deadlocked on 13 other counts against Raymond Buckey. Five months later, the state began a second trial against Raymond Buckey on those 13 counts. Mercifully, this second trial was a shorter one, and in July 1990 the second jury announced its verdicts: not guilty on all counts. An investigation that began with a single complaint in July 1983 was resolved almost seven years later.

Although this type of daycare case receives widespread publicity, there is a second type of charge that is far more frequent: the claim that a child has been sexually abused by a parent, another member of the family, or a family friend. What can forensic psychologists provide in the way of expertise in understanding both types of claims?

ROLES FOR PSYCHOLOGISTS

This section describes several roles for forensic psychologists in research and practice relating to child sexual abuse. Each role is introduced in this section and then described in detail in the remaining sections of this chapter.

Evaluating the Child

Sometimes, in the midst of a contested child custody case, one of the child's parents may claim that the other parent abused the child (e.g., Black, Schweitzer, & Varghese, 2011), which in some cases clearly is a false allegation (e.g., Neoh & Mellor, 2009). Or, as in many daycare cases, a parent may tell authorities of abuse at school reported by his or her child. Evaluating claims, whatever their source, is an exceedingly difficult task (see Bruck, Ceci, & Hembrooke, 1998; Faller & Nelson-Gardell, 2010; Neoh & Mellor, 2009; Yuille, 1988). No one feels comfortable discussing acts that invaded his or her privacy, and some young children may be limited in their ability to communicate what happened. However, if carefully interviewed, children are as capable of providing accurate accounts as are adults (e.g., Goodman & Melinder, 2007; Lamb et al., 2009; Yuille, 1988; Yuille, Marxsen, & Cooper, 1999). Psychologists should keep in mind that there are a number of factors, including being abused by a family member, being abused at a very young age, and being victimized numerous times, that may make the child less inclined to divulge the abuse (Smith et al., 2000).

Investigators, psychologists, and social workers use various approaches to assess the presence of abuse. Some of these approaches, such as the Step-Wise Interview technique developed by John Yuille and colleagues (Memon, Meissner, & Fraser, 2010; Yuille et al., 1993), have much validity in this context, as we discussed in Chapter 7. Other common approaches, such as the use of **anatomically detailed dolls,** are much more questionable (see Bruck, Ceci, & Francoeur, 2000; Ceci & Bruck, 1993; Lilienfeld & Landfield, 2008; Samra & Yuille, 1996).

Assessing Competency to Testify

Traditionally, it was assumed that children were not sufficiently competent witnesses to testify in court (see Ceci & Bruck, 1993; Goodman & Melinder, 2007). Based on British common law, it was believed that children could not distinguish fact from fantasy and were inherently unreliable. Beginning in the 1980s, new legislation in Canada (notably Bill C-15 and changes to the Canada Evidence Act) instituted progressive practices with child witnesses. For example, no longer was corroboration needed when a child made an allegation, and children could now provide evidence via closed-circuit television. As the Supreme Court of Canada noted in *R. v. W.(R.)* (1992):

First, the notion, found at common law and codified in legislation, that the evidence of children was inherently unreliable and therefore to be treated with special caution has been eliminated. Thus various provisions requiring that a child's evidence be corroborated have been repealed. Second, there is a new appreciation that it may be wrong to apply adult tests for credibility to the evidence of children. While the evidence of children is still subject to the same standard of proof as the evidence of adult witnesses in criminal cases, it should be approached not from the perspective of rigid stereotypes, but on a common sense basis. (summary para. 3)

Thus, at present, if a conclusion is made by police and the Crown prosecutor that sexual abuse likely did occur, and charges are laid, the child may be called upon to testify at the preliminary hearing and trial.

In Canada, before testifying, children under the age of 14 years are interviewed by the judge to determine whether they have the intelligence and moral capacity to give evidence. The law requires that a child witness must show that he or she understands the meaning of telling the truth, a lie, and an oath before being considered competent to testify. However, some researchers have criticized these requirements, because of the difficulty many child witnesses experience with them in court (Bala, Lee, Lindsay, & Talwar, 2001; Park & Renner, 1998). Queen's University researcher Nicholas Bala and his colleagues (2001) found that many complex moral and social issues are raised with children during this process, and that the questions are often abstract and beyond their cognitive abilities.

Preparing the Child to Testify

Some children face testifying—especially about abuse—with trepidation. (Other children may find that testifying is a source of catharsis or

Heather Price

Dr. Heather Price became interested in forensic psychology as an undergraduate at the University of Victoria when she was introduced to the study of eyewitness testimony. After completing her undergraduate degree, she entered Simon Fraser University's Psychology and Law program where she finished her Master's and Ph.D. She then undertook concurrent postdoctoral fellowships at the University of North Carolina at Chapel Hill and Wilfrid Laurier University before accepting her current position at the University of Regina in 2007.

Her research interests are generally focused on children as victims and witnesses. She conducts basic experimental research on children's memory and applied research on investigative interviews of children and evaluating children's credibility as witnesses. Dr. Price enjoys collaborating with colleagues around the world and has been very fortunate to have enthusiastic and talented graduate students who are also passionate about research. Dr. Price is currently working on several basic experimental projects on children's memory in an effort to better understand what children are capable of remembering about their autobiographical experiences and, by extension, abusive experiences. From an applied perspective, Dr. Price is currently investigating perceptions of children's credibility as alibi witnesses and how pre-interview biasing information can influence an interviewer's question selection, and is continuing work on understanding how judges make decisions in cases of alleged child sexual abuse.

Dr. Price also contributes to training programs for police officers and social workers in which she is able to present findings and offer recommendations from research related to investigative interviews of children. She thoroughly enjoys these teaching opportunities and the feedback she receives from those in the field. She often finds the questions raised by field investigators can lead to interesting lab work.

Dr. Price spends her free time on the floor at her children's gymnastics classes, dancing at her children's music classes, and splashing at her children's swimming lessons. As a family, she and her husband and children are particularly fond of exploring parks and lakes and collecting flowers and bugs.

vindication.) The Crown prosecutor may ask a psychologist to assist in making the apprehensive child as comfortable as possible. On a broader front, innovative procedures have been developed, such as closed-circuit television, to lessen the stress when a child testifies about sexual abuse. There are two types of closed-circuit television (CCTV): one-way CCTV and two-way CCTV. Using one-way CCTV involves allowing the victim to testify in a secure room with the judge, prosecutor, and defence attorney while the defendant and the jury watch from the courtroom. In one-way CCTV the victim cannot see the courtroom or the people in it (Landström & Granhag, 2010). Two-way CCTV, used more often in Australia, New Zealand, and the United Kingdom, also allows the victim to give testimony from a separate room. The difference is that the judge and the lawyers ask questions from the courtroom, and the victim can see the courtroom through a television monitor (Landström & Granhag, 2010). Psychologists can evaluate the strengths and limitations of these innovations, with regard to their stated goal of reducing trauma.

The importance of psychologists' involvement in the process of helping children prepare to act as witnesses is exemplified at The Centre for Children and Families in the Justice System formerly known as the **London Family Court Clinic** in Ontario (The Centre for Children and Families in the Justice System, 2011). This service is internationally renowned for its work with over 1000 child abuse victims and child witnesses. Staff members working at the clinic are experienced therapists who first conduct a thorough intake assessment focused on the child's particular situation, special needs, and concerns about testifying in court. In addition to the child interview, parents are interviewed and standardized psychometric tests are employed to evaluate the child's emotional functioning. Child witnesses then are given information about court procedures, taking an oath, and the meaning of various legal terms. The child witness is also trained in relaxation. The clinic states that there are two main goals for this type of court preparation with the child:

- To help the child witness provide a full and candid account of the experience (without compromising a defendant's right to a fair trial)
- To ensure that child witnesses are not traumatized further by the legal process itself.

This organization not only works directly with child victims and their families, but also publishes informational pamphlets and other resources to inform others about the issues that it deals with on a regular basis. In 2011, the centre published a guide entitled "Helping a Child be a Witness in Court: 101 Things to Know, Say, and Do" (Cunningham & Stevens, 2011). This is a great source of information for anyone dealing with child witnesses.

Testifying as an Expert Witness

Either the defence or prosecution could conceivably use a psychologist as an expert witness in a trial involving the sexual abuse of children. A Crown prosecutor could employ a psychologist to testify about research on the validity of children's memories in order to try to overcome the reluctance of many jurors to believe the testimony of children. The defence lawyer could use a psychologist to testify about the problems of eyewitness accuracy and the suggestibility of children. Each of these roles is described in subsequent sections of this chapter.

Assessing Allegations by a Child

Virtually any time parents report that they suspect their child was sexually abused by a teacher, relative, or other person, police will bring in psychologists or social workers to interview the child as part of the investigation.

Interviewing Techniques

The method used to interview a child is likely to have a significant influence on the responses the child gives (Sparling, Wilder, Kondash, Boyle, & Compton, 2011). One of the temptations in interviewing young children is the use of leading questions, or questions that assume a particular answer (as discussed in Chapter 7). The dilemma is that without the use of such questions, the child may be reluctant to respond at all, but the nature of the question may cause the child to answer in the suggested way, even if the answer does not reflect the child's real feelings or beliefs. On the other hand, the Step-Wise approach advocated by John Yuille offers a compromise, the initial use of completely nonleading questions, followed by progressively leading inquiries, but only as necessary.

The interviewing procedures used by the staff of Children's Institute International (CII) in the McMartin Preschool case have been criticized severely by several psychologists and social workers (Ceci & Bruck, 1995; Mason, 1991), and the availability of the transcripts of these interviews (thanks to the Department of Psychology at McGill University) has permitted the identification of specific problems. The following five procedures were identified as questionable by Wood, Garven, and their colleagues (Wood et al., 1997; Garven, Wood, Malpass, & Shaw, 1998).

1. *The use of suggestive questions.* This problem encompasses more than simply asking the child a set of leading questions. The technique of **suggestive questions** consists of "introducing new information into an interview when the child has not already provided that information in the same interview" (Garven et al., 1998, p. 348). For example, a CII interviewer asked a McMartin preschooler "Can you remember the naked pictures?" when no picture taking or nudity had been mentioned (quoted by Garven et al., 1998, p. 348). Suggestive questions reduce the accuracy level of children's reports (Ceci & Bruck, 1993); even the responses of adults are susceptible to being altered by such questions (Loftus, 1975).

2. *The implication of confirmation by other people.* The approach referred to by Wood et al. (1997) as the technique of "Other People" involves telling the child that the interviewer has already obtained information from another child or children regarding the topic at hand. For example, as one interview began, the CII staff member told the child that "every single kid" in a class picture had already talked to her about a "whole bunch of yucky secrets" from the school (quoted by Garven et al., 1998, p. 348). Such actions create conformity pressures in the respondent, as do similar police interrogation techniques, used with suspects and described in Chapter 7. As in the above example, the memory of adults as well as that of children can be substantially affected by the purported statements of another witness (Shaw, Garven, & Wood, 1997).

3. *Use of positive and negative consequences.* Wood et al. (1997) noted the frequent use of positive and negative reinforcement in the McMartin interviewing. The psychologists labelled the technique of giving or promising praise and other rewards as "Positive Consequences." For example, after a series of suggestive questions led to one child agreeing that a teacher had photographed some children while they were naked, the interviewer responded: "Can I pat you on the head … look at what a good help you can be. You're going to help all those little children because you're so smart" (quoted by Garven et al., 1998, p. 349). The technique called "Negative Consequences" reflected criticism of a statement by a child or a general indication that the child's statement was inadequate or disappointing. Garven and colleagues found striking examples in the transcripts. For example, one child denied any wrongdoing by the McMartin staff, and the interviewer's response was, "Are you going to be stupid, or are you going to be smart and help us here?" (quoted by Garven et al., 1998, p. 349). Although these psychologists noted that the effects of positive or negative reinforcement on children's accuracy have not been explored in forensic settings, wide acceptance exists for their general impact.

4. *Repetitious questioning.* Imagine if you were a child and the interviewer kept asking you a question you had unambiguously answered a few minutes before. Would this procedure cause you to change your answer? Wood and his colleagues called this the "Asked-and-Answered" procedure. Research generally has found that children will change their answers to repeated forced-choice questions but not to repeated open-ended questions; the interpretation is that children assume that their first answer to a forced-choice question was incorrect and so they change it to please the interviewer (Siegal, Waters, & Dinwiddy, 1988).

5. *Inviting speculation.* In the procedure that Wood et al. (1997) called "Inviting Speculation," the child was asked to "pretend" or "figure something out"; this technique was used by interviewers when other procedures had failed to produce confirmations of wrongdoing. (Again, it is remarkably similar to a technique used by police detectives with suspects, when they ask the suspects to role-play or answer a question such as, "Assume you did

kill her—how *would* you have done it?") In effect, this procedure lowered the threshold for producing incriminating statements that later could be "confirmed" by the use of some of the earlier-described procedures, especially positive reinforcement and repeated questioning.

Garven et al. (1998) investigated the impact of these techniques in a field experiment, using children ages three to six years. While at their daycare centre, the children had a visit from a storyteller; and were interviewed about it a week later. Even though the interview was brief (two to five minutes long), responses of many of the children were influenced by the use of reinforcement and social influence techniques. In fact, close to 60 percent of the children's responses reflected errors as a result of these interview techniques. Garven et al. concluded that techniques that effectively elicit false statements from children and adults "fall into four overlapping but distinguishable categories, represented by the acronym SIRR: (1) suggestive questions, (2) social influence, (3) reinforcement, and (4) removal from direct experience" (Garven et al., 1998, p. 355). The last of these refers to procedures such as "Inviting Speculation" (described above) and the interviewer's use of a puppet and a "pretend" instruction to question the child. The latter may provide the child an "escape hatch" when pressured to make false allegations; that is, the child can comply with the interviewer's insistence and still feel that he or she did not tell a lie.

In a classic study by Leichtman & Ceci (1995), the authors examined the memories of 176 children for a visit from a strange man named Sam. Three- to six-year-olds were interviewed on several occasions about the visit in one of the following conditions:

1. *Control*: no interviews contained suggestive questions.

2. *Stereotype*: participants were given information about the stranger before the visit.

3. *Suggestion*: interviews contained misleading suggestions about misdeeds committed by the man.

4. *Stereotype plus suggestion*: both pre- and post-visit manipulations were used with the child participants.

The authors found that 10 weeks later, control participants provided accurate reports, children exposed to the stereotypes gave a modest number of false reports, and misleading suggestions resulted in a substantial number of false reports. The children in the combined stereotype-plus-suggestion group provided very high levels of false reports.

The issues of children's understanding and memory of events, have been reviewed by several groups of psychologists (Goodman et al., 1999; Melton et al., 1995). Of special concern is the degree to which children are suggestible, because many judges and jurors assume that children are telling the truth when being questioned on the witness stand. The following conclusions seem appropriate:

1. Children are more susceptible to suggestion than adults, at least under some circumstances (Ceci & Bruck, 1993). However children are not as suggestible as many adults believe them to be, especially when questioned about salient events in their lives.
2. Qualities that lead to increased **suggestibility** in adults—a relatively weak memory to begin with, or a high-status interviewer—also lead to increased suggestibility in children (Ceci, Ross, & Toglia, 1987).
3. When initial memory is strong, age differences in suggestibility diminish or may not be a factor; even three-year-old children are quite capable of resisting false suggestions when their memory is solid (Goodman et al., 1999).

As mentioned, in optimal circumstances children can provide detailed, accurate accounts of their traumatic experiences. For example, Terr (1979) investigated the memories of 25 children, aged 5 to 14, who had been kidnapped on a school bus, driven around for 11 hours, and then buried underground in a tractor-trailer. After more than a day, part of the roof collapsed and the children dug their way to freedom. These children had intact and detailed memories of the incident after 13 months (Terr, 1979). In a follow-up study, Terr (1983) found that the children's memories for the event remained detailed four years later.

Nonetheless, while adults can certainly produce false memories when exposed to suggestive techniques and misleading information (e.g., Loftus, 2003a; Porter et al., 1999), young children are even more susceptible to such influences. As such, both investigators and counsellors must use nonleading interview techniques with children whenever possible. On a positive note, a series of studies conducted by Canadian researcher Heather Price (see earlier Canadian Researcher Profile box

on page 285) provides evidence that investigators can be effectively trained to properly interview child witnesses, and that there are a number of techniques to improve the investigator's child witness interviewing skills (Price & Roberts, 2011; Rischke, Roberts, & Price, 2011).

The Criterion-Based Content Analysis Technique

Often the purpose of the interview with a child who has alleged abuse appears to be encouraging the child to provide more information about the abuse, which some interviewers may already assume to have occurred. However, after an abuse allegation is reported, for other interviewers the credibility of the child complainant immediately comes into question. A study examining the credibility of abuse allegations revealed that children are deemed to be less credible than adults, although they were also rated as being more honest (Connolly, Price, & Gordon, 2010). We need to step back and acknowledge that allegations can be truthful or entirely manufactured (or something in between) (e.g., Yuille, Tymofievich, & Marxsen, 1995). For example, the Nova Scotia government awarded various sums of money to former residents of the Shelburne School for Boys after former residents made claims of sexual and physical abuse by staff. Many of these claims were later investigated as probable false allegations (see Porter et al., 2003a). In fact, it is possible for a child's account to be accurate, mistaken, or intentionally falsified. Do psychologists have procedures to distinguish between children's truthful statements and false ones?

Psychological researchers have attempted to find a way of discriminating true from false memories in the absence of corroboration (which is frequent in sexual abuse cases) (e.g., Blandón-Gitlin & Gerkins, 2010; Loftus & Pickrell, 1995; Marche, Brainerd, & Reyna, 2010; Otgaar et al., 2010; Payne, Neuschatz, Lampinen, & Lynn, 1997; Pezdek et al., 1997; Porter et al., 1999). Most of the literature has focused on adults recalling false events, sometimes from childhood. Pezdek and Taylor (2000) reviewed the literature and concluded that mistaken reports tend to contain less perceptual or sensory detail concerning the event, are described with more words, and tend to be held with less confidence. Porter et al. (1999) compared true and false childhood memory reports using a detailed coding procedure called the Memory Assessment Procedure (MAP). It was found that false memories tended to contain fewer details, were less coherent, and were recalled less confidently than true memories. A strong trend was also noted for false memories to be described from a "participant" perspective (own eyes), whereas most true reports were described from an "observer" perspective (like watching a video). However, true and false memories were similar on several content features, making them difficult to identify without a careful analysis. Collectively, these findings suggest that false memories may be distinguishable from true ones. However, as noted by Loftus (2003a), much more research is needed in this area before we apply these criteria in practice.

The **criterion-based content analysis technique** (CBCA) was developed as a clinical procedure in Germany to distinguish between children's truthful and fabricated allegations (Undeutsch, 1982, 1984, 1989; see Roma, Martini, Sabatello, Tatarelli, & Ferracuti, 2011; Vrij, 2001; Vrij, Granhag, & Porter, 2010b). The CBCA is one component of a more comprehensive procedure, called **statement validity assessment** (SVA), consisting of three parts: a structured interview with the child witness, the CBCA, and the application of the Statement Validity Checklist, which assesses other characteristics of the interview process, the witness, and the investigation (Raskin & Esplin, 1991). A description of these processes is as follows:

The structured interview portion consists of an extensive interview with the alleged child victim, without the use of leading questions. The purpose of this portion of the SVA is to create rapport and assess the child's cognitive, behavioral, and social skills. The second portion of the SVA consists of the CBCA. In this portion, a set of criteria is applied to the verbal content of the child's statement and used to provide an estimate of the statement's veracity. The presence of a criterion is an indication that the child is telling the truth. During this analysis, it may be important to consider the child's age, experience, and skill level when applying the criteria (e.g., younger children's verbal statements may contain less detail, which is one of the CBCA criteria) ...

The last portion of the SVA consists of applying the Statement Validity Checklist, which contains statement-related factors that assess the validity of several other characteristics related to the interview, the witness, and the investigation. These characteristics include, for instance, the child's psychological status and things about the interview that may have influenced the content. On the basis of the integration of the results of these three parts of the SVA, an overall evaluation is made of the statement's veracity. (Ruby & Brigham, 1997, p. 708)

A list of the criteria typically used is found in Box 12.1. The procedure has been used in more than 40 000 cases in Germany, where it is carried out by psychologists appointed as expert witnesses by the trial judge; it has been used in courts in the United States (Honts, 1994), and a version of statement analysis is currently used by the RCMP (RCMP, 2004). Some prominent psychologists, including Americans Charles Honts (1994) and David Raskin (Raskin & Esplin, 1991), and Canadian John Yuille (1988; Yuille, Marxsen, & Cooper, 1999), have encouraged its wider use, but two reviews of research on its validity, done by Steller and Koehnken (1989) and by Ruby and Brigham (1997), suggest the need for caution. The latter reviewers concluded that the technique "shows some promise in enabling raters to differentiate true from false statements" (Ruby & Brigham, 1997, p. 705) but that its validity still needs to be proven before it is applied to decisions about individual cases. A similar review conducted by Blandon-Gitlin, Pezdek, Rogers, and Brodie (2005) states that CBCA as a credibility assessment is of little utility to investigators (countered by the arguments of Roma et al., 2010; Vrij et al., 2010b).

There is some empirical evidence that certain CBCA criteria tend to be present more in truthful than untruthful accounts (e.g., Porter & ten Brinke, 2010; Vrij, 2008; Vrij, Akehurst, Soukara, & Bull, 2002). The results of a recent study testing the utility of CBCA showed that this credibility assessment tool was able to effectively differentiate between confirmed and unconfirmed cases of sexual abuse (Roma et al., 2011). However, there also is evidence that knowledge of the criteria can help liars, both children and adults, be more convincing in their stories. Vrij et al. (2002) had children of various ages and adult participants take part in a "rubbing the blackboard" event. In a subsequent interview, they either told the truth or lied about the experience. Some participants were taught about CBCA criteria prior to the interview while others were not. Overall, the CBCA scores discriminated between liars and truth-tellers in both children and adults. However, liars who were informed about CBCA got scores similar to those of truth-tellers.

University of British Columbia researchers David Marxsen, John Yuille, and Melissa Nisbet (1995) have suggested that 19 criteria are more likely to be found in truthful than untruthful statements. The first five below are considered essential; the remaining 14 add to the credibility of a sexual abuse allegation. They stated that "A common rule of thumb is that a credible statement must include the first 5 and any 2 of the remaining 14" (1995, p. 455). The criteria are the following:

1. Coherence: Does the statement make logical sense?
2. Spontaneous reproduction: Does the child's presentation of the account seem rigid and rehearsed, or is it reasonably natural?
3. Sufficient detail: Does the child give as much detail in discussing the abusive incident as he or she does in describing a nonabusive incident?
4. Contextual imbedding: Is the account embedded in a distinct spatial-temporal context?
5. Descriptions of interactions: Is there an account of interactions with other persons present during the event?
6. Reproduction of conversation: Is verbatim dialogue reported spontaneously?
7. Unexpected complications during the incident: Did an interruption or complication arise during the abuse?
8. Unusual details: Does the child spontaneously supply any details that would be considered unusual for a child to have made up?
9. Peripheral details: Does the child spontaneously include details peripheral to the abusive incident?
10. Accurate reported details misunderstood: Does the child spontaneously incorrectly describe a detail he or she misunderstood during the incident (e.g., saying that the abuser "peed white and sticky and that must have hurt 'cuz he groaned when it happened")?
11. Related external associations: Does the child spontaneously include something from outside the abusive event that is somehow connected to that event?
12. Accounts of subjective mental state: Does the child spontaneously describe his or her emotion and thought during the abusive event?
13. Attribution of perpetrator's mental state: Does the child spontaneously infer the abuser's emotion and thought during the abusive incident?
14. Spontaneous corrections: Does the child make any spontaneous corrections in his or her account?
15. Admitting lack of memory: Does the child spontaneously admit that he or she does not recall some details of the abusive event?
16. Raising doubts about one's own testimony: Does the child spontaneously express the unlikelihood of his or her own story?
17. Self-depreciation: Does the child spontaneously suggest that she may have some responsibility for the abuse taking place?
18. Pardoning the perpetrator: Does the child spontaneously attempt to excuse the abuser?
19. Details characteristic of the act: Does the child spontaneously describe the details of child sex abuse that may not be common knowledge? (Marxsen, Yuille, & Nisbet, 1995, p. 455)

Using Anatomically Detailed Dolls

In seeking to evaluate the reports of sexual abuse by children, psychologists and other mental health professionals have sought to use procedures beyond the usual interview, including the use of puppets, drawings, doll houses, and—especially—anatomically detailed dolls (sometimes called "anatomically correct dolls") (Conte, Sorenson, Fogarty, & Rosa, 1991; Hlavka et al., 2010; Samra & Yuille, 1996). Dolls were introduced in the late 1970s and eventually became "*the* assessment tool" (White, 1988, p. 472). They even received endorsement from the American Psychological Association's Council of Representatives to the effect that they "may be the best available practical solution" (Fox, 1991, p. 722) to the problem of validating allegations of abuse.

Anatomically detailed dolls include, typically, a mature male with a penis, scrotum, and pubic tresses; a mature female with developed breasts, a vagina, and pubic hair; a young male with a penis and scrotum but no pubic hair; and a young female with a vagina but without developed breasts and pubic hair (Skinner & Berry, 1993). Several companies have manufactured these dolls. The justification for the use of anatomically detailed dolls reflects not only a belief that they permit children to reveal aspects of abuse that they wouldn't reveal verbally, but also an assumption that sexually abused children will manifest "inappropriate" sexual behaviour when playing with such dolls—especially precocious play, that is, play that reflects an awareness that usually occurs only to older children—that is a result of abuse (Skinner & Berry, 1993, p. 401).

The research tests of this latter assumption have led to mixed results (e.g., Lilienfeld & Landfield, 2008; Skinner & Berry, 1993). On the one hand, the doll play of 25 nonabused children was found to differ from that of 25 sexually abused children; the latter were more likely to comment about specific sexual acts and demonstrate such acts (White, Strom, Santilli, & Halpin, 1986). Several studies indicated that the use of anatomically detailed dolls increased the reporting of genital contact when such contact had occurred. Gail Goodman and her colleagues (Goodman, Quas, Batterman-Faunce, Riddlesberger, & Kuhn, 1997) used the setting of a medical examination to determine whether three- to ten-year-olds who had been touched during the exam would indicate so when later questioned with the dolls. The researchers found that the children were more likely to disclose the touching with the dolls than when posed a free-response question. Another study that also used the setting of a medical examination found that use of the dolls increased reporting of touching of private parts but that some children who had not been touched reported that they had been when questioned with the dolls (Saywitz, Goodman, Nicholas, & Moan, 1991). Further, a study of two- to three-year-olds found that questions using the dolls did not generate more accurate responses than did questions that asked the children to demonstrate the touching on their own bodies (Bruck, Ceci, Francouer, & Renick, 1995). However, some comparisons of abused children and those who had not been abused found no differences in response to the dolls (Cohn, 1991; McIver, Wakefield, & Underwager, 1989).

A further limitation is demonstrated when the dolls are evaluated as a measuring instrument. The APA's Committee on Psychological Testing and Assessment has concluded that anatomically detailed dolls are "a psychological test and are subject to the standards [of test construction and validation] when used to assess individuals and make inferences about their behavior" (Landers, 1988, p. 25). How well does the doll procedure stack up psychometrically? Not well at all. For example, any valid test should be standardized; that is, the materials, testing conditions, instructions, and scoring procedures should remain constant. However, wide variation exists in the specific design of the dolls; as they became widely used, more than 15 firms began to manufacture and distribute them (White & Santilli, 1988). Furthermore, some psychologists use other dolls—genitally neutral dolls, such as Barbie dolls, or incompletely modified ones (e.g., Cabbage Patch dolls with breasts or a penis sewn on) (Skinner & Berry, 1993).

An additional problem is that no standardization exists in administration of the dolls—for example, whether to present them dressed or undressed, how to introduce them into the interview, and when to use them. No manual is available to provide scoring procedures. One study (Boat & Everson, 1988) found wide variation among examiners as to what was meant by particular types of responses (especially avoidance and anxiousness). It follows that no norms exist that permit psychologists to know the likelihood of certain types of responses.

Although a recent study argued that anatomically detailed dolls are beneficial as an investigative aid (Hlavka, Olinger, & Lashley, 2010) it should be clear that if anatomically detailed dolls are to be used at all, they should be used only with the greatest of caution (Everson & Boat, 1994). After reviewing a number of studies, Ceci and Bruck (1995) wrote:

Although the data, taken together, do not present persuasive evidence for the value of dolls in forensic and therapeutic settings, there are small pockets of data that would appear to provide some support for the validity of doll-centered interviews. ... However, we feel that these types of studies are not very relevant ... because these interviewing procedures bear little relationship to the procedures used in actual interviews with children suspected of sexual abuse. In the latter situation, children are rarely observed for over an hour in a free play situation, nor are these children merely asked to undress a doll and name its body parts. Rather, children are asked direct, leading, and misleading questions about abuse with the dolls, and they are often asked to reenact alleged abusive experiences. (p. 174)

Guidelines for the use of dolls include the following:

1. The dolls should not be used to make an initial diagnosis of abuse.
2. Mental health professionals who use the dolls should first be trained about proper interview techniques and the limitations of the procedure.

3. Investigators should be aware of the interpersonal factors, including the age of the child, his or her cultural background, and socioeconomic status, that can affect responses (Goodman et al., 1999; Koocher et al., 1995).

4. Videotaping interviews with the child and the administration of the doll technique has been suggested, so that independent fact finders can assess whether suggestive procedures were used.

Ultimately, anatomically detailed dolls are probably unnecessary as investigative aids, considering all the potential problems associated with their use, and since there are excellent interview techniques (such as the Step-Wise approach) available to ask children about their allegations.

Suggestions for Improving Child Interviewing Procedures

Each of the above procedures has been criticized, but what can be done to improve them? Excellent interviewing techniques that have not received the above criticisms are available (Poole, Bruck, & Pipe, 2011; Saywitz, Geiselman, & Bornstein, 1992; Saywitz & Snyder, 1996; Teoh & Lamb, 2011; Yuille, Hunter, & Harvey, 1990). Suggestions for an acceptable procedure have been offered by Saywitz and Dorado (1998):

Courtesy of Teach-a-Bodies, LLC <www.teach-a-bodies.com>

Although investigators often use anatomically detailed dolls in child sexual abuse investigations, the dolls may lead to responses from non-abused children that be misinterpreted as signs of abuse.

1. Interviewers must talk to children in language the children understand; thus the interviewer should listen to a sample of the child's speech to determine the language level. Subsequent questioning should reflect this language level.

2. Documentation is essential; if not taped, questions and answers should be recorded verbatim whenever possible. The CBCA categories *are* useful here, in judging the validity of the child's statements.

3. Questioning should begin with general open-ended questions. If a narrative results, interviewers can prompt children to elaborate, but highly leading questions should be avoided.

Children's Rights When Testifying

It can be argued that for any victim of sexual abuse or rape, whether an adult or a child, the experience of facing the alleged attacker in court is potentially stressful or even traumatic. The legal system, in recent years, has become increasingly concerned about the possible traumatic effects on children as witnesses in court. The trauma is compounded if opposing lawyers view children as especially susceptible to intimidation during cross-examination, and judges remain oblivious to efforts to "break down" the child on the witness stand. Some defence lawyers may use questions with complex grammatical structure in order to confuse the child; they may accuse the child of having been coached or use other "dirty tricks" to discredit the child. In the McMartin trial, one child who had been questioned for a half hour by the prosecutor was turned over to a defence lawyer for cross-examination, and then questioned for *15 and a half hours* by the defence. Although trial judges have great discretion to terminate or restrict cross-examination, this child was subjected to more than two days of questioning before being released from the witness box.

Do children possess any special rights to protection against these stresses? And if they do, can the defendant's rights to a fair trial still be preserved? Can psychologists who are advocates for children advise the courts about ways to preserve the child's self-esteem? In addressing these questions, many courts have instituted innovative procedures to protect children from undue traumatization. For example, courts have used child-sized witness chairs and even permitted children to testify while sitting on the floor (Walker, Brooks, & Wrightsman, 1998). Dolls or drawings have been allowed to supplement the child's oral testimony, screens have been introduced to shield the child from the defendant, and children have testified over closed-circuit television. Section 486 of the Criminal Code of Canada (2003) provides that a judge may permit a complainant under the age of 18 years to testify behind a screen if the judge is of the opinion that the use of a screen is "necessary to obtain a full and candid account of the acts complained of from the complainant."

PSYCHOLOGISTS AS EXPERT WITNESSES

In light of the recent publicity regarding numerous claims of sexual abuse—either within families or by child-care providers—the testimony of children probably does not receive the degree of skepticism it once did (Goodman, 1984). Yet publicity about such cases can vary; in the early 1980s a dominant theme was that children are victims, but more recent portrayals have once more cast doubt on the accuracy of memories, at least in cases of adults reporting recent awareness of abuses during their childhood (Berliner, 1998; Loftus, 2003a). Psychologists can play an important role as expert witnesses by being knowledge brokers in the courtroom and providing reviews of the scientific literature on topics of relevance (see Porter et al., 2003b). This is an important function, as potential jurors have been found to disagree significantly with psychological research findings on many items in a questionnaire designed to determine knowledge about sexual abuse (Morison & Greene, 1992). These include the greater tendency for jurors to assume that children generally tell the truth, can separate fact from fantasy, and avoid suggestions to answer as expected.

Testimony for the Prosecution

Berliner (1998) has identified several types of testimony by psychologists as expert witnesses in sexual abuse cases.

Social Frameworks Testimony

Social frameworks testimony is the "use of general conclusions from social science research in determining factual issues in a specific case" (Walker & Monahan, 1987, p. 570). (Such testimony also can be given in other types of cases covered in other chapters of this book, including rape

trauma and battered woman syndrome.) This type of testimony provides a context for evaluating the evidence in the case; it can "tell jurors something they do not already know or disabuse them of common but erroneous misconceptions" (Walker & Monahan, 1987, p. 583). Examples suggested by Berliner (1998) included the nature of sexual abuse of children, the reactions of victims, and the memory abilities and suggestibility of children. A law review article by Myers and his colleagues expanded on these issues (Myers et al., 1989). Courts have accepted as admissible this type of testimony in the interest of educating jurors or correcting misapprehensions.

Testimony about Similarities between the Child Witness and Sexually Abused Children

As Berliner noted, "Although the expert may rely on general social science knowledge, the opinion is specifically linked to the child witness" (1998, pp. 13–14). Here things get more questionable, as the following indicates.

Margaret Kelly Michaels was charged in June 1985 with sexually abusing 20 children at the Wee Care daycare centre in Maplewood, New Jersey, where she had worked, first as a teacher's aide and then as a teacher of a pre-kindergarten class. At her trial, several children testified to the following:

... having blades of knives inserted into their rectums, vaginas, and penises. Children also reported having had sticks and wooden spoons inserted into their various orifices. One child said that Michaels put a light bulb in her vagina. Others told of the tine end of forks being inserted into their vaginas while the back end of the silverware was inserted into their rectums. (Rosenthal, 1995, p. 252)

As part of the prosecution's case, Eileen Treacy, an expert witness described as an authority in child psychology and the treatment of sexually abused children, testified, despite objections by the defence. Treacy's letterhead stated that she provided "psychological and consultation services," but she did not have a doctoral degree and was not licensed to practise psychology (Rosenthal, 1995). She testified about an elaboration of **child sexual abuse accommodation syndrome**, which included five phases, or characteristics common to many situations of abuse—engagement, sexual interaction, secrecy, disclosure, and suppression.

She told the jury that if those five characteristics could be identified in cases in which abuse was suspected, the abuse had in fact occurred (Rosenthal, 1995). She based her testimony on her interviews with 18 of the Wee Care children and a checklist of 32 "behavioural symptoms" for each child. She told the jury that the existence of 5 to 15 of her indicators established the existence of sexual abuse. When she was asked by Michaels's defence lawyer how she had arrived at the "5 to 15" figure, the trial judge refused to allow the question (Rosenthal, 1995).

For Treacy the behavioural symptoms were evidence for the presence of the five phases of child sexual abuse accommodation syndrome; for example:

[W]here children denied that abuse occurred, Treacy instructed the jury that the denials were exhibitions of the "suppression phase." In fact, she found that all 19 of the children who testified at trial exhibited the suppression phase as well as the other four "phases." That the children initially told investigators and their parents that they liked Michaels, Treacy said, was evidence of the "engagement phase," during which the abuser ingratiates herself with the children. Statements elicited from the children regarding the alleged pile-up games and sexual contact between Michaels and the children were evidence of a "sexual interaction" phase. The "secrecy phase," she testified, was found in the absence of complaints or indications of abuse at Wee Care until the interviews with the children began. And, the statements elicited from the children during and about the interviews constituted the exhibition of the "disclosure phase." Treacy testified that, on the basis of her theories, every child's denials, recantations, and unresponsive answers were proof of victimization. (Rosenthal, 1995, pp. 259–260)

Treacy concluded that in all the children but one, the indicators were "consistent with" having been sexually abused. Although she acknowledged that other factors in children's lives could have caused some of the behavioural symptoms—for example, birth of new siblings, severe illness of family members, a turbulent relationship between parents—she was able to conduct a "confounding variable analysis," the results of which led her to conclude that for all but one of the children, these "confounding variables" could not have been responsible for the appearance of the "behavioural indicators."

Although Kelly Michaels was found guilty of 155 counts of sexually abusing these children and sentenced to 47 years in prison, her conviction was later negated by a New Jersey appellate court, which ruled that the expert went beyond acceptable limits in leaving an impression with the jury that particular children had been abused (*State v. Michaels,* 1993). After some delay, the district attorney decided not to retry Michaels, and she was released from custody. An *amicus curiae* brief by a group of social scientists played a role in the appeal of the conviction (see Box 12.2).

Is the type of testimony exemplified in this case effectively different from ultimate-opinion testimony? Psychologists Gary Melton and Susan Limber (1989) took the position that a psychologist testifying that a child has been abused is the same as testifying that the child is telling the truth. Similarly, the New Hampshire Supreme Court ruled that "We see no appreciable difference between [a statement that the children exhibited symptoms consistent with those of sexually abused children] and a statement that, in her opinion, the children were sexually abused" (*State v. Cressey,* 1993, p. 699).

Ultimate-Opinion Testimony

As in the case of determination of criminal responsibility, courts have generally been reluctant to admit **ultimate-opinion testimony** about the credibility of a particular witness—in this case, a child who has reported having been sexually abused. Still, Myers (1992) has distinguished between testifying on the ultimate legal issue (such as the guilt of the accused person) and on the ultimate factual issue (such as whether the child shows signs of abuse), which may be permitted. In *R. v. Marquard* (1993), the Canadian Supreme Court ruled that:

---

while expert evidence on the ultimate credibility of a witness is not admissible, expert evidence on human conduct and the psychological and physical factors which may lead to certain behaviour relevant to credibility, is admissible, provided the testimony goes beyond the ordinary experience of the trier of fact. This is particularly the case with evidence of children. (summary para. 11)

However, it remains very difficult for psychologists to assess whether sexual abuse took place; even physical evidence, such as a ruptured hymen, can

BOX 12.2 — THE *AMICUS CURIAE* BRIEF IN THE MICHAELS v. NEW JERSEY APPEAL

The conviction of Kelly Michaels was seen as an injustice by some journalists (Nathan, 1987; Rabinowitz, 1990) and by a number of social scientists. The journalists brought public attention to the case by publishing articles in widely read periodicals. The social scientists, led by Maggie Bruck and Stephen J. Ceci (1993), prepared an *amicus curiae* brief accompanying Michaels's appeal. The brief presented a summary of research findings on children's suggestibility and cited examples from interviews with the Wee Care children that increased the risk that the children's responses were more a function of suggestibility than reflective of accuracy. For instance, interviewers often began the interview with an assumption of guilt. Here are some other examples:

- "There's a couple of things I'd like to let you know before we start. Alright? That is, Kelly said a lot of things to scare kids and I think she might have said them to you, too."
- "All your friends that I told you about before were telling us that Kelly, the teacher we are talking about, was doing something they didn't like very much. She was bothering them in a kind of private way and they were all pretty brave and they told us everything, and we were wondering if you could help us out too, doing the same thing."
- "Some of your friends were hurt and they told us just about everything." (Bruck & Ceci, 1993, p. 284)

The procedures used by the interviewers in this investigation capitalized on intimidation and social influence, just as the ones in the McMartin case did.

---

occur in young girls through natural causes. No checklist of perfectly reliable indicators exists. In fact, a review of the literature found that no symptom was reported to be present in more than half of sexually abused children (Kendall-Tackett, Williams, & Finkelhor, 1993).

Testimony for the Defence

Most of the testimony by psychologists in child sexual abuse cases has been offered in support of the prosecution (Mason, 1998), but several aspects of such cases invite psychologists to be expert witnesses for the defence. Among these are the following:

1. An expert can testify about the suggestive nature of the questions in the interview, as illustrated in the description of types of questions asked by the Martensville interviewers. The expert could inform jurors about the influence of misleading information on the accuracy of a child's self-report (McAuliff & Kovera, 1998).
2. Psychologists can testify about research findings on the causes and extent of suggestibility in children and the sometimes-vulnerable nature of memory. In cases claiming repressed or recovered memory, a defence witness can testify about demonstrations of how false memories can be implanted in children and adults.

3. Psychologists can refute the testimony of prosecution witnesses, and, in particular, they can question whether the procedures used by prosecution experts meet the standards for admissibility of scientific testimony. For example, even the psychiatrist who first introduced child sexual abuse accommodation syndrome questioned its use to "prove a child was molested" (Summit, 1992, p. 160), and Treacy's use of "behavioural symptoms" and her procedure of doing a "confounding variable analysis" did not meet scientific standards of verifiability and validity.

GENERAL GUIDELINES FOR THE EVALUATION OF CREDIBILITY IN CHILD SEXUAL ABUSE CASES

Porter, Campbell, and colleagues (2003a) have provided a series of four major guidelines for the courts in evaluating the credibility of a complainant in a sexual abuse investigation. In general, they argue that psychologists can provide useful information about memory and the assessment of credibility that can help judges and juries interpret the evidence before them. Further, they argue that psychological or psychiatric testimony concerning memory for trauma would prove useful to inform legal decision making. They offer the following guidelines (for use with both children and adults):

1. The *context* in which the memory was recalled should be evaluated. Suggestive interviewing or other suggestive techniques (e.g., hypnosis) should raise suspicions about the validity of the allegation in question.
2. The *content* of the memory should be evaluated. As discussed, content differences have been found between real and mistaken memories.
3. *Individual differences* should be considered. The authors note that false memories are more likely in people with a greater susceptibility to suggestion in general and with a tendency toward dissociation.
4. *Corroboration* of the alleged event. A critical aspect of the evaluation process should focus on gathering evidence that either refutes or supports the claim based on the complainant's report.

Repercussions of Childhood Sexual Abuse

Childhood sexual abuse ranges widely in its physical severity, from nonviolent touching to the abuse culminating in murder (see Box 12.3 for a Canadian example of the latter). Experiencing a traumatic event such as sexual abuse at a young age can be severely detrimental psychologically and may affect the victim for the rest of his or her life. The type and severity of the trauma, as well as the age the trauma was experienced, and the length of time the trauma was endured is directly related to the likelihood of experiencing childhood PTSD, or trauma-related symptoms (although some children may not experience any of the negative symptoms related to being the victim of child sexual abuse; Beitchman, Zucker, Hood, & DeCosta, 1992; Perry, 2001, 2009). Specifically, childhood sexual abuse has been identified as one of the most traumatic events that a child can endure, and is most likely to result in trauma-related symptoms (see section on PTSD later in this chapter) (Elklit, 2002; Oddone Paolucci, Genuis, & Violato, 2001). The effects of childhood trauma are witnessed throughout all areas of the child's life. One area that may be significantly affected is the victim's brain, both physically and cognitively. Research has demonstrated that children who are subjected to trauma early in life experience physical changes in their brains and have issues with neurotransmitter regulation that can lead to aggression (De Bellis, Hooper, Woolley, & Shenk, 2010; Francati, Vermetten, & Bremner, 2007).

Further, traumatized children are likely to have academic difficulties and social difficulties (Amstadter et al., 2011; Margolin & Gordis, 2000). Similar to the effects of sexual assault seen in adults, children who have been the victim of sexual assault suffer from affective disturbances, somatic disturbances, high stress, and difficulty controlling anger (Anda et al., 2006).

There also exists a relationship between experiencing childhood sexual abuse and antisocial behaviour and delinquency (Apel & Burrow, 2011; Duke et al., 2010; Mueser, Rosenberg, & Rosenberg, 2009). Specifically, those who endured childhood sexual abuse as a child may be more likely to enter into abusive relationships as an adult (Gomez, 2011). Additionally, these victims may go on to sexually abuse other children (Menard, 2002). It should be noted that victims of childhood sexual abuse usually do not go on to become abusers themselves.

Thus, the effects of childhood trauma not only are salient in childhood but also may follow victims throughout their lifetime. Victims of childhood sexual abuse are more likely than others to experience mental health issues, substance abuse, self-injurious behaviour, and suicidality as adults (Balsam, Lehavot, & Beadnell, 2011; Beaver, Mancini, DeLisi, & Vaughn, 2011; Maniglio, 2011; McClain & Garrity, 2011). Further, those who experience a traumatic event in childhood are most likely to experience another, often violent, traumatic event later in life (McIntyre & Widom, 2011; Reese-Weber & Smith, 2011).

Fortunately, there are a number of trauma-related treatments available to help children who have been traumatized during childhood (e.g., Black, Woodworth, Tremblay, & Carpenter, 2011). Trauma-focused cognitive behavioural therapy is a treatment designed specifically for use with children who have experienced childhood sexual abuse. This treatment has proven effective at reducing trauma-related symptoms among children and helping them to go on to live a happy life (Cohen, Deblinger, & Mannarino, 2010).

THE PSYCHOLOGY OF ADULT SEXUAL ASSAULT VICTIMS

Background

It was established earlier that sexual violence is a significant problem in our society. Sadly, 10 to 25 percent of women report an adulthood

BOX 12.3 | THE TORI STAFFORD CASE

© THE CANADIAN PRESS/Dave Chidley

On April 8, 2009, Victoria "Tori" Stafford was kidnapped outside her elementary school in Woodstock, Ontario. Tori was eight years old when she was last seen, walking away from school with a woman in a white coat. The disappearance of Tori Stafford garnered international attention, with the case being profiled on an episode of *America's Most Wanted*. Although Tori's body was not found until July 19, 2009, three months after her disappearance, two suspects—Michael Rafferty and Terri-Lynne McClintic—were arrested and charged with her murder on May 20, 2009. Rafferty (28 years) was charged with first-degree murder and McClintic (18 years and Rafferty's girlfriend at the time) was charged with accessory to murder. Eight days later after an extensive interrogation, her charge was changed to first-degree murder, and she agreed to plead guilty. McClintic revealed that she lured Tori away from the schoolyard with the promise of seeing a dog and brought her to Rafferty, knowing that he would sexually assault her.

Soon after, Tori's body was found in a wooded area hidden under a pile of rocks. Due to the length of time that she had been exposed to the elements, her body was so severely decomposed that forensic specialists were unable to determine whether she had been sexually assaulted. However, due to the plea bargain that McClintic struck for her guilty plea, she was required to reveal the details of the crime and admitted to police that Rafferty had raped Tori in his car on the day that she was kidnapped. McClintic went on to say that Rafferty then physically assaulted Tori before he ultimately killed her. Despite McClintic's admission, Rafferty pleaded not guilty to all of the charges related to the case. In a dramatic twist, mere weeks before Rafferty's trial was set to begin, McClintic recanted her earlier testimony that Rafferty was responsible for the sexual assault and murder and claimed that she, in fact, had wielded the weapon that ultimately killed Tori Stafford. Regardless of the new confession, the prosecution believed that Rafferty had killed Tori and pursued the charges against him. On May 11, 2012, the jury found Rafferty guilty on the counts of first-degree murder, sexual assault causing bodily harm, and kidnapping. Rafferty was given a life sentence with no chance of parole for 25 years (CBC News, May 15, 2012; *National Post*, 2012).

rape experience (Koss, 1993; Lawyer, Resnick, Bakanic, Burkett, & Kilpatrick, 2010). According to the *Canadian Violence Against Women Survey* (Johnson, 1996), 39 percent of Canadian women experienced at least one incident of sexual assault (broadly defined, as per the Criminal Code of Canada stipulates) after the age of 15 years.

Historically, victims of sexual violence were not treated well within our legal system. In fact, Canadian rape laws served to protect men accused of the crime. For example, before legal reforms in the 1980s, husbands could not be prosecuted for sexually assaulting their wives. In addition, Canadian laws provided safeguards for men accused of rape. Prosecutors were allowed to present information about a complainant's sexual history to undermine her credibility, and judges instructed jurors about the dangers of convicting a defendant on the uncorroborated testimony of a complainant. Traditionally, it was unusual for courts to convict in a rape case in the absence of corroboration (e.g., Yuille, 1988).

These trends were problematic and discouraged crime victims from reporting offences. Fortunately, in the late 1970s and early 1980s the traditional rape laws and doctrines underwent major changes in the Canadian legal system. Under our current Criminal Code, we do not have a "rape" offence per se, but a broad category of "sexual assault," encompassing a wide range of crimes with a sexual component (as described earlier). Sexual assaults with a weapon or those that cause bodily harm (aggravated sexual assaults) warrant more severe sentences than other forms of sexual assault. Unlike many U.S. states, Canada has no statute of limitations, so charges can be laid at any time in an offender's lifetime after an offence takes place. Further, there are now important limitations on the kind of evidence about a complainant's sexual history that a defence lawyer can bring up in court. Before the last decade, the defence often obtained subpoenas that forced physicians, schools, therapists, and other third parties to produce their confidential files on a complainant, without even having to demonstrate they had any relevance in the case.

However, a 1995 Supreme Court judgment in the British Columbia case of Bishop Hubert O'Connor (*R. v. O'Connor*, 1995) led to stricter controls on the defence having access to such private records in sexual assault cases. The *O'Connor* decision established that the accused must first convince the judge that information in the files is likely to be relevant to the case. The judge can then review the files, and weigh the positive and negative consequences of their being entered as evidence. In October 2000, the Supreme Court of Canada unanimously upheld the constitutionality of the Criminal Code provisions that deal with the exposure of the sexual histories of complainants in trials. In two cases, *R. v. Darrach* (2000) and *R. v. Mills* (1999), the Supreme Court concluded that the legal system must be committed to balancing the right of an accused to a fair trial with the privacy rights of the sexual assault complainant (who usually is called as a witness at the trial).

The approach adopted by the Canadian legal system encouraged more victims to report sexual offences, as reflected in the increasing number of sexual assault convictions in Canada in the past two decades (e.g., Motiuk & Belcourt, 1997). There also has been an explosion of research on sexual violence and its psychological aftermath, in Canada and elsewhere. It is clear that the experience of sexual assault can have major psychological consequences. In fact, rape is among the most traumatic experiences one can go through, and it frequently leads to mental health problems (Bryant-Davis, Ullman, Tsong, Tillman, & Smith, 2010; Foa & Rothbaum, 1998). Further, such symptoms may constitute a "syndrome."

WHAT IS THE RAPE TRAUMA SYNDROME?

As Chapter 10 described, a **syndrome** is a set of symptoms that may co-occur, such that they may be considered to imply a disorder or disease. Not all the symptoms have to exist in every subject, and, in fact, the criteria for how many must be present are unclear.

About 30 years ago, a psychiatric nurse and a sociologist, Burgess and Holmstrom (1974), coined the term **rape trauma syndrome** to describe the collection of responses reported by 92 women who had been raped or subjected to other sexual abuses. Each of these victims was interviewed within 30 minutes of her admission to a hospital and reinterviewed a month later. Burgess and Holmstrom were struck by the fact that a variety of sources—self-reports by those raped, descriptions by psychotherapists and trained social service workers, and reactions by friends and family of those who have been attacked—showed great uniformity of responses. Some typical self-descriptions of those who survived a rape are reported in Box 12.4. (The vast majority of those raped are women; therefore, the clinical and empirical literature has focused on their reactions, and much less information is available on male survivors [Koss & Harvey, 1991].) With that said, it is important to acknowledge that males are victims of rape and the assault has many life-altering repercussions for males as well (e.g., Light & Monk-Turner, 2009).

It should be noted that not all rape survivors suffer from the same severity of symptoms. In support of this finding, Koss and Harvey (1991) used an ecological model of response to having been raped that emphasized that a variety of personal, event, and environmental factors could influence the recovery from a sexual assault. They wrote:

Person variables of particular relevance include the age and developmental stage of the victim; her or his relationship to the offender; the ability of the victim to identify and make use of available social support; and the meaning that is assigned to the traumatic event by the victim, by family and friends, and by others including police, medical personnel, and victim advocates with whom the victim has had contact in the immediate aftermath of trauma. Relevant event variables include the frequency, the severity, and the duration of the traumatic event(s) and the degree of physical violence, personal violation, and life threat endured by the victim. Environmental variables involve the setting where the victimization occurred, including home, school, workplace, or street. Other environmental variables are the degree of safety and control that are afforded to victims post-trauma; prevailing community attitudes and values about sexual assault; and the availability, quality, accessibility, and diversity of victim care and victim advocacy services. (p. 45)*

A middle-class college student who has been raised in a family that values daughters as much as sons and who is well informed about rape and

Each person who has been raped has a different story to tell, but they all share reactions of personal intrusion and lifelong impact. Each has to come to terms with being assaulted:

- "Early on, I realized the way to make the pain less was to separate my mind from my body and not permit myself to feel" (quoted by Kraske, 1986, p. 8A).
- "I can recall many landmarks in my recovery, beginning with the moment I picked myself up off the kitchen floor and got myself to a hospital. There was the first night, weeks after the attack, when I didn't wake up crying or screaming. I remember the first time I said to someone—outside of my close friends and family who knew me when the assault occurred—'I was raped.' And the first time I disclosed 'my secret' to a man with whom I was beginning a relationship" (Kaminker, 1992, p. 16).

- "For a long time I thought I could deal with my anger and hostility on my own. But I couldn't. I denied that it had affected me, and yet I was so frantic on the inside with other people: I needed to be constantly reassured. It wasn't until I started seeing myself self-destructing that I realized I needed help. To realize how angry I was and to ask for help—those were the stepping stones. There's a part of me that wants to be stoic and very strong. I had to realize that the attack wasn't directed at me, as Kelly. It was random. I was at the wrong place at the wrong time. That was the first step toward getting rid of all those hostile feelings I had about it. Still, when you're a victim of a violent crime—when somebody has taken control over your life, if only for a moment—I don't think you ever fully recover" (actress Kelly McGillis, quoted by Yakir, 1991, p. 5).

able to avail herself of the supportive resources of an active feminist community may respond to sexual assault quite differently than will a teenage girl whose pre-rape beliefs involved victim blaming and whose key support figures continue to believe that "an unwilling woman can't really be raped." Similarly, individuals who experience violence and abuse in isolation from others and who feel obliged to recover from their experience in continued isolation will adjust differently over time than will those individuals whose suffering has been shared and/or those who have access to and are able to make use of helpful support figures. (p. 44)*

* From Mary P. Koss and Mary R. Harvey, *The rape victim: Clinical and community interventions*, 2nd edition (p. 44, 45). Copyright © 1991 Sage Publications. All rights reserved.

A study of the psychological pain experienced by nearly 800 victims of sexual assault found that trauma also was related to the nature of the assault. Reproductively aged women experienced the greatest level of trauma in response to vaginal rapes (versus other forms of assault/penetration), while women who were not of reproductive age were similarly traumatized by their sexual assault experience regardless of whether penile-vaginal intercourse

occurred (Thornhill & Thornhill, 1991). While the authors interpreted these results as evidence for an evolutionary conceptualization of psychological pain (with trauma being directly related to potential loss of reproductive resources [the ability to procreate]), these findings also have implications for understanding and treating sexual assault survivors.

While there is a widespread assumption that traumatic sexual assault experiences often are "repressed" in memory—an idea first communicated by Freud, recent evidence indicates that such experiences persist in memory. Peace, Porter, and ten Brinke (2008) compared the characteristics of traumatic memories for sexual violence and two other emotional experiences among 44 women recruited from a sexual trauma agency. They found that memories for sexual trauma were not impaired or fragmented relative to other memories. Instead, memories for sexual trauma were associated with a remarkably high level of vividness, detail, and sensory components (also see Porter & Peace, 2007).

Burgess and Holmstrom (1974) divided rape trauma syndrome into two phases, an acute crisis phase and a long-term-reactions phase. The first phase may contain reactions that last for days or weeks, and these are likely to be quite severe. They can affect all aspects of the survivor's life, including physical, psychological, social, and sexual aspects. The second phase is a more reconstructive one, which includes survivors' coming to terms with their reactions and attempting to deal with the hurt and sadness in an effective way.

Phase I: Acute Crisis Phase

Initiated immediately after the act, the **acute crisis phase** is characterized by great disorganization in the survivor's life. It often is described by survivors as a state of shock, in which they report that everything has fallen apart inside. Many re-experience the attack over and over again in their minds. Even sleep, when it finally comes, does not re-energize; instead, it serves as a vehicle for nightmares about the rape. Those raped in their own beds are particularly affected by insomnia (Burge, 1988).

When victims are asked to complete a checklist of their reactions only two or three hours after having been raped, interviewers found high degrees of similarity in responses: 96 percent reported feeling scared, a similar percentage were anxious or worried, and 92 percent said they were terrified and confused (Veronen, Kilpatrick, & Resick, 1979). "Thoughts were racing through my mind," said more than 80 percent of those who had been attacked.

Cognitive accounts of anxiety were not the only frequent reactions; physiological exemplars of fear or anxiety often included the following:

- Shaking or trembling (reported by 96 percent of respondents)
- A racing heart (80 percent)
- Pain (72 percent)
- Tight muscles (68 percent)
- Rapid breathing (64 percent)
- Numbness (60 percent).

Although these manifestations of fear and anxiety are the most frequent, a number of other consequences are witnessed. Nearly one half of survivors scored as moderately or severely depressed on the Beck Depression Inventory (Frank & Stewart, 1984). One study reported suicide attempts by 19 percent of a community sample of women who had been raped (Kilpatrick, Best, Veronen, Amick et al., 1985b). The person's previous sense of invulnerability dissipates in a decrease of self-esteem. Allison and Wrightsman (1993), in reviewing reports, classified these phase-one reactions with the following characteristics.

Denial, Shock, and Disbelief

"This couldn't have happened *to me*" was a common response. One victim, later recounting her thoughts during the attack, said: "Thoughts pounded through my head as I tried to understand what was happening. Was this a joke? Was this someone I know being cruel? It couldn't be real" (Barr, 1979, p. 18). Survivors may question their family and friends about how the rape could have happened.

Disruption

Changes in sleeping and eating patterns are typical. To varying degrees, survivors may display personality disorganization (Bassuk, 1980). Some may appear to be confused and disoriented, whereas others do not exhibit such easily observable behavioural symptoms, but the latter type may be dazed and numb, and hence unresponsive to their environment. Disruption after rape can extend to all areas of life, including lost days at work (Annan, 2011).

Guilt, Hostility, and Blame

When learning that a friend has been raped, others may react by blaming the victim, by assuming that the rape could have been avoided, or by otherwise attributing responsibility for the rape to the person who was raped. Psychoanalytic theory unfortunately proposed that the essence of femininity included masochism. Thus it is not surprising that victims, too, respond with guilt and self-blame.

Janoff-Bulman (1979) has suggested that a **self-blaming response** may be the second most frequent one after fear. "If only I had locked that window" or "If only I had taken an earlier bus home" are examples of reactions in which the survivors blame their own actions for the rape, or at least imply that different behaviours on their part could have avoided it. A distinction has been made between this type of self-blame; behavioural self-blame; and characterological self-blame, which refers to attributions by the survivor to stable and uncontrollable aspects of the self and may be characterized by statements such as "I'm just the kind of person who gets raped" (Frazier, 1990; Janoff-Bulman, 1979). In some victims, self-blame can be so strong that they believe the rape was their fault or that the man cared for them. Cases are reported of survivors who even married the men who raped them (Warshaw, 1988).

Other survivors may direct their aggression and blame at men in general, or at society for permitting sexual assaults to occur. Meyer and Taylor (1986) reported that 11 percent of rape victims reacted in this manner, by agreeing to statements like "Men have too little respect for women" or "There is never a policeman around when you need him." In this sample of survivors, only a little more than half (56 percent) assigned blame to the rapist.

Regression to a State of Helplessness or Dependency

Persons who have been raped often report the feeling that they no longer are "independent". A sense of autonomy or competence is replaced with one of self-doubt. Survivors are overwhelmed with feelings that they no longer have control over their lives and what happens to them. They have to rely on those close to them to make even the most insignificant decisions. One told Warshaw (1988): "Deciding what to wear in the morning was enough to make me panic and cry uncontrollably" (p. 54).

Distorted Perceptions

Distrust and pessimism—and even paranoia—are frequent reactions to being the victim of a sexual assault. The world becomes a scary place in which to live. In one survey, 41 percent of a sample of college students who were acquaintance-rape survivors believed that they would be raped again (Koss, 1988).

Phase II: Long-Term Reactions

In the second phase of rape trauma syndrome, the **long-term reactions phase**, survivors face the task of restoring order to their lives and re-establishing a sense of equilibrium and the feeling of mastery over their world (Burgess & Holmstrom, 1985). This task is not an easy one; if, indeed, completion of the task occurs, it usually takes anywhere from a few months to years. Most of the improvement occurs somewhere between one and three months after the rape (Kilpatrick, Resick, & Veronen, 1981), but only 20 percent to 25 percent of survivors reported no symptoms one year after the attack. Burgess and Holmstrom (1985) reported that 25 percent of the women they studied had not significantly recovered several years after the rape. Regression can occur, with some reporting being worse on some measures one year after the rape, compared to six months afterward. Among the responses that may reoccur are specific anxieties; guilt and shame; catastrophic fantasies; feelings of dirtiness, helplessness, or isolation; and physical symptoms (Forman, 1980).

Thus, often life activities are resumed, but they are "undertaken superficially or mechanically" (Koss & Harvey, 1991, p. 54). One of the challenging quests during this phase is for survivors to understand what has happened to them and what they are feeling as a process of psychological

healing moves forward (Bard & Sangrey, 1979). Their cognitive development may be impeded by being "constantly haunted" by vivid, traumatic memories (Neiderland, 1982, p. 414). One survivor reported, "I can't stop crying … and sometimes I feel a little bit overwhelmed. All these things flashing, all these memories" (quoted by Roth & Lebowitz, 1988, p. 90). It is not uncommon for rape survivors to experience contradictory feelings: fears, sadness, guilt, and anger all at the same time. A temptation is to assume "Once a victim, always a victim." Four months after having been raped, a woman wrote, "I am so sick of being a 'rape victim.' I want to be me again" (Barr, 1979, p. 105). Following a cognitive explanation, Koss and Harvey (1991) noted a change of schema, or organizing structure, as the rape led to shifts in beliefs about trust, safety, and intimacy.

Allison and Wrightsman (1993) described the following as among the major symptoms of this second phase.

Phobias

A **phobia** is an irrational fear, which interferes with affective adaptation to one's environment. A one-year follow-up of women who had been raped found frequent reports that they were still expressing phobias and other manifestations of fear and anxiety (Kilpatrick, Resick, & Veronen, 1981). A recent review of the effects of sexual violence on women reported that 73 percent to 82 percent of women experience fear and/or anxiety after being the victim of sexual violence (Campbell et al., 2009). A rape can be viewed as a **classical conditioning stimulus**, and thus anything associated with the rape will come to be feared, as a result of the association (Kilpatrick et al., 1981). The phenomenon of stimulus generalization means that if a knife was used in the attack, the survivor may develop a negative reaction to all types of knives. Survivors of sexual assaults may become afraid of being alone, or of going out at night.

As Allison and Wrightsman observed:

These fears may force the victim into what seems to be a no-win situation. If she stays home alone, she is afraid. If she goes out, she is also afraid. Many victims leave the lights on in their homes 24 hours a day. Clearly the nature of the conditional associations to the rape leads victims to alter their lives in many ways. (1993, p. 156)

Disturbances in General Functioning

Carrying out routine aspects of life is often a challenge during the second phase. Changes in eating patterns and sleeping patterns remain a problem. For some, the quality of intimate relationships may deteriorate, as the survivor restricts opportunities to take advantage of what previously were seen as positive experiences. One survivor wrote:

Jon and I had known for months that he would have to make a business trip to California in December. Originally, before things had changed, we had all planned to go. I loved California, I wanted to go away with Jon, I didn't want to be left alone, but as the trip approached we had to face the reality … I didn't think I could leave the little security I found in my house, for strange motels. Camping was out of the question. We gave up the idea and I tried to think about how I would survive a week without Jon. (Barr, 1979, p. 83)

Sexual Problems

Having been sexually assaulted has a strong negative effect on the survivor's sex life (e.g., Vickerman & Margolin, 2009). But several studies concluded that the difference between women who had been raped and a comparable group who had not was not the frequency of sexual activities but rather the subjective quality of such experiences (Feldman-Summers, Gordon, & Meagher, 1979; Orlando & Koss, 1983). Sexual assault survivors reported that they did not enjoy sex with their partner as much as they had before they were raped, and this level of satisfaction was not as high as that of the control group for almost every type of intimate relationship. The only exceptions were of two types: activities considered primarily as affectional rather than sexual (such as hand holding or hugging) and masturbation; frequency and satisfaction for both of these types of activities was unaffected by the rape. But survivors reported less desire to engage in sexual activity (Becker, Skinner, Abel, Axelrod, & Treacy, 1984).

Changes in Lifestyle

Some survivors of a sexual assault may restructure their activities and change their jobs and their appearance (Warshaw, 1988). Changing their cell phone numbers is typical. Moving to another residence or even another city is not unusual.

The Relationship of Rape Trauma Syndrome to Posttraumatic Stress Disorder

Many people in society live and deal with painful recollections of a horrific traumatic experience, often with severe consequences for their mental health. Psychological "trauma" is an emotional experience resulting from exposure to an event that involved actual or threatened death or serious injury, or a threat to the physical integrity of self or others. The most extreme psychological outcome of a traumatic experience is **posttraumatic stress disorder** (PTSD), affecting about 9 percent to 15 percent of the population (e.g., Breslau et al., 1991). People with PTSD live with painful recollections of a horrific experience, typically characterized by extremes of recall: intrusive memories combined with avoidance of thoughts or feelings about the event. PTSD often occurs following experiences such as military combat, natural disasters, serious accidents, witnessing violent death, or violent personal attacks.

In Canada, PTSD has received a great deal of attention of late because of high-profile cases in the media. Romeo Dallaire, who commanded Canadian peacekeeping forces during the 1990s mass genocide in Rwanda, suffered extreme PTSD symptoms after he returned to Canada. He has since written about his continuing ordeal with PTSD symptoms in his book *Shake Hands with the Devil: The Failure of Humanity in Rwanda* (Dallaire, 2003). When SwissAir Flight 111 went down near Peggy's Cove, Nova Scotia, in September 1998, all 229 onboard were killed, leaving nothing but a scattering of body parts and debris in the ocean. Over the next few days, military and civilian personnel launched a massive effort to recover the remains of the victims from open waters and the nearby beaches. Dalhousie University psychologist Sherry Stewart and her colleagues (Stewart, Mitchell, Wright, & Loba, 2004) found that 46 percent of a sample of these volunteer workers met the criteria for PTSD several years later.

The type of horrific experience studied by Stewart and colleagues may be exceeded by few types of human experience in causing PTSD. However, one such experience is rape (e.g., Foa & Rothbaum, 1998). Several researchers have documented that PTSD is often present in victims of rape, and some have concluded that they are the largest single group of PTSD sufferers (Foa, Olasov, & Steketee, 1987, cited by Koss & Harvey, 1991;

Jordan, Campbell, Follingstad, 2010; Steketee & Foa, 1987) regardless of the victim's age (for a discussion of the sexual assault of elderly people see Box 12.5 below). Foa and Rothbaum (1998) estimate that the incidence of PTSD symptoms in rape victims is upward of 50 percent. The review conducted by Campbell et al. (2009) reported that 6 percent to 65 percent of women with a history of sexual abuse will develop PTSD, and 12 percent to 40 percent will experience generalized anxiety.

A number of researchers have pointed to many possible parallels between RTS and PTSD (Biggers & Yim, 2003; Follingstad, 1994a). The third edition of the *Diagnostic and Statistical Manual of Mental Disorders-Revised,* often referred to as "DSM-III-R," first recognized the presence of a psychological disorder that was a direct result of a stressful event; this disorder, termed posttraumatic stress disorder, was defined as "the development of characteristic symptoms following a psychologically distressing event that is outside the range of usual human experience" (American Psychiatric Association, 1987, p. 247). The *DSM-III-R* further suggested that PTSD is "apparently more severe and longer lasting when the stressor is of human design" than if it were a disaster of nature or war combat (1987, p. 248). The major or "primary" symptoms used to demonstrate the presence of PTSD are

(1) a repeated experiencing of the traumatic event (e.g., intrusive thoughts or recurrent nightmares) or, in contrast, an avoidance of situations, ideas, and feelings that were related to the traumatic event and (2) **a psychic numbing** or reduced responsiveness to the environment.

In addition to these primary symptoms, the *DSM-III-R* diagnosis specified that a person must experience at least two of the following:

1. Difficulty falling or staying asleep
2. Irritability or outbursts of anger
3. Difficulty concentrating
4. Hypervigilance
5. Exaggerated startle response
6. Physiological reactivity upon exposure to events that symbolize or resemble an aspect of the traumatic event (American Psychiatric Association, 1987). (The fourth edition of the DSM has maintained this description of PTSD; American Psychiatric Association, 2000.)

Horowitz, Wilner, and Alvarez (1979) developed the Impact of Event Scale (IES) to measure the level of trauma associated with a particular event in a particular individual. Later, Kilpatrick and Veronen (1984) administered this scale to rape victims whose violent experiences varied in time since occurrence (six to 21 days, three months, six months, one year, two years, or three years before).

| BOX 12.5 | SEXUAL ABUSE OF THE ELDERLY |

The abuse of elderly individuals is a growing problem. The elderly, similar to children, are a vulnerable population (due to the physical and cognitive impairments associated with aging; Jeary, 2005) and it appears that some individuals are quick to abuse the elderly in a number of ways including neglect, financial abuse, and physical abuse (Acierno et al., 2010). In a comprehensive study of elder abuse, Acierno and colleagues (2010) found that of their sample of 5777 individuals above the age of 60 years, 0.6 percent of them had been the victim of sexual assault. Further, only 16 percent of those sexually abused had reported the incident to the police. There are a number of reasons for the low rates of reporting including that the elderly feel that they will be perceived as senile and will not be believed. Further, a large proportion of the sexual abuse occurs in elder-care facilities and the victims may not know how to report it, or may be wary

of reporting the abuse if it was perpetrated by one of the staff (Jeary, 2005; Jones & Powell, 2006; Ramsey-Klawsnik, Teaster, Mendiondo, Marcum, & Abner, 2008).

Victims of elder sexual abuse are subject to the same deleterious symptoms as their younger counterparts. Documented symptoms of elder sexual abuse include trouble sleeping, nightmares, loss of weight, general anxiety, and anxiety related to leaving the house (Jeary, 2005). In addition to the usual symptoms associated with being the victim of a sexual crime, victims of elder sexual abuse may experience incontinence and long-lasting physical injuries that stem from the abuse that would not be as detrimental to a younger and healthier individual (Jeary, 2005). Elder abuse was once a grossly underrepresented area in the field of victim research but is becoming an increasingly researched topic.

Regardless of the length of time since the rape, most victims reported experiencing aspects of the first two primary symptoms listed above. With regard to the second symptom, the numbed responsiveness and reduced involvement with the environment, Kilpatrick et al. (1981) found in a longitudinal study that fear stemming from having been raped caused victims to restrict their daily activities and lifestyles dramatically.

With respect to the other PTSD criteria listed above, several studies have identified some or all these symptoms in specific victims of rape (Burgess & Holmstrom, 1985; Kilpatrick, Veronen, & Best, 1985). More frequently, the symptoms are avoidance behaviours, hypersensitivity, difficulties in maintaining concentration, and intensification of symptoms whenever exposed to rape-related cues. A comparison of rape trauma syndrome to PTSD revealed that individuals with rape trauma syndrome experience many symptoms of PTSD, but are also likely to endure long-term depression, feelings of humiliation, and sexual dysfunctions, symptoms not related to PTSD (McGowan & Helms, 2003).

In 1991, the Supreme Court of Canada explicitly recognized the traumatic consequences of sexual assault in *R. v. McCraw* (1991). The Court observed:

The psychological trauma suffered by rape victims has been well documented. It involves symptoms of depression, sleeplessness, a sense of defilement, the loss of sexual desire, fear and distrust of others, strong feelings of guilt, shame and loss of self-esteem. It is a crime committed against women which has a dramatic, traumatic impact. ... To ignore the fact that rape frequently results in serious psychological harm to the victim would be a retrograde step, contrary to any concept of sensitivity in the application of the law. (para. 84)

Why do some people who are sexually assaulted develop debilitating PTSD while the symptoms of others desist after a few weeks or months? Foa and Rothbaum (1998) proposed that PTSD is the outcome of a fear memory that contains mistaken evaluations, whereas a normal trauma memory that does not result in PTSD reflects evaluations that are closer to reality. In particular, those who develop PTSD come to recall their emotional responses and actions during the experience in a way that promotes an increasingly negative view of themselves ("I am a bad person"), thus interfering with their

psychological recovery. As such, a rape victim who blames herself or himself for what happened is more likely to develop the disorder. Another probable factor contributing to whether someone develops PTSD or rape trauma syndrome after a sexual assault is whether the traumatic experience is shared with others. The importance of discussing traumatic experiences such as rape in leading to positive health outcomes is widely recognized (see Foa & Rothbaum, 1998). Several studies have compared outcomes of victims who had written about their trauma to control trauma groups who wrote about unrelated events (e.g., Pennebaker & Beall, 1986). These studies consistently found more positive health outcomes (e.g., fewer doctor visits, self-reported health problems) in disclosure versus control groups. Pennebaker (1993) found that the simple act of writing out a traumatic memory had positive effects on physical and mental health.

WHAT CAN A PSYCHOLOGIST DO?

When a person reports having been sexually assaulted and becomes a witness in a criminal trial against the alleged attacker, one task for a forensic clinical psychologist is an assessment of the survivor's claims and responses. Later, at the trial, a forensic psychologist may be called on to testify about the presence of rape trauma syndrome in order to support the complainant's claim of sexual assault, especially if there is no corroborating evidence to support the claim (Follingstad, 1994a).

As an example, consider the Ontario Court of Appeal case *R. v. Fagundes* (1997). In the original case, Jose Fagundes was convicted of breaking into a woman's home and brutally sexually assaulting her. Forensic psychologist Dr. Lana Stermac was asked by the Crown to give expert testimony with respect to PTSD and, specifically, rape trauma syndrome. The Crown argued that such evidence was necessary to help the jury to understand the victims' inability to identify the accused until some time after the attack, and to explain her "unusual" psychological reactions following the attack. The trial judge considered these reactions:

She also testified about three other occurrences. She visualized the assailant as a blank styrofoam head. The type that would be in a store window with a hat or a wig on it. She was unable to visualize the particular features of her assailant. Another was that she would view the incident at times as a third

---

party, as if she was viewing the rape that was perpetrated on her. Another was that, she visualized that during the period of the rape she had been tied up although her memory is clearly that did not occur. She said it was almost as if she was watching a movie, that is how she would reflect upon it. Another circumstance is the fact that the threat that the complainant now testifies to was not disclosed until eight or nine months after the event. (*R. v. Fagundes*, 1997, para. 12)

The judge believed that the pattern of her memories was not something that jurors could easily understand. As such, he allowed expert testimony on PTSD and rape trauma syndrome as possibly beneficial, and in line with the requirements for admitting an expert set out in *R. v. Mohan* (1994).

In Canada, this type of expert testimony during the trial may be less common than during sentencing or in civil hearings. Here, victim impact statements, which may indicate the presence of RTS or PTSD, often are entered prior to sentencing to inform the judge's decision about an appropriate sentence. During civil hearings, the presence of rape trauma syndrome or PTSD can influence the nature of the financial settlement and whether the victim is entitled to monetary resources for counselling.

The potential roles of psychologists in the legal process in sexual assault cases are described in the next sections.

Assessment

Follingstad (1994a) has identified a number of activities for the psychologist in sexual assault cases:

1. Document the survivor's level of psychological, social, and physical functioning both before and after the sexual assault.
2. Assess the survivor's changes in identity, including loss of self-esteem and dignity, increased difficulty in decision making, and changes in feeling about her appearance.
3. Interview the survivor and administer self-report measures to determine the presence of phobias as well as generalized and specific fears.
4. Determine social adjustment, level of sexual functioning, coping mechanisms, and also identify other stressors around the time of the rape.

5. Interview others (family members, friends, roommates, spouse, or significant other) to corroborate the survivor's report, as well as obtain their evaluations of the survivor's truth telling.
6. Determine whether the survivor has experienced previous sexual assaults.

Great care needs to be given to the manner in which rape survivors are questioned. Dean Kilpatrick (1983) has urged that the psychologist not be judgmental and that an effort be made to normalize the experience. That is, recognizing that often survivors are reluctant to disclose or describe the assault, psychologists should give them support when interviewing them. Suggested introductory statements include "Sometimes very bad things happen to good people—sometimes bad sexual things."

A number of rating scales and self-report measures are available to document the victim's level of trauma. Follingstad (1994a) and Koss and Harvey (1991) have described the following instruments:

- *Sexual Assault Symptoms Scale* (Ruch, Gartrell, Amedeo, & Coyne, 1991). This 32-item self-report scale is administered to the survivor as soon as possible after the rape. It measures four factors, including Disclosure Shame, Safety Fears, Depression, and Self-Blame. A difficulty is that many survivors are unable to complete the scale because of their emotional state, exhaustion, or intoxication.
- *Clinical Trauma Assessment* (Ruch, Gartrell, Ramelli, & Coyne, 1991). This rating scale, completed by the clinical psychologist, is useful in assessing the severity of the trauma. The survivor first participates in a structured interview, then the psychologist rates him or her on each of 16 specific trauma symptoms. Examples include depression, tension/rigidity, and loss of trust in people. A factor analysis revealed three main factors, labelled as Controlled Emotional Trauma Style, Cognitive Trauma, and Expressed Emotional Trauma Style.
- *Rape Trauma Syndrome Rating Scale* (DiVasto, 1985). This scale is designed to assess the severity of eight symptoms of the trauma of sexual assault; ratings are done by the interviewers after they ask open-ended questions about each symptom (e.g., "Has your appetite changed in any way?"). The scale distinguishes between survivors and a control group of women who had not been raped.

- *Impact of Event Scale* (Horowitz, Wilner, & Alvarez, 1979). Previously mentioned, this is a 15-item self-report scale, separated into two sub-scales, designed especially to measure symptoms of intrusion and avoidance. Respondents think of the last week and rate the items according to how much trouble they have had. The IES was able to detect changes in distress in rape survivors after treatment (Kilpatrick & Amick, 1985).

Also, a number of clinical instruments are available to assess PTSD, including scales developed from the MMPI; these are reviewed by Wilson and Keane (1997). It should also be mentioned that there are therapies available, specifically cognitive and behavioral therapies, that help to reduce the trauma-related symptoms that rape victims often experience (Resick, Williams, Suvak, Monson, & Gradus, 2011).

Testimony as an Expert Witness

One justification for the testimony of a psychologist as an expert witness in a rape trial is that jurors do not fully understand the nature of rape; they may misinterpret the reactions of the survivor, and they may subscribe to a number of **rape myths**, or incorrect beliefs about the causes and consequences of rape (Suarez & Gadalla, 2010). Although specific myths abound, they may take three general forms: (1) women cannot be raped against their will, (2) women secretly wish to be raped, and (3) most accusations of rape are false (Brownmiller, 1975). While these myths are believed by many people in society, men are more likely to endorse them than are women (McGee, O'Higgins, Garavan, & Conroy, 2011; Suarez & Gadalla, 2010). Specific knowledge about rape trauma syndrome often is lacking. A survey of both laypersons and psychologists about rape and posttraumatic stress disorder found that the laypersons were relatively poorly informed on many relevant issues such as common psychological reactions in response to rape (Frazier & Borgida, 1988).

Consider a typical set of circumstances: A woman reports to the police that she has been raped and identifies her attacker. The prosecutor concludes that enough evidence exists to proceed to a trial. The defendant's position is that sexual intercourse occurred between the two parties but it was consensual. This set of events is fairly typical; most rapes are acquaintance rapes, not rapes by strangers. Thus, when the case goes to trial, the jury essentially must answer the question "Whom do you believe?" Given such circumstances, a forensic psychologist as an expert witness may be helpful to the prosecution with regard to several issues (Block, 1990), discussed next.

The Issue of Consent

Is a complainant's behaviour consistent with having been raped? Faigman, Kaye, Saks, and Sanders (1997) concluded that "by far the most accepted use of RTS in rape prosecutions" was to demonstrate that the alleged victim's behaviour was "consistent with that of victims in general" (p. 406). A number of courts have permitted psychologists and other mental health professionals to testify about trauma in the survivor as evidence of a lack of consent, or to refute defence claims that the alleged victim's behaviour was inconsistent with that of someone who had been raped. One of the first such cases in which admissibility was granted was the American case *State v. Marks* (1982). The defendant met a woman at a bar and persuaded her to return to his home, where—she later alleged—he drugged her, raped her, and forced her to have oral sex with him. The prosecution introduced the expert testimony of a forensic psychologist who had examined the survivor two weeks after the encounter and concluded "that she was suffering from the PTSD known as rape trauma syndrome" (*State v. Marks,* 1982, p. 1299). The defendant was convicted.

Questions about the Behaviour of the Alleged Victim

As noted earlier, some jurors may subscribe to myths about the nature of rape and survivors of rape. Survivors may delay in reporting the attack or, when they testify, they may make inconsistent statements or exhibit a lack of memory. The defence lawyer may use these behaviours to attack the credibility of the complainant; hence the testimony of a psychologist about the presence of rape trauma syndrome in the witness may educate the jury about the real reactions and feelings of rape survivors as well as disabusing jurors of misconceptions (Block, 1990). Thus, here, the expert would testify as a rebuttal witness, after the survivor's credibility has been challenged, either on cross-examination or during the defence's direct examination (McCord, 1985).

Supporting a Claim of Damages in a Civil Suit

In an increasing number of cases, a sexual assault survivor may sue an alleged attacker in a civil suit in order to recover damages, or a third party may be sued for failure to provide protection. As outlined by Kevin Douglas and his colleagues, Canadian civil courts have begun to acknowledge that someone who suffers psychological injuries because of another person may be entitled to financial compensation (Douglas, Huss, Murdoch, Washington, & Koch, 1999). For example, in one of the first such cases, a woman sued her father for damages arising from years of sexual assaults, and the infliction of mental distress. A jury found that the accused had sexually assaulted his daughter and inflicted psychological distress, and assessed tort damages of $50 000. This finding was reversed but later upheld in the Supreme Court of Canada (*M.[K.] v. M.[H.]*, 1992).

However, in general, Canadian courts have been reluctant to award damages for psychological harm in the absence of physical injury (Samra & Connolly, 2004). Joti Samra and Deborah Connolly at Simon Fraser University have examined the legal compensability of sufferers of PTSD in Canada. They describe four main concerns of the courts concerning the practice of compensating for psychological injuries:

1. There is a greater degree of diagnostic uncertainty in psychological versus physical injury cases.
2. The prospect of financial gain may have a conscious or an unconscious motivating effect on potential claimants.
3. By expanding the scenarios in which psychological injury may be compensated, the floodgates of litigation may be opened.
4. Liability for purely psychological harm may result in a widened burden of liability on civil defendants (Samra & Connolly, 2004).

Despite these concerns, Canadian courts are increasingly willing to award compensation for psychological damages to victims of sexual crimes, even in the absence of physical injuries. Numerous Aboriginal people who suffered sexual abuse during their forced attendance at residential schools have been so compensated, for example. In other cases, parents have been successfully sued by their children whom they sexually victimized. Some recent case examples include the following:

1. *Y. (S.) v. C. (F. G.)* (1997). This is a leading British Columbia case pertaining to damages in sexual assault cases. A stepfather had sexually assaulted his stepdaughter over a seven-year period. The judge awarded the stepdaughter $250 000 for general and aggravated damages,

and described several aggravating factors (making the crime more severe and leading to higher compensation) in such cases, including the nature, duration, and frequency of the assaults; the relationship between the plaintiff and the defendant; the defendant's lack of remorse; and the physical pain and psychological suffering associated with the sexual abuse.

2. *A. B. v. T. S.* (2000). In this case, sexual abuse had been perpetrated on a young girl by a family friend. The judge noted (para. 28) that although there was no violence, there was a very close relationship between the defendant and the plaintiff. The abuse took place over a period of approximately nine years, from infancy to early adolescence. The abuse involved fondling of her genitals and digital penetration of her vagina and anus, along with oral sex. In considering the psychological damages, the judge awarded the plaintiff $165 000.

3. *W. M. Y. v. Scott* (2000). In this case, a man alleged that he was sexually assaulted by his soccer coach about 15 times over three years, starting when he was nine years of age. A psychologist gave his expert opinion that the plaintiff did not meet the full criteria for PTSD, but was left with major psychological problems, such as low self-esteem, relationship difficulties, and substance abuse problems. The judge awarded the man $110 000 in general and aggravated damages.

Thus, Canadian courts have established that physical injuries are not necessary to award compensation in sexual assault cases. Further, whereas it is perhaps the most common diagnosis in such cases, PTSD is not a necessary diagnosis. Psychological damages have been interpreted liberally and, certainly, rape trauma syndrome is applicable.

When a civil claim for psychological damages does occur, a psychologist's testimony will typically be introduced to support the claim. Samra and Connolly (2004) describe several guidelines for psychologists who conduct assessments of PTSD in a civil litigation case. These include:

1. Use well-established diagnostic schemes, such as the DSM-IV.
2. Clearly address the issue of causation (i.e., the relation between the defendant's actions and the plaintiff's psychological problems).
3. Document specifically the functional limitations of PTSD on the specific individual.
4. Document the impact the disorder has on the person's quality of life.

5. Give an opinion of the severity of the disorder and prognosis.
6. Address the person's personality problems and how the traumatic event(s) are related to them.
7. Include an assessment of possible malingering and deception.

As Frazier and Borgida (1992) noted, one problem is that rape trauma syndrome refers to a loose collection of symptoms. Some critics have argued that its generality removes any meaning from the term (Lawrence, 1984). Further, it is a term that may have several specific definitions. Careful review of the scientific literature led Frazier and Borgida to conclude that the literature to that point, which relied on standardized assessment measures and carefully matched control groups, has established that "rape victims experience more depression, anxiety, fear, and social adjustment problems than women who have not been victimized … [and] that many victims experience PTSD symptoms following an assault" (1992, p. 301).

At the same time, experts need to be careful to limit their testimony to verifiable statements. One problem of expert testimony is that it sometimes is not an accurate reflection of the state of scientific knowledge. Expert witnesses have described symptoms that have not been documented empirically, and on occasion they have generalized findings from adults to children (Faigman et al., 1997). Frazier and Borgida also cited several examples of experts' claims that have not been found in research—for example, that it is "very common" for a victim to ask the rapist not to tell anyone about the rape. Boeschen, Sales, and Koss (1998) classified possible testimony into five levels. These are summarized in Box 12.6 and serve as a useful summary for the limits of testimony.

BOX 12.6   **LEVELS OF TESTIMONY BY AN EXPERT WITNESS**

Boeschen, Sales, and Koss (1998) proposed five levels of testimony in evaluating the appropriateness of admitting scientific testimony on the trauma of having been raped.

- *Level 1: Testimony on specific behaviours of rape survivors that are described as "unusual" by the defence.* "Testimony at this level is used by the victim's counsel in both criminal and civil trials to rebut the perpetrator's argument that a victim exhibited an unusual behavior following a rape" (Boeschen et al., 1998, p. 424). The courts generally have found this testimony helpful; it counteracts stereotypes held by some jurors, and empirical work has confirmed that such behaviours (delay in reporting a rape, failure to identify the attacker) are not that unusual.
- *Level 2: Testimony on the common reactions to rape and the general diagnostic criteria of rape trauma syndrome or PTSD.* The expert describes common reactions; he or she has not examined the alleged victim and does not discuss the specific victim's behaviours. This type of testimony is generally considered to be appropriate, with the qualifier that the term "rape trauma syndrome" is sometimes excluded because of its prejudicial nature.
- *Level 3: Expert gives an opinion about the consistency of a victim's behaviour or symptoms with rape trauma syndrome or PTSD.* Boeschen and her colleagues noted, "This type of testimony is much more

controversial than that of Level 1 or 2 because it permits the expert to go beyond the general, educational information and apply it to a specific case" (1998, p. 426). Some courts have found it too prejudicial, but these authors believe that it is a valid use of expert testimony, since the psychologist "does not appear to unfairly comment on the victim's credibility" (1998, p. 427).
- *Level 4: Testimony stating that the victim suffers from rape trauma syndrome or PTSD.* The expert describes the complainant's symptoms and states that these meet the criteria for a diagnosis of PTSD, but the expert does not state that she was raped. Some courts have permitted this level of testimony, noting that the defence is allowed to cross-examine this witness or provide its own expert witness. But resolution of the issue remains difficult, especially with RTS testimony. Any psychologist who is allowed to testify has the ethical obligation to state the limitations of the concepts he or she introduces.
- *Level 5: Expert opinion that goes beyond a diagnosis.* At this level, the expert testifies that the victim is telling the truth and that she was raped. This level of testimony will be generally excluded. As noted in Chapter 9 with regard to testimony on criminal responsibility, this is ultimate-opinion testimony that may trespass on the role of the fact finder.

THE SCIENTIFIC STATUS OF RESEARCH ON RTS

Given the sometimes-misleading testimony and inconsistent court decisions, what is the current status of research on rape trauma syndrome? In a section of the relevant chapter in the Faigman, Kaye, Saks, and Sanders (1997) handbook on scientific evidence, Frazier and Borgida (1992) have provided a useful review of recent research. The two central questions are "What symptoms do rape victims experience?" and "Do rape victims exhibit a different set of symptoms than do nonvictims?" The reviewers identified several symptoms, with the following conclusions:

- *Depression*. As noted earlier, depression is one of the most commonly reported psychological disorders in rape victims. The review identified seven studies that compared depressive symptoms of groups of rape victims and non-victims, with depression assessed through the highly regarded Beck Depression Inventory. All seven studies found the average scores of the rape victims to be significantly higher than those of the nonvictims. Across studies, between 18 percent and 45 percent of the victims were moderately to severely depressed, whereas only 4 percent to 23 percent of the subjects in the nonvictim control groups were (Faigman et al., 1997).
- *Fear*. Self-report studies using the Veronen-Kilpatrick Modified Fear Survey found differences between victims and nonvictims up to one year after the rape. One study found that recent rape victims were more fearful than victims of other crimes. However, the duration of the fear was unclear, with some studies reporting differences several years after the rape, whereas other studies concluded that rape victims' fear had subsided by then.
- *Anxiety*. Difficulties in concentrating and avoidance of certain situations because of anxiety were present more often in rape victims than in nonvictims, for at least one year after the rape. In one study, 82 percent of the rape victims met the criteria for a diagnosis of generalized anxiety disorder.

Despite the consistent findings for these specific symptoms, the question remains whether there is virtue or even validity to suggest the presence of a syndrome. The next section offers a substitute for the use of RTS in expert testimony.

SUBSTITUTING PTSD FOR RAPE TRAUMA SYNDROME

As we have seen, the concept of rape trauma syndrome was originally based on the commonly shared experiences of rape survivors interviewed in hospital emergency rooms. Its original purpose was to aid psychotherapists in treatment. Some experts (see Biggers & Yim, 2003; Frazier & Borgida, 1992; McGowan & Helms, 2003) believe that the evidence is sufficient that certain reactions differentiate women who have been raped from those who have not. But is this strong enough to justify introduction of rape trauma syndrome testimony in the courtroom?

Recently Boeschen, Sales, and Koss (1998) have proposed that PTSD be substituted for rape trauma syndrome in the courtroom. PTSD has the following advantages:

1. It is the primary trauma-related diagnosis included in the *Diagnostic and Statistical Manual of Mental Disorders*. (The term "rape trauma syndrome" is not found in the DSM-IV or in any earlier editions.)
2. As described earlier, a diagnosis of PTSD reflects six rather specific criteria, each with an understandable, operational definition.
3. The PTSD criteria reflect "the intense fear that many rape survivors experience, as well as the desire to avoid situations that are reminders of the rape experience" (Boeschen, Sales, & Koss, 1998, p. 418).
4. A variety of tools are available to assess PTSD, including objective tests, structured diagnostic interviews, and trauma-specific self-report measures (Wilson & Keane, 1997).
5. The use of PTSD in the courtroom avoids employing the word "rape" in the diagnosis. As noted, some courts have considered admitting testimony on RTS as too prejudicial.

However, it should be noted that many of the reactions common to sexual assault survivors—depression, anger, sexual dysfunction, and disruption of basic values—are not included in the PTSD criteria (Faigman, Kaye, Saks, & Sanders, 1997). Some have suggested a "complex PTSD categorization" (Herman, 1992a) that would create a consolidated diagnosis for those reacting to rape. While the interest in studying rape trauma syndrome has waned over recent years, the detrimental effects of rape continue to affect millions of women and men worldwide.

SUMMARY

Charges of the sexual abuse of children usually take one of two forms: that a number of children have allegedly been abused by a child-care provider or that an individual child has been abused by a member of the child's family or a close friend. In the latter type, it is sometimes adults reporting the abuse after they recall the childhood attack much later.

Psychologists can participate in several ways when charges of sexual abuse of children are advanced. They can assess the nature of the abuse (including whether, in fact, it did occur); they can advise the court about the child's competency to testify; they can assist the prosecutor in preparing the child to testify and, especially, make recommendations to the judge about whether the trauma of testifying justifies innovations in courtroom procedures; and they can testify as expert witnesses, either for the prosecution or the defence.

In assessing the validity of claims of abuse, psychologists face a challenging task. Sometimes, in order to gain information through interviews with the children, suggestive questions and other procedures are used that inspire legitimate questions about the accuracy of the children's answers. Although designed with good intentions, the use of anatomically detailed dolls lacks the precision required of psychometric instruments and should not be used to diagnose the presence of abuse.

Psychologists have testified on either side in trials of alleged abusers of children. For the prosecution, testimony in general is in support of the validity of claims of abuse, although ultimate-opinion testimony usually is not permitted. Psychologists testifying for the defence may focus on the inadequacies of interviews with children, the suggestibility of young children, or the limitations in the procedures used by the psychologists who concluded that abuse had occurred.

The term "rape trauma syndrome" was first developed about 40 years ago to account for the relative uniformity of responses by survivors of rape. Burgess and Holmstrom (1974) divided the RTS into two phases, an acute crisis phase and a long-term reactions phase. The first phase included cognitive and physiological reactions, including denial, disruption of normal activities, guilt, and regression to a state of helplessness or dependency. The second phase dealt with restoration to a sense of equilibrium and mastery over the world, but many problems continued or reoccurred in this second phase.

Two roles for psychologists are salient with regard to the use of rape trauma syndrome. First is the assessment of the complainant's claims and responses. In doing so, the psychologist interviews the survivor and others, and administers several self-report measures. Second, at the trial, the forensic psychologist may be called on to testify about the presence of rape trauma syndrome in order to support the survivor's claims, especially if there is no corroborating evidence to support the claim and the defendant counterclaims that consensual sexual intercourse occurred. Specifically, as an expert witness, the psychologist may testify about the presence of rape trauma syndrome, which is indicative of lack of consent, or in a civil suit the psychologist may testify to support a claim of psychological damages. At sentencing hearings, victim impact statements are used by judges when deciding upon appropriate sentences for sexual offenders, and rape trauma syndrome can play a role.

Because of problems with the conceptualization of rape trauma syndrome, it has been suggested that, instead, psychologists should testify in criminal trials about the applicability of posttraumatic stress disorder, which has some overlap with rape trauma syndrome but contains more clearly defined criteria. Relative to the criminal courts, Canadian civil courts have adopted a liberal approach in accepting expert psychological evidence on the outcomes of sexual abuse (including testimony on rape trauma syndrome) that can warrant financial compensation.

KEY TERMS

acute crisis phase, p. 300

anatomically detailed dolls, p. 284

child sexual abuse accommodation syndrome, p. 293

classical conditioning stimulus, p. 301

criterion-based content analysis technique, p. 289

London Family Court Clinic, p. 285

long-term reactions phase, p. 301

phobia, p. 301

posttraumatic stress disorder, p. 302

psychic numbing, p. 303

rape myths, p. 306

rape trauma syndrome, p. 298

self-blaming response, p. 300

social frameworks testimony, p. 293

statement validity assessment, p. 289

suggestibility, p. 288

suggestive questions, p. 286

syndrome, p. 298

ultimate-opinion testimony, p. 294

SUGGESTED READINGS

Bull, R. (2010). The investigative interviewing of children and other vulnerable witnesses: Psychological research and working/professional practice. *Legal and Criminological Psychology, 15*, 5–23.

This article provides a detailed description of vulnerable witnesses and the various problems they represent for interviewing. This review provides an overview of recent research findings in the field of investigative interviewing and the direct relation they have to the improvement of interviewing techniques.

Ceci, S. J., & Hembrooke, H. (Eds.) (1998). *Expert witnesses in child abuse cases*. Washington, DC: American Psychological Association.

This review includes a number of valuable contributed chapters, all devoted to issues relevant to the psychologist called to serve as an expert witness in child sexual abuse cases. It contains chapters by Michael Lavin and Bruce D. Sales, Margaret Bull Kovera and Eugene Borgida, Lucy McGough, and others. Highly recommended.

Faller, K. C. (2007). *Interviewing children about sexual abuse: Controversies and best practices*. New York: Oxford University Press.

This book, written by a leading expert in the field of child sexual abuse, critically analyzes the current practices used to interview children after they have been sexually abused. This is a great resource for expert witnesses, and a fascinating read for students.

Williamson, T., Milne, B., & Savage, S. P. (Eds.). (2009). *International developments in investigative interviewing*. Portland, OR: Willan Publishing.

This book covers the advancements in interviewing techniques in a number of countries, discussing specific cases and research that led to changes in their practices. This book also touches on interesting topics relevant to interviewing such as torture and deception detection. This book is a must-read for practitioners, academics, and students alike.

Psychopathy: History, Assessment, Etiology, and Its Association with Violence

> *"I advance that psychopathy is the purest and the best explanation of antisocial behavior. Indeed, psychopathy is the unified theory of crime ..."*
> *(DeLisi, 2009)*
>
> —Matt DeLisi, Ph.D., Coordinator of Criminal Justice Studies and Professor of Sociology at Iowa State University.

Psychopathy is a disorder that attracts major attention from the research community and media alike. It typically is paired with evil serial murderers and their heinous acts. From *Silence of the Lambs*, a movie about a manipulative and highly intelligent psychiatrist/serial killer, to *Dexter*, a TV series about the life of a good-hearted but murderous psychopath, psychopathy usually is portrayed in its extreme manifestations. The media goes out of its way to depict psychopaths as criminal, intelligent, devious, charming, and egocentric (Stevens, 2008). Additionally, these characteristics often are portrayed as stable characteristics of the individual that are unchangeable. But how accurate are these media portrayals of psychopaths? Are all psychopaths criminals? Are all murderers psychopaths? Are some psychopaths "successful" in the corporate or political world? Questions such as these are addressed in this chapter, which provides the prevailing definition of psychopathy, the developmental trajectories of psychopathy, the manner in which psychopathy is linked to crime, whether the construct of psychopathy can be applied to females and youth, and whether we can "treat" this destructive condition.

DEFINING PSYCHOPATHY

Psychopathy is a multifaceted personality disorder that has a long clinical history but will be (likely) officially included only in the next edition of DSM. The development of a clearly delineated set of criteria for this disorder has been a long struggle, as the concept of psychopathy has undergone extensive and repeated restructuring over the past two centuries. In general, the definition of psychopathy has changed from a morally neutral view in the 1800s (as expressed by Pinel, 1801/1962) to a morally charged portrayal of a socially aberrant individual (Kraepelin, 1915). Regardless of

historical background, psychopathy always has had a clear link to criminal and antisocial behaviour, making it an important concept in the area of forensic psychology.

THE HISTORY OF THE CONSTRUCT OF PSYCHOPATHY

Early discussions of psychopathy were descriptive, emphasizing symptoms or behaviours characterizing the disorder. Early in the 19th century, Pinel described a group of patients exhibiting ***manie sans délire*** (moral insanity) who committed inexplicable crimes but did not share most traits of insane patients (Millon et al., 1998; Porter, 1996). These patients seemingly were able to understand the irrationality of what they were doing, were not otherwise psychotic, and appeared to have normal cognitive abilities. Pinel (1801/1962) explained, "I was not a little surprised to find many maniacs who at no period gave evidence of any lesion of understanding, but who were under the dominion of instinctive and abstract fury, as if the faculties of affect alone had sustained injury" (p. 9).

Prichard (1837) argued that psychopathic individuals exhibited a deplorable defect in personality that warranted social exclusion. To better describe his perspective on this disorder, Prichard coined the term *moral insanity*, which he defined as "... a morbid perversion of the natural feelings, affections, inclinations, temper, habits, moral dispositions, and natural impulses, without any remarkable disorder or defect of intellect or knowing and reasoning faculties, and particularly without any insane illusion or hallucination" (1837/1973, p. 16).

Sociologists began to take an interest in this problem in the early 20th century, and, not surprisingly, saw social conditions as the critical contributing factors. Accordingly, they replaced the term "psychopath" with the descriptor "sociopath" coined by Partridge. Partridge (1930) argued that individuals with this psychopathic inferiority were exhibiting a "social" disorder and coined the term "sociopath," reflecting the idea that the condition involved an "antisociety" view of life (see Box 13.1 for a more in-depth discussion). Such views were eventually incorporated into the APA's first edition of the DSM in 1952, which described a "sociopathic personality disturbance, antisocial reaction."

The current conceptualization of psychopathy derives from the clinical observations of psychiatrist Hervey Cleckley. In his classic text *The Mask of Sanity* (1941) in which he described some of his rather unusual patients, Cleckley proposed that there are a number of defining characteristics of the disorder, including emotional, interpersonal, and behavioural elements. Cleckley observed that psychopaths had a major emotional deficit, such that deep emotion and anxiety were absent. In fact, he theorized that a lack of emotion was at the core of the disorder, with other symptoms following from this emotional shallowness. Cleckley suggested that psychopaths are interpersonally arrogant, grandiose, callous, superficial, and manipulative. Affectively, they are short tempered, unable to form strong emotional bonds with others, and lacking in empathy, guilt, and remorse. Behaviourally, they are impulsive, irresponsible, and prone to violate social and legal norms (as described in Hare, 2002; Hare & Neumann, 2006; Hart & Hare, 1997).

Indeed, the measurement of psychopathy is an area of long-standing debate. Psychopathy falls into a conceptual area of research that has had difficulty in establishing the relationship between personality deviation and deviant behaviour (including criminality). Just because an individual acts in a criminal way does not mean that he or she has a personality disorder, and just because an individual has a personality disorder (like psychopathy) it does not mean that he or she will behave in a criminal way. Behaviour clearly plays a pivotal role in the diagnosis of psychopathy, but we need to make sure to take other important factors into account (see Box 13.2 for more personality disorders that are related to antisocial behaviour).

The modern conception matches major political figures such as Nero, Stalin, Hussein, Pot, and many of the prominent Nazis in World War II. The central feature of the construct—lack of **empathy** and, hence, conscience (or "lovelessness and guiltlessness"; McCord & McCord, 1964)—represents a mystery that continues to baffle mental health professionals and the public. Clinicians have speculated that underpinning psychopathy is an impairment or inability to experience the emotional aspects of life (e.g., Wilson, Juodis, & Porter, 2011). While other tools have been developed to measure psychopathy, such as the Psychopathic Personality Inventory Revised (PPI-R; Lilienfeld & Widows, 2005), none have been as popular or reliable as the Psychopathy Checklist—Revised (Hare, 2003).

| BOX 13.1 | SOCIOPATH OR PSYCHOPATH: WHICH TERM IS CORRECT? |

You have probably heard the term "sociopath" used interchangeably with the term "psychopath," and are now wondering whether there is a difference between sociopaths and psychopaths. In order to address this common confusion, we need to turn to the year 1952, when the first edition of the DSM was written. During this time, Cleckley's conceptualization of psychopathy was hotly debated and it was argued that the social aspect of the disorder was not sufficiently apparent. Thus, in order to demonstrate a fusion between the psychiatric and social explanations of psychopathy, the DSM-I renamed the evolving construct **sociopathic personality disturbance** (Millon et al., 1998). They hoped that by highlighting this psychosocial perspective, it would make it apparent that these individuals are as much a product of their environment as other individuals, and are not simply empathy-lacking monsters. Largely still based on Cleckley's personality features and some criminal behaviour, this DSM-I conceptualization of sociopathy is actually much closer to the notion of psychopathy than the later behavioural criteria included in the DSM-III and DSM-IV (in which it was renamed again as Antisocial Personality Disorder). So the next time you hear a friend say that they believe that someone is a "sociopath," you can inform them that you are impressed by their comprehension of the social underpinnings of psychopathy, but that the new term is "psychopath." We might think of a "sociopath" as an individual who has an "antisociety" orientation, such that he or she does not adhere to societal rules but may still have a conscience of some sort.

People—usually males—matching the current understanding of the prototypical psychopath have surfaced since antiquity. For example, the ancient Greek philosopher Theophrastus described a "man without moral feeling" in one of his 30 character profiles of human nature (e.g., Porter, Black, & Korva, 2012). The famed writings of Niccolò Machiavelli (1469–1527) advocated for manipulative, amoral, and deceptive behaviour in achieving power in politics and society (Campbell, 2003). In *The Prince*, Machiavelli expressed this view in his description of the ideal qualities of a successful political ruler, and, based on his writings, the term *machiavellianism* has become synonymous with callous, manipulative, and deceptive personality characteristics (see Campbell, 2003). Machiavellianism, subclinical narcissism, and psychopathy make up the increasingly validated **Dark Triad** (e.g., Jones & Paulhus, 2011; Paulhus & Williams, 2002) developed at UBC-Vancouver. The Dark Triad is a constellation of personality characteristics that is particularly predictive of antisocial behaviour and has sparked research interest in recent years.

THE PSYCHOPATHY CHECKLIST— REVISED (HARE, 2003)

Robert Hare, from the University of British Columbia, developed the first set of empirically derived criteria for psychopathy. He developed the Psychopathy Checklist (PCL) for classifying individuals as psychopathic in 1980, followed by the **Psychopathy Checklist—Revised** (PCL-R) in 1991, and 2003, a refinement of the measure. The PCL and the PCL-R were developed to make Cleckley's (1941) concept of psychopathy operational and quantifiable for researchers. Hare collected data on male adults in forensic settings from 1978 to 1991 to ensure that the construct of psychopathy was reliably measured with the PCL-R. He went beyond describing psychopaths to creating a reliable way of assessing the disorder, and the PCL-R has since become the benchmark for measuring psychopathy.

The PCL-R is a 20-item measure that uses a scale of 0 (does not apply) to 2 (definitely applies) for each item. The PCL-R is an interview tool rather than a questionnaire, which means that item scores are decided by the interviewer. For example, an interviewer may decide that an individual meets the criteria for the item "conning or manipulative" because the individual uses deceit and deception to cheat, defraud, or manipulate others. The scoring of most items requires considerable judgment, and a score of two can be given even if only a few of the characteristics are displayed by the individual being assessed, as long as characteristics are sufficiently extreme in intensity, frequency, or duration. PCL-R items are rated on the basis of a person's lifetime functioning, not on the basis of a present state or relatively recent behavioural history, so that the items are scored based on typical functioning rather than extreme individual situations. Traditionally a total score greater than or equal to 30 was found to be sufficient for warranting a diagnosis of psychopathy. More recently, however, a total score as low as 25 has been shown to be sufficiently sensitive. The ultimate decision of whether or not an individual is deemed to be a psychopath is up to the evaluating clinician.

The two most common biases in evaluating the criteria are the "halo effect" and the "nice-guy or bad-guy" effect (Hare, 1998). The **halo effect** involves basing each item score on an overall impression of the individual, which can be influenced by the type of offences the individual being assessed has committed. The "nice-guy or bad-guy" bias involves rating all items high or all items low. In other words, if an individual has scored low on the first few items of the PCL-R, raters may be biased to score the other items low to retain consistency.

It is assumed that there are two major factors in psychopathy, but both a three- (e.g., Shariat et al., 2010) and a four-factor model have been proposed in recent years (see Skeem & Cooke, 2010). Indeed, the so-called *factor structure* of the PCL-R is a hotly debated topic at the moment. The two major and originally proposed factors are the interpersonal/emotional factor and the behavioural factor. While factor-one items are relatively stable over time (sometimes referred to as *static* factors), factor-two items can change to some extent over time (*dynamic* factors). All but three of the criteria for psychopathy fall under one of the two factors. Below is a general description of the PCL-R items with examples of characteristics seen for each item.

Factor One: Interpersonal/Emotional

1. *Glibness/superficial charm.* The individual shows displays of emotion that do not appear genuine (e.g., fake tears), attempts to portray him-/herself in a good light and tells unlikely stories, and uses technical language and jargon (often inappropriately). The individual likely also has engaging conversations and interpersonal behaviour around others.

2. *Grandiose sense of self-worth.* The individual has an inflated ego, is self-assured and opinionated, exaggerates status and reputation, and displays little concern for the future. The individual also considers the present circumstances (e.g., imprisonment) to be the result of bad luck or personal victimization by the justice system.

3. *Pathological lying.* The individual often fabricates elaborate lies, even though they can be easily checked; lies with ease; is seldom embarrassed when caught lying; has an explanation or excuse for everything. These lies are often motivated by extrinsic gain (such as money) but may also be motivated by an enjoyment derived from lying ("duping delight").

4. *Conning/manipulative.* The individual uses deceit and deception to cheat and manipulate others; uses scams that are motivated by personal gain; has no concern for the effect of the manipulation on others; and is cool, self-assured or brazen when engaging in the manipulation. This manipulation can include criminal (e.g., using bad cheques) and non-criminal activities (e.g., using family members for money).

5. *Lack of remorse or guilt.* The individual has a general lack of concern for negative consequences of actions on others, appears to have no conscience or sense of guilt, does not seem sincere when talking about remorse, and is concerned more with his or her own suffering than that of others (such as his or her victims).

6. *Shallow affect.* The individual does not seem able to experience the normal range of emotions (e.g., from happy to sad), seems unemotional and cold, and acts in ways that are inconsistent with displayed emotions. Emotions that are displayed appear insincere and are dramatic, shallow, and short lived.

7. *Callous/lack of empathy.* The individual has an insensitive and cruel disregard for the feelings, rights, and welfare of others, leading him or her to be cynical and selfish. Others are seen as objects to be manipulated, and appreciation of the suffering of others is merely abstract.

8. *Failure to accept responsibility for own actions.* The individual rationalizes and excuses deviant behaviour by placing the blame on victims or circumstance, denying accusations, and greatly minimizing or denying the consequences of harmful behaviour (e.g., suggesting that victims are exaggerating injuries).

Factor Two: Behavioural

9. *Need for stimulation/proneness to boredom.* The individual has a chronic and excessive need for novel and exciting stimulation, engages in risk-taking behaviour, may try and use many types of drugs, complains that school and/or work are boring, and is unwilling to work at the same job for a significant length of time.

10. *Parasitic lifestyle.* The individual is intentionally financially dependent on others, continually relying on family and friends for financial aid. By presenting as helpless or using threats and coercion, the individual successfully exploits victims' weaknesses and avoids having to seek gainful employment.

11. *Poor behavioural controls.* The individual can be described as short tempered and easily becomes angry and aggressive, often responding to frustration and criticism with violent behaviour or verbal abuse. Behaviour seems inappropriate given the context, but the inappropriate behaviour is often short lived.

12. *Early behavioural problems.* Before the age of 12, the individual had serious conduct problems, including persistent lying, cheating, theft, robbery, fire setting, truancy, disruption of classroom activities, substance abuse (including alcohol and glue sniffing), vandalism, violence, bullying, running away from home, and precocious sexual activities. These behaviours were more serious than those experienced by most children and may have resulted in complaints, suspension from school, or contact with the police.

13. *Lack of realistic, long-term goals.* The individual demonstrates an inability or unwillingness to formulate and carry out realistic long-term

plans, lives day to day, and changes plans frequently. If specific goals are mentioned, they are unrealistic.

14. *Impulsivity.* The individual acts in ways that lack reflection or forethought, failing to consider the consequences of actions. Often breaking off relationships, quitting jobs, and moving frequently without informing others, this individual has an overall impulsive lifestyle.

15. *Irresponsibility.* The individual has little or no sense of responsibility, routinely fails to fulfill obligations and commitments to others, and has no sense of loyalty or duty including to family and friends. This mentality may cause unnecessary hardship to others, and lead to poor business relations.

16. *Juvenile delinquency.* Before the age of 17, the individual has a history of serious antisocial behaviour, including charges and convictions for criminal and statutory offences. This item is scored differently from the other items, and is defined objectively by the number and type of formal contacts with the criminal justice system. A 2 is warranted for a history of serious offences (from murder to major theft), 1 for a history of minor offences (from possession of drugs to causing a disturbance), and a 0 for no history of arrest.

17. *Revocation of conditional release.* As an adult, the individual violated a conditional release or escaped from a correctional institution, including technical (noncriminal) breaches. Again, this scoring is different from previous items; a 2 is assigned for major violations (e.g., revocation of parole), 1 for minor violations (failure to appear in court), and 0 for no violations.

Independent Items

18. *Promiscuous sexual behaviour.* The individual seeks casual or impersonal sexual relations with others, frequently has one-night stands, may maintain several sexual relationships at the same time, and is willing to engage in a wide variety of sexual activities with a wide variety of partners. Unwilling sexual partners may be "persuaded" into sexual acts with the individual by using force or threats.

19. *Many short-term marital relationships.* The individual has multiple relationships that involve some degree of commitment from one or both partners, including formal and common-law marriages. Scoring is different from previous items; for those under age 30, a 2 is warranted for three or more relationships, 1 for two relationships, and 0 for one or none. For those over age 30, a 2 is warranted for four or more relationships, a 1 for three relationships, and 0 for two or less.

20. *Criminal versatility.* The individual has an adult criminal record involving charges or convictions for many different types of offences. Again, the scoring is different from other items. A 2 is assigned if the individual has committed six or more types of offences, 1 for four or five types of offences, and 0 for three or fewer types of offences.

At this point some of you might be wondering whether *you* meet the criteria for psychopathy. Remember that most people will meet *some* of the criteria, but only few will exceed the necessary threshold. That being said, you probably have met someone who scores in the 25+ range (thus meeting the criteria for psychopathy). Coid et al. (2009) conducted the first major study of psychopathy in the general population (638 adults in households in England, Wales and Scotland), using the PCL—Screening Version, and found that 0.6 percent of the population met diagnostic criteria. Psychopathy scores correlated with being male; violent behaviour, incarceration; drug dependence; histrionic, borderline, and adult antisocial personality disorders; and, interestingly, panic and obsessive–compulsive disorders. A much higher prevalence of psychopathy is found among incarcerated inmates. Depending on the security level and other factors, in general between 15 and 25 percent of male offenders in North American federal correctional settings (e.g., Porter, Birt, & Boer, 2001), although apparently lower levels of psychopathy are found in incarcerated British offenders (e.g., Coid et al., 2009; Cooke & Michie, 1999).

What does someone who has a high level of the PCL-R criteria above "look like" clinically? There is a wide variation in clinical presentations, as the first author of this textbook can attest from his clinical practice with more than 200 offenders (e.g., Porter & Porter, 2007). However, there are some general ways in which we can describe all psychopaths. They all show a selfish orientation and profound emotional deficit, as evidenced from studies of psychophysiology, neurology, and behaviour (see Hare, 2003). In lay

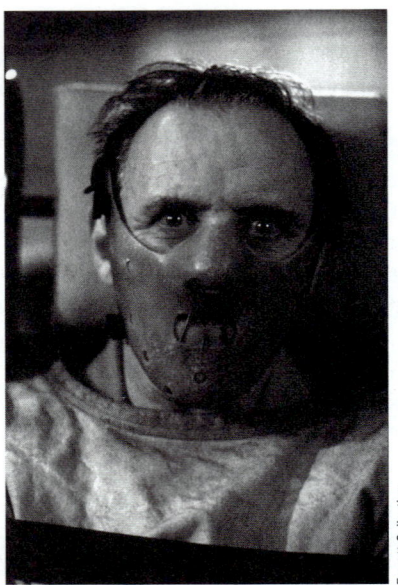

Hannibal Lecter

terms, they seem to have little or no "conscience" (Hare, 2006), although the cause of this deficit is controversial (see Skeem, Polaschek, Patrick, & Lilienfeld, 2011).

The psychopath's diminished capability for moral appreciation appears to have biological underpinnings; neuroimaging research indicates potential structural and functional abnormalities, including grey matter reductions in frontal and temporal areas (Oliveria-Souza et al., 2008), and anomalies in the prefrontal cortex, corpus callosum, amygdala, and hippocampus (e.g., Raine et al., 2004, 2003). Yet, psychopaths exhibit no apparent deficits in their intelligence (see Patrick, 2006). In fact, psychopaths typically are skilled conversationalists and use language to lie to and charm others for material gain, drugs, sex, or power (e.g., Hancock, Woodworth, & Porter, 2012). Canadian psychopathic offenders, for example, are 2.5 times more likely than other offenders to be successful in their applications for parole, despite a much higher rate of reoffending (Porter, ten Brinke, & Wilson, 2009). Some may even use their penchant for conning others to become cult leaders, corrupt politicians, or successful corporate leaders (Babiak & Hare, 2006, 2011).

The Language of the Psychopath

Sometimes the psychopath's emotional deficit is revealed through the manner in which he or she speaks. Some early studies indicated that psychopaths' language is less coherent than nonpsychopaths, which seems to contradict our contention that they have the "gift of the gab." Through case studies, Cleckley (1976) observed that the narratives of psychopaths were more likely to include a tangential and incoherent quality. Only two empirical studies examined the issue. Williamson (1993) analyzed the narratives of psychopaths and nonpsychopaths, finding that the former used more contradictory, logically inconsistent statements. Similarly, Brinkley, Newman, Harpur, and Johnson (1999) found that narratives by psychopaths contained fewer cohesive ties and more poorly integrated details, akin to the language of individuals with schizophrenia. A recent, more comprehensive study was the first to examine the specific qualities of psychopathic language by using more sophisticated statistical text analysis tools. Hancock, Woodworth, and Porter (2012) examined the language characteristics of the crime narratives of 14 psychopathic and 38 nonpsychopathic homicide offenders in describing their murders on three major characteristics: their instrumental nature, unique material and socioemotional needs, and the emotional deficit.

The authors speculated that even for powerful events such as murder, psychopaths would demonstrate in their language an "instrumental" worldview, in which the world was theirs for the taking. For example, nearly all (93.3 percent) of homicides by psychopaths are primarily instrumental (premeditated and motivated by an external goal) compared to 48.4 percent of those by nonpsychopathic offenders (Woodworth & Porter, 2002; also see Flight & Forth, 2007). Mokros et al. (2008) demonstrated the selfish, goal-driven, noncooperative nature of psychopaths in their propensity to exploit others while engaged in a Prisoner's Dilemma scenario. In the Hancock et al. study, psychopaths' instrumental orientation indeed was reflected in their speech in the form of more explanatory and causally framed language concerning their criminal actions, with a relatively high level of the usage of subordinating conjunctions (i.e., "because," "since," "as," "so that"). Secondly, the researchers found that psychopaths (relative to their counterparts) focused on material needs (food, drink, money), and contained fewer references to social needs (family, religion/spirituality) in their speech. Psychopaths' speech contained a higher frequency of "disfluencies" ("uh," "um") indicating that describing such a powerful, emotional event to another person was relatively difficult for them. Finally, psychopaths used more past-tense and fewer present-tense verbs in their narrative, indicating a greater psychological detachment from the incident, and their language was less emotionally intense and less pleasant.

Do you think you would be able to identify a psychopath now that you know the criteria? Perhaps. Hare (1999) argues that identifying psychopaths is important to your financial and personal well-being, but that their superficial charm may allow them to evade your radar. While this section of the chapter discussed the criteria for psychopathy in depth, a related construct called Antisocial Personality Disorder also warrants explanation.

DIFFERENTIATING ANTISOCIAL PERSONALITY DISORDER AND PSYCHOPATHY

Antisocial personality disorder (ASPD) is defined by the fourth edition of the *Diagnostic and Statistical Manual of Mental Disorders* (DSM-IV) as a disorder that "has also been referred to as psychopathy, sociopathy, or dissocial personality disorder" (p. 645, APA, 1994). However, over the course of various editions of the DSM, more than the name of the disorder has changed. Antisocial personality disorder is characterized today as "a pervasive pattern of disregard for and violation of the rights of others occurring since age 15, as indicated by 3 of the following; failure to conform to social norms, deceitfulness, impulsivity, irritability, reckless disregard for others, irresponsibility, lack of remorse." (APA, 1994). While ASPD was intended to provide a replacement for the diagnosis of psychopathy, ASPD is based almost purely on behavioural evidence, while psychopathy is identified through both behavioural and affective/interpersonal criteria (as were previous iterations of ASPD). This shift from a personality-based assessment of ASPD to a behavioural assessment was intentional, as the DSM-III Task Force felt that it was necessary to increase the reliability of the diagnosis (Arrigo & Shipley, 2001). By removing the necessary clinical inferences involved in assessing *why* deviant behaviours occurred, such as role of empathy and shallow affect, practitioners were able to base their diagnosis completely on observable characteristics. The difference in using purely behavioural criteria rather than using a mix of personality and behavioural criteria is so major that a significant

Savage Chickens by Doug Savage

ACCORDING TO THE TEST RESULTS, YOU DON'T HAVE ANTISOCIAL PERSONALITY DISORDER. IT TURNS OUT THAT YOU'RE ACTUALLY JUST AN ASSHOLE.

www.savagechickens.com © Doug Savage

While the definition of psychopathy includes core personality and emotional features associated with a lack of conscience, antisocial personality disorder is primarily defined by persistent observable behaviours deemed problematic by society.

proportion of offenders (of any kind) meet the criteria for ASPD (e.g., Arrigo & Shipley, 2001), but relatively few meet the criteria for psychopathy (e.g., Arrigo & Shipley, 2001). This is problematic, because it makes ASPD a diagnosis that provides little to aid in the differentiation of offenders, often rendering the diagnosis rather pointless. After much uproar about this problem from the academic community and practitioners, the DSM Task Force has announced that the DSM-V (expected to be released in 2013) will reinclude personality characteristics in this line of disorders, and change the name of ASPD into Psychopathy, or include psychopathy as a subtype of ASPD.

BORN OR RAISED? THE LIFESPAN TRAJECTORIES OF PSYCHOPATHS

Now that you are familiar with the construct of psychopathy, you are probably wondering how and why some people develop these psychopathic characteristics whereas most of us are concerned about others and try to adhere to societal rules (for example, in Canada, only about 10 percent of the population has a criminal record; Statistics Canada, 2000). Without getting into the philosophical argument of whether people in general are born with criminal characteristics or whether they are socialized to have them (the *blank slate* argument), this part of the chapter will explore the origins of psychopathy and the development of the disorder in individuals over time. While most researchers agree that the development of psychopathy is a combination of genetics and social environment, there are distinctly biological, environmental, and evolutionary theories that can help contextualize this disorder.

Biological Factors

Biological theories suggest that the origin of psychopathic characteristics lies in the biological makeup of the individual, including (among other explanations) genetic predispositions, and structural deficits that can happen after an individual experiences injury or trauma. While some biological theories assume that psychopathy is a stable characteristic, others simply suggest that physiological differences that develop over time can lead to the manifestation of psychopathy.

Genetics

Psychopathic characteristics, particularly callous-unemotional characteristics and antisocial behaviour, have a heritable component (e.g., Viding et al., 2005). This means that there is a genetic component to psychopathy, indicating that some individuals are predisposed to have deficits in emotionality from birth that they inherit from their parents. In fact, genetic factors are thought to account for 49 to 75 percent of the variance in the development of psychopathy, being more important than environmental factors (Waldman & Rhee, 2007; Viding et al, 2008). Most antisocial behaviour in adulthood has roots in childhood, and disorders with significant genetic contributions tend to manifest early in life, making psychopathy particularly interesting for those researching behavioural genetics (Gunter et al., 2010). Almost half of individuals with early-onset behavioural problems experience a persistence of symptoms into adulthood (Barker & Maughan, 2009), while those who develop it later in life often have short-lived antisocial episodes. This means that there appears to be a fundamental difference between those who are born with antisocial tendencies and those who develop them over time. This major difference lies in the emotionality (or lack thereof) found in early-onset antisocial individuals. Beaver et al. (2011) analyzed a sample of kinship pairs from the National Longitudinal Study of Adolescent Health to estimate the extent to which genetic factors relate to measures of psychopathic personality traits. The results of the analyses revealed that genetic factors explained between .37 and .44 of the variance in measures of psychopathy.

So, how exactly do genetics influence the development of psychopathy? In candidate gene studies, which investigate what part of an individual's genome accounts for differences between those with and without psychopathic traits, researchers have found that there is an association between the A+ genotype (blood type A positive) and elevated factor one psychopathy scores (Ponce et al., 2009). This means that individuals who have the blood type A positive are more likely to have the shallow emotions and lack of empathy associated with psychopathy than other blood types. Other ways that genes influence psychopathy are through metabolic pathways. It appears that a low-activity version of the enzyme responsible for breaking down neurotransmitters, **monoamine oxidase A (MAOA)**, has been associated with psychopathy trait scores (again, particularly factor 1) in adolescents (Fowler et al., 2009). MAOA is responsible for breaking down dopamine and serotonin (among others) and extreme abnormalities in this enzyme result in a condition called **Brunner syndrome**, which is characterized by severe impulsive behaviour. It is not surprising then that low-activity MAOA has been shown to form a vulnerability to antisocial spectrum disorders in adverse environments (Caspi et al., 2002). While all of these are significant results, it is important to understand that the MAOA variation accounts for only part of the variance in the risk for antisocial behaviour and psychopathic characteristics (Buckholtz & Meyer-Lindenberg, 2008). Epigenetic studies look at how genes develop into an individual's characteristics, also known as gene expression. In particular, there is ongoing research into how drug abuse impacts gene expression (Rutten & Mill, 2009) and how it leads to biologically significant differences in the brain tissue of psychopaths and nonpsychopaths. While this link is not yet fully understood, it appears that individuals who have nicotine, alcohol, or cannabis dependence have a different expression of MAOA and significant pathways in the brain than those who do not have substance dependence (Thalmeier et al., 2008). We still have a long road to travel before we truly understand how genetics impact psychopathy and antisocial behaviour, but there is strong evidence to suggest that particularly the emotional components of psychopathy have a genetic underpinning.

Neuroanatomy

The link between neuroanatomy and behaviour has interested researchers for centuries. Before the advent of neuroimaging tools such as FMRI, one of the only ways to examine the possible neural regions associated with behaviour was by observing behavioural and cognitive changes in individuals with damage to specific parts of the brain. While this method provides only indirect evidence of regions associated with a specific infliction, over time scientists were able to develop a primitive map of the brain. One of the most valuable cases for the study of psychopathology was that of Phineas Gage (Harlow, 1848), a railroad worker who survived an accident in which a large iron rod went completely through his head. This accident damaged a significant part of his prefrontal cortex (responsible for reasoning and higher-level thought), and his personality changed drastically. He went from a being a well-tempered man to showing characteristics now commonly associated with psychopathy: impulsivity, irresponsibility, sexual promiscuity, and verbal abusiveness (Kiehl, 2006). Further studies into the role of the prefrontal cortex in psychopathy suggest that the orbital frontal cortex (the part of your brain that is right above your eyes) specifically plays an important role in mediating psychopathic behaviours (see Kiehl, 2011). In fact, damage to the orbital frontal cortex can lead to a condition known as **pseudopsychopathy** (Blumer & Benson, 1975) or *acquired sociopathic personality* (Damasio, 1994). Patients suffering from this kind of damage have problems with empathy, impulsivity, irresponsibility, insight, behavioural inhibition, and planning, and may become prone to grandiosity and confabulation (Blumer & Benson, 1975; Malloy et al., 1993). Like psychopaths, these patients also have impaired ability to detect emotion in facial and vocal displays (Hornak et al., 2003), and that in turn impedes their decision-making ability in relation to how they respond to others (Bechara et al., 2000). While these symptoms map quite well onto the construct of psychopathy, the data suggest that patients with orbital frontal damage rarely show goal-directed or instrumental aggression and fail to display the callousness typically observed in true psychopaths (Blair, 2001). Thus, while the pseudopsychopathic symptoms mimic many of the symptoms found in true psychopathy, there are important differences between the two. This suggests that other areas of the brain likely also contribute to psychopathy.

One of these other structures is the amygdala, a part of the brain responsible for emotion recognition and regulation. In an effort to subdue patients with severe aggressive disorders **amygdalotomies** (intentional damage to the amygdala) have been performed periodically through history. Amygdalotomies were popular around the same time as the prefrontal lobotomies that you probably heard about in your intro-psych courses. Amygdalotmies successfully reduced the severity and frequency of aggressive behaviour and helped patients regain emotional control (Bagshaw et al., 1972), presumably because they removed the defective portion of the amygdala. These procedures were considered elective, meaning that patients chose to undergo the amygdala lesioning (although likely with strong encouragement from family and friends). While the overall effect was desirable, problems associated with amygdala damage include difficulty processing certain types of emotional stimuli. Patients often have difficulty recognizing faces and the emotions expressed on them (particularly fearful and angry faces), are more likely to consider strangers trustworthy, and have worse decision-making abilities (Kiehl, 2006). It appears then that certain kinds of targeted damage to the amygdala can lessen psychopathic symptoms, while damage from natural causes (developmental issues or accidents) may increase these symptoms.

Both the amygdala and the orbitofrontal cortex are part of the **paralimbic system** (also referred to as the mesocortex). Neuroimaging data, combined with the information gathered from patients with brain damage, indicates that this part of the brain is responsible for a gradual transition of signals from the primary limbic regions to higher neocortical regions. More specifically, it involves the orbital frontal cortex; medial (amygdala and parahippocampal gyrus) and lateral (anterior superior temporal gyrus) temporal lobe; and rostral, caudal, and posterior cingulate gyrus (Kiehl, 2006). Abnormalities in this system are said to be responsible for the structural foundations of psychopathy.

Environmental Predictors

Although brain impairments in psychopaths are largely believed to be caused by abnormal development, the contribution of environmental factors should not be overlooked. Early environmental and psychosocial predictors of psychopathy show the importance of the home environment on those who are predisposed to become psychopaths.

Family Background

Initial research into the role of family background found that children with psychopathic traits experience parental rejection (Partridge, 1928), rejection from mothers (Field, 1940), and early emotional deprivation (Bender, 1947). This means that children with psychopathic predispositions who grow up without strong emotional ties to their mothers are at risk for developing psychopathy. Besides attachment style, childhood physical abuse and parental alcoholism also appear to predict psychopathy (Pollak, Cicchetti, & Klorman, 1998). Children learn how others feel by watching those around them express feelings, and abusive or neglecting parents who spend little time communicating with their children may stunt the normal development of the ability to recognize the perspectives and emotions of others (Daversa, 2008). Additionally, chronic and harsh stress can also result in irreversible abnormalities in the amygdala, which leads to affective deficits (e.g., a lack of empathy). Stress can come from family instability, growing up in impoverished conditions, and having poor social support and coping mechanisms.

The **intergenerational cycle of crime** hypothesis suggests that family background plays an important role in genetically transmitting genetic vulnerability to develop antisocial behaviour and providing specific environmental interactions (Repo-Tiihonen et al., 2010). This means that parents will pass on their antisocial genes, and their interactions along with the environment they provide will form the child's antisocial personality. This was demonstrated in a study of 179 homicide offenders and their children. Forty-eight percent of the children of homicide offenders had a criminal history, with an average of 13 offences each. Those who were the children of psychopathic homicide offenders were more likely to be involved in crime against a person (e.g., violent offences), and they were prosecuted at an earlier age than children of nonpsychopathic parents. It appears that this intergenerational cycle plays an important role in facilitating the development of psychopathy. Why might this be the case? There have been several theories arguing that that early childhood abuse and neglect may contribute to certain psychopathic characteristics or even a subtype of psychopathy referred to as "secondary psychopathy."

For example, Porter (1996) theorized that primary psychopathy reflects a genetic emotional deficit, while secondary psychopathy reflects an acquired, environmentally based affective disturbance (e.g., Cook, Barese, & Dicataldo, 2010). Porter theorized that a specific environmental condition—namely extreme physical or sexual abuse by primary caretakers—results in a coping mechanism whereby some children learn to "turn off" their emotions and ultimately are unable to form or sustain significant interpersonal relationships based on positive affect. In support of this contention, several studies have found an association between abuse and psychopathy. Weiler and Widom (1996) examined the relationship between early childhood abuse, psychopathy, and violence in 652 previously abused and neglected individuals and 489 matched controls who were not victimized as children. These researchers found that individuals who experienced childhood abuse and/or neglect had significantly higher mean PCL-R scores than those in the control group. Several more recent studies have documented this relationship (e.g., Blackburn et al., 2008; Campbell, Santor, & Porter, 2004; Cima, Smeets, & Jelicic, 2008). Graham et al. (2011) examined the association between specific types of maltreatment (i.e., physical, emotional, sexual abuse, neglect) and PCL-R scores among a sample of 223 adult men convicted of sexual offences. Results indicate that childhood sexual abuse was associated with higher PCL-R total scores and facets tapping a grandiose and manipulative interpersonal style, impulsive-irresponsible lifestyle, and antisocial behaviour. While environmental influences on psychopathy have been discounted in favour of biological factors in recent years, we think that the influence of abuse on subtypes of psychopathy will be further substantiated with more research.

Evolutionary Perspectives

While most would argue that psychopathy is a mental disorder that causes considerable harm to the individual and those around him or her, others argue that psychopathy may actually be an evolved alternative approach to enhancing reproductive fitness, and that the coercive sexual behaviour typical of many psychopaths (see "Sexual Deviance" section below) may be more central to psychopathy than previously considered. The evolutionary approach suggests that male psychopaths adopt an alternative, reproductively viable strategy of attempting to pass on their genes through manipulation and coercion, including rape. Harris et al. (2007) argued that psychopaths adopt a "quantity-over-quality" strategy by engaging in sexual activity with a large number of females, either through lying and manipulation or direct aggression, and then abandonment, relying on the female's (perhaps victim's) sole investment for the upbringing of their offspring.

Despite remaining controversies, a growing body of research is consistent with this evolutionary conceptualization (see Glenn, Kurzban, & Raine, 2011). For example, compared to other sexual offenders, psychopaths engage in coercive sexual activities earlier in life, with reproductively viable females, and in ways that are more likely to result in pregnancy (i.e., genital-to-genital contact) (Harris et al., 2004; Quinsey et al., 1995). Thus, psychopaths are likely to father a (comparatively) large number of children than other men but then hold little to no investment in their children's upbringing.

These observations raise an interesting question; if psychopathy is actually an adaptive mechanism or alternative "mating" strategy, can we really still call it a disorder?

And how would this damaging lifestyle have evolved and been maintained in the modern gene pool specifically? Two evolutionary theories try to explain the origins of psychopathy.

Balancing Selection

Balancing selection suggests that psychopathic traits have been selected into our gene pool because they offer a fitness (survival/reproduction) advantage in certain environments (Glenn, Kurzban, & Raine, 2011). This suggests that because selection pressures (such as available food and mating preferences) change over time and across locations, selection can favour different types of personalities in different environments (Buss, 2009). In other words, for psychopathy to exist, the benefits of psychopathic traits must outweigh the costs in some environments. In our modern environment, for example, large cities where many interactions are one-time encounters may evoke or promote certain psychopathic traits. Individuals are likely to have many opportunities to be deceitful and manipulative in such anonymous environments without the risk of losing resources and reputation. For the individual, it may make sense to cheat and engage in antisocial behaviour in such situations as they might lead to higher personal and reproductive success. However, for this to work, psychopathic traits need to be maintained at a low frequency in the population. This is because a society cannot function properly if too many of its members adopt such parasitic lifestyles. If noticed, members of the larger group ostracize these individuals and stop sharing important resources with them. This theory has some support in the estimate that only about 0.6–1 percent of the population is psychopathic, and because many psychopaths appear to succeed in their domain of choice (e.g., crime or business) (Hare, 2003).

Deleterious Mutations

On the other hand, the **deleterious mutations** model suggests that psychopathy is a dysfunction that is a result of a series of mutations (Glenn, Kurzban, & Raine, 2011). We all carry mutations, some of which are new, but most of which are inherited and maintained through multiple generations. Mutations with very harmful effects are usually eliminated quickly from the gene pool (through death and lack of reproduction), but those with only mildly harmful effects often take much longer to remove. Over time our species has accumulated such mutations, and each of us carries a different number and type of them. This so-called mutation load is the source of some of the individual differences we observe between individuals, including differences in personality. In this framework, it has been hypothesized that psychopathy may be the result of a high mutation load of specific kinds of dysfunctions in brain development (including the amygdala). Supporting this idea of psychopathy as a dysfunction is that neurodevelopmental abnormalities and injuries tend to increase rather than decrease the risk of psychopathic traits (see Box 13.3 for a discussion of the role of neurology in psychopathy in the courtroom).

Both of these theories have received support by the literature, and ultimately it may be a combination of mutations and balancing selection that leads to the prevalence of psychopathy we see today. What do you think? Which of these theories do you think does a better job explaining this issue?

As with the application of evolutionary theory to almost any aspect of modern human behaviour, there are salient limitations in this context. For example, the evolutionary view of psychopathy is somewhat at odds with the sexual psychopath conceptualization proposed below, suggesting that the main motivation of psychopaths in perpetrating sexual crimes is thrill seeking, not reproduction.

BOX 13.3   SHOULD PSYCHOPATHS QUALIFY FOR THE NCRMD DEFENCE IN COURT?

Over the course of history psychopaths have been consistently seen as *bad* rather than *mad*, so legal institutions have not developed special considerations for them (Cooke, Forth, & Hare, 1995). If anything, psychopathy is seen as a risk factor for future crime and leads to generally harsher treatment by the legal system (e.g., Walsh & Walsh, 2006). But is this treatment still warranted now that we have accumulated significant evidence regarding the genetic and biological foundations of psychopathy? As behaviour becomes increasingly viewed as being biologically determined, legal systems generally assign less culpability to the individual. An individual who suffers from schizophrenia and commits a crime because of auditory command hallucinations ("voices" telling the individual to do something) would likely be seen as not legally culpable because the actions were driven by biological malfunction. Indeed, the legal system has safeguards in place to protect the mentally ill from unjust legal sanctions, including the NCRMD (not criminally responsible by reason of mental disorder) sentencing option. What differentiates psychopathy from other types of mental illness that might warrant an NCRMD decision is that psychopaths consistently have the mens rea (guilty mind or criminal intent), which is necessary for legal culpability.

This means that psychopaths understand the implications of their actions and they know that crime is illegal; they simply do not have the emotional systems that normally prevent people from committing crime (e.g., they lack empathy). While some argue that the fear processing deficits and neurobiological dysfunctions associated with psychopathy warrant mitigated criminal responsibility for the actions of psychopathic offenders, to date psychopathy has never been recognized as fulfilling the criteria for NCRMD in Canada (Freedman, 2008). In a recent *Scientific American* paper, noted neuroscientist Kent Kiehl and colleague Joshua Buckholtz (2010) seem to argue for an "understanding" approach with criminal psychopaths, and use the analogy of the psychopathic brain as being a "weak muscle" that should be a mitigating factor in sentencing. The problem with this argument is that psychopaths seem to have a good understanding of right and wrong, and understand ethical principles (e.g., Cima, Tonnaer, & Hauser, 2010); they simply don't "feel it." How can we have a criminal justice system in which we forgive callousness? This is a fascinating and complex intersection of psychology and law and one that we will be hearing more about and debating in coming years.

To elaborate, how can evolutionary theory explain the elevated incidence of sexual homicide found among sexual psychopaths with a reproductive goal (obviously killing the victim of one's sexual coercion guarantees no reproductive success), not to mention the targeting of "nonviable" victims such as children, animals, and other males (e.g., inmates).

THE LINK BETWEEN PSYCHOPATHY AND CRIME

Now that you are familiar with the criteria for psychopathy, it is probably quite clear how psychopathy might be linked to criminal behaviour. Psychopathy has been described as the most important forensic concept of the early 21st century (Monahan, 2006), "the most important and useful psychological construct yet discovered for criminal justice policies" (Harris, Skilling, & Rice, 2001, page number unavailable), and even "the unified theory of crime" (DeLisi, 2009, p. 256). The characteristics of psychopathy may even be considered a prescription for committing criminal acts. The lack of empathy combined with poor behavioural controls may result in both reactive violence and violence that is more predatory or premeditated in nature (Porter & Woodworth, 2006; Woodworth & Porter, 2002). Offenders with psychopathic features commit more crimes, commit a greater variety of crimes, and are more violent during the commission of their crimes (e.g. Hare, 2003). Interestingly, it appears that the impulsive and antisocial behavioural characteristics (PCL-R factor two) associated with psychopathy are most predictive of antisocial conduct (Leistico et al., 2008).

Violence

There is a well-defined relationship between psychopathy and violence (e.g., Porter & Woodworth, 2007). Because of this relationship, psychopathy has become one of the primary predictors used by clinicians to determine risk for future violence in the last two decades (Walsh & Walsh, 2006). Arguably because of the characteristics that make up the disorder, including manipulation, pathological lying, and a need for stimulation (among others), violence is high on the research agenda for those interested in psychopathy.

Research on psychopathy typically makes the distinction between instrumental violence and reactive violence. **Instrumental violence** is violence that is used to obtain a goal (e.g., to obtain money or drugs). This is different from reactive violence, which is violence in response to a perceived threat. Individuals who meet the criteria for psychopathy appear to have a higher incidence of instrumental violence than nonpsychopathic offenders. Indeed, the relationship between psychopathy and a calculating use of violence to achieve secondary personal goals is stable and consistent (Cooke et al., 2011; Cornell et al., 1996;

Flight & Forth, 2007; Porter & Woodworth, 2007; Walsh, Swogger, & Kosson, 2009; see the Canadian Researcher Profile for more information about Dr. Walsh). Even for extreme acts of violence such as murder, psychopathic individuals are more likely to kill for a personal gain rather than due to provocation; in fact, nearly all murders by psychopaths are carefully planned and are not reactive crimes (Woodworth & Porter, 2002). Part of the reason for this is the willingness of psychopaths to use others for personal gain, partly due to the callous, unemotional, and manipulative characteristics associated with PCL-R factor 1. A grandiose and manipulative interpersonal style might particularly contribute to this increased instrumental violence by reducing the fear of the consequences of violence, and using violence as a means of manipulation. With no emotional consequences of causing harm to another, the personal safeguards that normally prevent instrumental crime are removed.

CANADIAN RESEARCHER PROFILE

Zach Walsh

Zach Walsh received a Bachelor of Science with Honours in Psychology from the University of Winnipeg, and a M.A. and Ph.D. from the Chicago Medical School/Rosalind Franklin University. As a graduate student, Zach conducted research with jail inmates as a member of David Kosson's psychopathy lab. Following graduate school, Zach completed a CIHR Clinical Research Fellowship at the Brown University Center for Alcohol and Addiction Studies, where he worked with Gregory Stuart to examine the relationship between personality disorders, substance use disorders, and intimate partner violence. Zach also worked with Tracie Shea at the Brown University Department of Psychiatry and Human Behavior on the Collaborative Longitudinal Personality Disorder Study. Zach has been a member of the Centre for Advancement of Psychological Science and Law since joining the faculty of University of British Columbia in 2009. Zach is the proud owner of a pet capuchin monkey named Leary.

Zach's primary line of research focuses on specifying the relationship between psychopathic personality and violence. To this end, he has examined the consistency of the relationship between psychopathy and violence across levels of IQ, ethnicity, socioeconomic status, and neighbourhood disadvantage. This research has also involved dismantling psychopathy to examine interrelationships among narrow subcomponents of the psychopathic personality and specific classes of violent behaviour. In pursuing this line of research, Zach and his colleagues have examined patterns of relationship between subsets of psychopathic traits and instrumental aggression, intimate partner violence, and substance use. Recently, he has studied the moderating effect of psychopathy on the efficacy of substance abuse treatment for reducing partner violence, and the importance of psychopathic and normal personality traits for parsing heterogeneity among partner-violence perpetrators. In the coming years Zach plans to continue to focus his research on the complex interrelationships among personality disorders, substance use and violence, with a specific focus on psychopathy and intimate-partner violence. The ultimate goals of this research are to elucidate the factors that tie personality differences to propensity for violence, and to inform future clinical applications of the psychopathy construct.

Sexual Deviance

The relationship of psychopathy with each of sexual deviance and sexual violence has been heavily researched. Clearly, most sexual offenders are not psychopathic (e.g., Porter et al., 2000), and many psychopathic individuals may commit few or no acts of sexual violence. However, when considering some of the worst forms of sexual violence, psychopathy plays a major role. In particular, a combination of psychopathy and a predilection toward sexual aggression leads to horrific outcomes (e.g., Olver & Wong, 2006). For example, a disproportionate number of sexual homicides are perpetrated by psychopathic males (Myers et al., 2010; Porter et al., 2003). Further, Lawing, Frick and Cruise (2010) found that young sexual offenders with higher level of callous-unemotional traits (mapping onto adult psychopathy traits) had a greater number of sexual offence victims, used more violence with their victims, and engaged in more sexual offence planning than those low on these traits, similar to the findings with adults (e.g., see Porter, Demetrioff, & ten Brinke, 2010). Recently, Michael Williams, one of the perpetrators of the 2005 rape and murder of Nina Courtepatte in Edmonton, was found guilty of her first degree murder. Williams was described by the judge as a "frighteningly sadistic," "cold, cruel, callous, highly dangerous, very manipulative individual," who spoke of the rape and murder factually with little emotion (see our earlier discussion of the research by Hancock et al. (2012) on psychopathic language). Although such apparent callousness in behaviour and attitude seems incomprehensible and foreign to most, it is completely consistent with the features of psychopathic traits.

The Sexual Psychopath

But why do some psychopaths commit heinous sexual violence while others are content to victimize other people in nonviolent ways? The first author and colleagues (Porter et al., 2002, 2010) proposed the existence of a subgroup of sexual offenders they called *sexual psychopaths*, a psychological term not to be confused with the legal use of the term in various jurisdictions. Specifically, the sexual aggression by sexual psychopaths—unlike that of other sexual offenders—is associated with:

1. Diverse forms of sexual offending;
2. A primarily thrill-seeking motive (as opposed to anger or paraphilia); and
3. The use of excessive, gratuitous violence in the context of sex crimes.

The second point suggests that psychopaths who commit sexual crimes generally are not driven by a sexual deviancy but rather by "fun" or thrill seeking. This contradicts the idea that psychopaths are by nature sadistic monsters. In fact, recent research shows that psychopathy and sadism are not the same thing; they are independent conditions (Mokros et al., 2011). However, they sometimes co-occur in the same offender, which leads to a particularly high recidivism rate (see Harris & Rice, 1994). The correlation between psychopathy and deviant sexual arousal is a significant but modest one (about .20 to .28 in rapists and men convicted of sexually molesting children) (e.g., Firestone et al., 2000; Serin, Khanna, Malcolm, & Barbaree, 1994). In our view, thrill seeking rather than paraphilia is the dominant factor that spurs the psychopath to commit sex crimes. For example (e.g., Porter et al., 2010), psychopathic offender "Mr. C." most recently was convicted of the repeated sexual assaults of three teenage girls, incidents described as "master/slave" scenarios. He had previously been convicted of the serial rapes of adult females, sexual assaults on children, and even bestiality. His pattern was to target a certain victim group for a period of weeks or months and then to move to a different group. When he was asked to explain this unusual pattern, he laughed and said it was simply a matter of becoming "bored" and wanting to try out a new "experience." Not surprisingly then, when looking at the base rates of psychopathy in different kinds of sex offenders, those who commit sexual violence of various types (e.g., fondling and rape) and against various kinds of victims (e.g., children and adults) have an extremely high prevalence of psychopathy (Greenall, 2007; Olver & Wong, 2006).

In a fascinating study, Brown and Forth (1997) found that there was a significant *inverse* relationship between psychopathy and negative emotion immediately before the sexual offence. Thus, while feelings of anger, loneliness, rejection, guilt, or inadequacy may motivate many rapists, psychopathic rapists commit their crimes in a cool, unemotional manner. Psychopaths also were more likely than nonpsychopaths to experience *positive* affective states (excitement) before offending. In line with the link between psychopathy, sexual violence, and thrill seeking, psychopaths perpetrate more gratuitous violence during the commission of sexual offences (Gretton et al., 2001; Kosson, Kelly, & White, 1997; Meloy, 2000; Porter et al., 2003).

Famous Criminal Psychopaths

While there are successful and unsuccessful psychopaths, some are simply notorious. With media attention galore, some psychopaths will be in the history books as some of the most frightening individuals of all time. Ted Bundy, Robert Pickton, Clifford Olson, Joseph Fritzl, Jeffry Dahmer, and the crime duos Paul Bernardo and Karla Homolka (described in Chapter 2) and, most recently, Kruse Wellwood and Cameron Moffat (convicted in 2011 of killing Kimberly Procter and described later in the chapter [see Box 13.4 on page 330]) are just some of the infamous psychopaths who come to mind. In the interest of space, only the cases of Jeffrey Dahmer and Clifford Olson will be discussed.

Jeffrey Dahmer was an American sexual serial murderer in who killed 17 young men between the years 1978 and 1991. Dahmer typically picked up his victims at gay bars or other convenient locations, brought them to his home, and eventually murdered them. But it wasn't until 1991 that his killings became infamous. In the early morning of May 27, 1991, 14 year-old Konerak Sinthasomphone was discovered wandering naked on the street, heavily under the influence of drugs, and bleeding from his rectum. Two women from the neighborhood found the boy and called the police. Dahmer managed to catch up with his victim and tried to take him back to his house, but the women stopped him. When the police arrived, Dahmer explained that Sinthasomphone was his 19-year-old boyfriend, and that they had been in an argument while drinking. Against the protests of the two women who had called 911, police turned him over to Dahmer. That night, Dahmer killed and dismembered the boy, keeping his skull as a souvenir. For the victims to follow, Dahmer decided that he would attempt to turn them into zombies who would be completely submissive and eternally youthful sexual partners. He attempted to do so by drilling holes into their skulls and injecting hydrochloric acid into the frontal lobe of their brains with a large syringe while the victims were still alive. Dahmer was sentenced to 937 years in prison for rape, dismemberment, necrophilia, and cannibalism in 1994, and was murdered by a cellmate in 1994.

Dahmer was shown to have many of the characteristics associated with psychopathy, particularly manipulativeness, superficial charm, pathological lying, a lack of remorse, a lack of empathy, a need for stimulation, a parasitic lifestyle (he lived with his grandmother until age 29), poor behavioural controls, and promiscuous sexual behaviour. He also clearly displayed **sexual sadism** (sexual arousal derived from the infliction of pain, suffering, and/or humiliation on another individual) and necrophilia.

Clifford Olson, who died in 2011 much to the relief of the families of his many victims, was a Canadian serial killer who murdered at least 11 children and youths of both genders between 1980 and 1981. Four of these murders were committed while he was already under police surveillance as a suspect for the first seven murders. While the details of the assaults remain controversial because Olson appeared to exaggerate details (including claiming that he had murdered over 200 victims), he appeared to have a general procedure in his killings. His method of luring victims was to charmingly offer them a ride then explain that he was looking for someone to hire for a job. Posing as a construction contractor, he would take them to supposed work sites and gain their trust. Once in a secure location, Olson then offered his victims either drugs or alcohol; when the children were appropriately sedated, he beat, stabbed, or strangled them to death. While it is unclear whether he sexually abused his victims, his history of crime and persistent sexual assault against children makes sexual gratification one of the likely motivations for the murders. Possibly more notorious than his crimes is his aftermath in prison. Olson reportedly considered himself the ultimate serial killer with celebrity status akin to the famed fictional character Hannibal Lecter. He tormented the families of his victims with ongoing letters and provided a continuous stream of controversial media statements and publications from prison, until he died of cancer at the age of 71.

Olson was officially diagnosed as psychopathic while in prison, and had nearly all of the 20 main defining traits. Callous to the extreme, he was completely absent of any empathy or remorse, was extremely grandiose, and was a pathological liar who exaggerated the details of his crimes and displayed exceptional grandiosity. His superficial charm and lack of empathy were the keys to his ability to lure his victims. He also committed a wide range of crimes throughout his life, which make him high scoring on the behavioural traits associated with psychopathy. He was a prototypical psychopath preying on other Canadians in the most heinous way imaginable.

Corporate Psychopathy (Snakes in Suits)

Traditionally, most psychopathy research focused on incarcerated male violent offenders. However, over the last decade, there has been increasing attention on individuals who seem to possess the fundamental personality features of psychopathy but who may do quite well in the community for extended periods. These include in no particular order certain individuals who may thrive in corporate, political, or military settings. Many of the most powerful despots to have been successful in politics were psychopathic. For example, Stalin, who is thought to have caused the deaths of millions of people and who started off his career as a bank robber before moving into politics, fits the bill. With the current global economic crisis, key figures in the corporate world who contributed to the crisis have come under renewed scrutiny. Many of these were "white collar criminals", such as Bernie Madoff, who committed one of the largest financial frauds in history by defrauding thousands of investors of billions of dollars over the course of decades, and who seem to have some of the psychopathic features mentioned earlier. Hare has identified behaviours associated with **subclinical psychopathy,** which is a personality that meets many of the criteria for psychopathy, but not enough to warrant a full diagnosis of psychopathy (i.e., is under the 25 or 30 point cutoff). Such an individual may display callousness, a lack of empathy, greedy risk-taking behaviour, egocentricity, and superficial charm (Hare, 1993). These traits can be quite lucrative and beneficial in the cutthroat business world. Babiak and Hare (2006) have called these individuals snakes in suits, to highlight that although a psychopath may look like a well-heeled success story in business or politics, he or she is still a psychopath and will utilize any means necessary to achieve money and power. It has been argued that psychopathy:

> may be found among community groups, even high achievers, such as businessmen, politicians, doctors, lawyers and university students who, because of core features such as good social skills, high intelligence, and high socioeconomic status, may have escaped law enforcement agencies or have taken advantage of others without formally committing illegal acts. (p. 426, Salekin et al., 2001)

Are high-functioning psychopaths attracted to the business world? A study by Babiak, Neumann, and Hare (2010) indeed found that in a sample of American corporate professionals, the base rate of psychopathy was 4 to 9 times that of the general population. Researchers suggest that an increase in reports of individuals with psychopathic characteristics in the workplace has drawn more attention to this group, and it might reflect the fact that businesses place value on personal agendas consistent with the overarching business goals of increasing market share and profitability. In fact, corporations themselves have been likened to psychopaths, with their selfish profit-driven behaviour and a lack of inhibition to thwart people or other businesses that lie in their way. Some psychopathic traits may thus actually be desirable in Western society as they may help facilitate achieving the so-called American Dream. This is supported by research comparing individuals in positions of senior management with patients suffering from personality disorders. It appears that rates of the personality and interpersonal components of psychopathy (factor 1) actually exceed the rates found in the patient sample, and these traits are consistent with those identified as being important and beneficial for senior management roles (Board & Frizon, 2005).

But before psychopaths enter the workforce, some of them must go through university and obtain a degree. The chances that you have met a psychopath on campus are actually quite good. And your chances are best if you know students who are studying commerce or business. In a study of over 900 first-year students enrolled in various kinds of academic programs, students taking commerce scored significantly higher on self-report measures of psychopathy factor one scores than art, science, and law students (Wilson & McCarthy, 2011). Banking, finance, and media sectors appear particularly fertile areas for individuals with subclinical or full psychopathy to succeed. So-called **successful psychopaths** are individuals with psychopathic traits who function relatively normally in contexts such as university or business. These individuals are similar in many ways to criminal psychopaths, except that successful psychopaths have been able to remain on the right side of the law (Neumann, Hare, & Neumann, 2007), and may be more intelligent and nonviolent than the ones who end up in prison. These psychopaths have been described as manipulating others for their own personal gain in order to achieve high status within an organization, ruthless, and without a sense of personal responsibility (Boddy, 2006). Does this sound like anyone you know?

How are psychopaths able to so successfully fool and manipulate others for their own ends? Psychopaths are not only successful scam artists, but also appear to have a great ability to spot and then select vulnerable individuals around them (e.g., Wilson et al., 2008). In a sense, we are all potentially victims given our limited ability to detect deception (see Chapter 5). But in successfully duping others, psychopaths seem able to target people who are especially easy to manipulate. We might speculate that some relevant characteristics in these victims would include low self-esteem, low assertiveness, and increased depression, and anxiety (Egan & Perry, 1998). In a growing number of studies, psychopaths have shown a keen ability to detect these signs of vulnerability among others. In a fascinating study, Canadian researchers Book, Quinsey, and Langford (2007) found that psychopathic individuals are better able than nonpsychopaths to sense a lack of assertiveness after simply viewing a two-minute video of a vulnerable target. Wheeler, Book, and Costello (2009) showed that psychopaths are able to detect vulnerability based on walking style and other body language cues alone. Finally, Wilson, Demetrioff, and Porter (2008) discovered that men high in psychopathy had nearly *perfect* recall for sad and unsuccessful female characters—females who are likely to be highly vulnerable—but impaired memory for other less vulnerable characters, suggesting a truly predatory worldview in which they are seeking the "weakest gazelle." It is unknown at this time exactly how psychopaths detect vulnerability in others, but research will eventually shed more light on this phenomenon.

APPLICATIONS OF THE PSYCHOPATHY CONSTRUCT TO SPECIFIC GROUPS

Until now this chapter has focused on white male adult offenders, the sample for which the construct of psychopathy was originally developed. But does the construct of psychopathy apply equally well to other groups? Research has extensively investigated this issue and has established the validity and etiology associated with using the construct of psychopathy to help classify youth, females, and international samples.

Youth Psychopathy

Most psychopathy researchers assume that like all personality disorders, psychopathy is a lifelong condition. However, applying the construct of psychopathy to children and adolescents, along with stimulating a provocative body of research, has led to a heated academic debate. Some argue that is not possible to measure psychopathy, or any personality disorder, reliably before adulthood because of maturation and changes in personality (e.g., Vitacco & Vincent, 2006). In light of this, rather than calling young individuals "psychopaths," academics and professionals prefer to say that a young person is "displaying psychopathic traits," or having "callous-unemotional" traits. This nomenclature recognizes the potential malleability of these traits in childhood and adolescence.

Psychopathic traits can be found in children and youth, and these traits reliably predict adult psychopathy. Even children as young as three years of age can exhibit the classic characteristics of psychopathy (Glenn, Raine, Venables, & Mednick, 2007). The most important psychopathic traits identified in children and youth that predict adult psychopathy are **callous-unemotional traits (CU)**. CU traits include a lack of guilt, a lack of empathy, and the insensitive or cruel use of others. Youth with these kinds of CU features make up a group with a particularly severe, aggressive, and stable pattern of antisocial behaviour (Frick & White, 2008). Despite the high levels of stability, research also suggests that traits can still be somewhat malleable in these younger groups (Frick, et al., 2003).

Campbell and colleagues (2004) note that adolescents with a high level of psychopathic traits are more likely to have shown an earlier onset of conduct problems, to present with a greater variety and severity of delinquent behaviours, and to have symptoms of conduct disorder, narcissistic personality disorder, and oppositional defiant disorder (e.g., Murrie & Cornell, 2000). Recent Canadian research indicated that psychopathy has a moderate to high level of stability from childhood to adulthood (Lee, Klaver, Hart, Moretti, & Douglas, 2009).

While there are differences, childhood psychopathy generally "looks like" adult psychopathy. Even the antisocial and criminal behaviour committed by young children and youth with psychopathic traits parallel that of adult psychopaths. For example, Lawing, Frick, and Cruise (2010) found that offenders high on CU traits had a greater number of sexual offence victims, used more violence with their victims, and engaged in more sexual offence planning than those low on these traits, which is similar to the patterns found for adult sexual offenders. These kinds of patterns are especially important in light of the high base rates of psychopathy among young offender groups, which are estimated to lie between 15 percent and 37 percent (Kosson et al., 2002).

Partly because of the demonstrated stability of these constructs in youth, and partly to help practitioners identify youth at particular risk for future violence and offending, tools to assist in the discrimination of children and youth with psychopathic traits have been developed. The Childhood Psychopathy Scale (CPS; Lynam 1997) and the **Psychopathy Checklist—Youth Version** (PCL-YV; Forth, Kosson, & Hare, 2003), both heavily based on the PCL-R, particularly help experts and academics assess and screen for psychopathic characteristics in those who are too young to be diagnosed with the adult PCL-R.

Whether children and adolescents should be given a label of psychopathy remains a hotly debated topic, with many arguing that the stigma associated with being deemed a psychopath is detrimental to potential rehabilitation efforts. Just imagine the repercussions of a child or adolescent being labelled a psychopath. Schools, legal institutions, and even parents are likely to discriminate against the individual. A self-fulfilling prophecy might be set into motion, leading an individual who might have "grown out of it" to instead be doomed to a life with adult psychopathy. However, justification of the use of the psychopathy label for youth appears in the stability of the construct, which highlights the importance of early detection and intervention. Early detection would allow more appropriate correctional efforts and an increased knowledge regarding how to work with this population. While the stigma associated with the label may be detrimental in some aspects, the benefits associated with early intervention and possibly diminishing the psychopathic characteristics experienced by an individual arguably outweigh the potential costs.

Female Psychopathy

Is the construct of psychopathy applicable to delinquent females? Most of the research on psychopathy has focused on males, partly due to the

---

Young psychopaths pose an interesting challenge to the criminal justice system. Generally under the protection of laws that conceal their identity and make them eligible for lesser sentences than adults, individuals who commit crimes before the age of 18 (psychopathic or not) are granted a reasonable amount of leniency. In extreme cases, however, young offenders can be tried as adults. One of these extreme cases involves two psychopathic youth, Kruse Wellwood and Cameron Moffat from Colwood, British Columbia.

Wellwood and Moffat (who were 16 and 18 at the time) sexually assaulted and brutally murdered their female classmate, Kimberly Proctor, after which they mutilated her body with a knife. They then stored her body in a freezer overnight, placed the remains into a duffle bag, and put the body near a forest trail before setting it on fire. The boys had extensively planned the murder through text messages and online chats prior to

committing the offence. In line with the parental influences on psychopathy explained earlier in this chapter, Wellwood's father had also brutally killed a teenage girl after sexually assaulting her when Wellwood was a child. Indeed, the newspapers began talking about a potential "family reunion" as Wellwood was at one point scheduled to serve his adult sentence for murder in the same prison as his father.

According to the published psychological and psychiatric reports offered at sentencing, Wellwood and Moffat clearly met the criteria for psychopathy and sexual sadism. They lacked empathy, lacked remorse for their horrific crimes, had extensive histories of delinquency, were manipulative liars, and had narcissistic or grandiose traits. These traits became particularly apparent in a publicly released audio recording of the boys jokingly talking about the incident and the legal proceedings surrounding it.

---

underrepresentation of females in the correctional system. The few studies that have incorporated females into samples of psychopathic offenders have demonstrated that the construct is applicable across gender (e.g., Cale & Lilienfeld, 2002; Cook, Barese, & Dicataldo, 2010; Kreis & Cooke, 2011). However, female psychopathy has a lower base rate in correctional samples relative to male psychopathy (e.g., Forth et al., 1996). Similar to their male counterparts, psychopathic traits in females are predictive of violent behaviour and theft but, unlike males, psychopathy in females is unrelated to drug abuse (Vaughn et al., 2008). Additionally, specific traits such as a lack of planning and narcissism seem to play a more pivotal role in psychopathy for females. It has been suggested that female sex offenders come from more deprived backgrounds than other female offenders, and that they have often suffered extreme emotional, physical, and sexual abuse (e.g., Wijkman, Bijleveld, & Hendriks, 2010). Although psychopathy appears to be linked to male sexual offending (Quinsey, Lalumiere, Rice, & Harris, 1995), there is little support for psychopathy as a risk factor for female sex offending (Strickland, 2008).

Regarding the etiology of psychopathy for women, it appears that interpersonal and affective facets of psychopathy in adolescence are more important for the development of adult female psychopathy than male psychopathy. Researchers have looked at psychopathy and recidivism from adolescence to young adulthood, and have found that psychopathic female adolescents are less likely to reoffend than male adolescents (Salekin, 2008), but that the PCL-R is predictive of recidivism among both men and women (e.g., Coid et al., 2009). So, while it appears that there are some gender differences regarding the predictive value of psychopathy, it is valuable to view these within the larger context, which suggests that there are broader gender differences in patterns and motivation pertaining to crime and recidivism in general (e.g., Odgers, Moretti, & Reppucci, 2005), regardless of psychopathy designation. In other words, the same reasons females commit less crime in general might also be protective factors against developing psychopathic traits. Overall, psychopathic females are at an elevated risk for antisocial behaviour and recidivism compared to their female peers, but are at a lower level of risk than psychopathic males. Much more research is needed to help understand psychopathy in females, and how psychopathy and behaviour may be related differently for women than for men.

Together Paul Bernardo and Karla Homolka sexually assaulted and murdered three adolescent girls, including Homolka's own sister.

CAN PSYCHOPATHY BE TREATED?

In 1941 Cleckley, the grandfather of the modern construct of psychopathy, described psychopaths as neither benefiting from treatment nor forming the emotional bond to the therapist required for effective treatment. This certainly makes intuitive sense when we consider the biological factors and the types of traits that characterize psychopathy. It is presumably hard to rehabilitate someone who has no empathy, makes excuses for his or her actions, and does not have remorse for his or her crimes. And most importantly, he or she lacks any motivation to change! Additionally, developing a therapeutic relationship with an individual who is unemotional and a pathological liar is an exceptionally challenging task. But, considering the larger scope of the types of treatment forensic psychologists need to administer on a daily basis, *all* offenders probably have some characteristics that make them difficult to rehabilitate, regardless of whether or not they are psychopathic.

Treatment for psychopaths often is the same as treatment for any other kind of offender. Psychopathic offenders are typically placed into correctional programs, such as substance abuse programs or violence prevention programs, based on their behavioural (rather than emotional/cognitive) needs. These programs are typically conducted in groups of both psychopathic and nonpsychopathic individuals, and the psychopathic individual is not treated differently. In other words, most treatment programs to date are not tailored to meet the unique needs of psychopaths. There are many inherent problems with this kind of approach, but with the limited resources available in correctional facilities, this kind of treatment is often the only possibility. While there is a move by some researchers to tailor treatment to psychopaths and other high-risk offenders (e.g., Skeem, Polaschek, & Manchak, 2009), these types of programs are still very rare.

Not surprisingly, observations on the effectiveness of treatment with psychopaths have not been encouraging (Hare, 2003; Lösel, 1998; Rice, 1997; Rice, Harris, & Cormier, 1992). For example, Richards and colleagues (2003) evaluated the role of psychopathy in treatment response in a large sample of adult female offenders. Psychopaths showed poorer response to treatment in terms of noncompliance, violent and disruptive violations, avoidance of urinalysis testing, low attendance, and low therapist progress ratings. Using a sample of adult male offenders, Hobson, Shine, and Roberts (2000) found that higher psychopathy scores were associated with a higher incidence of misbehaviours (e.g., lying, verbal outbursts) in a treatment group. Probably the most referenced study on the treatability of psychopaths was conducted by Rice, Harris and Cormier in 1992. In this study, the researchers evaluated the efficacy of a maximum-security therapeutic community to reduce recidivism for 176 mentally disordered offenders, of whom some met the criteria for psychopathy. They found that treatment was effective in reducing violent recidivism for nonpsychopathic offenders to 22 percent compared to 45 percent in the control group. They also found that treatment was associated with a *higher* rate of violent

recidivism for psychopathic offenders compared to untreated psychopathic offenders, at 77 percent and 55 percent respectively. The authors suggested that because psychopaths learn interpersonal skills in treatment, treatment may actually make them more able to manipulate and exploit others, making them more likely to commit crime than before undergoing treatment. This study was widely adopted as indicating that efforts to treat psychopaths are futile and detrimental. Psychopaths gained the label "untreatable," which hindered research funding and interest in rehabilitation efforts aimed at psychopaths. Unfortunately, this study has been challenged for its methodological limitations and the authors were working with a very small subsample of high-risk psychopathic offenders (e.g., see D'Silva, Duggan, & McCarthy, 2004).

Initial misinterpretations of this study and apparent tunnel vision with regard to the treatability of psychopaths seems to have led to a common notion that psychopathic offenders cannot benefit from treatment. This notion is countered by the recent literature that has shown promising results regarding the treatability of psychopathic offenders. Most of the recent studies have made positive conclusions regarding reducing recidivism and violence for psychopathic offenders, suggesting that psychopaths do benefit from treatment. Although often effects are smaller for psychopathic program participants than nonpsychopaths, partly due to higher dropout rates and being expelled, small to moderate positive effects are typically observed for psychopaths who complete violence-reduction and substance abuse treatment (Burke, 2004; Skeem, Polaschek, & Manchak, 2009). These positive treatment effects appear to be similar for psychopathic individuals and violent individuals with other personality disorders (Wong, Gordon, & Gu, 2007). Canadian researchers Mark Olver and Steve Wong (2009) looked at the therapeutic responses of psychopathic sex offenders over a 10-year follow-up among 156 federally incarcerated sex offenders treated in a high-intensity sex offender program. Although psychopaths were more likely to drop out, almost 75 percent of them completed treatment. Further, psychopathic offenders who failed to complete treatment were more likely to recidivate violently than treatment completers. Positive treatment changes were associated with reductions in sexual and violent recidivism after psychopathy was controlled. The good news was that with a well-informed treatment program, most psychopathic offenders are able to complete treatment and some can even benefit in terms of showing a reduction in both sexual and violent recidivism.

Thus, even psychopaths who are sexual offenders have demonstrated positive improvements and reductions in recidivism through intervention (e.g., Abracen, Looman, & Langton, 2008). While there has only been limited research on sexual psychopaths, it has provided support for the effectiveness of sex offender treatment. In a review on the effectiveness of sex offender treatment for psychopathic offenders, Doren and Yates (2008) found that sex offender treatment does not appear to reduce serious recidivism for psychopaths to the same degree it does for nonpsychopaths and that individual differences in outcomes are larger for psychopathic groups. In other words, some psychopaths show significant reductions in sexual recidivism (at the same rates as non-psychopaths), while other psychopaths do not benefit from treatment as much. When these two groups of psychopaths are erroneously collapsed, the treatment seems wholly ineffective. Unfortunately, research has evaluated only the extent to which psychopaths benefit from treatment relative to nonpsychopaths, rather than how treated psychopaths fare compared to untreated psychopaths, making the treatment results hard to interpret. It seems that whether treatment benefits psychopathic sex offenders remains to be firmly established, but it is important to keep in mind that some studies have shown significant improvements and that there is hope that we can successfully rehabilitate at least some types of sexual psychopaths. Further, it has been demonstrated that the effort and time put into treatment makes a difference. Skeem, Monahan, and Mulvey (2002), for example, found that longer involvement in outpatient treatment (at least seven sessions) reduced the risk of violence among psychopathic individuals discharged from a nonforensic inpatient setting when compared to those who received fewer than seven sessions of treatment.

What about early intervention? Does treating young psychopaths show more clear results than treating adult psychopaths? While treating psychopathic youth poses significant issues, some studies have indicated small or moderate reductions in recidivism relating to treatment. Base rates of recidivism are high for psychopathic youth, with frequently reported rates around 64 percent for nonviolent offending, and 41 percent for violent offending (e.g., Salekin, 2008). With a sample of 64 youths enrolled in a substance abuse treatment program, researchers studied the impact of psychopathy

on treatment cooperation and treatment outcome (O'Neill et al., 2003). Youth scoring high on the PCL-YV attended the program for fewer days and participated less when they did attend. While the researchers found some clinical improvement, psychopathic youth demonstrated significantly less improvement over the course of treatment than their peers. These findings are similar to those mentioned earlier with regard to adults. In a well-designed study by Caldwell and colleagues (2006), 141 juvenile offenders with high scores on the PCL-YV were evaluated on their responsiveness to treatment. The psychopathic youth were assigned to either an intensive treatment program at a correctional institution, or treatment as usual (non-specialized generic treatment) in a conventional correctional setting. Youth who participated in the intensive treatment were half as likely to reoffend violently after two years as those receiving normal treatment. Additionally, intensive treatment was independently associated with relatively slower and lower rates of serious recidivism. These studies show promising advancements in the treatment of psychopathic youth, and point toward the value of programs tailored to dealing with the unique issues faced by psychopathic young offenders.

Ultimately, while the results are promising, most experts today would suggest that we simply don't know whether psychopaths can be treated. Conflicting evidence and controversy about the origins of psychopathy and how to approach rehabilitation has set the stage for passionate researchers who are set on finding out the answer. Today, the untreatability assumption continues to be widely and strongly held, and it has influenced public policy and law, as discussed in Box 13.5 on the death penalty and psychopathy. Regardless, it must be conceded that adult psychopaths represent a unique and challenging group of offenders who can be expected to be resistant to treatment. According to leading researchers, programs should focus on altering and managing *behaviour* rather than on changing the core personality characteristics of the psychopath (Quinsey et al., 2006; Wong & Hare, 2005). Often, intense supervision in the form of probation or parole with strict conditions will be needed and in the most extreme cases preventive detention may be warranted (i.e., long-term/indeterminate incarceration) (Quinsey et al., 2006). Finally, treatment providers must be especially careful not to be deceived into seeing progress (e.g., Porter et al., 2009; Seto & Barbaree, 1999) when what they really are observing is a performance worthy of an Academy Award.

With the notion of psychopathy being a stable characteristic that is strongly predictive of violence and future crime, and is potentially untreatable, its application to **death penalty** cases seems understandable even if morally questionable. In recent years, psychopathy assessments (most notably the PCL-R) have been introduced to death penalty cases in the United States to provide evidence for the clause that a defendant will *represent a continuing threat to society*, even if imprisoned for life (Edens, Petrila, & Buffington-Vollum, 2001). This would mean that, for example, an offender would continue to offend within the confines of prison or manage to escape and wreak havoc in the community. If an individual has committed a crime that is sufficiently severe and meets these dangerousness criteria, it should warrant capital punishment in the eyes of the law. While capital punishment trials have colloquially used the terms "psychopath" and "sociopath" to refer to defendants for centuries, the use of empirically validated measures to justify this designation changes the nature of its inclusion. The only possible argument for basing death penalty judgments on psychopathy scores is that *all* psychopaths are eternally offenders, which as the literature has demonstrated is clearly not the case. There is no empirical base for this kind of application, and it lends the designation superficial credibility. Introducing a defendant's psychopathy scores as a piece of evidence warranting capital punishment also biases jurors and fosters harsher sentences.

Note: This issue is directly contrary to recent attempts to introduce psychopathy as a mitigating factor in courts, as discussed in Box 13.3 on page 324.

SUMMARY

Psychopathy is a complex personality construct comprising two primary factors. Factor one features include interpersonal and emotional traits such as pathological lying and a lack of empathy and remorse, while factor two features include behaviour-oriented traits. The construct has changed in its definition and nomenclature over time, evolving from *manie sans délire* to sociopathy and to psychopathy. Most recently, the standardized Psychopathy Checklist—Revised, has made it easy to differentiate the diagnostic criteria for psychopathy versus other related constructs such as antisocial personality disorder. Defining and standardizing the measurement of psychopathy has made it easier to research the origins of psychopathy. These are still not well understood but certainly include genetics and biology (particularly in the prefrontal cortex and the amygdala), and also significant but as-yet unclear environmental factors. It also is possible that there are subtypes of psychopathy in terms of etiology and that some cases of psychopathy may result from chronic abuse early in life and other cases that may be primarily genetically driven. Psychopathy is associated with instrumental aggression and gratuitous violence, which appear to be associated with a thrill-seeking motive. Not all psychopaths are criminals; a recent research spotlight has been shining on white-collar psychopathy. The construct of psychopathy applies to each of children, youth, and females, although more research is required on each of these groups. Finally, treatment efforts aimed at psychopaths have shown some failures but some recent promising results, although the jury is still out on whether psychopathy can effectively be treated.

KEY TERMS

empathy, p. 314

halo effect, p. 315

instrumental violence, p. 325

intergenerational cycle
of crime, p. 322

manie sans délire (moral
insanity), p. 313

MAOA (monoamine oxidase A),
p. 320

paralimbic system, p. 321

pseudopsychopathy,
p. 321

Psychopathy Checklist—
Revised, p. 315

Psychopathy Checklist—Youth
Version, p. 330

sexual sadism, p. 327

sociopathic personality
disturbance, p. 314

subclinical psychopathy, p. 328

successful psychopaths, p. 328

SUGGESTED READINGS

Babiak, P., & Hare, R. D. (2006). *Snakes in suits: When psychopaths go to work*. New York: HarperCollins.

An interesting read on successful psychopaths.

Hare, R. D. (1993). *Without conscience: The disturbing world of the psychopaths among us*. New York: Guilford.

A classic read by the world's leading expert on psychopathy.

Hare, R. D., & Neumann, C. S. (2008). Psychopathy as a clinical and empirical construct. *Annual Review of Clinical Psychology, 4*, 217–246.

A great review of recent literature on psychopathy.

Skeem, J., Polaschek, D., Patrick, C., & Lilienfeld, S. (2011). Psychopathic personality: Bridging the gap between scientific evidence and public policy. *Psychological Science in the Public Interest, 12*, 95–162

A comprehensive review of psychopathy with an interesting discussion about treatment options.

CHAPTER

14

The Role of Psychology in Sentencing, Parole, and Dangerous Offender Hearings in Canada

> *Parole is intended for "a young man of good character, who may have committed a crime in a moment of passion ... [that] there is a good report on him while in confinement and it is supposed that if he were given another chance, he would be a good citizen."*
>
> —Prime Minister Wilfrid Laurier in introducing the basis of our modern parole system, An Act to Provide for the Conditional Liberation of Convicts, on August 11, 1899

In this chapter, we explore how the Canadian legal system deals with offenders who have been found guilty of a crime(s), and some of the major psychological factors that play a role in such decision making. Then we examine the prominent roles played by psychologists in facilitating these decisions.

Students should keep in mind that some dramatic changes may be occurring to our existing laws around sentencing and conditional release (perhaps they have already occurred by the time you read this!). There is much controversy over whether the current sentencing guidelines are appropriate and whether our parole system is working. The current (2013) Conservative government under Stephen Harper is taking a "tough on crime" approach, which includes major proposed changes to the current sentencing and parole frameworks. According to the Parliament of Canada website, the omnibus crime bill known as C-10 may restrict the use of conditional sentencing, increase the length of prison sentences, and place major prohibitions on those seeking a pardon. Some specific changes to the Criminal Code will include:

1. Mandatory minimum sentences: a large number of drug, sex, violent, and other serious offences will now have longer stipulated prison sentences, which will lead to a huge increase in numbers of federal offenders and the costs of their incarceration

2. More severe sentences for sexual offences against children

3. An end to house arrest (conditional sentences) for a large range of crimes

4. Longer sentences for violent and repeat young offenders

5. More rights for victims of crime to participate in parole decisions

6. More powers for correctional staff to penalize offenders for problematic institutional behaviour and for the police when parole conditions are violated.

Given the current majority status of the federal government, it is likely that these proposals will be realized in Parliament and become law. The trend toward American-style incarceration policies seems to be already in motion (Calverley, 2010). In Canada, from 2008 to 2009 there was a huge increase in government funding allocated to incarceration ($3.9 billion, or a 7 percent increase; Calverley, 2010).

PSYCHOLOGICAL FACTORS IN SENTENCING

In Canada, we, of course, rely upon the Criminal Code of Canada (2010) in which all of our codified offences are described and accompanied by various sentences, from probation to life in prison (capital punishment was abolished in 1976). For most indictable (more serious) offences, judges have a range of options for deciding on an appropriate sentence. For example, if one is found guilty of second-degree murder, he or she can be given a prison sentence ranging from 10 years to life, depending on the presence of **aggravating factors** (such as a breach of trust or domestic violence leading to a higher sentence) and **mitigating factors** (such as being a first-time offender, being remorseful, etc., leading to a lighter sentence).

In a given criminal case, both the prosecutor and defence have an opportunity to outline their views of an appropriate sentence and the judge then makes his or her decision, which can lean in one direction or the other, or be lower or higher than both of the lawyers' recommendations. A common outcome is for the judge to come down somewhere in the middle of the recommended sentences. The Criminal Code (section 718) outlines the primary principles of sentencing (also see a book on the topic by Honourable Justice Gilles Renaud, 2009), including **denunciation** or punishment, **deterrence** (specific to the offender and general to citizens who might contemplate a similar crime), **rehabilitation**, and the **promotion of responsibility**. In an individual case, the judge usually outlines his or her reasons for the chosen sentence, in accordance with these principles. In order for the judge to apply these principles and come up with the most appropriate sentence, it is increasingly common in Canada for the court to order a **presentence psychological report**, especially in cases involving violence or young offenders. The first author of this textbook has done many of these, and it is clear that judges take them seriously in formulating their sentencing decisions. In such reports, the psychologist addresses the following in making recommendations for appropriate sentencing: risk for reoffence, remorse/insight into the criminal behaviour, and potential for rehabilitation. Relevant information to inform such opinions includes criminal history, substance abuse history, education/employment history, mental health history, psychological testing, actuarial prediction of risk (using instruments such as the HCR-20, VRAG, and PCL-R as described in Chapters 10, 12, and 13 respectively), and clinical impressions of personality, sincerity, and motivation (e.g., see Melton, Petrila, Poythress, & Slobogin, 2007). We might refer to these considerations as "relevant psychological variables." And unique relevant variables will come up in individual cases. For example, in one presentence report conducted by the first author, a key issue was trauma and PTSD. The young offender had grown up in Rwanda; at the time of the 1994 genocide, he was 10, and had witnessed the machete slaughter of several of his immediate family members and friends. At this young age, he also had to kill an adult attacker in self-defence after he was chased by a group of killers for days. Now living in Canada, he was charged with a serious assault occurring when someone made a racial slur toward him. My report focused on his PTSD diagnosis and unique, tragic experiences in putting his crime into context; the judge agreed that these were mitigating circumstances.

Of course, as with deciding whether a defendant is guilty, judicial decisions about sentencing are influenced by a broad range of factors that, objectively, should be irrelevant (see Vidmar, 2011). There is a robust body of research showing that human decision making is subject to a host of biases to the extent that often it is completely irrational (e.g., Kahneman & Tversky, 1982). Although they no doubt try to stay objective, judges are not immune from such human biases. For example, research indicates that judges' sentencing decisions are heavily influenced by schemas based on their past experiences with defendants and complainants (e.g., Greenberg & Ruback, 1982; Konecni & Ebbesen, 1982). Further, like everyone else judges are susceptible to critical thinking errors and a reliance on false stereotypes (e.g., Granhag & Stromwall, 2004; Vrij, 2000, 2004; Vrij & Mann, 2004). And, not surprisingly, judges often are completely unaware of the influence of their biases in the courtroom (e.g., Kaufmann et al., 2003). Sporer and Goodman-Delahunty (2009) reviewed four categories of unconscious sources of potential bias in sentencing:

1. *Features associated with the judge.* These include gender, a "just world" outlook, and personal sentencing philosophy. For example, an archival study of 27 000 cases found that female judges were more severe than male judges in sentencing violent offenders (Myers & Talarico, 1987).

2. *Features associated with the defendant.* These include gender, facial characteristics such as baby-facedness, physical attractiveness, and emotional displays by the offender. For example, female defendants tend to receiver lighter sentences than men who commit similar crimes, and individuals who look baby-faced (e.g., Zebrowitz & McDonald, 1991) and/or physically attractive (e.g., Porter, Gustaw, & ten Brinke, 2010) tend to get more lenient sentences (e.g., Mazella & Feingold, 1994). As reviewed in chapter 8 Porter et al. (2010) found that mock jurors required less evidence to arrive at a guilty verdict and were more confident in this decision for untrustworthy-appearing defendants. Similarly, particular faces are viewed as being congruent with certain criminal offences. Thus, there are some faces that people agree "look like" that of a rapist, armed robber, or murderer (Bull & McAlpine, 1998), and if a defendant has a face that is considered to be consistent with the charged offence, he or she is more likely to be convicted than an individual with an "incongruent" face (Dumas & Teste, 2006; Macrae & Shepherd, 1989).

3. *Unanticipated or remote consequences of the offence such as severe injury to the victim (relative to a similar offence in which such injury did not occur).* For example, judges are

Savage Chickens

by Doug Savage

YOU'VE GOT VISITORS

www.savagechickens.com © Doug Savage

The trend in Canada toward the increasing use of minimum mandatory and stiffer sentences may result in the incarceration of many first-time offenders who previously would have received a conditional sentence or house arrest. What will be the impact of such measures on these individuals' family relationships and employment?

more severe in sentencing someone in a drunk driving case in which a victim was struck and killed versus being slightly injured.

4. *Contextual information at the time of the sentencing decision that heightens awareness of mortality.* When judges are prompted to think about their own death ("mortality salience") they tend to give more severe sentences (e.g., Kugler & Cooper, 2010).

Recent research even shows that simply having an empty stomach can profoundly influence judges' decisions. Danziger, Levav, and Avnaim-Pesso (2011) studied more than 1000 judicial decisions in Israeli courts and found that the percentage of favourable rulings for a defendant is dramatically lower right before a lunch break versus after the break!

UNCONSCIOUS RACISM AND SENTENCING DECISIONS

A recent review by Vidmar (2011), a major figure in research on judicial decision making, addressed the need for more research examining the manner in which judges formulate their trial and sentencing decisions. A recurring theme of his review is that judges are no better than laypersons at disregarding "non-relevant" factors in making decisions about guilt or sentencing. For example, he noted that **unconscious racism** often played a role in legal decision making. In one American study, Rachlinski, Johnson, Wistrich, and Guthrie (2009) found that judges were similar to lay-persons in that they were more punitive in sentencing black defendants versus those of other backgrounds. Other research he reviewed showed that defendants with more stereotypical black physical features were treated more harshly than other defendants; Eber-hardt, Davies, Purdie-Vaughns, and Johnson (2006) As reviewed in chapter 8 found that stereotypical-appearing black defendants in murder cases were more likely to receive the death penalty then defendants in similar cases. Given the gross overrepresentation of Aboriginal people in Canadian prisons, one must wonder whether such covert racism plays a role. Aboriginal people account for 13 percent of Canada's federal offenders, but only 3 percent of the Canadian population (Public Works & Government Services Canada, 1999; see Box 14.1 for more information). Given that they are so grossly overrepresented in Canadian prisons, one cannot help but wonder whether Aboriginals' nonverbal behaviour in the courtroom could be frequently and unfairly interpreted.

Brant (1993) discussed the nonverbal communication patterns of some Aboriginal groups that may be construed by non-Aboriginals as passive, difficult, and deceptive. In particular, Aboriginal people may, as predicated by their culture, suppress expressions of their emotions. Such flat affect may be considered inconsistent with the context at hand, and considered a sign of guilt, lack of remorse, or deception by decision makers (Kaufmann et al., 2003). Howard, Quinn, Blokland, and Flynn (1993) examined similar potential biases against Australian Aboriginal people, noting that:

There are major differences between Western and Aboriginal socio-linguistic etiquette; for example, in expectations about eye contact and the obligation to answer questions ... Many experienced judicial officers and counsel are aware of differing socio-linguistic etiquette that contribute to Aboriginal court-room demeanour. However, Aboriginal liaison officers also describe instances of Aboriginal defendants being berated by magistrates, or their own lawyers, for failure to participate as expected in court processes. Further, they report that there is the very real danger of Aboriginal court-room demeanour (not answering

According to section 718.2(e), the judge must consider all reasonable alternatives to prison before electing a period of incarceration, especially in the case of Aboriginal offenders. This resulted from the case of *R. v. Gladue* (1999) in which the Canadian court found that Aboriginal people have experienced a long-standing disadvantage in Canadian society and that the effects continue to be felt, leading to the dramatic overrepresentation of Aboriginal offenders in Canadian prisons (Statistics Canada, 2009). The landmark *Gladue* finding was controversial because of the seemingly light sentence given to the offender who was female, a mother, and Aboriginal. On September 16, 1995,

Jamie Tanis *Gladue* was celebrating her 19th birthday and drinking with a group of friends. Evidence indicated that she believed that her boyfriend was having a sexual relationship with her own older sister, Tara. During the evening, Gladue relayed specific threats that the victim was "going to get it." There was a confrontation during which the victim repeatedly insulted Gladue, after which she stabbed him in the chest. After being convicted of manslaughter, the judge considered her youth, her status as a mother, the absence of any serious criminal history, and her status as an Aboriginal person to be mitigating factors and sentenced her to three years in prison. What do you think of this approach?

---

questions, avoidance of eye contact, turning away from those attempting to communicate) being interpreted as indicating guilt, defiance or contempt. The Australian Law Reform Commission has noted the unreliability of demeanour as an indicator of truthfulness. Nevertheless demeanour continues to be used as an indicator of credibility of witnesses.

McDonald (1993) offered a number of observations concerning the communication styles of some Aboriginal people in Canada that may be relevant in the legal decision-making context:

1. In contrast to mainstream Canadian society where responses are quick, First Nations people may pause before offering a response.
2. First Nations people tend not to engage in "small talk." As a result, they may be judged as shy, reticent, or uncooperative by an interviewer when, in fact, the behaviour may actually indicate they feel that there is nothing worthwhile to say, so there is no reason to comment.
3. First Nations people may appear stoic or unconcerned because of a belief that it is improper to share personal feelings or information with a stranger.
4. Expect short and direct answers to questions. As well, there may be a cultural tendency not to volunteer information.
5. Lack of eye contact from First Nations people may mean respect for the interviewer/authority figure (Shebib, 2003).

The final point made by McDonald concerning eye contact is of particular relevance in the legal context. Brant (1993) observed that for most

Caucasian Canadians "people who do not provide direct eye contact are seen … as being shifty, devious, dishonest, crooks, slippery, untrustworthy, etc." (p. 261) (as we described in Chapter 5 on deception). In contrast, in most Aboriginal cultures in Canada, direct, sustained eye contact is seen as "rude, hostile, intrusive" (Brant, 1993, p. 261). That is, the Aboriginal custom of avoiding eye contact is intended as a sign of respect. Such behaviour may easily be construed as an indication of deception by individuals, including members of the judiciary, who adhere to the belief that liars avert their gaze (e.g., Global Deception Research Team, 2006; Stromwall & Granhag, 2003). In fact, research indicates that avoidance of eye contact is the number one sign of lying to which professionals and laypersons attend (Bond & Atoum, 2000; Porter & ten Brinke, 2010).

It is critical that judges or parole officers contemplate the manner in which they assess the credibility of an individual defendant or parole applicant, and whether his or her cultural background could be leading to a particular behaviour.

PSYCHOLOGICAL FACTORS IN PAROLE DECISION MAKING

As suggested by the quote at the start of the chapter, we've had a parole system in Canada for more than a century. This system of graduated release for federally incarcerated offenders (those with a sentence of at least two years) is by no means universal; for example, it is not practised in China and has been abolished in 16 American states. While Prime Minister Laurier implied that parole was originally intended for a "good" individual who made a single mistake in a fleeting moment of passion, our modern parole system is based on the contention that *most* offenders should be returned to the community with legally binding "conditions" prior to the end of their sentence. The intention is to support—and monitor—their reintegration into society gradually, as opposed to simply opening the prison gate at the end of the sentence with no further capacity to control the individual's behaviour.

With this system, the incarcerated offender is motivated by the possibility of early release to maintain positive institutional behaviour and take treatment programs, making the prison a safer place for staff and, in theory, promoting his or her rehabilitation. Secondly, after the offender is released into the community, the correctional system can set conditions, such as abstaining from alcohol and drugs, avoiding certain people or populations such as children, a curfew, or whatever the judge deems necessary. The offender's behaviour can be monitored on a regular basis by parole staff, and he or she can be reincarcerated for violating such conditions. Nowadays, only the very most dangerous offenders with determinate sentences complete their entire sentence to **warrant expiry**, an outcome requiring a "detention" hearing in which traditionally it must clearly be shown that the individual represents a high imminent risk for violence to the community. However, this is a major point of contention of the reigning Conservative government in Canada (see below) which passed a bill dictating that this will apply for an imminent risk for nonviolent crimes as well.

In reality, for several decades the Canadian corrections, policy essentially has been to "automatically" release federal offenders after two-thirds of their sentence on "statutory release" (this used to be called "mandatory supervision") (Correctional Service of Canada, 2008). Offenders automatically released are expected to follow specific conditions (depending on the nature of their criminal offence history including abstaining from alcohol and drugs, not being in the presence of a minor, etc.). If such conditions are violated, the offender will be returned to custody potentially until the end of his or her sentence. There are many other possibilities for early release prior to mandatory supervision. For example, many nonviolent offenders with a minimum three-year sentence are eligible to apply for early release after one sixth of their sentence on day parole. If granted day parole, the offender is released into the community during the daytime but must return to either a halfway house or prison at night (Cor-

rectional Service Canada, 2008). When an offender is granted full parole, he or she is allowed to live under supervision in the community, but again must adhere to a set of conditions that, if violated, can lead to re-incarceration.

Parole staff of the Correctional Service of Canada (CSC) which runs Canadian prisons, continue to oversee conditionally released offenders in the community and monitor their behaviour. However, the ultimate decision to grant parole is done by the National Parole Board of Canada, an independent administrative tribunal separate from CSC. The Parole Board has the authority to grant, deny, or revoke parole. Who serves on the Parole Board? Given the complexities of the task, one might expect it to be composed of judges and/or Ph.D.–level criminal justice staff and psychologists. However, the Parole Board is a diverse group of professionals and the minimum educational requirement (as listed on its website) is "A degree from a recognized university in one of the disciplines comprising the human sciences (law, criminology, social work, psychology, sociology, etc.) or an acceptable combination of relevant education, job-related training and/or experience" (Parole Board of Canada, 2011). Thus someone with an undergraduate degree (and criminal justice experience) or equivalent on-the-job experience could qualify. Whether

Savage Chickens   by Doug Savage

www.savagechickens.com © Doug Savage

Psychologists are studying the influence of emotional displays by offenders in sentencing and parole hearings, and whether decision-makers are able to discriminate true remorse and "crocodile tears."

this type of background is sufficient to make such complex decision is controversial. Our view is that there needs to be a public debate about the nature of experience and skills needed for this task, given the major consequences of parole decisions for both the offender and society at large.

SUBJECTIVITY IN PAROLE DECISIONS AND CONTROVERSIAL CASES

In Canada, there have been numerous instances in which questionable Parole Board decisions have led to tragic consequences. Among the most notorious cases is that of Robert Moyes in British Columbia, one that the first author often discusses in his training workshops on detecting deception (e.g., Porter et al., 2010). Moyes was granted day parole in 1995, while serving a life sentence for several armed robberies and after accruing almost 40 criminal convictions, including three attempted murders and three prison escapes. The National Parole Board had made more than 40 release decisions regarding Moyes over the years, and he had numerous previous parole violations. Within a year of his parole, Moyes had murdered seven people, including the brutal torture and killing of Eugene and Michelle Uyeyama. A subsequent investigation by the Parole Board concluded that there had been a "sound basis" for his conditional release from prison and that "it is unnecessary to offer any specific direction on change or amendment to policies, practices or procedures" (CTVNews.ca, 2006). However, the investigation did not examine how Moyes was able to fool the Parole Board into releasing him despite his numerous criminal convictions. According to a 2006 *Globe and Mail* report, when testifying in court, Moyes happily admitted that he lied repeatedly to parole and corrections officials for the past 30 years (www.globeandmail.com, 2006). In other chapters, we have explored some of the factors that may have played into Moyes' ability to fool the Parole Board, but we'll focus on one in particular a little later in this chapter: his ability to successfully feign remorse.

One thing is clear in examining patterns of parole decision making. Despite the best efforts of parole decision makers, it can be highly subjective, like all human decision making. However, in this context normal human biases and misperceptions can lead to terrible consequences, as with Moyes.

PSYCHOPATHY AND PAROLE DECISION MAKING

How do Parole Boards decide whether to release specific violent or sexual offenders? As described in Chapter 13, psychopathic offenders have high rates of reoffending and, relatively speaking, poor treatment prognoses (e.g., cf Skeem et al., 2012). Yet, few studies have focused on the role that psychopathy might play in parole decision making. One might expect that the powerful "psychopath" diagnosis/label would almost always lead to a negative outcome in various correctional contexts (e.g., Walsh & Walsh, 2006), which could be construed as an overly negative bias (e.g., Edens, 2006; Viljoen, MacDougall, Gagnon, & Douglas, 2010). For example, Edens et al. (2012) found that participants consistently were more likely to support executing a murderer if he was described as a psychopath in hypothetical cases. On the other hand, psychopathic individuals might be able to impress and deceive parole decision makers with the "gift of the gab," superficial charm, and false emotional displays (e.g., remorse) to fool prison staff (e.g., Porter & Woodworth, 2007). As we know, many psychopathic offenders have long criminal careers characterized by conning, defrauding, and scamming others; some even become cult leaders, corrupt politicians, or successful corporate leaders (e.g., Babiak, Neumann, & Hare, 2010; Boddy, 2010). In a well-known Canadian study, Michael Seto (profiled in Chapter 11) and Howard Barbaree (1999) found that the sex offenders who participated in a treatment program and received the most positive evaluations by the facilitators also had the highest PCL-R scores (leading to positive parole decisions) and the highest reoffence rates. It was likely such psychopathic sex offenders were chameleons who were able to play a convincing role of a motivated, remorseful, rehabilitated inmate during the program. As reviewed earlier Porter, ten Brinke, and Wilson (2009) conducted a file review of 310 Canadian male federal offenders, examining their entire criminal and conditional release histories. Psychopathic offenders (both sexual and nonsexual offenders) were about 2.5 times more likely to be granted conditional release than non-psychopathic offenders, and had a far higher recidivism rate. In other words, they were released by the Parole Board far more often despite their horrendous criminal and conditional release histories, and performed far worse in the community. This suggested that they may have been "Academy Award–winning actors" who were able to say all the right things and

© iStockphoto.com/Dieter Spears

feign remorse in the parole hearing. Similarly, Häk-känen-Nyholm and Hare (2009) examined the files of 546 Finnish offenders convicted of murder between 1995 and 2004. They found that psychopathic offenders with high scores were more likely to deny the charges, to be convicted for involuntary manslaughter rather than manslaughter or murder, and to receive permission from the Supreme Court to appeal their lower-court sentence. In other words, they seemed to be able to manipulate the system to their own ends. Porter and Woodworth (2007) examined the characteristics of violent actions (homicides) and the manner in which the violent acts were described by the perpetrators in interviews with correctional staff. They found that whereas psychopaths were far more likely than other murderers to have perpetrated primarily well-planned homicides, this difference disappeared when examining the self-report descriptions. Psychopaths were more likely to intentionally—and plausibly—characterize their murders as "crimes of passion" and to omit major details of their offences.

OFFENDER REMORSE AND SENTENCING/PAROLE DECISION MAKING

"I feel terrible for what happened." A major factor in both sentencing and parole decision making is the perceived **remorse** of the offender (e.g., Wood & MacMartin, 2007). In sentencing decisions,

judges are instructed to consider "the age of the victim, the duration and frequency of the [crimes], the criminal record of the offender, the effects on the victim and the presence or absence of ... remorse" (*R. v. B.,* 1990; *R. v. W.W.M.,* 2006). In the BC case, *R. v. Zeek* (2004), the judge observed (para. 24):

The part remorse plays in sentencing was explained by Taylor J.A. in *R. v. Anderson* 1992 CanLII 6002 (BC CA), (1992), 74 C.C.C. (3d) 523 (B.C.C.A.) at 535-36:

> The factor of "remorse" is often important. In so far as it might be suggested that the court should regard those who come before it in a submissive or contrite manner as deserving of more lenient treatment than those who accept their predicament with whatever fortitude they are able to summon, there would be little in this factor which could assist the sentencing judge. But to the extent that an accused person is able to demonstrate that he or she has, since the commission of the crime, come to realize the gravity of the conduct, and as a result has achieved a change in attitude or imposed some self-discipline which significantly reduces the likelihood of further offending, the existence of remorse in this sense obviously has much importance [emphases in original].

Thus, there is a "practical" assumption here that remorse can reduce recidivism, a theoretically sound idea. Further, defendants who communicate remorse for their actions are thought to be good candidates for treatment and rehabilitation: "[The defendant's] remorse, guilt, and shame should provide him with a strong motivation to work at changes that will prevent future acts of violence" (*R. v. Struve,* 2007). An important purpose of a parole interview is to allow the offender to show that his or her attitude has changed for the better since he or she went to jail or prison (e.g., Ruback & Hopper, 1986). However, data on criminal recidivism show that *expressed* remorse (as well as insight into the crime and offender distress) generally is unrelated to likelihood of reoffence (e.g., Hanson & Bussière, 1998). Why do you think would this be the case? Our strong suspicion is that true remorse will reduce the likelihood of reoffending, but that judges and juries are not proficient at distinguishing real and fake displays of remorse. Thus, when researchers examine the relation between remorse and recidivism, they find no relation because there is a mix of sincere and insincere emotion being used as a predictor.

Nonetheless, it is clear that impressions of remorse can influence the length of an offender's sentence and his or her likelihood of parole; offenders who show stronger emotion are less likely to be convicted and receive more lenient sentences than those who express little emotion (e.g., Heath, Grannemann, & Peacock, 2004). And, of course, many offenders have a keen awareness of this situation. Thus, a complex duel can occur in which, in the absence of genuine remorse, an offender may be highly motivated to fake regret for his or her actions, and the judge or parole board member may be motivated to detect "crocodile tears" (e.g., ten Brinke & Porter, 2012). In this context, it seems that deceptive offenders have a distinct advantage over legal decision makers, as suggested by the finding described above suggesting that psychopaths may often cry their way into being granted a conditional release (e.g., Häkkänen-Nyholm & Hare, 2009). Ruback and Hopper (1986) investigated assessments made by Parole Board staff regarding the offenders' success on parole both before and after an interview with the applicant. Prior to the interview, the Board had access to the offenders' files, detailing all relevant information required to make a decision regarding his or her release. During the interview, Parole Board members gained information concerning the offender's attitude and apparent level of remorse. Results indicated that decisions made after the interview became less accurate in predicting offenders' success upon subsequent release.

As hypothesized by Porter et al. (2010), one explanation for these findings is that the decision makers were duped by offenders during their interviews, persuaded by false displays of remorse. This may not be surprising given that observers generally are unable to discriminate real and false sadness facial expressions above chance (e.g., Porter & ten Brinke, 2008; Porter, ten Brinke, & Wallace, 2012), and psychopathic traits are associated with a proficiency in adopting false sadness expressions that mimic real ones (Porter, ten Brinke, Wallace, & Baker, 2012). Research has found that apologies accompanied by perceived remorse are more likely to be forgiven (Bornstein, Rung, & Miller, 2002). Although the impact of apologies on forgiveness and decision making is becoming more heavily studied (e.g., Corwin et al., 2012), more

research is needed on how other traits such as narcissism and extraversion play into the persuasiveness of such statements.

How do legal decision makers approach the task of evaluating remorse? Can true or false remorse be identified? Judges often refer to the defendant's demeanour: "The appellant's responses to questions posed him and his demeanour showed that his main concern was for himself ... I would have expected some show of distress or anguish for having raped a previously chaste young woman. The appellant showed no such signs" (*Balkissoon v. Canada [Citizenship and Immigration]*, 2001). Despite having such major applied relevance, remorse hardly has been studied empirically. Even the question of "what is remorse" is unanswered by science. While most of us feel remorseful for something, whether it be lying to a close friend or cheating on a partner, we know little scientifically of how remorse "looks," including what remorseful facial expressions might look like. We might define remorse, or guilt, as the negative feeling that results from the violation of a person's moral standards, and may arise from situations such as lying, neglecting a friend or family member, cheating, or failure at a particular duty (Keltner & Buswell, 1996; Tangney & Dearing, 2002). In a recent Ontario case (*Maureen Olivia Boldt v. Law Society of Upper Canada*, 2011), the court attempted to define remorse:

Remorse connotes a feeling of genuine sense of sorrow arising from recognition that one has done something wrong. A remorseful person appreciates the difference between right and wrong. Remorse connotes "moral or ethical strength," and incorporates the definition of "good character." It also states, in effect, "I was wrong and I deeply regret it."

---

ten Brinke, McDonald, Porter, and O'Connor (2012) conducted the first psychological study of how people behave during real versus faked remorse. They examined the facial, verbal, and body language behaviours accompanying videotaped accounts (nearly 300 000 frames) of people discussing true instances in which they had hurt another person. For one of the incidents, the participant felt no remorse but attempted to seem highly remorseful and for the other he or she truly felt intense remorse. The findings indicated that stories about falsified remorse were associated with a greater range of emotional expressions. Further, negative emotions were more commonly

Savage Chickens

by Doug Savage

www.savagechickens.com © Doug Savage

Psychological research indicates that a defendant's or witness' physical appearance and demeanour have major impact on his or her perceived credibility.

followed by other emotions—rather than a return to neutral emotion—in falsified versus sincere remorse. Participants also hesitated more in their speech while talking about deceptive relative to genuine remorse. In general, the findings showed that faked remorse is accompanied by an "emotionally turbulent display" of deliberate, falsified expressions and involuntary, genuine, emotional leakage. Participants also showed more speech hesitations while expressing deceptive versus real remorse. Other work suggests that high-stakes faked emotions in forensic contexts can be identified with informed attention to facial expressions as well (ten Brinke & Porter, 2012; ten Brinke, Porter, & Baker, 2012). Given its importance in legal settings, much more work is needed in this area.

DANGEROUS/LONG-TERM-OFFENDER DECISION MAKING: CRYSTAL BALL GAZING?

As discussed earlier, normally when a Canadian citizen is convicted of a crime, he or she will know the range of possible sentences that a judge could impose and then will be given a specific, **determinate sentence**, such as five years in prison with a likelihood of earlier conditional release. However, there is a single

piece of legislation in Canada—section 753 of the Criminal Code—that permits the court to lock up someone indefinitely for the risk he or she poses to society, rather than relating directly to the crime he or she has already committed. In other words, the court has to make extremely consequential predictions of future dangerousness, which can be fraught with uncertainty as described in Chapters 10 and 11 (e.g., Skeem & Monahan, 2011).

The **Dangerous (DO)** and **Long-Term Offender (LTO)** provisions of the Criminal Code are intended to protect Canadians from the most dangerous violent and sexual predators in the country. Individuals convicted of a series of violent and/or sexual offences—such as Paul Bernardo and Clifford Olson—can be given an indeterminate sentence if it is shown that there is an extremely high risk that they will commit future similar offences. In rare cases, a single brutal violent crime can be sufficient to lead to a DO or LTO finding. The main objective of protecting innocent Canadians from future harm is ensured by continued incarceration until the offender no longer poses such a high risk. In reality, this means that most DOs will never be released from prison. Before we examine the specific DO/LTO legislation, let's look at some basic features of such offenders. A 2002 report commissioned by the Correctional Service of Canada (Trevethan, Crutcher, & Moore, 2002) reported the following facts about DOs/LTOs:

1. Since January 1994, 274 offenders have been admitted to federal custody under the DO or LTO designation. Of these, 179 were DOs and 95 were sentenced as LTOs. Since 1997, the number of DOs has averaged about 24 per year.
2. DOs have a greater number of previous adult convictions than LTOs.
3. The majority of both DOs and LTOs have a current sexual offence, as well as previous sexual offences.
4. Relative to LTOs, DOs have a higher proportion of female youth and female adult victims.
5. DOs caused more injury, both physically and psychologically, to their victims and were more likely to use a weapon or threaten violence than LTOs.

According to the Correctional Service of Canada, there were 458 DOs as of April 2011. Although the DO provisions can apply to all criminals, most people who are given such designations are in custody for sexual offences. For example, 85 percent of DOs were sentenced for sexual assaults and 41 percent involved pedophilia. Renée Acoby is the only woman in Canada currently designated a DO. The Ontario attorney general requested that Acoby receive the designation after several violent incidents in prisons where she was incarcerated. Before Acoby, only two women had been given the designation. Marlene Moore committed suicide in prison in 1988. Lisa Neve had her designation lifted in 1999 and was freed after serving her sentence. The youngest person to be given the DO designation was a 17-year-old in British Columbia, Adam Laboucan, who had raped a three-month-old. According to a 2010 online CBC report, Adam Laboucan changed his name to Tara Desousa, and he has been diagnosed with borderline personality disorder. According to the report, while in prison he was caught prostituting himself to other prisoners, using drugs, and threatening to kill a female guard. Further, the report indicates that he confessed to killing a three-year-old child when he was 11.

While the provisions have been amended a number of times, the Criminal Code requirements for a DO finding are:

---

1. that the offense for which the offender has been convicted is a serious personal injury offense and that the offender constitutes a threat to the life, safety or physical or mental well-being of other persons on the basis of evidence establishing a pattern of repetitive behaviour by the offender, of which the offence for which he or she has been convicted forms a part, showing a failure to restrain his or her behaviour and a likelihood of causing death or injury to other persons, or inflicting severe psychological damage on other persons, through failure in the future to restrain his or her behaviour,
2. a pattern of persistent aggressive behaviour by the offender, of which the offence for which he or she has been convicted forms a part, showing a substantial degree of indifference on the part of the offender respecting the reasonably foreseeable consequences to other persons of his or her behaviour, or
3. any behaviour by the offender, associated with the offence for which he or she has been convicted, that is of such a brutal nature as to compel the conclusion that the offender's behaviour in the future is unlikely to be inhibited by normal standards of behavioural restraint;"
   or (for sexual offenders)
   that the offender, by his or her conduct in any

---

sexual matter including that involved in the commission of the offence for which he or she has been convicted, has shown a failure to control his or her sexual impulses and a likelihood of causing injury, pain or other evil to other persons through failure in the future to control his or her sexual impulses.

As of 2008, the Canadian government passed legislation that made it much easier for Crown prosecutors to obtain DO designations. The new law means that if someone is found guilty of a third conviction of a designated violent or sexual offence, he or she must prove that he or she does not qualify as a DO. According to the LTO legislation, offenders who meet the DO criteria but also show "a reasonable possibility of community management" may be ordered to serve a determinate sentence followed by a long-term supervision order up to 10 years. Thus, DO offenders serve indeterminate sentences without ready access to parole whereas LTO offenders serve determinate sentences with extended periods of community supervision. The key differences in the two findings is that—while risk for future serious violent crime is common for both—LTOs show some amenability to treatment. LTOs, unlike other offenders in Canada, can be monitored for an extended period beyond their original sentence. The judge must decide whether the offender might or rather probably will not benefit from treatment in the community with the outcome being reduced likelihood of violence. This is not an easy task. In fact, we might argue that the law makes it incredibly difficult to show that even the most dangerous offenders meet the criterion of "untreatability." As such, LTO findings are being far more common than DO findings (Seguin, Millson, & Robinson, 2009).

The role of psychologists and psychiatrists in DO/LTO hearings is a powerful one. The judge wants to know about the imminent risk for violence posed by the offender. As you may have guessed based on other chapters in this text, psychopathy and paraphilias (especially pedophilia) come up in most such hearings in Canada. Given their clear relation to risk for future violence and poor treatment prognosis (e.g., Shaw & Porter, 2012), this seems to make a lot of sense. However, Lloyd, Clark, and Forth (2010) caution that psychopathy (particularly scores on the PCL-R) may be applied inappropriately in this context. They examined judges' written or oral judgments in 136 DO hearings gathered from a publicly available legal database in Canada. They found that PCL-R scores were positively related to trial outcome. Specifically, psychopathy diagnoses were correlated to experts' ratings of treatment amenability, which in turn were related to hearing outcome. In addition, experts tended to show bias in the way they scored offenders on the PCL-R. On the other hand, in many DO/LTO hearings, the experts for the two sides are in remarkable agreement. To give an example, take the case of Ronald Berikoff, a prolific BC sexual offender (see website at the end of chapter for more information). The first author of this textbook was called as an expert in this case. Berikoff ultimately was found to be a DO with agreement from both sides that he was psychopathic and an extremely high risk to reoffend. The publicly available online court transcript conveys this and shows the types of information that the court examines in deciding on a DO/LTO application. Much of this information will sound familiar from other chapters in this text regarding risk assessment and psychopathy (and the acronyms such as VRAG and SARA have been described previously):

Dr. Lawson testified with respect to the prospects for treatment for individuals with very high scores on the PCL-R, who can be labelled psychopaths, such as Mr. Berikoff. In his opinion, it is not possible to say that any treatment will significantly reduce the rate of recidivism for these individuals. They are the most challenging subgroup of offenders to treat. There is some evidence that if they are treated with the current treatment programs available through the federal prison system, some psychopaths will actually become worse. This is considered to be due to the fact that psychopaths will learn, through the treatment process, to feign remorse, empathy and other skills, which will allow them to gain a foothold in the community. In Dr. Lawson's opinion, the prognosis of effective treatment for someone labelled a psychopath on the basis of the PCL-R is very, very poor. (Canadian Legal Information Institute, 2000)

The first author and another psychologist, interviewed Mr. Berikoff in March 1998 and prepared a psychological assessment report in preparation for a National Parole Board hearing. The major purpose of the report was to evaluate Mr. Berikoff's risk to reoffend if released into the community, and the secondary purpose was to provide an opinion as to what

sort of treatment programs may or may not benefit Mr. Berikoff.

Dr. Porter reviewed Mr. Berikoff's corrections files, consulted with his institutional parole officer, and interviewed Mr. Berikoff for approximately two hours. Dr. Porter noted that Mr. Berikoff's violence had been escalating through his adulthood, and appeared to have been out of control during the past few years. He also noted that Mr. Berikoff had traditionally denied or minimized the seriousness of his crimes, and that he tended to blame his victims and the legal system for his legal difficulties. Based on Dr. Porter's clinical judgment, Mr. Berikoff appeared to have little empathy for others, his emotional experience seemed limited, and he showed little insight into his criminal offending.

Dr. Porter then assessed Mr. Berikoff's risk for violent reoffending using the PCL-R, and two other tools, the Violence Risk Assessment Guide (VRAG) and the Spousal Assault Risk Assessment Guide (SARA). He described the PCL-R as a "well validated clinical tool which blends historical and clinical impressions to facilitate a judgment of a person's psychopathic tendencies." Mr. Berikoff scored 34, which is in the 94th percentile. The cutoff score in labelling someone as a psychopath is 30 out of 40. Numerous studies have indicated that a PCL-R score over 30 is one of the best predictors of future criminal and violent behaviour. The characteristics of people who score above 30 are different, in several ways, than people who score below 30. People who score over 30 tend to process emotional information in a different way, reoffend at a much higher rate, and are at a higher risk to engage in violent behaviour. They tend to be manipulative, have very little capacity to experience remorse or empathy, are unable to experience emotions that others experience, are often arrogant and overbearing, and show very little respect for others. In layman's terms, Dr. Porter described this as not really having a conscience. In terms of their behavioural characteristics, people who score over 30 on the PCL-R tend to be impulsive, are chronically antisocial, exercise poor control, are unable to form lasting relationships, and do not accept much responsibility.

His clinical impressions of Mr. Berikoff were consistent with the behavioural and personality traits normally associated with people scoring over 30 on the PCL-R. In Dr. Porter's opinion, Mr. Berikoff's score of 34 indicates a relatively high risk for both general recidivism and for violent recidivism. The next tool utilized by Dr. Porter was the VRAG, which is an actuarial predictive tool, incorporating the PCL-R score as one of its items.

Mr. Berikoff's VRAG score fell into the sixth of nine risk categories. According to Dr. Porter's report, offenders with similar scores have a 44 percent probability of violently reoffending within seven years of release, and a 58 percent probability of reoffending within a 10-year period. He described this as a moderate to high risk in statistical terms.

The final actuarial tool employed by Dr. Porter was the SARA. His findings in that regard were as follows:

On the SARA, Mr. Berikoff showed clear evidence for a high proportion of the risk factors (16/20). The suggested guidelines for summary risk ratings from the SARA manual indicate that offenders similar to Mr. Berikoff represent an EXTREMELY HIGH (the highest risk rating) risk to commit spousal violence in the future.

Although there has not been as much research on the SARA and recidivism as there has been on VRAG and recidivism, Dr. Porter equated "extremely high" risk as being more than an 80 percent chance.

Dr. Porter made recommendations for treatment for Mr. Berikoff, including the violent offender program, an anger management program, a substance abuse program, and a family violence program. In terms of treatment prospects, Dr. Porter testified that the effectiveness of treatment programs for psychopathic offenders is poor. In his opinion, such treatment programs generally have no positive effect. In one body of research he was aware of, there was some suggestion that offenders may get worse due to treatment, as a result of the program's facilitating an increase in criminal behaviour. At this point, he did not know whether existing programs in the corrections service would have any positive effect for Mr. Berikoff or not. At that time (and still today) the corrections service has not developed a program effective with psychopathic offenders so the picture for Mr. Berikoff's future rehabilitation was "pretty dismal" in Dr. Porter's opinion.

Dr. Porter testified that due to Mr. Berikoff's lack of remorse, his tendency to minimize, and his inability to feel empathy, he considered his assessment of Mr. Berikoff to be one of the most memorable assessments he has performed. To the date he assessed Mr. Berikoff, Dr. Porter had never done an assessment of an offender where the offender minimized his criminal behaviour to the extent Mr. Berikoff did. Dr. Porter also considered it to be one of the most profound cases of lack of remorse that he had seen.

The conclusion of his psychological assessment report, dated March 23, 1998, was as follows:

In my opinion, given his current clinical and actuarial features, his recent failure on statutory release, and his lack of therapeutic intervention, Mr. Berikoff's risk cannot be effectively managed in the community at this time. I would recommend that following his participation in the programs mentioned above, his risk to reoffend should be re-examined in an updated Psychological Assessment. If his risk for violence has not been substantially reduced, I would suggest that Mr. Berikoff should be considered as a possible Detention candidate (via a Commissioner's referral if necessary). However, should Mr. Berikoff be released into the community on parole, he should be closely monitored for relapse into substance abuse and violent behaviour in relationships. He should also be required to attend a Family Violence Program in the community. These needs would be best met under a Residency condition.

As a student of forensic psychology, you will be thinking about this kind of case and wondering how much certainty is required in deciding that

" I REALLY WANT THIS PAROLE... I'LL DO ANYTHING FOR IT... DO YOU WANT ANYBODY RUBBED OUT? "

While individuals deemed to be Dangerous Offenders in Canada are reviewed for conditional release on a regular basis, most spend a long period of time in prison and many are never released.

someone has such a damning label as DO/LTO and potentially locking him or her up forever. How can we be sure someone will reoffend? How can we be sure someone won't change for the better? These are the kinds of dilemmas confronting forensic psychologists all the time. Be prepared! Also, be aware of the unconscious biases that can influence legal decision making in this context.

For example, as with other types of hearings, Esses and Webster (1988) found that observers perceived physically unattractive sexual offenders as more likely to fulfill the DO criteria than average-looking and attractive sexual offenders. In particular, unattractive sexual offenders were viewed as less likely to restrain their behaviour in the future.

SUMMARY

In this chapter, we examined how the Canadian legal system deals with offenders in terms of sentencing and parole decisions. Further, we examined the only legislation in Canada that permits locking up offenders for crimes they are "likely" to do, and reviewed some of the assessments used to determine an offender's level of risk. We also reviewed some of the major psychological factors that play a role in such decision making and the major roles played by psychologists in assisting with these decisions, including the presentencing report.

We explored psychological factors in sentencing and parole and concluded that there are several

"official" factors and many that are unconscious, such as racism and covert attitudes regarding offenders and victims. Irrelevant factors relating to the judge, defendant, context, and outcome of the crime were described. The relevance of remorse displays and the presence of psychopathy in legal decision making was examined. Dangerous Offender and Long-Term Offender legislation was reviewed and the major psychological factors (e.g., type of crime and level of risk for reoffence) that contribute to such labelling were examined.

KEY TERMS

aggravating factor, p. 337

Dangerous Offender (DO), p. 345

denunciation, p. 338

determinate sentence, p. 345

deterrence, p. 338

Long-Term Offender (LTO), p. 345

mitigating factor, p. 337

presentence psychological report, p. 338

promotion of responsibility, p. 338

rehabilitation, p. 338

remorse, p. 343

unconscious racism, p. 339

warrant expiry, p. 341

SUGGESTED READINGS

Melton, G. B., Petrila, J., Poythress, N. G., & Slobogin, C. (2007). *Psychological evaluations for the courts: A handbook for mental health professionals and lawyers* (3rd Ed.). New York: Guilford Press.

This book is a great resource for anyone interested in psychological evaluations for the courts. It not only details the many types of psychological evaluations that are often required, but also provides descriptions of the assessment tools and detailed examples.

Sporer, S. L., & Goodman-Delahunty, J. (2009). Disparities in sentencing decisions. In M. E. Oswald, S. Bieneck, J. Hupfeld-Heinemann, M. E. Oswald, S. Bieneck, J. Hupfeld-Heinemann (Eds.), *Social psychology of punishment of crime* (pp. 379–401). New York: John Wiley & Sons.

This chapter expands on the sentencing disparities discussed in this chapter. It also provides recommendations as to how to reduce these disparities. A good read for anyone interested in the factors that influence judicial decision making.

Vidmar, N. (2011). The psychology of trial judging. *Current Directions in Psychological Science, 20,* 58–62.

This article provides a more in–depth look at a judge's decision making as well as the external constraints, such as precedent, that judges face when sentencing.

WEBSITE

R. v. Berikoff, 2000 BCSC 1024: **http://www.canlii. org/en/bc/bcsc/doc/2000/2000bcsc1024/ 2000bcsc1024.html**

The Promising Future of Forensic Psychology in Canada

> *Science knows no country, because knowledge belongs to humanity, and is the torch which illuminates the world. Science is the highest personification of the nation because that nation will remain the first which carries the furthest the works of thought and intelligence.*
>
> —Louis Pasteur (cited in Dubos, 1960, p. 145)

THE STATUS OF FORENSIC PSYCHOLOGY IN CANADA

Undergraduate and graduate students in forensic psychology courses and programs in Canada are enthusiastic and motivated to conduct top-notch research and apply their findings. Although what many of them want most is to become a criminal profiler as featured in many popular movies (Clarice Starling in *Silence of the Lambs* from 1991 or profilers in CBS's *Criminal Minds*), there is a high level of interest in most areas falling under the heading of forensic psychology, or psychology and law. We hope that this text has inspired some of you to continue on in the field and perhaps come up with your own new research and insights.

As a student of forensic psychology in Canada, there is much to be excited about in contemporary times. The impressive array of the types of work happening in our field by Canadians is described in Porter (2004) and Helmus et al. (2011). As evidenced throughout this book, Canada long has been a leader in the field, contributing some of its most important advances in both research and practice. To keep up with continuing progress, students may wish to periodically check the websites of the **Criminal Justice Section of the Canadian Psychological Association** (www.cpa.ca/aboutcpa/cpasections/criminaljusticepsychology), the **American Psychology-Law Society** (www.ap-ls.org), the **European Association of Psychology and Law** (www.eapl.eu), and the **Centre for the Advancement of Psychological Science and Law** (www.capsl.ca).

One reason that forensic psychology is becoming more popular in Canada is that lawyers, members of the judiciary, and other professionals in the legal system are seeing the value of psychology in their fields. As Munsterberg (1909) opined a century ago, and Ogloff (2004, 2011) has reiterated, the law needs psychology. Thankfully, the Canadian justice system is recognizing the value of psychology in its functioning. The basis of this positive recognition in recent years is decades of groundbreaking research, without which the foundations of application in the legal system would be weak. And, ultimately, when research effectively informs practice, psychologists are able to gain invaluable experience that then leads them to contribute to the effective training and education of others. This pedagogical mission occurs both with students like you and with staff who work on the front line in the legal system.

FORENSIC PSYCHOLOGY IN CANADA: THREE ACTIVITIES

Research

The legal system was created because of unacceptable human behaviour (i.e., crime) and is designed to control behaviour (Bartol & Bartol, 2011). As outlined by Ogloff (2004), this attempted control of human behaviour leads to assumptions of human nature, some of which may not be correct or have been untested. Consider, for example, a long-standing belief in our correctional system that all offenders have the potential to live as law-abiding citizens. Although this sounds good in principle (and most offenders, in fact, may have this capacity), forensic psychologists have shown that certain offenders, such as psychopaths, may not have this capacity (e.g., Olver & Wong, 2011; Shaw & Porter, 2012). Recent neuroimaging studies suggest possible functional or structural anomalies in the brains of psychopaths (e.g., Wahlund & Kristiansson, 2009; Yang & Raine, 2009) that could be related to the persistence of their antisocial and often violent behaviour (see Reidy, Shelley-Tremblay, & Lilienfeld, 2011). Interestingly, the current Conservative government's "tough on crime" approach seems to be founded on the opposite idea, that all offenders are deserving of a similar harsh punishment, and de-emphasizes rehabilitation relative to retribution. Yet, there is a great deal of research—much of it coming out of Canada—suggesting that certain treatment approaches work very well with certain kinds of offenders in reducing recidivism (e.g., Beggs & Grace, 2011; Dowden & Andrews, 2000; Hanson, Bourgon, Helmus, & Hodgson, 2009). Thus, psychological research has revealed that neither blanket assumption (that all criminals can change to become law-abiding citizens or that all criminals are beyond redemption) is correct and we need to focus intervention efforts on individuals with psychological features that allow the potential for prosocial change.

Another example of assumptions about human nature being challenged by psychological research in Canada is the frequent acceptance of "recovered" or "repressed" memory evidence by Canadian courts. Using archival data, SFU researchers (Connolly & Read, 2006) examined a sample of more than 2064 cases of sexual assault from the 1980s and 1990s and found that evidence for recovered or delayed memories has emerged in more than 5 percent of all sexual assault cases. There has been a vigorous debate over the accuracy of such recovered memories of alleged crimes (Loftus, 2004; Patry, Stinson & Smith, 2009; Peace, Porter, & Almon, 2012). In response to this controversy, memory distortion has become a prominent research focus in contemporary cognitive psychology and neuroscience. As we saw in earlier chapters, psychological research has established that many such reports are based on false memories (e.g., Loftus, 2003a; Loftus, 2011). Faulty eyewitness testimony has played a role in over 75 percent of wrongful convictions overturned by DNA evidence (Innocence Project, 2009). Substantial evidence reveals that even traumatic "events" can be completely falsely recalled or distorted in memory (Nourkova, Bernstein, & Loftus, 2004). And people who report likely false memories (i.e., those reporting memories of past lives) exhibit a greater propensity for false memories and score higher on measures of dissociation and personality features such as introversion and cooperativeness than others (Meyersburg, Bogden, Gallo, & McNally, 2009; Porter, Birt, Lehman, & Yuille, 2000; Zhu et al., 2010). Other Canadian researchers established that temporary

psychological states, such as being hypnotized, can lead to enhanced misinformation effects (Scoboria, Mazzoni, Kirsch, & Milling, 2002). Additionally, SFU researchers found that judges expressed an excessive interest in complainants' behaviour and emotions around the time of the alleged abuse and around the time of disclosure when evaluating the credibility of delayed reports of sexual abuse (Connolly, Price, & Gordon, 2009).

A third example pertains to the long-held assumption that people would not confess to a crime that they did not commit. Psychologists have conducted research that dispels some of the prominent myths and misconceptions around confessions in the legal system (see Loftus, 2011; Smith et al., 2010). These include (1) that false confessions do not happen or are extremely rare; (2) that only highly vulnerable people falsely confess; and (3) that there is little research on police interrogation and false confessions (Redlich & Meissner, 2009). Yet, as explored in Chapter 1, SMU researchers Smith et al. (2010) observed that judges in Canada have been reluctant to allow expert testimony on confession issues, a situation we think psychologists need to work to change. A step in this direction occurred in 2010 when the American Psychology-Law Society published a scientific review paper examining police interrogations and confessions (Smith et al. (2010). The paper represented not only the opinions of Kassin and his colleagues but also a consensus view of the members of the society, a significant proportion of whom are Canadian academics and their students.

As we can see, assumptions in the legal system must be tested scientifically. As the science of human behaviour, psychology is in the best position to fill this role. It has much to offer to the legal system by shedding light on people's actions as they relate to the law, from someone committing a crime to a witness testifying in court.

As we have witnessed throughout this book, Canada's track record in forensic research has been solid. While some of this work has been large-scale projects occurring in collaboration with researchers from other countries, much of it has been individual researchers "dogging it out" (often with their graduate students) until they find the answers to important psycho-legal questions. Pioneering research on eyewitness memory, criminal behaviour and risk assessment, victim behaviour, competency to stand trial, deception detection, and other areas has occurred here. Canadian researchers publish at a high rate in the leading academic journals in the field, such as ***Law and Human Behavior***, ***Behavioral Sciences and the Law***, and ***Criminal Justice and Behavior***.

Many of the luminaries in our field set the stage for this work starting in the 1960s and 1970s. For example, three obtained their Ph.D.s in the 1960s from the University of Western Ontario, which, interestingly, had little in the way of forensic training or research at the time. Dr. John Yuille, a professor emeritus at the University of British Columbia, has published widely on victim, witness, and suspect memory; trauma and memory; interviewing techniques; credibility assessment; and child sexual abuse. Dr. Robert Hare, a professor emeritus at the University of British Columbia, has written extensively about his research on psychopathy, created the major tool for measuring psychopathy, and wrote the 1993 bestseller *Without Conscience: The Disturbing World of the Psychopaths Among Us*. And Dr. Daniel Yarmey, a professor emeritus of the University of Guelph, has published numerous articles pertaining to eyewitness memory (as well as many other areas). As we saw earlier, he also wrote one of the first important texts on the psychology of eyewitnesses, *The Psychology of Eyewitness Testimony*, in 1979. Along with Dr. Donald Dutton, one of the leading experts on domestic violence, Yuille and Hare established the first formal forensic psychology program in Canada (at the University of British Columbia).

There are many other examples of people in our field who were trained in the 1960s and early 1970s who helped to set the stage for the excellent research currently happening in Canada (and inspired a passion for research in forensic psychology in generations of undergraduate and graduate students). Just to name a few:

- Dr. Don Read, current (at the time of writing) director of the Psychology and Law program at Simon Fraser University, obtained his Ph.D. in 1969 and went on to publish important articles on memory in forensic contexts, the recovered memory debate, eyewitness testimony, and other aspects of autobiographical memory. He also testified as an expert witness in some fascinating cases, including one in which the heavy-metal band Judas Priest was accused of planting subliminal messages about suicide in their songs.
- Dr. Phil Firestone at the University of Ottawa has conducted research on sexual offenders, diagnostic/intervention issues, and offender recidivism.

- Dr. Vernon Quinsey at Queen's University has conducted research on prediction, modification, and management of violent behaviour, and sexual offending.
- Dr. Chris Webster, professor emeritus at Simon Fraser University, has written about violence risk assessment and management.
- Dr. Don Andrews, who passed away in 2010, completed his doctorate degree at Queen's University in 1969, after which he joined the faculty at Carleton University, where he remained throughout his academic career. His academic work was devoted to the psychology of criminal conduct and he developed what became known as the "theory of correctional intervention," which has set the standard for successful intervention practices throughout the field of corrections worldwide.

As mentioned in Chapter 1, there are prominent programs of forensic research occurring at the University of Victoria, the University of British Columbia, Simon Fraser University, the University of Saskatchewan, Queen's University, the University of Toronto, Ryerson University, Université de Montréal, and the University of New Brunswick, largely the result of the seeds planted by people such as those described above. These programs are still thriving and in 2012 we would add to the list Carleton University, Memorial University of Newfoundland, and Saint Mary's University.

Students of forensic psychology need to strive to continue in this tradition of research excellence. But we need to expand the types of research we are doing; as noted by Ogloff (2011), the range of possible research topics in psychology and law is almost limitless since all areas of law make assumptions about human behaviour, most of which are untested. The vast majority of studies published in our field fall under one of the following categories (in order of frequency): jury decision making, eyewitness identification, scientific commentary, forensic assessment, legal attitudes, corrections, legal commentary, violence risk prediction, technical evidence, policing, expert witnesses, and psychological interventions in forensic contexts (Wiener et al., 2002). We need to expand our research questions to diverse areas of law and in relation to our changing laws in Canada. At present (2012), the Conservative government is introducing its "get tough on crime" bill, increasing minimum sentences for a host of crimes and reducing judicial discretion in sentencing. Despite Canada's declining violent crime rate, the government plans to exponentially expand and

"Americanize" the Canadian criminal justice system over the next five years, with changes to drug laws, sex offence laws, youth sentencing, the pardons system, parole, house arrest, and antiterrorism measures. One inevitable effect will be the incarceration of thousands more offenders, many of whom will be Aboriginal people, drug abusers, and mentally ill individuals. While in a sense these strategies ignore social science research, we will need to fully examine the implications of the new laws and more fully explore psychological factors influencing criminal behaviour, the effects of incarceration on recidivism (including in young offenders), and whether rehabilitation is possible in the context of increasing imprisonment. We also need to examine how such laws influence police behaviour, confessions, plea bargaining, and legal decision making. There are a host of other topics that are waiting to be studied. Further basic research on the nature of empathy, remorse, schadenfreude (enjoying other people's suffering), and sadism is waiting to happen. More research is needed on the factors that contribute to various specific types of crime. The nature of domestic violence, young offenders, female offenders, and the relation between neuroscience and the law require much more attention. Foundational issues such as neuroscience and its relation to criminal behaviour need far more attention, given their implications for criminal responsibility in the Canadian courts (e.g., Glenn, Raine, & Laufer, 2011).

Practice

Our field has a strong empirical basis because of ongoing research programs such as the ones mentioned above. This research foundation has led to the widespread application of psychology in the legal system, as we have seen throughout this text. At virtually every stage of the legal system in Canada, from the time a crime happens, psychologists are being consulted. For example, the RCMP and other police forces increasingly are relying on psychologists and other social scientists during their criminal investigations and interventions. These activities include helping with hostage negotiations, profiling serial offenders, planning interviews and interrogations, and offering counselling to officers who have gone through traumatic experiences (such as shooting a suspect).

If a suspect is apprehended and a trial is planned, psychologists are consulted for many reasons, including giving an opinion about evidence (such as a confession or another expert's report) or conducting assessments of criminal responsibility or fitness to stand trial. For example, at the Provincial Forensic Psychiatry Service in Nova Scotia and the Forensic Psychiatric Institute in British Columbia, psychiatrists and psychologists conduct assessments of defendants prior to trial. In the case of an NCRMD defence, they sometimes are called to give evidence about the accused person's psychological state at the time of the offence. Also, before a trial, psychologists may help to design programs to aid especially vulnerable witnesses to prepare for the possible ordeal of giving testimony (as The Centre for Children and Families in the Justice System in London, Ontario, does).

During the trial itself, a psychologist may be asked to give an expert opinion about a psychological issue if he or she meets the *Mohan* criteria, or about the defendant (such as the findings within a psychological assessment). For the purposes of sentencing and other pretrial hearings (such as a dangerous offender and long-term-offender hearings), a psychologist may be asked to conduct a risk assessment, commenting on an offender's likelihood of reoffending or potential for rehabilitation. After a defendant is designated an "offender" (by a guilty verdict) and placed in a correctional facility, psychologists, often full-time staff members in the institution (such as Dr. Diane Sirkia, profiled in Chapter 1), are heavily involved in the assessment of the person from the time he or she enters prison until that person is conditionally released or finishes the sentence. Sometimes, psychologists will be asked to provide assessment and intervention for an offender who may be suicidal. In fact, the Correctional Service of Canada is one of the largest employers of psychologists in Canada. When a person is found to be NCRMD or not fit to stand trial, he or she often is sent to a psychiatric facility such as the Forensic Psychiatric Institute in BC to be assessed by a psychologist such as Dr. Barry Cooper for ongoing assessment and treatment by psychologists.

Academic Training

As mentioned, there are two main kinds of training that forensic psychologists provide: teaching students like many of you, and training in the form of workshops, lectures, or supervision given to legal staff or psychologists in training. Some of you may have already decided that you would like to pursue a career in forensic psychology. At present, this can involve specific training at the undergraduate level and at the graduate level. If you wish to become a forensic psychologist who teaches and/or practises, you will need at least a Master's degree, but in most provinces a Ph.D. will be required in coming years.

As Ogloff (2004) reviewed, there is some good news for aspiring students. Earlier, he had conducted a survey of universities and law schools in Canada to examine what was then happening in psychology and law (Ogloff, 1990). He discovered that undergraduate courses in forensic psychology were being offered in five universities. However, when he looked at the situation in 2001, the number had increased to 25! In terms of graduate courses in the area, the number had risen from four to seven. And the number of formal programs in the field rose from none to four. This supports our observation that forensic psychology is thriving in Canada. However, Ogloff (2004) expressed some dissatisfaction that there were still few law schools offering courses in psychology and law. He concluded that "ongoing efforts must be made to provide systematic training to psychology graduate students in relevant areas of law and to ensure that some exposure of legal psychology is provided to students of law" (p. 85). In addition, because of a large number of faculty retirements, some formalized forensic psychology programs, such as the one at the University of British Columbia—Vancouver, have been phased out. Queen's University recently ended its renowned doctoral program in correctional/forensic psychology for such reasons. There are many unique challenges in conducting research on and working with forensic populations that cannot be met with standard training in clinical or experimental psychology. Further, there is still a huge demand for training in forensic psychology for students entering graduate school but still too few formal programs in the area (Helmus et al., 2011; Porter, 2004). For example, between 1995 and 2011 more than half of the departments in Canada had decreased their educational opportunities in forensic psychology (Helmus et al., 2011). Thus, Canadian universities must start to recognize and act upon the need for more formalized programs in this field. On the other hand, the program at SFU is thriving, and newer programs at Carleton University and at the UBC Okanagan campus offer unique opportunities to students in 2013 and beyond.

As of 2013, a large number of Canadian universities offer at least one course in forensic psychology, psychology and the law, or another similar class at the undergraduate level. These institutions include the University of British Columbia—Okanagan, Simon Fraser University, the University of Alberta, the University of Saskatchewan, the University of Winnipeg, Carleton University, Queen's University, the University of Toronto, Concordia University, the University of Waterloo, York University, the University of New Brunswick, Acadia University, Dalhousie University, St. Francis Xavier University, Saint Mary's University, University of Victoria, Simon Fraser University, the University of Saskatchewan, Ryerson University, Université de Montréal, and Memorial University of Newfoundland although this list is by no means complete.

To our knowledge, at the present time, there is only one university in Canada that has a formalized **undergraduate program in forensic psychology**: the University of British Columbia—Okanagan in Kelowna. A similar program started at Dalhousie University in 2002 and lasted until 2008, but relocated with the Dalhousie director (the first author of this textbook) to UBCO in 2008. Beginning in 2008, the specialization program in forensic psychology may be taken in conjunction with a four-year Bachelor of Science or Bachelor of Arts honours degree. This program provides exceptional undergraduate psychology students the opportunity to concentrate their studies in forensic psychology during the completion of their B.A. or B.Sc. Honours degree in Psychology. The program helps students to learn—through coursework, thesis, and practical experience—about the various roles that psychologists play in the legal system, psychological aspects of crime and criminal investigation, the assessment of risk for violence, and mental health issues/psychological interventions among both victims and offenders (see the UBC Okanagan Calendar for more information). As part of this program, students are required to complete two four-week (160-hour) placements within the criminal justice system, either working at a restorative justice facility, the John Howard Society, Kelowna Probation, Kelowna Parole, or the Elizabeth Fry Society. In addition, students are required to take two classes in forensic psychology, complete their honours research project on a forensic topic, and take several classes in sociology (such as criminology). The program recently has forged ties with international forensic programs and agencies; one of the recent graduates of the program, Brendan Wallace, completed a successful placement at a prison in Iceland in 2011.

If you are nearing completion of your undergraduate degree in psychology, you may be wondering where to go from here. Currently, several Canadian universities offer graduate-level training in forensic psychology, either in a formal program in the area or by allowing students to focus their training in that area while completing other programs (clinical, applied psychology, etc.). The graduate program at UBCO offers specialized training in either clinical-forensic or forensic research. For the clinical-forensic stream, students must complete a practicum within a forensic context, complete a portion of their internship at a forensic site, complete three of their option credits in forensic courses, and complete a Ph.D. thesis on a forensic topic.

Simon Fraser University offers two graduate-level programs in law and forensic psychology (see SFU Psychology website, http://www.psyc .sfu.ca). According to the website:

the Program in Law and Forensic Psychology offers experimental or clinical students unique research and applied experiences in the growing field of law and psychology. Students in both the Experimental Psychology and Law Stream and the Clinical-Forensic Stream enter the graduate training program in the psychology department through the normal procedures for the experimental and clinical training programs, respectively. In addition to the basic department requirements, students will enhance their experimental or clinical training by completing the requirements of the Clinical-Forensic or the Psychology and Law concentration, respectively. Students will be able to tailor the resources available through their respective concentrations to suit their intellectual and practical needs on an individual basis. In the experimental forensic program, students are required to take several courses in law and psychology, conduct a research project in law and psychology, and to complete a practicum in the area.

Carleton University does not have a specific graduate program in forensic psychology but students who are admitted to the graduate program

can take various courses in the forensic area, including "Sex Offenders," "Forensic Assessment," "Adult Offenders," "Witnesses, Victims, and Juries," "Youthful Offenders," and the "Psychology of Family Violence." Similar to Carleton, at UBCO, students can obtain specialized forensic training but there is no formalized forensic program per se.

PRACTICAL TRAINING

In recent years, psychologists have become increasingly active in offering training to Canadian legal decision makers. We have discussed many examples in this book. As mentioned in Chapter 1, in one of the most exciting developments in this area, the **National Judicial Institute (NJI)** based in Ottawa has invited psychologists to offer lectures and training to judges across the country. In light of the many well-known cases in which someone was falsely convicted, researchers in forensic psychology have been invited to educate the judiciary in areas such as eyewitness identification and credibility assessment. As Director George Thomson stated, such training is intended to educate judges on "the risk of over-reliance on certain factors, such as demeanour in findings of credibility" (Dotto, 2004, p. 49). He also noted that the NJI is considering having psychologists train judges in other areas.

Another type of training by psychologists has focused on deception detection or credibility assessment with Canadian psychologists, parole officers, judges, workers' compensation staff, private investigators, and human rights tribunals. Porter, Woodworth, and Birt (2000) combined training and research during a credibility assessment workshop with Correctional Service of Canada parole officers. The ability of officers to detect lying was looked at over two days of deception-detection training. On the first day, 32 officers judged whether 12 (six telling the truth, six lying) videotaped speakers were telling the truth, half of which were judged before and half judged after training. Five weeks later, 20 of the original participants judged the honesty of another 12 speakers (again, six telling the truth and six lying). In addition, three groups of undergraduate participants made judgments on the same 24 videotapes: (1) a feedback group, which received feedback on accuracy following each judgment they made; (2) a feedback plus cue information group, which was given feedback and

information on empirically based cues to lying; and (3) a control group, which received no feedback or cue information. It was found that at baseline all groups performed at or below the level of chance. However, overall, all groups, including the parole officers, became significantly better at detecting deception than the control group. By the final set of judgments, the parole officers were significantly more accurate (with an average of 76.7 percent) than their baseline performance (average of 40.4 percent). These results indicated that detecting lies is very difficult, but that training could help. More recent training (Porter et al., 2010) found that two hours of training helped workers' compensation staff increase their ability to identify both false emotional expressions (crocodile tears) and false stories about fictitious injuries.

There are many other examples of practical training in Canada. Psychologists such as John Yuille have trained many groups of police officers, lawyers, and social workers in appropriate interviewing techniques with children. For decades, Don Dutton has trained police officers in domestic violence intervention (as well as providing treatment to the abusers). Robert Hare and colleagues such as Adele Forth (at Carleton University) train legal staff in the use of the Psychopathy Checklist—Revised (2003). Other psychologists offer training in a variety of well-validated risk-assessment tools developed in Canada. For example, the **Mental Health, Law, and Policy Institute** in British Columbia (director: Dr. Ronald Roesch) is associated with the Simon Fraser psychology and law and criminology programs, and offers research and training in areas related to mental health law and policy (see SFU psychology website). Similarly, the mandate of the **Centre for Criminal Justice Studies** (director: Dr. Mary Ann Campbell) at the University of New Brunswick in Saint John is threefold: (1) to disseminate bodies of knowledge in the criminal justice area that meet the policy and practical needs of public and community-based organizations that address antisocial behaviour, (2) to provide consultation and training to legal professionals and community groups (e.g., parole, probation, prisons, policing, victim services, organizations involved in legislative and legal reform, etc.), and (3) to conduct research in areas with practical significance (see the University of New Brunswick psychology website, http://www.unb.ca/saintjohn/arts/depts/psychology/index.html).

SUMMARY

Canada has a tradition of excellence in forensic psychology. Beginning in the 1960s, academic researchers began to set the stage for new generations of researchers and practitioners in our field. While few of them were formally trained in forensic psychology, their research in diverse areas, including forensic aspects of memory, criminal behaviour, and forensic assessment, were pioneering and led to the generation of numerous fertile research programs across the country.

At present, forensic psychologists are having a great impact in Canada, in terms of research, practice, and training. Several Canadian universities offer formalized and less structured training in the field, at both the undergraduate and graduate levels. At the same time, Canadian universities need to create more such programs in light of the field's basic scientific importance, relevance in the legal system, and increasing interest from students hoping to pursue a career in forensic psychology.

KEY TERMS

American Psychology-Law Society, p. 352

Behavioral Sciences and the Law, p. 354

Centre for the Advancement of Psychological Science and Law, p. 352

Centre for Criminal Justice Studies, p. 358

Criminal Justice and Behavior, p. 354

Criminal Justice Section of the Canadian Psychological Association, p. 352

European Association of Psychology and Law, p. 352

Law and Human Behavior, p. 354

Mental Health, Law, and Policy Institute, p. 358

National Judicial Institute (NJI), p. 358

undergraduate program in forensic psychology, p. 356

SUGGESTED READINGS

Canadian Journal of Behavioural Science (April, 2004, Volume 36). Special Issue on Forensic Psychology.

This issue reports seven new empirical studies (six of them Canadian) in forensic psychology. This will give students an idea of the kind of interesting work happening in the field.

The following three papers by James Ogloff give an evolving historical and contemporary overview of graduate education in psychology and law, with attention to the Canadian context:

Ogloff, J. R. P. (1990). Law and psychology in Canada: The need for training and research. *Canadian Psychology, 31*, 61–73.

Ogloff, J. R. P. (1999). Graduate training in law and psychology at Simon Fraser University. *Professional Psychology: Research and Practice, 30*, 99–103.

Ogloff, J. R. P. (2000). Two steps forward and one step backward: The law and psychology movement(s) in the 20th century. *Law and Human Behavior, 24*, 457–483.

Glossary

Actuarial prediction

A judgment of future behaviour based on prespecified, empirically established assessments rather than subjective judgment. (p. 224)

Actuarial risk assessment

Based on statistical models that determine an offender's risk of reoffence based on the level of similarity between him or her and other offenders for whom the risk of reoffence is known. (p. 272)

Actus reus

"guilty act." In relation to criminal responsibility, it is the voluntary and wrongful act or omission that comprises the physical components of a crime. (p. 210)

Acute battering incident

Part of the cycle of abuse. The abuser explodes into an uncontrollable rage, leading to injuries to the partner. (p. 243)

Acute crisis phase

A state of mind immediately after being physically or sexually assaulted. This phase is characterized by great disorganization in the survivor's life; survivors often describe it as a state of shock, in which they report that everything has fallen apart inside. (p. 300)

Acute dynamic risk factors

Criminal factors that are able to change and are easily readjusted with intervention and treatment. (p. 272)

Advocate role

To take sides in a legal matter, potentially to become sympathetic to the arguments of the side that is paying the psychologist, and to slant the testimony in that direction. This shift toward partisanship may be subtle, even unconscious. (p. 27)

Aggravating factor

In relation to sentencing, it is a feature of the case that warrants a harsher sentence. (p. 337)

ALI standard

(also Brawner Rule) A policy that a person is not responsible for a criminal act if at the time of the crime, as a result of mental disease or defect, he or she lacked substantial capacity either to appreciate the criminality (wrongfulness) of his or her conduct or to conform his or her conduct to the requirements of the law. (p. 211)

American Psychology-Law Society (AP-LS)

The division of the American Psychological Association that is focused on topics at the intersection of psychology and law. (p. 352)

Amicus curiae briefs

Arguments by a third party (that is, an individual who is not part of the case) who acts as a "friend of the court," and informs judges on matters relevant to the dispute in a written testimonial. (p. 39)

Amydalotomy

A procedure that was performed to intentionally cause damage to the amygdala. This procedure was conducted to reduce the severity and frequency of aggressive behaviour and helped patients regain emotional control. (p. 321)

Anatomically detailed doll

A doll used in interviews with child complainants of sexual abuse. These dolls differ from other dolls in that they include (sometimes proportionally exaggerated) genitalia and other sexual organs. (p. 284)

Antiplaintiff bias

A preconceived negative opinion of the plaintiff that prevents a juror from impartially evaluating the facts of a case and generally leads to support for the defendant. (p. 190)

Antisocial personality disorder (ASPD)

A DSM-V personality disorder that is characterized by a pervasive pattern of disregard for and the violation of the rights of others occurring since the age of 15 years. To receive a diagnosis of ASPD, one must experience three of the following symptoms: a failure to conform to social norms, deceitfulness, impulsivity, irritability, reckless disregard for others, irresponsibility, or lack of remorse. (p. 319)

Assessment

Gathering information to assist in decision making. Psychological assessment can be conducted in two forms, formal or informal. Psychologists making formal assessments use well-validated measures and questionnaires while psychologists making informal assessments often use an unstructured interview and clinical intuition. (p. 25)

Assumption of risk

A civil defence aimed at proving that the plaintiff was aware of a dangerous condition and voluntarily exposed him- or herself to it. Particular actions by plaintiffs can be assigned values along a continuum ranging from 0 to 100 percent risk. (p. 198)

Authoritarianism

A trait characterized by favouring absolute obedience to authority. (p. 190)

Automatism

A Criminal Code defence that exists in two distinct forms: noninsane and insane automatism. Noninsane automatism refers to an involuntary action that is not caused by mental disorder (e.g., sleepwalking) whereas insane automatism refers to involuntary action caused by a disease of the mind (e.g., a psychotic break). (p. 212)

Baiting questions

Questions that are not necessarily accusatory in nature but still convey to suspects that some (false) evidence exists that links them to the crime. (p. 173)

Balancing selection

Suggests that psychopathic traits have been selected into our gene pool because they offer a fitness (survival/reproduction) advantage in certain environments. (p. 323)

Base rate

The relative frequency with which certain states or conditions occur in a population. A base rate is defined for and restricted to a specified population. (p. 224)

Battered woman defence

A defence used in court when a women murders her abuser. The defence can be used when a woman reasonably believed that her abuser was going to kill her. (p. 245)

Battered woman syndrome (BWS)

A set of distinct psychological and behavioural symptoms that result from prolonged exposure to situations of intimate partner violence. (p. 242)

Behavioral Sciences and the Law

A leading academic journal in the field of forensic psychology that is focused on publishing research at the intersection of law and the behvioural sciences. (p. 354)

Belief in a just world

A belief that the world is orderly and guided by justice. A perspective that individuals often adopt to justify the negative outcome of a situation (e.g., "she got what she deserved"). (p. 123)

Brunner syndrome

A condition that is characterized by severe impulsive behaviour. It results from extreme abnormalities in the MAOA enzyme. (p. 320)

Burnout

A psychological response to long-term exhaustion and diminished interest in life's activities. (p. 65)

California Psychological Inventory (CPI)

A psychological test similar in format to the MMPI, but whose subscales reflect personal traits such as dominance, sociability, and flexibility, in contrast to the diagnostic categories (e.g., Psychopathic Deviate, Hypomania) of the MMPI. (p. 55)

Callous-unemotional traits

The most important psychopathic traits identified in children and youth that predict adult psychopathy. These traits include a lack of guilt and empathy, and the insensitive or cruel manipulation of others. (p. 329)

Centre for the Advancement of Psychological Science and Law (CAPSL)

A research centre located at the University of British Columbia—Okanagan. The aim of the CAPSL is to produce innovative research on topics at the intersection of psychology and the legal system. (p. 352)

Centre for Criminal Justice Studies

A research centre located at the University of New Brunswick. The mandate of the CCJS

is threefold: (1) to disseminate bodies of knowledge in the criminal justice area that meet the policy and practical needs of public and community-based organizations that address antisocial behaviour, (2) to provide consultation and training to legal professionals and community groups (e.g., parole, probation, prisons, etc.), and (3) to conduct research in areas with practical significance. (p. 358)

Challenge for cause

A method of eliminating potential jury members used by attorneys in the legal system in the United States. (p. 204)

Child molesters

People who engage in sexual abuse against a child, including an array of sexual activities that ranges from fondling of the genitals to oral, vaginal, or anal penetration. There are a number of ways to categorize child molesters, the most common one referring to victim type (familial versus nonfamilial) or sexual interest (situational versus preferential). (p. 262)

Child pornography

Visual representation (whether it be a photograph or video), audio recording, or written description that depicts a person who is, or is made to appear, under the age of 18 years old engaged in explicit sexual activity. (p. 260)

Child sexual abuse accommodation syndrome

A syndrome to explain how children deal with ongoing sexual abuse. This syndrome includes five phases, or characteristics common to many situations of abuse—engagement, sexual interaction secrecy, disclosure, and suppression. (p. 293)

Classical conditioning stimulus

In relation to sexual assault, the classical conditioning stimulus is any type of sensory information that is associated with the sexual assault. The victim will likely fear these stimuli as a result of the association between him or her and the assault. (p. 301)

Client

The individual, agency, or public for whom forensic psychologists provide their services. (p. 49)

Clinical opinion

A judgment or perspective based on knowledge and experience in the field; it is most often proviced by a clinical psychologist. (p. 272)

Clinical prediction

A subjective judgment of an individual's future actions or outcomes derived from a psychologist's intuitive and impressionistic analysis of the case history. (p. 224)

Coerced-compliant false confession

When a suspect confesses as a result of coercion although fully aware that he or she is innocent (p. 164)

Coerced-internalized false confession

When the innocent suspect confesses and comes to believe that he or she truly is guilty. (p. 165)

Cognitive inconsistency

In relation to intimate partner violence, abused women often express two ideas that appear to be logically inconsistent with each other. For example, a woman might state that she was abused only when her partner was drunk but later describes an episode during which he was not drunk and yet abusive. (p. 243)

Cognitive interview

A formal questioning procedure, based on principles of cognitive and social psychology, used by police to enhance retrieval of information from the witness's memory. (p. 141)

Cognitive load theory

A psychological principle that states that the mind can focus on only a certain number of things at one time, and as the number of things that the mind is expected to focus on increases, performance decreases. In relation to deception, cognitive load refers to the large number of things that a liar must focus on when telling a lie. This includes controlling nonverbal behaviour such as facial expressions and body language as well as verbal behaviour (i.e., the lie). Because the mind has so much to focus on when lying, the theory of cognitive load stipulates that the liar will involuntarily leak cues to his or her deception. (p. 122)

Cognitive test of insanity

Consideration of the quality of the person's thought processes and perceptions of reality at the time of the crime (e.g., McNaughton Test). (p. 210)

Community policing

When the police department focuses on improving the quality of life and being responsive (even proactively) to citizens' concerns. (p. 71)

Competency to stand trial
The capacity of a person to understand the nature and purpose of court proceedings and to function and participate meaningfully within the process. (p. 220)

Compliance
Agreeing to a request made by another individual. May also refer to an inconsistency between one's public behaviour and one's private opinion. (p. 164)

Conduit-educator
A type of expert witness. The expert witness's own field becomes the first priority and he or she aims to provide a clear picture of all of the research in that field, as opposed to presenting a one-sided argument. (p. 38)

Confession
An admission of guilt by a suspect. A confession is among the most powerful evidence that can be presented at the defendant's trial. (p. 160)

Confidence game
Involves the well-developed use of deception and manipulation, and thus the betrayal of trust. (p. 174)

Confidentiality
Trial consultants keep all information about a particular case perpetually private and confidential, unless the consulting lawyer and client have agreed in writing to forego confidentiality or they are legally required via a court order to do so. (p. 33)

Confirmation bias
In relation to witness testimony, refers to the influence of observers' expectations on memory retrieval and reporting. (p. 148)

Conflict of interest
A divergence between the private concerns and the official responsibilities of a person in a position of trust. In relation to jury selection, a conflict of interest is a controversy that puts a juror at risk of being dismissed during a trial. (p. 187)

Consent
The voluntary agreement of both parties to engage in sexual activity. (p. 258)

Contrite phase
Part of the cycle of abuse in which the abuser's use of promises and gifts increases the abused spouse's hope that violence had occurred for the last time and that she would no longer be victimized. The abuser expresses regret and apologizes, often promising never to lose control again. (p. 243)

Control question technique (CQT)
A popular method in which a polygraph records changes in arousal when asked neutral, relevant, and probable-lie questions. (p. 117)

Correspondent inference theory
Deals with the decision to infer whether a person's actions reflect (or correspond to) an internal characteristic. (p. 179)

Countermeasures
Strategies used by examinees to manipulate their physiological arousal, distort the polygraph output and mislead the examiner. (p. 119)

Crime scene analysis
To examine evidence from the crime scene. This includes the analysis of physical evidence, victims, and witnesses in an attempt to construct an accurate description of the person or persons who perpetrated the crime. (p. 93)

Criminal harassment
The repeated unwanted, harassing, or threatening behaviours directed toward the victim over a period of time. (p. 253)

Criminal Justice and Behavior
A leading academic journal in the field of forensic psychology that promotes scholarly evaluations of assessment, classification, prevention, intervention, and treatment programs to help the correctional professional develop successful programs based on sound and informative theoretical and research foundations. (p. 354)

Criminal Justice Section of the Canadian Psychological Association
A section of the Canadian Psychological Association that represents members who work in various criminal justice and forensic settings, including corrections, law enforcement, the courts, hospitals, community mental health, and academic settings. (p. 352)

Criminal profile
A description of the person who is believed to have committed a particular crime. This description often includes the offender's age, sex, and race, as well as personality traits and his/her motivation for committing the crime. The profile may also include descriptions of the offender's behavioural patterns and tendencies. (p. 78)

Criminal profiling
The process of creating a profile of a criminal, most often conducted by a police investigator or psychological consultant who examines evidence from the crime scene, victims, and witnesses in an attempt to construct an accurate description of the person or persons who perpetrated the crime. (p. 75)

Criminal-profile generating process
A process with five main stages. Apprehension of a suspect is the goal and the final step in the process. (p. 94)

Criterion-based content analysis technique (CBCA)
A well-validated assessment of the truthfulness of written statements. CBCA can be used on the written statements of both children and adults and is often used in conjunction with other credibility assessments. (p. 289)

Cycle of abuse
The interactions between the abuser and his or her partner; a set of observable phases between abuser and his or her victim that culminates in abuse. (p. 243)

Danger Assessment
A risk assessment tool designed to predict risk for life-threatening IPV violence. (p. 252)

Dangerous Decisions Theory
Suggests that instantaneous impressions of trustworthiness based on facial appearance may play a major role in the assessment of credibility, guilt at trial, and various character traits. (p. 196)

Dangerous Offender (DO)
A designation given to an offender who the court concludes is a threat to the safety, physical and/or mental well-being, and lives of the public. This designation may lead to imprisonment for an indefinite amount of time. (p. 345)

Dangerousness
The likelihood that an individual will inflict serious physical injury or lasting physical harm to themselves or others; determined through risk factors, harm, and risk level. (p. 225)

Dark Triad
A constellation of three related but distinct personality traits (Machiavellianism, subclinical narcissism, and psychopathy) that all are associated with the use of manipulation and exploitation to better oneself. (p. 315)

Death penalty
Capital punishment; a death sentence given in many regions of the world when a convicted offender represents a continuing threat to society, even if imprisoned for life. (p. 334)

Deduction
The application of a general theory or rule to infer specific instances or occurrences. (p. 19)

Deep pockets
Abundant financial resources. (p. 198)

Delayed discovery
A legal doctrine that suspends the running of statutes of limitations during periods of time in which the plaintiff did not discover, or by the exercise of reasonable diligence, could not have discovered, the injuries that would lead to his or her causes of action against the defendant/perpetrator. (p. 151)

Deleterious mutations
Suggests that psychopathy is a dysfunction that is a result of a series of genetic mutations. The deleterious mutation hypothesis is supported by the evidence of physical differences in the brains of psychopaths versus nonpsychopaths. (p. 323)

Demand characteristics
Cues that suggest the nature of the response that is expected from the witness. (p. 140)

Denunciation
The act of providing incriminating information against someone. (p. 338)

Determinate sentence
Specific sentence, such as five years in prison, with a likelihood of earlier conditional release. (p. 345)

Deterrence
Something that discourages or is intended to discourage a person from committing an aversive act (e.g., committing a crime). (p. 338)

Disorganized criminal
The disorganized criminal does not plan his or her crime in advance and typically obtains victims randomly and then behaves haphazardly during the crime. Disorganized offenders are more apt to leave a weapon at the crime scene and depersonalize a body also called asocial criminals. (p. 94)

Domestic Violence Risk Appraisal Guide
An empirically derived instrument developed to assess IPV risk. (p. 252)

Domestic Violence Screening Instrument—Reviews
An empirically derived instrument developed to assess IPV risk. (p. 252)

Double-blind procedure
A lineup in which the administrator does not know which individual is the suspected culprit. It is designed to prevent any influence over witness identification decisions. (p. 150)

Dual relationship
When a psychologist enters into a personal relationship with a client or is engaged in more than one type of professional activity with a client. This type of relationship generally is unethical according to the CPA ethical guidelines. (p. 31)

Duping delight
The experience of enjoyment on the part of the deceiver when telling a lie. (p. 117)

DWB ("driving while black")
A sarcastically developed crime-classification expression for "Driving While Black" that reflects the tendency of some police officers to concentrate on minorities as likely offenders. (p. 50)

Ecological validity
The extent to which the conditions simulated in the laboratory reflect real-life conditions and the question of whether results found in the controlled environment also will occur and be applicable in real life. (p. 21)

Emotional arousal
The experience of strong emotions and emotional behaviour. (p. 117)

Emotional leakage
The expression of a genuine emotion when an individual is trying to conceal the emotion or mask it with another emotion. (p. 121)

Empathy
The ability to recognize and understand the feelings of others. (p. 314)

Empirical approach
Scientific explanations relying on or derived from experiment and direct observation. (p. 8)

Encoding
The first of three steps in the memory process. Encoding occurs when the item that is to be remembered is converted into a construct that the brain can store to later be retrieved. Encoding occurs in both short- and long-term memory. (p. 144)

Estimator variables
Variables that affect witness testimony but are not under the control of the criminal justice system. (p. 133)

European Association of Psychology and Law
An association based in Europe that embraces both researchers and practitioners interested in psychology and law. Its goals include the promotion of research, teaching, and the interchange of psychology and law. (p. 352)

Evaluation research
Scientific assessment of the effectiveness of policies, procedures, and approaches used in the criminal justice system. (p. 151)

Exhibitionists
People with the paraphilia of exhibitionism, characterized by becoming sexually aroused upon exposing one's genitals to a stranger. (p. 259)

Expert witness
A psychologist hired by one party to present expert testimony on a particular topic in an adversarial proceeding. (p. 26)

Fact witness
A witness who testifies about what he or she has observed or what knows as fact. (p. 34)

Factor analysis
A statistical procedure that examines relationships between responses to a variety of items and then identifies which items are theoretically and statistically related to each other. (p. 194)

False memories
Distorted or fabricated recollections of imagined experiences that may be vivid and held with high confidence. (p. 144)

False negative
In relation to the hiring of police recruits, a false negative is defined as an officer who is not hired because of his or her performance in the interview but who would have displayed an acceptable performance as an officer. (p. 54)

False positive
In relation to a polygraph test, a false positive is defined as physiological arousal

that an innocent individual experiences from stress, which is falsely interpreted as a sign of deception. (p. 118)

False positive
In relation to the hiring of police recruits, a false positive is defined as a recruit who is hired because of his or her performance in the interview but turns out to be a poor police officer. (p. 54)

Fitness-for-duty evaluation
An investigation of an officer's emotional stability following a traumatic event or a complaint lodged against him or her by another officer or a civilian. (p. 70)

Foils
The fillers in a police lineup; these are persons who are not suspects in the crime at hand but usually have similar physical characteristics to the reported suspect. (p. 138)

Forensic evidence
Evidence of a crime such as cause of death, the type of weapon used, the timeline of wounds/death, and whether sexual acts were performed both pre- and postmortem. (p. 96)

Forensic psychology
Any scientific inquiry at the intersection of psychology and the legal system, or the application of psychological knowledge in forensic contexts. (p. 2)

Frotteurs
Individuals with the paraphilia of frotteurism, characterized by becoming sexually aroused by touching or rubbing against a nonconsenting individual. This beahviour often occurs on public transportation. (p. 261)

Frye test
A standard for admissibility of proposed experts in court. Established in the U.S. more than 80 years ago, it stated that the well-recognized standards regarding principles or evidence for any particular field should determine the admissibility of expert testimony. (p. 38)

Fundamental attribution error
Accepting a dispositional attribution of a person's actions without fully accounting for the effects of situational factors. (p. 180)

Geographic profiling
A computer-based system developed by Professor Kim Rossmo that considers the pattern of documented crime scene locations to provide a statistical estimate of the probable residence or base of operations of a serial offender. (p. 78)

Grooming
The luring process; wherein the offender makes initial contact with the victim, befriends the potential victim and develops a relationship, encourages the exclusivity of their relationship, assures that the child is not at risk of telling their parents, and then introduces sexual content and acts to the child. (p. 261)

Group differences
The distinctions between the common features of one group of people with those of another. These features include racial/ethnic classifications, gender, and broad personality characteristics and attitudes. (p. 201)

Guilt
Legal culpability; requires not only the commission of an illegal act but also a state of mind reflecting awareness of its implications. (p. 210)

Guilty knowledge test (GKT)
A method of polygraph questioning which relies on orientation reflexes that occur when a relevant stimulus is presented to the individual being questioned. (p. 118)

Halo effect
Involves basing each item score on an overall impression of the individual, which can be influenced by the type of offences the individual being assessed has committed. (p. 315)

Harm
As a component of dangerousness, refers to the amount and type of violence being predicted. (p. 225)

High-stakes deception
A situation in which the consequences would be severe if the lie was exposed. An example of a high-stakes lie is a statement by an individual who has killed her or her relative but goes on television to plead for his or her return. If the lie is discovered, the individual likely would be charged with murder. (p. 112)

Hindsight bias
The tendency to view what has already happened as relatively inevitable and obvious without realizing that retrospective knowledge of the outcome is influencing one's judgment. (p. 154)

Hired gun
A psychologist willing to say whatever his or her hiring client needs to be said to aid his or her case. (p. 27)

Holistic process
In the context of eyewitness identification, a focus on the relationship of features and the general appearance as determinants in face recognition. (p. 151)

Hostage taker
An individual who holds another individual(s) against his or her will. Four basic types are differentiated in the law enforcement and clinical literature: the political activist or terrorist, the criminal, the mentally disturbed hostage taker, and the prisoner. (p. 66)

Hypervigilance
A symptom of posttraumatic stress disorder that is a state of sensory sensitivity in addition to extreme behavioural reactions in response to perceived threats in the environment. In relation to IPV, hypervigilance often takes the form of extreme scrutiny of the abuser's mood, language, and emotional expressions in anticipation of future abuse. (p. 243)

Ideal juror
The complete set of characteristics and traits that describe the individual most likely to rule in favour of the interested party. (p. 202)

Identikit
A collection of transparencies of various typical facial characteristics that can be superimposed on one another to build up a composite image of a person sought by the police. (p. 151)

Ilusion of transparency
A false idea that everything is clear-cut and works as it appears. (p. 123)

Immaturity index
An immaturity index consisting of a combination of three of the MMPI subscales of (Pd [Psychopathic Deviate], Ma [Hypomania], and the L Scale [a measure of social desirability]). This index is often a strong predictor of job termination among police officers. (p. 57)

Imminent danger
Impending threat of serious bodily harm or death. (p. 246)

Induction
The generation of rules or a theory based on several observed specific instances. (p. 19)

Inhibition hypothesis
A two-pronged hypothesis postulated by Darwin stating that (1) it is impossible to completely conceal true felt emotion on the face (due to a lack of control of the muscles associated with the emotion) and (2) it is impossible to fully feign emotional expressions when the emotion is not genuinely felt. (p. 121)

Instrumental violence
Violence that is used to obtain a goal (e.g., to obtain money or drugs). (p. 325)

Intergenerational cycle of crime
Suggests that parents pass on genes that make children vulnerable to antisocial behaviour. This genetic predisposition in addition to the environment that the child is raised in may help to form an antisocial personality disorder. (p. 322)

Intergenerationally predisposed type
A type of female sex offender: often works without a co-perpetrator and targets children opportunistically. Due to the opportunistic nature of these offences, the offender abuses both male and female children. This type of offender often was a victim of sexual abuse as a child and then turns the abuse on other children. (p. 265)

Internalization
Occurs when people come to believe that they committed acts that they, in fact, did not commit. (p. 170)

Internet lurers
Adults who contact children or adolescents online for sexual purposes. There are two types of Internet lurers, those who are driven to engage in sexual activity with the child or adolescent offline, and those who are driven solely by fantasy and choose only to engage in online sexual behaviour with the child. (p. 261)

Interrogation
A line of questioning conducted by the police with a suspect. The main goal of an interrogation is to secure a confession or gain information that furthers the investigation. (p. 171)

Interrogative suggestibility
The idea that because between some suspects are anxious or lack a strong self-concept, or for other reasons, they actually come to believe what the police are telling them. (p 176)

Interview
In the context of police selection, police officers (both local, provincial, and federal) who succeed in the PARE test (a measure of physical ability that includes running and lifting heavy items) then must participate in an interview to assess their communication and knowledge competencies as well as their potential to obtain a security clearance. (p. 53)

Intimate partner violence (IPV)
A form of abuse (physical, sexual, or emotional) between sexual partners. (p. 233)

Investigator bias
A lie bias that legal professionals experience due to an overwhelming suspiciousness stemming from their job experience. (p. 115)

Inwald Personality Inventory (IPI)
Developed to measure the suitability of personality attributes and behaviour patterns of law enforcement candidates. (p. 58)

Irresistible impulse exception
A criminal defence arguing that despite demonstrated cognitive knowledge of right or wrong, a defendant's free will was so overwhelmed that he or she lost the power to choose between right and wrong and therefor is not criminally responsible by reason of mental disorder. (p. 210)

Junk science
"Science" that is not backed by empirical data. (p. 36)

Juror bias
The assumption that each of us makes interpretations based on past experience and that these interpretations can colour a juror's verdict. (p. 190)

Juror stress
The mental, emotional, and physical tension and exhaustion that can affect jury members enduring sequestration, disturbing or complex evidence, and the desire to make the correct judgment. (p. 188)

Jury selection
The examination of prospective jurors in order to ensure a fair and impartial panel. The process focuses on eliminating potential jurors who show bias, prejudice, or some other inability to conduct their duties. (p. 200)

Jury tampering
The crime of attempting to influence a jury through any means other than presenting evidence and argument in court, including conversations about the case, offering bribes, making threats, or asking acquaintances to intercede with a juror. (p. 204)

Kernel-of-truth hypothesis
A position that group stereotypes may be unwisely generalized, but that some basic distinctions exist between groups and these distinctions form the foundation for group stereotypes. (p. 201)

Knowledge-bluff trick
When the interrogator pretends to have strong evidence (e.g., the suspect's fingerprints or DNA at the scene) when he or she does not. (p. 173)

L Scale
Detects a deliberate and unsophisticated attempt on the part of respondents to present themselves in a favourable light on the MMPI. (p. 57)

Law and Human Behavior
A leading academic journal in the field of forensic psychology that offers original research in the areas of criminal justice, law, psychology, sociology, psychiatry, political science, education, and communication, among others. It is the official journal of AP-LS. (p. 354)

Leading questions
Questions phrased in a manner that suggest to the witness the desired answer. (p. 140)

Learned helplessness
A response to having been exposed to painful stimuli over time, which one had no control over. Individuals with learned helplessness do not try to help themselves escape from aversive situations even if an avenue for escape exists. (p. 243)

Lineup
A criminal investigation technique in which the police arrange a number of individuals in a row and ask an witness to identify which, if any, of the individuals committed the crime. (p. 136)

Litigation explosion
The notion that there has been a rampant increase in often frivolous civil litigation in recent years. (p. 198)

London Family Court Clinic

Now referred to as the Centre for Children and Families in the Justice System. This centre, which helps child victims and witnesses prepare to testify in court, is internationally renowned for its work with over 1000 child abuse victims and child witnesses. (p. 285)

Long-Term Offender (LTO)

A designation that is given to an individual convicted of a "serious personal injury offence" and who a judge deems likely to reoffend. This designation results in a 10-year period of supervision upon the offender's release. (p. 345)

Long-term reactions phase

A state of mind after being sexually assaulted; a phase that involves the victim coming to terms with his or her reactions to the assault and attempting to deal with the hurt and sadness in an effective way. (p. 301)

Male-coerced type

A type of female sexual offender; this offender does not offend against children on her own, but partakes in the sexual abuse of children in the presence of a male co-offender. These offenders are characterized as codependent women who experienced sexual abuse themselves during childhood and are now in a dysfunctional relationship with a male who abuses them. (p. 266)

Malingering

The conscious fabrication or gross exaggeration of physical and/or psychological symptoms in order to achieve external goals such as avoiding prison or receiving monetary compensation. (p. 228)

Manie sans délire

"Moral insanity"; an early description of individuals who committed violent crimes but did not appear to possess the same symptoms of psychosis as the other mentally ill individuals. These individuals are seemingly able to understand the irrationality of what they were doing, were not otherwise psychotic, and appeared to have normal cognitive abilities. (p. 313)

MAOA (monoamine oxidase A)

A neurotransmitter responsible for breaking down dopamine and serotonin. (p. 320)

Mass murder

Three or more murders in one location and within a single criminal event. (p. 94)

Maximization

A scare tactic used by police that exaggerates the gravity of the offence and the magnitude of the charges; used to frighten the suspect into confessing. (p. 173)

McNaughton Rules

The foundation for the insanity criteria in many jurisdictions around the world. These rules provide the standard by which legal proof of insanity in the commission of a crime depends upon whether or not the accused knew the nature and quality of the act or that the act was wrong. (p. 210)

Memory testimony

The witness's statement of what he or she recalls of a prior event. Such statements may be influenced by far more than just memory processes. (p. 133)

Mens rea

"Guilty mind." In relation to criminal responsibility, it is defined as the criminal intention or knowledge that an act is wrong. (p. 210)

Mental Health, Law, and Policy Institute

An institute that offers research and training in topics related to mental health law and policy. This institute at Simon Fraser University maintains close ties with the psychology and law and criminology programs at this campus. (p. 358)

Microexpression

A brief leakage of genuine emotions that (according to Dr. Paul Ekman) manifests in the form of half- or full-face emotional expressions that can last for 1/25th to 1/5th of a second. (p. 121)

Minimization

A tactic used by police that is reflected in "soft sell" techniques in which the interrogator offers sympathy, face-saving excuses, or moral justification for the crime in an attempt to secure a confession. (p. 172)

Minnesota Multiphasic Personality Inventory (MMPI)

A psychological test that is the most popular measure of personality and psychopathology. It originally was designed in the early 1940s to identify persons with psychotic or neurotic problems, and continues to be used for that same purpose in many forensic contexts today. The MMPI is used by the police to assess the mental stability of applicants. (p. 55)

Mitigating factor

In relation to sentencing, it is a detail of the case that warrants a lighter sentence. (p. 337)

Mock jury approach

A jury research procedure that has participants assume the role of jurors tasked with determining an appropriate verdict or sentence based on either real or fictitious case materials. (p. 187)

Mode of death

The reason for death, be it natural, accidental, suicide, or murder. (p. 103)

Modus operandi

Directly translated as "method of operation." In relation to criminal acts, the modus operandi is the method used by the offender to commit his or her crimes. The modus operandi is the way in which the crimes are committed and should not be confused with the offender's signature. (p. 88)

Moral insanity

A morbid perversion of the natural feelings, affections, inclinations, temper, habits, moral dispositions, and natural impulses of humans, without any remarkable disorder or defect of intellect or knowing and reasoning faculties, and particularly without any insane illusion or hallucination. (p. 313)

Motivational impairment effect

Individuals most motivated to prevent detection of their lies are less successful in doing so. (p. 112)

Multiple cue method

The assessment of credibility that requires the evaluation of a large body of behavioural evidence (e.g., facial expressions, body language, language cues) prior to coming to a conclusion. (p. 124)

Mutt-and-Jeff tactic

An interrogation technique in which one detective comes across as hostile and relentless, while the other gains the suspect's confidence by being protective and supportive, sometimes known as "good-cop, bad-cop." (p. 174)

NASH classification

Whether a death could reliably be classified as natural, accidental, suicide, or homicide. (p. 104)

National Judicial Institute (NJI)

Based in Ottawa; it is an organization that facilitates the teaching and training of judges in forensic topics by trained psychologists and other professionals. The training is intended to educate judges on relevant topics such as the risk of overreliance on certain factors, such as demeanour, in findings of credibility. (p. 358)

National Sex Offender Registry (NSOR)
A list of convicted sex offenders who are living in Canada after having been released from jail or prison. Each offender profile includes a photograph of the offender's face; physical descriptors such as height, weight, hair, and eye colour; date of birth; known aliases; information about the offence itself; and the addresses for his or her home, place of work, and any other place frequented. (p. 277)

Necrophilia
A type of paraphilia defined by the DSM-IV-TR as the presence, over a period of at least six months, of recurrent and intense urges and sexually arousing fantasies involving corpses that are either acted upon or have been markedly distressing. (p. 216)

Not criminally responsible by reason of a mental disorder (NCRMD)
Canada's version of the insanity defence. It is a defence established by section 16 of the Criminal Code of Canada stating that "no person is criminally responsible for an act committed or an omission made while suffering from a mental disorder that rendered the person incapable of appreciating the nature and quality of the act or omission or of knowing that it was wrong." (p. 208)

Ontario Sex Offender Registry (OSOR)
A list of convicted sex offenders who are living in the community (in the province of Ontario) after having been released from jail or prison. Each offender profile includes a photograph of the offender's face; physical descriptors such as height, weight, hair, and eye colour; date of birth, known aliases, information about the offence itself, and the addresses for his or her home, place of work, and any other place frequented. (p. 277)

Ordeal
Historically, a prominent manner of detecting deception, involving torture and based on superstition and religious beliefs. (p. 115)

Organized criminals
Offenders who plan their crimes, target their victims (who usually do not know the perpetrator), and show self-control at the crime scene by leaving few clues. These individuals are apt to use a vehicle during the crime and use restraints. Also known as nonsocial criminals. (p. 94)

Parade
The British term for a police lineup. (p. 146)

Paralimbic system
Also called the mesocortex; is the part of the brain responsible for a gradual transition of signals from the primary limbic regions to higher neocortical regions. Abnormalities in this system are said to be responsible for the structural differences found in the brains of psychopaths. (p. 321)

Paraphilia
A DSM-IV-TR disorder that is characterized by becoming sexually aroused by deviant objects, situations, or under-aged or non-consenting persons. To be a diagnosed as paraphilia, symptoms must be distressing to the individual who experiences the sexual arousal or harmful to others. (p. 259)

Pedophilia
A paraphilia characterized by persistent fantasies, urges, thoughts, behaviours, and sexual desire for prepubescent children and a lack of sexual interest in other adults. (p. 260)

Peremptory challenge
A formal objection to the inclusion of a prospective juror in a jury that does not require counsel to assign a reason for the objection. (p. 199)

Philosopher-ruler/advocate
A type of expert witness; he or she takes a legal-adversary stance, in which he or she volunteers only research evidence that supports his or her side of the argument, de-emphasizes or omits possible flaws in the data, and/or refrains from discussing opposing evidence while on the stand. (p. 38)

Phobia
An irrational fear, the experience of which interferes with one's ability to function normally. (p. 301)

Photo array
Used in place of a live lineup, consists of a set of images substituted in place of actual persons. Also called a photo spread or six-pack. (p. 136)

Physical evidence
A primary type of evidence left at each crime scene. Physical evidence is the evidence that investigators can readily observe, such as blood spatter and methods of restraint, the position of the body, and the presence or absence of weapons as opposed to evidence from witnesses and victims. (p. 78)

Police corruption
The abuse of authority by police officers for personal gain. (p. 51)

Police selection
The screening of police candidates following predetermined criteria, including psychological and physical testing. (p. 51)

Police stress
Stress in police officers that often leads to mental health problems such as depression, substance abuse, burnout, or even suicide. (p. 49)

Polygraph
An investigative tool that measures changes in electrodermal activity including galvanic skin conductance, blood pressure, heart rate, and respiration for the purpose of deception detection. (p. 117)

Postevent misinformation paradigm
Modification of memories through the incorporation of misleading postevent information. (p. 144)

Posttraumatic stress disorder (PTSD)
The most extreme psychological outcome of a traumatic experience. People with PTSD, a disorder that will be retained in the DSM-V, can experience a variety of symptoms including intrusive memories or flashbacks, avoidance thoughts and behaviours, and hypervigilance. (p. 302)

Power and Control Wheel
An organizational tool that is often used in the assessment and treatment of domestic abuse. The wheel lists eight categories of abuse including (1) coercion and threats, (2) intimidation, (3) emotional abuse, (4) isolation, (5) minimization, denial, and blaming, (6) use of children to control the woman, (7) use of "male privilege," and (8) economic/resource abuse. (p. 244)

Precedent
A previous case or legal decision taken as a guide or justification for subsequent cases. (p. 19)

Presentence psychological report
A report that is conducted after an offender has been convicted but before he or she has been sentenced. The report often addresses the following in making recommendations for appropriate

sentencing: risk for reoffence, remorse/insight into the criminal behaviour, and potential for rehabilitation. Relevant information to inform such opinions includes criminal history, substance abuse history, education/employment history, mental health history, psychological testing, actuarial prediction of risk and clinical impressions of personality, sincerity, and motivation. (p. 338)

Primary negotiator
The person who is in direct contact with the hostage taker during hostage negotiations. The role of the negotiator is to build rapport with the hostage and eventually convince him or her to surrender. (p. 69)

Pro bono
Doing professional consultation or legal work for the public good without compensation. (p. 199)

Probability of commission
The likelihood that the defendant is the individual who committed the crime. (p. 192)

Pro-defendant bias
A predisposition or preconceived opinion supporting the defendant that prevents a juror from impartially evaluating the facts of a case. (p. 190)

Promotion of responsibility
To support or actively encourage a sense of accountability in offenders so that they may acknowledge the harm done to their victims as well as their community. (p. 338)

Pro-plaintiff bias
A predisposition or preconceived opinion supporting the plaintiff or complainant that prevents a juror from impartially evaluating the facts of a case. (p. 190)

Pseudopsychopathy
Also called acquired sociopathic personality. Patients suffering from damage to the orbital frontal cortex have problems with empathy, impulsivity, irresponsibility, insight, behavioural inhibition, and planning, and may become prone to grandiosity and confabulation. (p. 321)

Psychic numbing
A defence mechanism that is characterized by a reduced responsiveness to the environment after a traumatic event. (p. 303)

Psychological autopsy
The investigative method used by psychologists or other social scientists to help determine the mode of death in equivocal cases. This includes generating an understanding of the circumstances surrounding the death and the deceased's state of mind at the time of death. (p. 103)

Psychological profile
A criminal profile without demographic data. (p. 78)

Psychological self-defence
When battered women kill their abusers to protect themselves from being destroyed psychologically. (p. 247)

Psychopathic abusers
Domestic abusers who possess a number of traits commonly associated with psychopathy including impulsivity, a lack of empathy, and antisocial and violent behaviour. (p. 235)

Psychopathy
An aversive personality type that is characterized by an emotional void, impulsivity, a lack of guilt or remorse, pathological lying, manipulativeness, and a continual willingness to violate social norms. (p. 225)

Psychopathy Checklist—Revised (PCL-R)
The "gold standard" for measuring the concept of psychopathy in an operational and quantifiable way. It is a 20-item measure that uses a scale of 0 (does not apply) to 2 (definitely applies) for each item. The PCL-R is an interview tool rather than a questionnaire, which means that items are scored by the interviewer. (p. 315)

Psychopathy Checklist—Youth Version (PCL-YV)
A measure heavily based on the PCL-R; the PCL-YV is used to assess and screen for psychopathic characteristics in those who are too young to be diagnosed using the PCL-R. (p. 330)

Publication ban
A court-ordered prohibition by law or official decree that prevents the media or public from disseminating details about a legal proceeding. A publication ban is issued when the safety of the jurors, victim, or witness is at stake, or when the judge feels that the scrutiny and criticism from society will influence the jury's decision. (p. 189)

R. v. Lavallee
The pivotal Supreme Court of Canada case that set the precedent for battered woman syndrome. (p. 244)

R. v. Oickle
A landmark case in which the Canadian Supreme Court ruled that a confession will not be admissible if it is made under circumstances that raise a reasonable doubt as to voluntariness. (p. 160)

Racial profiling
Unjust victimization of minority groups by police officers based solely on race or cultural background. (p. 50)

Random sample of jurors
The selection of a set of potential jurors from the entire eligible population such that each member of the population has an equal probability of being chosen. This process is intended to produce a fair, impartial, and competent jury panel. (p. 186)

Rape myths
Incorrect beliefs about the victims, causes, and consequences of rape. (p. 306)

Rape trauma syndrome
A variation of posttraumatic stress disorder that is unique to victims of sexual assault. (p. 298)

Rapists
Those who sexually assault (most often specified to be vaginal penetration but any kind of penetrative offence) nonconsenting victims at least 16 years of age. (p. 262)

Rapport building
There interrogator builds a relationship with a suspect by showing sympathy, understanding, and respect. (p. 173)

RCMP Police Aptitude Test (RPAT)
A multiple-choice test designed to evaluate one's aptitude for police work. (p. 53)

Reasonable doubt
The standard of proof or threshold of certainty that must be surpassed to convict an accused in a criminal proceeding. (p. 192)

Recanted confession
When the suspect has made an incriminating statement to the police and later states that the confession was false. (p. 163)

Rehabilitation
The treatment of offenders to reduce the risk of them reoffending. (p. 338)

Relative judgment process
The natural tendency of a witness to consider lineup participants in comparison with one another, as opposed to a more direct comparison of each lineup member with the witness's memory of the culprit. (p. 148)

Reliability
The extent to which observations or measurements produce the same results on repeated trials over time. (p. 8)

Remorse
Deep regret or guilt for a committed act. (p. 343)

Replicability
The extent to which successive repetitions of a particular experiment produce similar results. (p. 8)

Retrieval
The third of the three steps in the memory process. Retrieval is the act of bringing the encoded and stored memory to the forefront of the mind. It is the act of "remembering." (p. 144)

Ride-alongs
When a civilian accompanies a police officer on patrol. (p. 62)

Risk
In relation to law, this means a danger of harm or loss from a plaintiff's action or behaviour. (p. 198)

Risk factors
A risk factor is something that increases the likelihood that an individual will commit a crime. A risk factor is a variable that is used to predict violence. (p. 272)

Risk level
As a component of dangerousness, refers to the probability that harm will occur. (p. 225)

Sadism
A paraphilia that is characterized by sexual arousal derived from the infliction of pain or humiliation on another human being. (p. 270)

Scan technique (scientific content analysis)
An interrogation technique that involves asking the subject to describe his or her activities the day of the crime, covering a period from several hours before to several hours after. This written description is then analyzed for verbal content, including the subject's use of pronouns and any changes in language use. (p. 178)

Science-translation brief
An objective summary of a body of research. Offered when the psychological body possesses knowledge the court otherwise might not have and that might assist the court in making ultimate decisions in a legal case. (p. 43)

Self-blaming response
A reaction to the sexual assault in which the victim blames his or her own actions for the rape, or at least implies that different behaviours on his or her part could have prevented it. (p. 300)

Self-defence
The use of equal force or the least amount of force necessary to repel danger when a person reasonably perceives that he or she is in imminent danger of serious bodily harm or death. Its key items include a reasonable perception of imminent danger and a justified use of lethal force. (p. 246)

Sequestered voir dire
A jury selection phase in which each of the potential jurors is questioned individually in the judge's chambers. (p. 203)

Serial murder
Three or more separate homicides with a cooling-off period between the crimes. (p. 77)

Sexual assault
Any nonconsensual sexual act committed by a male or a female against either a male or a female, regardless of the relationship between the individuals involved. (p. 257)

Sexual homicide
Sexual activity before, during, or after the commission of the murder. (p. 267)

Sexual sadism
Sexual arousal from the infliction of pain or humiliation on another human being. (p. 327)

Show-up
The live presentation of a criminal suspect to a victim or witness of a crime. Essentially a lineup composed of only one person. (p. 146)

Signature of a criminal
The unique, idiosyncratic aspects of the criminal act, often the reflection of a need to express violent fantasies. The signature is not necessary to complete the crime (i.e., not the *modus operandi*) but is an added act that the criminal feels compelled to do to receive satisfaction from the crime. (p. 88)

Situational tests
A test that simulates real-life police situations to evoke samples of the behaviour he or she will show on the job. (p. 60)

Social framework testimony
Use of general conclusions from social science research in determining factual issues in a specific case. This type of testimony provides jurors a context for evaluating the evidence in the case. (pp. 152, 293)

Sociopathic personality disturbance
The name given to psychopathy in the first edition of the DSM. The personality disorder was given this title in order to demonstrate a fusion between the psychiatric and social explanations of psychopathy. (p. 314)

Sociopsychological profile
A criminal profile with other sociological data such as the offender's occupation and level of education. (p. 78)

Sophonow inquiry
Thomas Sophonow is a Canadian who was wrongfully convicted of murder. The inquiry into his conviction, conducted in 2000, determined that faulty witness testimony and police interrogation techniques were major contributing factors. (p. 136)

Specialty designation
Recognition that a specific field of psychology has developed a substantial body of professional literature and specialized knowledge that distinguishes it from other specialties. Applied to specific training programs and not to individuals. (p. 4)

Spousal Assault Risk Assessment
A 20-item set of empirically based risk factors for use in the assessment of risk for spousal assault. It is most often used to determine the extent to which the offender is likely to commit violent acts in the future. (p. 252)

Spree murder
Killings at two or more locations with no emotional cooling-off period in between. (p. 94)

Stable dynamic risk factors
Behavioural and personality traits that are constant over time but are able to be changed or readjusted with intervention and treatment. (p. 272)

Stable risk factors
A risk factor that is historical and cannot change. (p. 271)

Stakeholders
People who have a special knowledge and interest, or a "stake," in an issue, such as running a police department. (p. 51)

Stalking
(or criminal harassment) Persistent unwanted attention from a perpetrator that causes a victim to fear for his or her safety or that of someone close to the victim. (p. 253)

Standard of reliability
Degree of consistency required in research findings. (p. 41)

Stare decisis
Directly translated to "let the decision stand." The legal principle of determining points in litigation according to previous cases (precedent). (p. 20)

Statement validity assessment
A deception detection approach relying on the complainant's statements; it consists of three parts: a structured interview with the child witness, the criterion-based content analysis technique, and the application of the Statement Validity Checklist, which assesses other characteristics of the interview process, the witness, and the investigation. (p. 289)

Statute of limitations
A law defining the period within which legal action may be taken after a crime has been committed. Once expired, offences cannot be prosecuted. (p. 151)

Stipulation
When detectives attempt to stifle attempts by the suspect to set down ground rules for the questioning during an interrogation. (p. 177)

Strategic use of evidence (SUE) technique
Evidence that is used strategically to catch the liar in a web of his or her deceit. (p. 125)

Subclinical psychopathy
A personality that meets many of the criteria for psychopathy, but not enough to warrant a full diagnosis of psychopathy. Such an individual may display callousness, a lack of empathy, greedy risk-taking behaviour, egocentricity, and superficial charm. (p. 328)

Successful psychopaths
Individuals with psychopathic traits who function relatively normally in contexts such as businesses. These psychopaths, like the less successful psychopaths, may ruthlessly manipulate others without guilt for their own personal gain in order to achieve high status within an organization. (p. 328)

Suggestibility
A state in which truth and falsehood become hopelessly confused in the suspect's mind. Suggestibility also refers to the ease with which an individual can be persuaded to believe something. (pp. 166, 288)

Suggestive questions
Introducing new information into an interview when the child has not already provided that information. Suggestive questions can lead witnesses to develop false memories of the crime. (p. 286)

Supplemental juror questionnaire
A list of questions that can be given to prospective jurors during a voir dire that is used to identify issues influencing legal decision making and individual attitudes and differences toward the legal system. (p. 205)

Sympathy for the defendant
Skepticism that the defendant truly committed the crime, or that the witness's testimony is truly accurate or that the confession was truly voluntary. (p. 42)

Syndrome
A collection of symptoms that frequently occur together, or, a condition characterized by a collection of symptoms. (p. 298)

System variables
Variables that affect witness testimony and are, or potentially can be, under the direct control of the criminal justice system. (p. 133)

Teacher-lover type
A type of female sex offender; prototypically a female teacher who sexually abuses a male student (or a female student, depending on the sexual orientation of the female teacher). This offender believes that she and the student are in love, and that the abuse is a positive and educational experience for the child. She does not believe that she is committing a criminal act. (p. 265)

Team policing
The assignment of police officers to particular neighbourhoods so that they become familiar with local concerns and priorities. (p. 48)

Tension-building phase
The first phase in the cycle of abuse; it is characterized by criticism, verbal bickering, increased strain, and sometimes minor physical abuse. (p. 243)

Testamentary capacity
The need to determine whether an individual was mentally competent at the time that his or her will was drawn. (p. 103)

Third-degree tactics
Interrogation tactics such as extreme deprivation, brutality, and torture, that were commonplace all over the world a century ago, and still occur in many countries today. (p. 164)

Trial consultant
Also known as a psycho-legal consultant. A psychologist hired by a trial lawyer to help him or her in preparing for and participating in the trial. This may include the manner in which a defendant should present him- or herself or how the lawyer should question witnesses. (p. 31)

Ultimate-issue testimony
Wrongful opinion evidence given by an expert witness that provides direct conclusions about a not-yet-decided legal issue that is sufficient to resolve the entire case (e.g., declaring a defendant to be not criminally responsible). (p. 218)

Ultimate-opinion testimony
Testimony given by an expert witness about the credibility of a particular witness. (p. 294)

Unconscious racism
A form of racism in which an individual cannot perceive the racial implications of his or her actions, nor perceive the causes of racially biased behaviour. The individual is not aware of his or her own racist attitudes. (p. 339)

Unconscious transference
An witness's misidentification of an innocent person as a criminal perpetrator due to the witness's previous exposure to the individual in another context. (p. 140)

Undergraduate program in forensic psychology

An undergraduate specialization program that was offered at Dalhousie University between 2002 and 2008. This program, which allowed undergraduates to gain hands-on experience in both research and forensic practice, has since been relocated to UBCO. (p. 356)

Values

Standards for decision making based on a society's established ideals for acceptable and unacceptable behaviour. (p. 7)

ViCAP

Violent Criminal Apprehension Program developed by the FBI. A computer program that helps investigators to link serial crimes across the United States. The VICAP system was used as a model for the ViCLAS system in Canada. (p. 97)

ViCLAS

Violent Crime Linkage Analysis System, a Canadian computer program that helps investigators to link serial crimes. After a violent crime is committed, police officers are required to complete a ViCLAS questionnaire that includes specific details of the crime. These details are then entered into the ViCLAS database by trained ViCLAS operators and the specifics of the crime are compared to the details of other crimes across the country to determine whether it it s similar to other crimes, and possibly committed by the same individual. (p. 78)

Victim blaming

Occurs when people blame the victim of abuse for the victimization. (p. 269)

Victimology

Collecting relevant information about a living or deceased victim such as age, physical characteristics, personality, reputation, potential criminal history, habits, hobbies, family structure, romantic relationships, location of residence, and occupation. (p. 96)

Voir dire

"To speak the truth"; it is the examination and selection of prospective jurors to form a fair and impartial jury. (p. 194)

Volitional aspect of insanity

The loss of ability to control one's behaviour. (p. 210)

Voluntary false confession

A false confession that is offered willingly, without elicitation. (p. 163)

Voyeurs

People with the paraphilia of voyeurism; characterized by becoming sexually aroused from secretly spying on others as they disrobe or engage in sexual behaviour. (p. 259)

Warrant expiry

The official end of a convicted offender's sentence. (p. 341)

Wellness training

Assisting police officers toward improving their lifestyle through learning new, health-enhancing behaviours and ideas. (p. 65)

Wizards

Individuals with abilities to detect deception with accuracy levels consistently higher than chance. (p. 115)

A. B. v. T. S. (2000). BCSC 976.

Abe, N. (2011). How the brain shapes deception: An integrated review of the literature. *The Neuroscientist.* Published online first. Retrieved November 10, 2011.

Abe, N., Fujii, T., Hirayama, K., Takeda, A., Hosokai, Y., Ishioka, T., et al. (2009). Do Parkinsonian patients have trouble telling lies? The neurobiological basis of deceptive behaviour. *Brain: A Journal of Neurology, 132*(5), 1386–1395.

Abel, G. G., & Rouleau, J. L. (1990). The nature and extent of sexual assault. In W. L. Marshall, D. R. Laws, H. E. Barbaree, W. L. Marshall, D. R. Laws, H. E. Barbaree (Eds.), *Handbook of sexual assault: Issues, theories, and treatment of the offender* (pp. 9–21). New York: Plenum Press.

Abracen, J., & Looman, J. (2005). Developments in the assessment and treatment of sexual offenders: Looking backward with a view to the future. *Journal of Interpersonal Violence, 20*(1), 12–19.

Abracen, J., Looman, J., & Langton, C. M. (2008). Treatment of sexual offenders with psychopathic traits: Recent research developments and clinical implications. *Trauma, Violence, & Abuse, 9*(3), 144–166.

Abramsky, T., Watts, C. H., Garcia-Moreno, C., Devries, K., Kiss, L., Ellsberg, M., et al. (2011). What factors are associated with recent intimate partner violence? Findings from the WHO multi-country study on women's health and domestic violence. *BMC Public Health, 11*, 109.

Acierno, R., Hernandez, M. A., Amstadter, A. B., Resnick, H. S., Steve, K., Muzzy, W., et al. (2010). Prevalence and correlates of emotional, physical, sexual, and financial abuse and potential neglect in the United States: The National Elder Mistreatment Study. *American Journal of Public Health, 100*(2), 292–297.

Acker, J. R., & Toch, H. (1985). Battered women, straw men, and expert testimony: A comment on *State v. Kelly. Criminal Law Bulletin, 21*, 125–155.

Ackerman, M. J., & Schoendorf, K. (1992). *Ackerman-Schoendorf Scales for Parent Evaluation of Custody (ASPECT): Manual.* Los Angeles: Western Psychological Services.

Acorn, A. (2011). Is insanity a demeaning defense? Examining the ethics of offender pathologization through the lens of the classics. *Journal of Forensic Psychology Practice, 11*(2–3), 204–231.

Adelson, R. (2004). Detecting deception. *Monitor on Psychology, 35,* 70.

Adler, T. (1993, September). APA files amicus brief in grant application case. *APA Monitor,* p. 26.

Adolphs, R. (2002). Trust in the brain. *Nature Neuroscience, 5*, 8–9.

Ainsworth, P. B. (1995). *Psychology and policing in a changing world.* Chichester, UK: Wiley.

Alberta Council of Women's Shelters. (2008). Annual statistics. Retrieved July 23, 2012, from http://www.acws.ca/annual_stats.php

Albini, J. L. (2001). Dealing with the modern terrorist: The need for changes in strategies and tactics in the new war on terrorism. *Criminal Justice Policy Review, 12*, 255–281.

Alder, K. (2007). America's two gadgets: Of bombs and polygraphs. *Isis, 98*, 124–137.

Alderden, M. A., & Ullman, S. E. (2012). Gender difference or indifference? Detective decision making in sexual assault cases. *Journal of Interpersonal Violence, 27*(1), 3–22.

Alexander, K. W., Quas, J. A., Goodman, G. S., Ghetti, S., Edelstein, R., & Redlich, A. (2005). Traumatic impact predicts long-term memory of documented child sexual abuse. *Psychological Science, 16,* 33–40.

Alicke, M. D., & Zell, E. (2009). Social attractiveness and blame. *Journal of Applied Social Psychology, 39*(9), 2089–2105.

Allen, S. W., Cutler, B. L., & Berman, G. L. (1993, August). *Analyses comparing various hostage negotiation techniques.* Paper presented at the meetings of the American Psychological Association, Toronto.

Allison, J. A., & Wrightsman, L. S. (1993). *Rape: The misunderstood crime.* Thousand Oaks, CA: Sage.

American Law Institute. (1962). *Model penal code.* Washington, DC: American Law Institute.

American Psychiatric Association. (1987). *Diagnostic and statistical manual of mental disorders—Revised* (3rd ed.). Washington: American Psychiatric Association.

American Psychiatric Association. (1994). *Diagnostic and statistical manual of mental disorders* (4th ed.). Washington, DC: American Psychiatric Association.

American Psychological Association. (2011). Specialty guidelines for forensic psychology. Retrieved May 15, 2012 from http://www.apa.org/practice/guidelines/forensic-psychology.aspx

Amstadter, A. B., Elwood, L. S., Begle, A. M., Gudmundsdottir, B., Smith, D. W., Resnick, H. S., et al. (2011). Predictors of physical assault victimization: Findings from the national survey of adolescents. *Addictive Behaviors, 36*(8), 814–820.

Anand, S., & Manweiller, H. (2005). Stress and the Canadian criminal trial jury: A critical review of the literature and the options for dealing with juror stress. *Criminal Law Quarterly, 50*, 403–440.

Anda, R. F., Felitti, V. J., Bremner, J., Walker, J. D., Whitfield, C., Perry, B. D., et al. (2006). The enduring effects of abuse and related adverse experiences in childhood: A convergence of evidence from neurobiology and epidemiology. *European Archives of Psychiatry and Clinical Neuroscience, 256*(3), 174–186.

Andrews, D. A., & Bonta, J. (2010). Rehabilitating criminal justice policy and practice. *Psychology, Public Policy, and Law, 16*(1), 39–55.

Annan, S. L. (2011). "It's not just a job. This is where we live. This is our backyard": The experiences of expert legal and advocate providers with sexually assaulted women in rural areas. *Journal of the American Psychiatric Nurses Association, 17*(2), 139–147.

Anson, R. S. (1998, July). The devil and Jeffrey MacDonald. *Vanity Fair,* pp. 46–68.

Apel, R., & Burrow, J. D. (2011). Adolescent victimization and violent self-help. *Youth Violence and Juvenile Justice, 9*(2), 112–133.

Archer, J. (2000). Sex differences in aggression between heterosexual partners: A meta-analytic review. *Psychological Bulletin, 126*, 651–680.

Arnett, P. A., Hammeke, T. A., & Schwartz, L. (1993, August). *Quantitative and qualitative performance on Rey's 15-item test.* Paper presented at the meetings of the American Psychological Association, Toronto.

Arnetz, B. B., Nevedal, D. C., Lumley, M. A., Backman, L., & Lublin, A. (2008). Trauma Resilience Training for Police: Psychophysiological and performance effects. *Journal of Police and Criminal Psychology, 24*, 1–9.

Aron, C. J. (1993, July 19). Women battered by life and law lose twice. *National Law Journal,* pp. 13–14.

Aronson, E. (1990, November). *Subtle coercion during police interrogation: The Bradley Page murder trial.* Invited address, Williams College, Williamstown, MA.

Aronson, E., Stephan, C., Sikes, J., Blaney, N., & Snapp, N. (1978). *The jigsaw classroom.* Thousand Oaks, CA: Sage.

Arrigo, B. A., & Purcell, C. E. (2001). Explaining paraphilias and lust murder: Toward an integrated model. *International Journal of Offender Therapy and Comparative Criminology, 45*(1), 6–31.

Arrigo, B. A., & Shipley, S. (2001). The confusion over psychopathy (I): Historical considerations. *International Journal of Offender Therapy and Comparative Criminology, 45*(3), 325–344.

Asch, S. E. (1956). Studies of independence and conformity: A minority of one against a unanimous majority. *Psychological Monographs, 70*, 1–70.

Ask, K., & Granhag, P. A. (2007). Motivational bias in criminal investigators' judgments of witness reliability. *Journal of Applied Social Psychology, 37*, 561–591.

Associated Press. (1992, February 23). FBI says 25 serial killers are still at large. *Lawrence Journal-World,* p. 13C.

Associated Press. (1993, November 4). Tape of therapy allowed in trial of two brothers. *The New York Times,* p. 7A.

Aubry, A., & Caputo, R. (1965). *Criminal interrogation.* Springfield, IL: Charles C Thomas.

Aubry, A., & Caputo, F. (1980). *Criminal interrogation* (3rd ed.). Springfield, IL: Charles C Thomas.

Augustin, D., & Fagan, T. J. (2011). Roles for mental health professionals in critical law enforcement incidents: An overview. *Psychological Services, 8,* 166–177.

Ax, R. K., Fagan, T. J., & Holton, S. B. (2003). Individuals with serious mental illnesses in prison: Rural perspectives and issues. In B. Stamm (Ed.), *Rural behavioral health care: An interdisciplinary guide* (pp. 203–215). Washington, DC: American Psychological Association.

Babchishin, K. M., Hanson, R., & Hermann, C. A. (2011). The characteristics of online sex offenders: A meta-analysis. *Sexual Abuse: Journal of Research and Treatment, 23*(1), 92–123.

Babcock, J. C., Green, C. E., & Robie, C. (2004). Does batterers' treatment work? A meta-analytic review of domestic violence treatment. *Clinical Psychology Review, 23*(8), 1023–1053.

Babiak, P., & Hare, R. D. (2006). *Snakes in suits: When psychopaths go to work.* New York, USA: HarperCollins.

Babiak, P., Neumann, C. S., & Hare, R. D. (2010). Corporate psychopathy: Talking the walk. *Behavioral Sciences and the Law, 28*(2), 174–193.

Bader, S. M., Schoeneman-Morris, K. A., Scalora, M. J., & Casady, T. K. (2008). Exhibitionism: Findings from a Midwestern police contact sample. *International Journal of Offender Therapy and Comparative Criminology, 52*(3), 270–279.

Bagby, R. M., Nicholson, R. A., Rogers, R., & Nussbaum, D. (1992). Domains of competency to stand trial: A factor analytic study. *Law and Human Behavior, 16,* 491–508.

Bagshaw, M. H., Mackworth, N. H., & Pribram, K. H. (1972). The effect of resections of the inferotemporal cortex or the amygdala on visual orienting and habituation. *Neuropsychologia, 102,* 153–162.

Baker, A., ten Brinke, L., & Porter, S. (2012, in press). Will get fooled again: Emotionally intelligent people are easily duped by high-stakes deceivers. *Legal and Criminological Psychology.*

Bala, N., Lee, K., Lindsay, R., & Talwar, V. (2001). A legal and psychological critique of the present approach to the assessment of the competence of the child witness. *Osgoode Hall Law Journal, 38*, 409–451.

Balkissoon v. Canada (Citizenship and Immigration) (2001). CanLII 26712 (I.R.B.).

Balsam, K. F., Lehavot, K., & Beadnell, B. (2011). Sexual revictimization and mental health: A comparison of lesbians, gay men, and heterosexual women. *Journal of Interpersonal Violence, 26*(9), 1798–1814.

Bar, M., Neta, M., & Linz, H. (2006). Very first impressions. *Emotion, 6*, 269–278.

Barbaree, H. E., & Seto, M. C. (1997). Pedophilia: Assessment and treatment. In D. Laws, W. T. O'Donohue, D. Laws, W. T. O'Donohue (Eds.), *Sexual deviance: Theory, assessment, and treatment* (pp. 175–193). New York: Guilford Press.

Barbaree, H. E., Seto, M. C., Langton, C. M., & Peacock, E. J. (2001). Evaluating the predictive accuracy of six risk assessment instruments for adult sex offenders. *Criminal Justice and Behavior, 28*(4), 490–521.

Barbaree, H. E., Seto, M. E., Serin, R. C., & Amos, N. L. (1994). Comparisons between sexual and nonsexual rapist subtypes: Sexual arousal to rape, offense precursors, and offense characteristics. *Criminal Justice and Behavior, 21*(1), 95–114.

Bard, M. (1970). *Training police as specialists in family crisis intervention.* NCJ 50. Washington, DC: U.S. Department of Justice, Law Enforcement Assistance Administration.

Bard, M., & Sangrey, D. (1979). *The crime victim's book.* New York: Basic Books.

Barker, E. D., & Maughan, B. (2009). Differentiating early-onset persistent versus childhood-limited conduct problem youth. *American Journal Psychiatry, 166*(8), 900–908.

Barr, J. (1979). *Within a dark wood.* Garden City, NY: Doubleday.

Barrett, G. V., & Morris, S. B. (1993). The American Psychological Association's amicus curiae brief in *Price Waterhouse v. Hopkins:* The values of science versus the values of the law. *Law and Human Behavior, 17*, 201–215.

Barrick, M. R., & Mount, M. K. (1991). The big five personality dimensions and job performance: A meta-analysis. *Personnel Psychology, 44*, 1–26.

Barrick, M. R., Shaffer, J. A., & DeGrassi, S. W. (2009). What you see may not be what you get: A meta-analysis of the relationship between self-presentation tactics and ratings of interview and job performance. *Journal of Applied Psychology, 94*, 1394–1411

Bartlett, F. (1932). *Remembering: A study in experimental and social psychology.* Cambridge, UK: Cambridge University Press.

Bartol, A. M., & Bartol, C. R. (2011). *Introduction to forensic psychology: Research and application.* Thousand Oaks, CA: Sage Publications.

Bartol, C. R. (1991). Predictive validation of the MMPI for small-town police officers who fail. *Professional Psychology: Research and Practice, 22*, 127–132.

Bartol, C. R., & Bartol, A. M. (1999). History of forensic psychology. In A. K. Hess & I. B. Weiner (Eds.), *Handbook of forensic psychology* (2nd ed., pp. 3–23). New York: John Wiley.

Basow, S. A., & Minieri, A. (2011). "You owe me: Effects of date cast, who pays, participant gender, and rape myth beliefs on perceptions of rape. *Journal of Interpersonal Violence, 26*, 479–497.

Bassuk, E. (1980). The crisis theory perspective on rape. In S. L. McCombie (Ed.), *The rape crisis intervention handbook* (pp. 121–129). New York: Plenum.

Batts, S. (2009). Brain lesions and their implications in criminal responsibility. *Behavioral Sciences & the Law, 27*(2), 261–272.

Beaber, R., Marston, A., Michelli, J., & Mills, M. (1985). A brief test for measuring malingering in schizophrenic individuals. *American Journal of Psychiatry, 144*, 1478–1481.

Beauregard, E., Proulx, J., Rossmo, K., Leclerc, B., & Allaire, J. (2007). Script analysis of the hunting process of serial sex offenders. *Criminal Justice and Behavior, 34*(8), 1069–1084.

Beauregard, E., Rebocho, M., & Rossmo, D. (2010). Target selection patterns in rape. *Journal of Investigative Psychology and Offender Profiling, 7*(2), 137–152.

Beauregard, E., Rossmo, D. K., & Proulx, J. (2007). A descriptive model of the hunting process of serial sex offenders: A rational choice perspective. *Journal of Family Violence, 22*(6), 449–463.

Beaver, K. M., Mancini, C., DeLisi, M., & Vaughn, M. G. (2011). Resiliency to victimization: The role of genetic factors. *Journal of Interpersonal Violence, 26*(5), 874–898.

Bechara, A., Tranel, D., & Damasio, H. (2000). Characterization of the decision-making deficit of patients with ventromedial prefrontal cortex lesions. *Brain, 123*(11), 2189–2202.

Becker, J. V., Skinner, L. J., Abel, G. G., Axelrod, R., & Treacy, E. C. (1984). Depressive symptoms associated with sexual assault. *Journal of Sex and Marital Therapy, 10*, 185–192.

Bedau, H. A., & Radelet, M. L. (1987). Miscarriages of justice in potentially capital cases. *Stanford Law Review, 40*, 21–179.

Beggs, S. M., & Grace, R. C. (2011). Treatment gain for sexual offenders against children predicts reduced recidivism: A comparative validity study. *Journal of Consulting and Clinical Psychology, 79*, 182–192.

Behavioral Sciences and the Law, 15, 307–320.

Behrman, B. W., & Davey, S. L. (2001). Eyewitness identification in actual criminal cases: An archival analysis. *Law and Human Behavior, 25*, 475–491.

Behrman, B. W., & Richards, R. E. (2005). Suspect/foil identification in actual crimes and in the laboratory: A reality monitoring analysis. *Law and Human Behavior, 29*, 279–301.

Beichner, D., & Spohn, C. (2005). Prosecutorial charging decisions in sexual assault cases: Examining the impact of a specialized prosecution unit. *Criminal Justice Policy Review, 16*, 461, 498.

Beitchman, J. H., Zucker, K. J., Hood, J. E., & DaCosta, G. A. (1992). A review of the long-term effects of child sexual abuse. *Child Abuse & Neglect, 16*(1), 101–118.

Bekerian, D. A., & Jackson, J. L. (1997). Critical issues in offender profiling. In J. L. Jackson & D. A. Bekerian (Eds.), *Offender profiling: Theory, research and practice* (pp. 209–220). New York: John Wiley.

Bell, V., Hemmens, C., & Steiner, B. (2006). Up skirts and down blouses: A statutory analysis of legislative responses to video voyeurism. *Criminal Justice Studies: A Critical Journal of Crime, Law & Society, 19*(3), 301–314.

Bender, L. (1947). Psychopathic behavior disorders in children. In R. M. Lindner & R. V. Seliger (Eds.), *Handbook of correctional psychology* (pp. 360–377). Oxford, UK: Philosophical Library.

Bennell, C. (2005). Improving police decision-making: General principles and practical applications of receiver operating characteristic analysis. *Applied Cognitive Psychology, 19*, 1157–1175.

Bennell, C., Corey, S., Taylor, A., & Ecker, J. (2008). What skills are required for effective offender profiling? An examination of the relationship between critical thinking ability and profile accuracy. *Psychology, Crime & Law, 14*(2), 143–157.

Bennell, C., Jones, N. J., & Corey, S. (2002). Does use-of-force simulation training in Canadian police agencies incorporate principles of effective training? *Psychology, Public Policy, and Law, 13*, 35–58.

Bennell, C., Jones, N. J., Taylor, P. J., & Snook, B. (2006). Validities and abilities in criminal profiling: A critique of the studies conducted by Richard Kocsis and his colleagues.

International Journal of Offender Therapy and Comparative Criminology, 50(3), 344–360.

Bennett Cattaneo, L. (2007). Contributors to assessments of risk in intimate partner violence: How victims and professionals differ. *Journal of Community Psychology, 35*, 57–75.

Bennett Cattaneo, L., & Goodman, L. A. (2003). Victim-reported risk factors for continued abusive behavior: Assessing the dangerousness of arrested batterers. *Journal of Community Psychology, 31*, 349–369.

Bennett, C., & Hirshhorn, R. (1993). *Bennett's guide to jury selection and trial dynamics in civil and criminal litigation*. St. Paul, MN: West.

Benokraitis, N. V., & Feagin, J. R. (1986). *Modern sexism: Blatant, subtle, and covert discrimination*. Englewood Cliffs, NJ: Prentice-Hall.

Ben-Shakhar, G. (2002). A critical review of the Control Question Test (CQT). In M. Kleiner (Ed.), *Handbook of polygraph testing* (pp. 103–126). San Diego, CA: Academic Press.

Ben-Shakhar, G. (2008). The case against the use of polygraph examinations to monitor postconviction sex offenders. *Legal and Criminological Psychology, 13*, 191–207.

Ben-Shakhar, G., & Furedy, J. J. (1990). *Theories and applications in the detection of deception*. New York: Springer-Verlag.

Ben-Shakhar, G., Bar-Hillel, M, & Kremnitzer, M. (2002). Trial by polygraph: Reconsidering the use of the guilty knowledge technique in court. *Law and Human Behavior, 26*, 527–541.

Benton, T. R., Ross, D. F, Bradshaw, E., Thomas, W. N., & Bradshaw, G. S. (2006). Eyewitness memory is still not common sense: Comparing jurors, judges and law enforcement to eyewitness experts. *Applied Cognitive Psychology, 20*, 115–129.

Benton, T., McDonnell, S., Ross, D. F., Thomas, W., & Bradshaw, E. (2007). Has eyewitness research penetrated

the American legal system? A synthesis of case history, juror knowledge, and expert testimony. In R. L. Lindsay, D. F. Ross, J. Read, M. P. Toglia, R. L. Lindsay, D. F. Ross, et al (Eds.), *The handbook of eyewitness psychology, Vol II: Memory for people*, 453–500. Mahwah, NJ: Lawrence Erlbaum Associates.

Berlin, F. S. (1994). Jeffrey Dahmer: Was he ill? Was he impaired? Insanity revisited. *American Journal of Forensic Psychiatry, 15*, 5–29.

Berliner, L. (1998). The use of expert testimony in child sexual abuse cases. In S. J. Ceci & H. Hembrooke (Eds.), *Expert witnesses in child abuse cases* (pp. 11–27). Washington, DC: American Psychological Association.

Bermant, G. (1986). Two conjectures about the issue of expert testimony. *Law and Human Behavior, 10*, 97–100.

Bernard, L. C., & Fowler, W. (1990). Assessing the validity of memory complaints: Performance of brain-damaged and normal individuals on Rey's test to detect malingering. *Journal of Clinical Psychology, 46*, 432–436.

Berresheim, A., & Weber, A. (2003). Structured witness interviewing and its effectiveness. *Kriminalistik, 57*, 757–771.

Berry, D. S., & McArthur, L. Z. (1986). Perceiving character in faces: The impact of age-related craniofacial changes on social perception. *Psychological Bulletin, 100*, 3–18.

Berry, D. S., & Zebrowitz-McArthur, L. Z. (1988). What's in a face? Facial maturity and the attribution of legal responsibility. *Personality and Social Psychology Bulletin, 14*, 23–33.

Bersoff, D. N. (1993, August). *Daubert v. Merrell Dow: Issues and outcome*. Paper presented at the meetings of the American Psychological Association, Toronto.

Beutler, L. E., Nussbaum, P. D., & Meredith, K. E. (1988). Changing personality patterns of police officers.

Professional Psychology: Research and Practice, 19, 503-507.

Biggers, J. R, & Yim, C. I. (2003). Rape trauma syndrome: An examination of standards that determine the admissibility of expert witness testimony. *Journal of Forensic Psychology Practice, 3*(1), 61-77.

Bigler, E. D., & Brooks, M. (2009). Traumatic brain injury and forensic neuropsychology. *The Journal of Head Trauma Rehabilitation, 24*, 76-87.

Birgden, A., & Perlin, M. L. (2009). "Where the home in the valley meets the damp dirty prison": A human rights perspective on therapeutic jurisprudence and the role of forensic psychologists in correctional settings. *Aggression and Violent Behavior, 14*, 256-263.

Bischoff, L. G. (1995). Review of Parent Awareness Skills Survey. In J. C. Conoley & J. C. Impara (Eds.), *Twelfth mental measurements yearbook* (pp. 735-736). Lincoln: University of Nebraska Press.

Black, F. A., Schweitzer, R. D., & Varghese, F. T. (2011). Allegations of child sexual abuse in family court: A qualitative analysis of psychiatric evidence. *Psychiatry, Psychology and Law, 1*, 1-15.

Black, P. J., Woodworth, M., Hancock, J., & Wollis, M. (July, 2012). The language of online sexual predation: A linguistic analysis of online predator grooming. Presented at the 24th Annual Convention of the Association of Psychological Science (APS). Chicago.

Black, P. J., Woodworth, M., Tremblay, M., & Carpenter, T. (2012, in press). A review of trauma-informed treatment for adolescents. *Canadian Psychology*.

Blackburn, R., Logan, C., Donnelly, J. P., & Renwick, S. D. (2008). Identifying psychopathic subtypes: Combining an empirical personality classification of offenders with the Psychopathy Checklist—Revised. *Journal of Personality Disorders, 22*(6), 604-622.

Blackman, J. (1986). Potential used for expert testimony: Ideas toward the representation of battered women who kill. *Women's Rights Law Reporter, 9* (3 & 4), 227-238.

Blackman, J., & Brickman, E. (1984). The impact of expert testimony on trials of battered women who kill their husbands. *Behavioral Sciences and the Law, 2*, 413-422.

Blagrove, M. (1996). Effects of length of sleep deprivation on interrogative suggestibility. *Journal of Experimental Psychology: Applied, 2*, 48-59.

Blair, R. J., (2001). Neurocognitive models of aggression, the antisocial personality disorders, and psychopathy. *Journal of Neurology, Neurosurgery and Psychiatry, 716*, 727-731.

Blandón-Gitlin, I., & Gerkens, D. (2010). The effects of photographs and event plausibility in creating false beliefs. *Acta Psychologica, 135*(3), 330-334.

Blandón-Gitlin, I., Pezdek, K., Rogers, M., & Brodie, L. (2005). Detecting deception in children: An experimental study of the effect of event familiarity on CBCA ratings. *Law and Human Behavior, 29*(2), 187-197.

Blandón-Gitlin, I., Sperry, K., & Leo, R. (2011). Jurors believe interrogation tactics are not likely to elicit false confessions: Will expert witness testimony inform them otherwise? *Psychology, Crime & Law, 17*(3), 239-260.

Blau, T. H. (1994). *Psychological services for law enforcement*. New York: John Wiley.

Block, A. P. (1990). Rape trauma syndrome as scientific expert testimony. *Archives of Sexual Behavior, 19*, 309-323.

Blumer, D., & Benson, D. F. (1975). Personality changes with frontal lobe lesions. In Benson, D. F., Blumer, D. (Eds.), *Psychiatric Aspects of Neurological Disease* (pp. 151-170). New York: Grune & Stratton.

Board, B. J., & Fritzon, K. (2005). Disordered personalities at work. *Psychology, Crime & Law, 11*(1), 17-32.

Boat, B. W., & Everson, M. D. (1988). Use of anatomical dolls among professionals in sexual abuse evaluation. *Child Abuse and Neglect, 12*, 171-174.

Bochnak, E. (Ed.). (1981). *Women's self defense cases: Theory and practice*. Charlottesville, VA: Michie Press.

Boddy, C. R. (2006). The dark side of management decisions: Organisational psychopaths. *Management Decision, 44*(10), 1461-1475.

Boddy, C. R. P. (2010). Corporate psychopaths and organizational type. *Journal of Public Affairs, 10*, 300-312.

Boeschen, L. E., Sales, B. D., & Koss, M. P. (1998). Rape trauma experts in the courtroom. *Psychology, Public Policy, and Law, 4*, 414-432.

Boland, P. L., & Quirk, S. A. (1994). At issue: Should child abuse be prosecuted decades after an alleged incident occurred? *American Bar Association Journal, 80*, 42.

Boldt v. Law Society of Upper Canada, SCC (2011).

Bolen, R. M., & Scannapieco, M. (1999). Prevalence of child sexual abuse: A corrective metanalysis. *Social Service Review, 73*, 281-313.

Bollingmo, G. C., Wessel, E. O., Eilertsen, D., & Magnussen, S. (2008). Credibility of the emotional witness: A study of ratings by police investigators. *Psychology, Crime & Law, 14*(1), 29-40.

Bond, C. F. Jr., & Uysal, A. (2007). On lie detection "wizards." *Law and Human Behavior, 31*, 109-115.

Bond, C. F., & DePaulo, B. M. (2006). Accuracy of deception judgments. *Personality and Social Psychology Review, 10*, 214-234.

Bond, C. F., Jr., & Atoum, A, O. (2000). International deception. *Personality and Social Psychology Bulletin, 26*, 385-395.

Bond, C. F., Jr., & DePaulo, B. M. (2008). Individual differences in judging deception: Accuracy and bias. *Psychological Bulletin, 134*, 477-492.

Bond, C. F., Kahler, K. N., & Paolicelli, L. M. (1985). The miscommunication of deception: An adaptive perspective. *Journal of Experimental Social Psychology, 21,* 331-345.

Bond, C. R., & DePaulo, B. M. (2006). Accuracy of deception judgments. *Personality and Social Psychology Review, 10*(3), 214-234.

Bond, G. D., & Lee, A. Y. (2005). Language of lies in prison: Linguistic classification of inmates' truthful and deceptive natural language. *Applied Cognitive Psychology, 19,* 313-329.

Bond, S. B., & Mosher, D. L. (1986). Guided imagery of rape: Fantasy, reality, and the willing victim myth. *Journal of Sex Research, 22,* 162-183.

Bonnie, R., & Slobogin, C. (1980). The role of mental health professionals in the criminal process: The case for informed speculation. *Virginia Law Review, 66,* 427-522.

Book, A. S., Quinsey, V. L., & Langford, D. (2007). Psychopathy and the perception of affect and vulnerability. *Criminal Justice and Behavior, 34*(4), 531-544.

Borchard, E. M. (1932). *Convicting the innocent: Sixty-five actual errors of criminal justice.* Garden City, NY: Doubleday.

Borgida, E. (Ed.), & Fiske, S. (Ed.). (2008). *Beyond common sense: Psychological science in the courtroom.* Malden: Blackwell.

Bornstein, B. H. & Greene, E. (2011). Jury decision making: Implications for and from psychology. *Psychological Science, 20*(1), 63-67.

Bornstein, B. H., Rung, L. M., & Miller, M. K. (2002). The effects of defendant remorse on mock juror decisions in a malpractice case. *Behavioral Sciences & The Law, 20*(4), 393-409.

Borum, R. (1988). A comparative study of negotiator effectiveness with "mentally disturbed hostage-taker" scenarios. *Journal of Police and Criminal Psychology, 4,* 17-20.

Borum, R., & Fulero, S. M. (1999). Empirical research on the insanity defense and attempted reforms: Evidence toward informed policy. *Law and Human Behavior, 23,* 117-135.

Bosco, D., Zappalà, A., & Santtila, P. (2010). The admissibility of offender profiling in courtroom: A review of legal issues and court opinions. *International Journal of Law and Psychiatry, 33*(3) 184-191.

Bothwell, R. K., Deffenbacher, K. A., & Brigham, J. C. (1987). Correlation of eyewitness accuracy and confidence: Optimality hypothesis revisited. *Journal of Applied Psychology, 72,* 691-695.

Bottoms, B. L., & Davis. S. (1993, September). Scientific evidence no longer subject to "Frye test." *APA Monitor,* p. 14.

Boudreau v. The King (1949), 94 C.C.C. 1 (SCC).

Bourque, J., LeBlanc, S., Utzschneider, A., & Wright, C. (2009). The effectiveness of profiling from a national security perspective. Canadian Human Rights Commission/Canadian Race Relations Foundation. Retrieved May 15 2012, from http://www.chrc-ccdp.ca/pdf/profilage_eng.pdf

Bovard, J. (1994, November). Drug-courier profiles. *Playboy,* pp. 46-48.

Bowman, J. (2007, December 3). Q&A: Selecting a jury for the Pickton trial. *CBC News.* Retrieved May 15, 2012, from http://www.cbc.ca

Bragg, R. (1995, July 18). Sheriff says prayer and a lie led Susan Smith to confess. *The New York Times,* pp. A1, A8.

Brainerd, C. J., Reyna, V. F., & Zember, E. E. (2011). Theoretical and forensic implications of developmental studies of the DRM illusion. *Memory & Cognition, 39*(3), 365-380.

Brandt, J. R., Kennedy, W. A., Patrick, C. J., & Curtain, J. J. (1997). Assessment of psychopathy in a population of incarcerated adolescent offenders. *Psychological Assessment, 9,* 429-435.

Brant, C. (1993). Communication patterns in Indians: Verbal and non-verbal. *Annals of Sex Research, 6,* 259-269.

Braswell, A. L. (1987). Resurrection of the ultimate issue rule: Federal Rule of Evidence 704(b) and the insanity defense. *Cornell Law Review, 72,* 620-640.

Brenner, M. (1997, February). American nightmare: The ballad of Richard Jewell. *Vanity Fair,* pp. 100-107, 150-165.

Breslau, N., Davis, G. C. D., Andreski, P., & Peterson, E. (1991). Traumatic events and posttraumatic stress disorder in an urban population of young adults. *Archives of General Psychiatry, 48,* 255-264.

Brewer, N., & Palmer, M. A. (2010). Eyewitness identification tests. *Legal and Criminological Psychology, 15,* 77-96.

Brewer, N., & Wells, G. L. (2006). The confidence-accuracy relationship in eyewitness identification: Effects of lineup instructions, foil similarity, and target-absent base rates. *Journal of Experimental Psychology, 12,* 11-30.

Brewer, N., & Wells, G. L. (2011). Eyewitness identification. *Current Directions in Psychological Science, 20,* 24-27.

Brewer, N., Keast, A., & Rishworth, A. (2002). The confidence-accuracy relationship in eyewitness identification: The effects of reflection and disconfirmation on correlation and calibration. *Journal of Experimental Psychology: Applied, 8*(1), 44-56.

Briere, J., & Conte, J. R. (1993). Self-reported amnesia for abuse in adults molested as children. *Journal of Traumatic Stress, 6,* 21-31.

Briggs, P., Simon, W. T., & Simonsen, S. (2011). An exploratory study of Internet-initiated sexual offenses and the chat room sex offender: Has the Internet enabled a new typology of sex offender? *Sexual Abuse: Journal of Research and Treatment, 23*(1), 72-91.

Brigham, J. C. (1971). Ethnic stereotypes. *Psychological Bulletin, 76,* 15-38.

Brigham, J. C. (1999). What is forensic psychology, anyway? *Law and Human Behavior, 23,* 273-298.

Brigham, J. C., & Bothwell, R. K. (1983). The ability of prospective jurors to estimate the accuracy of eyewitness identifications. *Law and Human Behavior, 7*(1), 19–30.

Brigham, J. C., & Wolfskeil, M. P. (1983). Opinions of attorneys and law enforcement personnel on the accuracy of eyewitness identifications. *Law and Human Behavior, 7,* 337–349.

Brigham, J. C., Bennett, L. B., Meissner, C. A., & Mitchell, T. L. (2007). The influence of race on eyewitness memory. In R. Lindsay, D. Ross, J. Read, & M. Toglia (Eds.), *Handbook of eyewitness psychology* (pp. 257–281). Mahwah, NJ: Lawrence Erlbaum & Associates.

Brigham, J. C., Maass, A., Snyder, L. D., & Spaulding, K. (1982). Accuracy of eyewitness identifications in a field setting. *Journal of Personality and Social Psychology, 42,* 673–681.

Bright, D. A., & Goodman-Delahunty, J. (2010). Mock juror decision making in a civil negligence trial: The impact of gruesome evidence, injury severity and information processing route. *Psychiatry, Psychology & Law, 19,* 1–21.

Briken, P., Habermann, N., Kafka, M. P., Berner, W., & Hill, A. (2006). The paraphilia-related disorders: An investigation of the relevance of the concept in sexual murderers. *Journal of Forensic Sciences, 51*(3), 683–688.

Bristow, A. R. (1984). *State v. Marks*: An analysis of expert testimony on rape trauma syndrome. *Victimology: An International Journal, 9,* 273–281.

Brown v. Board of Education of Topeka, 347 U.S. 483 (1954).

Brown v. Mississippi, 297 U.S. 278 (1936).

Brown, E., Deffenbacher, K., & Sturgill, W. (1977). Memory for faces and the circumstances of encounters. *Journal of Applied Psychology, 62,* 311–318.

Brown, J. E. (2004). Shame and domestic violence: Treatment perspectives for perpetrators from self psychology and affect theory. *Sexual and Relationship Therapy, 19*(1), 39–56.

Brown, L., & Willis, A. (1985). Authoritarianism in British recruits: Importation, socialization, or myth? *Journal of Occupational Psychology, 58,* 97–108.

Brownmiller, S. (1975). *Against our will: Men, women, and rape.* New York: Simon & Schuster.

Bruck, M., & Ceci, S. J. (1999). The suggestibility of children's memory. *Annual Review of Psychology, 50,* 419–439.

Bruck, M., Ceci, S. J., & Francouer, E. (2000). Children's use of anatomically detailed dolls to report on genital touching in a medical examination: Developmental and gender comparisons. *Journal of Experimental Psychology: Applied, 6,* 74–83.

Bruck, M., Ceci, S. J., & Hembrooke, H. (1998). Reliability and credibility of young children's reports: From research to policy and practice. *American Psychologist, 53,* 136–151.

Bruck, M., Ceci, S. J., Francouer, E., & Renick, A. (1995). Anatomically detailed dolls do not facilitate preschoolers' reports of pediatric examination involving genital touching. *Journal of Experimental Psychology: Applied, 1,* 95–109.

Brussel, J. A. (1968). *Casebook of a crime psychiatrist.* New York: Bernard Geis.

Bryant-Davis, T., Ullman, S. E., Tsong, Y., Tillman, S., & Smith, K. (2010). Struggling to survive: Sexual assault, poverty, and mental health outcomes of African American women. *American Journal of Orthopsychiatry, 80*(1), 61–70.

Brzozowski, J. (2004). "Spousal violence." In Brzozowski, J. (Ed.). *Family Violence in Canada: A Statistical Profile, 2004.* Catalogue no. 85-224. Ottawa: Statistics Canada.

Buckholtz, J. W., & Meyer-Lindenberg, A. (2008). MAOA and the neurogenetic architecture of human aggression. *Trends in Neurosciences, 31*(3), 120–129.

Buckhout, R. (1974). Eyewitness testimony. *Scientific American, 231,* 23–31.

Buckhout, R. (1983). Psychologist on the inside. *Psyc, 28,* 56–57.

Buckhout, R., & Friere, V. (1975). *Suggestibility in lineups and photospreads: A casebook for lawyers* (Center for Responsive Psychology Monograph No. CR-5). New York: Brooklyn College.

Bulkley, J. A., & Horwitz, M. J. (1994). Adults sexually abused as children: Legal actions and issues. *Behavioral Sciences and the Law, 12,* 65–87.

Bull, P. (2006). Detecting lies and deceit: The psychology of lying and the implications for professional practice. *Journal of Community and Applied Social Psychology, 16,* 166–167.

Bull, R., & McAlpine, S. (1998). Facial appearance and criminality. In A. Memon, A. Vrij, & R. Bull (Eds.), *Psychology and law: Truthfulness, accuracy and credibility* (pp. 59–76). London: McGraw-Hill.

Bull, R., & Soukara, S. (2010). Four studies of what really happens in police interviews. In G. Lassiter and C. A. Meissner (Eds.), *Police interrogations and false confessions: Current research, practice, and policy recommendations* (pp. 81–95). Washington, DC: American Psychological Association.

Bull, R., & Vine, M. (2003). Attractive people tell the truth: Can you believe it? Poster presented at the Annual Conference of the European Association of Psychology and Law, Edinburgh.

Bunting, L. (2007). Dealing with a problem that doesn't exist? Professional responses to female perpetrated child sexual abuse. *Child Abuse Review, 16*(4), 252–267.

Burge, S. K. (1988). Post-traumatic stress disorder in victims of rape. *Journal of Traumatic Stress, 1*(2), 193–209.

Burgess, A. W., & Holmstrom, L. L. (1985). Rape trauma syndrome and post-traumatic stress response. In A. W. Burgess (Ed.), *Research handbook on rape and sexual assault* (pp. 46– 61). New York: Garland.

Burgoon, J. K., & Buller, D. B. (1994). Interpersonal deception: III. Effects of deceit on perceived communication and nonverbal dynamics. *Journal of Nonverbal Behavior, 18,* 155–184.

Burke, H. (2004). Psychopathy and treatment outcome in incarcerated violent offender program participants. *Dissertation Abstracts International, 64.* Retrieved from PsycInfo database.

Burtt, H. (1931). *Legal psychology.* Englewood Cliffs, NJ: Prentice-Hall.

Buschman, J., Wilcox, D., Spreen, M., Marshall, B., & Bogaerts, S. (2008). Victim ranking among sex offenders. *Journal of Sexual Aggression, 14*(1), 45–52.

Buss, D. M. (2009). How can evolutionary psychology successfully explain personality and individual differences? *Perspectives on Psychological Science, 4,* 359–366.

Butcher, J. N., Dahlstrom, W. G., Graham, J. R., Tellegen, A., & Kaemmer, B. (1989). *The Minnesota Multiphasic Personality Inventory-2 (MMPI-2): Manual for administration and scoring.* Minneapolis: University of Minnesota Press.

Butler, B. (2007). The role of death qualification in capital trials involving juvenile defendants. *Journal of Applied Social Psychology, 37*(3), 549–560.

Butler, B. (2010). Moving beyond Ford, Atkins, and Roper: Jurors' attitudes toward the execution of the elderly and the physically disabled. *Psychology, Crime, and Law, 16,* 631–647.

Buxton, A. (1999). The best interest of children of gay and lesbian parents. In R. Galatzer-Levy, L. Krauss, & B. Leventhal (Eds.), *The scientific basis for custody decisions in divorce* (pp. 319–356). New York: John Wiley.

Buzawa, E. S., & Buzawa, C. G. (2003). *Domestic violence: The criminal justice response.* Thousand Oaks, CA: Sage.

Buzawa, E., Austin, T., & Buzawa, C. (1996). "Role of arrest in domestic versus stranger assault: Is there a difference?" In Buzawa, E. and Buzawa, C. (Eds.) *Do arrests and restraining orders work?* (pp. 150–175). Thousand Oaks, CA: Sage.

Byczynski, L. (1987, December 29). Is joint custody better? *Kansas City Times,* pp. A1, A4.

Cabeza, R., & St Jacques, P. (2007). Functional neuroimaging of autobiographical memory. *Trends in Cognitive Science, 11,* 219–227.

Caillouet, B. A., Boccaccini, M. T., Varela, J. G., Davis, R. D., & Rostow, C. D. (2010). Predictive validity of the MMPI-2 PSY-5 scales and facets for law enforcement officer employment outcomes. *Criminal Justice and Behavior, 37,* 217–238.

Caldwell, M., Skeem, J., Salekin, R., & Van Rybroek, G. (2006). treatment response of adolescent offenders with psychopathy features: A 2-year follow-up. *Criminal Justice and Behavior, 33*(5), 571–596.

Cale, E. M., & Lilienfeld, S. O. (2002). Sex differences in psychopathy and antisocial personality disorder. A review and integration. *Clinical Psychology Review, 22*(8), 1179–1207. Retrieved from EBSCO*host*.

Call, J. A. (2008). Psychological consultation in hostage/barricade crisis negotiation. In H. V. Hall (Ed.), *Forensic psychology and neuropsychology for criminal and civil cases* (pp. 263–288). Boca Raton, FL: CRC Press.

Calverley, D. (2010). Adult correctional services in Canada 2008/2009. Retrieved July 21, 2012, from http://www.statcan.gc.ca/pub/85-002-x/2010003/article/11353-eng.htm

Cameron, S. (2010). *On the farm: Robert William Pickton and the tragic story of Vancouver's missing women.* Toronto: Knopf Canada.

Campbell J. C. (2004). Helping women understand their risk in situations of intimate partner violence. *Journal of Interpersonal Violence, 19,* 1464–1477.

Campbell, J. C., Glass, N. E., Sharps, P. W., Laughon, K., & Bloom, T. (2007). Intimate partner homicide: Review and implications for research and policy. *Violence, Trauma & Abuse, 8,* 246–269.

Campbell, J. C., Webster, D. W., & Glass, N. E. (2009). The Danger Assessment: Validation of a lethality risk assessment instrument for intimate partner femicide. *Journal of Interpersonal Violence, 24,* 653–674.

Campbell, J. C., Webster, D., Koziol-McLain, J., Block, C., Campbell, D., Curry, et al. (2003). Risk factors for femicide in abusive relationships: Results from a multisite case control study. *American Journal of Public Health, 93,* 1089–1097.

Campbell, M. A., Porter, S., & Santor, D. (2004). Psychopathic traits in adolescent offenders: An evaluation of criminal history, clinical, and psychosocial correlates. *Behavioral Sciences and the Law, 22,* 23–47.

Canadian Centre for Justice Statistics. (2004). About family violence in Canada. Retrieved July 21, 2012, from http://www.justice.gc.ca/eng/pi/fv-vf/about-aprop

Canadian Mental Health Association, Citizens for Mental Health (2004). *Backgrounder: Justice and Mental Health.* Retrieved May 15, 2012, from http://www.cmha.ca/citizens/justice.pdf

Canadian Professional Police Association (n.d.). *The History of the Memorial Service.* Retrieved July 5, 2004, from http://www.cpa-acp.ca/memorial/history.htm

Canadian Psychological Association. (2000). Canadian code of ethics for psychologists: Third edition. Retrieved July 30, 2012, from http://www.cpa.ca/cpasite/userfiles/Documents/

Canadian%20Code%20of%20Ethics%20for%20Psycho.pdf

Canter, D. (2010). Offender profiling. In J. M. Brown, E. A. Campbell (Eds.), *The Cambridge handbook of forensic psychology* (pp. 236-241). New York: Cambridge University Press.

Canter, D., & Youngs, D. (2009). *Investigative psychology: Offender profiling and the analysis of criminal action*. New York: John Wiley & Sons.

Canter, D. V., & Wentink, N. (2004). An empirical test of Holmes and Holmes's serial murder typology. *Criminal Justice and Behavior, 31*(4), 489-515.

Canter, D. V., Alison, L. J., Alison, E., & Wentink, N. (2004). The organized/disorganized typology of serial murder: Myth or model? *Psychology, Public Policy, and Law, 10*(3), 293-320.

Caplan, L. (1984). *The insanity defense and the trial of John W. Hinckley, Jr.* New York: David R. Godine.

Carlson, H. M., & Sutton, M. S. (1975). The effects of different police roles on attitudes and values. *Journal of Psychology, 91*, 57-64.

Carr, C. (1994). *The Alienist*. New York: Random House.

Carr, C., (1997). *The Angel of Darkness*. New York: Random House.

Carroll, J. S. (1980). An appetizing look at law and psychology. *Contemporary Psychology, 25*, 362-363.

Carson, D. (1988). Risk: A four letter word for lawyers. In P. J. Hessing & G. Van den Heuvel (Eds.), *Lawyers on psychology and psychologists on law* (pp. 57-63). Amsterdam: Swets & Zeitlinger.

Carter, A. J., & Hollin, C. R. (2010). Characteristics of non-serial sexual homicide offenders: A review. *Psychology, Crime & Law, 16*(1-2), 25-45.

Caspi, A., Sugden, K., Moffitt, T. E., Taylor, A., Craig, I. W., Harrington, H., et al. (2003). Influence of life stress on depression: Moderation by a polymorphism in the 5-HTT gene. *Science, 301*(5631), 386-389

Cassell, P. G. (1996a). All benefits, no costs: The grand illusion of *Miranda's* defenders. *Northwestern University Law Review, 90,* 1084-1124.

Cassell, P. G. (1996b). *Miranda's* social costs: An empirical reassessment. *Northwestern University Law Review, 90,* 387-499.

Cassell, P. G. (1998). Protecting the innocent from false confessions and lost confessions—and from *Miranda. Journal of Criminal Law and Criminology, 78,* 497-556.

Cassell, P. G., & Hayman, B. S. (1996). Police interrogation in the 1990s: An empirical study of the effects of *Miranda. UCLA Law Review, 43,* 839-931.

Cattell, J. McK. (Ed.). (1894). *Proceedings of the American Psychological Association*. New York: Macmillan.

Cavanaugh, M. M., & Gelles, R. J. (2005). The utility of male domestic violence offender typologies: New directions, for research, policy, and practice. *Journal of Interpersonal Violence, 20,* 155-166.

CBC News Online (2004, July 23). Peel chief under fire for comments. Retrieved August 12, 2004, from http://toronto.cbc.ca/regional/servlet/View?filename=to_peelzhang20040723

CBC News. (1998, November 13). Teacher gets stiff jail sentence. Retrieved July 21, 2012, from http://www.cbc.ca/news/story/1998/02/06/teach980206a.html

CBC News. (2000a, November 11). Murrin acquitted in Mindy Tran Murder. Retrieved May 15, 2012, from http://www.cbc.ca

CBC News. (2000b, November 11). Murrin and juror say it's a professional relationship. CBC News. Retrieved May 15, 2012, from http://www.cbc.ca

CBC News. (2004, August 4). Teacher released after serving child rape sentence. Retrieved July 21, 2012, from http://www.cbc.ca/news/world/story/2004/08/04/letournea_freed040804.html

CBC News. (2006, November 22). Widow shocked by unconditional release of husband's killer. Retrieved July 21, 2012, from http://www.cbc.ca/news/story/2006/11/22/arenburg.html

CBC News (2006, December 13). Convicted wife-killer asks mother-in-law to raise daughter. Retrieved July 21, 2012, from http://www.cbc.ca/news/canada/edmonton/story/2006/12/14/white-kelly.html

CBC News. (2008, September 25). Ottawa sportscaster's killer jailed 2 years in U.S. for assault. Retrieved July 21, 2012, from http://www.cbc.ca/news/canada/ottawa/story/2008/09/25/ot-arenburg-080925.html

CBC News. (2010a, August 8). B. C. used penile teen sex text for decades. Retrieved July 21, 2012, from http://www.cbc.ca/news/canada/british-columbia/story/2010/08/08/bc-teen-sex-testing.html

CBC News. (2010, August 9). Pickton juror regrets taking part in trial. Retrieved from http://www.cbc.ca

CBC News. (2010, February 22). Schoenborn "not criminally responsible" for murders. Retrieved July 21, 2012, from http://www.cbc.ca/news/canada/british-columbia/story/2010/02/22/bc-schoenborn-verdict.html

CBC News (2012, May 15). Tori Stafford's mom says she will never forgive Rafferty. Retrieved July 21, 2012, from http://www.cbc.ca/news/canada/story/2012/05/15/tara-mcdonald-tori-stafford.html

CBC News Online (2004, January 19). Halifax police chief apologizes in discrimination case. Retrieved May 14, 2004, from http://www.cbc.ca/stories/2004/01/19/johnson040119

CBC News Online (2004, January 20). Documents detail Toronto drug squad corruption. Retrieved May 14, 2004, from http://www.cbc.ca/stories/2004/01/20/torontoprobe040120

CBC News. (2010b, October 21). Col. Russell Williams timeline. Retrieved July 21, 2012, from http://www.cbc.ca/fifth/2010-2011/abovesuspicion/timelinewilliams.html

CBC News. (2011, January 10). In the line of duty: Deaths of RCMP officers. Retrieved from http://www.cbc.ca

CBC News. (2011a, October 21). Scouts failed to stop sexual predator: CBC investigation. Retrieved July 21, 2012 from http://www.cbc.ca/news/canada/story/2011/10/20/scouts-turley-pedophile-list.html

CBC News. (2011b, January 18). Vatican letter on sex abuse from '97 revealed. Retrieved July 21, 2012, from http://www.cbc.ca/news/world/story/2011/01/18/vativan-letter-sex-abuse-ireland.html

Ceci, S. J., & Bruck, M. (1993). Suggestibility of the child witness: A historical review and synthesis. *Psychological Bulletin, 113,* 403–439.

Ceci, S. J., & Bruck, M. (1995). *Jeopardy in the courtroom: A scientific analysis of children's testimony.* Washington, DC: American Psychological Association.

Ceci, S. J., Ross, D. F., & Toglia, M. P. (1987). Suggestibility of children's memory: Psycholegal implications. *Journal of Experimental Psychology: General, 116,* 38–49.

Ceci, S. J., Toglia, M. P., & Ross, D. F. (Eds.). (1987). *Children's eyewitness memory.* New York: Springer-Verlag.

Center for Disease Control and Prevention. (2008). Adverse health conditions and health risk behaviors associated with intimate partner violence—United States 2005. Retrieved July 21, 2012, from http://www.cdc.gov/mmwr/preview/mmwrhtml/mm5705a1.htm

Centre for Children and Families in the Justice System (2011). Retrieved May 15, 2012, from http://www.lfcc.on.ca/

Chamallas, M. (1990). Listening to Dr. Fiske: The easy case of *Price Waterhouse v. Hopkins. Vermont Law Review, 15,* 89–124.

Chan, J. C. K., & LaPaglia, J. A. (2011). The dark side of testing memory:

Repeated retrieval can enhance eyewitness suggestibility. *Journal of Experimental Psychology: Applied, 17*(4), 418–432.

Chan, J. C. K., Thomas, A. K., & Bulevich, J. B. (2009). Recalling a witnessed event increases eyewitness suggestibility: The reversed testing effect. *Psychological Science, 20,* 66–73.

Chandler, J. (1990). *Modern police psychology.* Springfield, IL: Charles C Thomas.

Chapman, D. S., & Zweig, D. I. (2005). Developing a nomological network for interview structure: Antecedents and consequences of the structured interview selection. *Personnel Psychology, 58,* 673–702.

Chappell, D. (2010). Victimization and the insanity defence: Coping with confusion, conflict and conciliation. *Psychiatry, Psychology and Law, 17*(1), 39–51.

Chopra, S. R., & Ogloff, J. R. P. (2000). Evaluating jury secrecy: Implications for academic research and juror stress. *Criminal Law Quarterly, 44,* 190–222.

Christiansen, A. R., & Thyer, B. A. (2003). Female sexual offenders: A review of empirical research. *Journal of Human Behavior in the Social Environment, 6*(3), 1–16.

Christianson, S. A., & Hubinette, B. (1993). Hands up! A study of witnesses' emotional reactions and memories associated with bank robberies. *Applied Cognitive Psychology, 7,* 365–379.

Cima, M., Smeets, T., & Jelicic, M. (2008). Self-reported trauma, cortisol levels, and aggression in psychopathic and non-psychopathic prison inmates. *Biological Psychology, 78*(1), 75–86.

Cima, M., Tonnaer, F., & Hauser, M. D. (2010). Psychopaths know right from wrong but don't care. *Social Cognitive and Affective Neuroscience, 5*(1), 59–67.

Clark, K. B., & Clark, M. P. (1952). Racial identification and preference in Negro children. In G. E. Swanson, T. M. Newcomb, & E. L. Hartley (Eds.),

Readings in social psychology (Rev. ed., pp. 551–560). New York: Holt.

Clark, M. (1997). *Without a doubt.* New York: Viking Penguin.

Clark, S. E. (2005). A re-examination of the effects of biased lineup instructions in eyewitness identification. *Law and Human Behavior, 29,* 395–424.

Cleckley, H. (1941). *The mask of sanity* (1st ed.). St. Louis, MO: C. V. Mosby.

Clifford, B. R., & Hollin, C. R. (1981). Effects of the type of incident and the number of perpetrators on eyewitness memory. *Journal of Applied Psychology, 66,* 364–370.

Clifford, B. R., & Scott, J. (1978). Individual and situational factors in eyewitness testimony. *Journal of Applied Psychology, 63,* 352–359.

Clift, R. W., Rajlic, G., & Gretton, H. M. (2009). Discriminative and predictive validity of the penile plethysmograph in adolescent sex offenders. *Sexual Abuse: Journal of Research and Treatment, 21*(3), 335–362.

Cochrane, R. E., Tett, R. P., & Vandecreek, L. (2003). Psychological testing and the selection of police officers: A national survey. *Criminal Justice and Behavior, 30,* 511–537.

Cockburn, A., & Cockburn, P. (1999). *Out of the ashes: The resurrection of Saddam Hussein.* New York: HarperCollins.

Cohen, J. A., Mannarino, A. P., & Deblinger, E. (2010). Trauma-focused cognitive-behavioral therapy for traumatized children. In J. R. Weisz, A. E. Kazdin (Eds.), *Evidence-based psychotherapies for children and adolescents (2nd ed.)* (pp. 295–311). New York: Guilford Press.

Cohn, D. S. (1991). Anatomical doll play of preschoolers referred for sexual abuse and those not referred. *Child Abuse and Neglect, 15,* 567–573.

Coid, J., Yang, M., Ullrich, S., & Hare, R. D. (2009). Psychopathy among prisoners in England and Wales. *International Journal of Law and Psychiatry, 32,* 134–141.

Cole, M. & Petrunik, M. (2007) Sex offender registries. In W. Staples (Ed.), *Encyclopedia of Privacy* (Vol 2, pp. 493–496) Westport, CT: Greenwood Press.

Coleman, D. H., & Straus, M. A. (1986). Marital power, conflict, and violence in a nationally representative sample of American couples. *Violence and Victims, 1*, 141–157.

Collins, P. R. (2004). Friends of the court: Examining the influence of amicus curiae participation in U.S. Supreme Court litigation. *Law & Society Review, 38*, 807–832.

Connolly, D. A., & Read, J. D. (2003). Remembering historical child sexual abuse. *The Criminal Law Quarterly, 47*, 438–480.

Connolly, D. A., Price, H. L., & Gordon, H. M. (2009). Judging the credibility of historic child sexual abuse complainants: How judges describe their decisions. *Psychology, Public Policy, and Law, 15*, 102–123.

Connolly, D. A., Price, H. L., & Gordon, H. M. (2010). Judicial decision-making in timely and delayed prosecutions of child sexual abuse in Canada: A study of honesty and cognitive ability in assessments of credibility. Psychology, Public Policy and Law, 16, 177–199.

Connolly, D. A., & Read, J. D. (2006). Delayed prosecutions of historic child sexual abuse: Analyses of 2064 Canadian criminal complaints. *Law and Human Behavior, 30*, 409–434.

Conte, J. R., Sorenson, E., Fogarty, L., & Rosa, J. (1991). Evaluating children's reports of sexual abuse: Results from a survey of professionals. *American Journal of Orthopsychiatry, 61*, 428–437.

Cook, N. E., Barese, T. H., & Dicataldo, F. (2010). The confluence of mental health and psychopathic traits in adolescent female offenders. *Criminal Justice and Behavior, 37*(1), 119–135.

Cook, P. K. (2011). Comprehensive recidivism data from juvenile delinquents and juvenile sex offenders. *Dissertation Abstracts International, 72*.

Cook, S. W. (1979). Social science and school desegregation: Did we mislead the Supreme Court? *Personality and Social Psychology Bulletin, 5*, 420–434.

Cook, S. W. (1984). The 1959 social science statement and school segregation: A reply to Gerard. *American Psychologist, 39*, 819–832.

Cooke, D. J., Forth, A. E., & Hare, R. D. (1995). *Psychopathy: Theory, research and implications for society.* Dordrecht, Netherlands: Kluwer Academic Publishers.

Cooper, D. K., & Grisso, T. (1997). Five year research update (1991–1995): Evaluations for competence to stand trial. *Behavioral Sciences and the Law, 15*, 347–364.

Cormier, N. S., & Woodworth, M. T. (2008). Do you see what I see? The influence of gender stereotypes on student and Royal Canadian Mounted Police perceptions of violent same-sex and opposite-sex relationships. *Journal of Aggression, Maltreatment, & Trauma, 17*, 1–26.

Cornell, D. G., Warren, J., Hawk, G., Stafford, E., Oram, G., & Pine, D. (1996). Psychopathy in instrumental and reactive violent offenders. *Journal of Consulting and Clinical Psychology, 64*, 783–790.

Corrado, R. R., Vincent, G. M., Hart, S. D., & Cohen, I. M. (2004). Predictive validity of the Psychopathy Checklist: Youth Version for general and violent recidivism. *Behavioral Sciences & the Law, 22*(1), 5–22.

Correctional Service of Canada (1995). Federal offender family violence: Estimates from a national file review study. *Forum, 7*.

Correctional Service of Canada. (2008). Report on plans and priorities. Retrieved July 21, 2012, from http://www.csc-scc.gc.ca/text/ pblcsbjct-eng.shtml#community

Correctional Services Canada (2009a). Research report: 2009 victims questionnaire results. Retrieved July 21, 2012, from http://pbc-clcc. gc.ca/rprts/quest/quest09-eng.pdf

Correctional Services Canada (2009b). Community-based sexual offender maintenance treatment programming: An evaluation. Retrieved July 21, 2012, from http://www.csc-scc.gc .ca/text/rsrch/smmrs/rg/rg-r188/ rg-r188-eng.shtml

Corwin, E. P., Cramer, R. J., Griffin, D. A., & Brodsky, S. L. (2012). Defendant remorse, need for affect, and juror sentencing decisions. *Journal of the American Academy of Psychiatry and the Law, 40*(1), 41–49.

Court TV. (1992). *The insanity trial of Jeffrey Dahmer* (video). New York: Court TV.

Cox, G. D. (1991, October 28). Assumption of risks. *National Law Journal,* pp. 1, 24–25.

Cox, G. D. (1992, August 3). Tort tales lash back. *National Law Journal,* pp. 1, 36–37.

Crabbé, A., Decoene, S., & Vertommen, H. (2008). Profiling homicide offenders: A review of assumptions and theories. *Aggression and Violent Behavior, 13*(2), 88–106.

Crenshaw, M. (1986). The psychology of political terrorism. In M. G. Hermann (Ed.), *Political psychology* (pp. 379–413). San Francisco: Jossey-Bass.

Creswell, J., & Thomas, L. Jr. (January 24, 2009). The talented Mr. Madoff. Retrieved July 22, 2012, from http:// www.nytimes.com/2009/01/25/ business/25bernie.html

Crocker, P. L. (1985). The meaning of equality for battered women who kill men in self-defense. *Harvard Women's Law Review, 8*, 121–153.

Crossman, A. M., Scullin, M. H., & Melnyk, L. (2004). Individual and developmental differences in suggestibility. *Applied Cognitive Psychology, 18*(8), 941–945.

CTV News. (2005, May 21). Mary Kay Letourneau marries former student. Retrieved May 13, 2012, from http://www.ctv.ca/CTVNews/ CTVNewsAt11/20050522/ letourneau_wedding_050521

CTV News. (2009). Turcotte not criminally responsible for kids' stabbings. Retrieved May 13, 2012, from http://m.ctv.ca/topstories/20110705/turcotte-deaths-kids-110705.html

CTV News. (2011, May 31). Vince Li may get expanded hospital privileges. Retrieved May 13, 2012, from http://www.ctv.ca/CTVNews/Canada/20110531/vincent-li-may-get-expanded-hospital-privileges-11053

CTV News. (2012a, March 15). Man who killed his kids fit for release: Psychiatrist. Retrieved July 23, 2012, from http://www.ctv.ca/CTVNews/TopStories/20120315/guy-turcotte-psychiatrist-120314

CTV News. (2012b, May 14). Panel hears that Vince Li should get more freedom. Retrieved July 23, 2012, from http://www.ctv.ca/CTVNews/TopStories/20120514/bus-passenger-beheaded-120514

Culhane, S. E., Hosch, H. M., & Heck, C. (2008). Interrogation technique endorsement by current law enforcement, future law enforcement, and laypersons. *Police Quarterly, 11*(3), 366–386.

Cumming, G., & McGrath, R. (2005). *Supervision of the sex offender: Community management, risk assessment, and treatment (2nd ed.).* Brandon, VT: Safer Society Press.

Cunningham, A., & Stevens, L. (2011). *Helping a child be a witness in court: 101 things to know say and do.* London, ON: London Family Court Clinic.

Cunradi, C. B. (2007). Drinking level, neighborhood social disorder, and mutual intimate partner violence. *Alcoholism: Clinical and Experimental Research, 31,* 1012–1019.

Cunradi, C., Todd, M. Duke, M. & Ames, G. (2009). Problem drinking, unemployment and intimate partner violence among a sample of construction workers and their partners, *Journal of Family Violence, 24,* 63–74.

Cutler, B. (Ed.). (2009). *Expert testimony on the psychology of eyewitness identification.* New York: Oxford University Press.

Cutler, B. L., & Penrod, S. D. (1989). Forensically relevant moderators of the relation between eyewitness identification accuracy and confidence. *Journal of Applied Psychology, 74,* 650–652.

Cutler, B. L., & Penrod, S. D. (1995). *Mistaken identification: The eyewitness, psychology, and the law.* New York: Cambridge University Press.

Cutler, B. L., Berman, G. L., Penrod, S. D., & Fisher, R. P. (1994). Conceptual, practical, and empirical issues associated with eyewitness identification test media. In D. F. Ross, J. D. Read, & M. P. Toglia (Eds.), *Adult eyewitness testimony: Current trends and developments* (pp. 163–181). New York: Cambridge University Press.

Cutler, B. L., Moran, G., & Narby, D. J. (1992). Jury selection in insanity defense cases. *Journal of Research in Personality, 26,* 165–182.

Cutler, B. L., Penrod, S. D., & Martens, T. K. (1987). The reliability of eyewitness identification: The role of system and estimator variables. *Law and Human Behavior, 11,* 233–258.

D'Silva, K., Duggan, C., & McCarthy, L. (2004). Does treatment really make psychopaths worse? A review of the evidence. *Journal of Personality Disorders, 18*(2), 163–177.

Daftary-Kapur, T., Groscup, J. L., O'Connor, M., Coffaro, F., & Galietta, M. (2011). Measuring knowledge of the insanity defense: Scale construction and validation. *Behavioral Sciences & the Law, 29*(1), 40–63.

Dahl, J., Enemo, I., Drevland, G. B., Wessel, E., Eilertsen, D., & Magnussen, S. (2007). Displayed emotions and witness credibility: A comparison of judgements by individuals and mock juries. *Applied Cognitive Psychology, 21*(9), 1145–1155.

Dahlstrom, W. G., Welsh, G. S., & Dahlstrom, L. E. (1972). *An MMPI handbook: Vol. 1, Clinical interpretation.* Minneapolis: University of Minnesota Press.

Dallaire, R. (2003). *Shake hands with the devil: The failure of humanity in Rwanda.* Toronto: Random House Canada.

Damasio, A. R., (1994). *Decartes' error: error, reason, and the human brain.* New York: Grosset/Putnam.

Dane, F. C. (1985). In search of reasonable doubt: A systematic examination of selected quantification approaches. *Law and Human Behavior, 9,* 141–158.

Danziger, S., Levav, J., & Avnaim-Pesso, L. (2011). Extraneous factors in judicial decisions. *Proceedings of the National Academy of Sciences of the United States of America, 108,* 6889–6892.

Darwin, C. (1872/2005). The expression of the emotions in man and animals. In J. D. Watson (Ed.), *Darwin: The indelible stamp* (pp. 1066–1257). Philadelphia: Running Press.

Dattilio, F. M., Edwards, D. A., & Fishman, D. B. (2010). Case studies within a mixed methods paradigm: Toward a resolution of the alienation between researcher and practitioner in psychotherapy research. *Psychotherapy: Theory, Research, Practice, Training, 47,* 427–441.

Dauvergne, M., & Turner, J. (2010). Police-reported crime statistics in Canada, 2009. *Juristat: Canadian Centre for Justice Statistics, 30*(2). Retrieved May 15, 2012, from http://www.statcan.gc.ca/pub/85-002-x/2010002/article/11292-eng.htm

Davis, D., & O'Donohue, W. (2004). The road to perdition: Extreme influence tactics in the interrogation room. In W. O'Donahue (Ed.), *Handbook of forensic psychology* (pp. 897–996). San Diego: Academic Press.

Davis, J. D. (2006). *Perspectives and psychosocial characteristics of female sex offenders: Implications for counseling.* (Doctoral dissertation, Texas Southern University), Available from ProQuest Dissertations & Theses. (ProQuest Doc ID: 304958014).

Davis, J. H. (1989). Psychology and the law: The last 15 years. *Journal of Applied Social Psychology, 19,* 199–230.

Davis, J., & Gonzalez, R. (1996, February). *Relative and absolute judgments of eyewitness identification.* Paper presented at the meetings of the American Psychology-Law Society, Hilton Head, SC.

Davis, K. E., Ace, A., & Andra, M. (2000). Stalking perpetrators and psychological maltreatment of partners: Anger-jealousy, attachment insecurity, need for control, and break up context. *Violence and Victims, 15,* 407–425.

Davis, K. M., & Archer, R. P. (2010). A critical review of objective personality inventories with sex offenders. *Journal of Clinical Psychology, 66*(12), 1254–1280.

Davis, R. D., Rostow, C. D., Pinkston, J. B., Combs, D. R., & Dixon, D. R. (2004). A re-examination of the MMPI-2 Aggressiveness and Immaturity Indices in law enforcement screening. *Journal of Police and Criminal Psychology, 19,* 17–26.

Dawes, R. M. (1988). *Rational choice in an uncertain world.* San Diego: Harcourt Brace Jovanovich.

Dawes, R. M. (1994). *House of cards: Psychology and psychotherapy built on myth.* New York: Free Press.

Dawes, R. M., Faust, D., & Meehl, P. E. (1989). Clinical versus actuarial judgment. *Science, 243,* 1668–1674.

Dawson, M., & Dinovitzer, R. (2001). Victim cooperation and the prosecution of domestic violence in a specialized court. *Justice Quarterly, 18,* 539–622.

Dawson, M., V. Pottie Bunge, & Balde, T. (2009). National trends in intimate partner homicides: Explaining the decline, Canada, 1976–2001. *Violence Against Women, 15,* 276–306.

de Becker, G. (1997). *The gift of fear and other survival signals that protect us from violence.* New York: Dell.

De Bellis, M. D., Hooper, S. R., Woolley, D. P., & Shenk, C. E. (2010). Demographic, maltreatment, and neurobiological correlates of PTSD symptoms in children and adolescents. *Journal of Pediatric Psychology, 35*(5), 570–577.

de Fruyt, F., et al. (2009). Assessing the universal structure of personality in early adolescence: The NEO-PIR and NEO-PI-3 in 24 cultures. *Assessment, 16,* 301–311. (48 author team).

DeBoard-Lucas, R. L., & Grych, J. H. (2011). Children's perception of intimate partner violence: Causes, consequences, and coping. *Journal of Family Violence, 26,* 343–354.

Decker, S. H., & Wagner, A. E. (1982). Race and citizen complaints against the police: An analysis of their interaction. In J. R. Greene (Ed.), *Managing police work: Issues and analysis* (pp. 107–122). Newbury Park, CA: Sage.

Dedman, B. (1998, August 9). Study of assassins concludes there is no common profile. *Kansas City Star,* p. A15.

Deeley, P. (1971). *Beyond the breaking point.* London: Arthur Baker.

Deering, R., & Mellor, D. (2007). Female-perpetrated child sex abuse: Definitional and categorisational analysis. *Psychiatry, Psychology and Law, 14*(2), 218–226.

Deffenbacher, K. A., & Loftus, E. F. (1982). Do jurors share a common understanding concerning eyewitness behavior? *Law and Human Behavior, 6,* 15–30.

Deffenbacher, K. A., Bornstein, B. H., & Penrod, S. D. (2006). Mugshot exposure effects: Retroactive interference, mugshot commitment, source confusion, and unconscious transference. *Law and Human Behavior, 30,* 287–307.

Deffenbacher, K. A., Bornstein, B. H., Penrod, S. D., & McGorty, E. K. (2004). A meta-analytic review of the effects of high stress on eyewitness memory. *Law and Human Behavior, 28,* 687–706.

DeLisi, M. (2009). Introduction to the special issue on biosocial criminology. *Criminal Justice and Behavior, 36*(11), 1111–1112.

Delprino, R., & Bahn, C. (1988). National survey of the extent and nature of psychological services in police departments. *Professional Psychology, 19,* 421–425.

Denov, M. S. (2001). A culture of denial: Exploring professional perspectives on female sex offending. *Canadian Journal of Criminology, 43*(3), 303–329.

Denov, M. S. (2003a). To a safer place? Victims of sexual abuse by females and their disclosures to professionals. *Child Abuse & Neglect, 27*(1), 47–61.

Denov, M. S. (2003b). The myth of innocence: Sexual scripts and the recognition of child sexual abuse by female perpetrators. *Journal of Sex Research, 40*(3), 303–314.

Denov, M. S. (2004). The long-term effects of child sexual abuse by female perpetrators: A qualitative study of male and female victims. *Journal of Interpersonal Violence, 19*(10), 1137–1156.

Department of Justice Canada. (2012, July 9). Criminal Code of Canada. Retrieved July 15, 2012, from http://laws-lois.justice.gc.ca/eng/acts/C-46

Department of Justice. (2003). Family violence: Department of Justice Canada overview paper. Retrieved July 23, 2012, from http://www.justice.gc.ca/eng/pi/fv-vf/facts-info/fv-vf/fv3-vf3.html

Department of Justice. (2009). Family violence: Department of Justice Canada overview paper. Retrieved July 23, 2012, from http://www.justice.gc.ca/eng/pi/fv-vf/facts-info/fv-vf/index.html

DePaulo, B. M., & Kirkendol, S. E. (1989). The motivational impairment effect in the communication of deception. In J. C. Yuille (Ed.), *Credibility assessment* (pp. 51–70). Dordrecht, Netherlands: Kluwer.

DePaulo, B. M., Kashy, D. A., Kirkendol, S. E., Wyer, M. M., & Epstein, J. A. (1996). Lying in everyday life. *Journal of Personality and Social Psychology, 70,* 979–995.

DePaulo, B., Lindsay, J. J., Malone, B. E., Muhlenbruck, L., Charlton, K., & Cooper, H. (2003). Cues to deception. *Psychological Bulletin, 129,* 74–118.

Detrick, P., Chibnall, J. T., & Rosso, M. (2001). Minnesota Multiphasic Personality Inventory-2 in police officer selection: Normative data and relation to the Inwald Personality Inventory. *Professional Psychology Research & Practice, 32,* 484–490.

Devery, C. (2010). Criminal profiling and criminal investigation. *Journal of Contemporary Criminal Justice, 26*(4), 393–409.

Dickens, G., Sugarman, P., Edgar, S., Hofberg, K., Tewari, S., & Ahmad, F. (2009). Recidivism and dangerousness in arsonists. *Journal of Forensic Psychiatry & Psychology, 20*(5), 621–639.

Dietrich, J. F., & Smith, J. (1986). The nonmedical use of drugs including alcohol among police personnel: A critical literature review. *Journal of Police Science and Administration, 14,* 300–306.

Dillehay, R. C., & Nietzel, M. T. (1980). Constructing a science of jury behavior. In L. Wheeler (Ed.), *Review of personality and social psychology* (pp. 246–264). Newbury Park, CA: Sage.

Dingus, A. (1994, September). Wise blood. *Texas Monthly,* pp. 84–88.

Dion, K., Berscheid, E., & Walster, E. (1972). What is beautiful is good. *Journal of Personality and Social Psychology, 24,* 285–290.

Disclosure (2003, January 28a). *Inside the interrogation room: Technique critique.* Retrieved August 7, 2004, from http://www.cbc.ca/disclosure/archives/030128_confess/technique.html

Disclosure (2003, January 28b). *Inside the interrogation room: The Darrelle Exner murder.* Retrieved August 7, 2004, from http://www.cbc.ca/disclosure/archives/030128_confess/murder_print.html

DiVasto, P. V. (1985). Measuring the aftermath of rape. *Journal of Psychosocial Nursing and Mental Health Services, 23,* 33–35.

Dix v. Canada (A. G.). (2002). ABQB 580.

Dixon, L., & Browne, K. (2003). The heterogeneity of spouse abuse: A review. *Aggression and Violent Behavior, 8,* 107–130.

Dobash, R. E., Dobash, R. P., & Cavanagh, K. (2009). "Out of the blue." Men who murder an intimate partner. *Feminist Criminology, 4,* 194–225.

Dodge, K. A. (1991). The structure and function of reactive and proactive aggression. In D. J. Pepler & K. H. Rubin (Eds.), *The development and treatment of childhood aggression* (pp. 1–18). Hillsdale, NJ: Erlbaum.

Dolnik, A., & Fitzgerald, K. (2011). Negotiating hostage crises with the new terrorists. *Studies in Conflict and Terrorism, 34,* 267–294.

Donavant, B. (2008). *Efficacy of distance learning for professional development of police officers.* (Doctoral Dissertation).

Donovant, B. (2009). The new, modern practice of adult education: Online instruction in a continuing professional education setting. *Adult Education Quarterly, 59,* 227–245.

Doren, D. M., & Yates, P. M. (2008). Effectiveness of sex offender treatment for psychopathic sexual offenders. *International Journal of Offender Therapy and Comparative Criminology 52*(2), 234–245.

Dotto, L. (2004). Liar liar. *National Magazine, 13,* 44–49.

Douglas, J. E., & Munn, C. (1992, February). Violent crime scene analysis: Modus operandi, signature, and staging. *Law Enforcement Bulletin,* pp. 1–10.

Douglas, J. E., & Olshaker, M. (1995). *Mindhunter: Inside the FBI's elite serial crime unit.* New York: Charles Scribner's.

Douglas, J. E., Burgess, A. W., Burgess, A. G., & Ressler, R. (1992). *Crime classification manual.* Lexington, MA: Lexington Books.

Douglas, J. E., Ressler, R. K., Burgess, A. W., & Hartman, C. R. (1986). Criminal profiling from crime scene analysis. *Behavioral Sciences and the Law, 4,* 401–421.

Douglas, J., & Olshaker, M. (1997). *Journey into darkness.* New York: Pocket Star Books.

Douglas, J., & Olshaker, M. (1998). *Obsession.* New York: Charles Scribner's.

Douglas, K. S., & Reeves, K. A. (2010). Historical-clinical-risk management-20 (HCR-20) violence risk assessment scheme: Rationale, application, and empirical overview. In R. K. Otto, K. S. Douglas (Eds.), *Handbook of violence risk assessment* (pp. 147–185). New York: Routledge/Taylor & Francis Group.

Douglas, K. S., & Skeem, J. L. (2005). Violence risk assessment: Getting specific about being dynamic. *Psychology, Public Policy, and Law, 11*(3), 347–383.

Douglas, K. S., Guy, L. S., & Hart, S. D. (2009). Psychosis as a risk factor for violence to others: A meta-analysis. *Psychological Bulletin, 135*(5), 679–706.

Douglas, K. S., Huss, M. T., Murdoch, L. L., Washington, D. O. N., & Koch, W. J. (1999). Posttraumatic stress disorder stemming from motor vehicle accidents: Legal issues in Canada and the United States. In E. J. Hickling & E. B. Blanchard (Eds), *The international handbook of road traffic accidents & psychological trauma: Current understanding, treatment and law* (pp. 271–289). Oxford: Elsevier.

Douglas, K., Ogloff, J., Nicholls, T., & Grant, I. (1999). Assessing risk for violence among psychiatric patients: The HCR-20, Violence Risk Assessment Scheme, and the Psychopathy Checklist: Screening Version. *Journal of Consulting and Clinical Psychology, 67,* 917–930.

Dowden, C., & Andrews, D. A. (2000). Effective correctional treatment and violent reoffending: A meta-analysis. *Criminology, 42,* 449–467.

Doyle, A. C. (1891). A case of identity. In *The original illustrated Sherlock Holmes*. Secaucus, NJ: Castle.

Doyle, J. M. (2005). *True witness: Cops, courts, science, and the battle against misidentification*. New York: Palgrave MacMillan.

Dressing, H., Kuehner, C., & Gass, P. (2005). Lifetime prevalence and impact of stalking in a European population: Epidemiological data from a middle-sized German city. *British Journal of Psychiatry, 187*, 168–172.

Dreznick, M. T. (2003). Heterosocial competence of rapists and child molesters: A meta-analysis. *Journal of Sex Research, 40*(2), 170–178.

Drizin, S. A., & Leo, R. A. (2004). The problem of false confessions in the world. *North Carolina Law Review, 82*, 891–1007.

Duenwald, M. (2005, February 1). The physiology of facial expressions. Retrieved May 15, 2012, from http://discovermagazine.com

Duke, N. N., Pettingell, S. L., McMorris, B. J., & Borowsky, I. W. (2010). Adolescent violence perpetration: Associations with multiple types of adverse childhood experiences. *Pediatrics, 125*(4), e778–e786.

Dumas, R., & Testé, B. (2006). The influence of criminal facial stereotypes on juridic judgments. *Swiss Journal of Psychology/Schweizerische Zeitschrift Für Psychologie/Revue Suisse De Psychologie, 65*(4), 237–244.

Dunnette, M. D., & Motowidlo, S. J. (1976, November). *Police selection and career assessment*. Washington, DC: Law Enforcement Assistance Association, United States Department of Justice.

Durham v. United States, 214 F.2d 862 (D.C. Cir. 1954).

Duthie, B., & McIvor, D. L. (1990). A new system for cluster-coding child molester MMPI profile types. *Criminal Justice and Behavior, 17*, 199–214.

Dutton, D. G. (1981). *The criminal justice system response to wife assault*. Ottawa: Solicitor General of Canada, Research Division.

Dutton, D. G. (1988). *The domestic assault of women: Psychological and criminal justice perspectives*. Boston: Allyn & Bacon.

Dutton, D. G. (1995a). *The batterer: A psychological profile*. New York: Basic Books.

Dutton, D. G. (1995b). *The domestic assault of women: Psychological and criminal justice perspectives* (Rev. ed.). Vancouver: UBC Press.

Dutton, D. G., & Levens, B. R. (1977). Domestic crisis intervention: Attitude survey of trained and untrained police officers. *Canadian Police College Journal, 1*(2), 75–92.

Dutton, D. G., & McGregor, B. M. S. (1992). Psychological and legal dimensions of family violence. In D. K. Kagehiro & W. S. Laufer (Eds.), *Handbook of psychology and law* (pp. 318–340). New York: Springer-Verlag.

Dutton, D. G., & Nicholls, T. L. (2005). The gender paradigm in domestic violence research and theory: Part 1—The conflict of theory and data. *Aggression and Violent Behavior, 10*, 68–714.

Dutton, D. G., Hart, S. D., Kennedy, L. W., & Williams, K. R. (1992). Arrest and the reduction of repeat wife assault. In E. S. Buzawa & C. G. Buzawa (Eds.), *Domestic violence: The changing criminal justice response* (pp. 111–127). Westport, CT: Auburn House.

Dutton, D. G. (2007). The complexities of domestic violence. *American Psychologist, 62*, 708–709.

Dutton, D. G., Nicholls, T., & Spidel, A. (2005) Female perpetrators of intimate violence. In F. Buttell and M. Carney (eds.) *Special Issue, Journal of Offender Rehabilitation, 41*, 1–32.

Eastwood, J., & Snook, B. (2012). The effect of listenability factors on the comprehension of police cautions. *Law and Human Behavior, 36*(3), 177–183.

Ebberline, J. (2008). Geographical profiling obscene phone calls—A case study. *Journal of Investigative Psychology and Offender Profiling, 5*(1–2), 93–105.

Ebbinghaus, H. E. (1885). *Memory: A contribution to experimental psychology*. New York: Dover.

Eberhardt, J. L., Davies, P. G., Purdie-Vaughns, V. J., & Johnson, S. L. (2006). Looking deathworthy: Perceived stereotypically of black defendants predicts capital-sentencing outcomes. *Psychological Science, 17*, 383–386.

Edens, J. F. (2006). Unresolved controversies concerning psychopathy: Implications for clinical & forensic decision-making. *Professional Psychology: Research and Practice, 37*, 59–65.

Edens, J. F., Davis, K. M., Fernendez Smith, K., & Guy, L. S. (2012, in press). No sympathy for the devil: Attributing psychopathic traits to capital murderers also predicts support for executing them. *Personality Disorders: Theory, Research, and Treatment*.

Edens, J. F., Petrila, J., & Buffington-Vollum, J. K. (2001). Psychopathy and the death penalty: Can the psychopathy checklist-revised identify offenders who represent "a continuing threat to society?" *Journal of Psychiatry & Law, 29*(4), 433–481.

Edens, J. F., Poythress, N. G., & Lilienfeld, S. O. (1999). Identifying inmates at risk for disciplinary infractions: A comparison of two measures of psychopathy. *Behavioral Sciences and the Law, 17*, 435–443.

Egan, S. K., & Perry, D. G. (1998). Does low self-regard invite victimization? *Developmental Psychology, 34*(2), 299–309.

Egeth, H. E. (1993). What do we *not* know about eyewitness identification? *American Psychologist, 48*, 577–580.

Egger, S. A. (1984). A working definition of serial murder and the reduction of linkage blindness. *Journal of Police Science & Administration, 12*(3), 348–357.

Ehrensaft, M. K. (2008). Intimate partner violence: Persistence of myths and implications for intervention. *Children and Youth Services Review, 30*(3), 276-286.

Eke, A. W., Hilton, N. Z., Harris, G. T., Rice, M. E., & Houghton, R. E. (2011). Intimate partner homicide: Risk assessment and prospects for prediction. *Journal of Family Violence, 26*, 211-216.

Ekman, P. (1992). *Telling lies: Clues to deceit in the marketplace, politics, and marriage.* New York: W. W. Norton.

Ekman, P. (2003). *Emotions revealed: Recognizing faces and feelings to improve communication and emotional life.* New York: Owl Books.

Ekman, P. (2009). Darwin's contributions to our understanding of emotional expression. *Philosophical Transactions of the Royal Society B, 364*, 3449-3451.

Ekman, P., & Friesen, W. V. (1969). Nonverbal leakage and clues to deception. *Psychiatry: Journal for the Study of Interpersonal Processes, 32*, 88-106. Retrieved July 23, 2012, from http://psycnet.apa.org/psycinfo/1970-03731-001

Ekman, P., & O'Sullivan, M. (1991). Who can catch a liar? *American Psychologist, 46*, 913-920.

Ekman, P., Davidson, R. J., & Friesen, W. V. (1990). The Duchenne smile: Emotional expression and brain physiology: II. *Journal of Personality and Social Psychology, 58*, 342-353.

Ekman, P., Friesen, W. V., & O'Sullivan, M. (1988). Smiles when lying. *Journal of Personality and Social Psychology, 54*, 414-420.

Ekman, P., O'Sullivan, M., Friesen, W. V., & Scherer, K. R. (1991). Invited article: Face, voice, and body in detecting deceit. *Journal of Nonverbal Behavior, 15*, 125-135.

Elaad, E., Ginton, A., & Ben-Shakhar, G. (1994). The effects of prior expectations and outcome knowledge on polygraph examiners' decisions. *Journal of Behavioral Decision Making, 7*, 279-292.

Elbogen, E. B., & Johnson, S. C. (2009). The intricate link between violence and mental disorder: Results from the national epidemiologic survey on alcohol and related conditions. *Archives of General Psychiatry, 66*(2), 152-161.

Elklit, A. (2002). Victimization and PTSD in a Danish national youth probability sample. *Journal of the American Academy of Child & Adolescent Psychiatry, 41*(2), 174-181.

Elliott, I. A., Eldridge, H. J., Ashfield, S., & Beech, A. R. (2010). Exploring risk: Potential static, dynamic, protective and treatment factors in the clinical histories of female sex offenders. *Journal of Family Violence, 25*(6), 595-602.

Elliott, R. (1991). Social science data and the APA: The *Lockhart* brief as a case in point. *Law and Human Behavior, 15*, 59-76.

Elliott, R. (1993). Expert testimony about eyewitness identification: A critique. *Law and Human Behavior, 17*, 423-437.

Ellis, D., Choi, A., & Blaus, C. (1993). Injuries to police officers attending domestic disturbances: An empirical study. *Canadian Journal of Criminology, 35*, 149-168.

Ellis, H. D., Shepherd, J. W., & Davies, G. M. (1980). The deterioration of verbal descriptions of faces over different delay intervals. *Journal of Police Science and Administration, 8*, 101-106.

Ellison, K. W. (1985). Community involvement in police selection. *Social Action and the Law, 11*(3), 77-78.

Ellison, K. W., & Buckhout, R. (1981). *Psychology and criminal justice.* New York: Harper & Row.

Ellsworth, P. C. (1991). To tell what we know or wait for Godot? *Law and Human Behavior, 15*, 77-90.

Enayati, J., Grann, M., Lubbe, S., & Fazel, S. (2008). Psychiatric morbidity in arsonists referred for forensic psychiatric assessment in Sweden. *Journal of Forensic Psychiatry & Psychology, 19*(2), 139-147.

Englich, B., Mussweiler, T., & Strack, F. (2006). Playing dice with criminal sentences: The influence of irrelevant anchors on experts' judicial decision making. *Personality and Social Psychology Bulletin, 32*, 188-200.

Erickson, W. D., Luxenburg, M. G., Walbek, N. H., & Seely, R. K. (1987). Frequency of MMPI two-point code types among sex offenders. *Journal of Consulting and Clinical Psychology, 55*, 566-570.

Ernsdorff, G. N., & Loftus, E. F. (1993). Let sleeping memories lie? Words of caution about tolling the statute of limitations in cases of memory repression. *Journal of Criminal Law and Criminology, 84*, 129-174.

Erven v. The Queen (1979), 1 S.C.R. 926.

Esses, V. M., & Webster, C. D. (1988). Physical attractiveness, dangerousness, and the Canadian Criminal Code. *Journal of Applied Social Psychology, 18*, 1017-1031.

Ewing, C. P. (1990). Psychological self-defense: A proposed justification for battered women who kill. *Law and Human Behavior, 14*, 579-594.

Ewing, C. P., & Aubrey, M. R. (1987). Battered women and public opinion: Some realities about the myths. *Journal of Family Violence, 4*(2), 143-159.

Ewing, C. P., Aubrey, M., & Jamieson, L. (1986, August). *The battered woman syndrome: Expert testimony and public attitudes.* Paper presented at the meetings of the American Psychological Association, Washington, DC.

Faigman, D. (1986). The battered woman syndrome and self-defense: A legal and empirical dissent. *Virginia Law Review, 72*, 619-647.

Falkenbach, D. M., Poythress, N. G., & Heide, K. M. (2003). Psychopathic features in a juvenile diversion population: Reliability and predictive validity of two self-report measures. *Behavioral Sciences & The Law, 21*(6), 787-805.

Faller, K., & Nelson-Gardell, D. (2010). Extended evaluations in cases of child sexual abuse: How many sessions are sufficient? *Journal of Child Sexual Abuse: Research, Treatment, & Program Innovations for Victims, Survivors, & Offenders, 19*(6), 648–668.

Fawcette, J. M., Russell, E. J., Peace, K. A., & Christie, J. (2011). Of guns and geese: a meta-analytic review of the "weapon focus" literature. *Psychology, Crime & Law.*

Fazel, S., Sjöstedt, G., Grann, M., & Långström, N. (2010). Sexual offending in women and psychiatric disorder: A national case–control study. *Archives of Sexual Behavior, 39*(1), 161–167.

Federal Bureau of Investigation. (2012). Investigative programs: Critical incident response group. Retrieved July 19, 2012, from http://web.archive.org/web/20080109073451/http://www.fbi.gov/hq/isd/cirg/osb.htm

Feigenson, N., Park, J., & Salovey, P. (1997). Effect of blameworthiness and outcome severity on attributions of responsibility and damage awards in comparative negligence cases. *Law and Human Behavior, 21*, 597–617.

Fein, R. A., & Vossekuil, B. V. (1999). Assassination in the United States: An operational study of recent assassins, attackers, and near-lethal approachers. *Journal of Forensic Sciences, 44*, 321–333.

Felchlia, M. (1992). Construct validity of the Competency Screening Test. *Dissertation Abstracts International, 53*(1-B), 604.

Feldman, S. (2004). Reflections on the 40th anniversary of the Community Mental Health Centers Act. *Administration and Policy in Mental Health, 31*, 369–380.

Feldman-Summers, S., Gordon, P. E., & Meagher, J. R. (1979). The impact of rape on sexual satisfaction. *Journal of Abnormal Psychology, 88*, 101–105.

Felthous, A. R. (2010). Psychopathic disorders and criminal responsibility in the USA. *European Archives of Psychiatry and Clinical Neuroscience, 260*, S137–S141.

Ferguson, C. J., & Meehan, D. (2005). An analysis of females convicted of sex crimes in the state of Florida. *Journal of Child Sexual Abuse: Research, Treatment, & Program Innovations for Victims, Survivors, & Offenders, 14*(1), 75–89.

Ferguson, M., & Ogloff, J. R. P. (2011). Criminal responsibility evaluations: Role of psychologists in assessment. *Psychiatry, Psychology and Law, 18*(1), 79–94.

Fernandez, E. (1993, November 15). Dead letters. *People*, pp. 111–112.

Findley, K. A., & Scott, M. S. (2006). The multiple dimensions of tunnel vision in criminal cases. *Wisconsin Law Review, 2*, 291–397.

Finkel, N. J., Meister, K. H., & Lightfoot, D. M. (1991). The self-defense defense and community sentiment. *Law and Human Behavior, 15*, 585–602.

Finkelhor, D., Hotaling, G., Lewis, I. A., & Smith, C. (1990). Sexual abuse in a national survey of adult men and women: Prevalence, characteristics, and risk factors. *Child Abuse and Neglect, 14*, 19–28.

Finklehor, D., & Jones, L. (2006). Why have child maltreatment and child victimization declined? *Journal of Social Issues, 62*(4), 685–716.

Fiori, M. (2009). A new look at emotional intelligence: A dual-process framework. *Personality and Social Psychology Review, 13*, 21–33.

Firestone, P., Bradford, J. M., Greenberg, D. M., & Larose, M. R. (1998). Homicidal sex offenders: Psychological, phallometric, and diagnostic features. *The Journal of the American Academy of Psychiatry and the Law, 26*(4), 537–552. Retrieved July 23, from http://www.jaapl.org/content/26/4.toc

Firestone, P., Kingston, D. A., Wexler, A., & Bradford, J. M. (2006). Long-term follow-up of exhibitionists: Psychological, phallometric, and offense characteristics. *Journal of the American Academy of Psychiatry and the Law, 34*(3), 349–359.

Fisher, R. P. (1995). Interviewing victims and witnesses of crime. *Psychology, Public Policy, and Law, 1*, 732–764.

Fisher, R. P., & Geiselman, R. E. (2010). The cognitive interview method of conducting police interviews: Eliciting extensive information and promoting Therapeutic Jurisprudence. *International Journal of Law and Psychiatry, 33*, 321–328.

Fisher, R. P., & Schreiber, N. (2007). Interviewing protocols to improve eyewitness memory. In M. Toglia, J. Reed, D. Ross, & R. Lindsay (Eds.) *The handbook of eyewitness psychology: Volume One. Memory for events* (pp. 53–80). Mahwah, NJ: Erlbaum Associates.

Fisher, R. P., Geiselman, R. E., & Amador, M. (1989). Field test of the cognitive interview: Enhancing the recollection of actual victims and witnesses of crime. *Journal of Applied Psychology, 74*, 722–727.

Fisher, R. P., Geiselman, R. E., & Raymond, D. S. (1987). Critical analysis of police interview techniques. *Journal of Police Science and Administration, 15*, 177–185.

Fisher, R. P., Milne, R., & Bull, R. (2011). Interviewing cooperative witnesses. *Current Directions in Psychological Science, 20*, 16–19.

Fisher, R. P., Ross, S. J., & Cahill, B. S. (2010). Interviewing witnesses and victims. In P. A. Granhag (Ed.), *Forensic psychology in context: Nordic and international approaches* (pp. 56–74). Portland, OR: Willan Publishing.

Fiske, S. T., Bersoff, D. N., Borgida, E., Deaux, K., & Heilman, M. E. (1991). Social science research on trial: Use of sex stereotyping research in *Price Waterhouse v. Hopkins. American Psychologist, 46*, 1049–1060.

Fiske, S. T., Bersoff, D. N., Borgida, E., Deaux, K., & Heilman, M. E. (1993). What constitutes a scientific review? A majority retort to Barrett and Morris. *Law and Human Behavior, 17*, 217–233.

Fivush, R., & Schwarzmueller, A. (1995). Say it once again: Effects of repeated questions on children's event recall. *Journal of Traumatic Stress, 8,* 555-580.

Flight, J. I., & Forth, A. E. (2007). Instrumentally violent youths: The roles of psychopathic traits, empathy, and attachment. *Criminal Justice and Behavior, 34,* 739-751.

Flowe, H. D. & Humphries, J. E. (2011). An examination of criminal face bias in a random sample of police lineups. *Applied Cognitive Psychology, 25:* 265-273.

Foa, E. B., & Rothbaum, B. O. (1998). *Treating the trauma of rape: Cognitive behavioral therapy for PTSD.* New York: Guilford Press.

Foa, E. B., Olasov, B., & Steketee, G. (1987). *Treatment of rape victims.* Paper presented at the conference, State-of-the-Art in Sexual Assault, Charleston, SC.

Foley, L. A. (1993). *A psychological view of the legal system.* Madison, WI: Brown & Benchmark.

Follingstad, D. R. (1994a, March). *Rape trauma syndrome in the courtroom.* Workshop presented for the American Academy of Forensic Psychology, Santa Fe, NM.

Follingstad, D. R. (1994b, March 10). *The use of battered woman syndrome in court.* Workshop presented for the American Academy of Forensic Psychology, Santa Fe, NM.

Follingstad, D. R., Polek, D. S., Hause, E. S., Deaton, L. H., Bulger, M. W., & Conway, Z. D. (1989). Factors predicting verdicts in cases where battered women kill their husbands. *Law and Human Behavior, 13,* 253-270.

Forman, B. (1980). Psychotherapy with rape victims. *Psychotherapy: Theory, Research and Practice, 17,* 304-311.

Forth, A. E. & Book, A. (2010). Psychopathic traits in children and adolescents: The relationship with antisocial behaviors and aggression. In D. Lynam & R. Salekin (Eds.) *Handbook of youth psychopathy* (pp. 251-283). New York: Guilford.

Forth, A. E., & Mailloux, D. L. (2000). Psychopathy in youth: What do we know? In C. B. Gacono (Ed.), *The clinical and forensic assessment of psychopathy: A practitioner's guide* (pp. 25-54). Mahwah, NJ: Erlbaum.

Forth, A. E., Brown, S. L., Hart, S. D., & Hare, R. D. (1996). The assessment of psychopathy in male and female noncriminals: Reliability and validity. *Personality and Individual Differences, 20*(5), 531-543.

Forth, A. E., Kosson, D. S., & Hare, R. D. (2003). *The psychopathy checklist: Youth version.* Toronto: Multi-Health Systems.

Fowler, R., De Vivo, P. F., & Fowler, D. J. (1985). Analyzing police hostage negotiations: The verbal interaction analysis technique. *Journal of Crisis Intervention, 2,* 16-28.

Fowler, T., Langley, K., Rice, F., van den Bree, M. B. M., Ross, K., Wilkinson, L. S., et al. (2009). Psychopathy trait scores in adolescents with childhood ADHD: The contribution of genotypes affecting MAOA, 5HTT and COMT activity. *Psychiatric Genetics, 19,* 312-219.

Fox, K., Nobles, M., & Akers, R. L. (2011). Is stalking a learned phenomenon? An empirical test of social learning theory. *Journal of Criminal Justice, 39,* 39-47.

Fox, R. E. (1991). Proceedings of the American Psychological Association, Incorporated, for the year 1990. *American Psychologist, 46,* 689-726.

Francati, V. V., Vermetten, E. E., & Bremner, J. D. (2007). Functional neuroimaging studies in posttraumatic stress disorder: Review of current methods and findings. *Depression and Anxiety, 24*(3), 202-213.

Frank, E., & Stewart, B. D. (1984). Depressive symptoms in rape victims: A revisit. *Journal of Affective Disorders, 7,* 77-85.

Frank, G. (1966). *The Boston Strangler.* New York: Signet.

Frank, M. G., & Ekman, P. (1997). The ability to detect deceit generalizes across different types of high-stake lies. *Journal of Personality and Social Psychology, 72,* 1429-1439.

Franke, W. D., Collins, S. A., & Hinz, P. N. (1998). Cardiovascular disease morbidity in an Iowa law enforcement cohort, compared with the general Iowa population. *Journal of Occupational & Environmental Medicine, 40,* 441-444.

Franklin, B. (1994, August 22). Gender myths still play a role in jury selection. *National Law Journal,* pp. A1, A25.

Franklin, C. (1970). *The third degree.* London: Robert Hale.

Frazier, P. A. (1990). Victim attributions and postrape trauma. *Journal of Personality and Social Psychology, 59,* 298-304.

Frazier, P. A., & Borgida, E. (1988). Juror common understanding and the admissibility of rape trauma syndrome evidence in court. *Law and Human Behavior, 12,* 101-122.

Frazier, P. A., & Borgida, E. (1992). Rape trauma syndrome: A review of case law and psychological research. *Law and Human Behavior, 16,* 293-311.

Freedman, L. (2008). A cause for compassion: Understanding and applying neurobiological factors associated with psychopathy. Masters Thesis. Retrieved May 15, 2012, from http://gradworks.umi.com/MR/46/MR46874.html

Frei, A. (2008). Media consideration of sex offenders: How community response shapes a gendered perspective. *International Journal of Offender Therapy and Comparative Criminology, 52*(5), 495-498.

Frenda, S. J, Nichols, R. M., & Loftus, R. F. (2011). Current issues and advances in misinformation research. *Current Directions in Psychological Science, 20,* 20-23.

Freund, K. (1990). Courtship disorder. In W. L. Marshall, D. R. Laws, H. E. Barbaree, W. L. Marshall, D. R. Laws, H. E. Barbaree (Eds.), *Handbook of sexual assault: Issues, theories, and treatment of the offender* (pp. 195-207). New York: Plenum Press.

Frey, B. (1994). Development of a structured preference scale and a deductive preference scale. Unpublished Ph.D. dissertation, Department of Educational Psychology and Research, Lawrence, KS: University of Kansas.

Frick, P. J. (1998). *Conduct disorders and severe antisocial behavior.* New York: Plenum.

Frick, P. J., & Ellis, M. (1999). Callous-unemotional traits and subtypes of conduct disorder. *Clinical Child and Family Psychology Review, 2,* 149–168.

Frick, P. J., & White, S. F. (2008). Research review: The importance of callous-unemotional traits for developmental models of aggressive and antisocial behavior. *Journal of Child Psychology and Psychiatry, 49*(4), 359–375.

Frick, P. J., Bodin, S. D., & Barry, C. T. (2000). Psychopathic traits and conduct problems in community and clinic-referred samples of children: Further development of the Psychopathy Screening Device. *Psychological Assessment, 12,* 382–393.

Frick, P. J., Kimonis, E. R., Dandreaux, D. M., & Farell, J. M. (2003). The 4 Year Stability of Psychopathic Traits in Non-Referred Youth. *Behavioral Sciences & the Law, 21*(6), 713–736.

Frick, P. J., O'Brien, B. S., Wooton, J. M., & McBurnett, K. (1994). Psychopathy and conduct problems in children. *Journal of Abnormal Psychology, 103,* 700–707.

Friedland, N., & Merari, A. (1985). The psychological impact of terrorism: A double-edged sword. *Political Psychology, 6,* 591–604.

Friend, J., Langhinrichsen-Rohling, J., & Eichold, B. (2011). Same-day substance use in men and women charged with felony domestic violence offenses. *Criminal Justice and Behavior, 38*(6), 619–633.

Frowd, C. D., Bruce, V., Smith, A. J., & Hancock, P. J. B. (2008). Improving the quality of facial composites using a holistic cognitive interview. *Journal of Experimental Psychology: Applied, 14,* 276–287.

Fruyt, F., De Clercq, B. J., Miller, J., Rolland, J., Jung, S., Taris, R., et al. (2009). Assessing personality at risk in personnel selection and development. *European Journal of Personality, 23*(1), 51–69.

Frye v. United States, 293 F. 1013, 34 A.L.R. 145 (D. C. Cir. 1923).

Fulero, S. (1998, May 14). Personal communication via e-mail.

Fulero, S. M. (1988, August). *Eyewitness expert testimony: An overview and annotated bibliography, 1931–1988.* Paper presented at the meetings of the American Psychological Association, Atlanta.

Fulero, S. M., & Finkel, N. J. (1991). Barring ultimate issue testimony: An "insane" rule? *Law and Human Behavior, 15,* 495–507.

Fulero, S. M., & Penrod, S. (1990). The myths and realities of attorney jury selection folklore and scientific jury selection: What works? *Ohio Northern University Law Review, 17,* 229–253.

Fuselier, G. D. (1988). Hostage negotiation consultant: Emerging role for the clinical psychologist. *Professional Psychology: Research and Practice, 19,* 175–179.

Ganis, G., Rosenfeld, J. P., Meixner, J., Kievit, R. A., Schendan, H. E. (2011). Lying in the scanner: Covert countermeasures disrupt deception detection by functional magnetic resonance imaging. *Neurolmage, 55,* 312–319.

Gannon, M. (2005). "Crime Statistics in Canada, 2005," *Juristat* (Canadian Centre for Justice Statistics).

Garb, H. N. (1998). *Studying the clinician: Judgment research and psychological assessment.* Washington, DC: American Psychological Association.

Garry, M., Sharman, S. J., Wade, K. A., Hunt, M. J., & Smith, P. J. (2001). Imagination inflation is a fact, not an artifact. *Memory & Cognition, 29,* 719–729.

Garven, S., Wood, J. M., Malpass, R. S., & Shaw, J. S., III. (1998). More than suggestion: The effect of interviewing techniques from the McMartin Preschool case. *Journal of Applied Psychology, 83,* 347–359.

Gazzaniga, M. S. (2011). Neuroscience in the courtroom. *Scientific American, 304,* 54–59.

Geberth, V. J. (1981, September). Psychological profiling. *Law and Order,* pp. 46–49.

Geberth, V. J. (1990). *Practical homicide investigation: Tactics, procedures, and forensic techniques* (2nd ed.). New York: Elsevier.

Geiselman, R. E., & Callot, R. (1990). Reverse versus forward recall of script-based texts. *Applied Cognitive Psychology, 4,* 141–144.

Geiselman, R. E., & Padilla, J. (1988). Interviewing child witnesses with the cognitive interview. *Journal of Police Science and Administration, 16,* 236–242.

Geiselman, R. E., Fisher, R. P., MacKinnon, D. P., & Holland, H. L. (1985). Eyewitness memory enhancement in the police interview: Cognitive retrieval mnemonics versus hypnosis. *Journal of Applied Psychology, 70,* 401–412.

Genz, J. L., & Lester, D. (1976). Authoritarianism in policemen as a function of experience. *Journal of Police Science and Administration, 4,* 9–13.

George, J. R., & Robb, A. (2008). Deception and computer-mediated communication in daily life. *Communication Reports, 21,* 92–103.

George, R., & Clifford, B. R. (1992). Making the most of witnesses. *Policing, 8,* 185–198.

Gerard, H. (1983). School desegregation: The social science role. *American Psychologist, 38,* 869–872.

Germann, A. C. (1969). Community policing: An assessment. *Journal of Criminal Law, Criminology, and Police Science, 60,* 84–96.

Gershon, R. R. M, & Lin, S. (2002). Work stress in aging police officers. *Journal of Occupational & Environmental Medicine, 44,* 160–167.

Gershon, R. R. M., Barocas, B., Canton, A. N., Li, X., & Vlahov, D. (2009). Mental, physical, and behavioral outcomes associated with perceived work stress in police officers. *Criminal Justice and Behavior, 36*, 275–289.

Gilbert, G. (1754/1769). *The Law of Evidence 121-47*. London, His Majesty's Law Printers.

Gilbert, J. A. E., & Fisher, R. P. (2006). The effects of varied retrieval cues on reminiscence in eyewitness memory. *Applied Cognitive Psychology, 20*, 723–739.

Gill, M. and K. Pease (1998). Repeat robbers: How are they different? In M. Gill (ed.), *Crime at work: Studies in security and crime prevention*. Leicester, UK: Perpetuity Press.

Gill, M., & Matthews, R. (1994), Robbers on robbery: Offender perspectives. In M. Gill (ed.), *Crime at work*. Leicester, UK: Perpetuity Press.

Gillis, J., Diamond, S., Jebely, P., Orekhovsky, V., Ostovich, E. M., MacIsaac, K., et al. (2006). Systemic obstacles to battered women's participation in the judicial system: When will the status quo change? *Violence Against Women, 12*(12), 1150–1168.

Glancy, G. D., Regehr, C., Bryant, A. G., & Schneider, R. (1999). Another nail in the coffin of confidentiality. *The Canadian Journal of Psychiatry/La Revue Canadienne de Psychiatrie, 44*(5), 440.

Glenn, A. L., Kurzban, R., & Raine, A. (2011). Evolutionary theory and psychopathy. *Aggression and Violent Behavior, 16*(5), 371–380.

Glenn, A. L., Raine, A., & Laufer, W. S. (2011). Is it wrong to criminalize and punish psychopaths? *Emotion Review, 3*(3), 302–304.

Glenn, A. L., Raine, A., Venables, P. H., & Mednick, S. A. (2007). Early temperamental and psychophysiological precursors of adult psychopathic personality. *Journal of Abnormal Psychology, 116*, 508–518.

Global Deception Research Team (2006). A world of lies. *Journal of Cross-Cultural Psychology, 37*, 60–74.

Goffman, E. (1959). *The presentation of self in everyday life*. New York: Doubleday.

Golding, S. L. (1990). Mental health professionals in the courts: The ethics of expertise. *International Journal of Law and Psychiatry, 13*, 281–307.

Golding, S. L., & Roesch, R. (1987). The assessment of criminal responsibility: A historical approach to a current controversy. In I. B. Weiner & A. K. Hess (Eds.), *Handbook of forensic psychology* (pp. 395–436). New York: John Wiley.

Golding, S. L., Roesch, R., & Schreiber, J. (1984). Assessment and conceptualization of competency to stand trial: Preliminary data on the Interdisciplinary Fitness Interview. *Law and Human Behavior, 8*, 321–334.

Goldsmith, A. J. (2010). Policing's new visibility. *British Journal of Criminology, 50*, 914–934.

Goldstein, R. L. (1989). The psychiatrist's guide to right and wrong: Part IV: The insanity defense and the ultimate issue rule. *Bulletin of the American Academy of Psychiatry and the Law, 17*, 269–281.

Gómez, A. (2011). Testing the cycle of violence hypothesis: Child abuse and adolescent dating violence as predictors of intimate partner violence in young adulthood. *Youth & Society, 43*(1), 171–192.

Gondolf, E., & Heckert, A. (2003). Determinants of women's perceptions of risk in battering relationships. *Violence and Victims, 18*, (4) 371–386.

Gonzalez, R., Ellsworth, P. C., & Pembroke, M. (1993). Response biases in lineups and showups. *Journal of Personality and Social Behavior, 6*, 1–13.

Goodman, G. S. (1984). Children's testimony in historical perspective. *Journal of Social Issues, 40*(2), 9–31.

Goodman, G. S., & Melinder, A (2007). Child witness research and forensic interviews of young children: A review. *Legal and Criminological Psychology, 12*(1), 1–19.

Goodman, G. S., Quas, J. A., Batterman-Faunce, J. M., Riddlesberger, M. M., & Kuhn, J. (1997). Children's reaction to and memory for a stressful experience: Influences of age, knowledge, anatomical dolls, and parental attachment. *Applied Developmental Science, 1*, 54–75.

Goodman, G. S., Redlich, A. D., Qin, J., Ghetti, S., Tyda, K. S., Schaaf, J. M., et al. (1999). Evaluating eyewitness testimony in adults and children. In A. K. Hess & I. B. Weiner (Eds.), *Handbook of forensic psychology* (2nd ed., pp. 218–272). New York: John Wiley.

Goodwill, A. M., & Alison, L. J. (2007). When is profiling possible? Offense planning and aggression as moderators in predicting offender age from victim age in stranger rape. *Behavioral Sciences & the Law, 25*(6), 823–840.

Gough, H. G. (1975). *Manual for the California Psychological Inventory*. Palo Alto, CA: Consulting Psychologists Press.

Gould, K. (1995). A therapeutic analysis of competency evaluation requests: The defense attorney's dilemma. *International Journal of Law and Psychiatry, 18*, 83–100.

Gover, A. R., Paul D., & Dodge, M. (2011). Law enforcement officer' attitudes about domestic violence. *Violence Against Women, 17*, 619–636.

Government of Canada (2002). Intimate Partner Violence. Retrieved May 13, 2012, from http://www.canada.gc.ca/home.html

Grady, M. D., Brodersen, M., & Abramson, J. M. (2011). The state of psychological measures for adult sexual offenders. *Aggression and Violent Behavior, 16*(3), 227–240.

Graham, J. R. (1987). *The MMPI: A practical guide* (2nd ed.). New York: Oxford University Press.

Graham-Kevan, N., & Archer, J. (2003). Intimate terrorism and common couple violence: A test of Johnson's predictions in four British samples. *Journal of Interpersonal Violence, 18*(11), 1247–1270.

Granhag, P. A., & Strömwall, L. A. (Eds.). (2004). *The detection of deception in forensic contexts.* Cambridge, UK: Cambridge University Press.

Granhag, P. A., & Hartwig, M. (2008). A new theoretical perspective on deception detection: On the psychology of instrumental mind reading. *Psychology, Crime and Law, 14,* 189–200.

Greathouse, S. M., & Kovera, M. B. (2009). Instruction bias and lineup presentation moderate the effects of administrator knowledge on eyewitness identification. *Law and Human Behavior, 33,* 70–82.

Greely H., & Illes, J. (2007). Neuroscience-based lie detection: The urgent need for regulation. *American Journal of Law and Medicine, 33,* 377–431.

Greenberg, M. S., & Ruback, R. B. (1982). *Social psychology of the criminal justice system.* Monterey, California: Brooks/Cole.

Greene, E., Raitz, A., & Lindblad, H. (1989). Juror's knowledge of battered women. *Journal of Family Violence, 4*(2), 105–126.

Greenfield, D. P. (2009). Criminal responsibility from a clinical perspective. *Journal of Psychiatry & Law, 37*(1), 7–35.

Greenstone, J. L. (1995a). Hostage negotiations team training for small police departments. In M. I. Kurke & E. M. Scrivner (Eds.), *Police psychology into the 21st century* (pp. 279–296). Hillsdale, NJ: Lawrence Erlbaum.

Greenstone, J. L. (1995b). Tactics and negotiating techniques (TNT): The way of the past and the way of the future. In M. I. Kurke & E. M. Scrivner (Eds.), *Police psychology into the 21st century* (pp. 357–371). Hillsdale, NJ: Lawrence Erlbaum.

Greenwald, J. P., Tomkins, A. J., Kenning, M., & Zavodny, D. (1990). Psychological self-defense jury instructions: Influence on verdicts for battered women defendants. *Behavioral Sciences and the Law, 8,* 171–180.

Greenwood, P. W., & Petersilia, J. (1976). *The criminal investigation process.* Washington, DC: Law Enforcement Assistance Association.

Gretton, H. M., McBride, M., Hare, R. D., O'Shaughnessy, R., & Kumka, G. (2001). Psychopathy and recidivism in adolescent sex offenders. *Criminal Justice and Behavior, 28*(4), 427–449.

Grisso, T., & Saks, M. J. (1991). Psychology's influence on constitutional interpretation: A comment on how to succeed. *Law and Human Behavior, 15,* 205–211.

Grove, W. M., & Meehl, P. E. (1996). Comparative efficiency of informal (subjective, impressionistic) and formal (mechanical, algorithmic) prediction procedures: The clinical statistical controversy. *Psychology, Public Policy, and Law, 2,* 297–323.

Grubb, A. (2010). Modern day hostage (crisis) negotiation: The evolution of an art form within the policing arena. *Aggression and Violent Behavior, 15,* 341–348.

Gudjonsson, G. (1992). *The psychology of interrogations, confessions, and testimony.* Chichester, UK: Wiley.

Gudjonsson, G. H. (1984). A new scale of interrogative suggestibility. *Personality and Individual Differences, 5,* 303–314.

Gudjonsson, G. H. (1989). Compliance in an interrogation situation: A new scale. *Personality and Individual Differences, 10,* 535–540.

Gudjonsson, G. H. (1991). Suggestibility and compliance among alleged false confessors and resisters in criminal trials. *Medicine, Science, and the Law, 31,* 147–151.

Gudjonsson, G. H. (1997). *The Gudjonsson Suggestibility Scales Manual.* East Sussex, UK: Psychology Press.

Gudjonsson, G. H. (2003). *The psychology of interrogations and confessions: A handbook.* New York: Wiley.

Gudjonsson, G. H., & Copson, G. (1997). The role of the expert in criminal investigation. In J. L. Jackson & D. A.

Bekerian (Eds.), *Offender profiling: Theory, research and practice* (pp. 62–76). New York: John Wiley.

Gudjonsson, G. H., & Lebegue, B. (1989). Psychological and psychiatric aspects of a coerced-internalized false confession. *Journal of the Forensic Science Society, 29*(4), 261–269.

Gudjonsson, G. H., & Pearse, J. (2011). Suspect interviews and false confessions. *Current Directions in Psychological Science, 20*(1), 33–37.

Guéguen, H. (2008). The effect of a woman's smile on men's courtship behavior. *Social Behavior and Personality: An International Journal, 36,* 1233–1236.

Guidubaldi, J., & Cleminshaw, H. (1998, August). *The Parenting Satisfaction Scale: Development, validity, and applications.* Paper presented at the meetings of the American Psychological Association, San Francisco.

Gunter, T. D., Vaughn, M. G., & Philibert, R. A. (2010). Behavioral genetics in antisocial spectrum disorders and psychopathy: A review of the recent literature. *Behavioral Sciences & The Law, 28*(2), 148–173.

Gunter, T., Gurley, J. R., Marcus, D., Vaughn, M. G., & Philibert, R. A. (2010). Behavioral genetics in antisocial spectrum disorders and psychopathy: A review of the recent literature. *Behavioral Sciences & the Law, 28*(2), 148–173.

Gurley, J. R., & Marcus, D. K. (2008). The effects of neuroimaging and brain injury on insanity defenses. *Behavioral Sciences & the Law, 26*(1), 85–97.

Guterman, J. T., Martin, C. V., & Rudes, J. (2011). A solution-focused approach to frotteurism. *Journal of Systemic Therapies, 30*(1), 59–72.

Hadley, G. (2009). The identification of participation barriers associated with employment testing in the Ontario constable selection system. Retrieved May 15, 2012 from http://www.policecouncil.ca

Hafemeister, T. L., & Melton, G. B. (1987). The impact of social science research on the judiciary. In G. B. Melton (Ed.), *Reforming the law: Impact of child development research* (pp. 29–59). New York: Guilford.

Hageman, M. J. (1979). Who joins the force for what reason: An argument for "the new breed." *Journal of Police Science and Administration, 15,* 110–117.

Hagen, M. A. (1997). *Whores of the court: The fraud of psychiatric testimony and the rape of American justice.* New York: HarperCollins.

Häkkänen-Nyholm, H. & Hare, R. D. (2009). Psychopathy, homicide, and the courts: Working the system. *Criminal Justice & Behavior, 36*(8), 761–777.

Hale, M., Jr. (1980). *Human science and social order: Hugo Münsterberg and the origins of applied psychology.* Philadelphia: Temple University Press.

Hall, G. C. N. (1989). WAIS-R and MMPI profiles of men who have assaulted children: Evidence of limited utility. *Journal of Personality Assessment, 53,* 404–412.

Hall, G. C. N., Maiuro, R. D., Vitaliano, P. P., & Proctor, W. D. (1986). The utility of the MMPI with men who have sexually assaulted children. *Journal of Clinical and Consulting Psychology, 54,* 493–496.

Hall, N. (December, 2000). *Growing the problem: The second annual report of the Mental Health Advocate of British Columbia.* Victoria, BC: Author.

Hamberger, L. K., Lohr, J. M., Bonge, D., & Tolin, D. F. (1996). A large sample empirical typology of male spouse abusers and its relationship to dimensions of abuse. *Violence and Victims, 11,* 277–292.

Hancock, J., (2007). Digital Deception: When, where, and how people lie online. In K. McKenna, T. Postmes, U. Reips, & A. Joinson (Eds.), *Oxford handbook of internet psychology* (pp. 287–301). Oxford: Oxford University Press.

Hancock, J., Woodworth, M. T., & Porter, S. (2012, in press). Hungry like the wolf: A word pattern analysis of the language of psychopaths. *Legal and Criminological Psychology.*

Handler, M., Honts, C. R., Krapohl, J., Nelson, R., & Griffin, S. (2009). Integration of pre-employment polygraph screening into the police selection process. *Journal of Police and Criminal Psychology, 24,* 69–86.

Haney, C. (1980). Psychology and legal change: On the limits of a factual jurisprudence. *Law and Human Behavior, 4,* 147–199.

Hans, V. (1989). Expert witnessing. *Science, 245,* 312–313.

Hans, V. P. (1990). Attitudes toward corporate responsibility: A psychological perspective. *Nebraska Law Review, 69,* 158–189.

Hans, V. P., & Lofquist, W. (1992). Jurors' judgments of business liability in tort cases: Implications for the litigation explosion debate. *Law and Society Review, 26,* 85–115.

Hanson, R. (1997). How to know what works with sexual offenders. *Sexual Abuse: Journal of Research and Treatment, 9*(2), 129–145.

Hanson, R. K., & Morton-Bourgon, K. (2007). *The accuracy of recidivism risk assessment for sexual offenders: A meta-analysis (User Report No. 2007-01).* Canada: Public Safety and Emergency Preparedness. Retrieved May 15, 2012, from http://epe.lac-bac.gc.ca/100/200/301/psepc-sppcc/accuracy_of_recidivism-e/PS3-1-2007-1E.pdf

Hanson, R. K., Bourgon, G., Helmus, L. & Hodgson, S. (2009). The principles of effective correctional treatment also apply to sexual offenders: A meta-analysis. *Criminal Justice and Behavior, 36,* 865–891.

Hanson, R. K., Harris, A. J., Scott, T., & Helmus, L. (2007). *Assessing the risk of sexual offenders in the community: The dynamic supervision project (Cat. No.: PS3-1/2007-5).* Retrieved July 23, 2012, from http://www.publicsafety.gc.ca/res/cor/rep/_fl/crp2007-05-en.pdf

Hanson, R. K., Helmus, L. & Bourgon, G. (2007). *The validity of risk assessments for intimate partner violence: A meta-analysis.* (User Report No. 2007-07). Ottawa: Public Safety Canada.

Hanson, R., & Bussière, M. T. (1998). Predicting relapse: A meta-analysis of sexual offender recidivism studies. *Journal of Consulting and Clinical Psychology, 66*(2), 348–362.

Hanson, R., & Morton-Bourgon, K. E. (2005). The characteristics of persistent sexual offenders: A meta-analysis of recidivism studies. *Journal of Consulting and Clinical Psychology, 73*(6), 1154–1163.

Hanson, R., & Thornton, D. (2000). Improving risk assessments for sex offenders: A comparison of three actuarial scales. *Law and Human Behavior, 24*(1), 119–136.

Harding, H. H. & Helweg-Larsen, M. (2009). Perceived risk for future intimate partner violence among women in a domestic violence shelter. *Journal of Family Violence, 2,* 75–85.

Hare, R. (2003). *The Hare Psychopathy Checklist—Revised Manual* (2nd ed.). Toronto: Multi-Health Systems.

Hare, R. D. (1980). A research scale for the assessment of psychopathy in criminal populations. *Personality and Individual Differences, 1,* 111–119.

Hare, R. D. (1991). *The Hare Psychopathy Checklist—Revised.* Toronto, Canada: Multi-Health Systems.

Hare, R. D. (1993). *Without conscience: The disturbing world of the psychopaths among us.* New York: Simon & Schuster.

Hare, R. D. (1998). Psychopaths and their nature: Implications for the mental health and criminal justice systems. In T. Millon, E. Simonsen, M. Birket-Smith, & R. D. Davis (Eds.), *Psychopathy: Antisocial, criminal, and violent behavior* (pp. 188–212). New York: Guilford.

Hare, R. D. (1998). The Hare PCL-R: Some issues concerning its use and misuse. *Legal and Criminological Psychology, 3,* 101–122.

Hare, R. D. (1999). Psychopathy as a risk factor for violence. *Psychiatric Quarterly, 70*(3), 181–197.

Hare, R. D. (2002). Psychopathy and risk for recidivism and violence. In N. Gray, J. Laing, & L. Noaks (Eds.), *Criminal justice, mental health, and the politics of risk* (pp. 27–47). London: Cavendish Publishing.

Hare, R. D. (2006). Psychopathy: A clinical and forensic overview. *Psychiatric clinics of North America, 29*(3), 709–724.

Hare, R. D., & Jutai, J. (1983). Criminal history of the male psychopath: Some preliminary data. In K. T. Van Dusen & S. A. Mednick (Eds.), *Prospective studies of crime and delinquency* (pp. 225–236). Boston: Kluwer-Nijhoff.

Hare, R. D., & Neumann, C. S. (2009). Psychopathy: Assessment and forensic implications. *Canadian Journal of Psychiatry, 54*(12), 791–802.

Hargrave, G. E., & Hiatt, D. (1987). Law enforcement selection with the interview, MMPI, and CPI: A study of reliability and validity. *Journal of Police Science and Administration, 15*, 110–117.

Hargrave, G. E., Hiatt, D., Ogard, E., & Karr, C. (1993). *Comparison of the MMPI and the MMPI-2 for a sample of peace officers.* Unpublished manuscript cited by Blau, 1994.

Harlow, J., (1848). Passage of an iron rod through the head. *Boston Medical and Surgical Journal*, 34, 389–393.

Harris, G. T., & Rice, M. E. (1994). The violent patient. In M. Hersen, R. T. Ammerman (Eds.), *Handbook of prescriptive treatments for adults* (pp. 463–486). New York: Plenum Press.

Harris, G. T., Rice, M. E., Hilton, N., Lalumière, M. L., & Quinsey, V. L. (2007). Coercive and precocious sexuality as a fundamental aspect of psychopathy. *Journal of Personality Disorders, 21*(1), 1–27.

Harris, G. T., Rice, M. E., Quinsey, V. L., Lalumière, M. L., Boer, D., & Lang, C. (2003). A multisite comparison of actuarial risk instruments for sex offenders. *Psychological Assessment, 15*(3), 413–425.

Harris, G. T., Skilling, T. A., & Rice, M. E. (2001). The construct of psychopathy. *Crime and Justice, 28*, 197–264.

Harris, G., Rice, M., & Quinsey, V. (1993). Violent recidivism of mentally disordered offenders: The development of a statistical prediction instrument. *Criminal Justice and Behavior, 20*, 315–335.

Harris, T. (1981). *Red Dragon*. New York: Random House.

Harris, T. (1988). *Silence of the Lambs*. New York: Random House.

Harris, T. (1999). *Hannibal*. New York: Random House.

Hart, S. D., & Hare, R. D. (1997). Psychopathy: Assessment and association with criminal conduct. In D. M. Stoff, J. Breiling, & J. D. Maser (Eds.), *Handbook of antisocial behavior* (pp. 22–35). New York: Wiley.

Hart, S., & Hare, R. (1992). Predicting fitness for trial: The relative power of demographic, criminal, and clinical variables. *Forensic Reports, 5*, 53–54.

Hartman, J., & Belknap, J. (2003). Beyond the gatekeepers: Court professionals' self-reported attitudes about and experiences with domestic violence cases. *Criminal Justice and Behavior, 30*, 349–373.

Hartwig, M., Granhag, P. A., Strömwall, L. A., & Kronkvist, O. (2006). Strategic use of evidence during police interviews: When training to detect deception work. *Law and Human Behavior, 30*, 603–619.

Hasel, L. E., & Kassin, S. M. (2012). False confessions. In B. L. Cutler (Ed.), *Conviction of the innocent: Lessons from psychological research* (pp. 53–77). Washington: American Psychological Association.

Hassel, C. (1975). The hostage situation: Exploring motivation and cause. *The Police Chief, 42*(9), 55–58.

Hathaway, S. R., & McKinley, J. C. (1983). *The Minnesota Multiphasic Personality Inventory: Manual.* New York: Psychological Corporation.

Hauser, B. B. (1985). Custody in dispute: Legal and psychological profiles of contesting families. *Journal of American Academy of Child Psychiatry, 24*, 531–537.

Hays, G. (1992). *Policewoman one: My twenty years on the LAPD.* New York: Berkeley Books.

Hazelwood, R. R., & Burgess, A. W. (1995). *Practical aspects of rape investigation: A multidisciplinary approach.* (2nd ed.). Boca Raton, FL: CRC Press.

Hazelwood, R. R., & Douglas, J. E. (1980). The lust murderer. *FBI Law Enforcement Bulletin, 50*(7), 10–15.

Heath, W. P., Grannemann, B. D. and Peacock, M. A. (2004). How the defendant's emotion level affects mock jurors' decisions when presentation mode and evidence strength are varied. *Journal of Applied Social Psychology, 34*. 624–664.

Heffer, C. (2006). Beyond 'reasonable doubt': The criminal standard of proof instructions as communicative act. *The International Journal of Speech, Language and the Law, 13*, 159–188.

Heilbroner, D. (1993, August). Serial murder and sexual repression. *Playboy*, pp. 78, 147–150.

Heilbrun, K., & Brooks, S. (2010). Forensic psychology and forensic science: A proposed agenda for the next decade. *Psychology, Public Policy, and Law, 16*, 219–253.

Heilbrun, K., & Heilbrun, A. B., Jr. (1995). Risk assessment with the MMPI-2 in forensic evaluations. In Y. S. Ben-Porath, J. R. Graham, G. C. N. Hall, R. D. Hirschman, & M. S. Zaragoza (Eds.), *Forensic applications of the MMPI-2* (pp. 160–178). Thousand Oaks, CA: Sage.

Helmus, L., Babchishin, K. M., Camilleri, J. A., & Olver, M. E. (2011). Forensic psychology opportunities in Canadian graduate programs: An update of Simourd and Wormith's (1995) survey. *Canadian Psychology/Psychologie canadienne, 52*, 122–127.

Helmus, L., Thornton, D., Hanson, R. K., & Babchishin, K. M. (2012). Improving the predictive accuracy of Static-99 and Static-2002 with older sex offenders: Revised age weights. *Sexual Abuse: Journal of Research and Treatment, 24*(1) 64-101

Helweg-Larsen, M., Harding, H. G. & Kleinman, K. E. (2008). Risk perceptions of dating violence among college women: The role of experience and depressive symptoms. *Journal of Social and Clinical Psychology, 27,* 551-571.

Hemphill, J. F., Hare, R. D., & Wong, S. (1998). Psychopathy and recidivism: A review. *Legal and Criminological Psychology, 3,* 139-170.

Hemphill, J., Templeman, R., Wong, S., & Hare, R. D. (1998). Psychopathy and crime: Recidivism and criminal careers. In D. Cooke, A. Forth, & R. D. Hare (Eds.). *Psychopathy: Theory, research and implications for society* (pp. 374-399). Dordrecht, Netherlands: Kluwer.

Hendriks, J. J., & Bijleveld, C. H. (2006). Female adolescent sex offenders—an exploratory study. *Journal of Sexual Aggression, 12*(1), 31-41.

Henkel, J., Sheehan, E. P., & Reichel, P. (1997). Relation of police misconduct to authoritarianism. *Journal of Social Behavior and Personality, 12,* 551-555.

Henning, K. & Feder, L. (2005). Criminal prosecution of domestic violence offences: An investigation of factors predictive of court outcomes. *Criminal Justice and Behavior, 32,* 612-642.

Henning, K., Renauer, B. & Holdford, R. (2006). Victim or offender? Heterogeneity among women arrested for intimate partner violence. *Journal of Family Violence, 21,* 351-368.

Herbsleb, J. D., Sales, B. D., & Berman, J. J. (1979). When psychologists aid in the voir dire: Legal and ethical considerations. In L. E. Abt & I. R. Stuart (Eds.), *Social psychology and discretionary law* (pp. 197-217). New York: Van Nostrand Reinhold.

Herman, J. L. (1992). Complex PTSD: A syndrome in survivors of prolonged and repeated trauma. *Journal of Traumatic Stress, 5,* 377-392.

Hervé, H. F, Mitchell, D., Cooper, B. S., Spidel, A, & Hare. R. D. (2004). Psychopathy and unlawful confinement: An examination of perpetrator and event characteristics. *Canadian Journal of Behavioral Science, 36*(2), 137-145.

Hess, U., & Kleck, R. (1990). Differentiating emotional elicited and deliberate emotional facial expressions. *European Journal of Social Psychology, 20,* 369-385.

Hibler, N. S., & Kurke, M. I. (1995). Ensuring personal reliability through selection and training. In M. I. Kurke and E. M. Scrivner (Eds.), *Police psychology into the 21st century* (pp. 57-91). Hillsdale, NJ Lawrence Erlbaum Associates.

Hickman, M. J., Fricas, J., Strom, K. J., & Pope, M. W. (2011). Mapping police stress. *Police Quarterly, 14*(3), 227-250.

Hicks, S. J., & Sales, B. D. (2006). *Criminal profiling: Developing an effective science and practice.* Washington, DC: American Psychological Association.

Hightower, K. & Lush, T. (2011, October 25). Anthony jurors lay low after names released: Judge discloses identities after "cooling off period" following murder acquittal. Retrieved May 15, 2012, from http://www.cbc.ca

Hilton, N. Z., Harris, G. T., Rice, M. E., Houghton, R. E., & Eke, A. W. (2008). An indepth actuarial assessment for wife assault recidivism: The Domestic Violence Risk Appraisal Guide. *Law and Human Behavior, 32,* 150-163.

Hilton, N. Z., Harris, G. T., Rice, M. E., Lang, C., Cormier, C. A., & Lines, K. J. (2004). A brief actuarial assessment for the prediction of wife assault recidivism: The Ontario Domestic Assault Risk Assessment. *Psychological Assessment, 15,* 267-275.

Hines, D. A. (2007). Post-traumatic stress symptoms among men who sustain partner violence: A multi-national study of university students. *Psychology of Men and Masculinity, 8,* 225-239.

Hirschel, J. D., Hutchison, I. W., & Shaw, M. (2010). The interrelationship between substance abuse and the likelihood of arrest, conviction, and re-offending in cases of intimate partner violence. *Journal of Family Violence, 25,* 81-91.

Hlavka, H. R., Olinger, S. D., & Lashley, J. L. (2010). The use of anatomical dolls as a demonstration aid in child sexual abuse interviews: A study of forensic interviewers' perceptions. *Journal of Child Sexual Abuse: Research, Treatment, & Program Innovations for Victims, Survivors, & Offenders, 19*(5), 519-553.

Hobson, J., Shine, J., & Roberts, R. (2000). How do psychopaths behave in a prison therapeutic community? *Psychology, Crime & Law, 6*(2), 139-154.

Hodell, E. C., Dunlap, E. E., Wasarhaley, N. E., & Golding, J. M. (2011). Factors impacting juror perceptions of battered women who kill their abusers: Delay and sleeping status. *Psychology, Public Policy, and Law, 18*(2), 338-359.

Hoffman, L. E, Lavigne, B., Dickie, I., & Women Offender Sector, Correctional Service of Canada. (1998). Women convicted of homicide serving a federal sentence: An exploratory study. Retrieved May 19, 2004, from http://www.csc-scc.gc.ca/text/prgrm/fsw/homicide/toc_e.shtml

Hogan, R. (1971). Personality characteristics of highly rated policemen. *Personnel Psychology, 24,* 679-686.

Hoge, S., Bonnie, R., Poythress, N., & Monahan, J. (1992). Attorney-client decision making in criminal cases: Client competence and participation as perceived by their attorneys. *Behavioral Sciences and the Law, 10,* 385-394.

Hoge, S., Poythress, N., Bonnie, R., Monahan, J., Eisenberg, M., & Feucht-Haviar, T. (1997). The MacArthur Adjudication Competence Study:

Diagnosis, psychopathology, and adjudicative competence-related abilities. *Behavioral Sciences and the Law, 15,* 329–345.

Holbrook, S. H. (1957). *Dreamers of the American dream.* Garden City, NY: Doubleday.

Holmes, R. M., & Holmes, S. T. (1996). *Profiling violent crimes* (2nd ed.). Thousand Oaks, CA: Sage.

Holmes, R. M., & Holmes, S. T. (1998). *Serial murder* (2nd ed.). Thousand Oaks, CA: Sage.

Holtzworth-Munroe, A., & Stuart, G. L. (1994). Typologies of male batterers: Three subtypes and the differences among them. *Psychological Bulletin, 116,* 476–497.

Holtzworth-Munroe, A., Meehan, J. C., Herron, K., Rehman, U., & Stuart, G. L. (2000). Testing the Holtzworth-Munroe and Stuart (1994) batterer typology. *Journal of Consulting and Clinical Psychology, 68,* 1000–1019.

Honts, C. R. (1994). Assessing children's credibility: Scientific and legal issues in 1994. *North Dakota Law Review, 70,* 879–903.

Honts, C. R. (1994). Psychophysiological detection of deception. *Current Directions in Psychological Science, 3*(3), 77–82.

Honts, C. R. (1995). The polygraph in 1995: Progress in science and the law. *North Dakota Law Review, 17,* 987–1020.

Honts, C. R. (2004). The physiological detection of deception. In P. A. Granhag & L. A. Stromwall (Eds.), *Deception detection in forensic contexts* (pp. 103–123). Cambridge, UK: Cambridge University Press.

Honts, C. R., Raskin, D. C., & Kircher, J. C. (1987). Effects of physical countermeasures and their elecromyographic detection during polygraph tests for deception. *Journal of Psychophysiology, 1,* 241–247.

Horley, J., & Bowlby, D. (2011). Theory, research, and intervention with arsonists. *Aggression and Violent Behavior, 16*(3), 241–249.

Hornak, J., Bramham, J., Rolls, E. T., Morris, R. G., O'Doherty, J., Bullock, P. R., et al (2003). Changes in emotion after circumscribed surgical lesions of the orbitofrontal and cingulate cortices. *Brain, 126,* 1691–1712.

Horowitz, I. A., & Willging, T. E. (1984). *The psychology of law: Integrations and applications.* Boston: Little, Brown.

Horowitz, M. J., Wilner, N., & Alvarez, W. (1979). Impact of event scale: A measure of subjective stress. *Psychosomatic Medicine, 41,* 209–218.

Howard, D., Quinn, S., Blokland, J., & Flynn, M. (1993). Aboriginal hearing loss and the criminal justice system. *Aboriginal Law Bulletin, 3,* 9–11.

Howlett, D. (1995, November 13). He has eluded FBI and police for 17 years. *USA Today,* pp. 1A–2A.

Huber, P. (1988). *Liability: The legal revolution and its consequences.* New York: Basic Books.

Huff, C. R., Rattner, A., & Sagarin, E. (1996). *Convicted but innocent: Wrongful conviction and public policy.* Thousand Oaks, CA: Sage.

Huffington Post. (2012). Allan Schoenborn murders: B. C. to release report on children murdered by father. Retrieved July 23, 2012, from http://www.huffingtonpost.ca/2012/03/01/allan-schoenborn-murders_n_1312642.html

Humm, D. G., & Humm, K. A. (1950). Humm-Wadsworth Temperament Scale appraisals compared with criteria of job success in the Los Angeles Police Department. *Journal of Psychology, 30,* 63–75.

Huq, A. Z., Tyler, T. R., & Schulhofer, S. J. (2011). Why does the public cooperate with law enforcement? The influence of the purposes and targets of policing. *Psychology, Public Policy, and Law, 17,* 419–450.

Hurley, C. M., & Frank, M. G. (2011). Executing facial control during deception situations. *Journal of Nonverbal Behavior, 35,* 119–131.

Huss, M. T., & Langhinrichsen-Rohling, J. (2006). Assessing the generalization of psychopathy in a clinical sample of domestic violence perpetrators. *Law and Human Behavior, 30,* 571–586.

Hutchins, R. M., & Slesinger, D. (1928a). Some observations on the law of evidence—Spontaneous exclamations. *Columbia Law Review, 28,* 432–440.

Hutchins, R. M., & Slesinger, D. (1928b). Some observations on the law of evidence—Memory. *Harvard Law Review, 41,* 860–873.

Hutchins, R. M., & Slesinger, D. (1928c). Some observations on the law of evidence—The competency of witnesses. *Yale Law Journal, 37,* 1017–1028.

Hutchison, I. (2003). Substance use and abused women's utilization of the police. *Journal of Family Violence, 18,* 93–106.

Hyde, J. S., & DeLamater, J. D. (2003). *Understanding human sexuality.* (8th ed.). New York: McGraw-Hill.

Hyman, I. E., Husband, T. H., & Billings, F. J. (1995). False memories of childhood experiences. *Applied Cognitive Psychology, 9,* 181–197.

Iacono, W. G. (2008). Effective policing: Understanding how polygraph tests work and are used. *Criminal Justice and Behavior, 35,* 1295–1308.

Iacono, W. G., & Patrick, C. J. (1997). Polygraphy and integrity testing. In R. Rogers (Ed.), *Clinical assessment of malingering and deception* (2nd ed, pp. 252–281). New York: Guilford Press.

Iacono, W. G., & Patrick, C. J. (1999). Polygraph ("lie detector") testing: The state of the art. In A. K. Hess & I. B. Weiner (Eds.), *The handbook of forensic psychology* (2nd ed., pp. 440–473). New York: John Wiley.

Ibn-Tamas v. United States, 407 A.2d 626 (1979).

Ilfeld, F. W., Ilfeld, H. Z., & Alexander, J. R. (1982). Does joint custody work? A first look at outcome data of relitigation. *American Journal of Psychiatry, 139,* 62–66.

Inbau, F. E., & Reid, J. E. (1962). *Criminal interrogation and confessions*. Baltimore: Williams and Wilkins.

Inbau, F. E., Reid, J. E., & Buckley, J. P. (1986). *Criminal interrogation and confessions* (3rd ed.). Baltimore: Williams and Wilkins.

Inbau, F. E., Reid, J. E., Buckley, J. P. & Jayne, B. C. (2001). *Criminal interrogation and confessions* (4th ed.). Sudbury, MA: Jones and Bartlett Publishers.

Innocence Network. (2012). Innocence Network Exonerations 2011. Retrieved July 23, 2012, from http://www.innocencenetwork.org/annual-reports/innocence-network-report-2011

Innocence Project. (2009). Understanding the causes: Eyewitness identification. Retrieved May 11, 2012, from www.theinnocenceproject.org

Innocence Project. (2010). Innocence Project. Retrieved November 2010, from http://www.innocenceproject.org

Innocence Project website. (2011). Innocence project case files. Retrieved May 15, 2012, from http://www.innocenceproject.org/know

Inwald, R. (1990). *Fitness-for-duty evaluation guidelines: A survey for police/public safety administrators and mental health professionals*. Paper presented at the meetings of the American Psychological Association, Boston.

Inwald, R., & Shusman, E. (1984). The IPI and MMPI as predictors of academy performance for police recruits. *Journal of Police Science and Administration, 12,* 1–11.

Inwald, R., Knatz, H., & Shusman, E. (1983). *Inwald Personality Inventory Manual*. Kew Gardens, NY: Hilson Research.

Isikoff, M. (1994, March 21–27). The Foster case: Grist for the Whitewater rumor mill. *Washington Post National Weekly Edition*, p. 8.

Iverson, G. L., Franzen, M. D., & Hammond, J. A. (1993, August). *Examination of inmates' ability to malinger on the MMPI-2*. Paper presented at the meetings of the American Psychological Association, Toronto.

Jackman, M. R. (1978). General and applied tolerance: Does education increase commitment to racial integration? *American Journal of Political Science, 22,* 302–324.

Jackson, J. L., & Bekeran, D. A. (1997). Does offender profiling have a role to play? In J. L. Jackson & D. A. Bekerian (Eds.), *Offender profiling: Theory, research and practice* (pp. 1–7). New York: John Wiley.

Jackson, J. L., van den Eshof, P., & de Kleuver, E. E. (1997). A research approach to offender profiling. In J. L. Jackson & D. A. Bekerian (Eds.), *Offender profiling: Theory, research and practice* (pp. 107–132). New York: John Wiley.

Jacobs, R., Cushenbery, L., & Grabarek, P. (2011). Assessments for selection and promotion of police officers. In J. Kitaeff, J. Kitaeff (Eds.), *Handbook of police psychology* (pp. 193–210). New York: Routledge/Taylor & Francis Group.

Jaffe, P. G., & Juodis, M. (2006). Children as victims and witnesses of domestic homicide: Lessons learned from domestic violence death review committees. *Juvenile and Family Court Journal, 57*(3), 13–28.

Jaffe, P. G., Hastings, E., Reitzel, D., & Austin, G. W. (1993). The impact of police laying charges. In N. Z. Hilton (Ed.), *Legal responses to wife assault* (pp. 62–95). Newbury Park, CA: Sage.

Janik, J. (1993, August). *Pre-employment interviews of law enforcement officer candidates*. Paper presented at the meetings of the American Psychological Association, Toronto.

Janoff-Bulman, R. (1979). Characterological versus behavioral self-blame: Inquiries into depression and rape. *Journal of Personality and Social Psychology, 37,* 1798–1809.

Janofsky, J. S., Spears, S., & Neubauer, D. N. (1988). Psychiatrists' accuracy in predicting violent behavior on an inpatient unit. *Hospital and Community Psychiatry, 39,* 1090–1094.

Jeary, K. (2005). Sexual abuse and sexual offending against elderly people: A focus on perpetrators and victims. *Journal of Forensic Psychiatry & Psychology, 16*(2), 328–343.

Jenkins, P., & Davidson, B. (1990). Battered women in the criminal justice system: An analysis of gender stereotypes. *Behavioral Sciences and the Law, 8,* 161–170.

Jespersen, A. F., Lalumière, M. L., & Seto, M. C. (2009). Sexual abuse history among adult sex offenders and non-sex offenders: A meta-analysis. *Child Abuse & Neglect, 33*(3), 179–192.

Jobes, D. A., Berman, A. L., & Josselson, A. R. (1986). The impact of psychological autopsies on medical examiners' determination of manner of death. *Journal of Forensic Sciences, 31,* 177–189.

Johansson-Love, J., & Fremouw, W. (2006). A critique of the female sexual perpetrator research. *Aggression and Violent Behavior, 11*(1), 12–26.

Johansson-Love, J., & Fremouw, W. (2009). Female sex offenders: A controlled comparison of offender and victim/crime characteristics. *Journal of Family Violence, 24*(6), 367–376.

Johnson, A. (2008). *Organizational cynicism and occupational stress in police officers*. (Doctoral Dissertation).

Johnson, H. (1996). Violent crime in Canada. *Juristat, 16,* 6. Canadian Centre for Justice Statistics, Statistics Canada.

Johnson, H. (2006). *Measuring violence against women* (Report No. 85-570-XIE). Retrieved May 15, 2012, from http://www.statcan.gc.ca/pub/85-570-x/85-570-x2006001-eng.pdf

Johnson, I. M. (1990). A loglinear analysis of wives' decisions to call the police in domestic-violence disputes. *Journal of Criminal Justice, 18,* 147–159.

Johnson, J. (1994, May 16). Witness for the prosecution. *New Yorker*, pp. 42–51.

Johnson, K. (1998, April 16). New breed of bad cop sells badge, public trust. *USA Today*, p. 8A.

Johnson, L. B., Todd, M., & Subramanian, G. (2005) Violence in police families: Work-family spillover. *Journal of Family Violence, 20,* 3-12.

Johnson, M. P. (1995). Patriarchal terrorism and common couple violence: Two forms of violence against women. *Journal of Marriage and the Family, 57,* 283-294.

Johnson, R. R. (2011). Predicting officer physical assaults at domestic assault calls. *Journal of Family Violence, 26,* 163-169.

Jolliffe, D., & Farrington, D. P. (2004). Empathy and offending: A systematic review and meta-analysis. *Aggression and Violent Behavior, 9*(5), 441-476.

Jones, A. (1981). *Women who kill.* New York: Holt Rinehart.

Jones, A. (1994a, March 10). Crimes against women. *USA Today,* p. 9A.

Jones, A. (1994b). *Next time, she'll be dead: Battering and how to stop it.* Boston: Beacon Press.

Jones, D. A., & Belknap, J. (1996). Police responses to battering in a pro-arrest jurisdiction. *Justice Quarterly, 16,* 249-273.

Jones, E. E. (1990). *Interpersonal perception.* San Francisco: Freeman.

Jones, E. E., & Davis, K. E. (1965). A theory of correspondent inferences: From acts to dispositions. In L. Berkowitz (Ed.), *Advances in experimental social psychology* (Vol. 2, pp. 219-266). San Diego: Academic Press.

Jones, E. E., & Harris, V. A. (1967). The attribution of attitudes. *Journal of Experimental Social Psychology, 3,* 1-24.

Jones, H. H., & Powell, J. L. (2006). Old age, vulnerability and sexual violence: Implications for knowledge and practice. *International Nursing Review, 53*(3), 211-216.

Jones, J. W. (1995). Counseling issues and police diversity. In M. I. Kurke & E. M. Scrivner (Eds.), *Police psychology into the 21st century* (pp. 207-254). Hillsdale, NJ: Lawrence Erlbaum.

Jordan, C. E., Campbell, R., & Follingstad, D. (2010). Violence and women's mental health: The impact of physical, sexual, and psychological aggression. *Annual Review of Clinical Psychology,* 6607-6628.

Juodis, M., Woodworth, M., Porter, S., ten Brinke, L. (2009). Partners in crime: A comparison of individual and multi-perpetrator homicides. *Criminal Justice and Behavior, 36,* 824-839.

Jurgensen, K. (1994, October 20). Again, a "passion killer" gets away with murder. *USA Today,* p. 12A.

Jurow, G. L. (1971). New data on the effect of a "death qualified" jury on the guilt determination process. *Harvard Law Review, 84,* 567-611.

Kagehiro, D. K., & Stanton, W. C. (1985). Legal vs. quantified definitions of standards of proof. *Law and Human Behavior, 9,* 159-178.

Kahn, K. B., & Davies, P. G. (2011). Differentially dangerous? Phenotypic racial stereotypicality increases implicit bias among ingroup and outgroup members. *Group Processes and Intergroup Relations,* 14, 569-580.

Kahneman, D., & Tversky, A. (1982a). A reply to Evans. *Cognition, 12,* 325-326.

Kahneman, D., & Tversky, A. (1982b). On the study of statistical intuitions. *Cognition, 11,* 123-141.

Kahneman, D., & Tversky, A. (1982c). The psychology of preferences. *Scientific American, 246,* 160-173.

Kalven, H., & Zeisel, H. (1966). *The American jury.* Boston: Little, Brown.

Kaminker, L. (1992, November 16). An angry cry for mute voices. *Newsweek,* p. 16.

Kantor, G. K., & Straus, M. A. (1990). The "Drunken Bum" theory of wife beating. In M. A. Straus, & R. A. Gelles (Eds.), *Physical violence in American families* (pp. 203-234). New Brunswick, NJ: Transaction.

Kaplan, M. S., & Green, A. (1995). Incarcerated female sexual offenders: A comparison of sexual histories with eleven female nonsexual offenders. *Sexual Abuse: Journal of Research and Treatment, 7*(4), 287-300.

Kargon, R. (1986). Expert testimony in historical perspective. *Law and Human Behavior, 10,* 15-27.

Kassin, S. M. & Fong, C. T. (1999). "I'm Innocent!": Effects of training on judgments of truth and deception in the interrogation room. *Law and Human Behavior, 23,* 499-516.

Kassin, S. M. (1997a). False memories turned against the self. *Psychological Inquiry, 8,* 300-302.

Kassin, S. M. (1997b). The psychology of confession evidence. *American Psychologist, 52,* 221-233.

Kassin, S. M. (1998a). Clinical psychology in court: House of junk science? *Contemporary Psychology, 43,* 321-324.

Kassin, S. M. (1998b). Eyewitness identification procedures: The fifth rule. *Law and Human Behavior, 22,* 649-653.

Kassin, S. M. (2007). Internalized false confessions. In M. P. Toglia, J. Read, D. F. Ross, R. L. Lindsay, M. P. Toglia, J. Read, et al (Eds.), *The handbook of eyewitness psychology, Vol I: Memory for events* (pp. 175-192). Mahwah, NJ: Lawrence Erlbaum Associates Publishers.

Kassin, S. M. (2008). Confession evidence: Commonsense myths and misconceptions. *Criminal Justice and Behavior, 35,* 1309-1322.

Kassin, S. M., & Barndollar, K. A. (1992). The psychology of eyewitness testimony: A comparison of experts and prospective jurors. *Journal of Applied Social Psychology, 22*(16), 1241-1249.

Kassin, S. M., & Barndollar, K. A. (1992). The psychology of eyewitness testimony: A comparison of experts and prospective jurors. *Journal of Applied Social Psychology, 22,* 1241-1249.

Kassin, S. M., & Kiechel, K. L. (1996). The social psychology of false confessions: Compliance, internalization, and confabulation. *Psychological Science, 7,* 125-128.

Kassin, S. M., & McNall, K. (1991). Police interrogation and confessions: Communicating promises and threats by pragmatic implication. *Law and Human Behavior, 15,* 233-251.

Kassin, S. M., & Sukel, H. (1997). Coerced confessions and the jury: An experimental test of the "harmless error" rule. *Law and Human Behavior, 21,* 27-46.

Kassin, S. M., & Wrightsman, L. S. (1983). The construction and validation of a Juror Bias Scale. *Journal of Research in Personality, 17,* 423-442.

Kassin, S. M., & Wrightsman, L. S. (1985). Confession evidence. In S. M. Kassin & L. S. Wrightsman (Eds.), *The psychology of evidence and trial procedure* (pp. 67-94). Thousand Oaks, CA: Sage.

Kassin, S. M., Appleby, S. C., & Perillo, J. (2010a). Interviewing suspects: Practice, science, and future directions. *Legal and Criminological Psychology, 15*(1), 39-55.

Kassin, S. M., Drizin, S. A., Grisso, T., Gudjonsson, G. H., Leo, R. A., & Redlich, A. D. (2010b). Police-induced confessions: Risk factors and recommendations. *Law and Human Behavior, 34,* 3-38.

Kassin, S. M., Ellsworth, P. C., & Smith, V. L. (1989). The "general acceptance" of psychological research on eyewitness testimony: A survey of the experts. *American Psychologist, 44*(8), 1089-1098.

Kassin, S. M., Tubb, V., Hosch, H. M., & Memon, A. (2001). On the "general acceptance" of eyewitness testimony research: A new survey of the experts. *American Psychologist, 56*(5), 405-416.

Kassin, S., Goldstein, C. J., & Savitsky, K. (2003). Behavioral confirmation in the interrogation room: On the dangers of presuming guilt. *Law and Human Behavior, 27*(2), 187-203.

Kaufmann, G., Drevland, G. B., Wessel, E., Overskeid, G., & Magnussen, S. (2003). The importance of being earnest: Displayed emotions and witness credibility. *Applied Cognitive Psychology, 17*(1), 21-34.

Kaufmann, G., Drevland, G. C. B., Wessel, E., Overskeid, G., & Magnussen, S. (2003). The importance of being earnest: Displayed emotions and witness credibility *Applied Cognitive Psychology, 17,* 21-34.

Kebbell, M. R., & Wagstaff, G. F. (1997). Why do the police interview eyewitnesses? Interview objectives and the evaluation of eyewitness performance. *Journal of Psychology, 131,* 595-601.

Kebbell, M. R. and Milne, R. (1998), Police officers' perceptions of eyewitness performance in forensic investigations. *Journal of Social Psychology, 138,* 323-39.

Keleher, C. (2010). *The Repercussions of Anonymous Juries,* 44 U.S F. L. REV. 531.

Keller, S. R., & Weiner, R. L. (2011). What are we studying? Student jurors, community jurors, and construct validity. *Behavioral Sciences & the Law, 29,* 376-394.

Kelln, B., & McMurtry, C. M. (2007). STEPS—Structured tactical engagement process. *Journal of Police Crisis Negotiations, 7,* 29-51.

Kelly, J. F., & Wearne, P. K. (1998). *Tainting evidence: Inside the scandals at the FBI crime lab.* New York: Free Press.

Keltner, D., & Buswell, B. N. (1996). Evidence for the distinctness of embarrassment, shame, and guilt: A study of recalled antecedents and facial expressions of emotion. *Cognition and Emotion, 10,* 155-171.

Kendall-Tackett, K. A., Williams, L. M., & Finkelhor, D. (1993). Impact of sexual abuse on children: A review and synthesis of recent empirical studies. *Psychological Bulletin, 113,* 164-180.

Kennedy, M. A., & Yuille, J. C. (1999, November). *Recent complaint: The fallacy of raising a "hue and cry" after a sexual assault.* 48th Annual Conference of the Canadian Society of Forensic Science, Edmonton, AB.

Kent, J., & Leitner, M. (2007). Efficacy of standard deviational ellipses in the application of criminal geographic profiling. *Journal of Investigative Psychology and Offender Profiling, 4*(3), 147-165.

Kiehl, K. A. (2006). A cognitive neuroscience perspective on psychopathy: Evidence for paralimbic system dysfunction. *Psychiatry Research, 142*(2-3), 107-128.

Kihlstrom, J. F. (1996). The trauma-memory argument and recovered memory therapy. In K. Pezdek & W. P. Banks (Eds.), *The recovered memory/false memory debate* (pp. 297-311). San Diego, CA: Academic Press.

Kilpatrick, D. G. (1983, Summer). Rape victims: Detection, assessment and treatment. *Clinical Psychologist,* pp. 92-95.

Kilpatrick, D. G., & Amick, A. E. (1985). Rape trauma. In M. Hersen & C. G. Last (Eds.), *Behavior therapy casebook* (pp. 86-103). New York: Springer.

Kilpatrick, D. G., & Veronen, L. J. (1984). *Treatment of fear and anxiety in victims of rape* (Final report, NIMH Grant No. HMH29602). Rockville, MD: National Institute of Mental Health.

Kilpatrick, D. G., Best, C. L., Veronen, L. J., Amick, A. E., Villeponteaux, L. A., & Ruff, G. A. (1985). Mental health correlates of criminal victimization: A random community survey. *Journal of Consulting and Clinical Psychology, 53,* 866-873.

Kilpatrick, D. G., Resick, P., & Veronen, L. (1981). Effects of a rape experience: A longitudinal study. *Journal of Social Issues, 37*(4), 105-112.

Kilpatrick, D. G., Veronen, L. J., & Best, C. L. (1985). Factors predicting psychological distress among rape victims. In C. R. Figley (Ed.), *Trauma and its wake* (pp. 113-141). New York: Brunner/Mazel.

King, L., & Snook, B. (2009). Peering inside a Canadian interrogation room: An examination of the Reid model of interrogation, influence tactics, and coercive strategies. *Criminal Justice and Behavior, 36*(7), 674–694.

Kingshott, B. F. (2010). Serious crime: Managing the media. Academy Criminal Justice Sciences (ACJS) 2010 Conference. San Diego, CA.

Kingston, D. A., Seto, M. C., Firestone, P., & Bradford, J. M. (2010). Comparing indicators of sexual sadism as predictors of recidivism among adult male sexual offenders. *Journal of Consulting and Clinical Psychology, 78*(4), 574–584.

Kingston, D. A., Yates, P. M., Firestone, P., Babchishin, K., & Bradford, J. M. (2008). Long-term predictive validity of the Risk Matrix 2000: A comparison with the Static-99 and the Sex Offender Risk Appraisal Guide. *Sexual Abuse: Journal of Research and Treatment, 20*(4), 466–484.

Kitaeff, J. (Ed.). (2011). *Handbook of police psychology.* New York: Routledge/Taylor & Francis Group.

Klaver, J., Lee, Z., & Hart, S. D. (2007). Psychopathy and nonverbal indicators of deception in offenders. *Law and Human Behavior, 31,* 337–351.

Klippenstine, M. A., & Schuller, R. (2012). Perceptions of sexual assault: Expectancies regarding the emotional response of a rape victim over time. *Psychology, Crime & Law, 18*(1), 79–94.

Klippenstine, M., Schuller, R. A., & Wall, A-M. (2007). Perceptions of sexual assault: The role of alcohol and sexual experience. *Journal of Applied Social Psychology, 37,* 2620–2641.

Klostermann, K., Kelley, M. L., Mignone, T., Pusateri, L., & Fals-Stewart, W. (2010). Partner violence, and substance abuse: Treatment interventions. *Aggression and Violent Behavior, 15,* 162–166.

Kluger, R. (1976). *Simple justice.* New York: Alfred A. Knopf.

Knoll, J. (2010). Teacher sexual misconduct: Grooming patterns and female offenders. *Journal of Child Sexual Abuse: Research, Treatment, & Program Innovations for Victims, Survivors, & Offenders, 19*(4), 371–386.

Kocsis, R. N. (2007). *Criminal profiling: International theory, research, and practice.* Totowa, NJ: Humana Press.

Kocsis, R. N. (2010). Criminal profiling works and everyone agrees. *Journal of Forensic Psychology Practice, 10*(3), 224–237.

Kocsis, R. N., Middledorp, J., & Karpin, A. (2008). Taking stock of accuracy in criminal profiling: The theoretical quandary for investigative psychology. *Journal of Forensic Psychology Practice, 8*(3), 244–261.

Kolasa, B. J. (1972). Psychology and law. *American Psychologist, 27,* 499–503.

Konečni, V. J. & Ebbesen, E. B. (1982). An analysis of the sentencing system. In Konečni, V. J., & Ebbesen, E. B. (Eds.), *The criminal justice system: A social-psychological analysis.* (pp. 293–332.) San Francisco: W. H. Freeman.

Konecni, V. J., & Ebbesen, E. B. (1986). Courtroom testimony by psychologists on eyewitness identification issues: Critical notes and reflections. *Law and Human Behavior, 10,* 117–126.

Koocher, G. P., Goodman, G. S., White, C. S., Friedrich, W. N., Sivan, A. B., & Reynolds, C. R. (1995). Psychological science and the use of anatomically detailed dolls in child sexual-abuse assessments. *Psychological Bulletin, 118,* 199–222.

Korva, N., Porter, S., O'Connor, B., Shaw J., & ten Brinke, L. (2012, in press). Dangerous decisions: Influence of juror attitude and defendant appearance on legal decision-making. *Psychiatry, Psychology, and Law.*

Korva, N., Porter, S., O'Connor, B., Shaw, J., & ten Brinke, L. (2012, in press). Dangerous decisions: Influence of juror attitudes and defendant appearance on legal decision-making. *Psychiatry, Psychology and Law.*

Koss, M. P. (1988). Hidden rape: Incidence, prevalence, and descriptive characteristics of sexual aggression and victimization in a national sample of college students. In A. W. Burgess (Ed.), *Sexual assault* (Vol. II, pp. 3–25). New York: Garland.

Koss, M. P. (1993). Detecting the scope of rape: A review of prevalence research methods. *Journal of Interpersonal Violence, 8,* 198–222.

Koss, M. P., & Harvey, M. R. (1991). *The rape victim: Clinical and community interventions* (2nd ed.). Thousand Oaks, CA: Sage.

Kosson, D. S., Cyterski, T. D., Steuerwald, B., Neumann, C. S., & Walker-Matthews, S. (2002). The reliability and validity of the Psychopathy Checklist: Youth Version (PCL:YV) in nonincarcerated adolescent males. *Psychological Assessment, 14*(1), 97–109.

Kosson, D., Kelly, J., & White, J. (1997). Psychopathy-related traits predict self-reported sexual aggression among college men. *Journal of Interpersonal Violence, 12,* 241–254.

Kotlowitz, A. (1999, February 8). The unprotected. *New Yorker,* pp. 42–53.

Kraepelin, E. (1915). *Psychiatrie: Ein lehrbuch* (8th ed., Vol. 4). Leipzig, Germany: Barth.

Krafft-Ebing, R. von (1898/1965). *Psychopathia Sexualis.* (12th ed, F. Klaf, Trans.). New York: Bell Publishing Company

Krahenbuhl, S., Blades, M., & Eiser, C. (2009). The effect of repeated questioning on children's accuracy and consistency in eyewitness testimony. *Legal and Criminological Psychology, 14,* 263–278.

Kramer, G. M., & Gagliardi, G. J. (2009). Forensic evaluation of insanity: Assessing valid symptom report in defendants with major mental disorder. *Journal of Forensic Psychology Practice, 9*(1), 92–102.

Kramer, M. (1997, December 15). How cops go bad. *Time,* pp. 78–83.

Kraske, S. (1986, November 25). Victim of abduction, rapes recounts ordeal of terror. *Kansas City Star,* pp. 1A, 8A.

Kravitz, D. A., Cutler, B. L., & Brock, P. (1993). Reliability and validity of the original and revised Legal Attitudes Questionnaire. *Law and Human Behavior, 17,* 661–677.

Kreis, M. F., & Cooke, D. J. (2011). Capturing the psychopathic female: A prototypicality analysis of the Comprehensive Assessment of Psychopathic Personality (CAPP) across gender. *Behavioral Sciences & the Law, 29*(5), 634–648.

Kretschmer, E. (1925). *Physique and character.* New York: Harcourt.

Kroes, W., Margolis, B., & Hurrell, J. (1974). Job stress in policemen. *Journal of Police Science and Administration, 2*(2), 145–155.

Kropp, P. R. & Hart, S. D. (2000). The Spousal Assault Risk Assessment (SARA) guide: Reliability and validity in adult male offenders. *Law and Human Behavior, 24,* 101–118.

Kropp, P. R., & Hart, S. D. (1997). Assessing risk for violence in wife assaulters: The Spousal Assault Risk Assessment Guide. In C. D. Webster & M. A. Jackson (Eds.), *Impulsivity: Theory, assessment, and treatment* (pp. 302–325.) New York: Guilford.

Kropp, P. R., Hart, S. D., Webster, C. D., & Eaves, D (1995a). *Spousal assault risk assessment guide (SARA): Users Manual* (version 2). Vancouver: British Columbia Institute Against Family Violence.

Kropp, P. R., Hart, S. D., Webster, C. D., & Eaves, D. (1995b). *Manual for Spousal Assault Risk Assessment Guide* (2nd ed.). Vancouver, Canada: British Columbia Institute on Family Violence.

Kropp, P. R., Hart, S. D., Webster, C. W., & Eaves, D. (1998). *Spousal Assault Risk Assessment: User's guide.* Toronto: Multi-Health Systems.

Kugler, M. B., & Cooper, J. (2010). Still an American? Mortality salience and treatment of suspected terrorists. *Journal of Applied Social Psychology, 40*(12), 3130–3147.

Kulka, R. A., & Kessler, J. R. (1978). Is justice really blind? The effect of litigant physical attractiveness on judicial judgment. *Journal of Applied Social Psychology, 4,* 336–381.

Kurke, M. I., & Scrivner, E. M. (Eds.). (1995). *Police psychology into the 21st century.* Hillsdale, NJ: Lawrence Erlbaum.

Kwong, M. J., Bartholomew, K., & Dutton, D. G. (1999). Gender differences in patterns of relationship violence in Alberta. *Canadian Journal of Behavioural Science/Revue Canadienne Des Sciences Du Comportement, 31*(3), 150–160.

La Fon, D. S. (2008). The psychological autopsy. In B. E. Turvey (Ed), *Criminal profiling: An introduction to behavioral evidence analysis (3rd ed.)* (pp. 419–429). San Diego, CA: Elsevier Academic Press.

Labaton, S. (1993a, July 12). Pursuers grappling with smoke on bomber's long trail of fear. *New York Times,* pp. A1, A8.

Labaton, S. (1993b, October 7). Clue and $1 million reward in case of serial bomber. *New York Times, p.* A10.

Laboratory of Community Psychiatry. (1974). *Competency to stand trial and mental illness.* Northvale, NJ: Jason Aronson.

Labree, W., Nijman, H., van Marle, H., et al (2010) Backgrounds and characteristics of arsonists. *International Journal of Law and Psychiatry, 33,* 149–153

Lacayo, R. (1991, April 8). Confessions that were taboo are now just a technicality. *Time,* pp. 26–27.

Lalumière, M. L., & Quinsey, V. _. (1994). The discriminability of rapists from non-sex offenders using phallometric measures: A meta-analysis. *Criminal Justice and Behavior, 21*(1), 150–175.

Lamb, M. E., Orbach, Y., Sternberg, K. L., Aldridge, J., Pearson, S., Stewart, H. L., et al. (2009). Use of a structured investigative protocol enhances the quality of investigative interviews with alleged victims of child sexual abuse in Britain. *Applied Cognitive Psychology, 23*(4), 449–467.

LaMotte, V., Ouellette, K., Sanderson, J., Anderson, S. A., Kosutic, I., Griggs, J., et al. (2010). Effective police interactions with youth: A program evaluation. *Police Quarterly, 13,* 161–179.

Landers, S. (1988, June). Use of "detailed dolls" questioned. *APA Monitor,* pp. 24–25.

Landström, S., & Granhag, P. (2010). In-court versus out-of-court testimonies: Children's experiences and adults' assessments. *Applied Cognitive Psychology, 24*(7), 941–955.

Langer, W. C. (1972). *The mind of Adolf Hitler.* New York: Basic Books.

Langevin, R. (2003). A study of the psychosexual characteristics of sex killers: Can we identify them before it is too late? *International Journal of Offender Therapy and Comparative Criminology, 47*(4), 366–382.

Langevin, R., & Curnoe, S. (2004). The use of pornography during the commission of sexual offenses. *International Journal of Offender Therapy and Comparative Criminology, 48*(5), 572–586.

Langevin, R., & Curnoe, S. (2008). Assessing neuropsychological impairment among sex offenders and paraphilics. *Journal of Forensic Psychology Practice, 8*(2), 150–173.

Langevin, R., Paitich, D., Freeman, R., Mann, K., & Handy, L. (1978). Personality characteristics and sexual anomalies in males. *Canadian Journal of Behavioural Science, 10,* 222–238.

Langfeld, H. S. (1920). Psychophysical symptoms of deception. *Journal of Abnormal Psychology, 15,* 319–328.

Langleben, D. D. (2008). Detection of deception with fMRI: Are we there yet? *Legal and Criminological Psychology, 13*(1), 1–9.

Langleben, D. D. (2008). Detection of deception with fMRI: Are we there yet? *Legal and Criminological Psychology, 13*(1), 1-9.

Långström, N. (2010). The DSM diagnostic criteria for exhibitionism, voyeurism, and frotteurism. *Archives of Sexual Behavior, 39*(2), 317-324.

Långström, N., & Seto, M. C. (2006). Exhibitionistic and voyeuristic behavior in a swedish national population survey. *Archives of Sexual Behavior, 35*(4), 427-435.

Langton, C. M., Barbaree, H. E., Harkins, L., Arenovich, T., McNamee, J., Peacock, E. J., et al. (2008). Denial and minimization among sexual offenders: Posttreatment presentation and association with sexual recidivism. *Criminal Justice and Behavior, 35*(1), 69-98.

Larochelle, S., Diguer, L., Laverdière, O., & Greenman, P. (2011). Predictors of psychological treatment noncompletion among sexual offenders. *Clinical Psychology Review, 31*(4), 554-562.

Lassiter, Daniel G. G. (2010). Videotaped interrogations and confessions: What's obvious in hindsight may not be in foresight. *Law and Human Behavior, 34*(1), 41-42.

Lassiter, G. D., & Meissner, C. A. (Eds.). (2010). *Police interrogations and confessions: Current research, practice and policy*. Washington DC: American Psychological Association.

Lassiter, G. D., Ware, L. J., Lindberg, M. J., & Ratcliff, J. J. (2010). Videotaping custodial interrogations: Toward a scientifically based policy. In G. D. Lassiter & C. A. Meissner (Eds.), *Police interrogations and false confessions: Current research, practice, and policy recommendations* (pp. 143-160). Washington, DC: American Psychological Association.

Laufer, W. S., & Walt, S. D. (1992). The law and psychology of precedent. In D. K. Kagehiro & W. S. Laufer (Eds.), *Handbook of psychology and law* (pp. 39-55). New York: Springer-Verlag.

Lawing, K., Frick, P. J., & Cruise, K. R. (2010). Differences in offending patterns between adolescent sex offenders high or low in callous–unemotional traits. *Psychological Assessment, 22*(2), 298-305.

Lawrence, R. (1984). Checking the allure of increased conviction rates: The admissibility of expert testimony on rape trauma syndrome in criminal proceedings. *University of Virginia Law Review, 79*, 1657-1704.

Lawyer, S., Resnick, H., Bakanic, V., Burkett, T., & Kilpatrick, D. (2010). Forcible, drug-facilitated, and incapacitated rape and sexual assault among undergraduate women. *Journal of American College Health, 58*(5), 453-460.

Leal, S., & Vrij, A. (2010). The occurrence of eye blinks during a guilty knowledge test. *Psychology, Crime & Law, 16*, 349-357.

Lecci, L., & Myers, B. (1996, August). *Validating the factor structure of the Juror Bias Scale*. Paper presented at the meetings of the American Psychological Association, Toronto.

Lee, G. P., Loring, D. W., & Martin, R. C. (1992). Rey's 15-item visual memory test for the detection of malingering: Normative observations on patients with neurological disorders. *Psychological Assessment, 1*, 43-46.

Lee, Z., Klaver, J. R., Hart, S. D., Moretti, M. M., & Douglas, K. S. (2009). Short-term stability of psychopathic traits in adolescent offenders. *Journal of Clinical Child and Adolescent Psychology, 38*(5), 595-605.

Leichtman, M. D. & Ceci, S. J. (1995). The effects of stereotypes and suggestions on preschooler's reports. *Developmental Psychology, 31*, 568-578.

Leippe, M. R. (1995). The case for expert testimony about eyewitness memory. *Psychology, Public Policy, and Law, 1*, 909-959.

Leippe, M. R., Eisenstadt, D., & Rauch, S. M. (2009). Cueing confidence in eyewitness identifications: Influence of biased lineup instructions and pre-identification memory feedback under varying lineup conditions. *Law and Human Behavior, 33*, 194-212.

Leippe, M. R., Wells, G. L., & Ostrom, T. M. (1978). Crime seriousness as a determinant of accuracy in eyewitness identification. *Journal of Applied Psychology, 63*, 345-351.

Leistico, A. R., Salekin, R. T., DeCoster, J., & Rogers, R. (2008). A large-scale meta-analysis relating the Hare measures of psychopathy to antisocial conduct. *Law and Human Behavior, 32*(1), 28-45.

Leo, R. A. (1992). From coercion to deception: The changing nature of police interrogation in America. *Crime, Law, and Social Change, 18*, 35-39.

Leo, R. A. (1996a). The impact of *Miranda* revisited. *Journal of Criminal Law and Criminology, 86*, 621-692.

Leo, R. A. (1996b). Inside the interrogation room. *Journal of Criminal Law and Criminology, 86*, 266-303.

Leo, R. A. (1996c). *Miranda*'s revenge: Police interrogation as a confidence game. *Law and Society Review, 30*, 259-288.

Leo, R. A. (2008). *Police interrogation and American justice*. Cambridge, MA: Harvard University Press.

Leo, R. A., & Davis, D. (2010). From false confession to wrongful conviction: Seven psychological processes. *Journal of Psychiatry & Law, 38*(1-2), 9-56.

Leserman, J. (2005). Sexual abuse history: Prevalence, health effects, mediators, and psychological treatment. *Psychosomatic Medicine, 67*(6), 906-915.

Levine, L. J., & Pizzarro, D. A. (2004). Emotion and memory research: A grumpy overview. *Social Cognition, 22*, 530-554.

Levy, C. J. (1994, December 12). F.B.I. says fatal mail blast is work of serial bomber. *New York Times*, pp. A1, A12.

Lewis, A. (1993, April 23). After the buck stops. *The New York Times*, p. A19.

Lewis, C. F., & Stanley, C. R. (2000). Women accused of sexual offenses. *Behavioral Sciences & the Law, 18*(1), 73–81.

Liang, B., Williams, L. M., & Siegel, J. A. (2006). Relational outcomes of childhood sexual trauma in female survivors: A longitudinal study. *Journal of Interpersonal Violence, 21*(1), 42–57.

Lie, G., Schilit, R., Bush, R., Montagne, M., & Reyes, L. (1991). Lesbians in currently aggressive relationships: How frequently do they report aggressive past relationships? *Violence and Victims, 6*, 121–135.

Lieberman, J. D. (2011). The utility of scientific jury selection: Still murky after 30 years. *Psychological Science, 20*(1), 48–52.

Light, D., & Monk-Turner, E. (2009). Circumstances surrounding male sexual assault and rape: Findings from the National Violence Against Women Survey. *Journal of Interpersonal Violence, 24*(11), 1849–1858.

Lilienfeld, S. O., & Landfield, K. (2008). Science and pseudoscience in law enforcement: A user-friendly primer. *Criminal Justice and Behavior, 35*(10), 1215–1230.

Lilienfeld, S. O., & Widows, M. R. (2005). *Psychopathic Personality Inventory Revised (PPI-R). Professional Manual.* Lutz, FL: Psychological Assessment Resources.

Lindsay, D. S., & Read, J. D. (1994). Psychotherapy and memories of childhood sexual abuse: A cognitive perspective. *Applied Cognitive Psychology, 8*, 281–338.

Lindsay, R. C. L. (1994). Biased lineups: Where do they come from? In D. Ross, J. Read, & M. Toglia (Eds.), *Adult eyewitness testimony: Current trends and developments* (pp. 182–200). New York: Cambridge University Press.

Lindsay, R. C. L., & Wells, G. L. (1980). What price justice? Exploring the relationship of lineup fairness to identification accuracy. *Law and Human Behavior, 4*, 303–314.

Lindsay, R. C. L., Pozzulo, J. D., Craig, W., Lee, K., & Corber, S. (1997). Simultaneous lineups, sequential lineups, and showups: Eyewitness identification decisions of adults and children. *Law and Human Behavior, 21*, 391–404.

Lindsay, R. C. L., Wallbridge, H., & Drennan, D. (1987). Do the clothes make the man? An exploration of the effect of lineup attire on eyewitness identification accuracy. *Canadian Journal of Behavioural Science, 19*, 463–478.

Lindsay, R. C. L., Wells, G. L., & O'Connor, F. J. (1989). Mock-juror belief of accurate and inaccurate eyewitnesses: A replication and extension. *Law and Human Behavior, 13*, 333–339.

Lindsay, R. C. L., Wells, G. L., & Rumpel, C. (1981). Can people detect eyewitness identification accuracy within and across situations? *Journal of Applied Psychology, 66*, 79–89.

Lindsay, R. L., Mansour, J. K., Beaudry, J. L., Leach, A., & Bertrand, M. I. (2009). Beyond sequential presentation: Misconceptions and misrepresentations of sequential lineups. *Legal and Criminological Psychology, 14*(1), 31–34.

Lindsay, R. C. L., & Wells, G. L. (1985). Improving eyewitness identifications from lineups: Simultaneous versus sequential lineup presentation. *Journal of Applied Psychology, 70*, 556–564.

Lindsay, S., Read, D., & Sharma, K. (1998). Accuracy and confidence in person identification: The relationship is strong when witnessing conditions vary widely. *Psychological Science, 9*, 215–218.

Linedecker, C., & Burt, W. (1990). *Nurses who kill.* New York: Windsor.

Lipsey, M. W., Wilson, D. B., Cohen, M. A., & Derzon, J. H. (2002). Is there a causal relationship between alcohol use and violence? A synthesis of evidence. In M. Galanter (Ed.), *Recent developments in alcoholism, Vol. 13: Alcohol and violence—Epidemiology, neurobiology, psychology, family issues* (pp. 245–282). New York: Plenum.

Lipsitt, P. D., Lelos, D., & McGarry, A. L. (1971). Competency for trial: A screening instrument. *American Journal of Psychiatry, 128*, 105–109.

Lipton, J. P. (1977). On the psychology of eyewitness testimony. *Journal of Applied Psychology, 62*, 90–93.

Livingston, J. D., Wilson, D., Tien, G., & Bond, L. (2003). A follow-up study of persons found not criminally on account of metal disorder in British Columbia. *Canadian Journal of Psychiatry, 48*, 408–415.

Livingstone Smith, D. (2004). *Why we lie: The evolutionary roots of deception and the unconscious mind.* New York: St. Martin's Press.

Lloyd, C. D., Clark, H. J., & Forth, A. E. (2010). Psychopathy, expert testimony and indeterminate sentences: Exploring the relationship between Psychopathy Checklist—Revised testimony and trial outcome in Canada. *Legal and Criminological Psychology, 15*, 323–339.

Locke, D. and Code, R. (2001) "Canada's shelters for abused women, 1999–2000." *Juristat, 21.* Ottawa: Canadian Centre for Justice Statistics, Statistics Canada.

Loftus, E. (2003). Our changeable memories: Legal and practical implications. *Nature Reviews: Neuroscience, 4*, 231–234.

Loftus, E. F. (1975). Leading questions and the eyewitness report. *Cognitive Psychology, 7*, 560–572.

Loftus, E. F. (1976). Unconscious transference in eyewitness identification. *Law and Psychology Review, 2*, 93–98.

Loftus, E. F. (1979). *Eyewitness testimony.* Cambridge, MA: Harvard University Press.

Loftus, E. F. (1983). Silence is not golden. *American Psychologist, 65*, 9–15.

Loftus, E. F. (1993a). Psychologists in the eyewitness world. *American Psychologist, 48,* 550–552.

Loftus, E. F. (1993b). The reality of repressed memories. *American Psychologist, 48,* 518–537.

Loftus, E. F. (2003a). Make-believe memories. *American Psychologist, 58,* 867–873.

Loftus, E. F. (2003b). Memory in Canadian courts of law. *Canadian Psychology, 44,* 207–212.

Loftus, E. F. (2004). Dispatch from the (un) civil memory wars. *Lancet, 364,* 20–21.

Loftus, E. F., & Hoffman, H. G. (1989). Misinformation and memory: The creation of new memories. *Journal of Experimental Psychology: General, 118,* 100–104.

Loftus, E. F., & Ketcham, K. (1994). *The myth of repressed memory: False memories and allegations of sexual abuse.* New York: St. Martin's/ Griffin.

Loftus, E. F., & Pickrell, J. (1995). Formation of false memories. *Psychiatric Annals, 25,* 720–25.

Loftus, E. F., & Rosenwald, L. A. (1995). Recovered memories: Unearthing the past in court. *Journal of Psychiatry and Law, 23,* 349–361.

Loftus, E. F., Miller, D. G., & Burns, H. J. (1978). Semantic integration of verbal information into a visual memory. *Journal of Experimental Psychology: Human Learning and Memory, 4,* 19–31.

Loftus, E. F. (2011). Intelligence gathering post 9/11. *American Psychologist, 66,* 532–541.

Loh, W. D. (1981). Perspectives on psychology and law. *Journal of Applied Social Psychology, 11,* 314–355.

Lombroso, C. (1895). *L'homme criminel.* Paris: Felix Alcan.

London, K., Bruck, M., & Melnyk, L. (2009). Post-event information affect children's autobiographical memory after one year. *Law and Human Behavior, 33,* 344–355.

Loo, R. (1986). Suicide among police in a federal force. *Suicide and Life-Threatening Behavior, 16,* 379–88.

Looman, J. (2006). Comparison of two risk assessment instruments for sexual offenders. *Sexual Abuse: Journal of Research and Treatment, 18*(2), 193–206.

Looman, J., & Marshall, W. L. (2001). Phallometric assessments designed to detect arousal to children: The responses of rapists and child molesters. *Sexual Abuse: Journal of Research and Treatment, 13*(1), 3–13.

Lopez, A. (2011). *An examination of the reliability and validity of the officer evaluation: A behavioral rating scale.* (Doctoral Disseration).

Los Angeles Times. (1993, April 23). President defends Reno, calls for investigation. *Kansas City Star,* p. A1.

Lösel, F., & Schmucker, M. (2005). The effectiveness of treatment for sexual offenders: A comprehensive meta-analysis. *Journal of Experimental Criminology, 1*(1), 117–146.

Louisell, D. W. (1955). The psychologist in today's legal world. *Minnesota Law Review, 39,* 235–260.

Louisell. D. W. (1957). The psychologist in today's legal world: Part II. *Minnesota Law Review, 41,* 731–750.

Low, P. W., Jeffries, J. C., & Bonnie, R. J. (1986). *The trial of John W. Hinckley, Jr.: A case study in the insanity defense.* Mineola, NY: Foundation Press.

Lukacs, J. (1997). *The Hitler of history.* New York: Alfred A. Knopf.

Lukas, J. A. (1997). *Big trouble.* New York: Simon & Schuster.

Lunde, D. T., & Morgan, J. (1980). *The die song: A journey into the mind of a mass murderer.* New York: W. W. Norton.

Lundrigan, S., Czarnomski, S., & Wilson, M. (2010). Spatial and environmental consistency in serial sexual assault. *Journal of Investigative Psychology and Offender Profiling, 7*(1), 15–30.

Lupfer, M., Cohen, R., Bernard, J. L., Smalley, D., & Schippmann, J. (1985). An attributional analysis of jurors' judgments in civil cases. *Journal of Social Psychology, 125,* 743–751.

Lussier, P., Deslauriers-Varin, N., & Râtel, T. (2010). A descriptive profile of high-risk sex offenders under intensive supervision in the province of British Columbia, Canada. *International Journal of Offender Therapy and Comparative Criminology, 54*(1), 71–91.

Lykken, D. T. (1998). *A tremor in the blood: Uses and abuse of the lie detector.* New York: Plenum.

Lynam, D. R. (1997). Pursuing the psychopath: Capturing the fledgling psychopath in a nomological net. *Journal of Abnormal Psychology, 106,* 425–438.

Lynam, D. R. (2002). Fledgling psychopathy: A view from personality theory. *Law and Human Behavior, 26,* 255–259.

M. (K.) v. M. (H.), [1992] 3 S.C.R.

Macdonald, J. M., & Michaud, D. L. (1987). *The confession: Interrogation and criminal profiles for police officers.* Denver: Apache.

MacLaren, V. V. (2001). A quantitative review of the guilty knowledge test. *Journal of Applied Psychology, 86,* 674–683.

Macrae, C. N., & Shepard J. W. (1989). Do criminal stereotypes mediate juridic judgments? *British Journal of Social Psychology, 28,* 189–191

Magnussen, S., Melinder, A., Stridebeck, U., & Raja, A. Q. (2010). Beliefs about factors affecting the reliability of eyewitness testimony: A comparison of judges, jurors and the general public. *Applied Cognitive Psychology, 24,* 122–133.

Magnussen, S., Wise, R. A., Raja, A. Q., Safer, M. A., Pawlenko, N., & Stridbeck, U. (2008). What judges know about eyewitness testimony: A comparison of Norwegian and US judges. *Psychology, Crime and Law, 14,* 177–188.

Maher G. (1977). *Hostage: A police approach to a contemporary crisis.* Springfield, IL: Charles C Thomas.

Mahoney, T. H. (2008). Police-reported dating violence in Canada, 2008. *Juristat Article, 30,* 1–26.

Malcolm, P., Andrews, D. A., & Quinsey, V. L. (1993). Discriminant and predictive validity of phallometrically measured sexual age and gender preference. *Journal of Interpersonal Violence, 8*(4), 486–501.

Malle, B. F., Moses, L. J., & Baldwin, D. A. (2011). *Intentions and intentionality: Foundations of social cognition.* Cambridge, MA: The MIT Press.

Malloy, P., Bihrle, A., Duffy, J., & Cimino, C. (1993). The orbitomedial frontal syndrome. *Archives of Clinical Neuropsychology, 8,* 185–201.

Malpass, R. S., & Devine, P. G. (1980). Realism and eyewitness identification research. *Law and Human Behavior, 4,* 347–358.

Malpass, R. S., & Devine, P. G. (1981). Eyewitness identification: Lineup instructions and the absence of the offender. *Journal of Applied Psychology, 66,* 482–489.

Malpass, R. S., & Devine, P. G. (1983). Measuring the fairness of eyewitness identification lineups. In S. M. A. Lloyd-Bostock & B. R. Clifford (Eds.), *Evaluating witness evidence* (pp. 81–102). New York: John Wiley.

Malpass, R. S., Tredoux, C. G., & McQuiston-Surret, D. (2009). Public policy and sequential lineups. *Legal and Criminological Psychology, 14,* 1–12.

Maniglio, R. R. (2011). The role of child sexual abuse in the etiology of suicide and non-suicidal self-injury. *Acta Psychiatrica Scandinavica, 124*(1), 30–41.

Mann, S., Vrij, A., Leal, S., Granhag, P. A., Warmelink, L., & Forrester, D. (2011). *Look into my eyes: Deliberate eye contact as a cue to deceit.* Manuscript submitted for publication.

Manson v. Braithwaite, 432 U.S. 98 (1977).

Marche, T. A., Brainerd, C. J., & Reyna, V. F. (2010). Distinguishing true from false memories in forensic contexts: Can phenomenology tell us what is real? *Applied Cognitive Psychology, 24*(8), 1168–1182.

Margolin, G., & Gordis, E. B. (2000). The effects of family and community violence on children. *Annual Review of Psychology, 51,* 445–479.

Marin, J. C. (2003). *Analyse criminelle et analyse comportementale. Rapport du groupe de travail interministériel.* Paris, France: Ministère de la Justice.

Marsh, P. J., Odlaug, B. L., Thomarios, N., Davis, A. A., Buchanan, S. N., Meyer, C. S., et al. (2010). Paraphilias in adult psychiatric inpatients. *Annals of Clinical Psychiatry, 22*(2), 129–134. Retrieved July 23, 2012, from https://www.aacp.com/Pages.asp?AID=8602&issue=May%202010&page=C&UID=

Marshall, L. E., & Marshall, W. L. (2006). Sexual addiction in incarcerated sexual offenders. *Sexual Addiction & Compulsivity, 13*(4), 377–390.

Marshall, W. L. (2010). The role of attachments, intimacy, and loneliness in the etiology and maintenance of sexual offending. *Sexual and Relationship Therapy, 25*(1), 73–85.

Marshall, W. L., Eccles, A. A., & Barbaree, H. E. (1991). The treatment of exhibitionists: A focus on sexual deviance versus cognitive and relationship features. *Behaviour Research and Therapy, 29*(2), 129–135.

Martelli, M., Majib, J. M., & Pelli, D. G. (2005). Are faces processed like words? A diagnostic test for recognition by parts. *Journal of Vision, 5,* 58–70.

Martens, W. (2008). Introjective identification therapy for patients with antisocial personality disorders: A theoretical outline. *Annals of the American Psychotherapy Association, 11,* 10–16.

Marxsen, D., Yuille, J. C., & Nisbet, M. (1995). The complexities of eliciting and assessing children's statements. *Psychology, Public Policy, and Law, 1,* 450–460.

Mason, G. (2009, May 5). Police psychologist equates RCMP with Putin's Russia. *The Globe and Mail.*

Mason, M. A. (1991). The McMartin case revisited: The conflict between social work and criminal justice. *Social Work, 36,* 391–395.

Mason, M. A. (1998). Expert testimony regarding the characteristics of sexually abused children: A controversy on both sides of the bench. In S. J. Ceci & H. Hembrooke (Eds.), *Expert witnesses in child abuse cases* (pp. 217–234). Washington, DC: American Psychological Association.

Matthews, R., Matthews, J. K., & Speltz, K. (1989). *Female sexual offenders: An empirical study.* Orwell, VT: The Safer Society Press.

Mazzella, R., & Feingold, A. (1994). The effects of physical attractiveness, race, socioeconomic status, and gender of defendant and victims on judgments of mock jurors: A meta-analysis. *Journal of Applied Social Psychology, 24,* 1315–1344.

Mazzoni, G. A., & Scoboria, A. (2007). Cognition and false memories. In F. Durso (Ed.) *Handbook of applied cognition* (2nd ed.) (pp. 789–812). West Sussex, England: Wiley and Sons.

McAllister, H. A., Baiamonte, B. A., Ory, J. H., & Sherer, J. A. (2011). The effect of wanted posters on prospective and retrospective memory. *Law and Human Behavior, 35,* 104–109.

McAuliff, B. D., & Kovera, M. B. (1998, August). *Are laypersons' beliefs about suggestibility consistent with expert opinion?* Paper presented at the meetings of the American Psychological Association, San Francisco.

McCann, K., & Lussier, P. (2008). Antisociality, sexual deviance, and sexual reoffending in juvenile sex offenders: A meta-analytical investigation. *Youth Violence and Juvenile Justice, 6*(4), 363–385.

McCarron, M. E., & Stewart, D. W. (2011). A Canadian perspective on using vignettes to teach ethics in psychology. *Canadian Psychology/ Psychologie Canadienne, 52,* 185–191.

McClain, N. M., & Garrity, S. E. (2011). Sex trafficking and the exploitation of adolescents. *Journal of Obstetric, Gynecologic, & Neonatal Nursing: Clinical Scholarship for the Care of Women, Childbearing Families, & Newborns, 40*(2), 243–252.

McCleskey v. Kemp, 481 U.S. 279 (1987).

McCloskey, M., & Egeth, H. E. (1983). Eyewitness identification: What can a psychologist tell a jury? *American Psychologist, 38,* 550–563.

McConahay, J. B., & Hough, J. C. (1976). Symbolic racism. *Journal of Social Issues, 32,* 23–45.

McCord, D. (1985). The admissibility of expert testimony regarding rape trauma syndrome in rape prosecutions. *Boston College Law Review, 26,* 1143–1213.

McCord, W., & McCord, J. (1964). *The psychopath: An essay on the criminal mind.* Oxford, UK: D. Van Nostrand.

McCrae, R. R., & Costa, P. T. Jr (1997). Personality trait structure as a human universal. *American Psychologist, 52,* 509–516.

McGee, H., O'Higgins, M., Garavan, R., & Conroy, R. (2011). Rape and child sexual abuse: What beliefs persist about motives, perpetrators, and survivors? *Journal of Interpersonal Violence, 26*(17), 3580–3593.

McGowan, M., & Helms, J. L. (2003). The utility of the expert witness in a rape case: Reconsidering rape trauma syndrome. *Journal of Forensic Psychology Practice, 3*(1), 51–60.

McIntyre, J., & Spatz Widom, C. (2011). Childhood victimization and crime victimization. *Journal of Interpersonal Violence, 26*(4), 640–663.

McIntyre, J., & Spatz Widom, C. (2011). Childhood victimization and crime victimization. *Journal of Interpersonal Violence, 26*(4), 640–663.

McIver, W., Wakefield, H., & Underwager, R. (1989). Behavior of abused and non-abused children in interviews with anatomically correct dolls. *Issues in Child Abuse Accusations, 1,* 39–48.

McIvor, S. D., & Nahanee, T. (1998). "Aboriginal Women: Invisible Victims of Violence," in K. Bonnycastle and G. S. Rigakos, eds., *Unsettling Truths: Battered Women, Policy, Politics and Contemporary Research in Canada,* p. 65.

McMains, M. (1988). Psychologists' roles in hostage negotiations. In J. Reese & J. Horn (Eds.), *Police psychology: Operational assistance* (pp. 281–317). Washington, DC: U.S. Government Printing office.

McNally, R. J. (2003). *Remembering trauma.* Cambridge, MA: Belknap Press/Harvard University Press.

McNamara, J. (1967). Uncertainties in police work: The relevance of police recruits' backgrounds and training. In D. Bordua (Ed.), *The police: Six sociological essays* (pp. 163–252). New York: John Wiley.

McPoyle, T. J. (1981). The investigative technique of criminal profiling. *Your Virginia State Trooper, 3*(1), 87.

Meadows, R. J. (1987). Beliefs of law enforcement administrators and criminal justice educators toward the needed skill competencies in entry-level police training curriculum. *Journal of Police Science and Administration, 15,* 1–9.

Meddis, S. V. (1993, October 7). $1 million for clues to "Unabomber." *USA Today,* p. 3A.

Medwed, D. (2004). The zeal deal: Prosecutorial resistance to postconviction claims of innocence. *Boston University Law Review, 84,* 125–183.

Meehl, P. E. (1954). *Clinical versus statistical prediction: A theoretical analysis and a review of the evidence.* Minneapolis: University of Minnesota Press.

Meesig, R. & Horvath, F. (1995). A national survey of practices, policies and evaluative comments on the use of pre-employment polygraph screening in police agencies in the United States. *Polygraph, 24,* 57–136.

Meissner, C. A., & Kassin, S. M. (2002). "He's guilty!": Investigator bias in judgments of truth and deception. *Law and Human Behavior, 26,* 469–480.

Meissner, C. A., Horgan, A. J., & Albrechtsen, J. S. (2009). False confessions. In R. Kocsis' (Ed.), *Applied criminal psychology: A guide to forensic behavioral sciences* (pp. 191– 212). Springfield, IL: Charles C Thomas Publisher.

Meissner, C. A., Sporer, S. L., & Schooler, J. W. (2007). Person descriptions as eyewitness evidence. In M. P. Toglia, J. D. Read, D. R. Ross, & R. C. L. Lindsay (Eds.), *The handbook of eyewitness psychology* (Vol 2) (pp. 1–34). Mahwah, NJ: Erlbaum.

Melilli, K. 2009. *Disclosure of juror identities to the press: Who will speak for the jurors?* Retrieved July 23, 2013, from http://works.bepress .com/kenneth_melilli/1

Melinder, A., Alexander, K., Cho, Y., Goodman, G. S., Thorensen, C., Lonum, K., et al. (2010). Children's eyewitness memory: A comparison of interviewing strategies as realized by forensic professionals. *Journal of Experimental Child Psychology, 105,* 156–177.

Melnyk, L., & Bruck, M. (2004). Timing moderates the effects of repeated suggestive interviewing on children's eyewitness memory. *Applied Cognitive Psychology, 18,* 613, 631.

Melnyk, L., Crossman, A. M., & Scullin, M. H. 2007. The suggestibility of children's memory. In M. P. Toglia, J. D. Read, D. F. Ross, & D. F. Ross (Eds.), *The handbook of eyewitness psychology: Memory for events* (pp. 401–427). Mahwah, NJ: Lawrence Erlbaum.

Meloy, J. (2000). The nature and dynamics of sexual homicide: An integrative review. *Aggression and Violent Behavior, 5*(1), 1–22.

Meloy, J. R. (Ed.). (1998). *The psychology of stalking: Clinical and forensic perspectives*. San Diego: Academic Press.

Melton, G. B., & Limber, S. (1989). Psychologists' involvement in cases of child maltreatment: Limits of role and expertise. *American Psychologist, 44,* 1225–1233.

Melton, G. B., & Saks, M. J. (1990). AP-LS's pro bono amicus brief project. *American Psychology-Law Society News, 10,* 5.

Melton, G. B., Goodman, G. S., Kalichman, S. C., Levine, M., Saywitz, K. J., & Koocher, G. P. (1995). Empirical research on child maltreatment and the law. *Journal of Clinical Child Psychology, 24,* 47–77.

Melton, G. B., Petrila, J., & Poythress, N. G. (1987). *Psychological evaluations for the courts: A handbook for mental health professionals and lawyers.* New York,: Guilford Press.

Melton, G. B., Petrila, J., Poythress, N. G., & Slobogin, C. (1997). *Psychological evaluations for the courts* (2nd ed.). New York: Guilford Press.

Melton, G. B., Petrila, J., Poythress, N. G., & Slobogin, C. (2007). *Psychological evaluations for the courts: A handbook for mental health professionals and lawyers* (3rd ed.). New York: Guilford Press.

Melton, G. B., Weithorn, L. A., & Slobogin, C. (1985). *Community mental health centers and the courts: An evaluation of community-based forensic services.* Lincoln: University of Nebraska Press.

Memon, A., & Vartoukian, R. (1996). The effects of repeated questioning on young children's eyewitness testimony. *British Journal of Psychology, 87,* 403–415.

Memon, A., Meissner, C. A., & Fraser, J. (2010). The Cognitive Interview: A meta-analytic review and study

space analysis of the past 25 years. *Psychology, Public Policy, and Law, 16*(4), 340–372.

Metzl, J. M. (2004). Voyeur nation? Changing definitions of voyeurism, 1950–2004. *Harvard Review of Psychiatry, 12*(2) 127–131.

Meyer, C., & Taylor, S. (1986). Adjustment to rape. *Journal of Personality and Social Psychology, 50,* 1226–1234.

Meyersburg, C. A., Bogdan, R., Gallo, D. A., & McNally, R. J. (2009). False memory propensity in people reporting recovered memories of past lives. *Journal of Abnormal Psychology, 118,* 399–404.

Mezzo v. The Queen (1996), 1 S.C.R. 802.

Miccio-Fonseca, L. C. (2000). Adult and adolescent female sex offenders: Experiences compared to other female and male sex offenders. *Journal of Psychology & Human Sexuality, 11*(3), 75–88.

Michaud, P., St-Yves, M., & Guay, J. P. (2008). Predictive modeling in hostage and barricade incidents. *Criminal Justice and Behavior, 35,* 1136–1155.

Michaud, S. G. (with Hazelwood, R.). (1998). *The evil that men do: FBI profiler Roy Hazelwood's journey into the minds of sexual predators.* New York: St. Martin's Press.

Micheels, P. A. (1991). *Heat: The fire investigators and their war on arson and murder.* New York: St. Martin's Press.

Milano, C. (1989, August). Re-evaluating recruitment to better target top minority talent. *Management Review,* pp. 29–32.

Milgram, S. (1974). *Obedience to authority.* New York: Harper & Row.

Miller, H. A., Watkins, R. J., & Webb, D. (2009). The use of psychological testing to evaluate law enforcement leadership competencies and development. *Police Practice & Research: An International Journal, 10*(1), 49–60.

Miller, H. A., Watkins, R. J., & Webb, D. (2009). The use of psychological

testing to evaluate law enforcement leadership competencies and development. *Police Practice and Research, 10*(1), 49–60.

Miller, L. (2006). *Practical police psychology: Stress management and crisis intervention for law enforcement.* Springfield, IL: Charles C Thomas Publisher.

Miller, M. K., Flores, D. M., & Dolezilek A. N. (2007): Addressing the problem of courtroom stress. *Judicature, 91,* 60–69.

Millon, T., Simonsen, E., & Birket-Smith, M. (1998). Historical conceptions of psychopathy in the United States and Europe. In T. Millon, E. Simonsen, M. Birket-Smith, & R. D. Davis (Eds.), *Psychopathy: Antisocial, criminal, and violent behavior* (pp. 3–31). New York: Guilford.

Mills, J. F., Anderson, D., & Kroner, D. G. (2004). The antisocial attitudes and associates of sex offenders. *Criminal Behaviour and Mental Health, 14*(2), 134–145.

Mills, R. B., McDevitt, R. J., & Tonkin, S. (1966). Situational tests in metropolitan police recruit selection. *Journal of Criminal Law, Criminology, and Police Science, 57,* 99–104.

Milne, R., & Bull, R. (1999). *Investigative interviewing: Psychology and practice.* Chichester: Wiley.

Miranda v. Arizona, 384 U.S. 436 (1966).

Miron, M. S., & Douglas, J. E. (1979, September). Threat analysis: The psycholinguistic approach. *FBI Law Enforcement Bulletin,* pp. 1–8.

Mitchell, R. W. (1986). A framework for discussing deception. In R. W. Mitchell & N. S. Mogdil (Eds.), *Deception: Perspectives on human and nonhuman deceit* (pp. 3–40). Albany: State University of New York Press.

Modestin, J. (1998). Criminal and violent behavior in schizophrenic patients: An overview. *Psychiatry and Clinical Neurosciences, 52,* 547–554.

Mokros, A., Menner, B., Eisenbarth, H., Alpers, G. W., Lange, K. W., & Osterheider, M. (2008). Diminished cooperativeness of psychopaths in a prisoner's dilemma game yields higher rewards. *Journal of Abnormal Psychology, 117*(2), 406–413.

Mokros, A., Osterheider, M., Hucker, S. J., & Nitschke, J. (2011). Psychopathy and sexual sadism. *Law and Human Behavior, 35,* 188–199.

Monahan, J. (1992). Mental disorder and violent behavior: Perceptions and evidence. *American Psychologist, 47,* 511–521.

Monahan, J., & Steadman, H. (1994). Toward the rejuvenation of risk research. In J. Monahan & H. Steadman (Eds.), *Violence and mental disorder: Developments in risk assessment* (pp. 1–17). Chicago: University of Chicago Press.

Monahan, J., & Walker, L. (1988). Social science research in law: A new paradigm. *American Psychologist, 43,* 465–472.

Monahan, J., Steadman, H. Silver, E., Appelbaum, A., Robbins, P., Mulvey, E., et al. (2001). *Rethinking Risk Assessment: The MacArthur Study of Mental Disorder and Violence* (New York: Oxford University Press).

Monahan, J. (1997). Foreword. In C. D. Webster & M. A. Jackson (Eds.), *Impulsivity: Theory, assessment, and treatment* (pp. ix–xi). New York: Guilford.

Morabito, M. S. (2010). Understanding Community Policing as an Innovation: Patterns of Adoption. *Crime and Delinquency,* 56, 564–587.

Morales v. Artuz, [2002], S. R. C. 00-2730

Moran, G., & Comfort, J. C. (1982). Scientific jury selection: Sex as a moderator of demographic and personality predictors of impaneled felony juror behavior. *Journal of Personality and Social Psychology, 43,* 1052–1063.

Moran, G., & Cutler, B. L. (1989, August). *Dispositional predictors of criminal case verdicts.* Symposium paper presented at the meetings of the American Psychological Association, New Orleans.

Morison, S., & Greene, E. (1992). Juror and expert knowledge of child sexual abuse. *Child Abuse and Neglect, 16,* 595–613.

Morris, W. (1998). *The ghosts of Medgar Evers: A tale of race, murder, Mississippi and Hollywood.* New York: Random House.

Morrissey, J. P., Fagan, J. A., & Cocozza, J. J. (2009). New models of colloboration between criminal justice and mental health systems. *The American Journal of Psychiatry, 166,* 1211–1214.

Morse, S. J. (1978). Law and mental health professionals: The limits of expertise. *Professional Psychology, 9,* 389–399.

Morse, S. J. (1990). The misbegotten marriage of soft psychology and bad law: Psychological self-defense as a justification for homicide. *Law and Human Behavior, 14,* 595–618.

Morse, S. J. (2008). Psychopathy and criminal responsibility. *Neuroethics, 1*(3), 205–212.

Mossman, D. (1994). Assessing predictions of violence: Being accurate about accuracy. *Journal of Consulting and Clinical Psychology, 62,* 783–792.

Mossman, K. (1973, May). Jury selection: An expert's view. *Psychology Today,* pp. 78–79.

Motiuk, L. L., & Belcourt, R. I. (1997). *Homicide, sex, robbery, and drug offenders in federal convictions: An end of 1996 review.* Ottawa: Research Branch, Correctional Service of Canada.

Motiuk, L. L. & Belcourt, R. I. (1995). *A statistical profile of homicide, robbery, sex and drug offenders in federal corrections.* Ottawa: Solicitor General Canada Brief B-11.

Muchoki, S. (2011). Vocabulary used by sexual offenders: Meaning and implications. *Culture, Health & Sexuality, 13*(1), 101–113.

Mueser, K. T., Rosenberg, S. D., & Rosenberg, H. J. (2009). Trauma and posttraumatic stress disorder in vulnerable populations. In H. J. Rosenberg (Ed.), *Treatment of posttraumatic stress disorder*

in special populations: A cognitive restructuring program (pp. 9–35). Washington, DC: American Psychological Association.

Mullin, C. (1986). *Error of judgement.* London: Chatto & Windus.

Münsterberg, H. (1908a). *On the witness stand.* Garden City, NY: Doubleday.

Münsterburg, H. (1908b). *On the witness stand: Essays on psychology and crime.* New York: Doubleday.

Münsterburg, H. (1909). The field of applied psychology. *Psychological Bulletin, 6,* 49–50.

Murdock Hicks, M., Rogers, R., & Cashel, M. L. (2000). Predictions of violent and total infractions among institutionalized male juvenile offenders. *Journal of the American Academy of Psychiatry and the Law, 28,* 183–190.

Murphy, C. M., & O'Farrell, T. J. (1994). Factors associated with marital aggression in male alcoholics. *Journal of Family Psychology, 8,* 321– 335.

Murphy, C. M., O'Farrell, T. J., Fals-Stewart, W., & Feehan, M. (2001). Correlates of intimate partner violence among male alcoholic patients. *Journal of Consulting & Clinical Psychology, 69,* 528–540.

Murphy, L., Fedoroff, P., & Martineau, M. (2009). Canada's sex offender registries: Background, implementation, and social policy considerations. *Canadian Journal of Human Sexuality, 18*(1/2), 61–72. Retrieved May 15, 2012, from http://www.theroyal.ca/fedoroff/files/2011/07/2009_Murphy_Canadas-Sex-offender-Registries-Background-Implementation-and-Social-Policy-Considerations.pdf

Murphy, W. D., & Peters, J. M. (1992). Profiling child sexual abusers: Psychological considerations. *Criminal Justice and Behavior, 19*(1), 24–37.

Murray, D. M., & Wells, G. L. (1982). Does knowledge that a crime was staged affect eyewitness performance? *Journal of Applied Social Psychology, 12,* 42–53.

Murrie, D. C., & Cornell, D. G. (2000). The Millon Adolescent Clinical Inventory and psychopathy. *Journal of Personality Assessment, 75*(1), 110-125.

Myers, B., & Lecci, L. (1998). Revising the factor structure of the Juror Bias Scale: A method for the empirical validation of theoretical constructs. *Law and Human Behavior, 22,* 239-256.

Myers, J. E. B. (1992). *Legal issues in child abuse and neglect.* Thousand Oaks, CA: Sage.

Myers, J. E. B., Bays, J., Becker, J., Berliner, L., Corwin, D. L., & Saywitz, K. J. (1989). Expert testimony in child sexual abuse litigation. *Nebraska Law Review, 68,* 1-145.

Myers, M. A., & Talarico, S. M. (1987). *The social contexts of criminal sentencing.* New York: Springer-Verlag.

Nadel, L., & Jacobs, W. J. (1998). Traumatic memory is special. *Current Directions in Psychological Science, 7,* 154-157.

Nagel, T. W. (1983, October). *Tensions between law and psychology: Fact, myth, or ideology?* Paper presented at the meetings of the American Psychology-Law Society, Chicago.

Nakayama, M. (2002). Practical use of the concealed information test for criminal investigation in Japan. In M. Kleiner (Ed.). *Handbook of polygraph testing* (pp. 49-86). San Diego, CA: Academic Press.

Napier, M. (2005, September). The need for higher education. *Law and Order Magazine, 1,* 86-94.

Nash, R. A., & Wade, K. A. (2009). Innocent but proven guilty: Eliciting internalized false confessions using doctored-video evidence. *Applied Cognitive Psychology, 23*(5), 624-637.

Nathan, D. (1987). The making of a modern witch trial. *Village Voice, 33,* 19-32.

Nathan, P., & Ward, T. (2001). Females who sexually abuse children: Assessment and treatment issues. *Psychiatry, Psychology and Law, 8*(1), 44-55.

Nathan, P., & Ward, T. (2002). Female sex offenders: Clinical and demographic features. *Journal of Sexual Aggression, 8*(1), 5-21.

National Advisory Commission on Criminal Justice Standards and Goals. (1973). *Report on police.* Washington, DC: U.S. Government Printing Office.

Neiderland, W. G. (1982). The survivor syndrome: Further observations and dimensions. *Journal of American Psychoanalytic Association, 30,* 413-425.

Neil v. Biggers, 409 U.S. 188 (1972).

Neoh, J., & Mellor, D. (2009). Professional issues related to allegations and assessment of child sexual abuse in the context of family court litigation. *Psychiatry, Psychology and Law, 16*(2), 303-321

Neumann, C. S., Hare, R. D., & Newman, J. P. (2007). The super-ordinate nature of the psychopathy checklist-revised. *Journal of Personality Disorders, 21*(2), 102-117.

Newman, M. L., Pennebaker, J. W., Berry, D. S., & Richards, J. M. (2003). Lying words: Predicting deception from linguistic style. *Personality and Social Psychology Bulletin, 29,* 665-675.

Nicholson, R. (1999). Forensic assessment. In R. Roesch, S. D. Hart, & J. R. P. Ogloff (Eds.), *Psychology and law: The state of the discipline* (pp. 121-173). New York: Kluwer Academic/Plenum.

Nicholson, R. A., & Johnson, W. G. (1991). Prediction of competency to stand trial: Contribution of demographics, type of offense, clinical characteristics, and psychological ability. *International Journal of Law and Psychiatry, 14,* 287-297.

Nicholson, R. A., Briggs, S. R., & Robertson, H. C. (1988). Instruments for assessing competency to stand trial: How do they work? *Professional Psychology: Research and Practice, 19,* 383-394.

Nicole, A., & Proulx, J. (2007). Sexual murderers and sexual aggressors: Developmental paths and criminal history. In J. Proulx, É. Beauregard,

M. Cusson, A. Nicole (Eds.), *Sexual murderers: A comparative analysis and new perspectives* (pp. 29-50). New York: John Wiley & Sons.

Niederhoffer, A. (1967). *Behind the shield: The police in urban society.* Garden City, NY: Doubleday.

Nietzel, M. T., & Dillehay, R. C. (1986). *Psychological consultation in the courtroom.* New York: Pergamon Press.

Nikonova, O., & Ogloff, J. R. P. (2005). Mock jurors' perceptions of child witnesses: The

Noguchi, T. T. (with DiMona, J.). (1985). *Coroner at large.* New York: Simon & Schuster.

Norris, J. (1992). *Jeffrey Dahmer.* New York: Pinnacle Books.

Note. (1953). Voluntary false confessions: A neglected area in criminal investigation. *Indiana Law Journal, 28,* 374-392.

Nourkova V. V., Bernstein D. M., Loftus E. F. (2004) Altering traumatic memories. *Cognition & Emotion, 18,* 575-585.

Nunes, K. L., Babchishin, K. M., & Cortoni, F. (2011). Measuring treatment change in sex offenders: Clinical and statistical significance. *Criminal Justice and Behavior, 38*(2), 157-173.

Nunez, N., McCrea, S. & Culhane, S. E. (2011). Jury decision making research: Are researchers focusing on the mouse and not the elephant in the room? *Behavioral Sciences and the Law, 29,* 439-451.

O'Connor, T. (2005). *Police deviance and ethics.* Retrieved from Dr. O'Connor's Criminal Justice Megalinks.

O'Donohue, W. (2010). A critique of the proposed DSM-V diagnosis of pedophilia. *Archives of Sexual Behavior, 39*(3), 587-590.

O'Leary, D., Resnick-Luetke, S., & Monk-Turner, E. (2011). Holding out for a hero: Selecting a chief of police. *Police Practice and Research: An International Journal, 12,* 435-449.

O'Neill, M. L., Lidz, V., Heilbrun, K. (2003). Adolescents with psychopathic characteristics in a substance abusing cohort: Treatment process and outcomes. *Law and Human Behavior, 27*, 299-313.

O'Sullivan, M. (2003). The fundamental attribution error in detecting deception: The boy-who-cried-wolf effect. *Personality and Social Psychology Bulletin, 29*, 1316-1327.

O'Sullivan, M. (2005). Emotional intelligence and deception detection: Why most can't "read" others, but a few can. In R. E. Riggio & Feldman, R. (Eds.), *Applications of nonverbal communication.* Mahwah, NJ: Lawrence Erlbaum Associates Publishers.

O'Sullivan, M., & Ekman, P. (2004). The wizards of deception detection. In P. A. Granhag & L. A. Stromwall (Eds.), *Deception detection in forensic contexts* (pp. 269-286). Cambridge, UK: Cambridge University Press.

Oddone Paolucci, E., Genuis, M. L., & Violato, C. (2001). A meta-analysis of the published research on the effects of child sexual abuse. *Journal of Psychology: Interdisciplinary and Applied, 135*(1), 17-36.

Odgers, C. L., Moretti, M. M., & Reppucci, N. D. (2005). Examining the science and practice of violence risk assessment with female adolescents. *Law and Human Behavior, 29*, 7-27.

Odinot, G., Wolters, G., & Lavender, T. (2009). Repeated partial eyewitness questioning causes confidence inflation but not retrieval-induced forgetting. *Applied Cognitive Psychology, 23*(1), 90-97.

Ofshe, R. (1992). Inadvertent hypnosis during interrogation: False confessions due to dissociative state, misidentified multiple personality, and the satanic cult hypothesis. *International Journal of Clinical and Experimental Hypnosis, 40*, 125-156.

Ofshe, R. J., & Leo, R. A. (1997). The social psychology of police interrogation: The theory and classification of true and false confessions. *Studies in Law, Politics, and Society, 16*, 189-215.

Ofshe, R., & Watters, E. (1994). *Making monsters: False memories, psychotherapy, and sexual hysteria.* New York: Charles Scribner's.

Ogloff, J. (2001). Supreme Court refused to hear from CPA. *Psynopsis, 2*, 2-4.

Ogloff, J. P. (2011). A century of psychology and law: Successes, challenges, and future opportunities. In P. R. Martin, F. M. Cheung, M. C. Knowles, M. Kyrios, L. Littlefield, J. Overmier, J. M. Prieto (Eds.), *IAAP handbook of applied psychology* (pp. 362-385). Wiley-Blackwell.

Ogloff, J. R. P. (2004). Invited introductory remarks to the special issue. *Canadian Journal of Behavioural Science, 36*, 84-86.

Ogloff, J. R. P., & Otto, R. K. (1993). Psychological autopsy: Clinical and legal perspectives. *Saint Louis University Law Journal, 37*, 607-646.

Ogloff, J. R. P., & Vidmar, N. (1994). The impact of pretrial publicity on jurors: A study to compare the relative effects of television and print media in a child sex abuse case. *Law and Human Behavior, 18*, 507-525.

Ogloff, J. R., Roberts, C. F., & Roesch, R. (1993). The insanity defense: Legal standards and clinical assessment. *Applied & Preventive Psychology, 2*(3), 163-178.

Ogloff, J., Wong, S., & Greenwood, A. (1990). Treating criminal psychopaths in a therapeutic community program. *Behavioral Sciences & the Law, 8*, 81-90.

Oldfield, D. (1997). What help do the police need with their enquiries? In J. L. Jackson & D. A. Bekerian (Eds.), *Offender profiling: Theory, research and practice* (pp. 93-106). New York: John Wiley.

Oliveria-Souza, R., Ignácio, F., & Moll, J. (2008). The antisocials amid us. In W. Sinnott-Armstrong (Ed.), *Moral psychology, Vol 3: The neuroscience of morality: Emotion, brain disorders, and development* (pp. 151-158). Cambridge, MA: MIT Press.

Olson, W. K. (1991). *The litigation explosion: What happened when America unleashed the lawsuit.* New York: Dutton.

Olver, M. E., & Wong, S. (2011). Predictors of sex offender treatment dropout: Psychopathy, sex offender risk, and responsivity implications. *Psychology, Crime & Law, 17*(5), 457-471.

Olver, M. E., & Wong, S. P. (2006). Psychopathy, sexual deviance, and recidivism among sex offenders. *Sexual Abuse: Journal of Research and Treatment, 18*(1), 65-82.

Olver, M. E., & Wong, S. P. (2009). Therapeutic responses of psychopathic sexual offenders: Treatment attrition, therapeutic change, and long-term recidivism. *Journal of Consulting and Clinical Psychology, 77*(2), 328-336.

Olver, M. E., Preston, D. L., Camilleri, J. A., Helmus, L., & Starzomski, A. (2011). A survey of clinical psychology training in Canadian federal corrections: Implications for psychologist recruitment and retention. *Canadian Psychology/Psychologie Canadienne, 52*, 310-320.

Olver, M. E., Stockdale, K. C., & Wormith, J. (2011). A meta-analysis of predictors of offender treatment attrition and its relationship to recidivism. *Journal of Consulting and Clinical Psychology, 79*(1), 6-21.

Olver, M. E., Wong, S. P., Nicholaichuk, T., & Gordon, A. (2007). The validity and reliability of the Violence Risk Scale-Sexual offender version: Assessing sex offender risk and evaluating therapeutic change. *Psychological Assessment, 19*(3), 318-329.

Ones, D. S., Viswesvaran, C., Cullen, M. J., Dees, S. A., & Langkamp, K. (2003, April 11). Personality and police officer behavior: A comprehensive meta-analysis. In S. W. Spilberg and D. S. Ones (Chairs). *Personality work behavior of police officers.* Symposium conducted at the 18th annual meeting of the Society for Industrial and Organizational Psychology, Orlando, FL.

Ono, M., Sachau, D. A., Deal, W. P., Englert, D. R., & Taylor, M. D. (2011). Cognitive ability, emotional intelligence, and the Big Five personality dimensions as predictors of criminal investigator performance. *Criminal Justice and Behavior, 38,* 471–491.

Ontario Domestic Violence Death Review Committee. (2005). *Annual report to the chief coroner.* Toronto: Office of the Chief Coroner.

Orlando, J. A., & Koss, M. P. (1983). The effect of sexual victimization on sexual satisfaction: A study of the negative association hypothesis. *Journal of Abnormal Psychology, 92,* 104–106.

Orth, M. (1999). *Vulgar favors: Andrew Cunanan, Gianni Versace, and the largest failed manhunt in U.S. history.* New York: Delacorte.

Ostrov, E. (1985, August). *Validation of police officer recruit candidates' self-reported drug use on the Inwald Personality Inventory.* Paper presented at the meetings of the American Psychological Association, Los Angeles.

Ostrov, E. (1986). Police/law enforcement and psychology. *Behavioral Sciences and the Law, 4,* 353–370.

Otgaar, H., Candel, I., Merckelbach, H., Wade, K. A. (2009). Abducted by a UFO: Prevalence information affects young children's false memories for an implausible events. *Applied Cognitive Psychology, 23,* 115–125.

Otto, R. K., Edens, J. F., Poythress, N. G., & Nicholson, R. A. (1998, March). *Psychometric properties of the MacArthur Competence Assessment Tool-Criminal Adjudication (MacCAT-CA).* Paper presented at the meetings of the American Psychology-Law Society, Redondo Beach, CA.

Palermo, G. B., Kocsis, R. N., & Slovenko, R. (2005). *Offender profiling: An introduction to the sociopsychological analysis of violent crime.* Springfield, IL: Charles C Thomas Publisher.

Palmer, M. A., Brewer, N., & Weber, N. (2010). Postidentification feedback affects subsequent eyewitness identification performance. *Journal of Experimental Psychology, 16,* 387–398.

Paris, M. L. (1996). Trust, lies, and interrogation. *Virginia Journal of Social Policy and Law, 3,* 15–44.

Park, L. & Renner, K. (1998). The failure to acknowledge differences in developmental capabilities leads to unjust outcomes for child witnesses in sexual abuse cases. *Canadian Journal of Mental Health, 17,* 5–19

Parker, G. F. (2009). Impact of a mental health training course for correctional officers on a special housing unit. *Psychiatric Services, 60,* 640–645.

Partridge, G. E. (1928). A study of 50 cases of psychopathic personality. *American Journal of Psychiatry, 7,* 953–973.

Paterson, B., Claughan, P., & McComish, S. (2004). New evidence or changing population? Reviewing the evidence of a link between mental illness and violence. *International Journal of Mental Health Nursing, 13,* 39–52.

Paterson, E. J. (1979). How the legal system responds to battered women. In D. M. Moore (Ed.), *Battered women* (pp. 79–99). Newbury Park, CA: Sage.

Paterson, H. M., Kemp, R. I., & Ng, J. R. (2011). Combating co-witness contamination: Attempting to decrease negative effects of discuss on on eyewitness memory. *Applied Cognitive Psychology, 25,* 43–52.

Patrick, C. J. (2006). Back to the Future: Cleckley as a Guide to the Next Generation of Psychopathy Research. In C. J. Patrick (Ed.), *Handbook of psychopathy* (pp. 605–617). New York: Guilford Press.

Patrick, C. J., & Iacono, W. G. (1991). Validity of the control question polygraph test: The problem of sampling bias. *Journal of Applied Psychology, 76*(2), 229–238.

Patry, M. W., Stinson, V., & Smith, S. M., (2009). Supreme Court of Canada addresses admissibility of posthypnosis witness evidence: *R. v. Trochym* (2007). *Canadian Psychology, 50,* 98–105.

Paulhus, D. L., & Williams, K. M. (2002). The Dark Triad of personality: Narcissism, Machiavellianism and psychopathy. *Journal of Research in Personality, 36*(6), 556–563.

Paulsen, D. (2006). Human versus machine: A comparison of the accuracy of geographic profiling methods. *Journal of Investigative Psychology and Offender Profiling, 3*(2), 77–89.

Pavlidis, I., Eberhardt, N. L., & Levine, J. A. (2002). Seeing through the face of deception. *Nature, 415,* 35.

Payne, B. K., & Guastaferro, W. P. (2009). Mind the gap: Attitudes about *Miranda* warnings among police chiefs and citizens. *Journal of Police and Criminal Psychology, 24*(2), 93–103.

Payne, D. G., Neuschatz, J. S., Lampinen, J. M., & Lynn, S. J. (1997). Compelling memory illusions: The phenomenological qualities of false memories. *Current Directions in Psychological Science, 6,* 56–60.

Peace, K. A., & Porter, S. (2004). A longitudinal investigation of the reliability of memories for trauma and other emotional experiences. *Applied Cognitive Psychology, 18,* 1143–1159.

Peace, K. A., & Porter, S. (2011). Remembrance of lies past: A comparison of the features and consistency of truthful and fabricated trauma narratives. *Applied Cognitive Psychology, 25,* 414–423.

Peace, K. A., & Sinclair, S. M. (2012). Cold-blooded lie catchers? An investigation of psychopathy, emotional processing, and deception detection. *Legal and Criminological Psychology, 17,* 177–191.

Peace, K. A., & Sinclair, S. M. (2012). Cold-blooded lie catchers? An investigation of psychopathy, emotional processing, and deception detection. *Legal and Criminological Psychology, 17*(1), 177–191.

Peace, K. A., & Wells, K. M. (2012, in prep). *Beach parties and bleeding men: The misinformation effect as a function of emotional valence, psychopathy, and exposure duration.*

Peace, K. A., Brower, K. L., & Shudra, R. D. (2012). Fact or fiction?: Discriminating true and false allegations of victimization. In A. N. Hutcherson (Ed.), *Psychology of victimization* (pp. 1–79). Hauppauge, NY: Nova Science Publishers.

Peace, K. A., Porter, S., & Cook, B. L. (2010). Investigating differences in truthful and fabricated symptoms of traumatic stress over time. *Psychological Injury and Law, 3,* 118–129.

Peace, K. A., Porter, S., & ten Brinke, L. (2008). A within-subjects comparison of memories for sexual trauma with memories for non-sexual trauma and non-traumatic experiences in a clinical sample. *Memory, 16,* 10–21.

Peace, K., Porter, S., & Almon, D. (2012, in press). Sidetracked by emotion: Observers' ability to discriminate genuine and fabricated sexual allegations. *Legal and Criminological Psychology.*

Peak, K. J., & Glensor, R. W. (1996). *Community policing and problem solving: Strategies and practices.* Upper Saddle River, NJ: Prentice-Hall.

Pedersen, L., Kunz, C., Rasmussen, K., & Elsass, P. (2010). Psychopathy as a risk factor for violent recidivism: Investigating the Psychopathy Checklist Screening Version (PCL:SV) and the Comprehensive Assessment of Psychopathic Personality (CAPP) in a forensic psychiatric setting. *The International Journal of Forensic Mental Health, 9*(4), 308–315.

Pekkanen, J. (1976). *Victims: An account of rape.* New York: Popular Library.

Pence, E., & Paymor, M. (1985). *Power and control: Tactics of men who batter: An educational curriculum.* Duluth, MN: Minnesota Program Development.

Pennebaker, J. W., Francis, M. E., & Booth, R. J. (2001). *Linguistic inquiry and word count (LIWC): LIWC 2001.* Mahwah, NJ: Erlbaum.

Pennebaker, J. W. & Beall, S. K. (1986). Confronting a traumatic event: Toward an understanding of inhibition and disease. *Journal of Abnormal Psychology, 95,* 274–281.

Pennebaker, J. W. (1993). Putting stress into words: Health, linguistic, and therapeutic implications. *Behavior Research and Therapy, 31,* 539–548.

Pennington, N., & Hastie, R. (1981). Juror decision making models: The generalization gap. *Psychological Bulletin, 89,* 246–287.

Penrod, S. D., & Cutler, B. L. (1987). Assessing the competence of juries. In I. B. Weiner & A. K. Hess (Eds.), *Handbook of forensic psychology.* New York: John Wiley.

Penrod, S. D., Fulero, S. M., & Cutler, B. L. (1995). Expert psychological testimony on eyewitness reliability before and after Daubert: The state of the law and the science. *Behavioral Sciences and the Law, 13,* 229–259.

People v. Raymond Buckey et al., Los Angeles Sup. Ct. No. A750900 (1990).

People v. Torres, 128 Misc.2d 129, 488 N.Y.2d 358 (Sup. Ct. 1985).

Pereda, N., Guilera, G., Forns, M., & Gómez-Benito, J. (2009). The prevalence of child sexual abuse in community and student samples: A meta-analysis. *Clinical Psychology Review, 29*(4), 328–338.

Perez-Pena, R. (1994, December 12). Investigators describe a meticulous maker of bombs. *The New York Times,* p. A12.

Perillo, J. T., & Kassin, S. M. (2011). Inside interrogation: The lie, the bluff, and false confessions. *Law and Human Behavior, 35*(4), 327–337.

Perrott, S. B. & Kelloway, E. K. (2011). Scandals, sagging morale, and role ambiguity in the Royal Canadian Mounted Police: The end of a Canadian Institution as we

Perry, B. D. (2009). Examining child maltreatment through a neurodevelopmental lens:

Clinical applications of the neurosequential model of therapeutics. *Journal of Loss and Trauma, 14*(4), 240–255.

Peterson, C., & Parsons, B. (2005). Interviewing former 1- and 2-year-olds about medical emergencies five years later. *Law & Human Behavior, 29,* 743–754.

Peterson, C., Moores, L., & White, G. (2001). Recounting the same events again and again: Children's consistency across multiple interviews. *Applied Cognitive Psychology, 15,* 353–371.

Pezdek, K., & Banks, W. P. (Eds.). (1996). *The recovered memory/false memory debate.* San Diego: Academic Press.

Pezdek, K., & Taylor, J. (2000). Discriminating between accounts of true and false events. In D. F. Bjorklund (Ed.), *Research and theory in false-memory creation in children and adults* (pp. 69–92). Mahwah, NJ: Lawrence Erlbaum and Associates.

Pezdek, K., Finger, K., & Hodge, D. (1997). Planting false childhood memories: The role of event plausibility. *Psychological Science, 8,* 437–441.

Pigott, M. A., Foley, L. A., Covati, C. J., & Wasserman, A. (1998, March). Mock jurors' *perceptions of a male plaintiff in sexual harassment litigation.* Paper presented at the meetings of the American Psychology-Law Society, Redondo Beach, CA.

Pinel, P. (1962). *A treatise on insanity* (D. Davis, Trans.). New York: Hafner. (Original work published in 1801)

Pinizzotto, A. J. (1984). Forensic psychology: Criminal personality profiling. *Journal of Police Science and Administration, 12,* 32–40.

Pinizzotto, A. J., & Finkel, N. J. (1990). Criminal personality profiling: An outcome and process study. *Law and Human Behavior, 14,* 215–233.

Pirelli, G., Gottdiener, W. H., & Zapf, P. A. (2011). A meta-analytic review of competency to stand trial research. *Psychology, Public Policy, and Law, 17*(1), 1–53.

Pogrebin, M. R., Poole, E. D., & Regoli, R. M. (1986). Stealing money: An assessment of bank embezzlers. *Behavioral Sciences and the Law, 4,* 481–490.

Pokorny, A. D. (1983). Prediction of suicide in psychiatric patients: Report of a prospective study. *Archives of General Psychiatry, 40,* 249–257.

Pollak, S., Cicchetti, D., & Klorman, R. (1998). Stress, memory, and emotion: Developmental considerations from the study of child maltreatment. *Development and Psychopathology, 10,* 811–828.

Ponce, G., Perez-Gonzalez, R., Aragues, M., Palomo, T., Rodriguez-Jimenez, R., Jimenez-Arriero, M. A., (2009). The ANKK1 kinase gene and psychiatric disorders. *Neurotoxicity Research, 16*(1), 50–59.

Poole, D. A., & White, L. T. (1991). Effects of question repetition on the eyewitness testimony of children and adults. *Developmental Psychology, 27,* 975–986.

Poole, D., & Lindsay, D. (2002). Reducing child witnesses' false reports of misinformation from parents. *Journal of Experimental Child Psychology, 81*(2), 117–140.

Poole, D., Bruck, M., & Pipe, M. (2011). Forensic interviewing aids: Do props help children answer questions about touching? *Current Directions in Psychological Science, 20*(1), 11–15.

Pope, K. S., & Gutheil, T. G. (2009). Psychologists abandon the Nuremberg ethic: Concerns for detainee interrogations. *International Journal of Law and Psychiatry, 32,* 161–166.

Porter, S. & ten Brinke, L. (2008). Reading between the lies: Identifying concealed and falsified emotions in universal facial expressions. *Psychological Science, 19,* 508–514.

Porter, S. & ten Brinke, L. (2009). Dangerous decisions: A theoretical framework for understanding how judges assess credibility in the courtroom. *Legal and Criminological Psychology, 14,* 119–134.

Porter, S. & ten Brinke, L. (2010). The truth about lies: What works in detecting high-stakes deception? Invited Review in a Special Issue of *Legal and Criminological Psychology, 15,* 57–75.

Porter, S. (1996). Without conscience or without active conscience? The etiology of psychopathy revisited. *Aggression and Violent Behavior, 1,* 179–189.

Porter, S. (2004). Forensic psychology. *Canadian Journal of Behavioural Science, 36,* 81–83.

Porter, S., & Peace, K. A. (2007). "The scars of memory: A prospective, longitudinal investigation of the consistency of traumatic and positive emotional memories in adulthood": Erratum. *Psychological Science, 18*(7), 435–441.

Porter, S., & ten Brinke L. (2008). Reading between the lies: Identifying concealed and falsified emotions in universal facial expressions. *Psychological Science, 19* 508–514.

Porter, S., & ten Brinke, L. (2010). The truth about lies: What works in detecting high-stakes deception? Invited Review in a Special Issue of *Legal and Criminological Psychology 15,* 15–75.

Porter, S., & Woodworth, M. (2004, in press). Patterns of violent behavior in the criminal psychopath. In C. Patrick (Ed.). *Handbook of psychopathy.* New York: Guilford.

Porter, S., & Woodworth, M. (2006). Psychopathy and aggression. In C. Patrick (Ed.), *Handbook of psychopathy* (481–494). New York: Guilford.

Porter, S., & Woodworth, M. (2007). "I'm sorry ... but he started it: A comparison of the official and self-reported homicide descriptions of psychopath and non-psychopaths. *Law and Human Behavior, 31,* 91–107.

Porter, S., & Yuille, J. C. (1995). Credibility assessment of criminal suspects through statement analysis. *Psychology, Crime, and Law, 1,* 319–331.

Porter, S., Birt A. R., & Boer, D. P. (2001). Investigation of the criminal and conditional release histories of Canadian federal offenders as a function of psychopathy and age. *Law and Human Behavior, 25,* 647–661.

Porter, S., Birt, A. R., Yuille, J. C., & Hervé, H. (2001). Memory for murder: A psychological perspective on dissociative amnesia in forensic contexts. *International Journal of Law and Psychiatry, 24,* 23–42.

Porter, S., Birt, A. R., Yuille, J. C., & Lehman, D. (2000). Negotiating false memories: Interviewer and rememberer characteristics relate to memory distortion. *Psychological Science, 11,* 513–516.

Porter, S., Campbell, M. A., Birt, A. R., & Woodworth, M. T. (2003a). "He said, She said": A psychological perspective on historical memory evidence in the courtroom. *Canadian Psychology, 44,* 190–206.

Porter, S., Campbell, M. A., Birt, A. R., & Woodworth, M. T. (2003b). "We said, she said": A response to Loftus (2003). *Canadian Psychology, 44,* 213–215.

Porter, S., Campbell, M. A., Birt, A., & Woodworth, M. (2003). "He said, she said": A psychological perspective on historical memory evidence in the courtroom. *Canadian Psychology, 44,* 190–206.

Porter, S., Campbell, M. A., Woodworth, M., & Birt, A. R. (2001). A new psychological conceptualization of the sexual psychopath. In F. Columbus (Ed.) *Advances in Psychological Research (Vol. 7).* Huntington, NY: Nova Science Publishers.

Porter, S., Demetrioff, S., & ten Brinke, L. (2010). Sexual psychopath: Current understanding and future challenges. In Schlank, A. (Ed.), *The sexual predator—Volume IV* (p. 13-1-13-12). Kingston, NJ: Civic Research Institute.

Porter, S., Demetrioff, S., McDougall, A., ten Brinke, L., & Wilson, K. (2010). A prospective investigation of the vulnerability of positive and negative scenes to the misinformation effect.

Canadian Journal of Behavioural Science, 42, 55-61.

Porter, S., England, L., Juodis, M., ten Brinke, L. & Wilson, K. (2008). Is the face the window to the soul?: Investigation of the accuracy of intuitive judgments of the trustworthiness of human faces. *Canadian Journal of Behavioural Science, 40,* 171-177.

Porter, S., Fairweather, D., Drugge, J., Hervé, H., Birt, A., & Boer, D. P. (2000). Profiles of psychopathy in incarcerated sexual offenders. *Criminal Justice and Behavior, 27*(2), 216-233.

Porter, S., Gustaw, C., & ten Brinke, L. (2010). Dangerous decisions: The impact of first impressions of trustworthiness on the evaluation of legal evidence and defendant culpability. *Psychology Crime & Law, 16,* 477-491.

Porter, S., McCabe, S., Woodworth, M., & Peace, K. A. (2007). Genius is 1% inspiration and 99% perspiration ... or is it? An investigation of the impact of motivation and feedback on deception detection. *Legal and Criminological Psychology, 12*(2), 297-309.

Porter, S., Peace, K. A., & Emmett, K. (2007). You protest too much, methinks: Investigating the features of truthful and fabricated reports of traumatic experiences. *Canadian Journal of Behavioural Science, 39,* 79-92.

Porter, S., Peace, K., Douglas, R., & Doucette, N. (2011). Recovered memories in the courtroom. In J. Ziskin & D. Faust (Eds.), *Coping with psychological and psychiatric evidence.* Los Angeles: Law and Psychology Press.

Porter, S., ten Brinke, L., & Wallace, B. (2011, in press). Secrets and lies: Involuntary leakage in deceptive facial expressions as a function of emotional intensity. *Journal of Non-verbal Behavior.*

Porter, S., ten Brinke, L., & Wilson, K. (2009). Crime profiles and conditional release performance of psychopathic and non-psychopathic sexual offenders. *Legal and Criminological Psychology, 14,* 109-118.

Porter, S., ten Brinke, L., Baker, A., & Wallace, B. (2012). Would I lie to you? "Leakage" in deceptive facial expressions relates to psychopathy and emotional intelligence. *Personality and Individual Differences, 51,* 133-137.

Porter, S., Woodworth, M., & Birt, A. R. (2000). Truth, lies, and videotape: An investigation of the ability of federal parole officers to detect deception. *Law and Human Behavior, 24,* 643-658.

Porter, S., Woodworth, M., Earle, J., Drugge, J., & Boer, D. P. (2003). Characteristics of violent behavior exhibited during sexual homicides committed by psychopathic and non-psychopathic offenders.murderers. *Law and Human Behavior, 27,* 459-470.

Porter, S., Yuille, J. C., & Lehman, D. R. (1999). The nature of real, implanted and fabricated memories for emotional childhood events: Implications for the recovered memory debate. *Law and Human Behavior, 23,* 517-537.

Post, J. M. (1991). Saddam Hussein of Iraq: A political psychology profile. *Political Psychology, 12,* 279-289.

Potter, J. A., & Bost, F. (1995). *Fatal justice: Reinvestigating the MacDonald murders.* New York: Norton.

Powitsky, R. J. (1979). The use and misuse of psychologists in a hostage situation. *The Police Chief, 46*(6), 30-33.

Poythress, N. G. (1980). Assessment and prediction in the hostage situation: Optimizing the use of psychological data. *The Police Chief, 47*(8), 34-38.

Poythress, N., Bonnie, R., Hoge, S., Monahan, J., & Oberlander, L. (1994). Client abilities to assist counsel and make decisions in criminal cases: Findings from three studies. *Law and Human Behavior, 18,* 437-452.

Pozzulo, J. D., & Dempsey, J. L. (2009). Witness factors and their influence on jurors' perceptions and verdicts. *Criminal Justice and Behavior, 36,* 923-934.

Pozzulo, J. D., & Siobhan, M. (2006). Comparing identification procedures when the perpetrator has change appearance. *Psychology, Crime & Law, 12,* 429-238.

Pozzulo, J. D., Crescini, C., & Lemieux, J. M. T. (2008). Are accurate witnesses more likely to make absolute judgments? *International Journal of Law and Psychiatry, 31,* 495-501.

Prentky, R. A., & Knight, R. A. (1991). Identifying critical dimensions for discriminating among rapists. *Journal of Consulting and Clinical Psychology, 59*(5), 643-661.

Price, H. L., & Roberts, K. P. (2011). The effects of an intensive training and feedback program on police and social workers' investigative interviews of children. *Canadian Journal of Behavioural Science/ Revue Canadienne Des Sciences Du Comportement, 43*(3), 235-244.

Prichard, J. C. (1837/1973). *A treatise on insanity and other disorders affecting the mind.* New York: Arno.

Public Safety Canada Portfolio Corrections Statistics Committee. (2007). Corrections and conditional release overview. Retrieved July 23, 2012, from http://www.publicsafety.gc.ca/res/cor/rep/ccrso2007-eng.aspx

Public Works & Government Services Canada.(1999). Unintentional and intentional injury profile for aboriginal people in Canada. Retrieved July 23, 2012, from http://www.hc-sc.gc.ca/fniah-spnia/pubs/promotion/_injury-bless/2001_trauma/index-eng.php

Purcell, R., Pathé, M., & Mullen, P. E. (2002). The prevalence and nature of stalking in the Australian community. *Australian and New Zealand Journal of Psychiatry, 36,* 114-120.

Quen, J. M. (1981). Anglo-American concepts of criminal responsibility: A brief history. In S. J. Hucker, C. D. Webster & M. H. Ben-Aron (Eds.), *Mental disorder and criminal responsibility* (pp. 1–10). Toronto: Butterworths.

Quinsey, V. L., Arnold, L. S., & Pruesse, M. G. (1980). MMPI profiles of men referred for a pretrial psychiatric assessment as a function of offense type. *Journal of Clinical Psychology, 36*, 410–417.

Quinsey, V. L., Harris, G. T., Rice, M. E., & Cormier, C. A. (1998). *Violent Offenders: Appraising and managing risk*. Washington, DC: American Psychological Association.

Quinsey, V. L., Harris, G. T., Rice, M. E., & Cormier, C. A. (2006). Actuarial prediction of violence. In *Violent Offenders: Appraising and managing risk* (pp. 155–196). Washington, DC: American Psychological Association.

Quinsey, V. L., Rice, M. E., & Harris, G. T. (1995). Actuarial prediction of sexual recidivism. *Journal of Interpersonal Violence, 10*(1), 85–105.

R. v. Armstrong (1959), 125 C.C.C. 56.

R. v. B. (1990), 36 O.A.C. 307.

R. v. B. (K.G.), [1993] 1 S.C.R. 740.

R. v. Bain (1992), 1 S.C.R.

R. v. Béland, [1987] 2 S.C.R. 398.

R. v. Brown (2003), 64 O.R. (3d).

R. v. Burns, [1994] 1 S.C.R. 656.

R. v. Calderon (2004), Court of Appeal for Ontario, Docket C38499; C38500.

R. v. Chaulk, [1990] 3 S.C.R. 1303.

R. v. Darrach, [2000] 2 S.C.R. 443, 2000 SCC 46.

R. v. Fagundes (1997), Court of Appeal for Ontario, Docket c16059.

R. v. François, [1994] 2 S.C.R. 827.

R. v. Gladue (1999), 1 S.C.R. 688.

R. v. Henderson (2010), EWCA Crim 1269

R. v. Jabarianha, [2001] 3 S.C.R. 430.

R. v. Lavallee, [1990] 1 N.S.C.R. 852. (2010) O.N.C.A. 670.

R. v. Lifchus, [1997] 3 S.C.R. 320.

R. v. Malik & Bagri (2005), B.C.S.C. 350.

R. v. Malott, [1998] 1 S.C.R. 123.

R. v. Marquard, [1993] 4 S.C. R. 223.

R. v. McCraw (1991), 3 S.C.R. 72.

R. v. McIntosh and McCarthy (1997), 117 C.C.C. (3d) 385.

R. v. McLean (2003), Provincial Court of Newfoundland and Labrador. Docket: 130A-0001.

R. v. Mervyn (2003), Y.K.T.C. 34.

R. v. Miller (1985), 2 S.C.R. 613

R. v. Miller, (2000) B.C.C.A. 329

R. v. Mills (1999), BCCA 159.

R. v. Mohan, [1994] 2 S.C.R. 9.

R. v. N.S. (2010), O.N.C.A. 670.

R. v. Normore (2002), Provincial Court of Newfoundland. Docket 1301A-00470.

R. v. O'Connor, [1995] 4 S.C.R. 411.

R. v. Oickle (2000), S.C.C. 38, File no. 26535.

R. v. Oickle, [2000] 2 S.C.R. 3.

R. v. Osmar (2007), 44 CR.

R. v. Pan; R. v. Sawyer (2001), 2 S.C.R. 344, 2001 SCC 42.

R. v. Parks (1992), 75 C.C.C. (3d) 287.

R. v. Parks (1993), 84 C.C.C. (3d) 353.

R. v. Ranger (2003), Court of Appeal for Ontario. Docket C31117.

R. v. Redbreast (2004), ABQB 504.

R. v. Regan (1999), Nova Scotia Court of Appeal, Docket C.A.C. 147242.

R. v. Regan, [2002] 1 S.C.R. 297, 2002 SCC 12.

R. v. Roble (2004), CanLII 23106 (ON C.A.).

R. v. S. (R.D.) (1997), 3 S.C.R.

R. v. Samuel, 2004

R. v. Sawyer. [2001]. S. R. C. 344

R. v. Sterling (1995), S. J. No. 612 (C.A.).

R. v. Stone (1999), 2 SCR 290.

R. v. Struve (2007), BCSC 1316.

R. v. Swain, [1991] 1 S.C.R. 933.

R. v. W. (R.), [1992] 2 S.C.R. 122.

R. v. W.W.M. (2006), 206 O.A.C. 342.

R. v. Whynot (1983), 9 C.C.C. 449 (N.S.C.A).

R. v. Zeek (2004), B.C.C.A. 42.

Rabinowitz, D. (1990, May). From the mouths of babes to a jail cell: Child abuse and the abuse of justice. *Harper's Magazine,* pp. 52–63.

Rachlin, H. (1995). *The making of a detective*. New York: W. W. Norton.

Rachlinski, J. J., Johnson, S. L, Wistrich, A. J., & Guthrie, C. (2009). Does unconscious bias affect trial judges? *Notre Dame Law Review, 84*, 1195–1246.

Raine, A., Lencz, T., Taylor, K., Hellige, J. B., Bihrle, S., Lacasse, L., et al. (2003). Corpus callosum abnormalities in psychopathic antisocial individuals. *Archives of General Psychiatry, 60*, 1134–1142.

Ramsey-Klawsnik, H., Teaster, P. B., Mendiondo, M. S., Marcum, J. L., & Abner, E. L. (2008). Sexual predators who target elders: Findings from the first national study of sexual abuse in care facilities. *Journal of Elder Abuse & Neglect, 20*(4), 353–376.

Rappeport, M. (1993, October 11). Statistics fine-tune simple courtroom evidence. *National Law Journal,* 15–16.

Raskin, D. C., & Esplin, P. W. (1991). Statement validity assessment: Interview procedures and content analysis of children's statements of sexual abuse. *Behavioral Assessment, 13*, 265–291.

Rattner, A. (1988). Convicted but innocent: Wrongful conviction and the criminal justice system. *Law and Human Behavior, 12*, 283–293.

RCMP (2011). Truth verification. Retrieved July 23, 2012, from http://205.193.86.86/tops-opst/bs-sc/truth-sinc-ver-eng.htm

RCMP Watch. (2009). *Shannon Murrin settles civil suit with RCMP*. Retrieved from http://www.rcmpwatch.com

Re Moore and the Queen (1984), 10 C.C.C. (3d) 306.

Read, D., & Lindsay, S. D. (Eds.) (1997). *Recollections of trauma: Scientific evidence and clinical practice.* New York: Plenum.

Redlich, A. D., & Meissner, C. A. (2009). Techniques and controversies in the interrogation of suspects: The artful practice versus the scientific study. In J. Skeem et al. (Eds.), *Psychological science in the courtroom: Controversies and consensus* (pp. 124–148). Guilford Press.

Redlich, A. D., Quas, J. A., & Ghetti, S. (2008). Perceptions of children during a police interview: Guilt, confessions, and interview fairness. *Psychology, Crime and Law, 14,* 201–223.

Reese, J., Horn, J., & Dunning, C. (Eds.). (1991). *Critical incidents in policing.* Washington, DC: U.S. Government Printing office.

Reese-Weber, M., & Smith, D. M. (2011). Outcomes of child sexual abuse as predictors of later sexual victimization. *Journal of Interpersonal Violence, 26*(9), 1884–1905.

Regehr, C., & Glancy, G. (1995). Battered woman syndrome defense in the Canadian courts. *Canadian Journal of Psychiatry, 40,* 130–135.

Reich, J., & Tookey, L. (1986). Disagreements between court and psychiatrist on competency to stand trial. *Journal of Clinical Psychiatry, 47,* 616–623.

Reidy, D. R., Shelley-Tremblay, J. F., & Lilienfeld, S. O. (2011) Psychopathy, reactive aggression, and precarious proclamations: A review of behavioral, cognitive, and biological research. *Aggression and Violent Behavior, 16,* 512–524.

Reiser, M. (1972). *The police department psychologist.* Springfield, IL: Charles C Thomas.

Reiser, M. (1974). Some organizational stressors on policemen. *Journal of Police Science and Administration, 2,* 156–159.

Reiser, M. (1980). *Handbook of investigative hypnosis.* Los Angeles: LEHI.

Reiser, M. (1982a). Crime specific psychological consultation. *The Police Chief, 49*(3), 53–56.

Reiser, M. (1982b). *Police psychology: Collected papers.* Los Angeles: LEHI.

Reiser, M. (1982c). Selection and promotion of policemen. In M. Reiser (Ed.), *Police psychology: Collected papers* (pp. 84–92). Los Angeles: LEHI.

Reiser, M. (1985). Investigative hypnosis: Scientism, memory tricks, and power plays. In J. K. Zeig (Ed.), *Ericksonian psychotherapy: Vol. I. Structures.* New York: Brunner/Mazel.

Rendell, J. A., Huss, M. T., & Jensen, M. L. (2010). Expert testimony and the effects of a biological approach, psychopathy, and juror attitudes in cases of insanity. *Behavioral Sciences & the Law, 28*(3), 411–425.

Repo-Tiihonen, E., Tiihonen, J., Lindberg, N., Weizmann-Henelius, G., Putkonen, H., & Häkkänen, H. (2010). The intergenerational cycle of criminality association with psychopathy. *Journal of Forensic Sciences, 55*(1), 116–120.

Resick, P. A., Williams, L. F., Suvak, M. K., Monson, C. M., & Gradus, J. L. (2012). Long-term outcomes of cognitive-behavioral treatments for posttraumatic stress disorder among female rape survivors. *Journal of Consulting and Clinical Psychology, 80*(2), 201–210.

Ressler, R. K., & Shachtman, T. (1992). *Whoever fights monsters.* New York: St. Martin's Press.

Ressler, R. K., Burgess, A. W., Douglas, J. E., Hartman, C. R., & D'Agostino, R. B. (1986). Sexual killers and their victims: Identifying patterns through crime scene analysis. *Journal of Interpersonal Violence, 1,* 288–308.

Ressler, R. K., Burgess, A. W., Hartman, C. R., Douglas, J. E., & McCormack, A. (1986). Murderers who rape and mutilate. *Journal of Interpersonal Violence, 1,* 273–287.

Ressler, R., Burgess, A., & Douglas, J. (1988). *Sexual homicide.* Lexington, MA: Lexington Books.

Reynolds, K., & Miles H. L. (2009). The effect of training on the quality of HCR-20 violence risk assessments in forensic secure services. *Journal of Forensic Psychiatry and Psychology, 20,* 473–480.

Reynolds, M. (1994, November). The scariest criminal in America. *Playboy,* pp. 120–122, 128, 146–154.

Rice, M. E., & Harris, G. T. (1997). Cross-validation and extension of the Violence Risk Appraisal Guide for child molesters and rapists. *Law and Human Behavior, 21*(2), 231–241.

Rice, M. E., & Harris, G. T. (2011). Is androgen deprivation therapy effective in the treatment of sex offenders? *Psychology, Public Policy, and Law, 17*(2), 315–332.

Rice, M., & Harris, G. (1995). Violent recidivism: Assessing predictive validity. *Journal of Consulting and Clinical Psychology, 63,* 737–748.

Rice, M., Harris, G., & Cormier, C. (1992). An evaluation of maximum-security therapeutic community for psychopaths and other mentally disordered offenders. *Law and Human Behavior, 16,* 399–412.

Rider, A. O. (1980, June-August). The firesetter: A psychological profile. *F.B.I. Law Enforcement Bulletin,* pp. 2–23.

Ring, K. (1971). *Let's get started: An appeal to what's left in psychology.* Unpublished manuscript, Department of Psychology, University of Connecticut, Storrs, CT.

Rischke, A. E., Roberts, K. P., & Price, H. L. (2011). Using spaced learning principles to translate knowledge into behavior: Evidence from investigative interviews of alleged child abuse victims. *Journal of Police and Criminal Psychology, 26*(1), 58–67.

Risinger, D. M. (2007). Innocents convicted: An empirically justified factual wrong conviction rate. *The Journal of Criminal Law and Criminology, 97*(3), 761–800.

Roberts, A. R., & Roberts, B. (2005). *Ending intimate abuse: Practical guidance and survival strategies*. Oxford University Press, New York

Roberts, J. V., & Grossman, M.on, N., Davies, G. (1993). Sexual homicide in Canada: A descriptive analysis. *Annals of Sex Research, 6*(1), 5–25.

Roberts, K. A. (2011). Police interviews with terrorist suspects: Risks, ethical interviewing and procedural justice. *The British Journal of Forensic Practice, 13,* 124–134.

Roberts, W. T., & Higham, P. A. (2002). Selecting accurate statements from the cognitive interview using confidence ratings. *Journal of Experimental Psychology: Applied, 8,* 33–43.

Robertson, N., Davies, G., & Nettleingham, A. (2009). Vicarious traumatisation as a consequence of jury service. *The Howard Journal, 48,* 1–12.

Robinette, P. R. (1999). *Differential treatment of corporate defendants as a form of actor identity and evaluator expectations*. Unpublished doctoral dissertation, Department of Communication Studies, Lawrence, KS: University of Kansas.

Robinson, R., & Murdoch, P. (2003). *Establishing and maintaining peer support programs in the workplace* (3rd ed.). Elliot City, MD: Chevron.

Rodriguez, J. H., LeWinn, L. M., & Perlin, M. L. (1983). The insanity defense under siege: Legislative assaults and legal rejoinders. *Rutgers Law Journal, 14,* 397–430.

Roediger, H. L., III, & McDermott, K. B. (1995). Creating false memories: Remembering words not presented in word lists. *Journal of Experimental Psychology: Learning, Memory and Cognition, 21,* 803–814.

Roediger, H. L. (1996). Memory illusions. *Journal of Memory and Language, 35,* 76–100.

Roesch, R., & Golding, S. L. (1980). *Competency to stand trial*. Urbana: University of Illinois Press.

Roesch, R., & Golding, S. L. (1987). Defining and assessing competence to stand trial. In I. Weiner & A. Hess (Eds.), *Handbook of forensic psychology* (pp. 378–394). New York: John Wiley.

Roesch, R., Golding, S. L., Hans, V. P., & Reppucci, N. D. (1991). Social science and the courts: The role of amicus curiae briefs. *Law and Human Behavior, 15,* 1–11.

Roesch, R., Webster, C., & Eaves, D. (1984). *The Fitness Interview Test: A method for examining fitness to stand trial*. Toronto: Centre of Criminology, University of Toronto.

Roesch, R., Webster, C., & Eaves, D. (1994). *The Fitness Interview Test—Revised: A method for examining fitness to stand trial*. Burnaby, BC: Department of Psychology, Simon Fraser University.

Roesch, R., Zapf, P. A., & Eaves, D. (2006). *FIT-R: Fitness Interview Test—Revised. A structured interview for assessing competency to stand trial*. Sarasota, FL: Professional Resource Press/ Professional Resource Exchange.

Roesch, R., Zapf, P. A., Eaves, D., & Webster, C. D. (1998). *The Fitness Interview Test—Revised*. Burnaby, BC: Mental Health, Law, and Policy Institute, Simon Fraser University.

Roe-Sepowitz, D., & Hickle, K. (2011). Comparing boy and girl arsonists: Crisis, family, and crime scene characteristics. *Legal and Criminological Psychology, 16*(2), 277–288.

Rogers E. M. (2003). *Diffusion of Innovations*. New York: Free Press

Rogers, R. (1984). *Rogers Criminal Responsibility Assessment Scales (R-CRAS) and test manual*. Odessa, FL: Psychological Assessment Resources.

Rogers, R. (1986). *Conducting insanity evaluations*. New York: Van Nostrand Reinhold.

Rogers, R. (1988). Structured interviews and dissimulation. In R. Rogers (Ed.),

Clinical assessment of malingering and deception (pp. 250–268). New York: Guilford Press.

Rogers, R. (1990). Models of feigned mental illness. *Professional Psychology: Research and Practice, 21,* 182–188.

Rogers, R., & Cavanaugh, J. L. (1981). The Rogers Criminal Responsibility Assessment scales. *Illinois Medical Journal, 160,* 164–169.

Rogers, R., & Ewing, C. P. (1989). Ultimate opinion proscriptions: A cosmetic fix and plea for empiricism. *Law and Human Behavior, 13,* 357–374.

Rogers, R., & Ewing, C. P. (1992). The measurement of insanity: Debating the merits of the R-CRAS and its alternatives. *International Journal of Law and Psychiatry, 15,* 113–123.

Rogers, R., & Johansson-Love, J. (2009). Evaluating competency to stand trial with evidence-based practice. *Journal of the American Academy of Psychiatry and the Law, 37*(4), 450–460.

Rogers, R., & Sewell, K. W. (1999). The R-CRAS and insanity evaluations: A re-examination of construct validity. *Behavioral Sciences & the Law, 17*(2), 181–194.

Rogers, R., Cavanaugh, J. L., Seman, W., & Harris, M. (1984). Legal outcome and clinical findings: A study of insanity evaluations. *Bulletin of the American Academy of Psychiatry and the Law, 12,* 75–83.

Rogers, R., Dolmetsch, R., Wasyliw, O. E., & Cavanaugh, J. L. (1982). Scientific inquiry in forensic psychology. *International Journal of Law and Psychiatry, 5,* 187–203.

Rogers, R., Gillis, J. R., Bagby, R. M., & Monteiro, E. (1991). Detection of malingering on the Structured Interview of Reported Symptoms (SIRS): A study of coached and uncoached simulators. *Psychological Assessment: A Journal of Consulting and Clinical Psychology, 3,* 673–677.

Rogers, R., Johansen, J., Chang, J. J., & Salekin, R. (1997). Predictors of adolescent psychopathy: Oppositional and conduct-disorders symptoms. *Journal of the American Academy of Psychiatry and Law, 25,* 261-270.

Rogers, R., Sewell, K. W., & Goldstein, A. M. (1994). Explanatory models of malingering: A prototypical analysis. *Law and Human Behavior, 18,* 543-552.

Rogers, R., Wasyliw, O. E., & Cavanaugh, J. L. (1984). Evaluating insanity: A study of construct validity. *Law and Human Behavior, 8,* 293-303.

Roma, P., Martini, P., Sabatello, U., Tatarelli, R., & Ferracuti, S. (2011). Validity of Criteria-Based Content Analysis (CBCA) at trial in free-narrative interviews. *Child Abuse & Neglect, 35*(8), 613-620.

Roper, R., & Shewan, D. (2002). Compliance and eyewitness testimony: Do eyewitnesses comply with misleading "expert pressure" during investigative interviewing? *Legal and Criminological Psychology, 7,* 155-163.

Rosen, P. (1972). *The Supreme Court and social science.* Urbana: University of Illinois Press.

Rosenbaum, D. P., Graziano, L. M., Stephens, C. D., & Schuck, A. M. (2011). "Understanding Community Policing and Legitimacy-seeking Behavior in Virtual Reality: A National Study of Municipal Police Websites." *Police Quarterly, 14,* 25-47.

Rosenbaum, R. (1993, April). The F.B.I.'s agent provocateur. *Vanity Fair,* pp. 122-136.

Rosenbaum, R. (1998). *Explaining Hitler.* New York: Random House.

Rosenhan, D. L. (1973). On being sane in insane places. *Science, 179,* 250-258.

Rosenthal, R. (1995). *State of New Jersey v. Margaret Kelly Michaels:* An overview. *Psychology, Public Policy, and Law, 1,* 246-271.

Rossi, D. (1982). Crime scene behavioral analysis: Another tool for the law enforcement investigator. *The Police Chief, 49*(1), 152-155.

Rossmo, D. K. (1997). Geographic profiling. In J. L. Jackson & D. A. Bekerian (Eds.), *Offender profiling: Theory, research and practice* (pp. 159-175). New York: John Wiley.

Rossmo, D. K. (2000). *Geographic profiling.* Boca Raton, FL: CRC Press.

Roth, S., & Lebowitz, L. (1988). The experience of sexual trauma. *Journal of Traumatic Stress, 1*(1), 79-107.

Rowland, C. K. (1994, February 28). Personal communication.

Royal Canadian Mounted Police (2010, July 30). *Undercover operations.* Retrieved May 15, 2012 from http://bc.rcmp.ca/ViewPage.action?siteNodeId=154&languageId=1&contentId=691

Royal Canadian Mounted Police. (2004). *Truth verification.* Retrieved August 20, 2004, from http://www.rcmp.ca/techops/truth_ver_e.htm

Ruback, B., & Hopper, H. (1986). Decision making by parole interviewers: The effect of case and interview factors. *Law and Human Behavior, 10,* 203-214.

Ruby, C. L., & Brigham, J. C. (1997). The usefulness of the criteria-based content analysis technique in distinguishing between truthful and fabricated allegations: A critical review. *Psychology, Public Policy, and Law, 3,* 705-737.

Ruch, L. O., Gartrell, J. W., Amedeo, S. R., & Coyne, B. J. (1991). The Sexual Assault Symptom Scale: Measuring self-reported sexual assault trauma in the emergency room. *Psychological Assessment, 3,* 3-8.

Ruddy, C. (1997). *The strange death of Vincent Foster.* New York: Free Press.

Rudin, J. (2000, May 15). Aboriginal peoples and the criminal justice system. Retrieved May 15, 2012 from http://www.attorneygeneral.jus.gov.on.ca/inquiries/ipperwash/.../Rudin.pdf

Rutten, B. P., & Mill, J. (2009). Epigenetic mediation of environmental influences in major psychotic disorders. *Schizophrenia Bulletin, 35*(6), 1045-1056.

Ryan, C., Anastario, M., & DaCunha, A. (2006). Changing coverage of domestic violence murders: A longitudinal experiments in participatory communication. *Journal of Interpersonal Violence, 21,* 209-228.

Ryan, G., Miyoshi, T. J., Metzner, J. L., Krugman, R., & Fryer, G. E. (1996). Trends in a national sample of sexually abusive youths. *Journal of the American Academy of Child & Adolescent Psychiatry, 35*(1), 17-25.

Rye, B. J., & Meaney, G. J. (2007). Voyeurism: It is good as long as we do not get caught. *International Journal of Sexual Health, 19*(1), 47-56.

Saks, M. J. (1992). Normative and empirical issues about the role of expert witnesses. In D. K. Kagehiro & W. S. Laufer (Eds.), *Handbook of psychology and law* (pp. 185-203). New York: Springer-Verlag.

Saks, M. J. (1993). Improving APA science translation amicus briefs. *Law and Human Behavior, 17,* 235-247.

Salekin, R. T. (2008). Psychopathy and recidivism from mid-adolescence to young adulthood: Cumulating legal problems and limiting life opportunities. *Journal of Abnormal Psychology, 117*(2), 386-395.

Salekin, R. T., Rogers, R., & Sewell, K. W. (1996). A review and meta-analysis of the Psychopathy Checklist-Revised: Predictive validity of dangerousness. *Clinical Psychology Science and Practice, 3,* 203-215.

Salekin, R. T., Trobst, K. K., & Krioukova, M. (2001). Construct validity of psychopathy in a community sample: A nomological net approach. *Journal of Personality Disorders, 15*(5), 425-441.

Salfati, C. (2011). Criminal profiling. In B. Rosenfeld, S. D. Penrod (Eds.), *Research methods in forensic psychology* (pp. 122-134). Hoboken, NJ: John Wiley & Sons.

Salters-Pedneault, K., Ruef, A. M., & Orr, S. P. (2010). Personality and psychophysiological profiles of police officer and firefighter recruits. *Personality and Individual Differences, 49*(3), 210-215.

Samra, J., & Connolly, D. A. (2004). Legal compensability of symptoms associated with Posttraumatic stress disorder: A Canadian perspective. *International Journal of Forensic Mental Health, 3*, 55–66.

Samra, J., & Yuille, J. C. (1996). Anatomically-neutral dolls: their effects on the memory and suggestibility of 4- to 6-year-old eyewitnesses, *Child Abuse & Neglect 20*, 1261–1272.

Samuels, A., O'Driscoll, C., & Allnutt, S. (2007). When killing isn't murder: Psychiatric and psychological defences to murder when the insanity defence is not applicable. *Australasian Psychiatry, 15*(6), 474–479.

Sanders, L. (1981). *The Third Deadly Sin.* New York: G. P. Putnam's Sons.

Sattler, J. M. (1991). How good are federal judges in detecting differences in item difficulty on intelligence tests for ethnic groups? *Psychological Assessment, 3*, 125–129.

Saunders, D. (1992). A typology of men who batter women: Three types derived from cluster analysis. *American Journal of Orthopsychiatry, 62*, 264–275.

Saxe, L., Dougherty, D., & Cross, T. (1985). The validity of polygraph testing: Scientific analysis and public contravercy. *American Psychologist, 40*, 355–366.

Saywitz, K. J., & Dorado, J. S. (1998). Interviewing children when sexual abuse is suspected. In G. P. Koocher, J. C. Norcross, & S. S. Hill, III. (Eds.), *Psychologists' desk reference* (pp. 503–509). New York: Oxford University Press.

Saywitz, K. J., Goodman, G. S., Nicholas, E., & Moan, S. F. (1991). Children's memories of a physical examination involving genital touch: Implications for reports of child sexual abuse. *Journal of Consulting and Clinical Psychology, 59*, 682–691.

Saywitz, K., & Snyder, L. (1996). Narrative elaboration: Test of a new procedure for interviewing children. *Journal of Consulting and Clinical Psychology, 64*, 1347–1357.

Saywitz, K., Geiselman, R. E., & Bornstein, G. (1992). Effects of cognitive interviewing and practice on children's recall performance. *Journal of Applied Psychology, 77*, 744–756.

Schaer, J. (1999). *Suicide prevention in law enforcement.* Employee and Family Assistance Program: Toronto Police Service.

Schall v. Martin, 467 U.S. 253 (1984).

Schmalleger, F. (1995). *Criminal justice today* (3rd ed.). Englewood, Cliffs, NJ: Prentice Hall.

Schneider, E. M. (1986). Describing and changing: Women's self-defense work and the problem of expert testimony on battering. *Women's Rights Law Reporter, 9* (3–4), 195–222.

Schretlen, D. (1986). *Malingering: Use of a psychological test battery to detect two kinds of simulation.* Ann Arbor, MI: University Microfilms International.

Schubert, S. (2006, October). A look tells all. Retrieved May 15, 2012, from http://www.sciam.com

Schuller, R. A. & Hastings, P. A. (2002). Complainant sexual history evidence: Its impact on mock jurors' decisions. *Psychology of Women Quarterly, 26*, 252–261.

Schuller, R. A. & Klippenstine, M. (2004). The impact of complainant sexual history evidence on jurors' decisions: Considerations from a psychological perspective. *Psychology, Public Policy, and Law, 10*, 321–342.

Schuller, R. A. & Rzepa, S. (2002). Expert testimony pertaining to battered woman syndrome: Its impact on jurors' decisions. *Law and Human Behavior, 6*, 655–673.

Schuller, R. A. (1992). The impact of battered woman syndrome evidence on jury decision processes. *Law and Human Behavior, 16*, 597–620.

Schuller, R. A. (1994). Applications of battered woman syndrome evidence in the courtroom. In M. Costanzo & S. Oskamp (Eds.), *Violence and the law* (pp. 113–134). Thousand Oaks, CA: Sage.

Schuller, R. A., Smith, V. L., & Olson, J. M. (1994). Jurors' decisions in trials of battered women who kill: The role of prior beliefs and expert testimony. *Journal of Applied Social Psychology, 24*, 316–337.

Schuller, R. A., Wells, E., Rzepa, S., & Klippenstine, M. A. (2004). Rethinking Battered Woman Syndrome evidence: The impact of alternative forms of expert testimony on mock juror's decisions. *Canadian Journal of Behavioural Science, 36*, 127–136.

Schuller, R., & Vidmar, N. (2011). The Canadian criminal jury. *Chicago-Kent Law Review Forthcoming, 86*, 487.

Schulman, J., Shaver, P., Colman, R., Emrich, B., & Christie, R. (1973, May). Recipe for a jury. *Psychology Today*, pp. 37–44, 77–84.

Schulman, M. (1979). *A survey of spousal violence against women in Kentucky.* Washington, DC: Law Enforcement.

Scoboria, A., Mazzoni, G., & Jarry, J. L. (2008). Suggesting childhood food illness results in reduced eating behavior. *Acta Psychologica, 128*, 304–309.

Scoboria, A., Mazzoni, G., Kirsch, I. & Milling, L. S. (2002). Immediate and persisting effects of misleading questions and hypnosis on memory reports. *Journal of Experimental Psychology: Applied, 8*, 26–32.

Scogin, F., Schumacher, J., Howland, K., & McGee, J. (1989, August). *The predictive validity of psychological testing and peer evaluations in law enforcement settings.* Paper presented at the meetings of the American Psychological Association, New Orleans.

Sears v. Rutishauser, 466 NE.2d 210, Ill. (1984).

Seelau, S. M., & Wells, G. L. (1995). Applied eyewitness research: The other mission. *Law and Human Behavior, 19*, 319–324.

Seglins, D. (2008, April 28). CBC News investigation: The report that led to the charges and the Crown's problems. CBC News. Retrieved May 15, 2012, from http://www.cbc.ca

Seguin, S., Millson, B., & Robinson, D. (2009). Forum on corrections research. Retrieved May 13, 2012, from http://www.csc-scc.gc.ca/text/pblct/forum/e042/e042b-eng.shtml

Segura, L. (2009, November 29). Feeling nervous? 3000 behaviour detection officers will be watching you at the airport this Thanksgiving. Retrieved from alternet.org.

Selkin, J. (1987). *The psychological autopsy in the courtroom: Contributions of the social sciences to resolving issues surrounding equivocal deaths.* Denver: Self-published.

Selkin, J., & Loya, J. (1979, February). Issues in the psychological autopsy of a controversial public figure. *Professional Psychology,* pp. 87–93.

Sellbom, M., Fischler, G. L., & Ben-Porath, Y. S. (2007). Identifying MMPI-2 predictors of police officer integrity and misconduct. *Criminal Justice and Behavior, 34,* 985–1004.

Serin, R. C., & Amos, N. L. (1995). The role of psychopathy in the assessment of dangerousness. *International Journal of Law and Psychiatry, 18,* 231–238.

Serin, R. C., Mailloux, D. L., & Malcolm, P. (2001). Psychopathy, deviant sexual arousal and recidivism among sexual offenders: A psycho-culturally determined group defense. *Journal of Interpersonal Violence, 16*(3), 234–246.

Serota, K. B., Levine, T. R., & Boster, F. K. (2010). The prevalence of lying in America: Three studies of self-reported lies. *Human Communication Research, 36,* 2–25.

Seto, M. C., & Fernandez, Y. M. (2011). Dynamic risk groups among adult male sexual offenders. *Sexual Abuse: Journal of Research and Treatment, 23*(4), 494–507.

Seto, M. C., & Hanson, R. (2011). Introduction to special issue on Internet-facilitated sexual offending.

Sexual Abuse: Journal of Research and Treatment, 23(1), 3–6.

Seto, M. C., Cantor, J. M., & Blanchard, R. (2006). Child pornography offenses are a valid diagnostic indicator of pedophilia. *Journal of Abnormal Psychology, 115*(3), 610–615.

Seto, M. C., Hanson, R. K., & Babchishin, K. M. (2011). Contact sexual offending by men by men with online sexual offenses. *Sexual Abuse: A Journal of Research and Treatment, 23,* 124–145.

Seto, M. C., & Barbaree, H. E. (1999). Psychopathy, treatment behavior, and sex offender recidivism. *Journal of Interpersonal Violence, 14,* 1235–1248.

Shade, D. D. (1994). Computers and young children: Software types, social contexts, gender, age, and emotional responses. *Journal of Computing in Childhood Education, 5*(2), 177–209.

Shade, D. D. (1994). Computers and young children: Software types, social contexts, gender, age, and emotional responses. *Journal of Computing In Childhood Education, 5*(2), 177–209.

Shariat, S., Assadi, S., Noroozian, M., Pakravannejad, M., Yahyazadeh, O., Aghayan, S., et al. (2010). Psychopathy in Iran: A cross-cultural study. *Journal of Personality Disorders, 24*(5), 664–675.

Sharman, S. J., & Scoboria, A. (2009). Imagination equally influences false memories of high and low plausibility events. *Applied Cognitive Psychology, 23,* 813–827.

Sharn, L. (1993, November 4). Typical arsonist is young, unfulfilled. *USA Today,* p. 3A.

Sharps, M. J., Janigian, J., Hess, A. B., & Hayward, B. (2009). Eyewitness memory in contact: Toward a taxonomy of eyewitness error. *Journal of Police and Criminal Psychology, 24,* 36–44.

Shaw, J. S., III, & McClure, K. A. (1996). Repeated postevent questioning can lead to elevated levels of eyewitness confidence. *Law and Human Behavior, 20,* 629–653.

Shaw, J. S., III. (1996). Increases in eyewitness confidence resulting from postevent questioning. *Journal of Experimental Psychology: Applied, 2,* 126–146.

Shaw, J., & Porter, S. (2012). Forever a psychopath? Psychopathy and the criminal career trajectory. In H. Hakkanen-Nyholm & Nyholm, J. (Eds.), *Psychopathy and law* (p. 201–224). Wiley.

Shebib, B. (2003). *Choices: Counseling skills for social workers and other professionals.* New York: John Wiley and Sons.

Shneidman, E. S. (1981). The psychological autopsy. *Suicide and Life-Threatening Behavior, 11,* 325–340.

Shoemaker, D. J., South, D. R., & Lowe, J. (1973). Facial stereotypes of deviants and judgments of guilt or innocence. *Social Forces, 51,* 427–433.

Shorey, R. C., Brasfield, H., Febres, J., & Stuart, G. L. (2011). The association between impulsivity, trait anger, and the perpetration of intimate partner and general violence among women arrested for domestic violence. *Journal of Interpersonal Violence, 26,* 2681–2697.

Shuman, D. W., & Gold, L. H. (2008). Without thinking: Impulsive aggression and criminal responsibility. *Behavioral Sciences & the Law, 26*(6), 723–734.

Shuman, D. W., & Gold, L. H. (2008). Without thinking: Impulsive aggression and criminal responsibility. *Behavioral Sciences & the Law, 26*(6), 723–734.

Shusman, E. J., & Inwald, R. E. (1991). Predictive validity of the Inwald Personality Inventory. *Criminal Justice and Behavior, 18,* 419–426.

Shusman, E. J., Inwald, R. E., & Knatz, H. F. (1987). A cross-validation study of police recruit performance as predicted by the IPI and MMPI. *Journal of Police Science and Administration, 15,* 162–169.

Shusman, E., Inwald, R., & Landa, B. (1984). A validation study of correction officer job performance as predicted by the IPI and MMPI. *Criminal Justice and Behavior, 11,* 309–329.

Sickmund, M., Snyder, H. N., & Poe-Yamagata, E. (1997). *Juvenile Offenders and victims: 1997 update on violence.* Washington, DC: Office of Juvenile Justice and Delinquency Prevention.

Siegal, M., Waters, L. J., & Dinwiddy, L. S. (1988). Misleading children: Causal attributions for inconsistency under repeated questioning. *Journal of Experimental Child Psychology, 45,* 438–456.

Silverstein, J. M. (1985). The psychologist as panel member. *Social Action and the Law, 11*(3), 72–74.

Silverton, L., & Gruber, C. (1998). *Malingering Probability Scale (MPS) Manual.* Los Angeles: Western Psychological Services.

Silverton, L., Gruber, C. P., & Bindman, S. (1993, August). *The Malingering Probability Scale for Mental Disorders (MPS-MD): A scale to detect malingering.* Paper presented at the meetings of the American Psychological Association, Toronto.

Simmons, C. A., Lehmann, P., & Cobb, N. (2008). A comparison of women versus men charged with intimate partner violence: General risk factors, attitudes regarding using violence and readiness to change, *Violence and Victims, 22,* 571–585.

Simon, D. (1991). *Homicide: A year on the killing streets.* New York: Ivy Books.

Simpson, B., Jensen, E., & Owen, J. (1988, October). Police employee assistance program. *Police Chief,* pp. 83–85.

Singleton, G. W., & Teahan, J. (1978). Effects of job related stress on the physical and psychological adjustment of police officers. *Journal of Police Science and Administration, 6,* 355–361.

Sinha, M. (2009). *Collecting data on the involvement of adults and youth with mental health issues in the criminal justice system.* Statistics Canada, Canadian Centre for Justice Statistics.

Skeem, J. L. & Mulvey, E. P. (2001). Psychopathy and community violence among civil psychiatric patients: Results from the MacArthur violence risk assessment study. *Journal of Consulting and Clinical Psychology, 69,* 358–374.

Skeem, J. L., & Monahan, J. (2011). Current directions in violence risk assessment. *Current Directions in Psychological Science, 20*(1), 38–42.

Skeem, J. L., Golding, S. L., Cohn, N. B., & Berge, G. (1998). Logic and reliability of evaluations of competence to stand trial. *Law and Human Behavior, 22,* 519–547.

Skeem, J. L., Monahan, J. & Mulvey, E. P. (2002). Psychopathy, treatment involvement, and subsequent violence among civil psychiatric patients. *Law and Human Behavior, 26,* 577–603.

Skeem, J. L., Polaschek, D. L., & Manchak, S. (2009). Appropriate treatment works, but how?: Rehabilitating general, psychopathic, and high-risk offenders. In J. L. Skeem, S. O. Lilienfeld, K. S. Douglas, J. L. Skeem, S. O. Lilienfeld (Eds.), *Psychological science in the courtroom: Consensus and controversies* (pp. 358–384). New York: Guilford Press.

Skeem, J., Polaschek, D., Patrick, C., & Lilienfeld, S. (2011). Psychopathic personality: Bridging the gap between scientific evidence and public policy. *Psychological Science in the Public Interest, 12,* 95–162.

Skinner, L. J., & Berry, K. K. (1993). Anatomically detailed dolls and the evaluation of child sexual abuse allegations. *Law and Human Behavior, 17,* 399–421.

Skolnick, J. H. (1966) *Justice without trial: Law enforcement in a democratic society.* New York: John Wiley.

Skolnick, J. H., & Bayley, D. H. (1986). *The new blue line: Police innovation in six American cities.* New York: Free Press.

Skolnick, J. H., & Leo, R. A. (1992). The ethics of deceptive interrogation. In J. W. Bizzack (Ed.), *Issues in policing: New perspectives* (pp. 75–95). Lexington, KY: Auburn House.

Slobogin, C. (1996). Dangerousness as a criterion in the criminal process. In B. D. Sales & D. W. Shuman (Eds.), *Law, mental health, and mental disorder* (pp. 360–383). Pacific Grove, CA: Brooks/Cole.

Slobogin, C. (1997). Deceit, pretext, and trickery: Investigative laws by the police. *Oregon Law Review, 76,* 775–816.

Slobogin, C., Melton, G. B., & Showalter, C. R. (1984). The feasibility of a brief evaluation of mental state at the time of the offense. *Law and Human Behavior, 8,* 305–321.

Slovenko, R. (2006). Commentary: Deceptions to the rule on ultimate issue testimony. *Journal of the American Academy of Psychiatry and the Law, 34*(1), 22–25.

Slovic, P., & Fischhoff, B. (1977). On the psychology of experimental surprises. *Journal of Experimental Psychology: Human Perception and Performance, 3,* 545–551.

Smeets, T., Merckelbach, H., Horselenberg, R., & Jelicic, M. (2005). Trying to recollect past events: Confidence, beliefs, and memories. *Clinical Psychology Review, 25,* 917–934.

Smith v. Jones [1999]. S. R. C. 455.

Smith, D. H., & Stotland, E. (1973). A new look at police officer selection. In J. R. Snibbe & H. M. Snibbe (Eds.), *The urban policeman in transition* (pp. 5–24). Springfield, IL: Charles C Thomas.

Smith, D. W., Letourneau, E. J., Saunders, B. E., Kilpatrick, D. G., Resnick, H. S., & Best, C. L. (2000). Delay in disclosure of childhood rape: Results from a national survey. *Child Abuse & Neglect, 24*(2), 273–287.

Smith, G. P., & Burger, G. (1993, August). *Detection of malingering: A validation test of the SLAM Test.* Paper presented at the meetings of the American Psychological Association, Toronto.

Smith, S. M., Stinson, V., & Patry, M. W. (2009). Using the "Mr. Big" technique to elicit confessions: Successful innovation or dangerous development in the Canadian legal system?

Psychology, Public Policy, and Law, 15, 168-193.

Smith, S. M., Stinson, V., & Patry, M. W. (2010a). High risk interrogation: Using the "Mr. Big" technique to elicit confessions. Law and Human Behavior, 34, 39-40.

Smith, S., Stinson, V., & Patry, M. (2010b). Confession evidence in Canada: Psychological issues and legal landscapes. Psychology, Crime and Law, 18(3), 1-17.

Snook, B., & Keating, K. (2011). A field study of adult witness interviewing practices in a Canadian police organization. Legal and Criminological Psychology, 16, 160-172.

Snook, B., & Mercer, J. C. (2010). Modelling police officers' judgments of the veracity of suicide notes. Canadian Journal of Criminology and Criminal Justice, 52(1), 79-95.

Snook, B., Cullen, R. M., Bennell, C., Taylor, P. J., & Gendreau, P. (2008). The criminal profiling illusion: What's behind the smoke and mirrors? Criminal Justice and Behavior, 35(10), 1257-1276.

Snook, B., Eastwood, J., Gendreau, P., Goggin, C., & Cullen, R. M. (2007). Taking stock of criminal profiling: A narrative review and meta-analysis. Criminal Justice and Behavior, 34(4), 437-453.

Snook, B., Eastwood, J., Stinson, M., Tedeschini, J., & House, J. C. (2010). Reforming investigative interviewing in Canada. Canadian Journal of Criminology and Criminal Justice, 52, 203-218.

Snyder, C. J., Lassiter, G. D., Lindberg, M. J., & Pinegar, S. K. (2009). Videotaped interrogations and confessions: Does a dual-camera approach yield unbiased and accurate evaluations? Behavioral Sciences & the Law, 27, 451-466.

Sophonow Inquiry Report (2001). Retrieved July 23, 2012, from http://www.gov .mb.ca/justice/sophonow

Soskis, D. A. (1983). Behavioral sciences and law enforcement personnel:

Working together on the problem of terrorism. Behavioral Sciences and the Law, 1, 47-58.

Sotgiu, I., & Mormont, C. (2008). Similarities and differences between traumatic and emotional memories: Review and directions for future research. Journal of Psychology: Interdisciplinary and Applied, 142(5), 449-469.

Sparling, J., Wilder, D. A., Kondash, J., Boyle, M., & Compton, M. (2011). Effects of interviewer behavior on accuracy of children's responses. Journal of Applied Behavior Analysis, 44(3), 587-592.

Sparrow, M. K., Moore, M. H., & Kennedy, D. M. (1990). Beyond 911: A new era of policing. New York: Basic Books.

Spence, S. A. (2008). Playing devil's advocate: The case against fMRI lie detection. Legal and Criminological Psychology, 13(1), 11-25.

Spence, S. A., Hunter, M. D., Farrow, T. F. D., Green, R. D., Leung, D. H., & Hughes, C. J. (2004). A cognitive neurobiological account of deception: Evidence from functional neuroimaging. Philosophical Transactions of the Royal Society of London, 359, 1755-1762.

Spielberger, C. D. (Ed.). (1979). Police selection and evaluation: Issues and problems. Washington, DC: Hemisphere.

Spitzberg, B. H., & Cupach, W. R. (2007). The state of the art of stalking: Taking stock of the emerging literature. Aggression & Violent Behavior, 12, 64-68.

Spitzberg, B. H., Cupach, W. R., & Ciceraro, L. D. L. (2010). Sex differences in stalking and obsessive relational intrusion: Two meta-analyses. Partner Abuse, 1, 259-285.

Sporer, S. L. (1993). Eyewitness identification accuracy, confidence, and decision times in simultaneous and sequential lineups. Journal of Applied Psychology, 78, 22-33.

Sporer, S. L. (1981). Toward a comprehensive history of legal

psychology. Unpublished manuscript, University of Erlagen-Nürnberg.

Stanford, R. M., & Mowry, B. L. (1990). Domestic disturbance danger rate. Journal of Police Science and Administration, 17, 244-249.

Stark, R., & McEvoy III., J. (1970). Middle class violence. Psychology Today, 4. 52-65.

State v. Cressey, 628 A.2d 696 (N.H. 1993).

State v. Marks, 231 Kan. 647 P.2d 1292 (1982).

State v. Michaels, 625 A.2d 489 (N.J. Sup. Ct. App. Div. 1993).

Statistics Canada, Canadian Centre for Justice Statistics. (2009b). Family violence in Canada: A statistical profile. Ottawa: Ministry of Industry.

Statistics Canada. (2001a, 19 July). Crime statistics 2000. The Daily. Retrieved August 25, 2004, from http://www .statcan.ca/Daily/English/010719/ d010719b.htm

Statistics Canada. (2001b). Canada's shelters for abused women, 1999-2000. Juristat, 21(1), catalogue number: 85-002-XIE2001001.

Statistics Canada. (2001c). Spousal violence after marital separation. Juristat, 21(7), catalogue number: 85-002-XIE.

Statistics Canada. (2005). Family violence in Canada: A statistical profile. Retrieved July 23, 2012, from http://www .statcan.gc.ca/daily-quotidien/050714/ dq050714a-eng.htm

Statistics Canada. (2006). Shelters: A refuge from family violence. Retrieved July 23, 2012, from http:// www41.statcan.gc.ca/2006/2693/ ceb2693_003-eng.htm

Statistics Canada. (2009a). Spousal violence. Retrieved July 23, 2012, from http:// www41.statcan.gc.ca/2009/2693/ cybac2693_002-eng.htm

Statistics Canada. (2010). Police reported crime statistics in Canada. Retrieved July 23, 2012, from http://www.statcan.gc.ca/ pub/85-002-x/2011001/ article/11523-eng.htm

Statistics Canada. (2010). Violence against women. Retrieved July 23, 2012, from http://www41 .statcan.gc.ca/2007/2693/ ceb2693_002-eng.htm

Statistics Canada. (2011). Police reported crime statistics in Canada, 2010. Retrieved July 23, 2012, from http://www.statcan.gc.ca/pub/85-002-x/2011001/article/11523-eng.htm

Steadman, H. J., Robbins, P. C., Monahan, J., Appelbaum, P., Grisso, T., Mulvey, E. P., et al. (1996). The MacArthur Violence Risk Assessment Study. *American Psychology-Law Society News, 16*(3), 1-4.

Steblay, N. M. (1997). Social influence in eyewitness recall: A meta-analytic review of lineup instruction effects. *Law and Human Behavior, 21*, 283-297.

Steblay, N., Dysart, J., Fulero, S., & Lindsay, R. C. L. (2003). Eyewitness accuracy rates in police showup and lineup presentations: A meta-analytic comparison. *Law and Human Behavior, 27*, 523-540.

Steketee, G., & Foa, E. B. (1987). Rape victims: Post-traumatic stress responses and their treatment. *Journal of Anxiety Disorders, 1*, 69-86.

Steller, M., & Koehnken, G. (1989). Criteria-based statement analysis. In D. C. Raskin (Ed.), *Psychological methods in criminal investigation and evidence* (pp. 217-245). New York: Springer.

Stern, L. W. (1903). *Beiträge zur Psychologie der Aussage.* (Contributions to the Psychology of Testimony). Leipzig: Verlag Barth.

Stets, J. E., & Straus, M. A. (1990). Gender differences in reporting marital violence and its medical and psychological consequences. In M. A. Straus & R. J. Gelles (Eds.). *Physical violence in American families: Risk factors and adaptations to violence in 8, 145 families* (pp. 151-166). New Brunswick, NJ: Transaction.

Stets, J., & Straus, M. (1992a). Gender differences in reporting marital

violence. *Physical violence in American families* (pp. 151-166). New Brunswick, NJ: Transaction Publishers.

Stets, J., & Straus, M. (1992b). The marriage license as a hitting license. *Physical violence in American families.* pp. 227-244. New Brunswick, NJ: Transaction Publishers. Originally published 1989, *Journal of Family Violence, 4*.

Stevens, A. (2008). *Psychopathy in the media: A content analysis.* Masters Thesis. Retrieved from ProQuest Dissertations & Theses: http://gradworks.umi.com

Stevens, J. A. (1997). Standard investigatory tools and offender profiling. In J. L. Jackson & D. A. Bekerian (Eds.), *Offender profiling: Theory, research and practice* (pp. 76-91). New York: John Wiley.

Stewart, S. H., Mitchell, T. L., Wright, K. D., & Loba, P. (2004). The relations of PTSD symptoms to alcohol use and coping drinking in volunteers who responded to Swissair Flight 111 airline disaster. *Journal of Anxiety Disorders 18*, 51-68.

Stix, G., (2008). Lighting up the lies. *Scientific American, 299*, 18. Retrieved August 13, 2012, from http://www.tectrends.com/cgi/ showan?an=00170825

Storey, J. E., Gibas, A. L., Reeves, K. A., & Hart, S. D. (2011). Evaluation of a violence risk (threat) assessment training program for police and other criminal justice professionals. *Criminal Justice and Behavior, 38*, 554-564.

Storey, J. E., Hart, S. D., Meloy, J., & Reavis, J. A. (2009). Psychopathy and stalking. *Journal of Law and Human Behavior, 33*(3), 237-246.

Stovall v. Denno, 388 U.S. 293 (1967).

Stratton, J. (1978). The police department psychologist: Is there any value? *The Police Chief, 45*(5), 70-74.

Stratton, J. A. (1980). Psychological services for police. *Journal of Police Science and Administration, 8*, 31-39.

Straus, M. (2010a). Thirty years of denial of key research findings on partner violence: Implications for prevention and treatment.

Straus, M. (2010b, May 26). Mental health and violence between marital and dating partners across the life span and in 32 nations. *Paper presented at the International Association of Mental Health Services*, Vancouver, British Columbia, Canada.

Straus, M. A. (1979). Measuring family conflict and violence: The conflict tactics scale. *Journal of Marriage and the Family, 41*, 75-88.

Straus, M. A., & Gelles, R. J. (1986). Societal change in family violence from 1975 to 1985 as revealed by two national surveys. *Journal of Marriage and the Family, 48*, 465-479.

Strawbridge, P., & Strawbridge, D. (1990). *A networking guide to recruitment, selection, and probationary training of police officers in major police departments in the United States of America.* New York: John Jay College of Criminal Justice.

Strickland, S. M. (2008). Female sex offenders: Exploring issues of personality, trauma, and cognitive distortions. *Journal of Interpersonal Violence, 23*(4), 474-489.

Stromwall, L. A., Granhag, P. A., & Hartwig, M. (2004). Practitioners' beliefs about deception. In P. A. Granhag & L. A. Stromwall (Eds.), *Deception detection in forensic contexts* (pp. 229-250). Cambridge, UK: Cambridge University Press.

Stromwall, L., & Granhag, P. (2003). How to detect deception? Arresting the beliefs of police officers, prosecutors and judges. *Psychology Crime & Law, 9*, 19-36.

Stuart, G. L., Moore, T. M., Ramsey, S. E., & Kahler, C. W. (2003). Relationship aggression and substance use among women court-referred to domestic violence intervention programs. *Addictive Behaviors, 28*, 1603-1610.

Suarez, E., & Gadalla, T. M. (2010). Stop blaming the victim: A meta-analysis on rape myths. *Journal of Interpersonal Violence, 25*(11), 2010-2035.

Sullivan, K., & Sevilla, G. (1993, August 30–September 5). A look inside a rapist's mind. *Washington Post National Weekly Edition*, p. 32.

Sullivan, T. P. (2010). The wisdom of custodial recording. In G. D. Lassiter & C. A. Meissner (Eds.), *Police interrogations and false confessions: Current research, practice, and policy recommendations* (pp. 127-142). Washington, DC: American Psychological Association.

Summit, R. (1992). Abuse of the child sexual abuse accommodation syndrome. *Journal of Child Sexual Abuse, 1*(4), 153-161.

Sun, Z. T., Liu, C. X.; Wang, Y. (2006). A Follow-up study on MMPI in police recruitment. *Chinese Mental Health Journal, 20*, 517-519.

Swan, S. C., & Snow, D. L. (2002). A typology of women's use of violence in intimate relationships. *Violence Against Women, 8*, 286-319.

Swenson, W. M., & Grimes, P. B. (1969). Characteristics of sex offenders admitted to a Minnesota state hospital for pre-sentence psychiatric investigation. *Psychiatric Quarterly Supplement, 34*, 110-123.

Sylvestre, M. (2010). Policing the homeless in Montreal: Is this really what the population wants? *Policing & Society, 20*, 432-458.

Tanford, J. A. (1990). The limits of a scientific jurisprudence: The Supreme Court and psychology. *Indiana Law Journal, 66*, 137-173.

Tanford, J. A., & Tanford, S. (1988). Better trials through science: A defense of psychologist-lawyer collaboration. *North Carolina Law Review, 66*, 741-780.

Tangney, J. P., & Dearing, R. L. (2002). *Shame and guilt*. New York: Guildford Press.

Tapp, J. L. (1976). Psychology and the law: An overture. *Annual Review of Psychology, 27*, 359-404.

Tapp, J. L. (1977). Psychology and the law: A look at the interface. In B. D. Sales (Eds.), *Psychology in the legal process* (pp. 1-15). New York: Spectrum.

Tavris, C., & Aronson, E. (2007). *Mistakes were made (but not by me): Why we justify foolish beliefs, bad decisions and hurtful acts*. New York: Harcourt.

Taylor, R. (2009). Slain and slandered: A content analysis of the portrayal of femicide in crime news. *Homicide Studies: An Interdisciplinary & International Journal, 13*(1), 21-49.

ten Brinke, L. & Porter, S. (2011, in press). Cry me a river: Identifying the behavioural consequences of extremely high-stakes interpersonal deception. *Law and Human Behavior*.

ten Brinke, L., McDonald, S., Porter, S., & O'Connor, B. (2012). Crocodile tears: Facial, verbal and body language behaviour associated with genuine and fabricated remorse. *Law and Human Behaviour, 36*, 51-59.

ten Brinke, L., Porter, S., & Baker, A. (2012, in press). Darwin the detective: Observable facial muscle contractions reveal emotional high-stakes lies. *Evolution and Human Behavior*.

Tenney, E. R., Cleary, H. D., & Spellman, B. A. (2009). Unpacking the doubt in "beyond a reasonable doubt": Plausible alternative stories increase not guilty verdicts. *Basic and Applied Social Psychology, 31*(1), 1-8.

Teoh, Y., & Lamb, M. E. (2010). Preparing children for investigative interviews: Rapport-building, instruction, and evaluation. *Applied Developmental Science, 14*(3), 154-163.

Terman, L. M. (1917). A trial of mental and pedagogical tests in a civil service examination for policemen and firemen. *Journal of Applied Psychology, 1*, 17-29.

Terr, L. C. (1979). Children of Chowchilla. *Psychoanalytic Study of the Child, 34*, 547-623.

Terr, L. C. (1983). Chowchilla revisited: The effects of psychic trauma four years after a school-bus kidnapping.

American Journal of Psychiatry, 140, 1543-1550.

Tewksbury, R. (2004). Experiences and attitudes of registered female sex offenders. *Federal Probation, 68*(3), 30-33.

Thalmeier, A., Dickmann, M., Giegling, I., Schneider, B. A. M. H., Maurer, K., Schnabel, A. (2008). Gene expression profiling of post-mortem orbitofrontal cortex in violent suicide victims. *International Journal of Neuropsychopharmacology, 11*(2), 217-228.

Thornhill, N. W., & Thornhill, R. (1991). An evolutionary analysis of psychological pain following human (Homo sapiens) rape: IV. The effect of the nature of the sexual assault. *Journal of Comparative Psychology, 105*(3), 243-252.

Tjaden, P., & Thoennes, N. (1998). *Stalking in America: Findings from the National Violence Against Women Survey*. (NCJ 169592). Washington, DC: National Institute of Justice and Centers for Disease Control and Prevention.

Todorov, A., Baron, S. G., & Oosterhof, N. N. (2008). Evaluating face trustworthiness: A model based approach. *Social Cognitive and Affective Neuroscience, 3*, 119-127.

Tomkins, A. J., & Oursland, K. (1991). Social and social science perspectives in judicial interpretations of the Constitution: A historical view and an overview. *Law and Human Behavior, 15*, 101-120.

Tomkins, A. J., & Pfeifer, J. E. (1992). Modern social scientific theories and data concerning discrimination: Implications for using social science evidence in the courts. In D. K. Kagehiro & W. S. Laufer (Eds.), *Handbook of psychology and law* (pp. 385-407). New York: Springer-Verlag.

Tonkin, M., Bond, J. W., & Woodhams, J. (2009). Fashion conscious burglars? Testing the principles of offender profiling with footwear impressions recovered at domestic burglaries. *Psychology, Crime & Law, 15*(4), 327-345.

Tonkin, M., Woodhams, J., Bond, J. W., & Loe, T. (2010). A theoretical and practical test of geographical profiling with serial vehicle theft in a U.K. context. *Behavioral Sciences & the Law, 28*(3), 442–460.

Toobin, J. (1994, October 31). Juries on trial. *New Yorker,* pp. 42–47.

Toobin, J. (1996a, September 9). The Marcia Clark verdict. *New Yorker,* pp. 58–71.

Toobin, J. (1996b). *The run of his life.* New York: Simon & Schuster.

Toronto Star. (2010a). Col. Russell Williams: A serial killer like none police have seen. Retrieved July 23, 2012, from http://www.thestar.com/news/article/873244--col-russell-williams-a-serial-killer-like-none-police-have-seen?bn=1

Toronto Star. (2010b). Russell Williams wrote letters of apology. Retrieved July 23, 2012, from http://www.thestar.com/news/canada/article/878276--russell-williams-wrote-letters-of-apology

Torry, Z. D., & Billick, S. B. (2010). Overlapping universe: Understanding legal insanity and psychosis. *Psychiatric Quarterly, 81*(3), 253–262.

Toufexis, A. (1991, May 6). Mind games with monsters. *Time,* pp. 68–69.

Towl, G. (2011). Forensic psychotherapy and counselling in prisons. *European Journal of Psychotherapy and Counselling, 13*(4), 403–407.

Tremper, C. (1987). Organized psychology's efforts to influence judicial policy-making. *American Psychologist, 42,* 496–501.

Trevethan, S., Crutcher, N., & Moore, J.-P. (2002). *A Profile of Federal Offenders Designated as Dangerous Offenders or Serving Long-Term Supervision Orders.* Research Report No. R-125. Ottawa: Correctional Service of Canada

Trivers, R. (2011). *The folly of fools: The logic of deceit and self-deception in human life.* New York: Basic Books.

Trocmé, N., & Bala, N. (2005). False allegations of abuse and neglect when parents separate. *Child Abuse & Neglect, 29*(12), 1333–1345.

Trocmé, N., MacLaurin, B., Fallon, B., Daciuk, J., Billingsley, D., Tourigny, M., et al. (2001). *Canadian incidence study of reported child abuse and neglect (CIS): Final Report.* Ottawa, ON: Minister of Public Works and Government Services Canada.

Trojan, C., & Salfati, C. G. (2011) Linking criminal history to crime scene behavior in single-victim and serial homicide: Implications for offender profiling research. *Homicide Studies: An Interdisciplinary & International Journal, 15*(1), 3–31.

Trovillo, P. V. (1939). A history of lie detection. *Journal of Criminal Law and Criminology, 29,* 848–881.

Turner, M. (2008). Female sexual compulsivity: A new syndrome. *Psychiatric Clinics of North America, 31*(4), 713–727.

Turvey, B. (1999). *Criminal profiling: An introduction to behavioral evidence analysis.* London: Academic Press.

Tversky, A., & Kahneman, D. (1974). Judgment under uncertainty: Heuristics and biases. *Science, 185,* 1124–1131.

Tversky, A., & Kahneman, D. (1983). Extensional versus intuitive reasoning: The conjuction fallacy in probability judgment. *Psychological Bulletin, 90,* 293–315.

Tversky, A., Slovic, P., & Kahneman, D. (1990). The causes of preference reversal. *American Economic Review, 80,* 204–217.

Tyler, T. R., & Folger, R. (1980). Distributional and procedural aspects of satisfaction with citizen-police encounters. *Basic and Applied Social Psychology, 1,* 281–292.

UBC Law Innocence Project (2012). *UBC Law Innocence Project: What we do.* Retrieved July 23, 2012, from http://www.innocenceproject.law.ubc.ca

Uchida, C. D., Brooks, L. W., & Kopers, C. S. (1987). Danger to police during domestic encounters: Assaults on Baltimore County police, 1984–86. *Criminal Justice Policy Review, 2,* 357–371.

Ulrich, D., & Trumbo, D. (1965). The selection interview since 1949. *Psychological Bulletin, 63,* 100–116.

Underwood, III, J, H., Boudreaux, D. O., & Rao, S. (2009). Demographics in civil trials:

Undeutsch, U. (1967). Beurteilung der Glaubhaftigkeit von Aussagen. In U. Undeutsch (Ed.), *Handbuch der Psychologie Vol. 11: Forensische Psychologie* (pp. 26–181). Gottingen, Germany: Hogrefe.

Undeutsch, U. (1982). Statement reality analysis. In A. Trankell (Ed.), *Reconstructing the past: The role of psychologists in criminal trials* (pp. 27–56). Stockholm, Sweden: Norstedt & Somers.

Undeutsch, U. (1984). Courtroom evaluations of eyewitness testimony. *International Review of Applied Psychology, 33,* 51–67.

Undeutsch, U. (1989). The development of statement reality analysis. In J. C. Yuille (Ed.), *Credibility assessment* (pp. 101–120). Dordrecht, The Netherlands: Kluwer.

United States v. Hall, 93 F.3d 1337 (7th Cir. 1996).

Ustad, K. L., Rogers, R., Sewell, K. W., & Guarnaccia, C. A. (1996). Restoration of competency to stand trial: Assessment with the Georgia Court Competency Test and the Competency Screening Test. *Law and Human Behavior, 20,* 131–146.

Valentine, R., & Mesout, J. (2009). Eyewitness identification under stress in the London Dungeon. *Applied Cognitive Psychology, 23,* 151–161.

van den Bos, K., & Maas, M. (2009). On the psychology of the belief in a just world: Exploring experiential and rationalistic paths to victim blaming. *Personality and Social Psychology Bulletin, 35*(12), 1567–1578.

Van den Haag, E. (1960). Social science testimony in the desegregation cases:

A reply to Professor Kenneth Clark. *Villanova Law Review, 6,* 69–79.

Van der Kolk, B. A., & Fisler, R. (1995). Dissociation and the fragmentary nature of traumatic memories: Overview and exploratory study. *Journal of Traumatic Stress, 8,* 505–525.

Van Dongen, E. (2002). Theatres of the lie: "Crazy" deception and lying as drama. *Anthropology and Medicine, 9,* 135–151.

Van Hasselt, V. B., Baker, M. T., Romano, S. J., Schlessinger, K. M., Zucker, M.,

Vancouver Sun. (2012). Karla Homolka now a mother of three in the Caribbean. Retrieved July 30, 2012, from http://www.vancouversun.com/entertainment/Karla+Homolka+mother+three+Caribbean+says+ebook/6820329/story.html

Vandiver, D. (2003, January). Female sex offenders: An analysis of offending patterns and judicial processing characteristics. *Dissertation Abstracts International Section A, 63*

Vandiver, D. M., & Kercher, G. (2004). Offender and victim characteristics of registered female sexual offenders in Texas: A proposed typology of female sexual offenders. *Sexual Abuse: Journal of Research and Treatment, 16*(2), 121–137.

Vandiver, D. M., & Teske, R.(2006). Juvenile female and male sex offenders: A comparison of offender, victim, and judicial processing characteristics. *International Journal of Offender Therapy and Comparative Criminology, 50*(2), 148–165.

Vandiver, D. M., Dial, K., & Worley, R. M. (2008). A qualitative assessment of registered female sex offenders: Judicial processing experiences and perceived effects of a public registry. *Criminal Justice Review, 33*(2), 177–198.

Vaughn, M. G., Newhill, C. E., DeLisi, M., Beaver, K. M., & Howard, M. O. (2008). An investigation of psychopathic features among delinquent girls: Violence, theft, and drug abuse. *Youth Violence and Juvenile Justice, 6*(3), 240–255.

Vecchi, G. M., Van Hasselt, V. B., & Romano, S. J. (2005). Crisis (hostage) negotiation: Current strategies and issues in high-risk conflict resolution. *Aggression and Violent Behavior, 10*(5), 533–551.

Verhovek, S. H. (1993, May 5). Investigators puzzle over last minutes of Koresh. *The New York Times,* p. A10.

Vermunt, R., Blaauw, E., & Lind, E. A. (1998). Fairness evaluations of encounters with police officers and correctional officers. *Journal of Applied Social Psychology, 28,* 1107–1124.

Veronen, L. J., Kilpatrick, D. G., & Resick, P. A. (1979). Treatment of fear and anxiety in rape victims: Implications for the criminal justice system. In W. H. Parsonage (Ed.), *Perspectives on victimology* (pp. 148–159). Thousand Oaks, CA: Sage.

Vickerman, K. A., & Margolin, G. (2009). Rape treatment outcome research: Empirical findings and state of the literature. *Clinical Psychology Review, 29*(5), 431–448.

Viding, E., Blair, R. R., Moffitt, T. E., & Plomin, R. (2005). Evidence for substantial genetic risk for psychopathy in 7-year-olds. *Journal of Child Psychology and Psychiatry, 46*(6), 592–597.

Viding, E., Jones, A. P., Frick, P. J., Moffitt, T. E., & Plomin, R. (2008). Heritability of antisocial behaviour at 9: Do callous–unemotional traits matter? *Developmental Science, 11*(1), 17–22.

Vidmar, N. (1995). *Medical malpractice and the American jury.* Ann Arbor: University of Michigan Press.

Vidmar, N. (2011). The psychology of trial judging. *Current Directions in Psychological Science, 20,* 58–62.

Viljoen, J. L., MacDougall, E. A., Gagnon, N., & Douglas, K. (2010). Psychopathy evidence in legal proceedings involving adolescent offenders. *Psychology, Public Policy, and the Law, 16*(3), 254–283.

Viljoen, J. L., Slaney, K. L., & Grisso, T. (2009). The psychology use of

trial judging. *Current Directions in Psychological Science, 20,* 58–62.

Viljoen, J. L., Slaney, K. L., & Grisso, T. (2009). The use of the macCAT-CA with adolescents: An item response theory investigation of age-related measurement bias. *Law and Human Behavior, 33*(4), 283–297.

Vitacco, M. J., & Vincent, G. M. (2006). Understanding the Downward extension of psychopathy to youth: Implications for risk assessment and juvenile justice. *International Journal of Forensic Mental Health, 5*(1), 29–38.

Vollers, M. (1991, July). The haunting of the New South. *Esquire,* pp. 58–63, 120.

Vrij, A. & Baxter, M. (1999). Accuracy and confidence in detecting truths and lies in elaborations and denials: Truth bias, lie bias and individual differences. *Expert Evidence, 7,* 25–36.

Vrij, A. (2000). Telling and detecting lies as a function of raising the stakes. In C. M. Breur, M. M. Kommer, J. F. Nijboer, & J. M. Reintjes (Eds.), *New trends in criminal investigation and evidence II* (pp. 699–709). Antwerpen, Belgium: Intersentia.

Vrij, A. (2001). Implicit lie detection. *The Psychologist, 14,* 597–598.

Vrij, A. (2004). Why professionals fail to catch liars and how they can improve. *Legal and Criminological Psychology, 9,* 159–181.

Vrij, A. (2005). Criteria-based content analysis: A qualitative review of the first 37 studies. *Psychology, Public Policy, and Law, 11,* 3–41.

Vrij, A. (2006). Challenging interviewees during interviews: The potential effects on lie detection. *Psychology, Crime, & Law, 12,* 193–206.

Vrij, A. (2007). Deception: A social lubricant and a selfish act. In K. Fiedler (Ed.), *Frontiers of social psychology: Social communication* (pp. 309–342), New York; Psychology Press.

Vrij, A. (2008). Detecting lies and deceit: *Pitfalls and opportunities* (2nd ed.). New York: John Wiley & Sons.

Vrij, A. (2008). Nonverbal dominance versus verbal accuracy in lie detection: A plea to change police practice. *Criminal Justice and Behavior, 35,* 1323-1336.

Vrij, A., & Mann, S. (2001a). Who killed my relative? Police officers' ability to detect real-life high-stake lies. *Psychology, Crime, & Law, 7,* 119-132.

Vrij, A., & Mann, S. (2001b). Telling and detecting lies in a high-stake situation: The case of a convicted murderer. *Applied Cognitive Psychology, 15,* 187-203.

Vrij, A., & Mann, S. (2004). Detecting deception: The benefit of looking at a combination of behavioural, auditory and speech content related cues in a systematic manner. *Group Decision and Negotiation, 13,* 61-79.

Vrij, A., Akehurst, L., Soukara, S., & Bull, R. (2002). Will the truth come out? The effect of deception, age, status, coaching, and social skills on CBCA scores. *Law and Human Behavior, 26,* 261-283.

Vrij, A., Fisher, R. P., Mann, S., & Leal, S. (2008). A cognitive load approach to lie detection. *Journal of Investigative Psychology and Offender Profiling, 5,* 39-43. Retrieved July 23, 2012, from http://onlinelibrary.wiley.com/doi/10.1002/jip.82/abstract

Vrij, A., Granhag, P. A., & Porter, S. (2011). Pitfalls and opportunities in nonverbal and verbal lie detection. *Psychological Science in the Public Interest, 11,* 89-121.

Vrij, A., Granhag, P. A., Mann, S., & Leal, S. (2011a). Lying about flying: The first experiment to detect false intent. *Psychology, Crime, and Law, 25,* 212-218.

Vrij, A., Granhag, P. A., Mann, S., & Leal, S. (2011b). Outsmarting the liars: Towards a cognitive lie detection approach. *Current Directions in Psychological Science, 20,* 28-32.

Vrij, A., Leal, S., Mann, S., & Granhag, P. A. (2011). A comparison between lying about intentions and past activities: Verbal cues and detection accuracy. *Applied Cognitive Psychology, 25,* 212-218.

Vrij, A., Mann, S., Fisher, R., Leal, S., Milne, B., & Bull, R. (2008). Increasing cognitive load to facilitate lie detection: The benefit of recalling an event in reverse order. *Law and Human Behavior, 32,* 253-265.

Vrij, A., Mann, S., Leal, S., & Fisher, R. (2010). "Look into my eyes": Can an instruction to maintain eye contact facilitate lie detection? *Psychology, Crime, & Law, 16,* 327-348.

W. M. Y. v. Duncan Scott, B. C. Soccer Assoc. et al. (2000), BCSC 1294.

Wade, K. A., Garry, M., Read, J. D., & Lindsay, D. S. (2002). A picture is worth a thousand lies: Using false photographs to create false childhood memories. *Psychonomic Bulletin & Review, 9,* 597-603.

Wagenaar, W. A. (1988). *Identifying Ivan.* Cambridge, MA: Harvard University Press.

Wagenaar, W. A., & Groenewed, J. (1990). The memory of concentration camp survivors. *Applied Cognitive Psychology, 4,* 77-87.

Wagstaff, G. F. (2008) Hypnosis and the law: Examining the stereotypes. *Criminal Justice and Behavior, 35,* 1277-1294.

Wagstaff, G. F., MacVeigh, J., Boston, R., Scott, L., Brunas-Wagstaff, J., & Cole, J. (2003). Can laboratory findings on eyewitness testimony be generalized to the real world? An archival analysis of the influence on violence, weapon presence, and age on eyewitness accuracy. *The Journal of Psychology, 137,* 17-28.

Wahlund, K., & Kristiansson, M. (2009). Aggression, psychopathy and brain imaging: Review and future recommendations. *International Journal of Law and Psychiatry, 32,* 266-271.

Wakefield, H., & Underwager, R. (1998). Coerced or nonvoluntary confessions. *Behavior Sciences and the Law, 16,* 423-440.

Wald, M., Ayres, R., Hess, D. W., Schantz, M., & Whitebread, C. H. (1967). Interrogations in New Haven: The impact of *Miranda. Yale Law Journal, 76,* 1519-1648.

Waldman, I. D., & Rhee, S. H. (2007). Genetic and environmental influences on psychopathy and antisocial behavior. In C. Patrick (Ed.), *Handbook of psychopathy* (pp. 205-228). New York: Guilford.

Walker, C. M., & Woody, W. D. (2011). Juror decision making for juveniles tried as adults: The effects of defendant age, crime type, and crime outcome. *Psychology, Crime and Law, 17,* 659-675.

Walker, C. M., & Woody, W. D. (2011). Juror decision making for juveniles tried as adults: the effects of defendant age, crime type, and crime outcome. *Psychology, Crime and Law, 17,* 659-675.

Walker, C. M., & Woody, W. D. F., McGovern, S. K., Poey, E. L., & Otis, K. E. (2004). Treatment effectiveness for male adolescent sexual offenders: A meta-analysis and review. *Journal of Child Sexual Abuse: Research, Treatment, & Program Innovations for Victims, Survivors, & Offenders, 13*(3-4), 281-293.

Walker, D. F., McGovern, S. K., Poey, E. L., & Otis, K. E. (2004). Treatment effectiveness for male adolescent sexual offenders: A meta-analysis and review. *Journal of Child Sexual Abuse: Research, Treatment, & Program Innovations for Victims, Survivors, & Offenders, 13*(3-4), 281-293.

Walker, L. E. (1998, August). *Forensic psychology: Psychologists, Solomon, and child custody decisions.* Symposium introduction presented at the meetings of the American Psychological Association, San Francisco.

Walker, L. E. A. (1979). *The battered woman.* New York: Harper & Row.

Walker, L. E. A. (1992). Battered woman syndrome and self-defense. *Notre Dame Journal of Law, Ethics, and Public Policy, 6,* 321–334.

Walker, L. E. A. (1993). Battered women as defendants. In N. Z. Hilton (Ed.), *Legal responses to wife assault: Current trends and evaluation* (pp. 233–257). Thousand Oaks, CA: Sage.

Walker, L., & Monahan, J. (1987). Social frameworks: A new use of social science in law. *Virginia Law Review, 73,* 559–612.

Walker, N. E., Brooks, C. M., & Wrightsman, L. S. (1998). *Children's rights in the United States: In search of a national policy.* Thousand Oaks, CA: Sage.

Walsh, Z., & Kosson, D. S. (2007) Psychopathy and violence: A prospective study of the influence of socioeconomic status and ethnicity. *Law and Human Behavior, 31,* 209–229.

Walsh, Z., & Walsh, T. (2006) The evidentiary introduction of PCL-R assessed psychopathy in U.S. courts: Extent and appropriateness. *Law and Human Behavior, 30,* 493–507.

Walsh, Z., Swogger, M. T., & Kosson, D. S. (2009). Psychopathy and instrumental violence: Facet level relationships. *Journal of Personality Disorders, 23,* 416–424.

Walsh, Z., Swogger, M. T., O'Connor, B., Shonbrun, Y. C., Shea, M. T., & Stuart, G. L. (2010). Subtypes of partner violence perpetrators among male and female civil psychiatric patients. *Journal of Abnormal Psychology, 119,* 563–574.

Warling, D., & Peterson-Badali, M. (2003). The verdict on jury trials for juveniles: The effects of defendant's age on trial outcomes. *Behavioral Sciences and the Law, 21,* 63–82.

Warmelink, L., Vrij, A., Mann, S., Leal, S., Forrester, D., & Fisher, R. (2011). Thermal imaging as a lie detection tool at airports. *Law & Human Behavior, 35,* 40–48.

Warren, G., Schertler, E., & Bull, P. (2009). Detecting deception from emotional and unemotional cues. *Journal of Nonverbal Behavior, 33,* 59–69.

Warshaw, R. (1988). *I never called it rape.* New York: Harper & Row.

Waschbusch, D., Porter, S., Carrey, N., Kazmi, O., Roach, K., & D'Amico, D. (2004). A comparison of conduct problems in elementary age children. *Canadian Journal of Behavioural Science, 36,* 97–112.

Websdale, N. (2003). Reviewing domestic violence deaths. *National Institute of Justice, 250,* 26–31.

Webster, M. (2004). Do crisis negotiators practice what they preach? *The Canadian Review of Policing Research, 1.* Retrieved August 17, 2004, from http://crpr.icaap.org/issues/issue1/mwebster.html

Wecht, C. (1994). *Cause of death.* New York: Penguin.

Weiler, B., & Widom, C. (1996). Psychopathy and violent behaviour in abused and neglected young adults. *Criminal Behaviour and Mental Health, 6*(3), 253–271.

Weisman, J. (1980). *Evidence.* New York: Viking.

Weiss, W. U, Weiss, P. A., Cain, S., & Manley, B. (2009). Impression management in police officer candidacy on the MMPI-2. *Journal of Police and Criminal Psychology, 24,* 120–125.

Weisz, J. R., Hawley, K. M., Pilkonis, P. A.,Woody, S. R., & Follette,W. C. (2000). Stressing the (other) three Rs in the search for empirically supported treatments: Review procedures, research quality, relevance to practice and the public interest. *Clinical Psychology: Research and Practice, 7,* 243–258.

Wells, G. L. (1978). Applied eyewitness testimony research: System variables and estimator variables. *Journal of Personality and Social Psychology, 36,* 1546–1557.

Wells, G. L. (1984a). How adequate is human intuition for judging eyewitness testimony? In G. L. Wells & E. F. Loftus (Eds.), *Eyewitness testimony: Psychological perspectives* (pp. 256–272). New York: Cambridge University Press.

Wells, G. L. (1984b). The psychology of lineup identifications. *Journal of Applied Social Psychology, 14,* 89–103.

Wells, G. L. (1986). Expert psychological testimony: Empirical and conceptual analysis of effects. *Law and Human Behavior, 10,* 83–95.

Wells, G. L. (1993). What do we know about eyewitness identification? *American Psychologist, 48,* 553–571.

Wells, G. L. (1995). Scientific study of witness memory: Implications for public and legal policy. *Psychology, Public Policy, and Law, 1,* 726–731.

Wells, G. L., & Bradfield, A. L. (1998). "Good, you identified the suspect": Feedback to eyewitnesses distorts their reports of the witnessing experience. *Journal of Applied Psychology, 83,* 360–376.

Wells, G. L., & Hasel, L. E. (2007). Facial composite production by eyewitnesses. *Current Directions in Psychological Science, 16,* 6–20.

Wells, G. L., & Leippe, M. R. (1981). How do triers of fact infer the accuracy of eyewitness identification? Using memory for peripheral detail can be misleading. *Journal of Applied Psychology, 66,* 682–687.

Wells, G. L., & Loftus, E. F. (1984). Eyewitness research: Then and now. In G. L. Wells & E. F. Loftus (Eds.), *Eyewitness testimony: Psychological perspectives* (pp. 1–11). Cambridge, UK: Cambridge University Press.

Wells, G. L., & Olson, E. (2003). Eyewitness identification. *Annual Reviews of Psychology, 54,* 277–295.

Wells, G. L., & Quinlivan, D. S. (2009). Suggestive eyewitness identification procedures and the Supreme Court's reliability test in light of eyewitness science: 30 years later. *Law and Human Behavior, 33,* 1–24.

Wells, G. L., & Seelau, E. (1995). Eyewitness identification: Psychological research and legal policy on lineups. *Psychology, Public Policy, and Law, 1,* 765-791.

Wells, G. L., Lindsay, R. C. L., & Ferguson, T. (1979). Accuracy, confidence, and juror perceptions in eyewitness identification. *Journal of Applied Psychology, 64,* 440-448.

Wells, G. L., Malpass, R. S., Lindsay, R. C. L., Fisher, R. P., Turtle, J. W., & Fulero, S. M. (2000). From the lab to the police station: A successful application of eyewitness research. *American Psychologist, 55,* 581-598.

Wells, G. L., Rydell, S. M., & Seelau, E. P. (1993). On the selection of distractors for eyewitness lineups. *Journal of Applied Psychology, 78,* 835-844.

Wells, G. L., Seelau, E., Rydell, S., & Luus, C. A. E. (1994). Recommendations for properly conducted lineup identification tasks. In D. F. Ross, J. D. Read, & M. P. Toglia (Eds.), *Adult eyewitness testimony: Current trends and developments* (pp. 223-244). New York: Cambridge University Press.

Wells, G. L., Small, M., Penrod, S., Malpass, R. S., Fulero, S. M., & Brimacombe, C. A. E. (1998). Eyewitness identification procedures: Recommendations for lineups and photospreads. *Law and Human Behavior, 22,* 603-647.

Wells, G. L., Memon, A., & Penrod, S. D. (2006) Eyewitness evidence: Iimproving its probative value. *Psychological Science in the Public Interest, 7,* 45-75.

Wessel, I., van der Kooy, P., & Merckelbach, H. (2000). Differential recall of central and peripheral details of emotional slides is not a stable phenomenon. *Memory, 8,* 95-100.

Westbrook, L. (2009). Crisis information concerns: information needs of domestic violence survivors. *Information Processing and Management, 45,* 98-114.

Wheeler, S., Book, A., & Costello, K. (2009). Psychopathic traits and perceptions of victim vulnerability. *Criminal Justice and Behavior, 36*(6), 635-648.

Whipple, G. M. (1909). The observer as reporter: A survey of the "psychology of testimony." *Psychological Bulletin, 6,* 153-170.

Whipple, G. M. (1910). Recent literature on the psychology of testimony. *Psychological Bulletin, 7,* 365-368.

Whipple, G. M. (1911). The psychology of testimony. *Psychological Bulletin, 8,* 307-309.

Whipple, G. M. (1912). The psychology of testimony and report. *Psychological Bulletin, 9,* 264-269.

Whitaker, D. J., Le, B., Hanson, R., Baker, C. K., McMahon, P. M., Ryan, G., et al. (2008). Risk factors for the perpetration of child sexual abuse: A review and meta-analysis. *Child Abuse & Neglect, 32*(5), 529-548.

White, E. K., & Honig, A. L. (1995). The role of the police psychologist in training. In M. I. Kurke & E. M. Scrivner (Eds.), *Police psychology into the 21st century* (pp. 257-277). Hillsdale, NJ: Lawrence Erlbaum.

White, J. H., Lester, D., Gentile, M. & Rosenbleeth, J. (2011). The utilization of forensic science and criminal profiling for capturing serial killers. *Forensic Science International, 209,* 160-165.

White, S. (1988). Should investgatory use of anatomical dolls be defined by the courts? *Journal of Interpersonal Violence, 3,* 471-475.

White, S., & Santilli, G. (1988). A review of clinical practices and research data on anatomical dolls. *Journal of Interpersonal Violence, 3,* 430-442.

White, S., Strom, G., Santilli, G., & Halpin, B. (1986). Interviewing young sexual abuse victims with anatomically correct dolls. *Child Abuse and Neglect, 10,* 519-529.

Wiener, R. L., Hackney, A., Kadela, K., Rauch, S., Seib, H., Warren, L., et al. (2002). The fit and implementation of sexual harassment law to workplace evaluations. *Journal of Applied Psychology, 87,* 747-764.

Wiggins, E. C., & Brandt, J. (1988). The detection of simulated amnesia. *Law and Human Behavior, 12,* 57-78.

Wigmore, J. H. (1909). Professor Münsterberg and the psychology of testimony: Being a report of the case of *Cokestone v. Münsterberg. Illinois Law Review, 3,* 399-455.

Wijkman, M., Bijleveld, C., & Hendriks, J. (2010). Women don't do such things! Characteristics of female sex offenders and offender types. *Sexual Abuse: Journal of Research and Treatment, 22*(2), 135-156.

Wildman, R. W., II, Batchelor, E. S., Thompson, L., Nelson, F. R., Moore, J. T., Patterson, M. E., & et al. (1978). *The Georgia Court Competency Test: An attempt to develop a rapid, quantitative measure of fitness for trial.* Unpublished manuscript, Forensic Services Division, Central State Hospital, Milledgeville, GA.

Williams, K. (2007). *Our enemies in blue: Police and power in America.* Cambridge, MA: South End Press.

Williams, L. M. (1994). Recall of childhood trauma: A prospective study of women's memories of child sexual abuse. *Journal of Consulting & Clinical Psychology, 62,* 1167-1176.

Williams, W., & Miller, K. (1981). The processing and disposition of incompetent mentally ill offenders. *Law and Human Behavior, 5,* 245-261.

Williamson, S. (1993, June). Cohesion and coherence in the speech of psychopathic criminals. *Dissertation Abstracts International, 53,* 6579.

Willis, D. S. (2004). Juror privacy: The compromise between judicial discretion and the first amendment. *37 Suffolk U. L. Rev.* 1195.

Willis, J., & Todorov, A. (2006). First impressions: Making up your mind after a 100-ms exposure to a face. *Psychological Science, 17,* 592-598.

Wilson, J. P., & Keane, T. M. (Eds.). (1997). *Assessing psychological trauma and PTSD.* New York: Guilford Press.

Wilson, M., & Daly, M. (1993). An evolutionary psychological perspective on male sexual proprietariness and violence against wives. *Violence & Victims, 8*, 271–294.

Wilson, M., & McCarthy, K. (2011). Greed is good? Student disciplinary choice and self-reported psychopathy. *Personality and Individual Differences, 51*(7), 873–876.

Wilson, P., Lincoln, R., & Kocsis, R. (1997) Validity, utility and ethics of profiling for serial violent and sexual offenders. *Psychiatry, Psychology and Law, 4*, 1–11.

Wise, R. A., & Safer, M. A. (2004). What US judges know and believe about eyewitness testimony. *Applied Cognitive Psychology, 18*, 427–443.

Wise, R. A., Safer, M. A., & Maro, C. M. (2011). What U.S. law enforcement officers know and believe about eyewitness factors, eyewitness interviews and identification procedures. *Applied Cognitive Psychology, 25*, 488–500.

Wolak, J., Finkelhor, D., & Mitchell, K. (2011). Child pornography possessors: Trends in offender and case characteristics. *Sexual Abuse: Journal of Research and Treatment, 23*(1), 22–42.

Wolfgang, M. E., & Ferracuti, F. (1967). *The subculture of violence*. London: Tavistock.

Wolpe, P. R., Foster, K. R., & Langleben, D. D. (2005). Emerging neurotechnologies for lie-detection: promises and perils. *American Journal of Bioethics, 5*, 39–49.

Wong, S., Gordon, A., & Gu, D. (2007). Assessment and treatment of violence-prone forensic clients: An integrated approach. *British Journal of Psychiatry, 190* (Suppl 49), s66–s74.

Wong, S., Olver, M. E., Nicholaichuk, T. P., & Gordon, A. (2003). *The Violence Risk Scale—Sexual Offender Version (VRS–SO)*. Saskatoon, Saskatchewan, Canada: Regional Psychiatric Centre and University of Saskatchewan.

Wood, J. M., Schreiber, N., Martinez, Y., McLaurin, K., Strok, R., Velarde, L., (1997). *Interviewing techniques in the McMartin Preschool and Kelly Michaels cases: A quantitative analysis*. Unpublished paper, University of Texas at El Paso.

Wood, L. A., & MacMartin, C. (2007). Constructing the remorseful offender: Judges' sentencing decisions in child sexual assault cases. *Journal of Language and Social Psychology, 26*, 343–362.

Woodworth, M. & Porter, S. (1999). Historical foundations and current applications of criminal profiling in violent crime investigations. *Expert Evidence, 7*, 241–264.

Woodworth, M., & Porter, S. (2002). In cold blood: Characteristics of criminal homicides as a function of psychopathy. *Journal of Abnormal Psychology, 111*, 436–445.

Woodworth, M., Peace, K. A., O'Donnell, C., & Porter, S. (2003). Forensic community programs: Recommendations for the management of NCRMD patients in the community. *Journal of Forensic Psychology Practice, 3*, 1–22.

Woodworth, M., Porter, S., ten Brinke, L., Doucette, N. L., Peace, K., Campbell, M. A. (2009). A comparison of memory for homicide, non-homicidal violence, and positive life experiences. *International Journal of Law and Psychiatry, 32*, 329–334.

World Health Organization— Collaborating Centre for Evidence and Health Policy in Mental Health. (2001). *Comparative risk assessment: Child sexual abuse* (pp. 1–121). Sydney, Australia: St. Vincent's Hospital.

Wortley, S. & Owusu-Bempah, A. (2011). The usual suspects: police stop and search practices in Canada. *Policing and Society: An International Journal of Research and Policy 21*(4).

Wright, D. B., Memon, A., Skagerberg, E. M., & Gabbert, F. (2009). When eyewitnesses talk. *Current Directions in Psychological Science, 18*, 174–178.

Wright, L. (1994). *Remembering Satan*. New York: Alfred A. Knopf.

Wrightsman, L. S., & Heili, A. (1992, September). *Working paper— Measuring bias in civil trials*. Unpublished paper, Department of Psychology, Lawrence, KS: University of Kansas.

Wrightsman, L. S., & Kassin, S. M. (1993). *Confessions in the courtroom*. Thousand Oaks, CA: Sage.

www.rcmp-grc.ca. (2011). *Brochure— National sex offender registry*. Retrieved July 23, 2012, from http://www.rcmp-grc.gc.ca/tops-opst/bs-sc/nsor-rnds/broch-eng.htm

Y.(S.) v. C. (F.G.) (1997), 26 B.C.L.R. (3d) 155 (C.A.).

Yakir, D. (1991, February 24). I had to realize how angry I was. *Parade Magazine*, pp. 4–5.

Yang, Y., & Raine, A. (2009). Prefrontal structural and functional brain imaging findings in antisocial, violent, and psychopathic individuals: A meta-analysis. *Psychiatry Research, 174*, 81–88.

Yarmey, A. D. (1979). *The psychology of eyewitness testimony*. New York: Free Press.

Yarmey, A. D. (1984). Age as a factor in eyewitness memory. In G. L. Wells & E. F. Loftus (Eds.), *Eyewitness testimony: Psychological perspectives* (pp. 142–154). Cambridge, MA: Cambridge University Press.

Yarmey, A. D. (1986). Ethical responsibilities governing the statements experimental psychologists make in expert testimony. *Law and Human Behavior, 12*, 101–116.

Yarmey, A. D. (2001). Expert testimony: Does eyewitness memory research have probative value for the courts? *Canadian Psychology, 42*, 92–100.

Yarmey, A. D. (2003). Eyewitness identification: Guidelines and recommendations for identification procedures in the United States and Canada. *Canadian Psychology, 44,* 181–189.

Yarmey, A. D., & Jones, H. P. T. (1983). Is the psychology of eyewitness identification a matter of common sense? In S. M. A. Lloyd-Bostock & B. R. Clifford (Eds.), *Evaluating witness evidence: Recent psychological research and new perspectives* (pp. 13–40). Chichester, UK: Wiley.

Yarmey, A. D., Yarmey, M. J., & Yarmey, A. L. (1996). Accuracy of eyewitness identifications in showups and lineups. *Law and Human Behavior, 20,* 459–477.

Yllo, K., & Straus, M. (1990). Patriarchy and violence against wives: The impact of structural and normative factors. In M. Straus & R. Gelles (Eds.), *Physical Violence in American Families.* New Brunswick, NJ: Transaction Publishers.

Yonah, A., & Gleason, J. M. (Eds.). (1981). *Behavioral and quantitative perspectives on terrorism.* New York: Pergamon.

Yonge, K. C., & Jacquin, K. M. (2010). Criminal profile accuracy following training in inductive and deductive approaches. *American Journal of Forensic Psychology, 28*(3), 5–24.

Young, D. (1996). Unnecessary evil: Police lying in interrogations. *Connecticut Law Review, 28,* 425–477.

Youngstrom, N. (1991, October). Spotting serial killer difficult, experts note. *APA Monitor,* p. 32.

Yuille, J. C. (1980). A critical examination of the psychological and practical implications of eyewitness research. *Law and Human Behavior, 4,* 335–345.

Yuille, J. C. (1988). The systematic assessment of children's testimony. *Canadian Psychology, 29,* 247–262.

Yuille, J. C. (1989). Expert evidence by psychologists: Sometimes problematic and often premature. *Behavioural Sciences and the Law, 7,* 181–196.

Yuille, J. C. (1993). We must study forensic eyewitnesses to know about them. *American Psychologist, 48,* 572–573.

Yuille, J. C., & Cutshall, J. (1986). A case study of the eyewitness memory of a crime. *Journal of Applied Psychology, 71,* 291–301.

Yuille, J. C., Daylen, J., Porter, S., & Marxsen, D. (1996). Challenging the eyewitness expert. In J. Ziskin (Ed.) *Coping with psychiatric and psychological testimony* (5th ed., pp. 1266–1298). Los Angeles: Law and Psychology Press.

Yuille, J. C., Hunter, R., Joffe, R., & Zaparniuk, J. (1993). Interviewing children in sexual abuse cases. In G. Goodman & B Bottoms (Eds.), *Understanding and improving children's testimony: Clinical, developmental and legal implications.* Guilford Press.

Yuille, J. C., Marxsen, D., & Cooper, B. (1999). Training investigative interviewers: Adherence to the spirit, as well as the letter. *International Journal of Law and Psychiatry, 22,* 323–336.

Yuille, J. C., Ternes, M., & Cooper, B. S. (2010). Expert testimony on laboratory witnesses. *Journal of Forensic Psychology Practice, 10*(3), 238–251.

Yuille, J. C., Davies, G., Gibling, F., Marxsen, D. & Porter, S. (1994). Eyewitness memory of police trainees for realistic role plays. *Journal of Applied Psychology, 79(6),* 931–936.

Yuille, J. C., Hunter, R., & Harvey, W. (1990). A coordinated approach to interviewing in child sexual abuse investigations. *Canada's Mental Health, 38*(2–3), 14–17.

Yuille, J. C., Tymofievich, M. & Marxsen, D. (1995). The nature of allegations of child sexual abuse. In T. Ney (Ed.), *True and false allegations of child sexual abuse* (pp. 21–46). New York: Bruner Mazel.

Yun, M., & Roth, M. (2008). Terrorist hostage-taking and kidnapping: Using script theory to predict the fate of a hostage. *Studies in Conflict & Terrorism, 31,* 736–748.

Zapf, P. (1998, March). *An examination of the construct of competence in a civil and criminal context: A comparison of the MacCAT-T, the MacCAT-CA, and the FIT-R.* Paper presented at the meetings of the American Psychology-Law Society, Redondo Beach, CA.

Zapf, P., & Roesch. R. (1997). Assessing fitness to stand trial: A comparison of institution-based evaluations and a brief screening interview. *Canadian Journal of Community Mental Health, 16,* 53–66.

Zapf, P., Roesch, R., & Viljoen, J. L. (2001). Assessing fitness to stand trial: The utility of the Fitness Interview Test (Revised Edition). *Canadian Journal of Psychiatry, 46,* 423–432.

Zebrowitz, L. A., & McDonald, S. (1991). The impact of litigants' babyfacedness and attractiveness on adjudications in small claims courts. *Law and Human Behavior, 15,* 603–623.

Zebrowitz, L. A., Voinescu, L., & Collins, M. A. (1996). "Wide-eyed" and "crooked-faced": Determinants of perceived and real honesty across the life span. *Personality and Social Psychology Bulletin, 22,* 1258–1269.

Zhang, J. J., Wieczorek, W. W., Conwell, Y. Y., Tu, X. M., Wu, B. W., Xiao, S. S., & Jia, C. C. (2010). Characteristics of young rural Chinese suicides: A psychological autopsy study. *Psychological Medicine: A Journal of Research in Psychiatry and the Allied Sciences, 40*(4), 581–589.

Zhu, B., Chen, C., Loftus, E. F., Lin, C.,He, Q., Chen, C., et al. (2010).

Individual differences in false memory from misinformation: Personality characteristics and their interactions with cognitive abilities. *Personality and Individual Differences, 48,* 889-894.

Zimbardo, P. G. (1967). The psychology of police confessions. *Psychology Today, 1,* 17-27.

Zinzow, H., & Thompson, M. (2011). Barriers to reporting sexual victimization: Prevalence and correlates among undergraduate women. *Journal of Aggression, Maltreatment & Trauma, 20*(7), 711-725.

Ziskin, J. (1995). *Coping with psychiatric and psychological testimony* (Vol. 1-3, 5th ed.). Los Angeles: Law and Psychology Press.

Ziskin, J., & Faust, D. (1988). *Coping with psychiatric and psychological testimony* (4th ed., Vols. 1-3). Los Angeles: Law and Psychology Press.

Zizzo, F. (1985). Psychological intervention and specialized law enforcement groups. *Emotional First Aid: A Journal of Crisis Intervention, 2*(1), 25-27.

Name Index

Note: Boldface page numbers indicate information found in text boxes.

Johnson, H., 225, 238
Johnson, K., 51
Johnson, L. B., 70
Johnson, M. N., 318
Johnson, R. R., 64–65
Johnson, S. L., 190, 339
Jones, A., 242
Jones, E. E., 179–180
Jones, H. P. T., 153
Jones, J. W., 54
Jones, N. J., 63, 102
Josselson, A. R., 104
Juodis, M., 77–78, 98, 114, 196, 240
Jutai, J., 226

K
Kaemmer, B., 55
Kafka, M. P., 88
Kagehiro, D. K., 192
Kahler, K. N., 111
Kahn, K. B., 50
Kahneman, D., 20, 114, 153, 185, 196, 338
Kalven, H., 15
Kantor, G. K., 239
Kargon, R., 14
Karpin, A., 101
Karr, C., 55
Kashy, D. A., 112
Kassin, S.
    confessions, 163–164, 169, 180–181, 353
    identification process, 150
    interrogation, 115, 171–173, 353
    juror bias, 41, 192–193
    review of Hagen, 27
    testimony, 37, 153, 154
    wrongful convictions, 167, 178
Kaufmann, G., 168, 196, 338–339
Kaye, D. H., 306, 309
Keane, T. M., 306
Keast, A., 155
Keating, K., 139–140
Kebbell, M. R., 132
Keleher, C., 189
Keller, S. R., 21, 194
Kelln, B., 66, 68–69
Kelloway, E. K., 48–49
Kelly, J. F., 79
Keltner, D., 344
Kemp, R. I., 135
Kennedy, D. M., 72
Kennedy, M. A., 151
Kenney, J. S., 76
Kenning, M., 251
Kent, J., 106
Kessler, J. R., 196
Ketcham, K., 37
Kiechel, K. L., 169
Kihlstrom, J. F., 143

Kilpatrick, D., 303–305
King, L., 174, 181
Kingshott, B. E., 71–72
Kirkendol, S. E., 112
Kirsch, I., **149**, 353
Kitaeff, J., 53
Klaver, J. R., 123
Kleck, R., 121
Klippenstein, M., 187, 249, 281
Kluger, R., 40
Knatz, H., 58–59
Kocsis, R., 78, 84, 94, 99, 101
Koehnken, G., 289
Kolasa, B. J., 16
Konecni, V. J., 42, 154, 195, 338
Korva, N., 81, 197
Koss, M. P., 298, 305, **308,** 309
Kosson, D., 25, 67
Kotlowitz, A., 166
Kovera, M. B., 28, 136
Krafft-Ebing, R. von, 267–268
Krahenbuhl, S., 140–141, 150
Kramer, M., 51–52
Krapohl, J., 61
Kravitz, D. A., 190
Kremnitzer, M., 118
Kretschmer, E., 91
Kristiansson, M., 25, 352
Kroes, W., **65**
Kropp, P. R., 252
Kugler, M. B., 339
Kulka, R. A., 196
Kurke, M. I., 53–54
Kwong, M. J., 236

L
La Fon, D. S., 103–104
Labaton, S., 83
Labree, W., 82
Lacayo, R., 164–165
Lalumiere, M. L., 87, 274
LaMotte, V., 63
Landa, B., 59
Langer, W. C., 85
Langevin, R., 80, 87–88, 268, 270
Langfeld, H. S., 122
Langford, D., 329
Langhinrichsen-Rohling, J., 239
Langkamp, K., 58
Langleben, D. D., **127**
Lanning, K., 97
LaPaglia, J. A., 140–141, 150
Lassiter, G. D., 179
Laufer, W. S., **18**, 355
Lavin, M., 30
Lavender, T., 140
Lawing, K., 330
Lawlor, M. C., 31
Leal, S., 122, 124–125, 128
Lebegue, B., 166

LeBlanc, S., 76
Lecci, L., 194
Lee, A. Y., 127
Lee, K., 141
Lee, Z., 123
Lehman, D., 8, 145, 239, 353
Leichtman, M. D., 287
Leippe, M. R., 133, 146, 148, 152–154
Leitner, M., 106
Lelos, D., 221
Lemieux, J. M. T., 149
Leo, R. A., 167, 170, 174, 180
Lester, D., 52, 98
Levav, J., 339
Levens, B. R., 64–65
Levine, J. A., 125
Levine, L. J., 168
Levine, T. R., 112, 115
Levy, C. J., 83
LeWinn, L. M., 209
Lewis, A., 86
Li, X., 70
Lieberman, J. D., 201
Lightfoot, D. M., 251
Lilienfeld, S. O., 25, 353
Limber, S., 294
Lin, S., 70
Lincoln, R., 84
Lind, E. A., 50
Lindberg, M. J., 179
Lindsay, D. S., 143, 179
Lindsay, R. C. L., 6, 136, 146, 148, 150
Lindsay, S., 8, 139
Linedecker, C., 78
Linz, H., 114
Lipsey, M. W., 239
Lipsitt, P. D., 221
Lipton, J. P., 141
Liu, C., 56
Livingston, J. D., 212–213
Livingstone Smith, D., 111
Lloyd, C. D., 346
Lloyd-Bostock, S. M. A., 177
Loe, T., 93
Lofquist, W., 198–199
Loftus, E., 14, 16–17, 37, 144, 152, 289
Loh, W., 16
Lombroso, C., 13, 117
London, K., 144
Long, A., 28
Loo, R., 49
Lopez, A., 71
Louisell, D. W., 17
Louw, D. A., 218
Low, P. W., 210
Lowe, J., 114
Loya, J., 103
Lubbe, S., 81–82
Lublin, A., 70
Lukas, J. A., 15

Ogard, E., 55
Ogloff, J.
  forensic psychology in Canada, 4,
    352, 354, 356
  insanity cases, 214, 219
  juries, 188
  profiling, 103
O'Hara & O'Hara, 171, 172
Oldfield, D., 90
O'Leary, D., 51
Olshaker, M., **89,** 90, 93, 97–99
Olson, E., 133, 134
Olver, M. E., 252–253, 270, **275,** 332
Ones, D. S., 58
Ono, M., 51, 59
Orr, S. P., 60
Orth, M., 85
Ory, J. H., 133
Osterheider, M., 25
Ostrom, T., 133, 146
Ostrov, E., 53, 59
O'Sullivan, M., 9, 112, 115, 120–121,
  178, 196
Otgaar, H., 143
Otto, R., 103
Oursland, K., 20
Owen, J., **65**
Owusu-Bempah, A., 50

P
Padilla, J., 141
Paitich, D., 88
Palermo, G. B., 78, 217
Palmer, M. A., 134, 146
Palmiotto, M. J., 71
Paolicelli, L. M., 111
Paris, M. L., 181
Park, J., 198
Parker, G. F., 66
Parsons, B., 143
Partridge, G. E., 314
Paterson, B., 66
Paterson, E. J., 64
Paterson, H. M., 135
Patrick, C. J., 118
Patry, M. W., 10, 111, **166, 175, 180,**
  353
Paul, D., 242
Paulsen, D., 106
Pavlidis, B. K., 125
Payne, B. K., 170
Peace, K. A., **134,** 139, 143, 229, 281,
  299
Peacock, M. A., 344
Peak, K. J., 71
Pearse, J., 163, 169–170, 182
Pease, K., 80
Pelli, D., 120, 195
Pembroke, M., 146
Pennebaker, J. W., 127, 304

Penrod, S. D., 35, 133, 140, 145–146,
  147, 155, 200
Perez-Pena, R., 83
Perillo, J., 163, 172
Perkins, D. D., 41
Perlin, M. L., 26, 209
Perrott, S. B., 48–49
Peters, J. M., 87–88
Petersilia, J., 132
Peterson, C., 141, 143
Peterson-Badali, M., 194
Petherick, L., 100
Petrila, J., 208, 221, 338
Pezdek, K., 288–289
Pickrell, J., 144
Pinegar, S. K., 179
Pinel, P., 313
Pinizzotto, A. J., 84, 94, 100–101
Pinkston, J. B., 58
Pirelli, G., 220
Pizzarro, D. A., 168
Pogrebin, M. R., 80
Pokorny, A. D., 224
Poole, D. A., 141, 179
Poole, E. D., 80
Pope, K. S., 62, 66
Porter, S. (author),
  career, **119, 250**
  Centre for Advancement of
    Psychological Science and
    Law, 7
  NCRMD community programs, 229
  research
    courts, 15, 20
    credibility assessments,
      196–197
    dangerous/long term offender,
      347–348
    deception detection, 9, 111–118,
      121–125, 127
    homicide offenders, 97, 318,
      343
    memory accuracy, 145, 288, 299
    polygraph, 61
    profiling, 87, 95,
    psychopathy, 225–227, 268–269,
      322, 329 342
    remorse detection, 344–345
    sentencing, 338, 342
    sexual abuse, 281, 283, 295
    wrongful conviction, 168
  training, 358
Post, J. M., 86
Potter, J. A., 79
Powitsky, R. J., 69
Poythress, N. G., 69, 208, 220–221,
  338
Pozzulo, J. D., 134, 141, 149, 190
Price, H. L., 179, 190, **285,** 288, 353
Prichard, J. C., 313
Proctor, W. D., 88

Proulx, J., 77, 80, 106
Pruesse, M., 88
Purdie-Vaughns, V. J., 190, 339

Q
Quas, J. A., 181
Quen, J. M., 210
Quinlivan, D. S., 146, 151
Quinn, S., 339
Quinsey, V. L., 26, 88, 225, 274, 329,
  354
Quirk, S. A., 151

R
Rachlin, H., 178
Rachlinski, J. J., 339
Radelet, M. L., 167
Raine, A., 352, 355
Raja, A. Q., 153
Rao, S., 197
Rappeport, M., 21
Raskin, D., 289
Rassin, E., 82
Ratcliff, J. J., 179
Rattner, A., 164, 167
Rauch, S., 148
Raymond, D. S., 139–141
Rayna, V. F., 144
Read, D., 8, **134,** 135, 139, 354
Read, J. D., 132, 143, 353
Reavis, J. A., 80, 254
Redlich, A. D., 181, 353
Reese, J., **65**
Reeves, K. A., 63
Regehr, C., **44**
Regoli, R. M., 80
Reichel, P., 52
Reid, J. E., 171–177
Reidy, D. R., 25, 353
Reiser, M., 53, 61–62, **65,** 69, 111
Reitzel, D., 64–65
Renauer, B., 237
Reppucci, N. D., 40, 43
Resnick-Luetke, S., 51
Ressler, R., 80–81, 84, 87–89, 92–95,
  100
Reynold, K., 63
Reynolds, M., 83
Rhodes, W., 106
Rice, M., 225, 332
Richards, J. M., 127
Rider, A. O., 81
Riley, J. A., 223
Ring, K., 42
Rishworth, A., 155
Risinger, D. M., 167, 176
Robb, A., 112
Roberts, A. R., 238
Roberts, B., 238

Wilson, M., 106
Wilson, P., 84
Wise, R. A., 131, 153
Wistrich, A. J., 339
Wolfskeil, M. P., 153
Wolpe, P. R., 126
Wolters, G., 140
Wong, S., 88, 270, 332, 352
Wood, L. A., 286, 287, 343
Woodhams, J., 93–94
Woodworth, M., **250**
    Centre for Advancement of
        Psychological Science and
        Law, 7
    NCRMD community programs, 229
    research
        deception detection, 9, 115, 178
        homicide offenders, 25, 97, 318,
            343
            profiling, 87, 95,
            psychopathy, 225, 227, 318, 343
    training, 358
Woody, W. D., 194
Wormith, J. S., 6, 252–253
Wortley, S., 50
Wright, C., 76

Wright, D. B., 141
Wright, D. G., 135
Wright, L., 162–163, 166
Wrightsman, L. S. (author), 41, 163,
    192–193, 198–199, 300–301
Wundt, W., 14
Wyer, M. M., 112
Wygant, D. B., 220

Y
Yang, Y., 25, 352
Yarmey, A. D.
    career, 354
    expert witness, 36, 42
    eyewitness testimony, 17, 37,
        153
    police procedure, 135, 147–148
    research, 10, 17
    wrongful convictions, 133
Yarmey, A. L., 147
Yarmey, M. J., 147
Yates, P. M., 333
Yonah, A., 69
Young, D., 105–106, 180
Youngstrom, N., 78

Yuille, J.,
    criterion-based content analysis,
        289, 290
    eyewitnesses, 17, 134–135, 145
    interviewing, 143, 284, 286
    research, 17, 21, 354
    Step-Wise, 284, 286
    training, 151
Yun, M., 67

Z
Zaparniuk, J., 143
Zapf, P. A., 209, 220, 221
Zappala, A., 76
Zavodny, D., 251
Zebrowitz, L. A., 153, 196, 338
Zebrowitz-McArthur, L. Z., 114, 196
Zeisel, H., 15
Zember, E., 144
Zhang, J. J., 103
Zhu, B., 353
Zimbardo, P. G., 174
Ziskin, J., 215, 218
Zizzo, F., 70
Zweig, D. I., 54

Subject Index

Note: Boldface page numbers indicate information found in text boxes.

Unabomber, 82–84, 90
unconscious racism, 339–340
unconscious transference, 140
undergraduate program in forensic psychology, 356
unexpected or equivocal deaths, 103–104
United States v. Hall, 180
Université du Québec à Trois-Rivières, 6
University of Alberta, 82
University of British Columbia, **7**
  forensic consulting course, 32
  psychopathy research, 25
  training of police, 65
University of Guelph, 10, 17, 36
University of Liverpool, **68**
University of Virginia, 5
U.S. Drug Enforcement Administration, 100
U.S. National Commission on Law Observance and Enforcement, 172
U.S. Secret Service, 80
U.S. Supreme Court, 12–13, 37, 40–42, 100

V
values, 29–30
Vancouver Police Department, 33

VandenElsen, Carline, 66
variables, 133–135
Versace, Gianni, 85
victim blaming, 269, 299–300
victimology, 96, 104
victim psychology, 143–144
Viljoen, Jodi, **219**
violence in psychopaths, 324–325
Violence Risk Appraisal Guide, 26, 272
Violent Crime Linkage Analysis System, 78, 104–105
Violent Criminal Apprehension Program, 97, 104–105
visible minorities, 50–51
voir dire, 11, 194, 204
volitional aspect of insanity, 210–211
voluntary confessions, 179–180
voluntary false confessions, 163–164
voyeurs, 259–260, 277

W
W. [R.], R. v., 151
Walsh, Zach, **325**
warrant expiry, 341
wellness training, 64, **65**
White, Michael, **113**
white lies, 112, 123
Whitman, Charles, 94
Whynot, Jane, **235**

Williams, Russell, 78, **267**
Williams, Wayne, 98
witnesses. *See also* expert witnesses
  accuracy, 35–37
  children, 141, **142**, 144
  gathering useful information, 132–133
  memory errors, 131–133, 141, 152–153, **154**
  psychology, 131–135, 156
  questioning, 136, 139–143, **154**
  variables, 133–135
wizards, detection, 115
wrongful convictions, 167–169

Y
Yates, Robert, 103
youth psychopaths, 329–330

Z
Zaccardelli, Giuliano, 48